ISBN: 9781313104050

Published by:
HardPress Publishing
8345 NW 66TH ST #2561
MIAMI FL 33166-2626

Email: info@hardpress.net
Web: http://www.hardpress.net

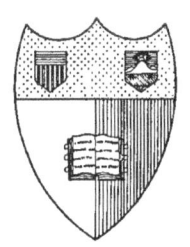

Cornell University Library
Ithaca, New York

BOUGHT WITH THE INCOME OF THE
SAGE ENDOWMENT FUND
THE GIFT OF
HENRY W. SAGE
1891

Cornell University Library
QE 461.H28 1904

The Tertiary igneous rocks of Skye.

3 1924 004 066 373

PLATE XIII.
(FRONTISPIECE.)

View up Loch Coruisk, showing part of the Cuillin range.

The mountains seen are as follows, from left to right: Sgùrr Dubh Bheag in the foreground; the top of Sgùrr Dearg (with the "Inaccessible Pinnacle") appearing over Sgùrr a' Coir' an Lochain (with vertical cleft); the broken ridge of Sgùrr na Banachdich; the double summit of Sgùrr a' Ghreadaidh in the centre; the four peaks of Sgùrr a' Mhadaidh; Bidein Druim nan Ramh (partly seen); and the Druim nan Ramh ridge bounding the valley on the right.

MEMOIRS OF THE GEOLOGICAL SURVEY
OF THE
UNITED KINGDOM.

THE
TERTIARY IGNEOUS ROCKS
OF
SKYE.

BY

ALFRED HARKER, M.A., F.R.S.,

WITH NOTES BY

C. T. CLOUGH, M.A., F.G.S.

PUBLISHED BY ORDER OF THE LORDS COMMISSIONERS OF HIS MAJESTY'S TREASURY.

GLASGOW:
PRINTED FOR HIS MAJESTY'S STATIONERY OFFICE
By JAMES HEDDERWICK & SONS
AT "THE CITIZEN" PRESS, ST. VINCENT PLACE.

And to be purchased, either directly or through any Bookseller, from
JOHN MENZIES & Co., ROSE STREET, EDINBURGH, and
90 WEST NILE STREET, GLASGOW; or
EDWARD STANFORD, 12, 13, and 14 LONG ACRE, LONDON, W.C.; and
HODGES, FIGGIS & Co., LTD., 104 GRAFTON STREET, DUBLIN.

1904.

Price, Nine Shillings.

PREFACE.

THE Tertiary Volcanic region of the West of Scotland is well known to be of exceptional interest from many points of view, and on this account my predecessor, Sir A. Geikie, determined that a typical portion of the region should be mapped and described in great detail. The district comprising the central mountain group of Skye was selected by him, and the services of Mr. Harker were secured in order that the actual survey and the petrographical work might be carried out by the same officer. The present memoir is, therefore, the result of work which was planned and in great part executed under the direction of Sir A. Geikie, who has himself contributed very largely to our knowledge of the selected area, and who has taken from first to last special interest in Mr. Harker's researches.

The district is one which has attracted the attention of many distinguished geologists from the days of Macculloch down to recent years. The main outlines of the geology are, therefore, familiar to students of the science, but in view of the publication of this volume some of the salient features of the development of research may here be referred to. Macculloch's classic work showed that the basalts of the plateaux and the eruptive masses pierce and overlie the Oolitic strata, and are therefore younger than the Jurassic rocks. The discovery of plant remains at Ardtun, in Mull, announced by the Duke of Argyll in 1851, marked an important advance, for they were regarded by Professor E. Forbes as proving the Tertiary age of the basalts with which they are associated. At the same time Forbes was led to the conclusion, from the evidence at Loch Staffin, in Skye, that the basaltic lavas are there contemporaneous with the Oolitic strata. Following the opinion of Professor Forbes, in his earliest investigations Sir A. Geikie inferred that the basaltic lavas of Skye are not younger than some late part of the Jurassic period, and he further contended that the gabbros of that island are of Archaean age from the striking resemblance of the banded types to some of the ancient gneisses of the North-West Highlands. In 1871 appeared Zirkel's valuable description of the petrology of the igneous rocks of Skye. In 1874 Professor Judd published his well-known paper, in which he maintained that in the West Highlands there are relics of five great extinct Tertiary volcanoes indicating three periods of igneous activity—the first marked by the extrusion of acid lavas and tuffs connected with plutonic masses of granite, the second by basaltic lavas related to deep-seated masses of gabbro, and the third by minor outflows of lava from sporadic cones. In 1888 Sir A. Geikie embodied the results of his prolonged study of the Tertiary Igneous Rocks of the West Highlands in his monograph, communicated to the Royal Society of Edinburgh, on "The History of Volcanic Action during the Tertiary Period in the British Isles." He therein maintains that the basaltic plateaux are probably due to fissure eruptions; that the basaltic lavas were subsequently pierced by laccolitic masses of gabbro, which produced a certain amount of contact alteration on the previously-erupted lavas; and, finally, that the basic rocks were disrupted by the protrusion of masses of granophyre. These conclusions have been confirmed by Mr. Harker.

In the following pages the rocks are described with reference to their field relations and petrographical characters, due regard being paid throughout to the fact that they form a connected series of igneous products. The area referred to is represented by Sheets 70 and 71 of the one-inch maps, together with parts of Sheets 80 and 81. Sheet 81 has been published, and Sheets 70 and 71 are now being prepared for publication. In view of the complexity of the district and the impossibility of adequately representing the geological features on the one-inch maps, it is proposed to publish four six-inch Sheets (Skye 38, 39, 44, and 45), embracing the most interesting portion of the area.

This memoir has been written by Mr. Harker, and is based principally on the area surveyed by him. During the years 1895-1901 he mapped in detail the central mountain group, a broad belt of the surrounding country, the basaltic plateaux to the west and north-west of the mountainous region, the large island of Scalpay and some of the smaller islands off the East Coast. Mr. Clough has surveyed the south-eastern part of Skye and the island of Soay, a region consisting of older stratified rocks which have been invaded by numerous minor intrusions belonging to the Tertiary series. Messrs. Woodward, Barrow, and Wedd have mapped other portions of Skye, especially those in which Jurassic rocks occur, but where Tertiary igneous rocks are also found. In the following pages Mr. Harker has freely availed himself of the information supplied by his colleagues as to the Tertiary igneous rocks of the areas surveyed by them, and has visited localities of interest which lie outside his own special district.

The petrographical descriptions are based on a large series of specimens, of which more than a thousand have been sliced for microscopical examination. Most of these specimens have been collected by Mr. Harker, but a considerable number have been supplied by Mr. Clough and a few by Mr. Woodward. They include also a number of specimens collected by Sir A. Geikie prior to the detailed survey. Dr. Pollard has made twelve complete and four partial analyses for the purpose of this memoir.

During the progress of the survey Professor Lebour generously placed at our disposal his own manuscript maps of the Broadford and Kyleakin districts, together with five analyses of rocks which had been made for him by Mr. T. Baker, of the Durham College of Science. We are also indebted to Mr. Archibald Livingstone, of the Antrim Iron Ore Company, for the results of the chemical examination of some of the clays in the basaltic series; to Mr. J. H. Player for the partial analysis of another clay; to Professor Sollas for isolating and examining the constituents of some of the rocks; and to Sir J. Norman Lockyer, K.C.B., for photographs of the spectra of certain rocks.

The photographic views given as plates were taken by Mr. R. Lunn, save the frontispiece, which is reproduced by the kind permission of Messrs. Wilson & Co., Photographers, Aberdeen. One sketch was very kindly made for us by Mr. Colin B. Phillip. The other illustrations, including the micro-sections, are by the author; but many of the text figures have been re-drawn by J. D. Bowie, who has also prepared the sketch map prefixed to this volume.

Our thanks are due to the proprietors of estates in Skye, more particularly to Macleod of Macleod and Mr. R. L. Thomson of Strathaird, who have afforded every facility for the survey, and also to numerous residents of humbler station who have given kindly and intelligent help. To Mr. T. A. Falcon, as a frequent companion in camping and climbing in the Cuillins, the author desires to express his indebtedness in many ways. Mr. Falcon's photographs of the mountains have proved of value in deciphering their structure.

J. J. H. TEALL,
Director.

GEOLOGICAL SURVEY OFFICE,
   28 JERMYN STREET,
     LONDON, 12th *April* 1904.

CONTENTS.

CHAPTER.		PAGE.
I.	Introduction, and General Relations of the Volcanic Series,	1
II.	Volcanic Agglomerates, Tuffs, and Conglomerates,	15
III.	Basic Lavas: General Petrography,	29
IV.	Basic Lavas: Alterations and Metamorphism,	41
V.	Rhyolitic and Trachytic Lavas and Tuffs,	55
VI.	Peridotites (Earlier Group),	63
VII.	Gabbros: Field-Relations,	82
VIII.	Gabbros: Petrography,	102
IX.	Granites and Granophyres: Field-Relations,	126
X.	Granites and Granophyres: Petrography,	152
XI.	Invasion of Basic Rocks by the Granite-Magma,	169
XII.	Composite Sills and Dykes: General Features,	197
XIII.	Composite Sills and Dykes: Detailed Description,	215
XIV.	Basic Sills: the Great Group,	235
XV.	Basic Sills: Minor Groups,	254
XVI.	Minor Acid Intrusions,	271
XVII.	Basic Dykes: Field-Relations,	291
XVIII.	Basic Dykes: General Petrography,	315
XIX.	Basic Dykes: Tachylytic Selvages,	333
XX.	Basic Dykes: Xenoliths,	351
XXI.	Basic Dykes and Sheets of the Cuillins,	364
XXII.	Later Peridotites,	374
XXIII.	Trachyte and Trachy-Andesite Dykes,	386
XXIV.	Augite-Andesite and Pitchstone Dykes,	399
XXV.	General Review of Tertiary Igneous Activity in Skye,	411
XXVI.	Physical Features and Scenery,	434
Appendix.	Bibliography of the Tertiary Igneous Rocks of Skye,	453
Explanation of plates of micro-sections,		466
Index,		473

LIST OF ILLUSTRATIONS.

LIST OF FIGURES IN THE TEXT.

			PAGE
Fig.	1.	Sketch-map to show the distribution of Tertiary igneous rocks in the British Isles,	3
,,	2.	Section in the southern part of the Isle of Scalpay,	8
,,	3.	Section to illustrate the structure of the basalt plateaux,	9
,,	4.	Section across the volcanic vent of Kilchrist,	16
,,	5.	Contrasted outlines of volcanic agglomerate and granite,	17
,,	6.	Cliff-section at Camas Bàn, Portree Harbour,	23
,,	7.	Micro-section: olivine-basalt lava,	34
,,	8.	Section along Allt Dearg Mòr, near Sligachan,	39
,,	9.	Diagrammatic representation of the relations of the trachytic and rhyolitic rocks,	57
,,	10.	Section along the Sgùrr Dubh ridge,	63
,,	11.	Dykes or veins of gabbro traversing peridotite,	65
,,	12.	Block of banded peridotite enclosed in gabbro,	65
,,	13.	Micro-section: dunite, rich in picotite,	72
,,	14.	Micro-section: peridotite,	72
,,	15.	Sketch-map to show the shape of the gabbro laccolite,	86
,,	16.	Section through Gars-bheinn,	89
,,	17.	Sketch-map showing the distribution of banded structures in the gabbro,	91
,,	18.	Section across Druim an Eidhne,	93
,,	19.	Ground-plan of a sheet of gabbro and its dyke-feeder at Eas Mòr, Allt Coire na Banachdich,	95
,,	20.	Map showing a part of the Broadford gabbro boss with patches of the Cambrian limestones enclosed,	98
,,	21.	Micro-section: olivine-gabbro, showing the ophitic structure,	115
,,	22.	Micro-section: "granulitic gabbro," probably a highly metamorphosed basaltic lava,	115
,,	23.	Dykes of banded gabbro in glen south of Allt a' Chaoich,	119
,,	24.	Secondary twin-lamellation in the felspar of the gabbros,	124
,,	25.	View from Bealach a' Leitir, showing granite underlying gabbro,	128
,,	26.	Section across Glen Sligachan, from Sgùrr nan Gillean to Marsco,	129
,,	27.	Section through Marsco and Ruadh Stac,	130
,,	28.	Section through Lochain Beinn na Caillich and towards Broadford,	131
,,	29.	Map of part of the Beinn an Dubhaich granite, showing its relation to the Cambrian limestones,	133
,,	30.	Section from Loch Kilchrist to Glen Boreraig,	134

			PAGE.
Fig. 31.	Relations of granite and marble on the lower slopes of Beinn an Dubhaich,		135
,, 32.	Section along Beinn na Cro,	-	138
,, 33.	Section in the south-western part of Scalpay,		139
,, 34.	Some rarer minerals of the granophyres (from micro-sections),		159
,, 35.	Section across the deep gully on the N.W. slope of Marsco,		177
,, 36.	Sketch-map to illustrate the relation of the enclosed bodies of gabbro, etc., on the slopes of Marsco,		179
,, 37.	Outlines of Glamaig and Beinn Dearg, with Sròn a' Bhealain,		188
,, 38.	Section from Sron a' Bhealain to Allt Daraich and Glamaig,		189
,, 39.	Section through Glamaig and to the Sligachan estuary,		190
,, 40.	Ground-plan of part of Allt Daraich, near Sligachan,		193
,, 41.	Granophyre crowded with xenoliths of marscoite, from Allt Daraich,		194
,, 42.	Section through Cnoc Càrnach, showing composite triple sills,		205
,, 43.	Section of triple composite sill at Camas na Geadaig, Scalpay,		207
,, 44.	Section of quintuple composite laccolite at Allt an' t-Sithean, near Sligachan,		209
,, 45.	Section across the composite sill of Carn Dearg, near Suishnish,		211
,, 46.	Sketch-map of a small area in the interior of Scalpay,	-	212
,, 47.	Altered phenocrysts and xenocrysts in the basalt of the composite sills (from micro-sections),		220
,, 48.	Section of composite sill at Rudh' an Eireannaich, Broadford Bay,	-	225
,, 49.	Enlarged section of composite sill of Rudh' an Eireannaich,		226
,, 50.	Ideal curve of variation of magnesia,	-	232
,, 51.	Ideal curve of variation of lime,		232
,, 52.	Sketch-map illustrating the distribution of the basic sills and of the multiple basic dykes,		238
,, 53.	Section through Monadh Meadale and Beinn Totaig,		239
,, 54.	Preshal More, near Talisker, seen from the south-west,		244
,, 55.	Section through Druim na Creiche,	- -	257
,, 56.	Geological map of Roineval,		258
,, 57.	Section through Roineval,		259
,, 58.	Sketch-map illustrating the distribution of certain groups of acid intrusions,	-	273
,, 59 and 60.	Sections across circus north of Rudha Chinn Mhòir, Scalpay,		274
,, 61.	Micro-section: rhyolitic dyke, Druim an Eidhne,		285
,, 62.	Ground-plan in Tairneilear, showing dykes terminating abruptly against volcanic agglomerate,	-	293
,, 63.	Sketch-map illustrating the bearings of the basic dykes in Skye,		301
,, 64 to 66.	Ground-plans on shore west of Broadford Bay, to show lateral shifting of dykes,		303, 304

			PAGE.
Fig. 67.	Ground-plan on shore west of Broadford Bay, to show a number of dykes sharply deviated,		304
,, 68.	Micro-section: diabase dyke, Ben Aslak,		323
,, 69 and 70.	Sheaths and cores on surface of a basaltic sheet, Cnoc a' Chàise, near Knock,		336
,, 71.	Micro-section: margin of small basalt dyke, Ben Lee, near Sligachan,		346
,, 72.	Sketch-map to illustrate the distribution and inclination of the inclined basic sheets of the Cuillins,		367
,, 73.	Section across the gabbro area to show the vertical distribution of the inclined sheets,		368
,, 74.	Section to illustrate the shifting of an inclined basic sheet, Loch Scavaig,		369
,, 75.	Sketch-map to illustrate the distribution of the peridotites, older and younger,		375
,, 76.	Sketch-map to show the distribution of some trachytic and other dykes,		387
,, 77.	Diagram to show the varying inclination of the "rodding" in the dykes of the Broadford and Sleat districts,		392
,, 78.	Dyke with "rodded" structure, near Coire-chatachan,		393
,, 79.	Terraced hills on the west side of Glen Varragill,		437
,, 80.	Outlines of hills on the west side of Glen Brittle,		439
,, 81.	View of Blath bheinn from Kilchrist,		441
,, 82.	The "Inaccessible Pinnacle" of Sgùrr Dearg,		447
,, 83.	Outlines of the Alaisdair group of mountains,		448
,, 84.	Contrasted outlines of the gabbro and granite mountains,		449

LIST OF PLATES.

			To face Page
Plate	I.	Exposed surface of volcanic agglomerate, Druim an Eidhne,	21
,,	II.	Banded structure in the peridotite group, An Garbh-choire,	75
,,	III.	Brecciated appearance, due to xenolithic structure, in the peridotite group, An Garbh-choire,	77
,,	IV.	Veined structure in the peridotite group, An Garbh-choire,	78
,,	V.	Strongly banded structure and felspathic veins in gabbro, Druim an Eidhne,	90
,,	VI.	Banded structure, showing curvature, in gabbro, Druim an Eidhne,	90
,,	VII.	Crushed granite, from the shore between Allt Fearna and Strollamus Lodge, $2\frac{1}{2}$ miles N.W. of Broadford. Natural size. The lower figure is from a typical specimen, while the upper one shows an earlier stage in the process of brecciation,	167
,,	VIII.	Marsco, from the north-west,	176

			* To face Page
Plate	IX.	Part of the northern face of Preshal More, near Talisker, showing curvature of columns in a dolerite sill,	244
,,	X.	Columnar sill of dolerite forming the cliff at Rudha Buidhne, near Braes,	244
,,	XI.	Weathered surface of acid dyke, Druim an Eidhne, showing crowded spherulites : natural size,	283
,,	XII.	Weathered surface of acid dyke, Druim an Eidhne, showing tortuous flow-structure : natural size,	284
,,	XIII.	View up Loch Coruisk, showing part of the Cuillin range,	Frontispiece.
,,	XIV.	View of Clach Glas from Garbh-bheinn, showing the northward prolongation of the Blath-bheinn ridge,	445
,,	XV.	View from Coire na Creiche. In the foreground is Sgùrr na Fheadain, the termination of a branch ridge running out from the triple-peaked Bidein Druim nan Ramh. It shows well the inclined sheets dipping to the left (east) and the fissures due to dykes running in the direction of the branch ridge itself. The four peaks of Sgùrr a' Mhadaidh are seen to the right,	446
,,	XVI.	View of the Pinnacle Ridge of Sgùrr nan Gillean. The notches and gullies, with other vertical fissures, are due to dykes. The outcrops of the inclined sheets of dolerite are seen running nearly horizontally along the steep slopes,	446
,,	XVII. to XXVII.	Micro-sections of rocks. The explanation of these is given, with the plates, at the end of the volume.	

THE TERTIARY IGNEOUS ROCKS OF SKYE.

CHAPTER I.

Introduction, and General Relations of the Volcanic Series.

As a region of igneous rocks the Western Isles of Scotland, with neighbouring parts of the Scottish mainland and of Ireland, have engaged attention since the early days of modern geology; and a considerable literature dealing with the various districts severally or collectively has grown up during the last hundred years. The special features of the region are the grand scale on which igneous activity has here operated, the completeness of the record, and the manner in which the inner mechanism of igneous action has been brought to light by profound erosion. The clear recognition of the Tertiary age of the whole has added a further feature of interest, more especially as regards the rocks of deep-seated origin. In few other parts of Europe is there any similar exhibition of plutonic rocks of this comparatively late geological date, and the study of the British area has contributed in no small degree to dispel the misconception of radical differences supposed to distinguish pre-Tertiary from Tertiary igneous rocks. In all the aspects indicated Skye is fully equal, and in some particulars superior, to other parts of the region in the advantages which it offers to the geologist, and the island has received a corresponding amount of attention at the hands of observers.

In view of the frequent references contained in the following pages and the full Bibliography given as an appendix, no formal review of the literature of the subject is called for. Among the earlier writers Macculloch may claim the chief place. His great work, published in 1819, is a monument alike of accurate observation and of acute generalisation, and it contains much which, after more than eighty years, is still valuable. Boué's "Essai géologique sur l'Ecosse" (1820) should also be mentioned, and a memoir published in 1829 by von Oeynhausen and von Dechen. A brief but

A

important paper by J. D. Forbes in 1845 marked a decided advance in the geology of the Skye mountains. The results of Sir A. Geikie's earliest geological work in Skye were presented to the Geological Society in 1857, and forty years later he embodied in his "Ancient Volcanoes of Great Britain" the results of many valuable researches in the same district. Professor Zirkel was the first to apply to the igneous rocks of Skye, in 1870, the methods of modern petrology; while our fuller knowledge of this side of the subject is due principally to an important series of memoirs from the pen of Professor Judd. The mineralogy of Skye, as of Scotland in general, owes most to the late Professor Heddle, whose many contributions are collected in his posthumous publication "The Mineralogy of Scotland" (1901).

In this chapter we shall offer a few introductory remarks upon the Tertiary igneous rocks of Britain in general, and also some observations concerning the general relations of the volcanic rocks of Skye, which here, as elsewhere in the region, constitute the earliest members of the whole suite. It should be mentioned that in the south-eastern part of Skye there are igneous rocks of much greater antiquity, with which we shall have no concern. Apart from those older than the Moine crust-movements, and accordingly much disguised in character, there are various pre-Tertiary dykes both acid and basic, the latter chiefly of lamprophyric affinities. Few of these are found beyond the limits of the Sleat district. The most north-westerly example observed is a much decayed mica-lamprophyre dyke intersecting the Cambrian limestones in Coire Beithe, on the south side of Beinn na'Caillich, near Broadford.

Although the immediate subject-matter of this memoir is limited to the Isle of Skye, it is important to bear in mind constantly that the Tertiary igneous rocks of Britain have a much wider distribution. Bedded basalts comparable with those which build the plateaux of Skye occur in many other parts of the Inner Hebrides, besides some patches on the adjacent coast of Scotland and a large area in the north-east of Ireland (*see* sketch-map, Fig. 1); the Tertiary age of these rocks being proved in several localities by the discovery of an Eocene flora in intercalated bands of tuff and lignite.* On petrographical and other grounds it seems probable that the area of distribution of Tertiary igneous rocks in Britain may be further extended to include the gabbros and granites of St. Kilda, Arran, the Mourne Mountains, Carlingford, and perhaps other districts.† There is moreover a very numerous system of basic dykes throughout the western and southern parts of Scotland and the northern parts of Ireland and England,

* See especially Starkie Gardner, *Proc. Roy. Soc.*, vol. xxxviii., pp. 14-23 : 1885, and vol. xxxix., pp. 412-415 : 1886.

† The intrusions at Carrock Fell, in Cumberland, may possibly come in here. Mr. T. Davies made a like suggestion for the granite of Lundy, off the north coast of Devon (see Judd, *Quart. Journ. Geol. Soc.*, vol. xxx., p. 275 : 1874); but the specimens of this rock which we have examined lend no support to the supposition.

which are with good reason inferred to belong to the same general period of igneous activity.* Such an inference seems to be warranted by the petrographical characters of the dykes, their bearing and behaviour in the field, and the fact that some of them traverse Mesozoic strata. Thus the Cleveland dyke near Whitby (about 300 miles from Skye) cuts through the Oolites;

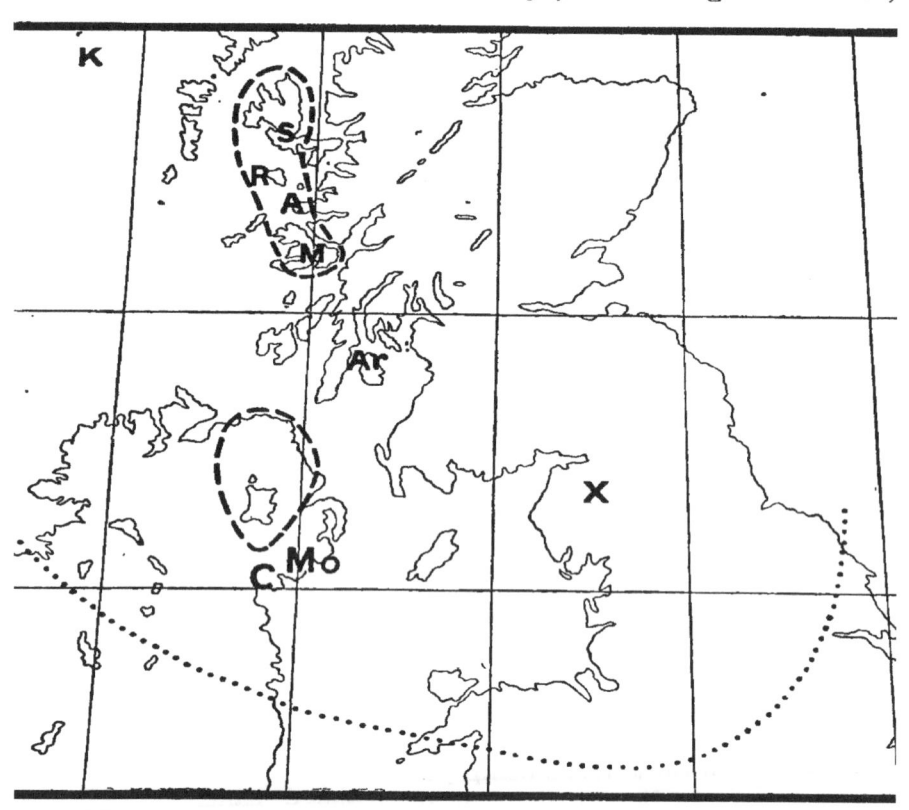

FIG. 1.—Sketch-map to show the distribution of Tertiary igneous rocks in the British Isles.

The broken lines enclose the areas in the west of Scotland and the north-east of Ireland where Tertiary volcanic rocks are preserved.
The dotted line marks the southern limit in England, Wales, and Ireland of basic dykes believed to be of Tertiary age.
The situations of the principal plutonic intrusions of Tertiary age are indicated by letters, as follows: K, St. Kilda; S, Skye; R, Rum; A, Ardnamurchan; M, Mull; Ar, Arran; Mo and C, Mourne Mts and Carlingford. The letter X marks the situation of the gabbro and granophyre intrusions of Carrock Fell, possibly of Tertiary age, but only proved to be post-Silurian.

* See map by Sir A. Geikie in *Trans. Roy. Soc. Edin.*, vol. xxxv., Pl. I.: 1888. The later dykes of Anglesey are also referred, with considerable probability, to a Tertiary age (Greenly, *Geol. Mag.*, 1900, pp. 160-164).

and, since no igneous outburst is known to have occurred between Permian and Eocene times, this fact affords a strong probability of the Tertiary age of the dyke.*

The British area thus embraced is still but a small fraction of the whole "petrographical province," which extends northward for more than two thousand miles, to far within the Arctic Circle, and includes not only Iceland and the Färöer, but Jan Mayen, a portion of Greenland, Spitzbergen, Franz Josef Land, etc. Throughout this great area the volcanic rocks are marked by common characteristics, such as the great preponderance of basic lavas, the prevalence of the fissure type of eruption, and other features, geological as well as petrographical. At certain centres, notably in Iceland, volcanic activity has been prolonged down to the present time, or, as some geologists would prefer to say, has been revived upon the old lines and with the old characteristics. The southern and western boundaries of this "Brito-Icelandic province" are probably rather sharply defined, for on Rockall, some 250 miles west of Skye, and at the Wolf Rock, off the Cornish coast, we meet with igneous rocks of a very different kind. Although the Tertiary age of these two occurrences cannot be proved, their petrographical nature leads us to attach them to another great province, characterised especially by rock-types rich in alkalies, which embraces most of the Atlantic basin.

Subsequently to the cessation of igneous activity within the British area, the volcanic tract has been subjected to extensive crust-movements, generally in the sense of subsidence, and to erosion on an enormous scale; and it has thus been reduced essentially to a certain number of islands rising from the hundred-fathom continental platform. Some of the larger questions on which we might desire to have assurance have thus become matters of speculation; among others the question to what extent basaltic districts now separated by the sea have once been continuous. Professor Judd is of opinion that the lavas were poured forth from great central volcanoes comparable with Etna at the present day. Of these he has specified five, in Mull, Skye, Rum, Ardnamurchan, and St. Kilda, their sites being marked by the occurrence of considerable masses of plutonic rocks, which in his view represent the denuded cores or basal wrecks of these hypothetical volcanoes. The detailed survey of Skye has led to quite other conclusions, and has endorsed the view, first enunciated by Sir A. Geikie in 1880, that the basaltic lavas issued, not from great volcanic vents, but from innumerable small fissures. There would thus be no narrow limit to the possible extent of a continuous lava-field. That of the Snake River Plains in Idaho stretches for much more than 300 miles, the total area being still undetermined, while the "Deccan traps" in India cover at least 200,000 square miles. There is therefore nothing of inherent improbability in the supposition that a basaltic tract once extended continuously from Antrim to Skye and much farther.

* On this question, see more particularly Sir A. Geikie, *Trans. Roy. Soc. Edin.*, vol. xxxv., p. 30 : 1888.

The *volcanic** phase, doubtless representing in itself a prolonged lapse of time, was followed by a *plutonic* phase, in which the manifestations of igneous activity assumed a new form. The energy, instead of being diffused over a vast region, became localised about certain centres within that region, and one such plutonic centre or focus was situated in what is now the mountain district of Skye, including the Cuillins and the Red Hills. Here large bodies of molten magma, first of basic (including ultrabasic) and afterwards of acid composition, were intruded immediately below and among the volcanic rocks, and consolidated beneath a very considerable superincumbent mass. There is evidence that this was effected by many distinct intrusions, and the building up of these complex plutonic masses must have been a gradual and prolonged process.

To the plutonic phase there succeeded a third and final phase of activity characterised by *minor intrusions* in the form of sills, sheets, and dykes. This third phase embraced numerous distinct episodes, the history of which has been partly, but not in every case completely, deciphered. We shall show that certain groups of these minor intrusions are probably common to the whole great region or "petrographical province"; others affect a very large area of that region, including Skye or a considerable portion of Skye; while others again stand in relation to the special centre of activity already established during the plutonic phase, and have a distribution limited accordingly. The groups which fall into this last category are as a rule very definitely characterised, and it has been found possible to follow out the succession of events connected with the special Skye focus in sufficient detail. The rocks belonging to groups of regional extension present much less variety in their petrographical characters; and, for this and other reasons, it is not possible to decipher their succession in any thorough fashion.

The succession of events from the breaking out of igneous action in the area considered to its final extinction implies a very extended length of time, but its actual duration is a question concerning which we have little certain knowledge. The only precise datum is supplied by the botanical evidence which assigns the volcanic rocks to some part of the Eocene. Since the volcanic phase covers only a fraction of the whole time demanded, we might be led to suggest that succeeding events were prolonged into some of the later divisions of Tertiary time.† Against this, however, we have to set the consideration of the enormous amount of erosion‡ which has

---

* Throughout this memoir we use the term "volcanic" in its strict sense, *i.e.* limited to eruptions at the surface of the earth's crust. The plutonic and later intrusions in our area had no connection with volcanoes, other than the lax connection which unites all the extrusive and intrusive rocks as members of one great suite, for which we may infer a remote common parentage.

† Prof. Judd, in his earlier papers, dealing with the Western Isles as a whole, referred the latest igneous eruptions to the Pliocene. This, however, was when the flora of the basaltic group was believed to be of Miocene age. (See *Quart. Journ. Geol. Soc.*, vol. xxx., p. 274 : 1874.)

‡ On this point, see Judd, *l.c.*; also Geikie, *Quart. Journ. Geol. Soc.*, vol. lii., pp. 402-405 : 1896.

affected our Tertiary igneous districts, and which was mainly accomplished before the Glacial Epoch. The lavas, it is true, may have been undergoing erosion concurrently with the later phases of igneous activity; but the great basic sills intercalated among the lavas, and belonging to a much later episode, expose their truncated edges throughout a thickness of rocks amounting to hundreds and indeed thousands of feet. The gabbro, too, which must certainly have consolidated under a considerable cover,* has been carved into lofty mountains. Such considerations dispose us to throw back the period of igneous activity so far as is consistent with the varied developments of which the record gives evidence, and without further knowledge the balance of probability cannot be more precisely stated.

In describing the various rocks, geologically and petrographically, we shall treat them, so far as is possible, in chronological sequence. As regards the dykes, however, the imperfection of the record, or of our reading of it, sometimes precludes such orderly treatment, and the account will then be given in a more collective form. For convenience, and to avoid repetition, certain features of special interest will be discussed in separate chapters; and some general considerations, which turn upon a comprehensive review of the observations recorded, will find their most appropriate place near the end of the volume. In accordance with this plan, the volcanic rocks will be first described, then in due sequence the several plutonic rocks and, partly in chronological order, the various minor intrusions of the area.

The *volcanic rocks* still preserved in Skye, together with the numerous sills of basic rocks intruded amongst them, occupy, roughly speaking, the whole of the north-western half of the island, *i.e.* all the country to the north and west of the central mountains, which consist essentially of gabbro and granite. It is quite clear, morever, that they have once had a considerable extension south-eastward; for, besides numerous patches of the volcanic rocks enclosed in the plutonic masses of the mountain district, we find outliers of some extent in the Strathaird peninsula, and other areas both north and south of the Beinn na Caillich massif, the most easterly of the granitic or "Red" Hills. These last-mentioned relics of the volcanic group are let down by faults, and owe partly to this cause their preservation from destruction. Prior to the great erosion of later Tertiary times these rocks must have overspread the greater part, if not the whole, of Skye. Nor is it to be supposed that even this area, nearly 50 miles in length, represents the full extent of country which they covered; for there

* Michel-Lévy's remarks on this point (*Structures et classification des roches éruptives*, Paris, 1889, p. 9) seem to be based on a misunderstanding of Sir A. Geikie's writings. The same conception, that the gabbros and granites of the Hebrides can be explained as extrusive rocks, has also been put forward by Reyer upon a misunderstanding of Judd's description (*Theoretische Geologie*, Stuttgart, 1888, pp. 369-372).

is nowhere any sign of thinning away of the group, and the truncated edges of the basalt sheets are seen, often to a thickness of many hundreds of feet, in the precipitous cliffs which form the coast-line in the north and west of the island.

Apart from local variations, the volcanic group has, throughout the large continuous area which it occupies in the north-western half of Skye, a *general dip to westward* or to some point south of west. In accordance with this we find that, while on the east side Jurassic rocks are almost everywhere seen beneath, and are exposed near Broadford and Portree to some distance inland, on the west coast the volcanic rocks descend in most places below sea-level, though probably to no great depth.* But although the general decline of the base westward, and the principal exceptions to this, are the results of subsequent disturbance, many of the minor irregularities are to be attributed to the unevenness of the old land-surface upon which the earliest volcanic rocks were erupted. Prior to the volcanic epoch the pre-Tertiary strata had been both disturbed and deeply eroded. The volcanic rocks thus repose in different places on different members of the Jurassic and older systems. In the north of the island they rest on the Oxfordian group and the Great Estuarine Series; farther south on the Lower Oolites, and then on the Lias. At Sconser on one side of the island, and near the Sound of Soay on the other, they pass from Jurassic strata to Torridon Sandstone: then to the east of Blaven they rest on Jurassic rocks again, and in the Strathaird peninsula on higher members of the Jurassic. At Creag Strollamus, north of Beinn na Caillich, the volcanic rocks are again seen on Torridon Sandstone, and in some of the patches enclosed in the Beinn na Caillich granite there are little outliers resting on the Cambrian limestones. Only three-quarters of a mile from Creag Strollamus, on the opposite side of the Sound of Scalpay, the bedded basalts lie on strata of Cretaceous age, and this is the case also, as Mr Clough has discovered, at one point on the Sound of Soay.

The volcanic series of Skye, so far as it is preserved, consists almost wholly of lavas of *basic and sub-basic composition*. At one place only, on the northern border of the Cuillins, do we find the relics of a group of sub-acid and acid lavas and tuffs. Excluding these from present consideration, the uniformity of general characters from base to summit of the series is very striking. At the base of the whole, certain local accumulations of volcanic agglomerates and tuffs prove that the volcanic era was ushered in, in places, by outbursts of a paroxysmal kind; but the great succession of lavas above is practically unbroken by any pyroclastic deposits worthy of notice.

The *thickness of the group*, or rather of that portion of it which has survived the energetic erosion of later Tertiary times, must be very considerable; but there are serious difficulties in the way of framing

* On Loch Harport Jurassic sandstones were brought up as cores in boring for the foundations of the new pier, about 500 yards beyond the Talisker Distillery at Carbost. The spot is covered by about 21 feet of water at high tide, and the borings were only 6 or 7 feet deep.

even an approximate estimate of it. These difficulties arise chiefly from the monotony of lithological characteristics, which makes it by no means easy to detect the faults which certainly intersect and displace the rocks, and impossible in general to determine the throw of such faults. If we could overcome this obstacle and calculate the thickness of the whole pile which builds the moorland plateaux, we should still have to restore in imagination the portion removed, and then to deduct from the total the aggregate thickness of the intruded sills, which in many parts of the district surpass in importance the lavas themselves. From the altitudes attained by the group in such places as the Quiraing, the Storr Rock, etc., we may at least infer that the total thickness of lavas and sills together considerably exceeds 2000 feet, and of the lavas alone 1000 feet. This is not the full thickness of the group, and there are places, such as the Isle of Scalpay (fig. 2), where lavas free from sills mount up to a thickness of 1500 or 1600 feet.

The impossibility of compiling any estimate from horizontal

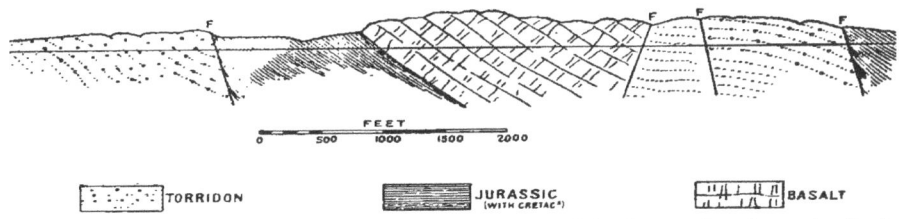

FIG. 2.—Section in the southern part of the Isle of Scalpay, showing a faulted area of the basaltic lavas, resting on Jurassic and Cretaceous strata and thrown against the Torridonian. Scale, 3 inches to a mile.

sections may easily be made apparent. The base of the volcanic series is exposed at Peinchorran and Balmeanach, north of Loch Sligachan. From thence, following the direction of dip, viz. W. by S., we arrive at Carbost pier on Loch Harport in about 9¾ miles. The dips along this line vary usually between 10° and 20°, with an average of about 16°, and hence, if the succession were an unbroken one, we should have crossed a thickness of some 14,000 feet. Nevertheless, at Carbost pier the base is again found only a few feet below sea-level. Making any reasonable allowance for the uneven form of the old land-surface on which the lavas were poured out, it is still manifest that in the traverse specified we must have crossed faults with a downthrow towards the east amounting in the aggregate to many thousands of feet. A section across the northern part of the island would bring out the same point, for it is evident that the observed dips would, if the succession were unbroken, carry the basalts far below sea-level on the west coast. The faults, the existence of which is thus proved, may often evade notice in mapping, owing to the impossibility of distinguishing horizons in the series and to the concealment of much of the ground by drift and peat. Along the coast northward from Loch Sligachan, where Jurassic strata are exposed below the basalts, such faults as occur can of course be verified and their effect estimated; but, since this coast runs nearly along the strike of the volcanic rocks, it contributes no information germane to the question. In places where the circumstances are most favourable to investigation, as in the Talisker district, numerous strike-faults can be verified, the downthrow being in general towards the east (fig. 3); and it is safe to assume that the essential structure of the whole plateau country is that of a succession of gently tilted strips separated in this way by strike-faults. This is the type to which Powell* has given the name of "Kaibab Structure."

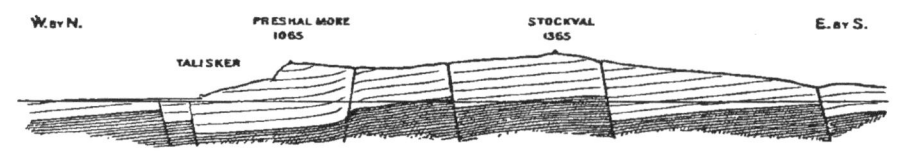

Fig. 3.—Section from Talisker Bay through Preshal More and Stockval to the Eynort River, to illustrate the structure of the basalt plateaux. The general dip is westerly, while the important faults usually throw down to the east. It is probable that the base of the volcanic series is in no place very far below sea-level. Scale, 1 inch to a mile.

The same reasons which make it impossible to frame a just estimate of the thickness of the volcanic series also preclude its subdivision. Excepting only some rather important accumulations of volcanic agglomerate which occur at the base of the series in the central mountain district, all intercalations of pyroclastic and stratified deposits among the lavas are minor and strictly local incidents which cannot be correlated with one another. The lavas themselves show on the whole a remarkable uniformity of general characters, and such varieties as occur we have not been able to connect with different horizons in the series. Even the division into a Lower and an Upper group, well marked in Antrim, cannot be made out in Skye. More accurately, it can be made out in one locality only, where a group of acid volcanic rocks is interposed in the midst of the basalts, and may possibly correspond with the rhyolites, etc., which in Antrim occur between the two divisions of the basalts.

It has long been recognised that the British Tertiary volcanic rocks were *of subaërial origin.* Professor Judd and Sir A. Geikie have both pointed out in more than one place the abundant evidence of this offered in all parts of the region; and the contrast with undoubted submarine volcanic series, such as those of Lower Palæozoic age in North Wales and elsewhere, is sufficiently marked. In the Tertiary area we find on the one hand no marine deposits interbedded among the lavas, and on the other hand, what is even more convincing, the direct evidence that at many stages, which represent short pauses in the long succession of eruptions, individual flows remained as actual land-surfaces for sufficient time to allow of the formation of a soil and the growth of terrestrial vegetation. The only detrital and sedimentary accumulations which occur are

* *Amer. Journ. Sci.* (3), vol. xii., p. 419 : 1876.

certain river-gravels and lacustrine deposits, always of local distribution.

The evidence of terrestrial conditions afforded by the contemporaneous weathering of the basalts and the growth of vegetation is particularly well marked in Antrim; and in that district a continuous group of clays, lithomarges, pisolitic iron-ores, etc., including a tuff with good plant remains, is traceable throughout a large part of the area. In Skye, where the lavas are perhaps thicker, they seem to have been poured out with fewer, or at least shorter, pauses. Clays are found, however, in some parts of the area, as will be noticed below, and vegetable remains are also known in numerous places. The plant-beds of Skye have not yielded specimens comparable in perfection with those from Ballypallidy in Antrim, Ardtun Head in Mull, and the Isle of Canna, by which the Eocene age of the volcanic series has been determined;[*] but thin beds of lignite and coal are found not infrequently in some parts of the island. Coal has been worked at Portree Harbour, Camastianavaig, Strathaird, etc.,[†] but only on a small scale, the beds, though sometimes as much as a foot thick, having no great lateral extent. The coal is usually impure, but this is not always the case; at An Ceannaich, south of Dunvegan Head, for instance, Sir A. Geikie has remarked a seam of coal, about a foot thick, of remarkable purity. He cites this as an example of a mode of occurrence not infrequent, the carbonaceous band forming the highest member of a small group of sediments intercalated between two flows of basalt.[‡]

Concerning the accumulations of vegetable origin, we have nothing to add to the brief accounts given by Macculloch,[§] Sir A. Geikie,[||] and others. It is a fact perhaps worthy of notice that the carbonaceous deposits associated with the basalt group are quite as much mineralised as some of those in the Jurassic strata (*see* analyses), and seams from 1 to 3

	I.	A.
Water,	10·00	11·494
Gas,	36·40	35·077
Residual Carbon,	50·16	45·183
Ash,	3·44	8·246
	100·00	100·000
Specific gravity,	...	1·373

I. Lignite, Ardmore Point, Vaternish; "in a bed 18 inches thick, mostly tree trunks, overlaid by a bed of amygdaloid, with an intervening bed of red clay one foot thick": anal. Heddle, *Mineralogy of Scotland*, vol. ii., p. 183: 1901.

A. Lignite, Brora, Sutherland; in Jurassic strata: *ibid.*

[*] See Starkie Gardner and von Ettingshausen, *Monograph of the British Eocene Flora*, vol. ii., *Palæontograph. Soc.*: 1883-1886.

[†] At several places in Skye, including Strathaird, inconstant seams of coal in the Jurassic have also been worked.

[‡] *Quart. Journ. Geol. Soc.*, vol. lii., p. 341: 1896.

[§] *Descr. of West. Isl. Scot.*, vol. i., pp. 360-362: 1819.

[||] *Quart. Journ. Geol. Soc.*, vol. lii., pp. 341, 342: 1896.

inches thick in some places consist of very pure coal. Coal of less pure nature may form beds of six inches or even a foot in thickness. These carbonaceous deposits are often associated with thin stratified (lacustrine) tuffs, or again with volcanic (fluviatile) conglomerates, as already noticed.

It has been stated above that the basic lavas were poured forth, not from large orifices, with their external apparatus of cone and crater, such as in popular parlance are connoted by the term volcano, but from *fissures*, the insignificance of which individually was more than compensated for by their vast number. The grounds for this statement are, in brief: the enormous volume and extent of the extravasated lavas as a whole, in contrast with the limited dimensions of the several flows which collectively build up the pile; the almost total absence of the pyroclastic accumulations which are the chief products of most volcanic vents of the central type; and the fact that the lavas, as a group, show no indication whatever of thickening towards particular centres and dying out as we recede from such points. They show, indeed, as has been remarked above, no sign of dying out at all: the area which they now occupy in Skye is certainly only a part of their original extent, and probably but one relic among others of a continuous lavafield of vastly greater dimensions.

It is necessary to say a few words about the supposed basal wrecks of large central volcanoes, upon which Professor Judd has laid much stress in developing his views of British Tertiary vulcanicity. One of these is situated in Skye, and consists of the large masses of gabbro and granite which constitute the mountain tract, these representing, in that geologist's view, the core of a volcano which once rose 12,000 or 15,000 feet above a base about thirty miles in diameter. Professor Judd's papers, as well as those by Sir Archibald Geikie combating his conclusions, are cited in the Appendix. It will be sufficient in this place to say that our survey proves these plutonic rocks, both gabbro and granite, to be *younger* than any extravasated lavas in Skye. Partly they break abruptly through the older strata, though without any indication that their molten magmas ever found exit at the surface above; partly, and more usually, they are intruded as large irregular sheets or lacolites at or near the base of the volcanic group. In both modes of occurrence they produce intense metamorphism in the volcanic rocks in their neighbourhood, and enclose numerous patches of those rocks, also in a highly metamorphosed condition. We shall have occasion to remark below that there are both gabbros and granites, nowhere exposed at the surface, belonging to an earlier date; but, as the evidence for the existence of these is their occurrence as fragments in the agglomerates at the base of the volcanic series, they are manifestly *older* than any of the volcanic rocks. If, as is possible, there do exist plutonic rocks of the same general age as the basaltic and other lavas, representing the unexhausted portion of a great subterranean reservoir from which those lavas were drawn, they must be situated at a great depth, and must have an enormously greater extent than the gabbro and granite masses of the Skye mountains. Also, in view of the great predominance of basic types among the lavas both of Skye and of other parts of the "petrographical province," it is clear that, among such hypothetical plutonic masses, granite can play at most a very subordinate rôle.

We may picture the channels through which the lavas rose to the then surface as ordinarily straight vertical fissures, which would naturally be occupied, when volcanic activity finally died out, by the latest uprise of the molten magma: in other words, they must be represented now by dykes of the same general composition as the extravasated lavas themselves. Such dykes are often seen in profusion where the lavas have been stripped by erosion from the adjacent rocks. They are of moderate width, a few feet at most, running in nearly straight lines in directions which do not vary much from N.N.W.–S.S.E., or N.W.–S.E., and composed of basalt and dolerite. It is not to be assumed that all dykes in the district answering to this description represent feeders of the lava-flows: we shall have to point out below that some were possibly feeders of the intrusive sills, while very many—probably the majority—are of still later date. Generally speaking, the number of dykes which traverse the lava-series becomes smaller, in any given locality, as we pass upward. This is very largely due to the resistance offered by the often massive intruded sills to the passage of later dykes; but no doubt it is owing also in some degree to the fact that those dykes which represent the feeders of the lavas necessarily terminate each at its appropriate flow.

It would be satisfactory to verify in some instances by ocular demonstration the presumed continuity of dyke and lava-flow, but no undoubted example of this has come under our notice. There would be in any case small chance of the relation being often displayed, and it is to be remembered that the lavas, in consequence of their proneness to disintegration under subaërial agencies, are rarely well exposed. All the salient features in the basalt country are formed by the intrusive sills, and for long distances the lavas themselves are never seen except perhaps in the bed of an occasional burn.

It appears that the form of the upward channels, while in the great majority of cases a straight fissure, was liable to some modification in form in traversing certain rocks. An interesting illustration of this occurs to the south of Creag Strollamus, in the Broadford district. The base of the lavas is here seen resting on the Torridon Sandstone, which in this part of Skye is a massive, close-grained grit, and very near this spot passes locally into quartzite. This rock, as we shall have occasion to note in a later chapter, is of a singularly obdurate nature as regards admitting the passage of dykes. At this place, extending for 500 yards along the N.W. side of Allt Fearna, we have a surface of Torridon Sandstone from which the lavas have been stripped away. With the sandstone we see little patches of basalt, the largest not much over a hundred yards in length. They resemble the lavas which come on in force a short distance away, but they are not outliers of them. They do not lie on the surface of the sandstone, but traverse it and are involved with it in an intricate fashion. The larger outcrops are long in comparison with their breadth, and their long axes have the direction of the dykes of the district. They are too irregular in outline to be termed dykes, but we must regard them as the analogues of the dykes seen in other kinds of country-rock, and as representing the channels by which the lavas rose through the Torridon Sandstone at this place. It is noteworthy that in this neighbourhood, *e.g.* N.E. of Loch Cùil na Creag, the lavas occasionally enclose fragments of sandstone. In general the lavas of the district are remarkably free from inclusions of any kind.

Another locality which exhibits remarkable relations between the lavas and the rocks through which they have been erupted is the northern slope of Creagan Dubha,* the basaltic crags immediately north of Beinn Dearg Mhòr (of Strath). Here several small patches of grit, probably Liassic, are involved in the lavas. As they are found up to about 200 feet from the base of the lava-group, their presence is not easily explained.

The *thickness and extent of the individual flows* is a question of importance with reference to the hypothesis of fissure-eruptions. The evidence on this point is chiefly of an indirect kind, for it is not always possible to determine by inspection the actual line of junction of two flows, and, as has been said, exposures showing any considerable total thickness of the lavas are rare. A criterion often applicable in other regions, viz. the vesicular or scoriaceous character of the upper and lower surfaces of a flow, fails us here, because the lavas are as a rule vesicular throughout. This fact is perhaps sufficient in itself to suggest that the flows are thin and numerous, and more positive testimony to the same effect is not wanting. We shall describe later the important group of dolerite sills which are intruded with remarkable regularity along the bedding of the lavas. In some places these sills are of small thickness, and are intruded at short intervals in the vertical succession. If we assume that the lava between two such sills represents in each case a single flow, we find that the average thickness of the flows may be about 20 feet or somewhat less. This is probably an over-estimate, for we are scarcely warranted in assuming that every divisional surface between the lava-flows has been injected with the sill-magma.

In one place, as will be shown later, we get a more definite insight into the manner in which the great mass of basalts is built up by many small overlapping flows. This is in An Fhionn-choire, on the northern border of the Cuillins, where we have intercalated among the basic lavas a group of rhyolitic and other rocks which are very different from them. Here it is seen that these acid rocks dovetail into the basalts in a fashion which proves that the latter, as well as the former, are of very complex constitution, consisting

* The Ordnance Survey does not place the name correctly : on the six-inch map the crags are called Coire Garbh, this name belonging to the corrie on the east.

of many comparatively thin sheets which rapidly thin out in a lateral direction (*see* Fig. 9, below).

In other places, and especially in the Talisker district, the individual flows may be picked out by the effects of contemporaneous atmospheric weathering, which has produced advanced decomposition in the upper surface of one flow before it was covered by another. Here again we find ample confirmation of the statement that the great thickness and extent of the basalt group results only from the superposition and overlapping of a vast number of separate flows, each of which is of very insignificant dimensions.

CHAPTER II.

Volcanic Agglomerates, Tuffs, and Conglomerates.

In this and the three chapters next following we shall describe in detail the volcanic rocks of Skye. Departing to some extent for convenience from strict chronological order, we shall treat these rocks as follows:—First, the pyroclastic accumulations, which, though not confined to one horizon, have their principal representatives at the base of the whole series; second, the basic lavas which make up the greater part of the succession; and third, the trachytic and rhyolitic rocks intercalated in the midst of the sequence. While the basic lavas have what may be termed a *regional* distribution, and there is no reason other than the geographical one for treating separately those of the Isle of Skye, the other rocks enumerated represent purely *local* episodes connected with the special focus of igneous activity of Central Skye. This distinction is essential to an understanding of the true relationship of the several groups of rocks, and, as already intimated, we shall apply it also to the various groups of intrusions to be dealt with subsequently.

Disregarding for the present the rhyolitic and trachytic rocks to be treated in Chapter V., one of the most striking features of the volcanic series of Skye taken as a whole is the *comparative scarcity of fragmental accumulations*. Throughout the greater part of its extent, so far as the detailed survey has gone, the succession of basic lavas is found to be almost unbroken by any intercalation of volcanic tuff, breccia, or agglomerate. Only occasionally, and as a rule at a low horizon, do we meet with a thin and inconstant bed among the lavas which tells of a local outburst of a more energetic kind; and only at or near the actual base of the series do we encounter pyroclastic accumulations of any important magnitude and extent. The general absence of fragmental volcanic rocks is quite in accord with the tranquil welling out of the extravasated material which characterises fissure-eruptions in other countries; and it is also consistent with what is known of like cases that such an extensive and long-continued outpouring of lava should be ushered in by eruptions of a more vigorous and indeed violently explosive nature. The vast fissure-eruptions of Wyoming and Idaho, for example, were preceded by explosive outbursts which gave rise to the breccias of the Absaroka Range. The extreme violence of these early eruptions in Skye is attested by the tumultuous accumulations of shattered blocks and fragments of all sizes, which in two or three places rest on the Jurassic and other strata and attain a thickness of many hundreds of feet. We obtain additional evidence, and also some insight into the nature of these eruptions, from the *actual vents* which are still to be detected in more than one instance. It will be convenient to notice the largest and most important of these vents before proceeding to describe the more or less clearly bedded pyroclastic accumulations.

The largest area of volcanic agglomerate in Skye lies immediately south of the eastern Red Hills of Strath and *north-west of Loch Kilchrist*, about $2\frac{1}{2}$ miles from Broadford. It is bounded on the north side by the subsequently intruded granite of Beinn Dearg Bheag, etc., and its precise relations to the neighbouring stratified rocks, Cambrian limestones and Lias, are in some other places obscured by other intrusions and by faults; but there is sufficient evidence to show that, excluding the narrow strip extending north-westward, the agglomerate cannot be regarded as a bedded or lenticular mass. The main body breaks abruptly through the adjacent strata, and must have a highly inclined or quasi-vertical boundary with a roughly cylindrical form (Fig. 4). Its extent,

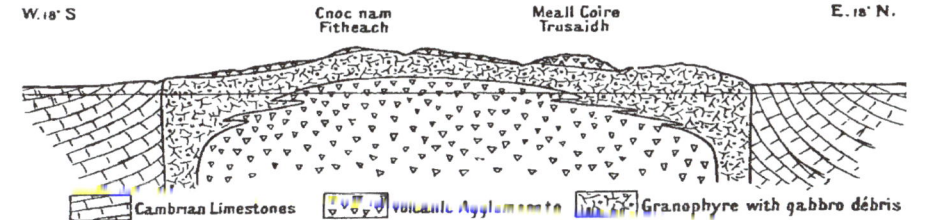

FIG. 4.—Section across the volcanic vent of Kilchrist; showing the volcanic agglomerate breaking through a sharp anticline of Cambrian limestone, and itself invaded by a later intrusion of a peculiar granophyre, full of débris of gabbro, to be described later. Scale, $1\frac{1}{2}$ inch to a mile.

measured north-eastward from the high-road at Kilbride, is more than $2\frac{1}{4}$ miles, but it is clear that its northern portion has been cut off by the subsequent intrusion of the granite, which sharply truncates the boundary of the agglomerate as shown on the map. The surface of the mass is broken into small irregular hills, rounded, but with a characteristic "knobby" appearance, contrasting equally with the smooth slope of the granite above and the scar-like spread of the limestones on the opposite side of the strath (Fig. 5).

The agglomerate forming the large mass[*] consists of material partly volcanic, partly non-volcanic, closely commingled. Of the recognisable elements basic lavas are the most abundant, in pieces ranging in size from small fragments to blocks a foot or more in diameter, and in some places as much as five or six feet. They seem in all cases to be derived from the breaking up of pre-exist-

[*] Its true nature was first recognised by Prof. Judd, *Quart. Journ. Geol. Soc.*, vol. xxx., p. 255 : 1874. It has been described by Sir A. Geikie, *Trans. Roy. Soc. Edin.*, vol. xxxv., pp. 108-110 : 1888.

ing masses, true bombs not being recognised. Sandstones also figure largely among the fragments. Most of them are probably from Jurassic rocks, but the Torridonian seems also to be represented, sometimes in the form of quartzite. Jurassic shales are occasionally found. Other rocks occur only sparingly, and it is remarkable that the Cambrian limestones are rarely met with. The few pieces of these latter were found in the western portion of the mass only. All these larger elements, usually constituting a large proportion of the whole, are embedded in a fine-textured matrix of a dull dark green colour. Nowhere is there any indication of stratification or of any sorting of the coarser and finer materials; although there are places where no conspicuous fragments meet the eye, so that the rock might be described petrographically as becoming a tuff rather than an agglomerate.

Embedded in the mass at various spots are patches of basic lavas 100 or 200 yards in length, which we cannot suppose to have been thrown up in an explosion. They have a lenticular shape, and are sometimes bounded by lines which might be laid

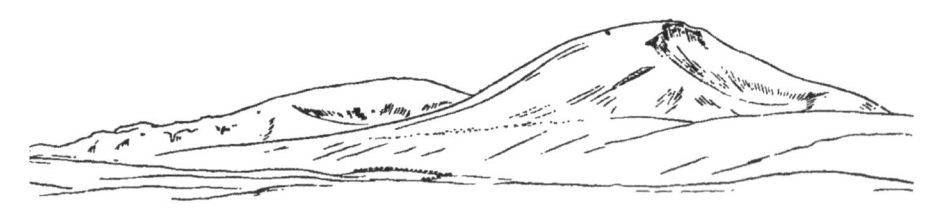

FIG. 5.—Contrasted outlines of volcanic agglomerate and granite, as seen from Broadford.
The low broken hills to the left mark the situation of the Kilchrist vent, and are composed of volcanic agglomerate. The smooth outline of the granite is seen in Beinn Dearg Bheag and Beinn na Caillich, which form part of the Red Hills. In one place on Beinn na Caillich this smooth outline is broken by the outcrop of a large dyke intersecting the granite.

down on the map as faults, but are not to be traced farther. In one place, just N.W. of Meall Coire Trusaidh, a patch of Torridonian quartzite nearly 100 yards long is included in the same fashion. These relatively large enclosed patches must be explained by supposing that the vent has been enlarged by successive stages, and that portions of the bounding wall which fell in have sometimes escaped destruction by later outbursts. It is important to notice that the large blocks in the agglomerate and a considerable proportion of the fragments of medium size must have been derived not from below but *from above*. They came from the breaking up of rocks, now removed, which were traversed by the upward prolongation of the funnel. This appears from the large amount of basalt obviously derived from the shattering of some old *coulée*, and equally from the composition of the non-volcanic element in the agglomerate. As regards the latter, the map shows that the vent, as we now see it, is drilled through the Cambrian limestones almost exclusively, touching the

B

Jurassic only for a short distance at the western edge: still Jurassic rocks are, after basalt, the most important constituent of the agglomerate, while the limestones are practically not represented. It is clear that the Jurassic sandstone of the agglomerate, like much of the basalt, came from overlying strata now removed. The occasional presence of fragments of granite and other acid igneous rocks raises a different question, to be discussed later.

The finely divided material which forms the matrix seems to be in the main of basaltic composition. In part it may have been produced by the mutual concussion and friction of the blocks and fragments, which are now mostly of sub-angular shape; in part it probably represents true volcanic dust thrown up directly by the eruptions. To this later origin also we may ascribe many of the smaller fragments of basalt, and especially those having a highly vesicular or scoriaceous texture.

It is interesting to note the close resemblance between the Kilchrist vent and that, of similar large dimensions and doubtless of the same age, in the central part of the Isle of Arran.* In the latter, as in the former, the enclosed fragments embrace various sedimentary as well as igneous rocks; and some of them, including patches of large extent, must have fallen into the vent from above. There are also, as in Skye, fragments of plutonic rocks identical in character with those which at a later epoch were intruded in the immediate vicinity. The matrix of the Arran agglomerate contains much more non-igneous material (quartz-grains, etc.) than that of Kilchrist, but there is the same ultimate base of finely-divided basaltic tuff. A curious point of similarity is the fact that the Arran vent is surrounded by a partial ring of later intrusive rocks, chiefly a granite which in places is greatly modified by basic xenoliths. The corresponding phenomena in the case of the Kilchrist vent will be described in their place below (Chap. XI.).

Of the material ejected from the great Kilchrist vent over the surrounding country but scanty relics remain, owing to the subsequent invasion of granite and to the extensive erosion which has affected the whole district in later times. A strip of bedded agglomerate, however, runs along the south-western border of the granite, and is continuous on the map with the agglomerate filling the vent. It overlies Jurassic strata with only a small thickness of basalt intervening. Its full thickness is not seen, owing to its being cut off by the granite, but its evident prolongation northward, along the western base of Creagan Dubha, is at first some hundreds of feet thick, rapidly thinning away. It probably did not extend much farther, and, as Sir A. Geikie has pointed out, at An Carnach, in the Strathaird peninsula, only two miles west of the vent, a thick series of basaltic lavas rests directly on the Jurassic. The relics of volcanic rocks enclosed in the granite on the N.E. side of Beinn na Caillich prove in like manner that the agglomerate has not extended

* Peach and Gunn, *Quart. Journ. Geol. Soc.*, vol. lvii., pp. 226-229 : 1901 ; Gunn, *The Geology of North Arran* (*Mem. Geol. Sur. Scot.*), pp. 79-83 ; and Harker, *ibid.*, pp. 103, 104 : 1903.

more than 1½ mile from the vent in a northerly direction. This rapid thinning away of very thick accumulations of volcanic agglomerate is quite in accord with what is seen elsewhere in the district; and the outburst thus indicated, the earliest manifestation of volcanic activity in this neighbourhood, may well have been one of important magnitude. That activity was renewed at this vent at a later time is not improbable in itself, and seems necessary to account for the profusion of basalt blocks and fragments in the volcanic pipe; but any direct evidence of such later eruptions in the form of bedded agglomerates has been destroyed by erosion. By analogy we may infer that the chief outbursts were comprised within the earlier part of the volcanic period.

Another locality in Skye where the actual form and relations of a volcanic vent are partially displayed is on the *Sound of Soay*. Along this part of the coast-section the base of the volcanic series rises above sea-level, and for some distance a strip of Mesozoic strata intervenes between the basalts and the underlying Torridonian. It is of special interest as one of the few places in the Western Isles where deposits of Cretaceous age are to be seen. This strip of coast was surveyed by Mr Clough, who has supplied the notes which follow. It will be seen that this vent is of much smaller dimensions than that of Kilchrist. Its position is marked by a small mass of agglomerate about 700 yards west of the mouth of Allt nan Leac, beneath the basalts, which pass over it unbroken. "It is about 40 yards broad, and has nearly vertical boundaries, both on the west and on the east. In all probability it belongs to a small volcanic vent or blowhole, which has broken through the adjacent Cretaceous and Liassic beds . . . . The materials in this agglomerate comprise blocks of soft red sandstone, some of them broken and angular and several yards long, which are probably of Cretaceous age; also many lumps of chert, containing sponge spicules and foraminiferæ like those in the Cretaceous cherts found *in situ* near at hand, and a few pieces of quartzite and soft green sandstone. Some of the pieces of chert contain red cores, the nature of which has not been determined. No fragments of igneous rock were noticed; but, besides the basalt which overlies the agglomerate, there were an extensive sheet of basalt at the bottom and a thin basalt dyke at the west side."

On the east side of the mass just described is a bedded agglomerate underlying the basalts and possibly ejected from the same vent, though the occurrence of fragments of igneous rock presents an interesting point of difference. "It is in places 20 feet thick, but in others only two or three feet, or even not represented at all. In it are noticed many pieces of highly vesicular decomposed igneous rock and others of Torridonian grit, red sandstone, and limestone, the two last-mentioned rocks having apparently been derived from Cretaceous and Liassic beds like those which occur below. The agglomerate is injected with various thin irregular squirts of basalt; and in one inaccessible cliff there is a remarkable aggregation of pieces of limestone, some of them six feet long, lying in a matrix which seemed from below as if it might be basalt."

It is clear that the explosive outburst to which these accumulations of coarse agglomerate are to be attributed belongs to the very earliest stage of volcanic activity at this place. The occurrence of fragments of fossiliferous Mesozoic rocks recalls the large volcanic vent of Arran, which has preserved in the same way the only direct evidence of the former existence in that island of Rhætic, Liassic, and Cretaceous strata.

We pass to those pyroclastic accumulations which, in contradistinction to the contents of the vents, we have called bedded. By this term we do not imply the existence of a visible stratified disposition, but merely that the deposits in question occupy a definite horizon in the volcanic succession, usually at or near the base of the series. They have, as a rule, an evidently lenticular shape, sometimes thinning away rapidly from a central point.

The bedded agglomerate seen on the south-west and west border of the eastern Red Hills of Strath has already been mentioned, and calls for no detailed description. Generally speaking it consists of a dull green matrix of basaltic composition enclosing abundant fragments of lava. Comparing it with the agglomerate of the great vent close by, we miss the large basalt blocks and the profusion of sandstone fragments which characterise the latter; a circumstance which might be anticipated after the remarks made above.

Farther to the north-east, near the high-road which there follows the coast-line, in a strip of country much broken by faults, we find certain agglomerates which are worthy of passing remark. Their relations are obscured by intrusions as well as by faulting; and a further difficulty, experienced also in some other parts of the district, arises from brecciation due to mechanical causes. For instance, a rock on the shore north-east of Creag Strollamus, taken at first as a volcanic agglomerate composed of acid igneous rocks, proved upon closer examination to be merely a crushed and brecciated granite (see Plate VII.), and specimens from several other localities gave a like result, while others did not permit of any certain conclusion. Nevertheless, the existence of agglomerates containing abundant fragments of acid rocks is easily established, these being in places free from any effects of crushing, especially when they are caught up as patches in the gabbro and granite of the district. One specimen sliced [6836] shows numerous irregularly shaped fragments of pink granophyre, up to an inch or two in diameter, set in a dark greenish grey matrix. The matrix itself is chiefly of acid material also, with abundant chips of felspar and minute rock-fragments; but there is also some admixture of basic tuff-material, besides a few recognisable fragments of basalt. Rocks of this type, containing granite, granophyre, etc., occur at several localities.

An area of volcanic agglomerate and tuff, with an extent of more than one mile and a half, is seen in the upper parts of *Coire Coinnich and Coire na Seilg*, and forms the north-western spur of Belig. Its original relations are nowhere displayed, except to the

PLATE I.

Exposed surface of volcanic agglomerate, Druim an Eidhne.

north-east of Belig, where it dips under the basaltic lavas. Farther west it is covered by gabbro, and everywhere it is underlain by granite, both of later age. It seems highly probable, however, that the upper and lower surfaces of the lenticular mass have themselves determined in great part the horizons at which the two plutonic rocks were intruded; so that little of the agglomerate is cut off, and the maximum thickness seen, some 1000 or 1200 feet, represents approximately the original total. Where thickest, the material consists of the usual dirty-green matrix enclosing abundant fragments which range in size up to blocks of more than two feet in diameter. In addition to basalt, gabbro is extremely abundant, while in some parts quartz-porphyry and granite are well represented. In places the agglomerate gives way to a grey tuff of acid composition without conspicuous fragments. It is especially noticeable that the large fragments become fewer as the deposit thins out westward and dies away (or is obliquely cut off) on the ridge of Garbh-bheinn.

The other principal mass of volcanic agglomerate and tuff in the district is exposed above Strath na Creitheach in the slope leading up to *Druim an Eidhne.* This also is overlain by gabbro and underlain by granite, but in this case the intrusive rocks have evidently cut into the agglomerate much more than in the former, and what is left probably does not adequately represent the original dimensions. The broad spread occupying the rough slope to the north-west of Loch na Creitheach has a diameter of about a mile and a thickness of probably 300 or 400 feet; in addition, a narrow strip extends for another mile just below the gabbro of Druim an Eidhne. The greater part of the mass may fairly be termed agglomerate, since it contains abundant fragments of various sizes set in a greyish green or dull green matrix of finer material (Plate I.). Among the fragments gabbro figures largely, as well as basalt. In places we find instead of agglomerate a fine-textured tuff, thoroughly compacted, with conspicuous bands of darker and lighter grey. From the irregular distribution of this tuff, and the conflicting dips which it shows, it seems probable that it has been broken up by some outburst from below or by an uneven settling down, suggesting that the actual vent of eruption is concealed below. The agglomerate is not perceptibly less coarse in the narrow strip along Druim an Eidhne than in the broad area below; and the same remark applies to an isolated patch a quarter of a mile wide and more than a mile in length wholly enclosed in the gabbro farther west. Here the pieces of gabbro and basalt are sometimes three or four feet across. These facts may be taken to indicate that the agglomerate actually seen is only the relics of a more extensive mass.

It may be noted, without going further into detail, that numerous small patches of agglomerate, breccia, and tuff occur entangled in the gabbro throughout the Cuillins, often in a highly metamorphosed state. They occur not only near the boundary of the gabbro area, but far in the interior, and at various altitudes. The highest summit of all, for example, is formed by a metamorphosed volcanic breccia.* Many of these patches are associated with basaltic lavas, but otherwise their original relations are lost. All these pyroclastic rocks in the mountains seem to be of basic composition; the recognisable fragments are of basalt and often abundant gabbro.

Although the relics of the volcanic rocks in the mountain tract are severed from their original associations, the structure of the great gabbro mass in which they have been entangled, to be described later, permits us to assert that the disturbance caused by its intrusion was restricted within certain limits. We cannot suppose that the small patches of volcanic breccia and agglomerate now seen high up in the northern and western Cuillins have been brought up from the base of the whole volcanic series. These patches must belong to various horizons in that series; and we learn that explosive eruptions, though not equal in magnitude and violence to the earliest ones, *recurred at various epochs* among the fissure-eruptions of basic lavas. These small outbursts were principally confined to what is now *the mountain-district*. Here the earliest paroxysmal eruptions were chiefly concentrated, and attained their greatest violence, and here too minor eruptions of like type were resumed locally and occasionally during the volcanic period. The area which was subsequently to be affected by the great plutonic intrusions was already marked out as a special centre of igneous activity.

It is highly probable from the observed field-relations that the two last-mentioned large masses of volcanic agglomerate, that of Coire Choinnich and Coire na Seilg and that of Druim an Eidhne and Loch na Croitheach mark the sites of concealed volcanic vents similar to that of Loch Kilchrist and perhaps not inferior in size. This appears from the lenticular forms of the masses, which reach a great thickness in the centre and rapidly thin away in every direction. It is suggested equally by the large size of many of the enclosed blocks and, we may add, by the occurrence among the other fragments of pieces of plutonic rocks, often in great abundance. There are, however, in Skye fragmental volcanic accumulations, seemingly remote from any large vent, which have a more decidedly bedded habit, and do not thin away so rapidly. These show in many places an evident stratification, though usually of a rude kind. They do not enclose such large blocks as are found in the localities already noticed, and the fragments in them do not present the same variety, gabbro and granite in particular being absent.

The best example of those truly bedded tuffs and agglomerates is that exposed along the coast *between Portree and the Braes*. Sir A. Geikie estimates its maximum thickness at about 200 feet on the south side of Portree Harbour, but it is usually much less. It is probably continuous at the same horizon, at or near the base of the whole volcanic series, to as far as Eilean Tioram at least, four miles S.S.E. from the former locality; but in this neighbourhood it is only a few feet thick. The section at Camas Bàn, Portree

* This point, Sgùrr Alaisdair, 3275 feet, is not named on the Ordnance map : it is 200 yards N.E. by E. from the summit of Sgùrr Sgùmain.

Harbour, is shown on Fig. 6. The general mass of the rock is a basic tuff of a dull dirty-green colour or, in the upper part, red and ferruginous, probably from contemporaneous weathering. This deeply weathered rock recalls in its general appearance some of the volcanic clays of Antrim. A specimen from Leac Agamnha, examined by Mr Player, yielded about 30 per cent. of alumina. In the upper part of the Camas Bàn section conspicuous enclosed fragments are scattered only sparingly, but lower down they are more numerous, and include blocks of several inches diameter. Bedding is more or less evident in the finer portion of the accumu-

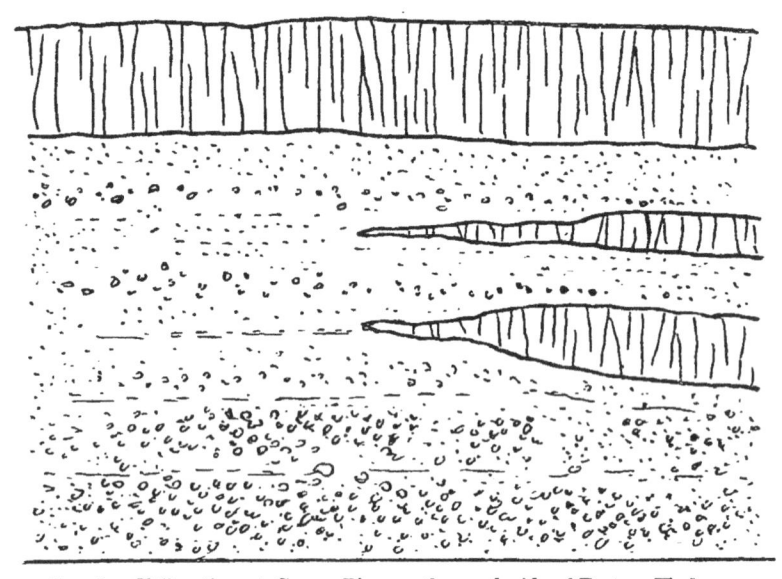

FIG. 6.—Cliff-section at Camas Bàn, on the south side of Portree Harbour; about 60 or 70 feet high. This shows the pyroclastic deposit covered by an intrusive sill of dolerite and invaded by two others.

lation; and even in the coarser, which may be termed agglomerate, a certain stratification is apparent in the distribution of the enclosed blocks. The blocks and smaller fragments consist almost, if not quite, wholly of basaltic rocks, some compact but many scoriaceous, vesicular, amygdaloidal, or pumiceous. Only one specimen was examined microscopically. "The slice [6662] shows it to be essen- "tially a brown glass with only occasional microscopic crystals of a "basic plagioclase. It has been highly vesicular, and the vesicles "are now filled by various secondary products, including a chloritic "mineral, nearly colourless and singly refracting in thin section, and "a zeolite."* At one locality on the coast of Portree Harbour larger enclosed blocks occur, and Sir A. Geikie places here the vent of eruption. We have not traced the deposit in the northward

* *Quart. Journ. Geol. Soc.*, vol. lii., p. 348 : 1896.

direction. Large blocks are sometimes found in places where the accumulation is of small thickness: they occur, for instance, up to a foot in diameter on the shore at Eilean Tioram. Here, too, are broken seams of coal, two or three inches thick, in the agglomerate, a feature observed at some other localities.

It is necessary here to make some remark on the occurrence of *gabbro and granite as fragments in the volcanic agglomerates of the large vents.* All these pyroclastic accumulations are demonstrably much older than any gabbro or granite intrusions seen in Skye. The conclusion is inevitable that there exists, or has existed, in this district *an earlier suite of plutonic rocks, both gabbro and granite, which have nowhere been brought to light by erosion.* Any data concerning these concealed plutonic masses, other than the proofs of their existence, are naturally scanty, but are not entirely lacking. Firstly, we find that they were petrographically the prototypes of the later plutonic masses, which we can observe directly in the same district. The gabbros are not distinguishable from those which build the Cuillins; the acid rocks are hornblende-granites and granophyres identical in characters with those forming the Red Hills, and having similar spherulitic, felsitic, and porphyritic modifications in places. Further, fragments of these rocks are nowhere found, so far as our observations go, in the breccias and agglomerates occurring outside the mountain tract; which suggests that the areal distribution of the earlier concealed plutonic masses has a general correspondence with that of the later and exposed ones. We may even extend this remark to the gabbro and the granite severally, for each is found in the agglomerates only in the neighbourhood of visible intrusions of its own kind: gabbro fragments are never found in the eastern Red Hills, nor granite fragments in the Cuillins; while in the Coire Choinnich and Belig patch, on the border-line between the Red Hills and the gabbro mountains, both rocks are represented. Finally, it is of interest to find in this last-named locality many fragments of gabbro veined by granite; from which we may infer that in the earlier, as in the later, suite of plutonic rocks the basic rock preceded the acid one in order of formation.

Among the basaltic rocks which occupy the extensive tract to the west and north of the Cuillins, pyroclastic accumulations play but a very insignificant part. In the area mapped there are indeed only three or four localities that require notice. One of these is Sgùrr an Duine, on the coast between Loch Brittle and Loch Eynort, where a small patch of volcanic agglomerate is seen. Since it forms the top of a practically vertical cliff of 600 feet, and is covered by drift, its actual relations are not easily made out; but its lateral extension is not more than about 200 yards, and its maximum thickness perhaps 60 or 80 feet, its form being apparently lenticular. The material is wholly basaltic, including subangular blocks up to a foot or more in diameter. Two other occurrences are to be noted between Loch Eynort and Talisker. One is on

Beinn Bhreac, the highest point in this part of the plateau country. The summit is formed by a patch of volcanic agglomerate, some 300 yards long, composed of small basalt fragments, with some up to six inches diameter, often rounded, in an iron-stained matrix. The other locality is the conspicuous hill named Preshal Beg, about a mile and a half south of Talisker. This hill is built of a fine group of columnar dolerite sills, to be noticed in a later chapter, and immediately under these occurs a bed of volcanic agglomerate. Although probably not more than 25 feet thick, it can be traced right round the base of the hill, which is about 800 yards long. The best exposures are on the north side. The fragments are all of basalt, some as much as a foot in diameter, but mostly smaller. They are subangular or sometimes well rounded, especially in the case of the larger blocks. Although this agglomerate seems to have more of the form of a continuous bed than some others, it certainly does not extend far: Preshal More, barely a mile to the north, is made by the same group of columnar sills, but the agglomerate below has disappeared. In all these pyroclastic accumulations outside the mountain tract no single fragment of gabbro or granite has been found: the material consists wholly of volcanic rocks. This is in marked contrast with the agglomerates of the Cuillins and the Red Hills, and also with the deposits, not purely of pyroclastic origin, which we proceed to discuss.

The last fragmental rocks to be noticed in this place are *volcanic conglomerates*, and these, within the area surveyed, have a very restricted occurrence. A good place to study them is about two or three hundred yards north-east of Glen Brittle House, where they occur interbedded among the basaltic lavas a short distance up the two small burns which unite near the sheep-fold. A small cliff-section shows conglomerates with intercalated beds of laminated fine tuff, lying nearly horizontally. In the upper part the pebbles, with diameters up to two or three inches, are of basaltic lava, sometimes amygdaloidal, sandstone, and exceptionally granite. In the lower part they are sometimes more than six inches in diameter, and are chiefly of fine-grained grey gabbro and grit. All the pebbles have a thoroughly rounded shape, and are undoubtedly waterworn. They are thickly set in a greyish fine-textured matrix, apparently a basic tuff. The whole group has no great thickness, and cannot be followed far along the outcrop; being obliquely cut off both ways by the gabbro, which, as seen in Allt Coire na Banachdich, near the foot-bridge, has greatly metamorphosed the conglomerate. The same rocks, however, are seen in Allt a' Mhuillin, the next burn to the south, with a thickness of over 100 feet, though the top is cut off by the gabbro. They reappear half a mile further, again on the border of the gabbro, the pebbles here being almost wholly of sandstone. These three localities are in a N.N.W.-S.S.E. line, the last and highest being 500 feet above sea-level. This conglomerate has not been certainly detected elsewhere, except as a small patch enclosed in the gabbro of Coire Labain a mile farther east.

The curiously limited distribution of this conglomerate and the well-worn form of the pebbles point to the conclusion that we have here a portion of an old river-channel contemporaneous with the basaltic lavas; and this is in accord with the various facts which lead us to assign a subaërial origin to the whole volcanic group. It is also to be remarked that in the Isle of Canna, only 13 miles to the south-west, Sir A. Geikie* has found clear evidence of a powerful river which flowed westward over the lava-plains from a source in the mountains of Inverness-shire. The Glen Brittle conglomerate does not, like those of Canna, contain pebbles of rocks foreign to the island; but its pebbles are largely of rocks which, it is almost certain, could not be exposed to erosion in the neighbourhood at the date of the conglomerate; viz. the Jurassic and possibly Torridonian sandstones, which were already buried, and the earlier gabbro and granite, which have never been brought to light. The pebbles then must be derived at second hand, though almost contemporaneously, from a volcanic agglomerate or from more than one such source; a conclusion arrived at also by Sir A. Geikie for the local pebbles in the Canna conglomerates. That the materials reached Glen Brittle from some source to the east is quite in accord with what we have already seen of the petrographical characters of the agglomerates. That there are here no pebbles from still farther east is accounted for by the stream being a small one, possibly a tributary of the river of Canna.

Another equally interesting but less easily accessible occurrence is seen in the cliff a little south of Dùnan Earr an Sgùirr, between Loch Brittle and Loch Eynort. Here the little ravine of Allt Geodh' a' Ghamhna shows a section some 30 feet in height with the following succession, in descending order:

Basaltic lavas, with sills, above.	
Coal-seam, ...	0—3 in.
Pale yellowish grey coarse tuff, ...	1 ft.
Coal-seam, ...	0—3 in.
Conglomerate with tuff matrix, ...	6—7 ft.
Dull yellowish grey tuff without pebbles, with impure coal-seam (6 to 8 inches) in lower part, ...	5—7 ft.
Conglomerate with tuff matrix, ...	5—6 ft.
Tuff, as before, without pebbles, ...	2½—3 ft.
Conglomerate with tuff matrix, ...	about 9 ft.
Basaltic lavas, with sills, below.	

All the pebbles are well rolled. In the highest band of conglomerate they are closely set, and range up to 4 or 6 inches in diameter, consisting in about equal proportions of granite (with felsite) and a reddish quartzose grit (? Torridonian). In the two lower bands of conglomerate the pebbles range up to 10 or 12 inches in diameter, and are almost all of the grit. Here there is a rather larger proportion of matrix, and the conglomerate passes rather irregularly into the tuff devoid of pebbles.

* *Quart. Journ. Geol. Soc.*, vol. lii., pp. 354-373 : 1896. Similar fluviatile conglomerates occur at Fionn-chro in Rum and on the coast W. of Carsaig in Mull.

One other locality may be mentioned where conglomerates occur among the lavas. This is in the neighbourhood of Loch Cùil na Creig, a little west of Creag Strollamus and about 1½ mile north of Beinn na Caillich. The conglomerates occur at two horizons, but both very near the base of the group, which here rests on Torridon Sandstone. There seems to be no difficulty in supposing that the sandstone pebbles, which form the most conspicuous element of the deposit, were in this case derived from the near vicinity. They range up to as much as a foot in diameter. It is very interesting to find that in this locality, situated to the east of the central mountains, the conglomerates contain no fragments of gabbro, while they do contain abundantly in places fragments of granite and other acid rocks, some porphyritic, similar to those of later date in the immediate vicinity. These are found, together with abundant basalt, in the conglomerate of the higher horizon, exposed in and near Allt an Doire. The lower conglomerate, seen near the tarn, is wholly of Torridon sandstone pebbles with very little matrix.

The various pyroclastic accumulations in the vicinity of the large plutonic intrusions exhibit very marked effects of *thermal metamorphism*, and this is notably the case where patches of these rocks are completely enveloped in the gabbro of the Cuillins or the granite of the Red Hills. A summary account of these metamorphic phenomena will suffice in this place.

The fine-textured basic tuffs and the matrix of the volcanic agglomerates show in the more altered examples a partial recrystallisation. Perhaps the most characteristic change, however, is the production of minute flakes of brown mica, and this is often found in an early stage of the metamorphism.* A slice [7463] may show little angular red-brown patches, which are chips of lava, and owe their colour to a dense aggregate of minute biotite-flakes of metamorphic origin. Where fragments of felspar-crystals are enclosed in the tuff, they often have a very limpid appearance, as if cleared by the heat from their minute inclusions. The inclusions which they do contain are of relatively large size and of rounded shape.

The metamorphism of the distinct rock-fragments in the agglomerates needs no description in this place, since the alterations produced in the several rocks will be described in succeeding chapters. The pieces of basalt, for instance, show the same metamorphic changes that will be detailed below under the head of the basaltic lavas, including the conversion of zeolites to felspars in the amygdules and the frequent production of hornblende. The gabbro-fragments exhibit uralitisation of the augite and other familiar effects. Fragments of Liassic grits, when highly metamorphosed, are converted into quartzites with various accessory minerals, such

* The phenomena are generally comparable with those described in andesitic and basaltic tuffs of Lower Palæozoic age near the Shap granite in Westmorland. See Harker and Marr, *Quart. Journ. Geol. Soc.*, vol. xlvii., pp. 299, 300 : 1891 ; and vol. xlix., p. 361, Pl. xvii., Fig. 5 : 1893.

as biotite, zoisite, and perhaps sillimanite. These and some other phenomena may be well studied in the metamorphosed volcanic conglomerate seen in Allt Coire Banachdich, about 300 yards above the Glen Brittle road and just below a small foot-bridge.

In consequence of mechanical disturbances of a later date the volcanic agglomerates seem in some places to have suffered a considerable degree of *crushing and brecciation*; but, from the nature of these accumulations, it is not often possible to obtain very satisfactory evidence. It is very clear in a few places, where considerable strips of basalt and other rocks occur enclosed in the agglomerate. A good instance is seen in the upper part of the Allt Leth-pheiginne glen, to the north of Kilbride. Here an enclosed strip of the basaltic lavas, 70 or 80 yards wide and more than 200 yards in length, is brecciated throughout. Immediately to the south is a similar strip of felsite or fine granophyre, also brecciated and crushed. Other instances might be cited, but there is always some doubt as to how far the shattering of these enclosed patches may be referable to the epoch of the agglomerate itself.

CHAPTER III.

Basic Lavas: General Petrography.

We have now to consider more particularly the basic lavas, which are incomparably the most important products of the volcanic phase of activity, and in many respects constitute the most important group in the whole suite of Tertiary igneous rocks in our area. Their field-relations and their place in the succession have been sufficiently discussed. We have seen that in order of time they immediately follow the principal volcanic agglomerates and tuffs, and that probably with little or no interval, for in places fragmental accumulations are intercalated in the lower part of the lava group. These, however, at least outside the mountain tract, are of small extent and importance, and the most striking feature of the group is the great succession of basic lavas, broken, as a rule, only by innumerable intrusive sills of later date. The lavas rest then on the bedded volcanic agglomerates and tuffs where these occur; but in most places where the base is seen it reposes directly upon the old pre-Tertiary land-surface. We proceed to describe the essential petrographical characters of the basic lavas, reserving for the following chapter an account of the subsequent changes which they have undergone under the operation of various agencies.

We have to remark at the outset that the published descriptions of these basaltic lavas in Skye, and presumably in other parts of the British Tertiary province, require to be read with some discrimination, owing to the fact that the great prevalence of sill-formed intrusions in the lava group has not hitherto been sufficiently recognised. It is highly probable that for this reason the dolerite sills, of later date, have sometimes been treated as constituent parts of the succession of lavas. These sills, as we shall show hereafter, not only make up a large part of the total thickness, but form all the salient features of the plateau country (see Fig. 79, below). Except where good sections are exposed in some of the streams, it is possible to walk many miles over the peat-clad moors without seeing anything of the lavas, and a collection of specimens made in such a traverse might include only sill-rocks. In a better selected locality a considerable proportion of the intrusive rocks would still be collected with the extrusive.

The lavas are constantly of fine texture, and in most places, though not everywhere, amygdaloidal. The sills, on the other hand, usually show a more evidently crystalline texture, and rarely exhibit any conspicuous amygdaloidal character. The ophitic structure is much more commonly met with in the latter rocks than in the former, though it does not afford a conclusive test. Professor Judd has stated* that "ophitic varieties .... abound in, though they are not confined to, intrusive rocks; while rocks of granulitic structure . . . . are especially abundant among the lavas." In a later memoir† he speaks of the ophitic structure as one "characteristically exhibited by the basaltic lavas of Western Scotland." The former quotation expresses what is also the result of our own observations. The ophitic structure is certainly found in many of the lavas, but it is not characteristic of them as a group.

As seen in the field or in hand-specimens, only a small proportion of the lavas show conspicuous porphyritic crystals. The greater part of the rocks are amygdaloidal, the vesicular cavities, now occupied by zeolites, chlorites, calcite, quartz, etc., being usually from $\frac{1}{8}$ to $\frac{1}{2}$ inch long, though smaller ones are also found, and exceptionally some as much as two or three inches long. The smaller are often nearly spherical; the larger are ovoid. The contents of these amygdules will be considered below. The largest ones often have a vacant space in the interior, into which some of the secondary minerals project with good crystal-faces; but the vesicles of moderate and small size are rarely or never empty except from the destruction of their contents by weathering. The general mass of the rock is never of coarse texture. The freshest examples show a finely crystalline appearance and a nearly black colour; the more altered rocks are of dull aspect, with a dark-grey or greenish-grey tint, and more advanced decay may obscure the character of the rock further by a development of chloritic and ferruginous matter. The more amygdaloidal varieties are usually the more decomposed. Olivine, even when present in some abundance, is rarely to be detected by eye: in this respect the rocks differ from many European basalts and also from many of the basaltic dykes of Skye.

Although, as we have intimated, the lava series includes rocks with a considerable range of composition, from thoroughly basic types, often rich in olivine, to andesites, sometimes of highly felspathic nature, we have found it impossible to distinguish the several types systematically in the field and so to subdivide the group on the map. It had been hoped that the difficulty might be mastered by making use of the specific gravity of the rocks, which, with Walker's balance, can be estimated without great labour. In practice this has not been found to afford a sufficient criterion, although it enables us to separate the most basic types on the one hand and some of the least basic on the other. The amygdaloidal varieties, which prevail almost everywhere, must in all cases be rejected. Even in compact non-amygdaloidal rocks the same secondary changes which are partly answerable for the monotonous uniformity of appearance have often altered

* *Quart. Journ. Geol. Soc*, vol. xlii., p. 75 : 1886.
† *Quart. Journ. Geol. Soc.*, vol. xlv., 195 : 1889.

the density very sensibly, and in a manner for which we cannot make allowance. It may be remarked, however, that of lavas without conspicuous amygdules and not greatly decomposed the majority have specific gravities between 2·80 and 3·00, with an average of about 2·90. Ten specimens out of seventy gave figures above 3·00, the highest being 3·11. Those which fell below 2·80 include no doubt most of what might fairly be named augite-andesites, which are apparently not very numerous ; but they certainly include also some truly basic lavas of which the density has been reduced by partial decay.

There are no earlier published chemical analyses of the basic lavas of Skye, and this seems to be true also of the whole British Tertiary " province." Streng's* analysed rocks from Fingal's Cave in Staffa and the Giant's Causeway in Antrim may perhaps be lavas, but are more probably sills. An average example of the Skye basaltic lavas was selected for analysis, and Dr Pollard obtained the result given below. The rock was fresh, and contained

SiO_2	46·61
TiO_2	1·81
Al_2O_3	15·22
Cr_2O_3	trace.
Fe_2O_3	3·49
FeO	7·71
NiO and CoO	trace.
MnO	0·13
MgO	8·66
CaO	10·08
Na_2O	2·43
K_2O	0·67
H_2O { above 105°	2·07
{ at 105°	1·10
CO_2	trace.
P_2O_5	0·10
	100·08
Specific gravity	2·87

Olivine-Basalt lava [8185], near bridge over Allt Fionnfhuachd, Drynoch : anal. W. Pollard, *Summary of Progress Geol. Sur.* for 1899, p. 174. The rock contains only a few small amygdules, which are included in the material analysed. It consists of olivine-grains with only incipient serpentinisation, magnetite either in imperfect octahedra or enwrapping the felspar, labradorite in crystals of tabular habit parallel to the brachypinacoid, with albite-lamellation, and granules of augite, very pale in a slice, with occasionally a little chloritic alteration. (See Plate XVII., Fig. 3, A.)

* *Pogg. Ann.*, vol. xc., p. 114 : 1853.

only infrequent amygdules, and those of small size. The analysis shows it to be a thoroughly basic rock, rich in iron, magnesia, and lime. As compared with other basalts of like silica-percentage, however, there is perhaps a slight deficiency of magnesia. Probably analyses of some of the other basaltic lavas of our area would show a more marked deficiency in magnesia with a correspondingly high figure for the iron-oxides; for in some examples which must be of thoroughly basic composition olivine is wanting, and magnetite unusually abundant. A noticeable point in the analysis given is the rather high content of titanic acid.

Sir J. Norman Lockyer has made a spectroscopic examination of this and several others of the basic igneous rocks of Skye, taking photographs of the arc-spectra between silver poles; and he has very kindly placed these photographs at our disposal, after identifying a number of the lines shown. They reveal the presence of some elements not usually estimated in chemical analyses. In addition to the commoner constituents, the spectrum of this lava shows strong chromium lines and distinct lines of titanium and vanadium, while strontium is more faintly indicated.

The percentage mineral composition of the rock cannot be calculated without further knowledge of the composition of the several minerals, and in particular of the augite. If this were assumed to be a diopside, we should have about 54 per cent. of labradorite, 29 of augite, 9 of olivine, and 8 of iron-ores (largely titano-magnetite). Since the augite is probably an aluminous one, the proportion of that mineral must be greater than that thus found and the proportion of felspar less. Apatite amounts to about 0·2 per cent. of the rock.

The minerals just enumerated are the constituent minerals of this group of rocks in general, with the reservation, however, that olivine is often wanting. In a few cases we find a rhombic pyroxene in addition to the monoclinic. Further there are the secondary minerals, of which a long list might be made out. We proceed to notice briefly the several primary constituents.

The felspar of the true basalts appears to be in all cases some variety of *labradorite*, though with a certain range of composition in different rocks. It builds crystals of tabular habit parallel to the brachypinacoid, giving the usual elongated rectangular sections, commonly from $\frac{1}{100}$ to $\frac{1}{50}$ inch in length, but in some fine-textured rocks as small as $\frac{1}{500}$ inch. The narrowest crystals are often simple, but others are twinned on the albite law, once or with repetition according to the width of the crystals. Sometimes one individual of a twin projects slightly beyond its neighbour, imparting something of a stepped appearance to the termination of the crystal as seen in section. The only inclusions found are minute glass-cavities and occasionally a needle of apatite or granule of magnetite.

When porphyritic crystals of larger size occur, these, too, are of labradorite. They have usually the same tabular habit, but with a length of $\frac{1}{4}$ to $\frac{1}{2}$ inch, and they are twinned on the carlsbad as well as the albite law. The principal inclusions are glass- and stone-cavities and small scraps of augite or granules of magnetite. Some basalts in the Talisker district contain porphyritic felspars with a very unusual crystallographic habit, giving a rhomb-shaped outline.

The *augite* occurs either in granules packed into the interspaces between the felspars or in little sub-ophitic patches partially enwrapping the felspar crystals; only exceptionally in the form of ophitic plates of any extent. It is a brown, as distinguished from a green augite, but becomes very pale or almost colourless in thin slices. Twinning has not been observed. Though we have no direct information concerning the composition of the mineral, it is doubtless, as usual in such rocks, an aluminous variety. This may be inferred from the fact that the common decomposition-product is a mineral of the chlorite group. It occurs as definite pseudomorphs after augite, as well as in the form of a lining to amygdaloidal cavities and as veinlets traversing the felspar, etc. It takes the form of an aggregate of little scales, usually without any definite arrangement in the case of pseudomorphs. It has a green colour, though varying in depth of tint in different cases, and is strongly pleochroic. Where, however, the scales are of very minute size, so that they overlap one another in the thickness of the slice, the characteristic optical properties are lost, and such an aggregate is quite dark between crossed nicols.

A few of the rocks [*e.g.* 8697, from Allt Coire Labain, etc.] contain scattered porphyritic crystals of augite, usually of imperfect form and apparently corroded. These contain relatively large glass-inclusions, as was remarked by Zirkel.*

One type of basalt is characterised by *hypersthene*, in addition to the monoclinic pyroxene. This mineral has not been found in the fresh state, but is represented by the unmistakable pseudomorphs of green pleochroic bastite. These are idiomorphic, though not very perfectly shaped, and they show the usual delicate fibrous structure parallel to the vertical axis.

The *olivine* of the basaltic lavas may build well-shaped crystals, but more usually they are imperfect and often rounded or corroded to the form of shapeless grains. The grains have usually diameters of $\frac{1}{50}$ to $\frac{1}{20}$ inch, rarely as much as $\frac{1}{10}$. This small size and the frequent secondary alteration of the mineral are the reasons why olivine is rarely to be identified clearly upon a hand-specimen. In some rocks it is fresh or only slightly serpentinised, but in many others it is more or less completely pseudomorphed. The replacing substances often observed in various slides are pale green serpentine, dark brown or red iron-oxide, and some mineral of the rhombohedral carbonate group (magnesite, dolomite, or calcite, not discriminated). Two or all of these substances usually occur together. The iron-oxide, which seems to be amorphous hæmatite in various stages of conversion to limonite, forms always the marginal zone of such a composite pseudomorph, the interior occupied by a serpentine or a carbonate, or both (*see* Fig. 7). In

* *Unters. über die mikrosk. Zusammensetzung und Structur der Basaltgesteine*, p. 13: 1870.

C

some examples again the pseudomorphs are composed mainly of some undetermined mineral of which several varieties have been noticed, sometimes with the general appearance of a mica and recalling in some respects the iddingsite of Lawson.* Here again there is a copious separation of red iron-oxide, which forms a dense marginal crust, and occupies little veins running into the interior (Plate XVII., Fig. 1). The substance which forms the bulk of these pseudomorphs, though often with patches of serpentine enclosed, is usually of a very pale tint or almost colourless in a thin slice, and gives about the same interference-colours as augite. It has a strong cleavage, parallel to the brachypinacoid of the olivine, and extinguishes straight, or very nearly straight, with reference to this, the least axis of the ellipsoid of elasticity being that perpen-

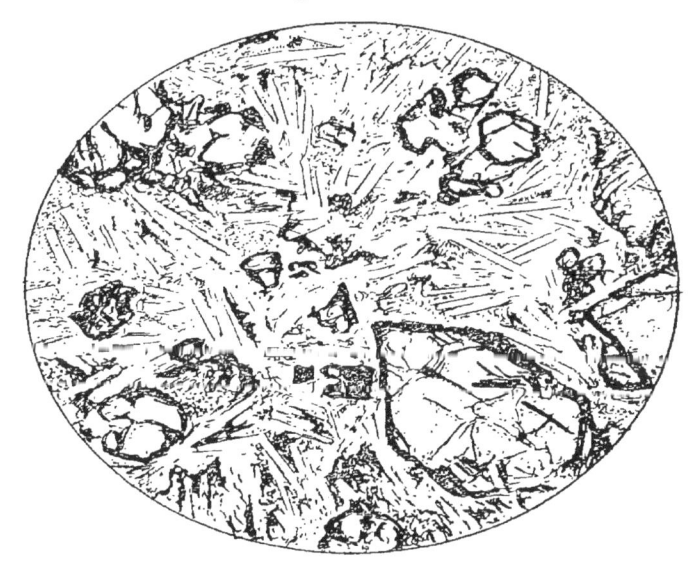

FIG. 7.—[9359] × 20. Olivine-Basalt lava, in Allt Dearg Mòr, about 2 miles S.W. of Sligachan : showing pseudomorphs after olivine, composed of carbonates with a border of iron-oxide.

dicular to the cleavage. Another variety of pseudomorph of this class shows a more perfect and regular cleavage, like that of a mica, which it also resembles in its interference-colours (Plate XVII., Fig. 2). Here the extinction is decidedly oblique, sometimes to the extent of 10° or 12°. The greatest axis of the ellipsoid of elasticity is the one most nearly perpendicular to the cleavage, and vibrations in this direction give a pale reddish yellow colour, those perpendicular to it a pale green. The first stage in the alteration of the olivine in almost all our basalts is the separation of iron-oxide, and the mineral is presumably of a variety somewhat rich in iron. At a late stage both serpentinous pseudomorphs and those

* *Bull. Dept. Geol. Univ. Calif.*, vol. i., pp. 31, etc., : 1893.

of the class which we have likened to iddingsite sometimes absorb part of the iron-oxide again, becoming of a deep green colour with strong pleochroism. We find also pseudomorphs with a deep red-brown colour, which probably belong to what Professor Heddle[*] has named ferrite.

Almost all the rocks contain, though in varying amount, an opaque black mineral of the *iron-ore* group. This is usually in distinct crystals, sharply bounded or with rounded edges and angles, and with a diameter of 0·001 to 0·002 inch. Sometimes, and especially in the less fine-textured basalts, the iron-ore occurs in shapeless patches, tending to enwrap the felspar crystals, and here the diameter may be as much as 0·01 inch. We have not made any direct chemical examination of these minute crystals and grains, and their true nature remains in some doubt. Wherever any crystallographic outline is shown, as is usually the case, the shape is always the familiar octahedral one of magnetite: no form suggestive of ilmenite has been observed. On the other hand, the rock analysed yielded 1·81 per cent. of titanic acid, and appears to be a typical example, though much of its iron-ore is in rather shapeless granules. If we admit the octahedral mineral titanomagnetite (Fe_2TiO_4), isomorphous with magnetite (Fe_2FeO_4), as the rhombohedral ilmenite ($FeTiO_3$) is isomorphous with hæmatite ($FeFeO_3$), we may conjecturally represent the iron-ore in this rock as an isomorphous mixture in nearly equal proportions of titanomagnetite and magnetite. The trace of chromic oxide found in the analysis must also be reckoned to the iron-ore: the manganese, nickel, and cobalt belong presumably to the ferro-magnesian silicates.

Minute slender needles of *apatite* were observed in some of the slides, and this mineral is probably generally distributed, though not always easily detected.

There remain only secondary minerals due to alteration of the primary constituents. Those most usual in the general mass of the rocks—as distinguished from the amygdules—are chlorite, serpentine, calcite, and red iron-oxide. This last is quite abundant in some of the more decomposed lavas, being derived from the destruction of olivine and perhaps of augite, as well as by oxidation of magnetite. It is commonly amorphous, but the minute flakes of hæmatite which Zirkel[†] notes as abundant in certain basalts of this region are perhaps also of secondary origin.

The partial decomposition which has affected so large a proportion of these basic lavas somewhat obscures the question of the occurrence in them of some residual glassy base. It may safely be stated that the majority of the rocks have been holocrystalline, and that very few of the more typical basalts can have contained more than a small amount of vitreous matter. There are, however, among the finer-textured microlitic rocks, especially those whose affinities seem to be rather with the pyroxene-andesites than with

[*] *Min. Mag.*, vol. v., p. 29 : 1882.
[†] *Unters. über die mikrosk. Zusammensetzung und Structur der Basaltgesteine*, p. 71 : 1870.

the basalts proper, some showing an interstitial base which may have been glassy or partly glassy. It is to be presumed that the several lava-flows, as poured forth, formed each at its upper surface a scoriaceous crust, probably rich in glassy matter, but we have not found any case in which such crust is preserved in a recognisable condition. This we may probably attribute to the subaërial origin of the lavas, each flow, as soon as formed, becoming at once subject to atmospheric degradation, and the scoriaceous crust of a basalt being exceptionally easily destroyed.

The sequence of crystallisation of the several primary minerals, excepting only the iron-ores, is always the same; viz. apatite, olivine or hypersthene (these two not being found together), felspar, augite. The iron-ore is sometimes, and perhaps most commonly, idiomorphic towards the felspar, sometimes moulded upon it. This may perhaps be connected with the varying composition of the iron-ore (whether more or less titaniferous); but it is also possible that the iron-ore always began to separate out before the felspar, and in some cases continued to crystallise after it. We have found no evidence of two distinct generations of the iron-ore. It seems to be in general later than the olivine, and is always earlier than the augite.

The rocks show differences of *micro-structure* which are to be correlated partly with the preponderance of one or other of the two chief constituent minerals, felspar and augite, partly with the circumstances in which the consolidation took place. The most evident distinction is that between the "*granulitic*" and the *ophitic* varieties. Both types of structure are found in rocks of various degrees of fineness of texture, and also in connection with different relative proportions (within certain limits) of the constituent minerals. The difference must therefore be dependent upon the circumstances attending consolidation, and in particular, as Professor Judd* has urged, upon the stage at which differential movement within the rock ceased. If the lava-flow had come to rest prior to the crystallisation of the augite, that mineral was able to build spreading plates, moulded upon the earlier-formed felspar crystals: if on the other hand movement continued to a late stage, such ophitic plates could not be formed, or were immediately broken up. and the augite consequently occurs in granules. So far as our observations go, the "granulitic" type of structure (Pl. XVII., Fig. 3, A) is the more common among these rocks, and especially in the amygdaloidal varieties; but the ophitic type (Pl. XVII., Fig. 3, B) is certainly more common than experience of other basaltic lavas would lead us to expect. We incline to attribute this to the subaërial eruption of the Skye lavas and the small size of the individual flows. Among those examples which we here group under the ophitic type, only a minority show the structure in its most typical development: many are better described as sub-ophitic, the augite tending to enwrap the felspar crystals but

* *Quart. Journ. Geol. Soc.*, vol. xlii., p. 76 : 1886. We follow Prof. Judd in using the term "granulitic," although it is open to objection, not being the structure met with in the rocks named granulites.

not wholly enclosing them. In the rare case where the augite freely encloses the little felspars [2705], the rock resembles pretty closely a fine-textured micro-ophitic type met with in some of the sills [cf. 9249].

In varieties rich in augite the micro-structure sometimes becomes modified in other ways. One curious type has the augite partly in a rather finely granular form, but largely in irregular shafts or blades roughly radiating from certain centres, giving a kind of ocellar structure (Plate XVII., Fig. 3, C). Varieties rich in felspar and of fine texture assume a different character. In the fine-textured rocks the felspar generally takes the form of slender microlites (Plate XVII., Fig. 3, D), and both the granulitic and the ophitic type of structure are met with among such rocks; but when there is a marked preponderance of felspar over augite, the microlites tend to pack together and assume a rude parallelism, and the rock thus acquires a more special character. This seems to be found rather among the rocks of andesitic affinities than among the typical basalts, and with it there may be a certain amount of interstitial base.

There remain the conspicuously *porphyritic* basalts, which, though not the prevalent type, are well represented in some parts of the area. The best examples which we have examined come from the inaccessible cliffs of Talisker. Numerous fallen blocks of the lavas (besides others of the sill-rocks) are strewn along the beach, and are well known to mineralogists for the beautiful crystals of various zeolitic minerals which are contained in their drusy cavities. Where these latter occur, the rock is always much decomposed, but in other parts—often on the same block—it is perfectly fresh. Here it is a dark basalt, with fine-textured ground, enclosing abundant phenocrysts of felspar and showing also little yellow grains of olivine. The felspars, up to about ¼-inch in length, have a peculiar crystal-habit. They are of flat tabular shape, and present the outline of a rhomb, resembling in this respect, though otherwise widely different, the well-known rhomb-porphyries of Norway. The angles, however, are in this case quite sharp. We have not been able to isolate the crystals or to make any satisfactory crystallographic determination of their forms. Slices [9803] show that they are of medium labradorite, with a maximum extinction-angle of about 38° in sections perpendicular to the twin-lamellæ. They have carlsbad- as well as albite-twinning, and a slight zonary banding between crossed nicols. The little elongated felspars of the ground-mass are also striated; the pale brown augite has the "granulitic" habit; round grains of fresh olivine and little octahedra of magnetite are present in moderate amount.

In another variety from the Talisker district the porphyritic felspars (medium labradorite) have the usual habit. The felspars of the ground are of more slender shape, and the augite, less abundant than before, is ophitic. This rock is very rich in olivine, and magnetite is present in fair amount·[9804].

In the tract surrounding the Cuillins porphyritic basalts are exceptional. They make some spread, however, along Allt Coire

Labain, below the mouth of the corrie. Here the rock contains a large amount of epidote, principally replacing the porphyritic felspars; and this is possibly, though not necessarily, to be regarded as a metamorphic effect due to the neighbouring gabbro intrusion.

A conspicuously *amygdaloidal* character is, as has already been remarked, generally prevalent. It is found in most parts of the basalt tract, and in most of the separate flows, and usually affects the whole thickness of a flow. In some cases a more highly vesicular and scoriaceous structure marks the upper surface of a flow, but in most instances the scoriaceous crust which probably formed the surface of the freshly consolidated lava seems to have been destroyed before it was covered by the next outpouring. Where it has not been removed, it is always found to have suffered greatly from atmospheric decomposition, and is in great part converted into an obscure ferruginous material, too fragile and incoherent to admit of slicing. Good examples may be studied at many localities on the coast, *e.g.* near the Stack at the southerly point of Talisker Bay.

Although we have not found it practicable to map the basic lavas except as a whole, it is easy to see that they present considerable differences in mineralogical, and doubtless in chemical, composition, and in this respect fall under different heads. Such a classification is largely independent of micro-structure, which, as we have seen, is determined in great part by other considerations. There are firstly the *olivine-basalts*, which are probably the most prevalent type. These are of thoroughly basic composition. We do not, however, take the presence or absence of olivine as a criterion to discriminate between the basic and the sub-basic lavas. Many of our rocks devoid of that mineral are probably quite as basic in composition as some of those with olivine. These *basalts without olivine* consist of a medium or basic labradorite, abundant augite, and often a rather large amount of iron-ore. Further there are the *hypersthene-basalts* (Plate XVII., Fig. 3, B), in which the rhombic pyroxene may be regarded as in some sense taking the place of olivine. These rocks rather closely resemble some which are widely distributed in the Lower Palæozoic volcanic district of the English Lake Country. Finally, there are the less basic rocks, some at least of which may on petrographical grounds be styled *augite-andesites*. Here, not only is olivine absent, but magnetite is only a minor accessory, and felspar predominates decidedly over augite. In some cases at least this felspar is of a more acid variety than in the preceding types. Judged by its extinction-angles in the slices, it is in some cases andesine and even oligoclase. In rocks containing felspar of these relatively acid kinds augite is only sparingly present, and the mass consists chiefly of a plexus of small narrow felspar crystals giving a structure comparable with that of many trachytes. There is, however, a considerable amount of magnetite in minute grains, and often abundant little specks of secondary ferric oxide. Andesites of this type, both amygdaloidal and non-amygdaloidal, come from Allt Dearg Mòr, near Sligachan, and other places [2624, 2625, etc.].

Not only have we found it impracticable to map out subdivisions of the lava-group based on the sequence of different petrographical types, but such information as we have gained on this point from the sliced specimens and from specific gravity determinations renders it very doubtful whether any simple sequence could be made out even from a much larger mass of data. It appears that more and less basic lavas are intimately associated, and alternate with one another. The lowest lavas were specially examined in this connection, as belonging to an easily defined horizon, though not necessarily the same in different localities. In most places where the base of the group is exposed the lowest lavas are decidedly basic, but sub-basic rocks are in some cases associated. Thus at Creagan Dubha, near Beinn Dearg Mhòr (of Strath), the lowest of all are andesites, then follow typical basalts, but above these andesitic lavas come on again. At other horizons in the series we find a similar alternation of different types, and the difficulty is much increased by the fact that the amygdaloidal lavas, which in most parts largely predominate, are often too

Fig. 8.—Section along Allt Dearg Mòr. near Sligachan: scale, 1½ inch to a mile. The general direction is N.E.-S.W., but the line is made to follow the principal bends of the stream. A number of dykes and a few thin sills are shown, the latter indicating the general dip of the lava-group.

  A. Amygdaloidal lavas, usually much decayed.
  B. Hypersthene-Basalt.
  C. Amygdaloidal Andesite.
  D. Basalt, very rich in olivine.

much decomposed to permit their being referred confidently to recognised types (*see* Fig. 8).

One negative characteristic of the basic lavas of Skye deserves notice. Professor Judd[*] has pointed out an interesting difference between these basaltic lavas of the Brito-Icelandic province and those, also of late geological age, in Bohemia, the Eifel, Auvergne, etc. The foreign basalts frequently enclose nodular crystalline patches of olivine, or of olivine and enstatite. Whether they be early crystalline segregations floated up from the deep-seated source of the lavas or actual fragments detached from concealed rock-masses—a distinction which in some circumstances may be more apparent than real—these nodules may be regarded as foreign bodies enclosed in the basalts: they are what Lacroix[†] styles "enclaves homœgènes." Such inclusions are not met with

[*] *Quart. Journ. Geol. Soc.*, vol. xlii., p. 70: 1886.
[†] A. Lacroix, *Les enclaves des roches volcaniques*, Macon, 1893, p. 8.

in the British lavas. Further, the lavas in our area do not, so far as our observations go, carry inclusions of other rocks—troctolite, anorthosite, and especially gabbro and granite—such as are found abundantly in some of the neighbouring intrusive rocks. With this negative characteristic of our basaltic lavas we may perhaps correlate another, viz. the comparative rarity of conspicuous porphyritic crystals. This subject will be more fully discussed in the chapter devoted to xenolithic inclusions. Even enclosed fragments accidentally picked up (the " enclaves énallogènes " of Lacroix) are very rare in the basaltic lavas of Skye, and when they are found it is in association with special circumstances. We have already mentioned one locality, a little N.E. of Loch Cùil na Creig, near Strollamus, where little fragments of sandstone occur rather abundantly. This is not far from a place where the lavas are seen to have broken in an irregular fashion through the Torridon Sandstone. It is also worthy of note that the lavas here rest upon a conglomerate (a river-gravel of the volcanic epoch) composed wholly of material from the Torridon Sandstone; which suggests another possible source for the unusual occurrence of enclosed fragments in the basalt.

CHAPTER IV.

Basic Lavas: Alterations and Metamorphism.

The first subject which calls for notice under this head is the *partial decay* which has affected in varying degree the greater part of our basaltic lavas. Indeed very few of these rocks can be considered as absolutely in their pristine condition, consisting wholly of products from igneous fusion. There are good reasons for believing that only a part of the alteration observed is attributable to what may be strictly termed "weathering," *i.e.* the agency of surface waters percolating the rocks and carrying the atmospheric gases and other substances in solution. We have at least to consider the possibility, and indeed probability, that many of the effects may be *due to the action of water of volcanic origin* held, in vesicles and otherwise, in the lavas themselves; and possibly too of other "mineralising agents," although these have left little clear trace of their presence.* Such action, conducted presumably at relatively high temperatures, and not long subsequent to the outpouring of the lavas, would properly be regarded rather as the final phase of vulcanicity than as a later and independent event.

The question here raised is one having a far wider bearing than is implied in its application to the Skye basalts, and a general discussion of it would not be in place here. It is worthy of note, however, that a comparison of these Tertiary lavas with similar ones of Palæozoic age in various parts of Britain does not bring out any apparent relation between the antiquity of the several rocks and their state of preservation. It is instructive, too, to observe that the intrusive sills intercalated among the Skye lavas, and the dykes which intersect them, are always in a fresher condition than the lavas themselves, although the mineral composition is similar and no very great difference of age can in some cases be presumed. Still more striking is a comparison between the ordinary basaltic lavas of the plateau country and their metamorphosed representatives bordering the large plutonic intrusions. It is clear from the phenomena to be described below that the latter were at the time of these intrusions in the same altered condition as the former are now; while it is also evident that since the metamorphism, which transformed the decomposition-products into new substances, largely of species identical

* No datolite or other boron mineral has been recorded from the Tertiary volcanic districts of Britain. Some apophyllites contain a small amount of fluorine, and this is the case in the only specimen from Skye yet analysed.

with the original igneous minerals of the basalts, these rocks have suffered no further noticeable change. We may fairly infer from this that the alteration, of the kind here considered, in the plateau basalts as now seen, has been effected almost wholly within a quite limited time immediately following their extrusion. Without pursuing the question farther, we shall, for convenience of description at least, endeavour to separate two kinds of alteration in the basaltic lavas: one belonging to the closing phase of volcanic activity and effected by the agency of heated water; the other, still in progress, due to atmospheric action and properly described by the term weathering.

Alteration of the former kind is everywhere observable, except where its effects have been obliterated by subsequent thermal metamorphism; but it is most notable in those rocks which are most conspicuously amygdaloidal. Doubtless these are the lavas which held most water when they solidified. The process has consisted mainly in the abstraction of material from the body of the rock, and especially from the felspars, to fill or partially fill the vesicles, fissures, or other vacant spaces. Such material is deposited in the vesicles and other cavities in new forms, viz. as minerals, usually, into the constitution of which the water itself enters. In this way the vesicles of the lava have become *amygdules* and the larger cavities *druses*. The smaller spaces are always filled, the larger ones partially filled or only lined: where empty vesicles are found it is only because subsequent weathering has removed the contents.

It is the amygdules and druses in the basalts that have made many places in Skye famous with mineralogists. We reproduce here, from various sources, chemical analyses of a number of the minerals.

    I. Thomsonite, near Steinscholl : anal. Heddle, *Min. Mag.*, vol. v., p. 119 : 1883. Lost 0·848 per cent. moisture at 100° C.
    II. Ditto, Storr : *ibid.*, p. 120.
    III. Ditto (Faroëlite), Storr : anal. Heddle, *Phil. Mag.* (4), vol. xiii., p. 53 : 1857.
    IV. Ditto, Portree : *ibid.*
    V. Ditto, Uig : *ibid.*, p. 54.
    VI. Ditto, Uig, another specimen : *ibid.*
    VII. Ditto, Old Man of Storr : anal. Thomson, cit. Heddle, *Min. of Scot.*, vol. ii., p. 111.
    VIII. Scolezite, Portree : anal. Heddle, *ibid.*, p. 106.
    IX. Ditto, Storr : *ibid.* The total is there given as 95·55.
    X. Mesolite, Talisker : anal. Heddle, *Phil. Mag.* (4), vol. xiii., p. 51 : 1857.
    XI. Ditto, Storr : *ibid.*, p. 52.
    XII. Ditto, Kilmuir : *ibid.*
    XIII. Ditto, near Steinscholl : anal. Heddle, *Min. Mag.*, vol. v., p. 118 : 1883. Lost 0·9 per cent. moisture at 100° C.
    XIV. Uigite, near Uig : mean of duplicate analyses by Heddle, *Min. Mag.*, vol. v., p. 27 : 1882.
    XV. Laumontite, Snizort : anal. Connell, cit. Hintze, Heddle, and others.
    XVI. Ditto, Storr : anal. Scott, *Edin. New Phil. Journ.*, vol liii., p. 284 : 1852.

Analyses of Secondary Minerals in the Basic Lavas.

	I.	II.	III.	IV.	V.	VI.	VII.	VIII.	IX.	X.	XI.	XII.	XIII.	XIV.	XV.	XVI.	XVII.	XVIII.	XIX.
SiO_2	39·696	39·016	41·32	41·20	43·172	43·21	40·33	45·61	45·92	46·714	46·724	46·20	45·615	46·150	52·04	53·048	53·96	51·98	51·09
Al_2O_3	29·949	28·125	28·44	30·00	29·30	29·03	29·00	25·91	25·32	26·617	26·696	26·48	24·465	21·638	21·14	22·943	20·13	20·34	21·29
Fe_2O_3	...	3·281	...	...	...	...	...	...	...	...	...	...	1·428	...	...	...	...	0·59	0·32
FeO	1·43	...	...	...	...	...	...	...	...	...	...	...	...	...	...	...	...	...	...
MnO	0·076	...	...	...	...	...	...	...	...	...	...	...	0·384	...	...	...	...	...	...
MgO	...	0·646	...	...	...	...	...	...	...	...	...	...	0·461	...	...	...	...	...	...
CaO	10·076	10·733	11·54	11·40	9·816	10·35	12·12	13·38	18·43	9·078	8·902	10·00	6·116	16·256	10·62	9·076	12·36	11·55	11·49
Na_2O	5·511	3·709	5·77	4·88	5·326	5·16	5·33	3·00	3·52	5·389	5·404	4·98	6·905	4·801	...	...	...	...	0·31
K_2O	0·378	1·01	...	...	...	...	...	...	...	...	...	...	0·567	...	...	...	0·87	...	...
H_2O	13·073	18·985	13·26	13·20	12·40	12·46	13·22	12·56	12·36	12·831	12·925	13·04	12·246	11·731	14·92	14·039	12·42	15·78	15·37
	100·189	100·506	100·33	100·18	100·014	100·21	100·00	100·46	100·55	100·629	100·653	100·76	100·178	100·466	98·72	100·300	100·23	100·24	99·87
Specific gravity	...	2·147–2·131	...	...	...	...	...	...	...	...	...	...	2·103	2·284	...	...	2·252	...	...

	XX.	XXI.	XXII.	XXIII.	XXIV.	XXV.	XXVI.	XXVII.	XXVIII.	XXIX.	XXX.	XXXI.	XXXII.	XXXIII. XXXIV.	XXXV.	XXXVI.	XXXVII.
SiO_2	51·74	56·54	52·40	43·18	48·72	48·81	47·48	49·17	55·95	50·70	51·2	52·007	53·820	46·28 54·22	41·411	42·504	40·329
Al_2O_3	21·77	16·43	17·98	21·77	17·68	18·73	20·21	18·92	20·72	1·48	...	1·820	{ 2·728 }	4·14 0·68	9·075	5·065	8·717
Fe_2O_3	...	...	...	...	...	0·08	...	...	...	...	1·09	...		... ...	2·054	0·852	1·972
FeO	...	...	...	1·38	...	...	...	...	1·00	...	0·09	...		... ...	...	...	...
MnO	...	...	0·36	...	...	...	...	...	...	...	0·3	...		... ...	0·107	0·224	0·131
MgO	...	...	9·97	9·25	9·36	8·01	...	...	...	0·18	0·5	0·396		... 27·22	22·8	23·954	21·71
CaO	12·21	8·90	1·40	3·44	0·6	1·9	4·68	12·9	1·68	33·24	23·13	32·554	29·860	30·63 1·02	1·80	3·274	2·8
Na_2O	...	0·46	0·03	0·95	1·22	0·08	4·58	trace.	12·62	...	0·37	7·670	9·551	1·68 ...	...	0·45	...
K_2O	...	...	17·83	20·20	21·88	23·07	1·71	19·73	0·57	...	5·49	...	...	... ...	...	0·171	...
H_2O	14·68	17·05	...	...	...	...	20·30	...	8·54	14·18	17·02	5·058	3·760	15·69 10·04	23·433	23·679	24·338
	100·40	99·38	99·07	100·12	99·46	100·68	98·96	100·72	99·50	99·78	99·80	99·805	99·739	100·42 99·78	100·722	100·136	99·998
Specific gravity	...	...	...	...	...	...	...	...	2·248	...	...	2·784	...	2·198 2·246	2·296	...	...

XVII. Ditto, Skye : anal. Mallet, *Amer. Journ. Sci.* (2), vol. xxii., p. 179 : 1856.
XVIII. Ditto, Storr : anal. Heddle, *Min. of Scot.*, vol. ii., p. 91 : 1901.
XIX. Ditto, Storr : *ibid.*
XX. Ditto, ? Skye : mean of duplicate analyses by Babo and Delffs, *Pogg. Ann.*, vol. lix., p. 341 : 1843.
XXI. Stilbite (Sphærostilbite), Storr : anal. Heddle, Greg and Lettsom's *Manual*, p. 164 : 1858.
XXII. Ditto (Hypostilbite), Skye : anal. Haughton, *Phil. Mag.* (4), vol. xiii., p. 509 : 1857.
XXIII. Levyne, Quiraing : anal. Heddle, *Min. of Scot.*, vol. ii., p. 96 : 1901.
XXIV. Chabasite, blue, Talisker : anal. Heddle, *ibid.*, p. 93.
XXV. Ditto, white, Talisker : *ibid.*
XXVI. Acadialite (Chabasite), Talisker : *ibid.*
XXVII. Gmelinite, ? Skye : anal. Berzelius, cit. Heddle, *ibid.*, p. 96.
XXVIII. Analcime, Talisker : anal. Heddle, *ibid.*, p. 97.
XXIX. Gyrolite, Storr : anal. Anderson, *Phil. Mag.* (4), vol. i., p. 113 : 1851.
XXX. Apophyllite, Storr : anal. Heddle, *Min. of Scot.*, vol. ii., p. 81 : 1901. With 0·7 of fluorine.
XXXI. Pectolite, Storr : anal. Scott, *Edin. New Phil. Journ.*, vol. liii., p. 280 : 1852.
XXXII. Ditto, Talisker : anal. Heddle, *Phil. Mag.* (4), vol. ix., p. 253 : 1855.
XXXIII. Okenite, An Leth Allt, Loch Brittle : anal. Stuart Thomson, *Trans. Geol. Soc. Glasg.*, vol. ix., p. 251 : 1893.
XXXIV. Ditto, Dunan Earr an Sguirr : anal. Heddle, *ibid.*
XXXV. Saponite, olive, Storr : anal. Heddle, *Trans. Roy. Soc. Edin.*, vol. xxix., p. 100 : 1879. Lost 13·652 per cent. moisture at 100° C.
XXXVI. Ditto, white, Quiraing : *ibid.* Lost 15·536 per cent. moisture at 100° C.
XXXVII. Ditto, yellow, Quiraing : *ibid.*, p. 101. Lost 15·132 per cent. moisture at 100° C.

The minerals which contribute to fill the amygdaloid and geodic cavities of the basalts are very numerous. Most common of all are *zeolites* in great variety, several occurring together in the large amygdules of certain localities. In addition to radiating fibrous aggregates, which often occupy the smaller and more spherical cavities, chabasite, analcime, and stilbite are very frequently recognised. From mineralogical works a long list might be compiled,* including thomsonite, mesolite, faroëlite, laumontite, gyrolite, pectolite, apophyllite (with tesselite), prehnite scolezite, gmelinite, levyne, heulandite, epistilbite, sphærostilbite, acadialite, and uigite. Some of the last-named are of rare and exceptional occurrence. Among localities known to collectors for the variety and beauty of their crystals are Talisker Bay, the Storr, the Quiraing, and a spot about a mile north of the last. Where two or more zeolites occur in the same cavity, they form successive coats more or less regularly disposed. The larger cavities are often not completely filled, the central space being either empty or occupied by water giving an alkaline reaction.

* For our present purpose, such hydrous silicates as apophyllite, pectolite, and gyrolite may be loosely grouped with the zeolites.

While zeolites and allied minerals are usually the chief, and often the sole, contents of the amygdules, they are frequently accompanied by other substances, and sometimes give place to them entirely. Among these may be mentioned chloritic minerals, which seem to belong to Heddle's division of the saponites as distinguished from the chlorites proper: indeed he has identified the species saponite from more than one locality. Calcite is not infrequent, and in some places occur chalcedony and onyx, less frequently crystalline quartz. Epidote is locally abundant, especially near the gabbro border, where it may possibly be connected with metamorphism due to that rock. In a few places iron-oxides (hæmatite and limonite) occur in quantity. Finally bitumen or asphalte is known, though not common, and Heddle states that calcite sometimes contains a considerable amount of this substance, while petroleum partly fills cavities at Talisker.*

It can scarcely be doubted that the contents of the amygdules are, generally speaking, derived from the rocks themselves, and carried to the cavities, where they occur, dissolved in water, which need not have had any extensive circulation. The characteristic minerals are all such as might be expected from such a source. It is noticeable that the zeolites are mostly lime-zeolites or such soda-lime-zeolites as have lime for their principal base, the soda-zeolite analcime being almost the only exception.† It is reasonable to suppose that the original composition of the basalt, save as regards water, is represented by an analysis of the rock *inclusive* of the amygdules. The partial decomposition of some of the original minerals and the transference of derived materials to the vesicles were, it seems highly probable, carried on at somewhat high temperatures; the process being not an accident of "weathering" long posterior to and independent of the extrusion of the lavas, but rather a final result of the volcanic energy itself. The partial unmaking of these basaltic rocks and the concurrent infilling of their vesicles and other cavities may have begun as soon as the lavas were solid, and continued throughout their cooling.‡ We know at least that the process was complete prior to the next events of which we have record in the district, the intrusions of the peridotites and gabbros; for the amygdules are metamorphosed in common with the rest of the rock in the vicinity of the peridotite, gabbro, and granite masses.

If the filling of the vesicles by zeolites and other minerals took place during the cooling of the lavas, and was a process requiring a prolonged time, it follows that the earlier-formed minerals must have crystallised at higher temperatures than those which followed.

---

* See Heddle, *Mineralogy of Scotland*, 1901. From the same work we may add the sulphide tetrahedrite and, of very rare occurrence, native copper coated with malachite.

† Even the analcime, in the only specimen analysed, contains a notable amount of lime. The absence of natrolite is especially to be remarked.

‡ *Cf.* Sir A. Geikie, *Ancient Volcanoes of Great Britain*, vol. ii., p. 189: 1897.

The data are wanting which would enable us to apply this test. We might expect the content in water of the various compounds to afford some clue, and J. D. Dana,* writing many years ago on this subject, with special reference to the Lake Superior region, remarked that the earlier minerals in general contain less water in their composition than the later. This rule, however, holds good only partially in Skye. Quartz and calcite are, as might be expected, always the earliest minerals in the amygdules in which they respectively occur, but the chloritic minerals come next, before even the least hydrous of the zeolites. Of the latter, too, chabasite, with as much as 20 per cent. of water, has usually crystallised first of all, though it is exceptionally found on both stilbite and analcime. Apophyllite is found crystallised on gyrolite, this on mesolite and thomsonite, and mesolite on analcime, all in accordance with their percentages of water; but elsewhere analcime occurs on mesolite and even on apophyllite. It is clear that more than one factor goes to determine the particular mineral formed at any epoch, one being probably the relative proportions of lime and soda in solution.

The changes in progress in the rocks at the time when the amygdules were filled were evidently of a kind which resulted in the production chiefly of zeolites. In these minerals the molecular ratios

$$CaO + Na_2O : Al_2O_3 : SiO_2$$

vary from 1 : 1 : 2 (thomsonite, mesolite, etc.) to 1 : 1 : 4 (analcime and laumontite), or exceptionally 1 : 1 : 6 (stilbite); thus corresponding generally, excepting the water, with the composition of the felspars from which they are derived. It appears, therefore, that the lime and soda, alumina, and silica have been abstracted from the felspars in the same proportions as they present in those minerals. This is very different from what occurs in ordinary weathering, and points to different conditions, of which high temperature is doubtless one.†

Turning now to *true weathering*, the contrast becomes very apparent. The results here are, in the earlier stages, a partial chloritisation of the augite, serpentinisation of the olivine, carbonatisation of the felspars, etc., with some separation of silica. In the later stages we find complete disintegration of the rock, the original minerals being totally destroyed. This has happened to some extent during the volcanic period itself, whenever any noteworthy pause occurred in the outpouring of the lavas, the surface of the last solidified flow being thus exposed to subaërial agents of destruction until it was covered by a new outburst. These old

---

* *Amer. Journ. Sci.*, vol. xlix., pp. 49–64 : 1845.
† The well-known occurrence of zeolites formed from thermal waters in Roman masonry at Plombières, etc., has an obvious bearing on this question, and the processes by which zeolitic minerals have been artificially produced are equally instructive. See Daubrée, *Études synthétiques de géologie expérimentale*, 1879.

land-surfaces are marked by ferruginous, or siliceous and ferruginous, clays of composition very different from that of the basalts. The change consists, besides hydration, in the removal of a large part of the substance of the original rock, and the several ingredients have been removed in very different proportions. The alkalies and most of the lime are readily carried off; and part of the silica, and usually of the iron, goes also, the behaviour of these two constituents differing in different cases. This results in a relative enrichment in alumina, a substance which does not enter into easily soluble compounds, and the rock is reduced to a clay, siliceous or ferruginous according to the proportions of silica and iron-oxide which remain. The process, ideally complete, would give rise to a clay consisting practically of hydrated alumina; but this final stage does not seem to have been reached in the basaltic district of Skye. Here in the most altered deposits the alumina is probably still combined with silica.

Several writers have remarked the occurrence of *beds of clay*, usually more or less ferruginous, interbedded among the basalts in the northern and western parts of Skye. Macculloch* noticed them especially in the great Talisker cliff (Beinn nan Cuithean), where the number of beds varies from eight or nine to twelve, fifteen, or even more in the precipitous face of 900 feet. Boué mentioned a reddish or purplish "bolar" substance in the same neighbourhood. In 1882 Heddle noticed a similar ferruginous clay, usually of a deep red colour, forming layers one or two feet thick at the Quiraing, and occurring also in a repeated series of beds at the Storr. He gave an analysis of the substance (column I. below), and pointed out its identity with the so-called plinthite of Antrim. The latter (A) had been regarded by Thomson as a distinct mineral, but is only a type of many clays in the Antrim district. The substance examined by Heddle is doubtless of similar nature to that at Talisker, for elsewhere he remarks at this place "bands of plinthite, of some inches in thickness, zoning the cliffs horizontally from bottom to top at distances of about 40 feet." †

In 1896 Sir A. Geikie drew attention again to the clays intercalated among the basalt-flows between Lochs Brittle and Dunvegan, and especially to the cliff at Rudha nan Clach, north of Talisker Bay, where "some conspicuous bands of lilac and red are interspersed among the basalts."‡ He suggested that they might be worth examination from the economic point of view, as a possible source of aluminium; the clays of the basaltic district of Antrim being well known to include some of the bauxite type, which have been utilised for that industry. The analysis B, furnished by the Antrim Iron Ore Company, represents one of these Irish clays of such a grade as can be worked profitably as bauxite, and C a less siliceous sample which, in the dry state, must consist to the extent

---

* *Description of the Western Islands of Scotland*, vol. i., pp. 376, 377: 1819.
† *Min. Mag.*, vol. iv., p. xiii.: 1880.
‡ *Quart. Journ. Geol. Soc.*, vol. lii., pp. 339, 340: 1896.

	I.	A.	B.	C.	D.
SiO_2	29·547	30·88	14·50	3·26	50.75
TiO_2	..	..	..	4·53	..
Al_2O_3	19·027	20·76	47·60	46·68	20·87
Fe_2O_3	28·013	26·16	2·30	2·74	15·90
FeO	3·251	..	.	.	..
MnO	0·844	.	.	..	..
CaO	2·234	2·60	..	..	0·72
H_2O (combined)	10·704	19·60	18·00	25·13	10·50
(moisture)	6·687		17·00	17·00	
	100·307	100·00	99·40	99·34	98·74
Specific gravity	..	2·342	..	..	..

I. Ferruginous clay ("plinthite"), Quiraing, Skye: anal. M. F. Heddle, *Min. Mag.*, vol. v., p. 26: 1882.
A. Ferruginous clay, brick-red ("plinthite"), Antrim: anal. Thos. Thomson, *Outlines of Mineralogy*, vol. i., p. 323 (in 7th ed., 1836).
B. Bauxite clay, Antrim.
C. Bauxite clay, less siliceous, Ballynure, Antrim.
D. Ferruginous and siliceous clay, bluish grey, southern part of Antrim: anal. Apjohn, see Delesse, *Ann. des mines*, (5th ser.), vol. xii., p. 419: 1857.

of 86 to 89 per cent. of the mineral bauxite, $H_6Al_2O_6$. More than 20 per cent. of silica or 3 per cent. of iron is detrimental to the purpose in view, and consequently material such as that analysed by Heddle would be without value. The Company named have had partial analyses made of samples of clays from Skye, which appeared to be promising for the bauxite industry, but the results were of a disappointing kind. The General Manager, Mr Arch. Livingstone, has kindly communicated the particulars, as below. The specimens were from Rudha nan Clach, from Talisker, and from near the Talisker Distillery at Carbost on Loch Harport. Each gave about 17 per cent. of moisture.

	SiO_2	Fe_2O_3
Rudha nan Clach (from "Iron Ore Bed")	32·37	19·09
Do. (under the "Iron Ore Bed")	33·45	17·68
Stream above Talisker Farm	34·86	15·60
Quarry above Talisker Distillery	51·88	12·95
Do., another sample	46·11	14·36
At or near the same place	45·85	14·35

The first three are evidently of the "plinthite" type, and are both too siliceous and too ferruginous for use; while the other three depart still further from the bauxite standard. These latter resemble in their content of silica another type of clay from Antrim, occurring at the base of the volcanic series (*see* column D).

Distribution of Plinthite and other Clays.

Mr H. B. Woodward, who mapped the basalts in the vicinity of Portree for the Geological Survey, collected in 1894 a specimen bearing much apparent resemblance to the Irish bauxite from Leac Aghamnha, on the south side of Portree Harbour, and has supplied a note on the subject: "A sample was sent to Mr J. Hort Player, who very kindly examined it and made a partial analysis: this showed that the rock contained only about 30 per cent. of alumina, and it was evidently a somewhat altered volcanic ash—possibly a material from which bauxite might ultimately be produced by natural causes. The occurrence of bands of hardened red clay among the bedded basalts is well known. Bands of this nature, approaching to lithomarge, occur at Ben Tianavaig and other localities."

It will be seen that our present knowledge scarcely warrants any expectation that workable bauxite-clays of importance will be found in Skye. Further, although the samples of clays examined contain enough iron-oxide to render them unsuitable for this purpose, we have not discovered among the Skye basalts any important bedded iron-ores such as accompany the Irish clays, and have been worked concurrently with them. An important difference between the two districts is to be noted in this connection. While the basaltic group of Skye appears to be indivisible, that of Antrim falls into two well-marked sub-groups, separated in time by an interval which may have been very considerable. During this interval, while the Lower Basalts remained for a long time an exposed land-surface, the pisolitic iron-ores, the bauxites, lithomarges, and boles, and the associated plant-beds were formed, and they now divide the Upper from the Lower Basalts. In addition there are in Antrim minor beds of ferruginous clays intercalated among the basalts at various horizons, and it is with these, not with the main deposits, that the occurrences in Skye are to be paralleled.

Brick-red ferruginous clays, resulting from the decomposition of the basaltic lavas and doubtless of the same general character as the "plinthite" analysed by Heddle, are widely distributed, especially in the western part of the area surveyed, and may often be observed running as narrow bands along the face of the precipitous cliffs between Loch Brittle and Loch Harport. In a few cases, where they are associated with decomposed tuffs and impure carbonaceous seams, these clays may have been formed in shallow pools into which the material was washed, but in general they are to be regarded as due to the decomposition of the lava in place. This is often shown by the occurrence of intermediate stages of decay, giving a gradual transition from ordinary basalt to typical "plinthite"; and in some cases amygdules are evident in a rock which is otherwise completely converted to red clay. As a rule the seams do not exceed a very few inches in thickness, but there are exceptions to this rule. The thickest mass which we have observed reached between three and four feet. This is in Fiskavaig Burn, about 700 yards above the hamlet: its lateral extent cannot be traced. Basalts showing various stages of this kind of alteration, down to typical plinthite, may have a thickness of 10 or 15

D

feet, as in the burn above Drynoch Farm, near Loch Harport, and the Glen Caladale burn, west of the mouth of Loch Eynort.

The basaltic lavas in the vicinity of the large gabbro and granite intrusions invariably show the effects of *thermal metamorphism* in greater or less degree. In some places on the west side of the Cuillins the transformation they have suffered is such that to ordinary inspection the true nature of the rocks is almost completely disguised; but in general the altered lavas are still easily recognisable as such, though manifestly changed to some extent. They assume a dark grey colour, and are tougher and more compact than the unaltered rocks, breaking with a more splintery fracture. The amygdules, instead of perishing more rapidly, are now more durable than the body of the rock, and are prominent on a weathered face.

It is always found that the first indications of change appear in the chloritic and other alteration-products of the basalts and the contents of the amygdules.* In other words, products formed at relatively low temperatures were affected more readily than minerals originally crystallised from igneous fusion. Indeed, many observations, in this district and elsewhere, point to the fact that hydrous compounds with part of their water only loosely held, and carbonates in the presence of available silica, enter into new combinations on a quite moderate elevation of temperature. With progressive metamorphism the essential minerals of the rock become in turn unstable, the augite being transformed before the felspar.

The most conspicuous secondary minerals in the general mass of the metamorphosed rocks are a greenish or yellowish-green rather fibrous hornblende and a brown biotite, separately or often together. Epidote is often found, and to considerable distances from the intrusions, in rocks showing but little other change; but it cannot be assumed that this mineral is always a product of thermal metamorphism. Of the hornblende and biotite, the former comes usually from direct transformation of the augite, a kernel of which is often left unchanged in the partially metamorphosed rocks. The biotite, on the other hand, seems from its disposition to be derived in great part from chloritic and other alteration-products of the original rock: for example, it occurs as minute flakes disseminated through the felspar [2709]. Presumably the presence of alkalies and a deficiency of lime in spots where chloritic material was collected would tend to determine the formation of biotite rather than hornblende. It is clear, however, that the latter mineral too may sometimes be formed from the alteration-products, for we find it occupying little veins [2699], or as actinolitic needles embedded in an aggregate of yellowish-green chloritic material [2701]. Many of the slides show biotite forming in preference to hornblende in immediate proximity to grains of magnetite, which have probably furnished some iron for the purpose [7128, etc.].

* A few examples have been described in *Quart. Journ. Geol. Soc.*, vol. lii., pp. 386, 387 ; 1896.

The felspar of the basalt is often quite unchanged in the less metamorphosed rocks, although the augite may be far advanced towards total replacement by the minerals already mentioned. The earliest change seen in the felspar is a clearing of the crystals from the slight turbidity which they often show in the non-metamorphosed rocks: in the most altered rocks the felspars are completely re-crystallised, and little trace may remain of the original micro-structure of the rock. It is doubtful to what extent the original magnetite of the basalt is also recrystallised.

The most interesting metamorphic effects are found in connection with the amygdules. We have seen that these, in a very large proportion of the Skye basalts, consist of zeolites, two or more being often associated within the same cavity. In the metamorphosed rocks the amygdules present a dead-white aspect not unlike that seen in many of the unchanged lavas, but they are notably harder, and on examination are found to be of felspar. This *conversion of lime- and lime-soda-zeolites into lime-soda-felspars* by thermal metamorphism is one that might be expected on chemical grounds, although it does not appear to have been recorded from other districts. In many cases it must involve little more total chemical change than the expulsion of the water, and it is indeed merely a restoration of the original minerals of which the zeolites are the degraded representatives.

The felspars in these metamorphosed amygdules (Pl. XVII., Figs. 4 and 5) form an aggregate of interlocking crystals or allotriomorphic crystal-grains with a somewhat dusty appearance in thin slices. Often they are apparently untwinned, but fine twin-lamellation is also very frequently seen. Measurements of extinction angles in different cases indicate oligoclase, andesine, and andesine-labradorite, besides more basic varieties, and more than one of these may occur in intimate association. Probably the kind of felspar formed in any particular part of an amygdule depended upon the composition of the zeolitic substance at that spot, for we have reason to believe that in ordinary thermal metamorphism interchange of material is restricted within very narrow limits.*
That the transformation of the zeolites into felspars took place very readily, *i.e.* did not demand a very elevated temperature, appears from the fact that it has occurred in specimens which exhibit no other sign of metamorphism [7460]. Further, we have found little indication of the replacement being a gradual process, for only rarely do a few patches of unchanged zeolite remain in the heart of the new-formed felspar [7127].

Felspars are often the only contents of the metamorphosed amygdules, but in other cases we find various minerals in addition, doubtless when the zeolites have occupied the original cavity in company with chloritic material, calcite, etc. Epidote is a not infrequent associate of the felspar, in grains or imperfect crystals— always at or near the boundary of the amygdule, and sometimes form-

* See Harker and Marr, *Quart. Journ. Geol. Soc.*, vol. xlix., pp. 368, 369 : 1893.

ing a continuous border, which lies mainly within the boundary but may also encroach slightly upon the general mass of the rock. It is of earlier crystallisation than the new felspar, which is often seen to be moulded upon it (Plate XVII., Fig. 5). The epidote is nearly colourless in thin slices. Its bi-refringence is very variable, and some of the crystals appear to be rather zoisite than epidote. Probably the mineral formed at any spot depended upon the relative quantities of lime and iron available for its composition. Occasionally a few rose-coloured grains indicate some content of manganese, and may be termed withamite [7461]. In other slices an augite mineral, perhaps malacolite, and a fibrous faint-green hornblende occur as constituents of the metamorphosed amygdules. They may be intimately associated with felspar to build a crystalline aggregate of fine texture. They have crystallised before the latter mineral, and needles and fibres of the hornblende are seen penetrating both the felspar and certain small patches of clear quartz which occur only sparingly.

Summarily, these metamorphosed basic lavas have the same general characteristics as have been described for similar rocks elsewhere—e.g., for those of Lower Palæozoic age near the granites of Shap and Eskdale in the English Lake District; but the Skye basalts present a special feature of interest in the abundant formation of felspars at the expense of zeolites in the amygdaloidal cavities.

The effects described are the most usual results of thermal metamorphism in the basalts, and may be observed in various stages of development to distances of half a mile or more from the boundaries of the large plutonic masses. In some places, however, changes of a more radical kind mark a higher grade of metamorphism, in which the basalts may almost lose all semblance to the appearance of their unaltered representatives. This most extreme stage of metamorphism, involving complete reconstitution of the rocks, is found in some of the basaltic lavas in contact with the gabbros and peridotites on the western and south-western fringe of the Cuillins. A good locality for studying the effects is near a little tarn to the N.E. of An Sgùman, not far from the boundary of the gabbro. Here are dark-grey finely crystalline rocks with amygdules often indicated by small lighter ovoid patches or light rings with a dark interior. A thin slice [8731] shows that the component minerals, olivine, magnetite, augite, and felspar, with the possible exception of the first, are all new-built. The micro-structure is precisely that of the rocks termed pyroxene-granulites* by the German petrographers. The augite forms rounded granules, and the magnetite, though sometimes with an indication of the octahedral form, is also rounded (*see* Plate XVIII., Fig 1). Olivine is abundant, though not evenly distributed. The felspar (labradorite), with albite and carlsbad twinning, is moulded upon all the other minerals, and shows little crystal-outline of its own. The minerals composing the meta-

* Not the "granulitic" structure of Judd.

morphosed amygdules are simply augite and felspar, the olivine and magnetite not entering, though grains of these may trench on the margin. There is a border of augite grains enclosing an aggregate of felspar, and sometimes (as in the figure) an inner ring of augite concentric with the other. This augite, and less clearly that in the body of the rock, has a faint reddish tint in the slice, with slight pleochroism. In this as in many other points the rock recalls the pyroxene-granulites* of Saxony, and there is a resemblance, possibly suggestive, between the highly altered amygdules and some of the curious eye-like structures found in the latter rocks. The amygdules doubtless consisted before metamorphism of a lime-soda-zeolite with an outer layer of some chloritic mineral and sometimes a second layer of the same. The zeolite has given rise to a felspar, as in the other occurrences noted above, while the chloritic mineral has, in these most highly metamorphosed lavas, been transformed, not into hornblende, but into augite. Further, there is in this extreme grade of metamorphism no uralitisation of the augite in the body of the rock, but only recrystallisation.

In specimens of such a rock as this there is nothing to suggest its true nature and origin except the amygdules, which are themselves much disguised, and have lost something of the sharpness of their outline. In extremely metamorphosed basalts from other localities, where the amygdaloidal structure was wanting, only close examination of the field-relations enables us to assign the rocks to their proper place. This is especially the case where, as we shall observe later, portions of the basaltic lavas have been, quite locally, fused in contact with the gabbro magma and partially incorporated in it. The most highly metamorphosed examples are sometimes quite as coarse in texture as many of the larger dykes and sills of dolerite in the district.

Metamorphism imparts to the basalts a quality of hardness and durability which they lack in other conditions, and it is only in this state that they form strong features. The summit of Glamaig is an example. Here, as has been described in another place,† the rocks are highly magnetised in a manner which we shall have to note as characteristic much more generally of the gabbro of the mountains and the dolerite sills of the plateaux.

In conclusion, it may be mentioned that the basaltic lavas in numerous isolated places have become *brecciated* as a result of crushing. Usually these crushed basalts present the appearance of a conglomerate rather than a breccia, the several fragments being rounded as if they had been rolled over and ground together. Good examples are seen along Allt nam Meirleach, a branch of the Tungadal River. Other places where the basalt has locally the

---

* Some rocks in the neighbourhood of Druim an Eidhne, which are probably metamorphosed lavas of this kind, have not been separated on the map from the gabbros. They are mentioned under the head of "granulitic gabbros" in Chap. VIII., and their structure is illustrated in Fig. 22.
† Harker, *Proc. Camb. Phil. Soc.*, vol. x., pp. 270-272, Pl. XI. : 1890.

appearance of a conglomerate are—Inver Meadale; Coire nan Sagart, on the slope of Broc-bheinn ; and Allt a' Choire Gaisteach, a tributary of the Vikisgill Burn. Some of the sections suggest that the breaking up of the rock in this way may have been facilitated by a certain spheroidal parting with incipient exfoliation. The intrusive sills associated with the lavas are not crushed. This must be attributed to the superior rigidity of these rocks, for it cannot be supposed that the brecciation of the lavas was earlier than the intrusion of the sills.

CHAPTER V.

RHYOLITIC AND TRACHYTIC LAVAS AND TUFFS.

Lavas of acid and sub-acid composition—rhyolites, dacites, trachytes, etc.—play but a very subordinate part among the British Tertiary volcanic rocks. The "felstone-lavas," to which Prof. Judd in his first account (1874) assigned a prominent place, have since been relegated by that author (1889, 1890) mainly to the family of augite-andesites. Some of the rocks he still retains as rhyolites, dacites, and sanidine-trachytes; but from his generalised treatment it is not possible to be sure whether true lava-flows of acid and sub-acid composition are intended. Rhyolites, including obsidians, are recognised in the Antrim area,[*] even after excluding such intrusive types as the quartz-porphyry of Tardree ; and it appears that they were poured out, though only sparingly, about the middle of the volcanic period, *i.e.* between the lower and upper groups into which the basalts of the Irish district divide.[†] The pitchstone of the Sgùrr of Eigg and Oighsgeir, regarded as a glassy lava of trachytic or perhaps dacitic composition, is referred, on the other hand, to a much later epoch,[‡] and perhaps some of the rocks of Ardnamurchan, described by Prof. Judd,[§] also belong here. Sir A. Geikie's "pale group" of Beinn Mòr in Mull,[||] which is underlain by a great thickness of basalts, is described as highly felspathic, and may prove on closer examination to include trachytic or even rhyolitic lavas ; while the existence of an older group of trachytes is proved by their occurrence as pebbles in the gravel at Ardtun Head in the same island.[¶]

This is but a scanty record in comparison with the vast outpouring of basic lavas belonging to the same great suite of eruptions, and our investigations in Skye serve further to emphasise this enormous preponderance of basic over acid material among the British Tertiary volcanic rocks. In one small area only, situated on the northern border of the Cuillins, has a group of rhyolitic and trachytic rocks been discovered. These rocks form much of the ground below Fionn Choire, and extend for some little distance up Bruach na Frithe at its northern end. The area which

---

[*] See especially Cole, *Sci. Trans. Roy. Dubl. Soc.* (2), vol. vi., pp. 77-114 : 1896.
[†] McHenry, *Geol. Mag.*, 1895, pp. 261-264.
[‡] Geikie, *Quart. Journ. Geol. Soc.*, vol. xxvii., pp. 303-309 : 1871 ; and vol. lii., p. 371 : 1896.
[§] *Quart. Journ. Geol. Soc.*, vol. xlvi., p. 378 : 1890.
[||] *Trans. Roy. Soc. Edin.*, vol. xxxv., p. 93 : 1888.
[¶] Cole, *Quart. Journ. Geol. Soc.*, vol. xliii., p. 277 : 1887.

they occupy has a length of a mile in a W.S.W.-E.N.E. direction and a maximum width of about ⅓ mile. It is very conspicuous as seen from the Sligachan and Glen Brittle foot-path, owing to the bare surface of the rocks and their pale colour, often with a tint of lilac or lavender. No further extension of this group of rocks has been detected, excepting at one or two places about 1½ to 1¾ mile to the south-west, and within the gabbro tract. Here a few relics of laminated rhyolite and acid breccia are preserved. Associated with these are some strips of a biotite-bearing felsite (not a lava) to be referred to again below. The locality is on the slopes of Sgùrr Thuilm.

Three divisions of the group may be recognised for convenience of description; the first and lowest consisting chiefly of trachytic lavas, the second of rhyolitic tuffs and breccias, and the third of rhyolitic lavas. The strike is on the whole east and west, being more E.S.E.-W.N.W. at the eastern end and E.N.E.-W.S.W. at the western; and the general dip is southerly, though variable in direction as well as in amount. Most of the northern, or rather N.N.W., border of the area is a fault, throwing down to the south, against which the lower members of the group are obliquely cut off; and in some parts, especially to the north of Tobar nan Uaislean, the rocks are invaded by numerous tongues of gabbro. These accidents partly obscure, but do not conceal, the real extent of the group and its relations to the basalts, which are of a remarkable kind.

Owing partly to the arrangement described, the lowest or trachytic division is found only in the eastern part of the area. Here it is clearly underlain by amygdaloidal basalts. Further, the several members of the division die out eastward, dove-tailing with flows of amygdaloidal basalt which die out westward; thus making it clear that the trachytic and associated rocks are contemporaneous with that portion of the basaltic group exposed immediately to the east (Fig. 9). Again, they are surmounted in Meall Odhar by more massive basaltic rocks, much invaded and metamorphosed by gabbro above, these basalts being apparently on the same horizon as the rhyolitic rocks seen farther west. The trachytes, etc., either die out westward before reaching the boundary fault, or are cut off by a parallel fault a little north of the main one, for in this place we find rhyolitic tuffs on the line of strike of the trachytic lavas. On the former alternative, which seems the more probable on the ground, it would appear that, although the acid fragmental rocks are in the main newer than the lavas mentioned, they are in part contemporaneous; and this supposition is perhaps strengthened by the occurrence of two or three thin bands of rhyolitic breccia and tuff interstratified with the trachytes. It is possible that a similar relation holds between the middle (fragmental) division and the upper (rhyolitic lavas), but the irregularities of dip and strike and the want of exposures in critical places leave this point in doubt. It is at least certain that both the lower and the middle division die out rapidly towards the west, for beyond Allt Mòr an Fhinn Choire the rhyolitic lavas rest with unbroken junction upon amygdaloidal basalts. The rhyolites themselves, with certain agglomeratic beds mainly of acid material which form the summit of the group, die out on the western face of Bruach na Frithe, dovetailing, as before described for the trachytes, with amygdaloidal basalts (Fig. 9); while metamorphosed basalts like those of Meall Odhar overlie the group again about Tobar nan Uaislean and upward.

It thus appears that the stratigraphical position of all these rocks is *in the midst of the basalt series*, a considerable thickness of the basic lavas occurring both below and above. In this we seem to trace both an analogy and a contrast with the corresponding succession in the Irish area. We have already remarked that in Antrim the basalts fall into two divisions, which must have been separated by a very considerable interval of time; and, according to Mr McHenry, the acid lavas and breccias belong to this interval between the Lower and the Upper Basalts. In Skye the basic lavas present practically an unbroken succession, and there is no direct proof to show that they represent both divisions of the Antrim basalts. If, however, we

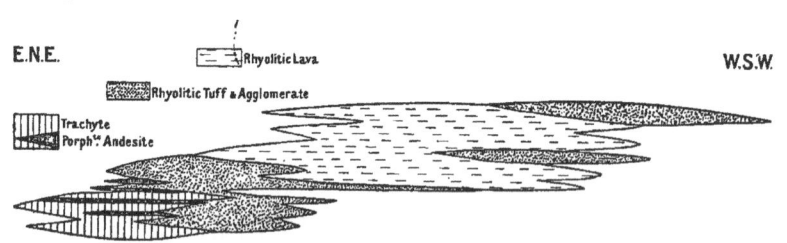

FIG. 9.—Diagrammatic representation of the relations of the trachytic and rhyolitic rocks to one another and to the basalts. The figure is an ideal general section of the group, not drawn to true scale.

may correlate the acid volcanic rocks of Skye with those of Antrim, we obtain the missing evidence on this question. It then appears that our basaltic lavas are the equivalents of both the Lower and the Upper Basalts of Ireland; but in our area there was no pause between the two, and they cannot be separated except in the very limited district where the trachytic and rhyolitic rocks interpose to mark the division.

The field-relations, as described above and illustrated diagrammatically in Fig. 9, prove firstly that this group of rocks is of *extremely local* distribution, and is contemporary with a part of the basaltic lavas; and secondly that *the centre of eruption gradually shifted westward or south-westward*, so that the successive divisions of the group overlap one another in that direction, and are in turn overlapped by the massive basalts of Meall Odhar and Bruach na Frithe. Incidentally the manner of occurrence of these trachytic and rhyolitic rocks throws light upon the nature of the great accumulation of basaltic lavas, which is here revealed as an aggregate of comparatively thin flows, each of small extent and rapidly wedging out.

The fact that the volcanic rocks of acid and sub-acid composition consist to the extent of fully one-half of tuffs and breccias suggests that, unlike the basalts, they were ejected from a true volcanic vent, or from vents belonging to a definite volcanic centre; and the limited distribution of the rocks is quite in accord with this supposition. It is also worthy of note in this connection that there are no acid or sub-acid dykes in the vicinity, and indeed none in the district which can be referred to this early epoch. Activity must have been prolonged at this centre for a considerable time, for the total thickness of rocks seen is not less than 2000 feet.

Turning to the *petrographical characters* of the rocks, we take first the *trachyte*, which forms the bulk of the lowest division of the group, and is seen in the eastern part of the area, viz. N. and N.W. of Meall Odhar. It is a rock of uniform appearance, light grey in colour, and of very fine texture, presenting little of a crystalline aspect to the eye. It contains flattened green and greenish yellow amygdules (chloritic and epidotic) and some smaller ones of quartz, and has evidently suffered somewhat from secondary changes. A fairly fresh specimen gave the specific gravity 2·53. A slice [9260] shows this rock to consist essentially of minute crystals of orthoclase, mostly less than $\frac{1}{1000}$ inch in length, closely packed with a fluxional arrangement. Minute octahedra of magnetite are also found in subordinate quantity. In this ground-mass are enclosed, quite sparingly, decayed flakes of biotite and other pseudomorphs which by their form suggest augite. The secondary products, in addition to the quartz in the vesicles, are disseminated chloritic matter and granular epidote. Another specimen, taken at a rather higher horizon, has rather more of the mica, though this is still a very subordinate element. It appears, to the eye, as little black specks with a parallel disposition; and a slice [7839] shows that these are flakes of biotite which have been altered by the so-called "resorption" and subsequently chloritised. There are also in this specimen a few scattered alkali-felspars, up to $\frac{1}{10}$ inch in diameter, embedded in the fine-textured trachytic ground-mass.

Intercalated in the trachytic division are four flows of a *porphyritic andesite*, a rock of very striking appearance owing to the presence of abundant large felspars, sometimes as much as two inches long. The specific gravity of the rock is 2·72. The andesites stand out a little in relief from the trachytic lavas, and the second and thickest flow makes a conspicuous small escarpment at the foot of Meall Odhar. Immediately beneath it is a thin band of a curious *volcanic agglomerate*, mainly of gabbro material. This has in the field the appearance of a crystalline rock, but is seen to enclose fragments of gabbro up to several inches in diameter. In a slice [7840] the principal elements are seen to be shattered crystals of labradorite, doubtless derived from a gabbro, with a few alkali-felspars, probably from a granite: there are also chloritic and serpentinous substances replacing destroyed augite.

The acid fragmental accumulations, which occur principally in the middle division of the group, consist essentially of rhyolitic material. They are in general *rhyolite-tuffs* of fine texture enclosing scattered larger fragments, though in some beds the coarser material is in such quantity as to warrant the term *rhyolite-breccia*. The breccias are well seen along a strip adjoining the northern border of the area, between Allt an Fhionn-choire and the next burn to the west. There are also two lenticular accumulations of breccia in the upper part of the succeeding division of rhyolitic lavas: one of these is on the spur of Bruach na Frithe marked by an Ordnance Survey cairn (1681·5 ft.), and the other occurs a little higher up, running for some distance along the western flank of the mountain. It is to be noticed that the rhyolitic tuffs and breccias, as well as the rhyolitic lavas, are, to a much greater extent than the lower division of the group, invaded by offshoots from the gabbro of the Cuillins, chiefly in the form of tongues and wedges which tend to follow the bedding of the volcanic rocks. If these latter have suffered in consequence any considerable thermal metamorphism, the effects of this are masked by other secondary changes. What is seen in other regions would lead us to anticipate much less mineralogical transformation from the influence of heat in these acid rocks than in the basalts. The whole group is traversed too by the same N.N.W. basic dykes which intersect also the basalts and the gabbro, and there are inclined intrusive sheets (not sills) of basic rocks in addition.

The acid pyroclastic rocks show little variety except as regards the varying proportion of larger fragments which they contain. The finely-divided matrix is always of pale colour, either white or light greenish from disseminated chloritic matter. In it are little chips and broken crystals of felspar, besides rock-fragments. These latter are angular, sub-angular, or rounded, and mostly less than an inch in diameter, though larger in some beds. The majority are of rhyolite; some seem to be of trachyte; while darker fragments, more conspicuous though less abundant, are of a microlitic andesite and a vesicular basalt, stained a deep brown colour and recalling palagonite [7837, 7838].

The *rhyolites* constitute, as has been said, the uppermost of the three divisions of the group, and make up about a half of the total thickness. The breccias towards the summit, already mentioned, indicate some recurrence of explosive eruptions towards the close of the rhyolitic phase. The most extensive exposures of the acid lavas occur in the neighbourhood of Allt Mòr an Fhinn-choire, the burn coming down from the fine group of springs named Tobar nan Uaislean; but here, and generally throughout the area, these rocks are greatly altered by secondary changes. Better specimens, which may be taken as representing fairly closely the unaltered condition of the rocks, are to be found in the little isolated patches associated with the biotite-felsite and gabbro on the south-western slope of Sgùrr Thuilm.

The prevalent type[*] appears in hand-specimens as a compact-

[*] A preliminary account of these rocks was published in the *Summary of Progress* for 1897, pp. 131-135, and is here reproduced with some modifications and additions.

looking rock of light grey to pale lavender colour. A specific gravity determination on an average specimen gave 2·596. Though there is no conspicuous porphyritic structure, a few small scattered crystals of felspar are visible, which are found to be orthoclase, turbid from incipient decomposition. A strongly marked flow-structure, exaggerated by secondary mineralogical changes, imparts a laminated appearance and often a highly fissile structure. This lamination is shown by alternating narrow bands of lighter and darker grey, with fine lines of a dark green colour and slender strings of quartz. In thin slices [7830–7836] it is seen that these bands correspond with slight differences in the nature of the general ground-mass of the rock; differences partly original, but partly due to, or accentuated by, secondary changes. The texture is in general very fine; in some bands of rather confused appearance, though evidently a felspar-quartz aggregate; in others more definite, with many minute felspars set parallel to the direction of flow. The ferro-magnesian element of the rock has been quite subordinate, and is in no case preserved unaltered. The least changed specimens show under the microscope small yellow-green chloritised prisms, representing destroyed augite, and more rarely a flake of altered biotite. Of iron-ore minerals there are minute cubes of pyrites, usually converted to limonite, and sometimes grains of magnetite. In many specimens both augite and iron-ore have disappeared, and there is only chloritic or ferruginous matter disseminated through the rock or tending to collect in cloudy patches. It is interesting to note that, in those specimens which contain most of the pseudomorphs after augite, there are rather abundant little prisms of apatite, associated with the ferromagnesian mineral and the magnetite.

Specimens from different horizons on the hill-side east of Allt Mòr an Fhinn-choire show no noticeable variations excepting such as are due to the varying advance of secondary changes, indicated especially by the development of quartz. In slices of the less altered examples the lighter bands are seen to be rich in this mineral, which tends to form a mosaic, and in this kind of occurrence is doubtless of secondary origin. The distinct strings of quartz, already mentioned as visible in hand specimens, are not essentially different. They sometimes swell into little lenticles, and it is clear that they are not merely veins filling fissures, but replace portions of the ground-mass. The little pseudomorphs supposed to represent augite, as well as the small crystals of pyrites, are sometimes embedded in the clear quartz-mosaic. Other specimens illustrate what may be regarded as a further stage, the little strings of quartz passing in places into knots up to half an inch in diameter, while locally there occur nodules of quartz up to an inch or more. In the examples which have suffered most alteration we find not only these knots or nodules of quartz but also druses, often an inch or two inches in diameter, and of irregular shape. These are lined with quartz crystals in the form of the hexagonal prism with pyramid termination, coated with a yellow ferruginous skin. The flow-lines of the rhyolite tend to wind round these drusy cavities, but are sometimes cut off by the larger ones, the appearances indicating that there has been an original cavity, but that it has been in some degree extended in connection with the process by which the new quartz was produced. The rocks in some places give evidence of a certain amount of crushing, and are indeed locally brecciated, this mechanical modification being clearly posterior to the chemical alteration which gave rise to the fine strings, knots, and druses of quartz.

The degree to which these lavas have been altered by replacement by secondary quartz—for which we must postulate in part an extraneous origin—leaves the true nature of the rocks, taken by themselves, a question of some obscurity. Having regard, however, to their general characters, and especially to the paucity of porphyritic elements, the strongly marked fluxion-structure, and certain peculiarities in some bands which suggest a devitrified glass, the affinities of these lavas seem to be very decidedly with the rhyolites. This conclusion is placed beyond doubt by an examination of the fresh examples preserved under exceptional conditions.

Like the Icelandic rhyolites, which they resemble in many respects, these Skye rocks show in general no tendency to spherulitic structures. If microspherulitic varieties are represented, their distinctive characters have been obliterated by secondary processes. At one place, however, quite at the base, or more accurately in the highest part of the underlying pyroclastic division, there is a thin flow of rhyolite composed in great part of large spherulites. This is exposed in the little ravine of Allt an Fhionn-choire. As is usual in these coarsely spherulitic rocks, the structure is obscured by later changes, and there is indeed a close resemblance to certain "nodular" rhyolites of Lower Palæozoic age in North Wales and Westmorland. Again, at a place a little east of Allt Mòr an Fhinn-choire the rhyolite at the base of the division shows what is possibly a spherulitic structure on a smaller scale; but this is too much affected by secondary changes to be made out clearly under the microscope.

In conclusion we have to notice the *intrusive biotite-felsite*, already mentioned, on the slopes of Sgùrr Thuilm. It occurs in several detached but neighbouring outcrops along a strip about $1\frac{1}{2}$ mile long, which are surrounded by gabbro. The exposures are not good enough to show clearly whether the gabbro has broken up and enveloped an earlier mass of felsite, or has been penetrated by intrusions of a later felsite; but the shape of the outcrops, so far as it can be determined, rather suggests the former interpretation. It is also worthy of remark that the gabbro is not traversed by any dykes or veins of acid rock, which might be apophyses from a later intrusion. It is therefore possible, and not improbable, that we have here the relics of an intrusive mass of acid rock older than the gabbro of the Cuillins, and so belonging to some part of the stage of volcanic eruptions. This suggests a possible connection between the felsite and the rhyolitic rocks of Fionn Choire and Bruach na Frithe, only about a mile distant. Such suggestion is strengthened by the occurrence, at one or two places among the felsite, of volcanic rocks allied to those described from Fionn Choire. At one spot is found a laminated rhyolite and at another spot a small patch of rhyolitic breccia. Their relations to the felsite are not clearly exhibited, but they are presumably enveloped in it.

The petrographical characters of the felsite of Sgùrr Thuilm are consistent with the idea that it is genetically related to the rhyolites. It is a dull, compact, light grey rock, enclosing numerous little yellowish felspars and some bronzy flakes of mica, sometimes as much as $\frac{1}{4}$ inch in diameter. The porphyritic felspars, which embrace orthoclase and oligoclase, have more or less rounded outlines, and are usually very turbid. The mica is considerably altered, sometimes completely bleached, sometimes chloritised. There are also grains of magnetite and prisms of apatite, the latter penetrating both mica and iron-ore. These various minerals tend to occur in groups or patches. The groundmass is of a common "felsitic" type, very fine-textured, but not cryptocrystalline : the felspathic element is partly in the form of minute prisms [8195, 8196.]

It is possible, and perhaps probable, that this rock represents a volcanic plug or "neck" connected with the acid lavas and tuffs, its form and relations obscured by a subsequent invasion of gabbro; but the evidence does not warrant us in insisting strongly upon this view. Apart from this, the very limited distribution of this highly interesting group of volcanic rocks, and the largely fragmental character of the rocks themselves, sufficiently prove them to be the products of central volcanic eruptions. That these were demonstrably contemporaneous with fissure-eruptions of widely different petrographical nature in the immediate vicinity, clearly indicates that there was no immediate relationship between the two groups. During the volcanic phase of activity at least, the "regional" and the "local" events followed independent lines, and must have been provoked by two different sets of causes. (*See* Chapter XXV.)

CHAPTER VI.

Peridotites (Earlier Group).

The plutonic phase of igneous activity in the Skye area was initiated by the intrusion of a magma of ultrabasic composition, which consolidated to form rocks rich in olivine. The intrusion assumed the laccolitic habit, and was effected at several places within what is now the south-western part of the Cuillin Hills, and also at one place in the neighbouring Isle of Soay. Except in the last case, the horizon was in the basaltic lavas, and not far from the base of that group. The geological relations of the peridotite laccolites of the Cuillins are, however, obscured in some measure by the gabbro which, in the form of one great complex laccolite, builds the greater part of this group of mountains. The gabbro magma, intruded immediately after the peridotic, has enveloped and invaded the ultrabasic rocks in a very remarkable manner. Some advantage of description might be gained by treating the gabbros before the peridotites, but the chronological order seems on the whole to be the more convenient.

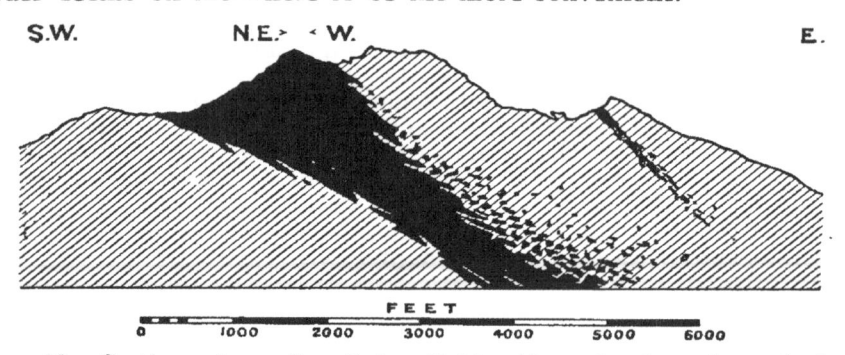

Fig. 10.—Section along the Sgùrr Dubh ridge, showing the principal laccolitic mass of peridotite and a smaller one to the east, and representing diagrammatically the partial destruction of the peridotite by the gabbro magma in which it became enveloped.

The principal mass of ultrabasic rocks is that which we shall designate the *Sgùrr Dubh laccolite*. It forms the whole of the western peak of the ridge of that name, known to climbers as Sgùrr Dubh na Dabheinn, and attains there its greatest thickness. In the col between this peak and the higher one to the east (Sgùrr Dubh Mhòr) the peridotite mass passes under the gabbro of the latter mountain, the irregular surface of junction having a steep dip to N.E. or E.N.E. (Fig. 10). On the Coir' a'

Ghrunnda side it extends down into the corrie, the boundary which corresponds with the under side of the laccolite passing through the middle of the tarn. The inclination here, judged by the dip of the flow-banding in the peridotite, is much less, not exceeding 30°. From Sgùrr Dubh na Dabheinn the outcrop of the laccolitic mass may be traced both eastward and northward, though with diminished thickness. In the former direction the peridotites form the floor of An Garbh-choire, and extend nearly as far as to the shore of Loch Scavaig. The trend corresponds roughly with the line of the valley, and the inclination, as indicated by fluxion-banding, is to some point of north, usually at a high angle. The thickness of the laccolite, which at its maximum reaches more than 1500 feet, is here reduced to 500 or 600 feet. Farther east, in consequence of the form of the ground and the varying inclination of the mass, the belt of ground occupied by the peridotite expands, and extends for some distance southward up Coire Beag. Beyond this the mass is so much invaded and broken up by gabbro that its continuity is lost. The northward prolongation of the laccolitic body from Sgùrr Dubh na Dabheinn crosses the col connecting the two mountains known as Sgùrr Mhic Choinnich and Sgùrr a' Coir' an Lochain, and extends down Coireachan Ruadha towards the head of the Coruisk valley. In this latter part of its course it is deeply cut into by the gabbro and divided into tongue-like strips. The whole outcrop has a roughly semicircular form, extending from Allt a' Chaoich, near Loch Scavaig, to the foot of Coireachan Ruadha, a distance of three miles. The concave boundary, representing the upper surface of the mass, is presented to the north-east; the convex boundary, representing the lower surface, to the south-west. The irregular form of the outcrop arises partly from original departure from the ideal lenticular shape of a laccolite, partly from subsequent tilting and flexure, but chiefly from the partial destruction of the mass by the later intrusions of gabbro, in which it was completely involved.

The *partial destruction of the peridotite laccolite by the gabbro magma* is most marked along the upper or concave side, and especially towards the terminations eastward and northward. The best place for observing the phenomena is near the eastern end, about Allt a' Chaoich (the "Mad Burn") and the stream immediately south of it. Here the whole mass of the peridotite is intersected by offshoots from the neighbouring gabbro. These are partly in the form of straight dykes, partly a network of irregular veins; and the dykes often serve as the origin of veins, which branch out from them and connect them (Fig. 11). In places the gabbro within the peridotite area swells into larger masses, which enclose detached blocks of peridotite (Fig. 12). By increase in the amount of gabbro as compared with peridotite, we pass insensibly from peridotite full of ramifying veins of gabbro to gabbro crowded with blocks of peridotite, the boundary being one which defies mapping. Outside the main area of peridotite there are still isolated portions of considerable size seen along the side of Allt a' Chaoich and on

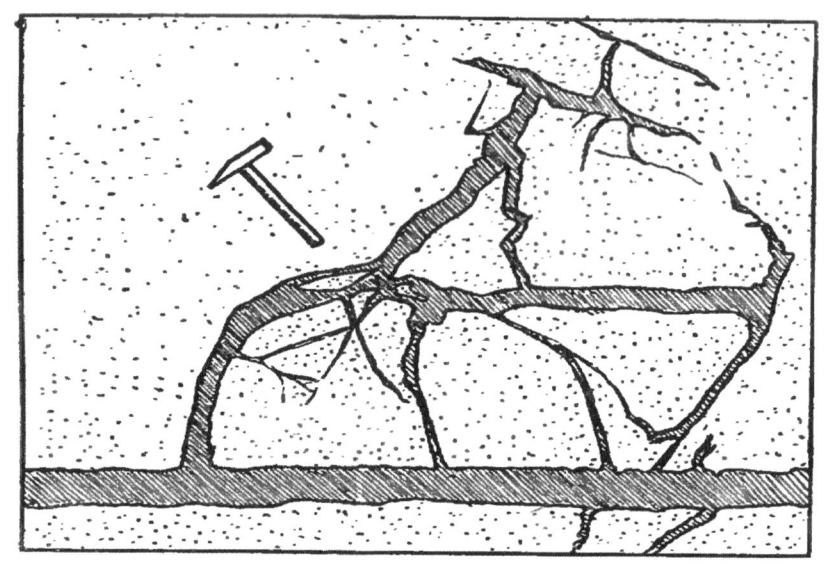

Fig. 11.—Dykes or veins of gabbro traversing the peridotite group, in glen south of Allt a' Chaoich, Loch Scavaig : seen in ground-plan.

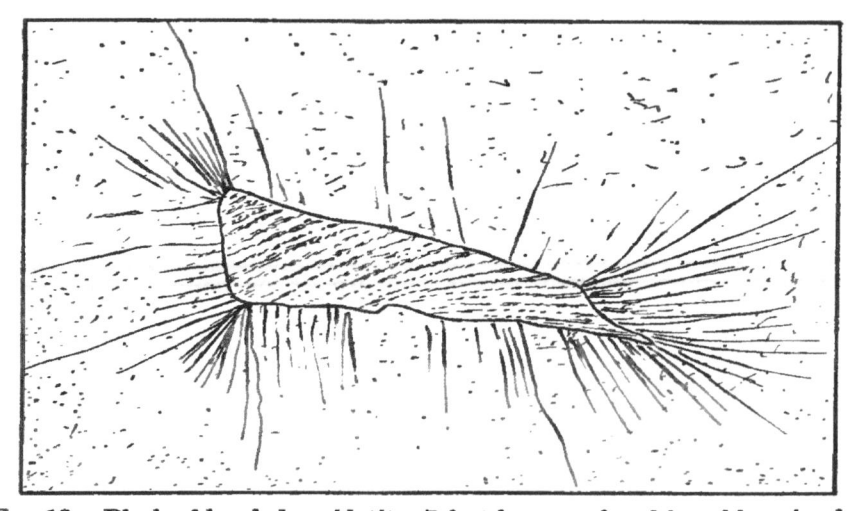

Fig. 12.—Block of banded peridotite, 7 feet long, enclosed in gabbro, in glen south of Allt a' Chaoich, Loch Scavaig : seen in ground-plan. The gabbro is traversed by numerous fissures radiating from the enclosed block.

the flanks of Meall na Cuilce. Farther east and north these become more broken up, but blocks of peridotite several feet in diameter are still found embedded in the gabbro as far as the shores of Loch Scavaig and Loch Coruisk and even on some of the islets of the latter. A similar destructive action of the gabbro upon the peridotite laccolite, though in a less marked degree, may be seen in Coireachan Ruadha. On the south-western or under side of the laccolite these extreme effects are not perceived; but the fact that the peridotite is often traversed by gabbro veins, while the reverse relation is never found, is sufficient to prove that the gabbro on this side also is newer than the ultrabasic rocks.

As regards the relative ages of the peridotites and the gabbros, it is proper to observe that the great gabbro mass of the Cuillins is the product of a number of successive intrusions, and only those portions which come into juxtaposition with the peridotite laccolite can be positively proved to be younger than it. The component parts of the gabbro mass seem, however, to be so intimately bound up together that nothing less than direct evidence could make it reasonable to regard them as partly earlier and partly later than the very distinct intrusion of ultrabasic magma. For this reason we consider the peridotites in question to have preceded all other plutonic intrusions in the district. To be sharply distinguished from these *older* peridotites of plutonic habit are certain *younger* peridotites, mostly in the form of dykes, which belong to a very much later epoch, and will be considered in a subsequent chapter (XXII.).

Besides the large Sgùrr Dubh laccolite already noticed, we refer to the earlier or plutonic set of peridotites now under discussion certain *smaller laccolitic masses* which will now be enumerated. With a single exception, they occur within, or in one case on the actual edge of, the gabbro of the Cuillins. One thin laccolite or sheet of small dimensions is seen in the dip between Sgùrr Dubh Mhòr and Sgùrr Dubh Bheag, the lower peak to the east (Fig. 10). This Sgùrr Dubh Bheag intrusion is the only one occurring at a higher horizon (having regard to the inclination of both peridotites and gabbros) than the large mass. It dips rather steeply to the east or north-east. Another small laccolitic mass, about 250 feet thick but rapidly tapering, crops out along the face of the buttress from Sgùrr na Banachdich which divides the upper part of Coireachan Ruadha into two smaller corries. Its rusty orange tint, contrasting with the darker gabbro above and below, makes it a conspicuous object as seen from Coruisk. A still smaller mass is intersected by the stream which drains the northerly branch of the same corrie. There are two small masses of irregular laccolitic form on the southern slope of Gars-bheinn, at altitudes of about 1500 and 1000 feet respectively. The lower of these, though partly enveloped by gabbro, rests upon the metamorphosed basaltic lavas below. Finally, a small mass of irregularly laccolitic habit occurs at An Dubh-sgeire on the east coast of the Isle of Soay, about two miles south of the last-mentioned locality. This, the most outlying intrusion of the group, occurs in the Torridonian grits, and therefore occupies a position below, but not necessarily much below, the base of the basalts. The distribution of these older peridotites is shown on a sketch-map in a later chapter (Fig. 75).

These various laccolitic intrusions, large and small, have been supplied, like other laccolites, *through fissures*, in which the magma finally consolidated to form *dykes*. It might be expected that all trace of these dykes would be destroyed by the later invasion of gabbro magma which enveloped the whole; but this is not always the case. Portions of some of the dykes are preserved, and in more than one case their actual connection with the laccolites which they fed is demonstrated. These dykes are seen to the east and south of Gars-bheinn in several places. They have a N.N.W.–S.S.E. direction and may be traced for considerable distances through the gabbro and the wedge-like portions of the basaltic lavas which here dove-tail with the gabbro. In the lavas the dykes are of course continuous; in the gabbro they are liable to be interrupted, and so occur in detached lengths. In places they are abundantly veined by the surrounding gabbro. They range in width up to as much as 40 or 50 feet; but usually they are less, partly perhaps in consequence of their being attacked by the gabbro magma.

One place where the actual connection of one of these dykes with the largest peridotite laccolite may be observed is in the lower part of Coire Beag, on the south-eastern side of the valley. The dyke can be traced at intervals for nearly 1000 yards in a S.S.E. direction from this place. It is doubtless a feeder of the large mass, but it is not to be supposed that it is the only one. Indeed there are at least two other places along the southern boundary of the laccolite where tongues project into the gabbro, which are probably of a similar nature, though they cannot be followed for more than a short distance. A more interesting case is presented by the two small Gars-bheinn intrusions. The lower of the two is in visible continuity with a dyke below, which runs S.S.E., cutting the basaltic lavas and the underlying Torridon Sandstone; but the mass is also prolonged upward into another dyke, having the same direction and nearly on the same line. This latter dyke runs up the hill-side, with breaches of continuity where it has been destroyed by the gabbro, and terminates at the upper and smaller laccolite, of which it is evidently the feeder. It appears then that we have here two laccolitic intrusions of ultrabasic rock, at different levels, supplied from the same source; the relations being still clearly indicated despite the interference of the subsequent and much more voluminous intrusion of gabbro.

To avoid possible confusion, before proceeding to the petrographical description of these various laccolites and their dyke-feeders, we will specify those younger ultrabasic rocks which are excluded from this place for later consideration. They are, as stated, mostly dykes, and dykes which are not the feeders of larger masses but independent intrusions. Sill-formed intrusions also occur, at least in the Isle of Soay. In addition there is an abrupt boss-like body of considerable size forming the hill An

Sgùman on the south-western edge of the gabbro of the Cuillins. The reasons for assigning this to the later group of peridotites are that it clearly breaks through the gabbro, and is connected with dykes referable to the later group, while its petrographical characters also point to the same conclusion. Finally there are a small mass near the summit of Glamaig and an isolated intrusion of irregular form, partaking of the nature both of a dyke and of a sheet, in the Lias near Suishnish Point, between Lochs Slapin and Eishort. All these younger rocks will be described in a later chapter.

Of the rocks now under discussion we have no chemical analyses, but it is very evident without such aid that they are all of ultra-basic composition. We have spoken of them collectively as peridotites, using that term in a broad sense. The commonest type is a picrite, in which augite and felspar are fairly well represented in addition to the dominant olivine; but there are other varieties of frequent occurrence, including very typical peridotites, in which the characteristic mineral occurs almost to the exclusion of all others.

The *constituent minerals* of these ultrabasic rocks are not many, and the various well-marked petrographical types arise from different associations of these minerals or associations of them in different proportions. Most important of all is olivine, which is found in all the rocks, and, except in the rare "norite," is the principal constituent, making up from one-half to practically the whole of the bulk in different types. Owing to this abundance of olivine, which is of a highly ferriferous variety, all the rocks assume on an exposed surface an orange to reddish-brown colour which at once arrests the eye. When augite or diallage is present, the small lustrous faces are visible here and there upon the rusty surface or upon a fractured specimen, where the olivine appears as a very dark or almost black crystalline aggregate. In the "troctolites" the white felspar interrupting the rusty film on the surface of the rock gives it a paler aspect. The rocks are of medium grain and of extreme hardness and toughness, giving a ringing metallic sound under the hammer. A certain heterogeneity in the composition of the rocks on a small scale, and the frequency of xenoliths which weather out more or less freely than their matrix, impart to exposed surfaces of the rocks a remarkably rough and often pitted character. Owing to this and to the soundness and toughness of the rocks, they lend themselves in an eminent degree to climbing, even on very steep faces.

The *olivine* occurs in crystals or crystals-grains varying from $\frac{1}{20}$ to $\frac{1}{8}$ inch in diameter. They are the earliest product of crystallisation, with the exception of the spinellids, and are thus idiomorphic, except when in the form of a granular aggregate they make up almost the whole bulk of the rock. They do not, however, usually show good crystal outlines. The mineral almost constantly contains inclusions of the type which Professor Judd has described, viz. flat rectangular cavities partly occupied by magnetite in branching or dendritic forms. When these are largest they vary from $\frac{1}{500}$ to $\frac{1}{300}$ inch in length (*cf.* Pl. XXV., Fig. 4, B), but usually they are much smaller, and then impart a peculiar dusty appearance to the thin slices. The little cavities are much more abundant here than in the olivine-gabbros to be described below, and often the magnetite occupies a larger space in each cavity, or almost fills it in some instances. We may infer that the olivine (including its minute interpositions) is in these ultrabasic rocks of a variety richer in iron than that in the gabbros.* The mineral is nevertheless sensibly without colour in thin slices.

The *augite*, which always forms allotriomorphic grains and patches, is sometimes colourless, sometimes light brown with a diallage structure (Fig. 14). In some cases again it shows in thin slices a faint green tint, perhaps due to the presence of chromium. There is then no diallage-structure, but only occasional bands of inclusions, the rule being apparently that the bands are parallel to one of the prismatic cleavages and the inclusions themselves to the other.

A rhombic pyroxene is an occasional accessory in the true peridotites and in some few examples predominates over the monoclinic species, while in the exceptional rock which we shall refer to as norite it constitutes fully one-half of the mass. Being sensibly colourless and without pleochroism in thin slices, it may perhaps be termed *enstatite*, but this criterion is of doubtful value when, as in this case, much of the contained iron is concentrated in the form of minute "schiller" inclusions. The mineral occurs in idiomorphic crystals, giving rectangular sections $\frac{1}{20}$ to $\frac{1}{10}$ inch long, with a marked schiller-structure parallel to the macropinacoid. Intergrowths with the monoclinic pyroxene are found.

When felspar occurs in the rocks, it is always *anorthite*. Only exceptionally does it tend to idiomorphism, with rectangular sections: usually it has an interstitial arrangement. It shows carlsbad and albite twinning, and less frequently a few lamellæ according to the pericline law.

The minerals of the iron-ore and spinel group, which are never wanting and sometimes abundant, belong to more than one variety. The most common is opaque in ordinary thin slices, and forms small octahedral crystals, invariably the earliest product of crystallisation and usually enclosed in the olivine. It has the appearance of magnetite, and is probably a *chrome-magnetite* or chromite, but has not been tested chemically. In some rocks we find, accompanying or replacing the opaque crystals, a translucent mineral of deep brown colour, usually in irregular grains, and this we may set down as *picotite*. At one place such a mineral occurs in relatively large crystals, which have been isolated and analysed. This is in the banded dunite to be described below, where the picotite is found in unusual abundance, making in some places narrow seams of practically pure material. It forms here well-shaped octahedra, black and lustrous, usually between $\frac{1}{100}$ and $\frac{1}{20}$

* In olivine from a peridotite in the Isle of Rum Heddle found Fe_2O_3 2·933 and FeO 18·703 : *Min. Mag.* (1884), vol. v., p. 16.

inch in diameter, and is distinguished from either magnetite or chromite by the fact that it scratches quartz. In thin slices it becomes transparent with a strong brown or greenish brown colour [9229, etc.]. A carefully conducted analysis by Dr Pollard gave the result shown in column I. There is a fair correspondence with the picotite of Lake Lherz (column A.), though the Skye mineral is notably richer in chromium. The only analysed mineral from the Western Isles which can be quoted for comparison is from near the summit of Askival in the Isle of Rum. The analysis is by the late Dr Heddle, and is confessedly imperfect, the investigation of minerals of this group presenting peculiar difficulties. The figures (B.) are, however, sufficient to show that the mineral is rather a chromite than a picotite, the alumina being much lower and the iron higher than in the first column.

	I.	A.	B.	I a.	I b.
SiO_2	1·19	2·00	6·543	·0197	··
TiO_2	0·34	··	··	·0042	··
Al_2O_3	46·54	56·00	17·957	·4554	·6083
Cr_2O_3	17·55	8·00	26·304	·1153	
Fe_2O_3	6·01	··	not det.	·0376	
FeO	10·10	24·90	34·239	·1403	·6059
NiO, CoO	0·24	··	··	·0032	
MnO	trace.	··	0·869	··	
MgO	18·35	10·30	13·913	·4547	
CaO	0·43	··	6·573	·0077	
	100·75	101·20	106·398		
Spec. grav.	(3·78)	4·08	4·163		

I. Picotite, from seam in banded dunite, glen south of Allt a' Chaoich, Loch Scavaig: anal. W. Pollard. (The specific gravity was taken on a hand-specimen, including a little olivine and serpentine, and is therefore too low.)

A. Picotite, Lake Lherz, Ariège: anal. A. Damour, *Bull. soc. géol. Fra.* (2), vol. xix., p. 414: 1862.

B. Chromite, seam in peridotite near summit of Askival, Isle of Rum: anal. M. F. Heddle, *Trans. Roy. Soc. Edin.* vol. xxx., p. 461: 1882. "The iron is *conjectured* to be in the ferrous state."

I a. and I b. Molecular ratios from analysis I. These give very closely the formula RO, R_2O_3, where RO stands for MgO and FeO with a little CaO, NiO, etc., while R_2O_3 stands for Al_2O_3 and Cr_2O_3 with some Fe_2O_3.

It seems probable that the brown translucent mineral in our other rocks is not essentially different from that analysed, and we may name it picotite without fear of error; but the nature of the opaque octahedra is not certainly determined. It must be admitted that the rough test of transparency or opacity in thin slices is not a very satisfactory criterion; but it also appears that the distinction between picotite and chromite is a rather arbitrary one, and has not been clearly defined. It is at least established that some picotites contain ferric as well as ferrous iron, while of the large number of published analyses of chromite (terrestrial) only two do not show alumina and magnesia.* The facts suggest that the spinels and the magnetites constitute not two but one group of isomorphous compounds of the general type RO,R_2O_3. If, as practical requirements may demand, we distinguish two sub-groups according to the predominance of alumina or ferric oxide among the sesquioxides, the varieties rich in chromic oxide occupy an ambiguous position, since Cr_2O_3 may be regarded as replacing either Al_2O_3 or Fe_2O_3. This is perhaps an argument for placing the highly chromiferous varieties in a third sub-group with some collective name. Here would be included most of the minerals which have been named chromite and some of those styled picotite, *e.g.* that from the original dunite of New Zealand with 56·54 per cent. of chromic oxide.

At a place very near to that which furnished the picotite analysed, the dunite contains instead another mineral of the spinel group. Unlike the picotite close by, but like the picotite in many of our rocks, it forms grains of irregular shape with little indication of crystal form. In thin slices it is transparent with a deep green colour, and it may be referred to *pleonaste*. It makes up in this place from one-third to one-half of the rock, but we have not observed it elsewhere.

The only other constituents of the rocks are rare scraps of brown *hornblende* and red-brown *biotite*, found occasionally in close association with the augite. Sometimes the biotite is intergrown with diallagic augite, its basal plane being parallel to the orthopinacoid of that mineral [9234].

The rocks consisting of various associations of the minerals enumerated present a considerable range of petrographical characters. As might be anticipated, they have much in common with the peridotites of Rum and the Shiant Isles, as described by Prof. Judd.†

Coming to the description of the rocks themselves, we may distinguish as the principal types peridotite in the narrower sense, picrite, and troctolite, and as an exceptional type norite.

Under the head of *peridotite* in the strict sense we include those rocks in which olivine predominates very decisively over all other constituents. Such rocks occur in considerable force in the large Sgùrr Dubh laccolite, especially in the eastern part of it. The type *dunite*, consisting wholly of olivine except for a usually very subordinate proportion of a spinellid mineral, is well represented. Locally, and especially in the small nameless glen a little south of Allt a' Chaoich, the spinellid mineral becomes a more prominent constituent; though it does not, except in particular bands of rock, equal in amount the olivine (Fig. 13). As the little octahedra of picotite become more numerous, they become transparent in the thin slices, and this presumably indicates a more chromiferous

* Pratt, *Amer. Journ. Sci.* (4), vol. vii., p. 284 : 1899. A large number of analyses are collected by Wadsworth in his *Lithological Studies* (Cambridge, Mass., 1884).
† *Quart. Journ. Geol. Soc.*, vol. xli., pp. 354-416. Pl. X.-XIII.

variety than the usual opaque mineral. In certain bands green pleonaste occurs richly instead of picotite. Specific gravity determinations of three specimens of dunites gave:—

[8726]	Lower part of Coire Beag	3·21
[9231]	Below An Garbh-choire	3·29
[9229]	Glen south of Allt a' Chaoich	3·32

The last is from a band rich in picotite. A specimen very rich in pleonaste, from the same neighbourhood, gave 3·435.

In the other peridotites, while the mineral which plays the title-rôle still makes up considerably more than half of the rock, it is accompanied by augite or felspar, or both, in addition to the usual small amount of magnetite, chromiferous magnetite, or picotite. The augite is usually a brown diallage (Fig. 14). The felspar, which

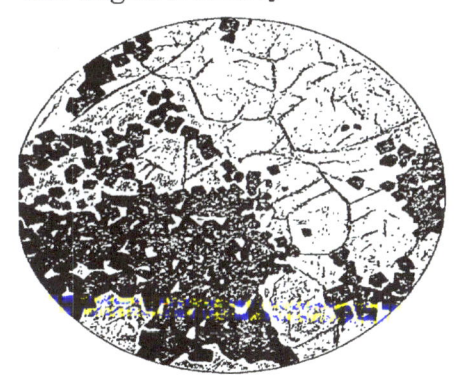

Fig. 13.—[9228] × 20. Dunite, rich in picotite, from the banded peridotites in the glen a little S. of Allt a' Chaoich, Loch Scavaig: consists wholly of fresh olivine and octahedra of picotite.

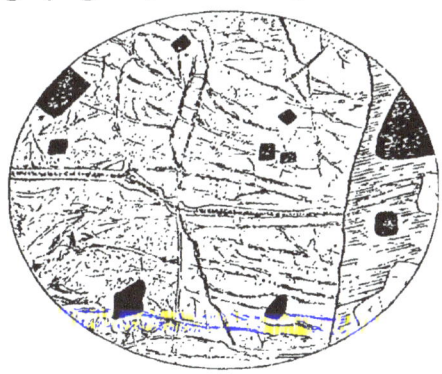

Fig. 14.—[9234] × 20. Peridotite, S.E. slope of Sgùrr Dubh na Dabheinn: chiefly of olivine (showing incipient serpentinisation), with some diallage and felspar (to the right) and opaque octahedra probably of chrome-magnetite.

is often quite as important a constituent, is always anorthite. Both minerals occur in little interstitial patches. These augite- or diallage- peridotites and anorthite-peridotites are connecting links with the picrites and troctolites, into which they graduate by diminution of the excessive proportion of olivine. An average peridotite from near the mouth of Coireachan Ruadha gave the specific gravity 3·26. An enstatite-peridotite, with only a small amount of diallage, seems to be of restricted occurrence.

The *picrite*, which is on the whole the prevalent type in the large laccolite, and is the essential rock of the smaller masses, differs from the peridotites proper in having a less marked preponderance of olivine, implying therefore a less extreme basic composition. Olivine still makes up fully one-half of the rock, and sometimes as much as three-fourths, the other principal minerals being augite and anorthite. As regards structural characters, there is little variety. The augite is in interstitial patches, or it may form spreading plates, each enclosing numerous grains of olivine, thus giving the "pœcilitic" structure of Williams. Where felspar and augite come together, the former mineral is idiomorphic towards the latter. The specific gravity of these rocks ranges up to 3·15, but, with increase in the proportion of felspar relatively to augite, may fall to 3·00 or less.

The third chief type, composed essentially of olivine and anorthite, will, in default of a more precise name, be spoken of as *troctolite*. It is to be observed, however, that this term (with its German equivalent Forellenstein) is currently applied to two very distinct rock-types, which are varietal forms of gabbro and peridotite respectively. The one has labradorite as its felspathic element (*e.g.* Coverack in Cornwall and Volpersdorf in Silesia), while the other, besides being usually richer in olivine, has anorthite *(e.g.* Allival in Rum). The former type is found, though rarely, among the Skye gabbros; but the rocks with which we are now concerned, intimately associated with true peridotites, belong to the second type. The felspar, by its optical properties as tested in the thin slices, seems to be always anorthite. In confirmation of this, Prof. Sollas has kindly determined the specific gravity of the felspar from one of our troctolites [9237] by means of his diffusion-column. The figures found were 2·735 to 2·74, with a mean of 2·737, and cleavage-flakes of specific gravity 2·74 gave extinction-angles of 36°. and 37°. The rocks are always rich in olivine, and their petrographical as well as geological affinities are clearly with the peridotites, not the gabbros.

Troctolites of this kind occur in some force in Coire Beag and near the foot of An Garbh-choire, and the same type is rather widely distributed in the form of enclosed patches and lumps in the picrites and peridotites and also as streaks and veins traversing those rocks. Anorthite makes up from 40 to 60 *per cent.* of the mass, or sometimes less. The remainder is chiefly fresh olivine, but there may be in addition augite or diallage in quite subordinate quantity. Brown translucent picotite is sometimes a rather conspicuous element. The only noticeable variety among the troctolites arises from a difference—more apparent than real—in the mutual relations of the two principal constituents. In the common type the olivine forms crystals and grains $\frac{1}{16}$ to $\frac{1}{4}$ inch in diameter, set in a framework of felspar [9236, etc.]. Sometimes, on the other hand, it is the latter mineral that forms conspicuous crystal-grains, often with partly rounded outlines, up to $\frac{1}{4}$ inch in diameter. The microscope shows, however, that here also the olivine is of prior crystallisation, for its grains encroach upon the edge of the felspars, and are occasionally enclosed in them [9237, 9238]. The peculiarity is most striking on a weathered face, where the felspars, always in relief, appear like white spherules in a black matrix. Under the microscope this appearance is lost (Plate XVIII., Fig. 2). An average specimen of the troctolites gave a specific gravity of 3·07. The somewhat similar rocks of Allival in the Isle of Rum are often more felspathic: one of these was found to have a specific gravity

2·88, corresponding with about 72 per cent. of anorthite to 28 of olivine.

In addition to rocks consisting essentially of anorthite and olivine in fairly equal proportion, we find varieties in which olivine preponderates, affording transitions to those peridotites (in the stricter sense) which we have termed anorthite-peridotites. On the other hand the coming in of augite offers connecting links with the picrites. Such variations may be found in what is apparently a single body of rock. This seems to be the case in the laccolite of An Dubh-sgeire on Soay, from which Mr Clough has collected a series of specimens. One from near the middle of the mass is a picrite with rather more felspar and less augite than usual [9973]. Abundant xenoliths in this are of troctolite, composed simply of olivine and felspar in about equal parts [9975]. Near the southern end of the intrusion the matrix of the mass, as Mr Clough remarks, nearly resembles the xenoliths at the other locality. It is indeed an olivine-felspar-rock with only accessory augite [9976], and, while petrographically a troctolite, is presumably a variety of the picrite. Again a specimen from the east side of the mass has for its essential minerals (in order of importance) olivine, felspar, and augite [9990]; and the preponderance of the first-named element brings this rock near to the typical peridotites. This intrusion, though of no great dimensions, thus illustrates the variability characteristic of the rocks of this group, as well as the close relationship existing between the xenoliths and their enclosing matrix.

The remaining rock-type to be noticed is one which for convenience we have termed *norite*: but we may make here a remark similar to that made in the case of the troctolites. The rock in question is not only closely connected with the peridotites as forming part of the Sgùrr Dubh laccolite, but also its mineralogical constitution links it with these rocks and severs it from the types of norite or hypersthenite which occur in some regions (but rarely in Skye) as associates of gabbro. In short, rocks composed essentially of a felspar and a rhombic pyroxene, like the felspar-olivine-rocks, seem to fall most naturally into two divisions, for which it would be useful to have two distinct names. The ultrabasic affinities of our rock are shown petrographically by the preponderance of the ferro-magnesian element, and presumable richness in magnesia, and by the extreme basic nature of the felspar, implying the absence of alkalies. In such a rock we may regard the rhombic pyroxene as substituted for olivine quite as much as for augite.

This type has been found in one locality only,[*] on the northern slope of the prominent peak called by climbers Sgùrr a' Coir' an Lochain, which guards the corrie of that name on its western side. It consists essentially of enstatite and anorthite, the former preponderating; while olivine occurs only in subordinate quantity, and diallage, magnetite (or possibly chrome-magnetite), and picotite are minor accessories (Plate XVIII., Fig. 3). The rhombic pyroxene is colourless in thin slices, and its birefringence weak: it must be

[*] Very beautiful rocks of this kind occur in Rum, occupying a considerable area to the north of Harris.

Banded structure in the peridotite group, An Garbh-choire.

referred to enstatite rather than bronzite or hypersthene. The crystals, which are idiomorphic towards the felspar, have a longitudinal striation indicating something of the "schiller" structure, but this is not of a very pronounced kind. Parallel intergrowths of enstatite and diallage are found.

Having noticed the petrographical characters of the principal types met with, we must devote some attention to the fashion in which these types, and varieties of them, are associated together. The most striking feature of the outcrops as seen in the field is their *heterogeneity*, which is carried to such an extreme that in some places it is scarcely possible to take a large hand-specimen consisting of only a single variety of rock. The heterogeneous nature of the mass is displayed chiefly in three ways—viz., in the interbanding of different kinds of rock, in the occurrence of débris of one kind enclosed in a matrix of another, and in the abundance of veins which are partly of the nature of segregation-veins.

A more or less noticeable *banding* affects the greater part of the rocks composing the several laccolitic masses, but it varies in the degree of its accentuation (Plate II.). Often the alternating bands are merely varieties of picrite differing somewhat in the relative proportions of the constituent minerals. The structure may in this case be almost imperceptible, except where it is revealed by a fluted appearance on a weathered face. The several bands are often not more than an inch or two in width, and are not very sharply divided from one another. It is quite clear that they are not separate injections, but that the structure is due to fluxion in a magma which was heterogeneous at the time of its intrusion. Elsewhere more pronounced differences in composition distinguish successive and alternate bands, more felspathic and more pyroxenic types, both rich in olivine, occurring in intimate association. At many places in An Garbh-choire, in the upper part of Coir' a' Ghrunnda, and elsewhere, bands of pale troctolite are thus associated with the darker picrite; and at other points, as in the vicinity of Allt a' Chaoich, more typical peridotites, *i.e.* rocks composed mainly of olivine, enter into the complex. The alternations occur on a rather large as well as on a small scale, so that in their general aspect on a weathered face the exposures may simulate the bedding as well as the lamination of stratified rocks. The narrower banding is undoubtedly a true flow-structure of the kind already indicated. It is not impossible, on the other hand, that the larger alternations are in part to be explained as distinct injections. Apart from the veins to be noticed below, however, we have found little or no evidence of one rock-type cutting transgressively into or across another; and we infer that, in so far as successive injections are responsible for the phenomena, they followed one another very closely, so that the earlier one was still fluid when the later was forced in beside it. Where an already consolidated rock was invaded by a new accession of molten magma, the former was apt to be broken up, and there resulted not banded but brecciated and xenolithic structures.

Among the most interesting phenomena of banding, and among those certainly due to segregation and fluxion, not to separate intrusions, are seams rich in minerals of the spinellid group. The best example of this, already referred to above, is the dunite in the small glen south of Allt a' Chaoich. Here, along some bands or streaks, picotite becomes a very prominent constituent of the rock; and certain black seams, following the general direction of the banding at this locality, consist simply of picotite in relatively large crystals, with only a very small proportion of interstitial olivine. These seams are really elongated lenticles, not being continued for any considerable distance. They are commonly from $\frac{1}{2}$ inch to 1 inch thick, exceptionally 2 or 3 inches. Seams very rich in a black mineral, probably chromite or chrome-magnetite, occur in the upper part of An Garbh-choire and near the head of Coir' a' Ghrunnda; but a spinellid mineral in an almost pure state has been found only in the glen first mentioned. One of the seams composed essentially of picotite (the mineral analysed above) gave the specific gravity 3·78.*

That phenomena of banding in the Tertiary peridotites of Britain are not confined to Skye, is evident from the accounts which have been published of some of these rocks in the neighbouring Isle of Rum. It appears even that seams consisting of spinellid minerals are not wanting in the latter island. Heddle describes his chromite from Askival, already referred to, as forming "a vein about one-quarter of an inch in thickness, embedded in a granular brown belt of rock, in augitic trap." He states that the brown belt was apparently chiefly olivine, and doubtless the "augitic trap" was in reality a peridotite, for such, as remarked by Professor Judd, is the nature of Macculloch's "augite rock" in Rum.

The banded arrangement of the peridotite group is not often accompanied by any very noticeable fluxional orientation of the crystals in the rocks themselves; but this is sometimes found, and in places near Allt a' Chaoich a decided parallelism of the crystals imparts a certain fissile character to the rocks. In the "troctolites" of Rum, mentioned above, this parallel orientation is sometimes much more highly developed.

The inclination of the banding varies considerably in different places, as is well seen in the Sgùrr Dubh laccolite. At the western border or base, as exposed near Loch Coir' a' Ghrunnda, the dip is easterly at 30° or less. Farther eastward the strike of the banding gradually changes, until along An Garbh-choire it is not very different from E.-W. The dips here are often at very high angles, or actually vertical, but lower angles are observed in some parts, always towards some point of north. In Coire Beag and near Allt a' Chaoich the banding dips northward at angles of 30° to 60°.

* Prof. Judd has described an almost pure picotite-rock (sp. gr. 3 90), which is stated to occur as a dyke in a mass of serpentine at Bingera, in New South Wales (*Min. Mag.*, vol. xi., p. 63 : 1895). This would imply that a rock-magma may exist with the composition of picotite. The circumstances, however, lead to a suspicion that this "dyke" may really be a contemporaneous seam in a peridotite, since serpentinised, and such suspicion is perhaps strengthened by the occurrence of another "dyke" composed of grossularite.

PLATE III.

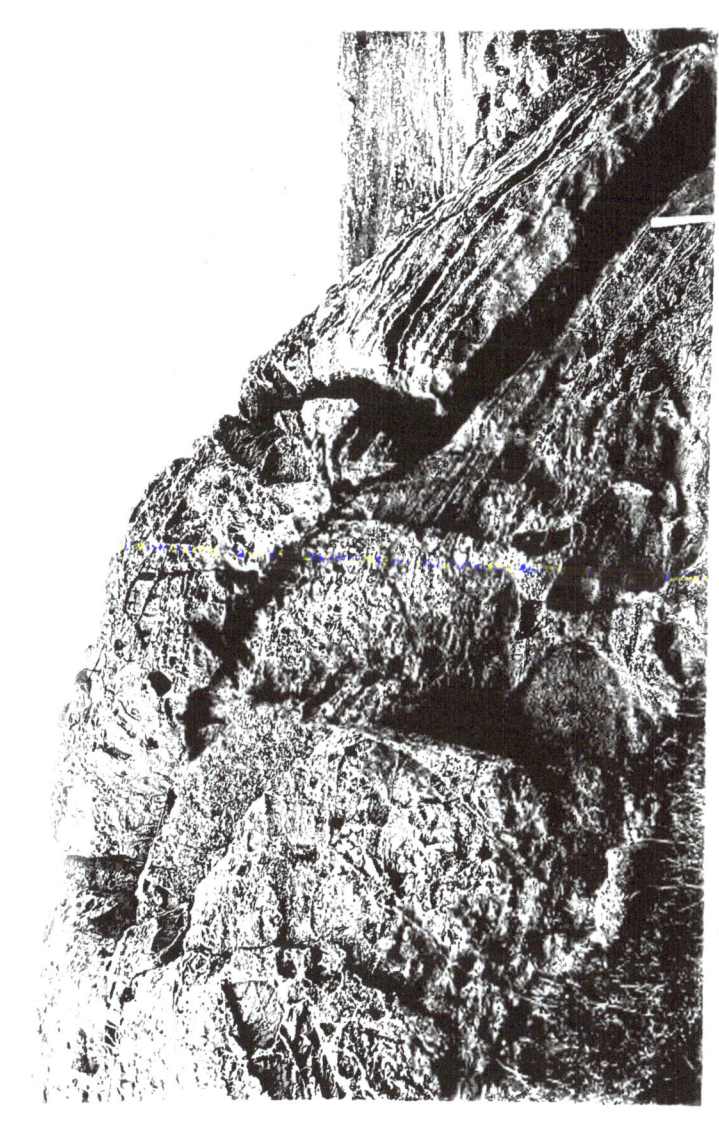

Brecciated appearance, due to xenolithic structure, in the peridotite group.
An Garbh-choire.

Everywhere the inclination of the structure corresponds in direction with that of the mass as a whole. Probably it corresponds approximately also as regards the angle of dip, though it is not necessary to suppose an accurate parallelism with the base of the laccolite at every place.* The smaller laccolitic intrusions are much less disturbed than the large one, and here the banding has a low and regular inclination. In the two Gars-bheinn intrusions it dips northward at about 10°. The dyke-feeders do not show any noteworthy banding.

Equally important with the prevalent banding, as impressing on these plutonic rocks of the peridotite group a highly peculiar aspect in the field, is the *xenolithic*† *structure*. This affects the great majority of the rocks, and is found in the dyke-feeders as well as in the laccolites themselves. The phenomenon consists simply in the occurrence of numerous, and sometimes crowded, inclusions of one rock in a matrix of a different rock, both inclusions and matrix being of types belonging to the peridotite group in the sense here understood. As in the case of the banding, the difference may be more or less pronounced. In some cases it is slight, xenoliths and matrix, *e.g.*, being of not very different varieties of picrite; and the heterogeneous nature of the mass may be betrayed only by the curiously pitted aspect of a weathered surface. In other cases the two rocks involved may differ widely, a common appearance on the weathered exposures being that of lumps of pale troctolite standing prominently out from a matrix of picrite or peridotite. Troctolite and picrite, the latter often banded, are the most frequent types occurring as xenoliths. They are of rounded to sub-angular shape, and commonly range in diameter from an inch to a foot. A place where the phenomena can be studied in rich variety is the lower part of An Garbh-choire (*see* Plates III. and IV.).

Two explanations seem to be *a priori* possible. An earlier rock, already consolidated, may have been broken up prior to, or in connection with, the intrusion of a new accession of magma, which then penetrated the interstices and enveloped the fragments; or the xenoliths may represent the débris of a rock previously solidified at some lower level and carried up in the form of fragments in a magma derived from the same or a neighbouring source. The fact that the xenoliths are usually much inferior in bulk to the enclosing matrix would seem to point to the latter explanation, as would also the rounded form of the xenoliths, indicative of a certain amount of corrosion by the magma. In some cases, however, there are circumstances which are more easily understood on the former hypothesis. The occurrence of strong banding in the xenoliths in some places is one such point; for, while this structure is highly characteristic of these laccolitic

---

* It will be shown below that banding in the gabbro laccolite of the Cuillins may be inclined at a considerable angle to the base of the laccolite itself (see Fig. 18, below).

† The term *xenolith* was first used by Sollas to denote a fragment of extraneous origin enclosed in an igneous rock. It corresponds with "enclave" as used by Lacroix and others.

intrusions, it is scarcely to be expected in rocks consolidated in some deep-seated reservoir. Again, although as a rule the xenoliths show no appearance of fitting together (having indeed more or less rounded outlines), and those which exhibit banding have not a common orientation, there are exceptions to this rule. In some places the xenoliths more than equal the matrix in bulk, and, although displaced and partly rotated, they present unmistakably the appearance of a rock broken up in place and injected in the interstices by a later magma (Plate IV.). The relations are indeed not unlike those of the peridotite and gabbro near Allt a' Chaoich, as described above (p. 64).

The two suppositions which we have stated as alternatives are not mutually exclusive, and the difference between them is perhaps less absolute than appears from the terms in which they are enunciated. If we are at liberty to imagine that the magma which the xenoliths represent in a given case was in part intruded as a member of the laccolite and there consolidated, in part solidified in the parent-reservoir or in the connecting conduit, and that the later intrusion was derived from the same source, we find place for both suggested explanations. In any case we must believe that the two rocks involved were of closely cognate origin, and were divided by no considerable interval of time. A high temperature in the earlier consolidated rock at the time when the later magma came in contact with it would promote a certain amount of solution and absorption of the former by the latter, of which we have evidence in the rounded form of the xenoliths.

A feature less widely developed than the banded and xenolithic structures, but still very frequently observed among our peridotites, is the occurrence of *segregation-veins* traversing the dominant rock in a given place. They are commonly about an inch or two in width, with the ramifying and irregularly tapering form characteristic of such veins in plutonic rocks of all kinds. They have too the usual relation to the dominant rock as regards composition, being invariably less basic, and in particular more felspathic: in most places they are of the troctolite type. In texture they are somewhat coarser than the rock which they traverse. In these respects they compare with the common pegmatite veins in granites and corresponding veins in other plutonic rocks, usually regarded as representing the final injection of residual magma, always more acid in composition than the general body of the rock. They are to be distinguished from ordinary veins of intrusion, with more sharply defined edges, which are also common in some places, and do not hold the same relation to the rock which they traverse (Plate IV.).

In their extreme variability and heterogeneity, in the prevalence of banded structures, in the occurrence of seams rich in chrome-bearing minerals, and in other respects, touching both their manner of occurrence and their petrographical characteristics, our rocks illustrate many of the observations of Vogt[*] in his study of peridot-

[*] Beiträge zur genetischen Classification der . . . Erzvorkommen (first part), *Zeits. für prakt. Geol.*, vol. ii., pp. 381-399 : 1894.

Veined structure in the peridotite group, An Garbh-choire.

ites and of the genesis of chrome-iron-ores; and the occurrences in the Cuillins present indeed a fairly close parallel to those of Hestmandö-Feld, in the north of Norway, which that geologist has described as a type. We shall see that there are also many points of resemblance between the peridotites of the Cuillins and the gabbros of the same district, to be described next. These latter show considerable heterogeneity within a single intrusive body, but it is not so prevalent, nor is it carried to such extremes, as in the peridotites.

A point of some interest in connection with the ultrabasic intrusions relates to the *nature of their contact* with the rocks among which they were intruded. The several masses which occur in the Cuillins, enveloped as they are by the later gabbro, afford no information under this head. The lower of the small laccolites on the slope of Gars-bheinn does indeed seem to impinge at its under surface upon the basaltic lavas, but no exposures of the junction have been observed. The intrusion of An Dubh-sgeire in Soay, however, occurring among Torridonian sandstones, presents in places visible contacts with the sedimentary rocks, and specimens have been examined. In one [9974], taken from the upper surface, near the middle of the reef, the igneous rock, normally an average picrite, becomes fine-textured at the edge, and the dividing line between it and the metamorphosed gritty rock is not sharply defined to the eye. The modification of the picrite extends inward for about half an inch from what may be taken as the surface of junction; and the microscope shows that this modification is not of the nature of an ordinary chilled selvage, but is due to the igneous rock having, to that depth, enclosed foreign material, which has been also in some measure absorbed into the ultrabasic magma and has so affected the composition of the edge of the laccolite. Quartz-grains are present abundantly in this marginal band, and are always deeply corroded, as is evident from their irregular shapes and ill-defined boundaries. Between the derived grains of quartz and the minerals proper to the picrite there is always interposed a brownish substance with confused structure, often imperfectly spherulitic, due to mutual reactions between the ultrabasic magma and the foreign matter (quartz with some alkali-felspar). This substance encloses the quartz-grains, and penetrates to some small distance among the olivine, anorthite, and augite of the picrite. It resembles in appearance some altered pitchstones, and has probably been in part vitreous, but later changes have obscured its true nature. Plentifully scattered through the brownish interstitial material are very slender felspar rods, about $\frac{1}{100}$ inch long, which are not anorthite but some less basic variety. In places there are pseudomorphs of a yellow serpentinous substance replacing idiomorphic crystals of relatively large size—$\frac{1}{10}$ inch or more in length. They have not the shape of olivine, but probably represent a rhombic pyroxene. This latter mineral is not one proper to the picrite, and the mode of occurrence of the pseudomorphs in the slice indicates that the mineral which they replace was connected with the special reactions in question. A mineral of the hypersthene group might indeed be expected from a peridotic magma locally acidified by absorbing extraneous silica.

In addition to the felspar-microlites, the brownish quasi-vitreous areas enclose. others in the form of little dark rods, which seem to represent some ferro-magnesian mineral destroyed. These are better seen in slices of other contact-specimens. In these the brown substance is in places reduced in amount while the enclosed crystallitic growths become more abundant and closely packed. They also increase in size, being sometimes as much as $\frac{1}{40}$ or $\frac{1}{30}$ inch in length. They are mostly slender felspar crystals, tending to fan-like and sheaf-like groupings; and their constantly low extinction-angles prove that they are alkali-felspars, probably both orthoclase and oligoclase, the alkalies being doubtless derived from the abundant felspathic grains in the contiguous Torridonian rock [10,042]. With the felspar rods there occur abundantly others, green and pleochroic, which are probably to be regarded as pseudomorphs after hypersthene.

Finally, a few remarks should be made relative to the *alteration* of the peridotites due to secondary changes. Incipient decomposition of the constituent minerals is found, as a rule, only in very slight degree, and most of the peridotites are entirely unchanged. In thin slices the felspar (when present) is perfectly clear, the pyroxene gives no clear evidence of secondary alteration, and even the olivine, one of the most susceptible of the rock-forming minerals, usually shows little or nothing of the familiar serpentinous transformation. The only rocks which are serpentinised in any important degree are those which have suffered crushing. This has given rise to a system of sub-parallel cracks, which are marked by narrow veinlets of colourless or yellowish serpentine (black in the hand-specimens) [9232, 9234]. There is a considerable amount of secondary magnetite-dust, mostly collected in the form of dense strings along the median line of each serpentine veinlet. It is evident that the earliest change in the olivine has been the separation of much of the iron in the form of oxide. At a later stage this may be in part reabsorbed into the serpentine, giving a yellowish colouration.

Equally interesting is the question of the *thermal metamorphism* of the peridotites by the later intrusions of gabbro, but on this point we have not gathered much information. A slice has been prepared, however, from one of the detached blocks of peridotite involved in the gabbro near the shore of Loch Scavaig, and this shows a micro-structure quite different from that of the normal rocks [9239]. Mineralogically the rock may be termed a picrite, but it consists mainly of a granulitic aggregate of olivine and felspar, in which the former occurs as rounded granules and the latter with allotriomorphic habit. There are even little areas free, or almost free, from olivine, recalling the "ocellar" structure common in the "pyroxene-granulites" of German petrographers. It seems not improbable, though by no means proved, that this structure is connected with recrystallisation in the process of thermal metamorphism. The diallage, however, which is the third but subordinate constituent, presents the ordinary characters of that mineral. In view of the comparatively simple mineralogical constitution of the peridotites, it is not to be expected that thermal metamorphism will give rise to important recombinations.

CHAPTER VII.

Gabbros: Field Relations.

For purposes of description we shall include under the name gabbro, not only the typical rocks so styled by petrographers, but also varietal forms which may be regarded as derived from that type by modifications either mineralogical or structural. Thus, variations in the relative proportions of the constituent minerals give, though only very locally and exceptionally, anorthosites, pyroxenites, troctolites, and picrites. Textural and structural modifications are more frequent and widespread, and give rocks which, taken apart from their actual associations and classed according to petrographical characters alone, might be named diabases, pyroxene-granulites, gabbro-aplites, and gabbro-pegmatites. All these are so intimately associated on the ground with the gabbros proper that no separation has been found practicable in the course of the mapping.

Gabbro, understood in this comprehensive sense, is a rock of great importance in the geological constitution of central Skye, and especially of the loftiest and most rugged mountains of the district. Its distribution, as shown on the map, may be summarised as follows. It forms the "country" rock of the whole of the *Cuillins* proper, and extends thence across the Camasunary valley at Loch na Creitheach, and so in a N.N.E. direction to form the *Blaven range*, viz. Blaven (Blath-bheinn*) itself, Garbh-bheinn, and part of Belig. This main gabbro tract measures about $8\frac{1}{2}$ miles from east to west and 6 miles from north to south, being, however, encroached upon from the north-east by the granite of the Red Hills. The isolated occurrences of the rock are not numerous. The largest of them is a patch about two miles long and one mile broad lying to the north-west of Broadford, where it is associated with the Cambrian Limestones and Torridon Sandstone. Some small patches occur on the north-west slopes of Belig, near the boundary of the main area, and a little boss about 150 yards in extent is seen on the moorland west of Glamaig, not far from the high-road. To these may be added a few very small patches near

* Although the older place-names in Skye, whether of the more prominent physical features or of settlements, are of Norse origin, the majority of names are Gaelic, and for these we follow in general the Gaelic spelling, as given on the Ordnance maps. A few names, however, are current in anglicised form, roughly transliterated, and some are so given on the maps, *e.g.* Coruisk and Quiraing. In some cases Norse names have been disguised in a Gaelic dress. If, as is probable, this is the case with "Blath-bheinn" (Blaaval, blue mountain), the English spelling of the guide-books is to be preferred to the Gaelic which appears on the map.

the south coast of Scalpay and the whole of Guillamon, a rocky islet about ¼ mile long to the north-west of Broadford Bay.*

It remains to be said, however, that numerous patches and strips of gabbro occur enclosed in the later granitic intrusions, indicating that the rock in question has had originally a somewhat wider distribution. These relics of destroyed gabbro are in places highly metamorphosed and otherwise modified, and will be described below. The most interesting is the broken series of narrow strips which runs from Glen Sligachan to Coire na Seilg along the flanks of Marsco. The northern half of Beinn na Cro is formed by a large patch of the bedded basaltic lavas, traversed by thick irregular sheets of gabbro, the whole enveloped in the main granite mass of the Red Hills. Small patches of gabbro are entangled in the granite at the north-west base of Blaven and the eastern base of Belig, on the moorland north of Beinn na Caillich, and in other localities.

The actual forms assumed by the gabbro intrusions, and their relations to the bedded and other rocks among which they have been intruded, are subjects which necessitate a few remarks of a general kind, and these remarks will be in great measure applicable also to the granite intrusions to be described later. Concerning the true shapes and essential geological relations of large bodies of plutonic rocks geologists have been to some extent divided. The tendency of general opinion at the present time is to regard these large masses as not differing essentially, but only in their greater magnitude and less perfect regularity, from smaller intrusive rock-bodies which are easily recognised as sheets and laccolites, dykes and "plugs." With this view the results of a survey of the gabbro and granite areas of Skye are wholly in accord. We may say further that the more extensive bodies of plutonic rocks are generally of the nature of sheets or laccolites rather than plugs or bosses, and this remark also is probably one of wide application. Indeed, the only alternative would require us to suppose that the igneous magma has not merely displaced but *re*placed (by actually incorporating) the rocks into which it has been forced; and, although we have in Skye itself abundant evidence of such action on a limited scale, its general application is negatived by chemical and other considerations sufficiently conclusive.†

Confining our attention then to Skye, we find that the plutonic rock-bodies, whether of gabbro or of granite, fall under two heads. Firstly there are those which have, allowing for minor irregularities, the general habit of *sheets or laccolites*, inclined at no high angle to the horizon, overlying older rocks and overlain (where

---

* A rock intrusive in Jurassic strata between Allt Leth Slighe and Glen Boreraig, in the neighbourhood of Loch Slapin, is petrographically a gabbro, but probably belongs to a much later group of intrusions. It will be considered below (Chapter XXI.).

† The argument has been very cogently stated by Brögger in the second part of his *Eruptivgesteine des Kristianiagebietes* (*Vidensk. Skrifter, Math. naturv. Klasse*, 1895, No. 7, pp. 116-153).

erosion has not removed the covering) by other older rocks. Such plutonic masses are the analogues of the smaller sheet-like or sill-like and laccolitic intrusions, composed usually of hypabyssal rocks, which may be directly observed as such in this and other districts. The only difference is that the large bodies are usually too extensive for their true forms and relations to be displayed in any one view, while the irregularity of their boundaries on a small scale often renders any single section inconclusive or misleading. The second category of plutonic masses is that which includes *stocks or bosses*, which break abruptly through the bedded or other rocks into which they have been intruded. Their analogues among minor intrusions are found in certain plug-like masses, or again (when there is a tendency to linear extension and straight boundaries) in dykes.

Corresponding in a general sense with the two kinds of habit just discriminated, there are two contrasted types of junction between the plutonic rock and contiguous rocks. The first type is usually gently inclined or quasi-horizontal, the igneous rock underlying or overlying that with which it is in contact at a low angle, and, if the latter be a bedded rock, cutting across it only gradually and obliquely or preserving a general parallelism with it. The second type of junction is usually approximately vertical and always clearly transgressive, the igneous rock cutting sharply across its neighbour, and, if the latter be a bedded rock, truncating the beds abruptly. Among minor intrusions of hypabyssal and volcanic rocks the sheet-like habit is almost always associated very regularly with the quasi-conformable type of junction and the plug-like and dyke forms with the transgressive junction, but in the case of the plutonic masses this correspondence is less complete. It may happen that a large body of gabbro or granite which from its general behaviour is clearly to be referred to the first mode of occurrence exhibits for some distance along its border a junction of the second type, while the converse case is also to be noted, though less frequently. In this way arise the irregularities which disguise in some degree the true nature of these large intrusive masses, and especially of those having a general sheet-like or laccolitic shape; and it follows that the true form and relations of such masses are to be made out, not from the examination of single sections, but from the boundary as laid down on a contoured map. It should be remarked, moreover, that we may have intrusive bodies of plutonic rock of the two different habits in direct continuity with one another, and such seems to be the case at more than one place in the district. The relation here indicated is doubtless that which among minor intrusions is often shown to subsist between a sill and the dyke which represents its feeder.

Certain other characteristic features seem to belong to the two modes of occurrence of the plutonic rocks, respectively, or, again, to the two different types of junction; and although these distinctions are more marked with the granites than with the gabbros, they may be briefly mentioned in this place. Along a junction of the gently inclined type the plutonic rock is frequently found to assume a finer texture and to develope porphyritic or spherulitic structure or some other modification, and at the same time there may be very little metamorphism produced in the adjacent rocks. Along a junction of the transgressive type, on the other hand, there is rarely any modification of the plutonic rock of a kind indicative of rapid cooling, while the metamorphism of the adjacent rocks may be very intense. In the latter case too the plutonic rock often encloses material derived from its bounding wall, and may even be considerably altered in bulk composition from this cause; a phenomenon not usually observable at the borders of sheet-like or laccolitic intrusions. To this rule there are, however, important exceptions.

The two contrasted modes of occurrence of plutonic rocks are well exemplified by the two principal gabbro masses of Skye, respectively. The large mass which builds *the Cuillins and Blaven*, considered as a whole (*i.e.* disregarding for the present its highly complex constitution), is of the nature of *a great sheet or laccolite*. and its junction with adjacent older rocks is in most places a gently inclined one. The laccolitic nature of the mass was recognised many years ago by J. D. Forbes in a paper which deserves to be better known. Writing in 1846, he points out that the gabbro clearly overlies the basaltic lavas in visible sections, and remarks in conclusion : " The whole phenomena of junctions and superpositions . . . . leads us to consider the hypersthene [gabbro] as *a vast bed*, thinning out both ways, and inclined at a moderate angle towards the S.E., or parallel to Loch Coruisk."*

The detailed mapping of the ground entirely confirms Forbes' statements, but the inclination of the base of the laccolite is only roughly expressed in the words quoted. As we follow round the outer boundary of the gabbro, we find that the dip is almost always inward, towards the mountains. To this rule there are, however, exceptions, the inclination in some places being nearly parallel to the boundary, but never outward. The altitude of the base of the laccolite varies from about 2500 feet above the sea to below sea-level. By taking points along the boundary corresponding with certain heights above sea-level (say at intervals of 500 feet), and drawing lines in the direction of local strike of the gabbro base, we obtain portions of contour-lines on the lower surface of the laccolite. These lines may be prolonged and connected up conjecturally, taking account of the obvious condition that neither inside nor outside the gabbro area must they cross the corresponding contour-lines of the surface of the ground. The large and deep interior valleys make this a much more determinate problem than might be expected, and the result given in the accompanying sketch-map (Fig. 15) must represent the general shape of the lower surface of the gabbro with a rough accuracy quite sufficient for our purpose.

It will be seen that a sharp anticline occurs at the northern or

* *Edin. New Phil. Mag.*, vol. xl., p. 86 : 1846.

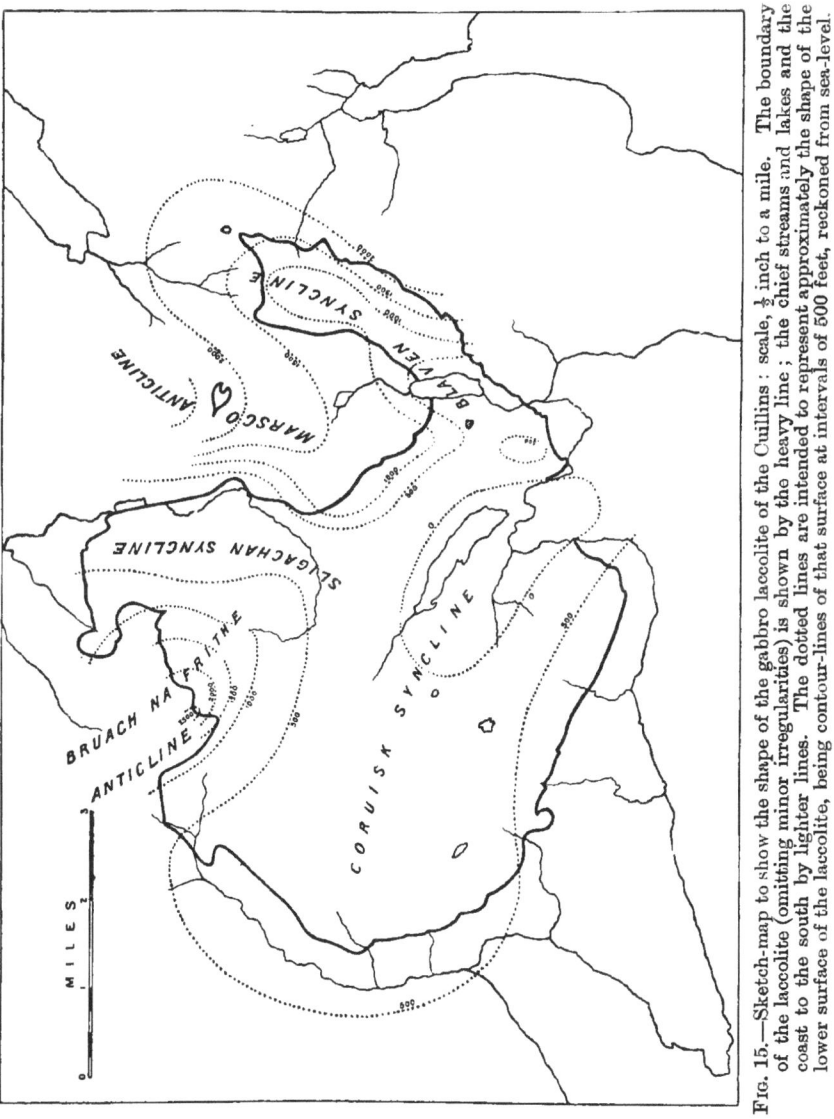

Fig. 15.—Sketch-map to show the shape of the gabbro laccolite of the Cuillins: scale, ½ inch to a mile. The boundary of the laccolite (omitting minor irregularities) is shown by the heavy line; the chief streams and lakes and the coast to the south by lighter lines. The dotted lines are intended to represent approximately the shape of the lower surface of the laccolite, being contour-lines of that surface at intervals of 500 feet, reckoned from sea-level.

north-western border, about Bruach na Frithe, and to the south-west of the axis of this a broad shallow syncline. The north-eastern part of the area is occupied by a very marked anticline corresponding with the later intrusion of granite, and the axis of this is prolonged in a S.S.W. direction to Sgùrr na Stri, overlooking Loch Scavaig. Between this anticline and the other one lies a syncline coinciding with the valley of the Sligachan River; while the south-eastern and almost detached portion of the gabbro, which builds the Blaven range, has also a sharply synclinal arrangement. There is a very evident relation between the form of the laccolite as thus roughly defined and the present surface-relief of the ground, and this will be referred to more fully below (Chap. XXVI.). One point very clearly illustrated by the sketch-map is that over considerable stretches in the interior the base of the gabbro must be at no great distance beneath the surface. This is true not only of low-lying portions of the surface such as Glen Sligachan and Harta Corrie, Coruisk, and the lower part of the Camasunary valley, but also for the more elevated Druim an Eidhne and Coire Riabhach and for portions of the northern mountains. Although only partially true, as Forbes believed, of the western range, it is true of the northern Cuillins and of the Blaven ridge, that much of their elevation is due not to the thickness of the gabbro but to the underlying rocks.

Although the shape of the base of the laccolite is in the main original and connected with the circumstances of the intrusion, some features of it must be ascribed to subsequent deformation. This is notably the case with what we have styled the Marsco anticline, which seems to be related to the intrusion of the granite beneath.

Concerning the shape and position of the top of the great laccolite the data directly observable are very scanty, the overlying rocks having escaped the effects of erosion only in a few small patches, if at all. The highest rocks in the Cuillins, forming the summits of the peaks known to climbers as Sgùrr Alaisdair, Sgùrr Tearlach, and Sgùrr Mhic Choinnich, to the east of Coire Labain, are not gabbro but basaltic lavas with some breccias. They are highly metamorphosed, and penetrated by tongues from the underlying gabbro. These rocks may possibly be only a patch of the volcanic group caught in the gabbro, like others at lower altitudes; but from their position and extent it seems very probable that they mark approximately the original summit of the gabbro mass. If so, the thickness of the laccolite in this place would be not far short of 3000 feet, and in the centre might perhaps be as much as 3500 feet, or about one-tenth of the probable average diameter. This kind of proportion is not unlike that observed in laccolitic intrusions in other parts of the world. The classical examples in the Henry Mountains of Utah have on the average a maximum thickness one-seventh of the diameter, and for more basic rocks, consolidated doubtless from a less viscous magma, a lower ratio is to be expected. Such a laccolite, indeed, may with equal propriety be regarded as a thick sheet tapering to the edge. From this point of view it is reasonable to suppose that the vanished upper surface corresponded in general form with the lower surface, the shape of which we have examined; and this would be the case whether the form is due to irregularity of intrusion or to subsequent disturbance.

The base of the gabbro does not correspond with a defined geological horizon. Approximately, however, the great laccolite occurs not far from the base of the volcanic series. This is true at least on the southern and eastern sides, where the thickness of basaltic lavas below is never great, and in one place the gabbro rests on Jurassic strata. Again, the agglomerate along which the gabbro is intruded at Loch na Creitheach and Druim an Eidhne is probably, like that of Coire Coinnich and Belig, at the very base of the volcanic rocks. On the western and north-western sides the gabbro is at a somewhat higher horizon, though here, too, the thickness of basalt beneath need not be very great.

We have hitherto treated the gabbro laccolite as a single body of rock; but this is far from representing adequately its actual constitution. What we have styled for convenience of reference the gabbro mountains consist in fact of a great complexity of basic igneous rocks, of which gabbro is the most prevalent. A glance at the geological map shows that there are entangled and enveloped in the gabbro a great number of patches of older rocks, viz. basic lavas and agglomerates; and further that the gabbro and the patches enclosed in it are alike traversed by innumerable dykes and sheets of later rocks, also of basic composition. But the complexity now specially referred to is of a different kind, arising from the heterogeneous constitution of the gabbro itself, which consists of very *many separate intrusions*, often of different petrographical varieties. This composite structure is not indicated on the map, the small size of many of the component masses and their intricate relations to one another rendering this impossible. In very many parts of the mountains different types of gabbros, coarse and fine, granular and diabasic, paler and darker, are seen to succeed one another or alternate, the nature of their junctions often being such as to demonstrate that they represent distinct intrusions. As a rule they are associated together with some approach to a parallel disposition in stratiform masses or sheets; but this regularity often breaks down, and the various masses are seen to undulate, to wedge out or fringe out, or to intersect one another obliquely. In other cases it is not possible to distinguish separate masses from variations, which undoubtedly occur, in individual masses. It is to be supposed that successive intrusions often took place through the same fissures, and further that intrusions from different fissures invaded and interlaced with one another. It is not difficult to understand how, in such conditions, the tendency to form rough sheets parallel with the general extension of the whole complex would be modified by many circumstances tending to introduce irregularities. The several intrusions clearly differed much in bulk. Some, especially the typical coarse gabbros in the interior

Complex Structure of Gabbro Laccolite. 89

of the area, are found to extend for many hundreds of feet across their strike; while others, usually of more aberrant varieties, are only a few feet thick.

The numerous *patches of basaltic lavas and agglomerates, mostly of lenticular form, enclosed* in the compound laccolite are in general not enveloped by individual gabbro intrusions, but caught between distinct intrusions. In accordance with this they have almost always an inclination more or less inward, *i.e.* towards the interior of the gabbro area, corresponding with the general structure of the composite laccolite itself. In some places not far from the boundary of the gabbro on the map occur patches of the volcanic rocks which were probably not wholly surrounded by gabbro, but have become isolated as the result of erosion. The gabbro mass fringing out into a number of sheets has intercepted wedge-like portions of the lavas, which, prior to the denudation of the district, were continuous with the main body beyond. This is especially the case on Garsbheinn, as illustrated by the section (Fig. 16), and on the north ridge of Bruach na Frithe and its vicinity. It is in accordance

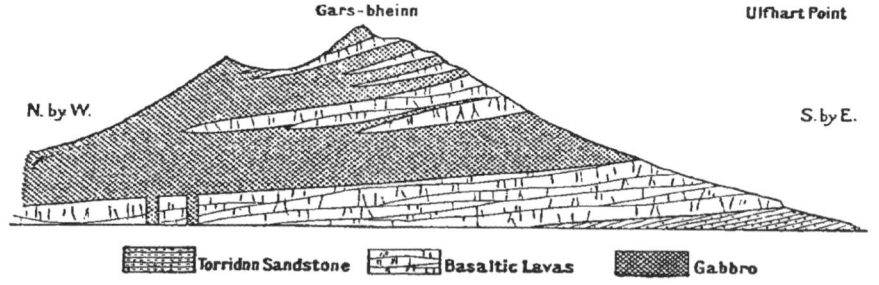

Fig. 16.—Section through Gars-bheinn, to illustrate alternations of basaltic lavas and gabbro, due to the successive intrusions of the latter rock having followed different bedding-planes in the lavas. Scale, 2 inches to a mile.

with the general stratiform arrangement of the gabbro mass, as a whole and in its component elements, that it sometimes passes at the edge into sheets, but never gives off dykes. These sheet-like apophyses, however, are not a very general feature, and never extend for any great distance. It is especially noticeable that the base of the laccolite is usually an unbroken surface. The map shows that the outcrop of the base is, round the greater part of the circumference, a continuous line. The only important exceptions to this, on a large scale, are seen above the upper part of Glen Brittle and on and about the northern ridge of Bruach na Frithe.

The gabbro laccolite, being formed by numerous distinct intrusions, is therefore not all exactly of one age, and it is of interest to inquire whether any law is apparent in the sequence of its component parts. Did successive intrusions spread out beneath those already injected, as at a later time the granite magma forced its way under a part of the whole gabbro laccolite? Or was the composite laccolite built up from below upward, the newer portions breaking through the older and spreading above them? These two alternatives are, of course, not exhaustive: we might conceive, for instance, that the highest and lowest portions represent the first intrusions, later ones having forced their way between and among the earlier. We have not been able to arrive at any conclusion on this point from actual observations demonstrating the priority of one component sheet to another, but other considerations may perhaps afford some clue. It is noteworthy that the gabbro magma has effected much more serious inroads upon the upper than upon the lower surface of the large pre-existing laccolite of peridotite. The only apparent explanation of this is that the peridotite was still at a high temperature when the overlying gabbro was intruded, but had cooled before the intrusion of the underlying. This would indicate that here the upper portion of the gabbro is older than the lower portion. If such be the general rule, it removes a difficulty which is otherwise pressing, viz. the fact that the conduits by which the higher portions of the gabbro mass were supplied are rarely to be detected.

The gabbro of the Cuillins and the Blaven range is not only complex as consisting of many distinct intrusions; the rocks of these individual intrusions themselves are often not of uniform characters. In many localities *patches and streaks* are seen, which differ mineralogically or in texture from the surrounding rock, but are not distinctly separable from it. They are not to be confused with the inclusion of actual xenoliths of one type in a matrix of another type, but are clearly referable either to segregation in place or to the magma being heterogeneous at the time of its intrusion. Only occasionally is there any great petrographical difference between the patches or streaks and the general body of the rock: in some cases the former are unusually rich in augite or in iron-ores.*

Usually the patches are more or less drawn out into narrow lenticles or bands, with a general parallelism at any given spot, and this may be carried so far that a very conspicuous *banded or ribboned structure* results. Banded gabbros are intercalated among and between rocks of the more normal massive kind, or in places occupy alone considerable stretches of ground. They are especially well developed round Loch Coruisk and from there north-eastward to Druim an Eidhne (Fig. 17), and it is in the latter place that the most remarkable exhibition of banding in the gabbros is found. The rocks here have been described by Sir A. Geikie and Mr Teall,[†] and their appearance in the field is well shown in the accompanying Plates V. and VI.

It appears from the small sketch-map appended that, disregarding a few local irregularities, the inclination of the

* Probably of this nature was the lump of magnetite found loose by Heddle on Druim nan Ramh. "It consisted of interlocked crystals, about the size of peas, and might have weighed forty pounds or more." *Trans. Roy. Soc. Edin.*, vol. xxx., p. 453 : 1882.

† *Quart. Journ. Geol. Soc.*, vol. l., pp. 645-659, Pl. XXVI-XXVIII : 1894. See also Plate XIII. in the same volume.

Strongly banded structure and felspathic veins in gabbro, Druim an Eidhne.

Banded structure in gabbro, Druim an Eidhre.

Banding in Gabbro Laccolite. 91

banding follows a general law, the structure dipping inwards towards the interior of the gabbro area. More accurately, it dips towards a point situated somewhat to the north-east of the centre and where a portion of the gabbro laccolite is wanting owing to the subsequent invasion of granite. The angle of dip is usually between 30° and 70°.

The significance of the banded structure will be more properly discussed in connection with the petrographical characteristics of the banded rocks. It may be remarked here, however, that the phenomenon is doubtless, as Sir A. Geikie and Mr Teall have

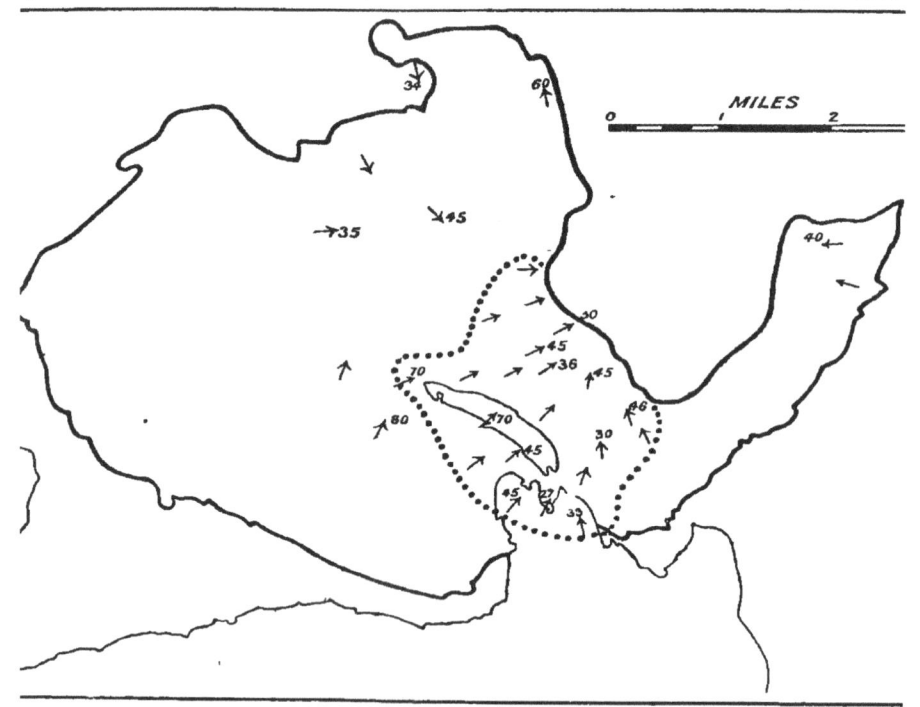

FIG. 17.—Sketch-map showing the distribution of banded structures in the gabbros of the Cuillins. The strong line indicates the boundary of the gabbro itself: the dotted line encloses the area within which banding is most prevalent. The dip of the banding is shown by arrows. Scale, ½ inch to a mile.

indeed proved, of the nature of an original flow-structure, and has a special interest with reference to the origin of some banded gneisses of much greater geological antiquity. The bands have thus a general parallelism with the upper and lower surfaces of the individual sheets of gabbro which exhibit the structure; but it does not follow, and it is evidently not the fact, that the banding is parallel to the lower surface of the complex laccolite as a whole. This appears from a consideration of the dips as recorded, and is very clear in what may be regarded as the typical locality, viz. the strip of gabbro on the border of the area at Druim an Eidhne (Fig. 18).

The bands, though usually straight and preserving a common direction in any given exposure, are seen in places to be winding or puckered (Plate VI.), and the finer seams are sometimes bent sharply upon themselves at an acute angle.

An interesting question refers to the *channels by which the gabbro magma ascended* before spreading laterally in the form of sheets. Analogy would lead us to expect that the molten material rose through more or less vertical fissures, which, filled by the latest uprising magma consolidating in them, are to be looked for in the form of dykes. That this was the case we have abundant evidence. The exposures of the base of the laccolitic mass belong in most places to its peripheral parts; but the north-eastern portion of the laccolite has been removed, partly by erosion, partly by the destructive agency of the granitic intrusion, and here we are able to obtain a glimpse of the mechanism by which the uprise of the gabbro magma was effected. On Druim an Eidhne a number of irregular dyke-like intrusions of gabbro are seen intersecting the volcanic agglomerate which there underlies the laccolite, and some of them are visibly continuous with the latter. The fissures which they fill are not straight nor of a uniform width: they suggest rather that the rocks on which the laccolite rests in its central part were at the time of the intrusion broken by a plexus of irregular curved and branching crevices, through which the successive bursts of molten magma ascended. Another place where a series of curving and in places bifurcating dykes can be traced is along a line from Glen Sligachan to the head of Coire na Seilg, passing over Marsco. This case has a peculiar interest, since the dyke-like strips of gabbro are enclosed in, and partially destroyed by, the granite: their remarkable features will be described in Chapter XI.

If the higher sheets of the gabbro laccolite were in any case intruded after the lower, their fissures of supply must have intersected these, and we should expect to find gabbro dykes cutting the gabbro mass itself. Not many instances of this have been detected. One such dyke runs along the western slope of Bruach na Frithe, where it may be followed by its dark colour contrasting with the somewhat paler rocks which it intersects. Two large dykes are conspicuous objects on the western slope of Gars-bheinn as seen from Coire nan Laogh. There they traverse one of the large enclosed patches of volcanic rocks, and their actual connection, if any, with the overlying gabbro is concealed by screes. In the tract immediately bordering the gabbro of the mountains gabbro dykes are seen in several places. Near the termination of the Blaven range, to the east and south of Loch na Creitheach, they are visibly continuous with the main body of gabbro.* Some of these have the irregular branching form of the

---

* The relation is further emphasised in one case by both the dyke and the contiguous portion of the laccolite enclosing quartz-pebbles, probably picked up by the dyke from a conglomerate a little lower down.

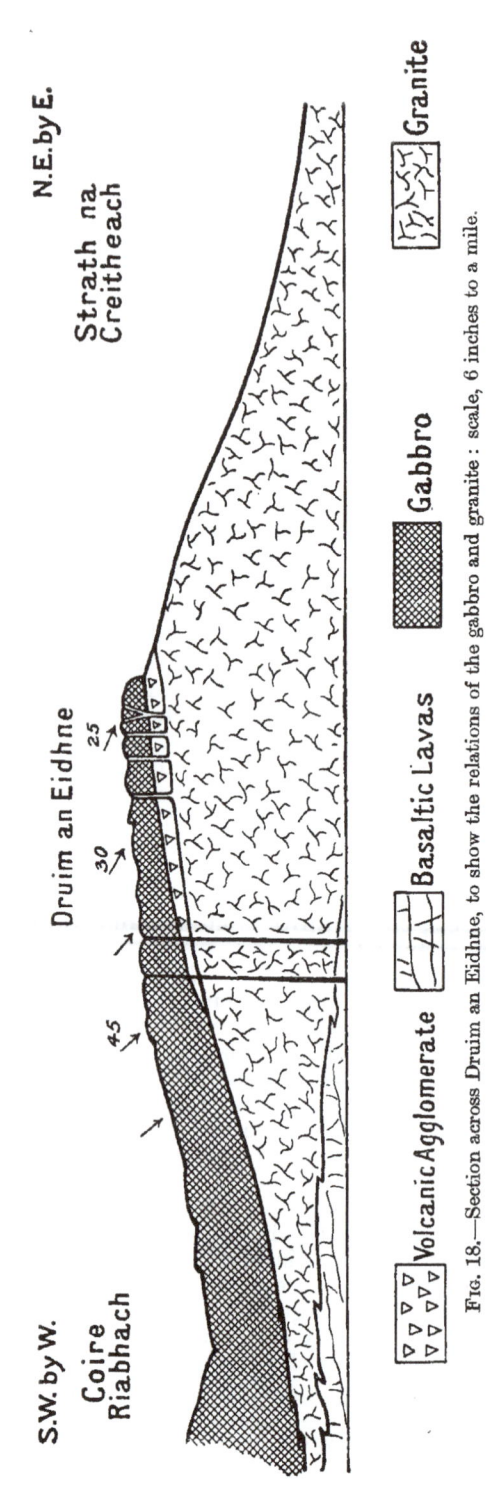

FIG. 18.—Section across Druim an Eidhne, to show the relations of the gabbro and granite: scale, 6 inches to a mile. The arrows mark the inclination of the banding in the gabbro at this place.

Druim an Eidhne dykes, but others run in straight lines for a certain distance, with the N.W.–S.E. direction common to most of the dykes of the district, both earlier and later than the gabbro. It will be pointed out in a subsequent chapter that there are in Skye certain dykes of coarse diabase often indistinguishable from gabbro in the field, but belonging to an epoch long posterior. Where a dyke of gabbro-like aspect is not in visible continuity with the gabbro laccolite there may thus exist a doubt, only to be solved by more minute study of the rock. The dyke which crosses the Blath-bheinn ridge itself in this neighbourhood, at about 1100 feet altitude, is, on petrographical grounds, to be referred to the later set, and the same is perhaps true of other large dykes on An Stac and Slat-bheinn. Those, however, which are seen, to the number of five or six, on the coast south of Sgùrr na Stri, though they have not been examined microscopically, we place here, for at least one of them can be traced up into continuity with the great gabbro mass.

The few actual exposures of dykes continuous with the overlying gabbro mass may be taken to indicate that the fissures of supply are for the most part concealed beneath the interior portion of the laccolite, and the general inward dip of the component sheets of the laccolite is in harmony with this supposition. In one place at least in the interior of the area the connection of a sheet of gabbro with its dyke of supply is clearly visible. This is at Eas Mòr, on Allt Coire na Banachdich, the most considerable water-fall in this part of Skye. The ordinary coarse gabbro is here in a very decayed state; but in it occurs a sheet of finer gabbro [8729] in a much sounder condition, and this, by its superior durability, has determined the fall. The sheet is of lenticular form, and probably does not extend far, though the thick cover of drift prevents the accurate tracing of it. For some distance it forms the upper part of the walls of the gorge below Eas Mòr (*see* Fig. 19), the coarse gabbro appearing beneath it. Nearly a hundred yards below the fall a broad dyke of fine-grained gabbro crosses the burn in a N.N.E. direction, intersecting the coarse gabbro, and this dyke is in visible continuity with the sheet above.

It remains to make a few remarks concerning the *nature of the junctions* between the gabbro of the great laccolite and the older rocks among which it was intruded. Excepting for a short distance to the south-east of Blath-bheinn, where it invades the Lias, and excepting also its junction with the granite, to be described in connection with the latter rock, the gabbro is everywhere in contact with members of the volcanic series. In these rocks it has produced metamorphism more or less intense, the phenomena of which have already been described. It should be remarked, however, that the effects are not everywhere equally extended, nor have they always attained the same degree at equal short distances from the gabbro. Perhaps one reason for this is connected with the fact that the gabbro mass, especially in its lower portion, is built up of successive sheet-like intrusions. If we may suppose that in some places a newer intrusion forced its way between an earlier one and the underlying rock, already metamorphosed, the latter would presumably be raised to a higher temperature, and might be so maintained for a prolonged time, and the effects might be expected to be correspondingly more pronounced.

The junction with the volcanic agglomerate is in general a clean-cut line. In some places, however, and especially in the case of some of the enclosed patches of that rock, the precise boundary is more difficult to draw. There is then room for a suspicion that the finely divided matrix of the agglomerate has been to some slight extent absorbed and incorporated in the gabbro magma. In such places there are often xenoliths of a somewhat different kind of gabbro enclosed in the prevalent type, which may perhaps represent fragments in the agglomerate set free in this fashion.

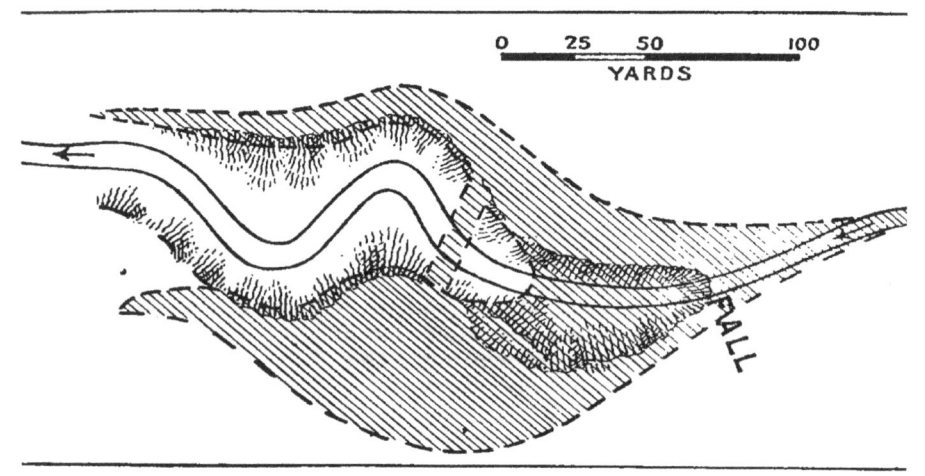

Fig. 19.—Ground-plan of a sheet of fine-grained gabbro and its dyke-feeder, at Eas Mòr, on Allt Coire na Banachdich. Scale, 24 inches to a mile.

The junction with the basaltic lavas has a rather different character. If it departs, as it occasionally does, from the simple type of contact, it is usually by the gabbro sending small veins into the immediately adjacent basalt. These veins may be numerous and minute. This, however, is apparently not so common a feature with the gabbro as with the granite. It is seen in a few places in the Cuillins, and is well exhibited at the boundaries of the irregular sheet of gabbro which forms the conspicuous buttresses at the north end of Beinn na Cro.

There are places where the relations between the basaltic lavas and the gabbro are of a more remarkable character, and there is little doubt that the former rocks have been to a limited extent actually fused and incorporated in the gabbro-magma. This is found at numerous localities on the western and south-western slopes of the Cuillins: *e.g.* in parts of Coire na Banachdich* and Coire Labain and on the flanks of Sgùrr nan Eag and Gars-bheinn. An easily accessible place for study is a flat knoll in the lower part of Coire Labain, about 580 yards E.S.E. of Loch an Fhir-bhallaich.† The phenomena are found only in connection with patches of lava actually enveloped in the gabbro mass or caught between sheet-like prolongations of it. They are rarely observable in other parts of the Cuillins, *e.g.* at one or two spots on Druim nan Ramh. The eye is caught at once by conspicuous amygdules, comparable with those seen in the metamorphosed lavas, but here occurring in what has otherwise the appearance of a normal gabbro. Sometimes the amygdules stand out prominently, and are found to be of quartz, perhaps with a black border of hornblende; sometimes we see the dead white colour of felspar, representing metamorphosed zeolites. Where the amygdules have been formed in the main of more perishable minerals, they have weathered into little cavities, and impart a curiously pitted appearance to a surface on which they are numerous.

Thin slices confirm the statement that the enclosing rock has the character of an ordinary gabbro. They also make it certain that the amygdules are enclosed foreign bodies, not patches of secondary minerals occupying druses in the gabbro. Their shape is always rounded, and in the smaller amygdules spherical. The quartz, probably derived from chalcedony, has clearly crystallised under metamorphic influence, for it is penetrated by fine needles of actinolite, and encloses imperfect crystals of light-green actinolitic (fibrous) hornblende and sometimes crystal-grains of yellow epidote [8700, 8701]. Other amygdules consist of an aggregate of felspar precisely like that described in the metamorphosed amygdaloidal basalts. As a rule the amygdules are immediately surrounded by the gabbro matrix, the basalt to which they belonged having wholly disappeared; but this is not always the case. Thus an amygdule may be invested by a relatively fine-textured rock, which must be regarded as a metamorphosed basalt, the little felspars bordering the amygdule being set tangentially to it in the customary fashion: as seen in the slice, this basalt gives place rapidly, though not at a perfectly defined line, to the enveloping gabbro [8699]. Here we have enclosed in the gabbro a small relic of basaltic lava, which itself encloses an amygdule.

Two alternative explanations are not inconsistent with the facts as so far stated. We might suppose that the amygdaloidal gabbro represents the extreme phase of metamorphism of amygdaloidal basalt, all the original characters of the rock except the amygdules having been obliterated; or, on the other hand, that the basalt has actually passed into a state of fusion and mingled with the gabbro magma, only the amygdules surviving. Further consideration,

* The pitted surface of these peculiar rocks when slightly weathered has probably given this corrie its name, signifying small-pox
† Following the usual track from Glen Brittle House, a conspicuous erratic of Matterhorn shape is seen close on the left: the knoll mentioned is then immediately on the right.

however, makes the former hypothesis scarcely tenable. The gabbro presents features (*e.g.* in some cases schiller-structures in the augite) which are highly distinctive of true plutonic rocks, and are not to be expected in any product of thermal metamorphism. Even more convincing is the fact that similar amygdules are locally found in the ultrabasic rocks already described, and present the same indications of a foreign origin. Since no metamorphism could convert a basaltic lava into a picrite or peridotite, it is clear that in that case at least the lava, with the exception of its amygdules, must have been fused, and moreover must have become sufficiently fluid to diffuse through the ultrabasic magma, mingling freely with it.

We conclude then that the amygdules in the gabbro are of the nature of xenoliths, set free from their original matrix by the complete fusion of the latter. There is no evidence that the process has operated on any extensive scale. The amygdaloidal gabbros occur in small patches or along bands rarely as much as 100 yards wide, and usually much less, always in the immediate neigbourhood of metamorphosed lavas. In strictness the zone of fusion must be supposed to stop at a definite line; but in actual mapping it is not always easy to divide sharply the amygdule-bearing gabbro from a highly-metamorphosed amygdaloidal basalt.

The relations of the gabbro to the large peridotite laccolite which it envelopes have been described in the preceding chapter. Not only does the later rock penetrate the earlier in the form of an intricate system of dykes and veins extending for some distance from the boundary; but about Allt a' Chaoich and Meall na Cuilce and down to the shores of Lochs Coruisk and Scavaig the gabbro encloses abundant blocks and fragments of picrite and other rocks belonging to the ultrabasic group. It is to be remarked that these enclosed fragments are of fairly angular shape, and there is little or no indication of the gabbro magma having absorbed material from the débris which it took up. Further, there is little clear indication of thermal metamorphism (at least as regards new minerals) in the enclosed blocks and fragments. The difference in these respects between the ultrabasic rocks and the basaltic lavas can only be attributed to the different petrographical natures of the two groups of rocks.

Turning now to the second considerable mass of gabbro in Skye, that exposed to the *north-west of Broadford*, we find that it offers in every respect a remarkable contrast to the larger mass of the mountain tract, its form and habit being those of a *boss*. It occupies most of the ground to the north-east of the Beinn na Caillich granite as far as the high-road, where it and the rocks with which it is associated are cut off by a fault bringing on the Lias. It is intruded chiefly into the Cambrian Limestones (Balnakiel group); but this statement does not adequately express what is seen on the ground, for, excepting an area of about 1400 by 500 yards, much invaded by gabbro, the limestone is seen only in the form of small detached portions enclosed in the igneous

G

98 *Cambrian Limestones enclosed in Gabbro Boss.*

rock (Fig. 20). There are about fifty of these enclosed patches, varying in dimensions from 300 to 20 yards, besides others, down to 10 feet or less in diameter, which are too small to be mapped. In ground-plan they always present convex outlines to the gabbro, and the smallest ones are circular. The larger are of irregular outline, with sharp indentations occupied by processes of the gabbro; and where these latter completely intersect the limestone, we have two or more ovoid patches lying close together, representing the relics of one larger patch. They are easily recognised,

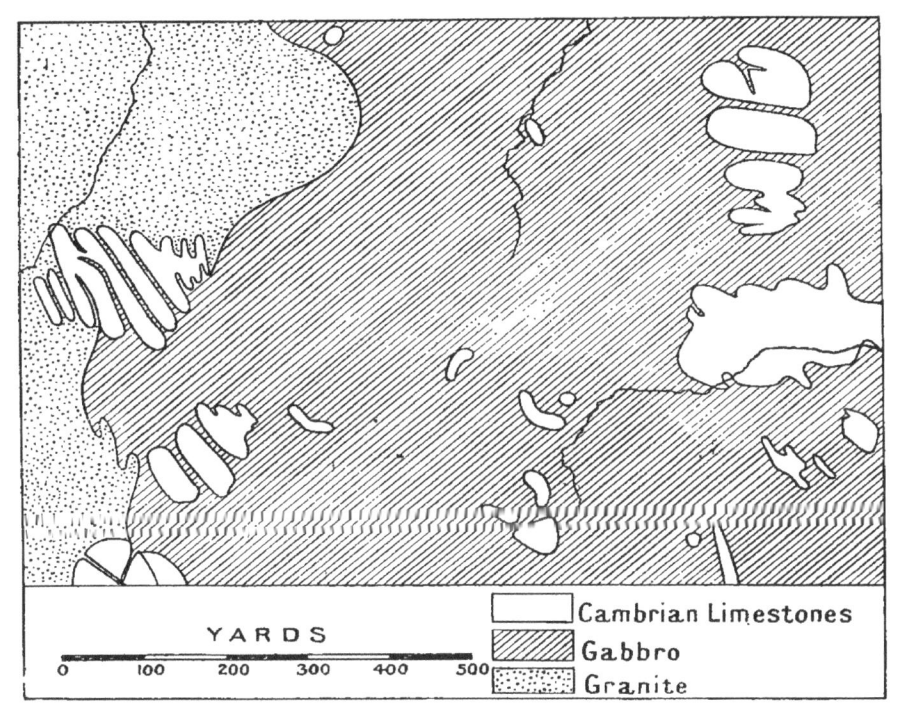

FIG. 20.—Map showing a part of the Broadford gabbro boss and a small part of the Beinn na Caillich granite, with patches of the Cambrian limestones enclosed in the igneous rock-masses.

The area shown lies immediately N.E. of Lochain Beinn na Caillich. For explanation, see text.

even where no rock is visible, by a depression due to the more rapid weathering of the limestone, and by the bright green growth of bracken contrasting with the peaty or heather-clad surface of the gabbro. The junction of the two rocks is often well exhibited, and is found to be *everywhere a vertical one*, the gabbro standing up as a perpendicular wall a few feet higher than the surface of the limestone. This is true all along the sinuous outline of the larger limestone patches, and it is true of patches only a few yards in diameter.

The gabbro has cut sharply across the limestone, the latter being cut out as if it had been annihilated, saving that columnar portions of it have been left standing surrounded by the igneous rock. It is not possible to explain the phenomena by supposing that the enclosed patches of limestone seen are resting upon gabbro below, and there is no evidence that they have been disturbed by the intrusion. It is true that they show dips in various directions and sometimes at high angles, but this seems to be due to folding of a much earlier date, connected with the over-thrusting of the Torridon Sandstone. Similar dips are observed in the larger and more independent area of limestone mentioned above, the strata there being greatly disturbed and in places vertical, while outliers of Torridon Sandstone rest almost horizontally upon them. Along the exposed western boundary of this area, too, the limestone does not dip away from the gabbro, but towards it at high angles. It is curious to notice that the gabbro shows no tendency to force its way along the thrust-plane, though the later intrusion of granite has often done so.

It can scarcely be doubted that this remarkable behaviour of the gabbro, so totally at variance with what is seen in the Cuillins, is in some measure due to the fact that the country-rock here is a limestone. The circumstantial evidence for this hypothesis is at least very strong. All intrusive rocks in the district, whether basic or acid, which occur in limestones, have a strong tendency to assume the forms of bosses, plugs, or dykes, with vertical walls; and the larger bodies exhibit curiously irregular and sinuous outlines in ground-plan. Intrusions which have been running as more or less regular sills or sheets in other "country" rocks, break abruptly across and lose all regularity as soon as they enter limestones. We shall have to revert to this matter in connection with the granites and minor intrusions of the district. At present it will suffice to note as a significant fact that this gabbro boss, at its north-western end, on Creag Strollamus, where it enters the Torridon Sandstone and basaltic lavas, at once takes the form of a sheet.

The mechanism of such an intrusion as the Broadford gabbro boss presents a physical problem of considerable difficulty. Where gabbro now appears on the map was once limestone, and this limestone has vanished as completely as if it had been annihilated. It can only have been removed either in blocks and fragments or in solution in the gabbro magma, and neither of these hypotheses, nor a combination of them, is easily applied. We may perhaps conceive the gabbro magma as forcing its way along joint-fissures of the limestone, detaching blocks and loose fragments of that rock, and floating them upwards; but, in view of the probably small difference in specific gravity between the limestone and the fluid magma, it is difficult to account on this supposition for the entire absence of detached pieces of limestone in the gabbro as now exposed. It is also necessary to assume that the intrusion has been prolonged upward with the same boss-like form through the once-overlying Torridon Sandstone, Cambrian quartzites, etc., an assumption not in itself probable. Even if the chief bulk of the limestone can have been carried away in fragments, as suggested, the smooth rounded form of the junctions compels us apparently to admit a certain amount of solvent action. Any noteworthy amount of solution and absorption of this dolomitic limestone by the basic magma would betray itself in the chemical composition of the gabbro by an unusually high percentage of lime and magnesia, and such data as we have on this point do not afford any support to the supposition. The following figures are taken from analyses given in full below:—

	Silica.	Lime.
Gabbro of Cuillins (I.)	46·39	15·29
Do. (II.)	47·28	13·42
Do. (III.)	48·12	15·43
Gabbro of Broadford boss (IV.)	50·78	10·28
Offshoot of the same, traversing limestone (V.)	47·18	11·59

It appears from these figures that the Broadford gabbros are not richer, but actually poorer, in lime than those of the Cuillins, intruded among basaltic lavas. This must of course be ascribed to different composition of the magma as intruded; but it is evident that in no case can any important absorption of lime be postulated. The figures in the last line refer to a dyke-like apophysis of the boss, cutting through the limestone, and they show it to be poorer in silica and rather richer in lime than the main body. This, however, if the two are really parts of one intrusion, only increases the difficulty; for it proves that any dissolved lime was not freely diffused through the magma, and free diffusion is essential to any explanation of the facts on the lines suggested. We are compelled, therefore, to leave the question unsolved.

Although the boundary of the gabbro boss is a highly sinuous one in ground-plan, and processes which might be called short dykes extend out from the main body, the junction is on the small scale a regular and clean-cut one. The gabbro does not send out veins into the limestone. The latter rock is highly metamorphosed, and is in the condition of a crystalline marble often carrying various silicates, etc. The metamorphism is quite of the same kind and degree as that produced by the Beinn an Dubhaich granite, two or three miles farther south, and we shall defer any detailed account of it until the latter is discussed (Chap. IX.).

Where the gabbro is in contact with Torridon Sandstone, on Creag Strollamus, the junction is of a different type. The intrusive mass has here a more irregular boundary, in the sense of sending out small veins into the neighbouring rock. In places these veins are numerous, minute, and ramifying; and the sandstone, for a few inches from the general line of junction, has been injected or impregnated with the gabbro magma, which has even insinuated itself in narrower threads between the grains of the clastic rock.

The gabbro boss of Broadford differs from the great laccolite of the Cuillins not only in general shape but in detailed structure. We are not able to assert that it represents a single effort of intrusion, but it certainly shows no clear indication of the complex constitution of the laccolitic mass, and exhibits much less range of petrographical diversity, while the banded, xenolithic, and other special structures are not met with.

The several *smaller masses of gabbro* in Skye do not call for particular notice. Both the stratiform and the boss-like modes of occurrence are represented among them. A small patch on the north-western spur of Belig is merely an outlier of the main laccolite, and the same is probably true for a patch on the main ridge of Marsco. The gabbro which runs with sheet-like habit along the west ridge of Beinn na Cro, and forms conspicuous buttresses at the northern end of the hill, may not impossibly represent the thin edge of the great laccolite, but the granite which has isolated this patch of basalt and gabbro has destroyed the evidence on this point. Some quite small sill-formed intrusions of gabbro on the southern and eastern slopes of the Blaven range, never far from the great laccolite but at lower horizons, belong probably to the same focus of intrusion. One or two other small masses seem to have the boss-like habit, *e.g.* one which breaks through the basaltic lavas on An Stac, about a mile east of Blath-bheinn.

We may mention also that Mr Clough has mapped two small bosses of gabbro in the Moine Schists of Sleat, about $\frac{1}{2}$ mile N.W. of Knock. This is about 9 miles S.S.E. of the Broadford boss. He has also noted two small bosses on the other side of the Sound of Sleat, which are possibly to be attached to the Skye group. One is a little south of Glenelg Pier and the other farther south, near Sandaig.

CHAPTER VIII.

Gabbros: Petrography.

In describing the petrographical characters of the gabbro group we shall discuss first what may be regarded as the *normal types*, reserving for later notice the aberrant varieties which occur chiefly in the form of bands, seams, and veins. These normal gabbros are typical basic rocks, varying in texture from coarse to fine. That they also vary within certain limits as regards the relative proportions of their component minerals is evident to the eye, and the different specific gravities of specimens tested indicate in a general way this range of composition. Twenty-five examples from different parts of the area gave a mean specific gravity of 2·927, the extreme figures being 2·85 and 3·03.

To illustrate the *chemical composition* of the normal gabbros two specimens have been subjected to careful analysis by Dr Pollard, and the results are shown below in columns I. and II. To these we are able to add an already published analysis by the late Professor Haughton (III.). All three are from the laccolitic mass of the Cuillins, and they exhibit a rather close resemblance to one another. They present a general similarity also to the Tertiary gabbros of Carlingford, of which Haughton has given two analyses, showing 47·52 and 48·80 per cent. of silica respectively.* We are also able to give an unpublished analysis of a gabbro from the Broadford boss (IV.) made by Mr T. Baker of the Durham College of Science and kindly communicated by Professor G. A. Lebour. This, as will be seen, is a rock of slightly more acid composition. Mr Player's analyses of the banded gabbros will be quoted in their proper place.

As compared with the average of gabbros from other regions, the Cuillin rocks analysed are rather poor in iron and magnesia and rich in lime.

Dr Pollard did not find metallic iron in the rocks examined, though it has been found in Skye gabbros by Mr Buchanan[†] and by Professor Tilden.[‡] Another interesting observation by the latter relates to the gases enclosed in the minute cavities of the crystals of the rock. A gabbro from Loch Coruisk yielded 3½ times

---

* *Quart. Journ. Geol. Soc.*, vol. xii., p. 197 : 1856 ; *Journ. Roy. Geol. Soc. Irel.*, vol. iv., p. 99 : 1876.

† Judd, *Quart. Journ. Geol. Soc.*, vol. xli., p. 374 : 1885.

‡ "On the Gases Enclosed in Crystalline Rocks and Minerals," *Proc. Roy. Soc.*, vol. lx., pp. 453-457 : 1897.

Analyses of Gabbros.

	I.	II.	III.	IV.	V.
SiO_2	46·39	47·28	48·12	50·78	47·18
TiO_2	0·26	0·28	. .	. .	. .
Al_2O_3	26·34	21·11	23·40	17·16	. .
Cr_2O_3	trace	. .	. .	. .	. .
Fe_2O_3	2·02	3·52	. .	3·15	. .
FeO	3·15	3·91	3·28	7·61	. .
MnO	0·14	0·15	1·68	. .	. .
MgO	4·82	8·06	5·31	7·16	. .
CaO	15·29	13·42	15·43	10·28	11·59
Na_2O	1·63	1·52	1·86 }	2·61 {	. .
K_2O	0·20	0·29	0·03 }		. .
H_2O { above 105°	0·48	0·53 }	0·48	1·20 (ign.) {	. .
at 105°	0·10	0·13 }			0·10
P_2O_5	trace	trace	. .	. .	. .
	100·82	100·20	99·59	99·95	. .
Specific gravity	2·85	2·90	. .	2·82	. .

I. Olivine-Gabbro of Cuillin laccolite, west bank of Sligachan River, just below Allt Coire Riabhaich [8043]: anal. W. Pollard, *Summary of Progress of Geol. Sur.* for 1899, p. 173. See Fig. 21, below.

II. Olivine-Gabbro of Cuillin laccolite, floor of Coir' a' Mhadaidh [8194]: anal. W. Pollard, *ibid.*, p. 174.

III. Gabbro of Cuillin laccolite, Loch Scavaig [probably olivine-gabbro; specimen not seen]: anal. S. Haughton, *Dubl. Quart. Journ. Sci.*, vol. v., p. 94: 1865. Analyses of the felspar and augite of this rock are quoted below.

IV. Gabbro of Broadford boss, near mouth of Allt Mhic Leanain, 1½ mile N.W. of Broadford [8950]: anal. T. Baker.

V. Gabbro of offshoot from Broadford boss, traversing the dolomitic limestone, west bank of Lochain Beinn na Caillich [8692]: partial anal. by W. Pollard.

s own volume of mixed gases, of which 21·6 per cent. was found be carbon dioxide and the rest chiefly hydrogen, with some rbon monoxide, nitrogen, and marsh gas. These figures are uivalent to about 0·02 in a percentage analysis of the rock. elium was sought spectroscopically but not detected.
In Sir J. Norman Lockyer's spectra of our gabbros, I. and II., the romium lines are very prominent, while vanadium and strontium e more faintly but distinctly indicated. The titanium lines are stinct, but not so strong as in some other rocks (especially the trusive sills to be described later), in which a relatively high rcentage of that element has been directly estimated. A comrison of the several photographs shows indeed that spectroscopic alysis under given conditions has a certain quantitative as well qualitative value.

The first three columns in the Table show decided differences in some particulars; and a comparison of thin slices enables us to see how variation in chemical composition has given rise to variation in the relative proportions of the constituent minerals. The significant figures in this connection are those for alumina, magnesia, and alkalies; for the two chief minerals of the rocks, viz. labradorite and augite, do not differ much in their content of silica and of lime, and any excess of iron-oxides can be disposed of in the form of magnetite. Thus the first rock is more felspathic than the second. By the kindness of Professor Sollas we are able to give the results of a direct mineral analysis made by him with the apparatus and methods which he has devised.* The percentage mineral composition of the first rock [8043] is as follows:—

Labradorite, sp. gr. 2·735 to 2·74	79·50
Augite and olivine, 3·21 to 3·335	16·18
Enstatite, 3·0	2·10
Magnetite -	2·40
	100·18

It is worthy of remark that the occurrence of a second pyroxene, which had escaped detection in the microscopical examination, was first established by this direct isolation of the mineral. The second rock [8194], owing to the presence of serpentine and other alteration-products, presented more difficulty in its mechanical analysis. Professor Sollas found:—

Labradorite, sp. gr. 2·737	65·96
Augite, sp. gr. 3·280	32·43
Magnetite	1·61
	100·00

The Skye gabbros have a quite simple mineralogical composition. A plagioclase felspar, usually labradorite, and augite are the constant, and sometimes the only noteworthy constituents. Olivine and magnetite occur very frequently, but not often in any great abundance; while hypersthene, hornblende, biotite, sphene, apatite, ilmenite, pyrite, garnet, orthoclase, and quartz are only of exceptional occurrence. To these may be added the common alteration-products of the minerals named, although most of the rocks are in a good state of preservation.†

Those petrologists who lay stress on the presence or absence of olivine would place the Skye gabbros under two heads accordingly, but such a subdivision does not appear to us to offer any advantages

---

* *Quart. Journ. Geol. Soc.*, vol. lviii., pp. 163-176 : 1902. In the paper as published there are certain clerical errors, which are here corrected.
† Good coloured plates of olivine-gabbros from Loch Coruisk are given in Teall's *British Petrography*, Pl. XVIII., Fig. 1, and XXV. : 1888. A general account of the gabbros of the Western Isles of Scotland is contained in papers by Professor Judd (1885, 1886), and examples from Skye had previously been described by Professor Zirkel (1871).

in this case. The presence or absence of olivine, except where it occurs in abundance, does not seem to be very closely connected with other petrographical characters in the rocks. In the very complex mass building the Cuillins and their branch ridges gabbros with and without olivine are intimately associated, the former, perhaps, predominating: the rock forming the smaller mass to the north-west of Broadford is, at least in the main, free from that mineral. In the description which follows we shall generally treat the rocks as a whole, whether they occur in laccolitic or sheet-like form, as in the Cuillins, or with boss-like habit as in the Broadford district. As regards the most common types, the same description will apply in general to all the occurrences. As regards varietal forms, however, there are differences which may be significant. The rocks are much more variable in the Cuillins (including the Blaven range) than elsewhere. Not only does the great laccolite consist of numerous distinct intrusive sheets which often differ from one another, but these also display in some cases considerable variation in the parts of one mass. The Broadford boss is much more uniform, and indeed shows very little variation except a transition to the diabasic type. Unlike the Cuillin mass, it is in general free from olivine. Of the smaller intrusions, it may be mentioned that the irregular sheets on Beinn na Cro have more variety of character than the boss just referred to, but without the extreme modifications met with in the great laccolite: olivine was found in one specimen only, a rock with "eyes" of coarser texture seen in the lowest exposure on the Strath Mòr side. The smaller intrusions of the district exhibit a general uniformity of petrographical characters.

We shall first describe severally the component minerals of the rocks.

In most of the gabbros the *felspar* has partially idiomorphic outlines with the usual crystal-habit. The carlsbad, albite, and pericline twin-laws are found, often in combination. In a large proportion of the more typical gabbros the crystals constantly show the albite-lamellation and very commonly the carlsbad twin in addition, while pericline lamellæ occur less generally, usually in the larger and broader crystals, often affecting only a portion of the crystal or not passing completely across it. Many examples have been observed, however, in which only pericline, or pericline with carlsbad, twinning is present, or in which the albite-lamellation is subordinate to the other; and it is never safe to assume that a single set of lamellæ in a crystal, or the more prominent and constant of two intersecting sets, is necessarily that corresponding with the albite-law. If the crystal is twinned on the carlsbad law, the albite and pericline lamellæ are of course easily distinguished; in other cases the discrimination can often be made by reference to the optical orientation, using a quartz-wedge or a quarter-undulation plate. Neither the direction of elongation of the section nor the parallelism of twin-lamellæ with cleavage-traces affords a criterion that can be trusted. It has been found necessary to bear this point constantly in mind in taking observations of extinction-angles in rock-slices with the view of identifying the various kinds of felspar.

The most usual inclusions in the felspars are merely of the earlier-crystallised minerals of the rock, but fluid-cavities are also found, sometimes with mobile bubbles.

	I.	II.	III.	A.	B.
SiO_2	53·60	49·155	50·811	47·90	45·87
Al_2O_3	29·88	29·62	29·48	31·30	34·73
Fe_2O_3	. .	1·152	0·252	trace	. .
FeO	0·20	. .	. .	. .	. .
MgO	0·07	0·911	0·124	1·16	1·55
CaO	11·02	15·309	12·69	11·22	17·10
Na_2O	4·92	2·914	3·922	3·96	. .
K_2O	0·80	0·695	0·552	0·98	. .
H_2O	0·48	0·73	2·481	1·54	. .
	100·97	100·486	100·292	98·06	99·25
Spec. grav.	. .	. .	2·715	. .	. .

I. Labradorite, Loch Scavaig: anal. S. Haughton, *Dubl. Quart. Journ. Sci.*, vol. v., p. 94: 1865. From the gabbro of which a bulk-analysis is given above (p. 103).

II. "Labradorite," Harta Corrie: anal. M. F. Heddle, *Trans. Roy. Soc. Edin.*, vol. xxviii., p. 253: 1877. In the original the total is erroneously given as 100·386.

III. Labradorite, near head of Loch Scavaig: anal. M. F. Heddle, *ibid.*

A. Labradorite, Beinn Mòr, Mull: anal. J. F. Brooks, *Quart. Journ. Geol. Soc.*, vol. xlii., p. 64: 1886.

B. Anorthite, Carlingford: anal. S. Haughton, *Quart. Journ. Geol. Soc.*, vol. xii., p. 196: 1856.

The common varieties of felspar in the Skye gabbros are, as a rule, labradorite. This is illustrated by the three analyses quoted, although the second one (evidently made on material not quite free from augite) falls rather between labradorite and bytownite.* The optical properties, however, are sufficient to show that there is, in different rocks, a considerable range of composition. In some of the more basic types bytownite and anorthite occur, though they are far less common than labradorite. On the other hand, the light-coloured veins which often traverse the more normal gabbros usually have more acid felspars. In some of them labradorite is accompanied by oligoclase or andesine, while in others oligoclase becomes the dominant constituent, and more basic felspars may be wanting. In these veins too, and not elsewhere among the gabbros, we sometimes find orthoclase.

* The three analyses correspond approximately with Ab_8An_9, Ab_3An_7, and Ab_3An_5, respectively. For the felspar of a gabbro in the lower part of Allt Coire na Banachdich the specific gravity, carefully determined by Prof. Sollas, is 2·708, and the extinction-angle on the basal cleavage 21°, corresponding with bytownite of composition Ab_1An_4.

Not infrequently the marginal portion of the crystal is of a somewhat different composition from the interior, and in that case always less basic. The difference is as a rule small, but in a few cases considerable—e.g., labradorite bordered by andesine, as shown by the extinction-angles. The zonary banding seen between crossed nicols does not on rotation disappear at the same time as the twin-lamellation, and therefore is not due merely to ultra-microscopic or molecular twinning.

We shall notice below that both albite and pericline lamellation have occasionally been brought about as secondary effects, due to the stresses which have operated on the rock-masses.

The common ferro-magnesian element of the Skye gabbros is *augite*. It is always present, and usually to the exclusion of rhombic pyroxenes, original hornblende, and biotite. Very often, and especially in the rocks of coarser texture, it is more or less affected by the so-called "schiller"-structures, and has in consequence a sub-metallic lustre. This peculiarity led Macculloch and other early writers to regard the mineral as hypersthene, and to style the rocks in question hypersthene-rocks or hypersthenites. Modern methods of optical examination have proved that the pyroxene is not a rhombic but a monoclinic one. Des Cloizeaux,* writing in 1862, says:—"A specimen labelled hypersthene from the Isle of Skye, from the Museum at Paris, gave me all the characters of a [monoclinic] pyroxene, with cleavages parallel to the faces m, h^1, and g^1 [the prism and the two pinacoids], and obliquity of the system of rings as seen through h^1." Subsequently Zirkel and Judd found that this monoclinic pyroxene is the dominant one, the rhombic mineral being of exceptional occurrence. This indeed might be inferred from the content of lime. The analyses I. to VI., quoted below, show that the lime makes about 20 per cent., while the magnesia is 14 to 16 per cent., and the ferrous oxide ranges from 9 to 14: further, that the alumina is quite low. The dominant pyroxene of the gabbros is therefore a malacolite with a moderate amount of iron. The molecular ratios

$$FeO : MgO : CaO$$

range in the six analyses from

$$0\cdot55 : 1\cdot05 : 1\cdot00$$
to $\quad 0\cdot34 : 1\cdot11 : 1\cdot00,$

and it is noticeable that they do not give

$$FeO + MgO = CaO,$$

as required by Tschermak's formula.†

---

* *Manuel de minéralogie*, vol. i., p. 58.

† Compare Teall's remarks on the augite of the Whin Sill, a rock presenting numerous analogies with the Skye gabbros. *Quart. Journ. Geol. Soc.*, vol. xl., pp. 648, 649 : 1884.

	I.	II.	III.	IV.	V.	VI.	VII.
SiO_2	51·30	50·80	53·046	51·362	51·936	49·268	..
TiO_2	..	..	..	..	0·38	..	..
Al_2O_3	0·76	3·00	4·816	1·662	1·322	0·222	11·45
Fe_2O_3	..	..	..	..	..	2·17	—
FeO	13·92	9·61	11·389	8·968	13·9	12·15	14·17
MnO	0·25	1·08	0·078	0·332	0·25	0·381	..
MgO	14·85	15·06	11·576	16·471	13·85	14·812	..
CaO	20·15	19·35	19·808	20·837	19·363	20·256	..
Na_2O	..	0·44	..	..	..	..	..
K_2O	-	0·22	..	..	..	..	..
H_2O	0·21	0·60	0·626	0·54	0·2	0·719	..
	101·44	100·16	101·339	100·172	101·252	99·978	
Sp. gr.	3·34	..	3·3293	3·329	3·335	3·321	..

I. "Diallage, Skye": anal. G. vom Rath, *cit.* Rammelsberg, *Handbuch der Mineralchemie*, p. 465 : 1860.

II. Augite, Loch Scavaig: anal. S. Haughton, *Dubl. Quart. Journ. Sci.*, vol. v., p. 95: 1865. From gabbro of which bulk-analysis is given, p. 103.

III. Augite, "in large lustrous greyish-green crystals," Coire na Creiche: anal. M. F. Heddle, *Trans. Roy. Soc. Edin.*, vol. xxviii., p. 479: 1879.

IV. Augite, "in large green crystals which weather pale, and assume on an outer film a lustre which is metallic and somewhat bronzy," Harta Corrie: anal. M. F. Heddle, *ibid*.

V. Augite, "slightly weathered, with a brownish-green colour, and a slightly bronzy lustre," Druim nan Ramh: anal. M. F. Heddle, *ibid.*, p. 480.

VI. Augite, "large, dark-green, cleavable masses," from near the shores of Loch Scavaig: anal. M. F. Heddle, *ibid*.

VII. "Diallage," Skye: anal. F. Herwig, *Programm des k. Gymnasium Saarbrücken*, 1884 ; *cit. Zeits. f. Kryst.*, vol. xi., pp. 67, 68 : 1886. [It is not stated that this mineral was from the gabbro.]

The augite crystals are as a rule allotriomorphic, and often tend to enwrap the felspars. Twinning parallel to the orthopinacoid is found, but not very frequently. The prismatic cleavage is occasionally supplemented by others, much less perfect, parallel to the two pinacoidal forms. Exceptionally a parting parallel to the orthopinacoid almost supersedes the ordinary augite-cleavage, and this is associated with a sub-metallic lustre on the planes of parting (diallage). Zirkel describes the examples collected and examined by him as for the most part diallagic. Professor Judd, speaking of the peridotites and gabbros of the Western Isles collectively, recognises both augite proper and diallage, and ascribes the peculiar nature of the latter to a system of "schiller"-inclusions arranged parallel to the orthopinacoid. He adds that in the central portion of the Skye gabbro the augite exhibits a still further modification. "In addition to the enclosures along the planes parallel with the orthopinacoid, other enclosures make their appearance in planes cutting these at an angle of 87½° [? 90°], or parallel with the clinopinacoid. . . . Frequently another set of enclosures may be detected as making their appearance along a third set of planes, which appear to be parallel to the basal plane."* For this variety he adopts Dana's term pseudo-hypersthene. It does not appear from our study of the Skye gabbros that the diallage-structure, though it is often found (Plate XVIII., Fig. 5), is the most usual modification of the augitic constituent. Much more common is what may be called the salite-structure, which appears in thin slices as a delicate striation parallel to the basal plane (Plate XVIII., Fig. 4). The same remark applies to some other British gabbros, including those of Carrock Fell and St David's Head. The basal striation is described by Mr Teall in the Whin Sill, and has been noted in other rocks by many observers. The structure has been variously explained as due to a minute parallel intergrowth of two different minerals, to exceedingly fine twin-lamellation, or to a system of minute parallel inclusions. A large number of slices of the Skye gabbros have not enabled us to establish any conclusion as regards the true nature of the structure. A parallel intergrowth of augite and hypersthene would accord well with the chemical composition of the mineral, which shows a striking deficiency in lime as compared with the ideal formula of a malacolite; but the perfectly normal optical orientation of the crystals seems to negative such a supposition. In many of our rocks the basal striation is accompanied by a set of microscopic inclusions, also parallel to the basal plane; but in other cases such inclusions, if they exist, are so minute as to evade observation, and there is nothing to suggest that the striation is necessarily dependent upon them. Professor Judd's view† seems to be that a fine lamellar twinning is first produced, parallel to the basal plane, and that this direction thereupon becomes a "solution-plane" or plane of chemical weakness, along which "schillerisation" is subsequently set up.

The geologist just named holds the schiller-inclusions to be of secondary origin. Without entering into a complete discussion of this question, we may briefly express our opinion that the arguments advanced in support of this theory by no means carry conviction. The fact that the peculiarity in question often affects only a portion of a crystal, sometimes with a capricious distribution, does not seem to be inconsistent with the primary origin of the phenomenon. Again, although it is true that the alteration of augite along cleavage- and other cracks sometimes gives rise to minute inclusions, these are not, in the examples which we have examined, of a kind comparable with those under discussion. The bronzy lustre sometimes seen in the field is, however, due to a surface-tarnish.

The augite of the gabbros proper (as distinguished from diabasic varieties) usually has a more or less evident striation, either basal,

* *Quart. Journ. Geol. Soc.*, vol. xli., p. 379 : 1885.
† *Min. Mag.*, vol. ix., pp. 192-196 : 1890.

or less frequently orthopinacoidal, or sometimes both. The structure is most pronounced in the coarser-textured rocks, and especially in the interior of the great gabbro mass, though it is not invariably very marked there. This, as Professor Judd remarks, implies that it is, in some measure and in some manner, connected with the depth at which the rocks were originally situated. When either the salite-structure or the diallage-structure is strongly developed, the mineral exhibits in hand-specimens a sub-metallic lustre, often with a bronzy colour. Otherwise it has the ordinary appearance of augite, black, or dark green, or with a rusty tinge.

We have observed nothing which seems to prove a secondary origin for either salite- or diallage- structure, or for the schillerisation which may accompany them: on the other hand, there are various circumstances which lead us to regard them as original. One point only may be noticed here. Crystals of augite picked up from the gabbro by a granitic magma, and thereby converted into hornblende, are found exhibiting the traces of basal striation, marked out by a schiller-structure.* Since the intrusion of the granite, according to all the evidence, followed the gabbro after only a short interval, this goes far towards establishing the structures in question as of primary origin.

In thin slices the augite is pale brown to nearly colourless, without sensible pleochroism. The extinction-angle $c\ \mathfrak{c}$ is 39° or 40°. Herwig found for a "diallage" from Skye the abnormally high angle 51° 25', but the specimen, if from the gabbro, was evidently an exceptional one, as appears from the partial analysis quoted above (VII.). In a large number of cases tested the axis of elasticity nearest to the vertical axis has always been found to be $\mathfrak{c}$, not $\mathfrak{a}$.

The augite is not often chloritised or serpentinised. Magnetite-dust or some other finely divided opaque matter disseminated through the crystals, or through parts of them, is sometimes found, and is probably a result of alteration. The most common change in the mineral, however, is a partial or even total conversion to hornblende, green, or greenish-yellow, or greenish-brown. Whether fibrous or compact, this is always formed in the usual crystallographic relation to the augite, viz. with the b and c axes common and the basal planes (as usually taken) inclined in opposite directions. Thus in a clinopinacoidal section the extinction-angles, 39° or 40° for the augite and 14° to 16° for the hornblende, are on the same side of the vertical. A brown hornblende, which seems to be original, is occasionally found in small patches intergrown with the augite according to the same law. Biotite seems to be wholly wanting among the normal rocks, though it is found near contacts with basalt, etc., and in some of the metamorphosed gabbros.

Although Macculloch and others, working without the advantage of modern methods of precision, erred in regarding the dominant pyroxene of the Cuillins as *hypersthene*, they were not without

* *Quart. Journ. Geol. Soc.*, vol. lii., p. 324 ; Pl. XIII., Fig. 3 : 1896.

warrant in recording the occurrence of that mineral. This is proved by the analysis quoted below, which is clearly that of a hypersthene belonging to the highly ferriferous variety for which Professor Judd has revived vom Rath's name amblystegite. Professor Judd has himself recorded this mineral from the gabbros of Loch Coruisk.*

SiO_2	-	51·318
FeO		33·924
MgO	- -	11·092
CaO	-	1·836
H_2O	- -	0·500
		98·700
Specific gravity	-	3·338

Hypersthene (amblystegite), Cuillins: anal. Thos. Muir, Thomson's *Outlines of Mineralogy*, vol. i., p. 202: 1836. [In the paper by von Oeynhausen and von Dechen (Karsten's *Archiv für Mineralogie, etc.*, vol. i., p. 74: 1829) this analysis is wrongly ascribed to Thomson. Further, the item Al_2O_3 1·300 is inserted, apparently in order to make up the 100 per cent., although the total is still given as 98·700.]

The molecular ratio $FeO : MgO + CaO$ given by this analysis is about 1·52 : 1·00.

The rhombic pyroxene seems to be rather rare in the Skye gabbros. In some other parts of the Western Isles it appears, according to Professor Judd, to be more widely distributed, though it is perhaps more frequently associated, with ultrabasic than with basic rocks. Only one of our specimens, from Coire na Banachdich [2637], has hypersthene as the dominant pyroxenic constituent. The crystals are idiomorphic, though not perfectly bounded. Two varieties occur side by side; the one clear and showing pale tints in thin slices; the other deeply coloured, with a strong "schiller" structure parallel to the orthopinacoid, and also densely charged at the margin and along cracks with finely-divided magnetite, evidently due to secondary alteration. The pleochroism-scheme, so far as it can be made out, is:—

	Pale crystals.	Deeply coloured.
$\mathfrak{a} = a$ -	Pale rose.	Deep brown (with a greyish tone).
$\mathfrak{b} = b$	Very pale.	Reddish brown.
$\mathfrak{c} = c$ -	Very pale apple-green.	?

A rhombic pyroxene occurs as a subordinate accessory mineral in some other gabbros examined from the Cuillins. In the analysed

* *Quart. Journ. Geol. Soc.*, vol. xli., pp. 380, 413; Pl. XI., Figs. 7, 8: 1885.

rock [8043], where it forms 2 *per cent.*, it is an enstatite, as appears clearly from its low specific gravity (3·0).

Olivine is a very frequent constituent of the Skye gabbros, though less constant than might be expected from the accounts given by Zirkel and Judd.* As usual, it is strictly idiomorphic, but with a strong tendency to rounded outlines. There is rarely any appearance of regular cleavage-cracks. The commonest inclusions are minute flat rectangular cavities containing dendritic growths of magnetite.† There is often also a copious separation of magnetite dust in cracks and at the margin of a crystal, this being evidently a secondary phenomenon (Fig. 21). It may be taken as indicating that the olivine is a variety rich in iron, and, although there are no published analyses of Skye olivines, this is borne out by the high density of the mineral in our gabbros. The olivine of the analysed rock [8043] sinks in a liquid of specific gravity 3·44. An olivine analysed by Heddle‡ from the neighbouring island of Rum, with 18·7 per cent. of ferrous oxide and 2·9 of ferric, gave the specific gravity 3·327: this was from the peridotite group.

The olivine is often fresh, and then sensibly colourless in thin slices. The commonest change is the separation of iron-oxide already mentioned. Complete destruction of the mineral sometimes gives rise to pseudomorphs of green or yellow or brown serpentine, the secondary magnetite being largely reabsorbed. In other rocks round pseudomorphs of fibrous (pilitic) hornblende seem to represent vanished grains of olivine. A third kind of transformation is of rarer occurrence: *e.g.* slide [2636] from Coire na Banachdich. This results in pseudomorphs of which the chief element is a mica-like mineral of yellowish-brown colour with one strong cleavage and sensibly straight extinction. The pleochroism is strong, vibrations parallel to the cleavage giving the deeper absorption. Embedded in this substance are rounded patches with a more confused structure: these too are pleochroic, but the stronger absorption is for transverse vibrations. These pseudomorphs recall some described from the olivine-diabases of Derbyshire,§ and are in some respects comparable with the iddingsite of Lawson.

Original *iron-ores* are present in most of the gabbros, though never abundant in the normal rocks and often wanting. They occur usually in irregular shapeless grains, often moulded upon the felspar crystals and sometimes on the augite, proving that they are not very early products of consolidation. When there is anything of crystal-outline to indicate the nature of the mineral the forms

---

* These writers, it must be noted, deal with a wider region than the Isle of Skye, and both appear to have paid special attention to the rocks of Mull. Zirkel states that the Skye rocks are poorer in olivine than those of Mull. Prof. Judd, however, believes that "all the gabbros in their unaltered condition contained olivine, though in very varying proportions." (*Quart. Journ. Geol. Soc.*, vol. xlii., p. 62 : 1886.)

† See Judd, *Quart. Journ. Geol. Soc.*, vol. xli., Pl. XII., Fig. 5 : 1885.

‡ *Min. Mag.*, vol. v., p. 16 : 1884.

§ Arnold-Bemrose, *Quart. Journ. Geol. Soc.*, vol. l., pp. 613 *et seq.* : 1894.

are almost always those of magnetite, and this may be inferred to be the common iron-ore in this group of rocks. The characteristic skeleton crystals of ilmenite are rarely observed [e.g. 2635], but the discrimination of the two minerals in rock-slices leaves much to be desired. Petrologists are not agreed as to the existence of "titaniferous magnetite," as distinct from a mixture of magnetite and ilmenite, and some have suggested the possibility of ultra-microscopic intergrowths. We have not observed any appearance of visible intergrowth, and the iron-ore of the highly ferriferous seams on Druim an Eidhne, which analysis shows to have the composition of a mixture of the two minerals, behaved as a homogeneous substance when etched by hydrochloric acid, the solution obtained containing titanic acid.* Chromite has not been detected in the microscopic examination of the rocks.

It is a curious fact that the gabbros, even when they do not usually contain any large proportion of iron-ore minerals, are capable of becoming highly magnetised. This may be verified on almost any prominent peak or ridge of the Cuillins, and accounts for the fact that the indications of the compass are in such situations wholly untrustworthy. The effects observed must be ascribed to atmospheric electricity, but the peculiar distribution of permanent magnetism in the rocks is not easily accounted for. It may be roughly described as equivalent to a number of magnetic poles of both kinds scattered through the mass of the rock without appearance of order or regularity, usually only a few inches or at most a few feet apart.†

In this connection it may be remarked that Sir A. Rücker‡ has determined in his laboratory the magnetic susceptibility of a number of Skye gabbros. Eleven specimens from Loch Coruisk gave from ·00049 to ·00684, with a mean of ·00237. Four other Skye gabbros gave from ·00246 to ·00747, the mean for the fifteen being ·00323. The Skye basalts were not tested, but thirteen from Mull gave a mean of ·00163 : it is not clear whether these rocks were lavas or sills.

Apatite is never an abundant mineral in the Skye gabbros, and does not occur in most of the slides. Specially remarkable is its absence from such highly basic modifications as the seams rich in iron-ore, just referred to ; while it is found frequently, though locally and in no great amount, in more acid members of the group, including the felspathic gabbro veins which traverse the seams in question.

One or two exceptional rocks, probably segregation-veins, contain *quartz* [2635]. As usual in quartz-gabbros, this mineral occurs as a constituent of micropegmatite, intergrown with felspar which, in part at least, is orthoclase.

Macculloch recorded the occurrence of abundant *garnet* in one

---

* Geikie and Teall, *Quart. Journ. Geol. Soc.*, vol. l., p. 652 : 1894.
† Harker, *Proc. Camb. Phil. Soc.*, vol. x., pp. 268-278, Pl. XI., XII. : 1900.
‡ *Proc. Roy. Soc.*, vol. xlviii., p. 521 : 1890.

locality.* Although Zirkel throws doubt on the statement, and we have not succeeded in verifying it on the ground, it is doubtless correct. Cohen† has given a photograph of a garnet, enclosing other small garnets, from a "granulite" in Skye, doubtless one of the "granulitic gabbros" of the Cuillins, and probably from Druim an Eidhne. We shall see reasons, however, for doubting whether these rocks really form part of the gabbro group.

The *special mineralogical variations* met with among the rocks require only a few remarks. Among the Skye gabbros varieties departing very notably from the average as regards mineralogical constitution are of quite rare occurrence, except in connection with the banded structure to which we have adverted. A few of these exceptional occurrences are worthy of mention. One variety is so rich in olivine as to be petrographically almost a peridotite. Such a rock, with specific gravity 2·925, occurs on the right bank of the Scavaig River. A thin slice shows that more than half of it consists of fresh olivine. The next abundant constituent is labradorite (not anorthite as in the troctolites in the peridotite group). Augite, of light brown colour and with some diallagic structure, is in rather subordinate amount, forming spreading crystal-plates which enclose the olivine in pœcilitic fashion. There are a few little octahedra of opaque black iron-ore, apparently magnetite. Next, a rock from Coire na Banachdich, already mentioned, is a norite, consisting of felspar, idiomorphic crystals of hypersthene, some strongly schillerised and others quite clear, and a small amount of interstitial augite [2637]. It is noticeable again that the felspar is labradorite, as in the normal gabbros : the norites belonging to the peridotite group have anorthite.

The *texture and micro-structure* of the rocks exhibit considerable variations. Among the normal gabbros a large number of examples have crystals measuring about $\tfrac{1}{10}$ inch, or ranging from $\tfrac{1}{20}$ to $\tfrac{3}{20}$ inch, but much coarser rocks also occur, especially in the heart of the mountains, the individual crystals being sometimes as much as an inch in length, or exceptionally two inches. In the pegmatoid veins and lenticles occasionally intercalated in the normal massive gabbros crystals of augite sometimes attain a length of six or eight inches. The mutual relations of the two principal constituents of the gabbros are not always the same. As a rule the felspar tends to be idiomorphic towards the augite, and may be said to be of earlier crystallisation (Fig. 21). It may be remarked, however, that the "order of crystallisation" should properly signify the order in which the several minerals *began* to separate from the molten magma, while the manner in which the crystals fit together can only indicate the order in which they *ceased* to form. The fact that the relations vary sometimes in one

* *Description of the Western Islands of Scotland*, vol. i., p. 419 : 1819. The text says "in the hill Scuir na Streigh," but Macculloch included under that name not only the Sgùrr na Stri of the Ordnance Survey, but also Sgùrr an Eidhne and Druim an Eidhne.
† *Sammlung von Mikrophotographien der mikroskopischen Structur von Mineralien und Gesteinen*, 3rd ed., Pl. V., Fig. 4 : 1899.

and the same thin slice leads to the conclusion that the periods of crystallisation of the several minerals (including the magnetite) overlapped considerably. In some of the coarser rocks the augite is very distinctly idiomorphic towards the felspar, and this is notably the case in many of the pegmatoid veins and streaks. In some of the coarse and most of the finer-textured rocks, on the other hand, the augite tends to wrap round the felspar, and there are diabasic varieties in which the structure is frankly *ophitic*. These are found in general only in the marginal portions of the complex. Taken apart from their associations, such rocks would be styled diabases, but from the point of view adopted they are regarded as modified forms of the gabbros.

Sharply distinguished from gabbros proper and diabases are the

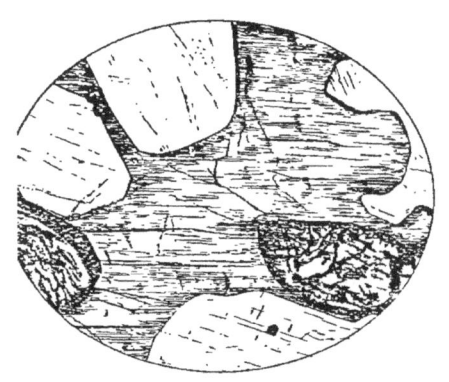

Fig. 21.—[8043] × 20. Olivine-Gabbro, west bank of Sligachan River, just below Allt Coire Riabhach; showing the ophitic structure. This is the rock analysed (I. above), and consists of labradorite, diallage, olivine with secondary magnetite, and a few small crystals of original magnetite.

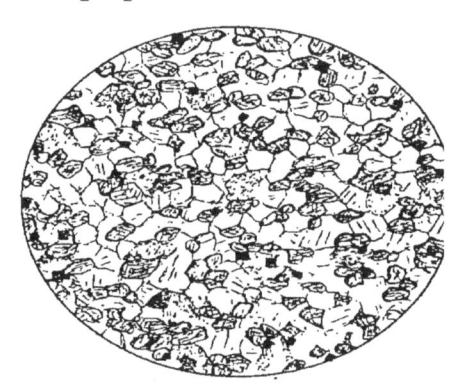

Fig. 22.—[5369] ×20. "Granulitic Gabbro," Druim an Eidhne; probably a highly metamorphosed basaltic lava. It consists essentially of a granulitic aggregate of labradorite and augite, with little octahedra of magnetite.

"*granulitic* gabbros" or, as Continental petrographers would name them, "pyroxene-granulites." They are dark, dense, rather fine-grained rocks, the individual crystals having diameters up to about $\frac{1}{100}$ inch only, consisting of labradorite and augite (with basal striation), with little octahedra of magnetite. The micro-structure is of the granulitic kind, and, when either of the principal constituents shows an approach to idiomorphism, it is the augite, not the felspar (Fig. 22). The true nature of these rocks is a matter of some uncertainty, and it is not improbable that they are highly altered representatives of basic lavas entangled in the gabbro complex. The occurrence of oval spots like much-changed amygdules lends colour to this idea. Sir A. Geikie and Mr Teall[*]

[*] *Quart. Journ. Geol. Soc.*, vol. l., p. 647 : 1894.

were disposed to discard this opinion in view of the micro-structure of the rocks; but the occurrences since examined and mapped in the western Cuillins prove that very radical transformations are possible in the metamorphism of the basaltic lavas by the gabbros. In no case have the granulitic rocks in question been observed to intersect the gabbros proper, though the converse relation is frequently verified. It may be that two distinct rocks have been confused together, viz. a granulitic variety of the gabbro and metamorphosed lava closely simulating it. Only those rocks have been mapped as metamorphosed basalts which afforded some positive evidence of that origin, the rest being thrown in with the gabbro. Rosenbusch's suggestion* that Judd's granulitic gabbros correspond with the "beerbachite" of Chelius (an aplitic rock occurring as small dykes and veins in gabbro) seems to be based on a misunderstanding. We have not observed any rock comparable with beerbachite in Skye, the veins which traverse the gabbro being of quite other types.

The gabbro contains in many places irregular veins and streaks of coarse texture, which we may term *pegmatoid gabbro*. They are not very sharply bounded against the normal rock, and are doubtless to be regarded as quasi-contemporaneous segregation-veins. Unlike most of the gabbro, they have augite idiomorphic towards felspar, sometimes in imperfectly-built crystals six or eight inches long. These pegmatoid streaks have been observed chiefly in the heart of the gabbro laccolite. A specimen was examined from Coire na Banachdich; a coarse rock with augite crystals two inches long. In a thin slice [2635] this augite is pale brown, with basal striation, and there are in addition pseudomorphs after a rhombic pyroxene. The felspar seems to be a somewhat acid labradorite. The iron-ore is titaniferous, and there are also a few little crystals of light brown sphene. The rest of the interspaces between the felspar and augite crystals is occupied by a delicate micropegmatite. A point of some interest is the presence of rather numerous little needles of apatite, a mineral comparatively rare in our gabbros, though it is found generally in the granites and granophyres of the district.

In many parts of the mountains the gabbro is traversed by pale veins of finer texture, which cut it sharply (*see* Plate VI.). They cut all varieties of the gabbro, but never any of the many dykes and sheets of various later ages by which the gabbro is intersected. This may be taken to indicate that the veins are closely bound up with the gabbros, and belong to the close of the gabbro-epoch, their magma being presumably a highly specialised derivative from the gabbro-magma, or representing its residual portion. They are very considerably more acid, and have in consequence a very different mineralogical constitution. Two types of veins are to be recognised, both to be distinguished from the true acid veins (granite and granophyre), which belong to the succeeding epoch, and to which they sometimes bear a resemblance at first sight.

* *Mikroskopische Physiographie der Massigen Gesteine*, 3rd ed., p. 492: 1896.

There are firstly *veins of felspathic gabbro*, found in some places traversing the darker and more pyroxenic normal rocks. Besides a paler colour, they have a somewhat finer texture, though not so fine as the other kind of veins to be mentioned. They are less common, and are usually seen to be in connection with rather larger sheet-like bodies of similar rock, from which they are offshoots. Veins of this kind on Druim an Eidhne have been described by Sir A. Geikie and Mr Teall.* Petrographically they are gabbros of a type poor in the ferro-magnesian silicates and iron-oxides. Further, they have oligoclase in some abundance, in addition to labradorite. The scanty augite seems to be in part proper to the rock, in part picked up from the normal gabbros. Apatite is a very noticeable constituent.

Secondly, there are *white felspathic veins*, which are more widely distributed than the preceding. Their width is often about an inch, but they range up to a foot or more in places, and also sink to very minute dimensions. They frequently ramify and anastomose; and exceptionally, when this is carried to an extreme, the gabbro looks like a breccia of angular fragments set in a matrix of the white felspathic rock. The veins are white or cream-coloured and of relatively fine texture, having often a saccharoid appearance. In some cases there are also little crystals up to $\frac{1}{8}$ inch. One specimen gave the specific gravity 2·58, indicating a composition very different from that of a gabbro. Slices show that the rocks consist essentially of oligoclase and orthoclase, in about equal quantity or the latter predominating [7847]. Quartz is never present. A little augite or uralitic hornblende and magnetite may occur, but these are, at least mostly, derived from the country rock. The felspars are often more turbid than is usual in the felspars of the gabbro. Epidote is occasionally found in granules, or again in little crystals about $\frac{1}{40}$ inch long [8046].

These light-coloured veins are not equally common in different parts of the area. They are especially characteristic of the eastern half of the Cuillin mass, including the Blaven range.

We have already alluded to the heterogeneous appearance not infrequently observed in the Cuillins in what must still be regarded as a geological unit, a sheet-like mass of gabbro the product of a single intrusion. The heterogeneity may show itself in two ways, by a patchy, or more frequently a banded, structure and by the occurrence of true xenoliths. The distribution and arrangement of the banded structure in the gabbros of the Cuillins have already been pointed out: we have now to consider briefly the *petrographical character of these banded rocks*. In this there is not much to be added to the description given by Sir A. Geikie and Mr Teall of the typical examples on Druim an Eidhne.

As seen in the field, the appearance is simply that of alternating layers and seams differing in texture and in the relative proportions of the component minerals. The latter difference, when noteworthy,

* *Quart. Journ. Geol. Soc.*, vol. l., pp. 650, 654 : 1894.

is made evident by difference of shade, lighter and darker bands corresponding with a preponderance of the felspathic and the pyroxenic constituents respectively (*see* Plates V. and VI., above). The differences may be slight or very considerable, and the width of the individual bands may vary within rather wide limits. When this is so, the greatest contrasts in petrographical constitution are found in connection with the narrowest bands, and the extreme variation, resulting in a nearly black variety very rich in augite and iron-ores, is found in thin seams only. In these respects the rocks are comparable with the banded peridotites already described.

Conspicuous banding in the gabbros is not confined to the sheet-formed intrusions which compose the great laccolitic mass: it is found also in some of the dyke-formed offshoots from the gabbro, which intersect the earlier peridotite group as already described. The phenomena are well seen in the glen immediately to the south of Allt a' Chaoich, near Loch Scavaig. The apophyses of the gabbro at that place are partly in the form of straight vertical dykes, partly a system of irregular ramifying veins, and it is the former only that display banding. These *dykes of banded gabbro* (Fig. 23) are instructive for comparison with the banded sheets. A single dyke shows considerable differences of composition in successive bands parallel to the bounding walls. Further, it may show considerable differences of texture, becoming more fine-grained towards the edge, and presenting a thoroughly close-textured selvage indicative of comparatively rapid chilling. This character, however, is not always found, and it may occur on one side of the dyke only: such an asymmetric dyke is illustrated in the figure (A). Since the dyke is not insinuated between two different members of the peridotite group, but cuts across the banded ultrabasic complex at a high angle, it is clear that a single intrusion of the gabbro magma would have cooled evenly at its two edges; and we are led to the conclusion that this dyke is the result of more than one injection, the right (eastern) portion being somewhat younger than the left (western), though following it so closely that no very well defined division is to be perceived between them.

It is worthy of note that in this dyke the banded structure is more sharply marked in the earlier (left-hand) half. The left and right portions do not perhaps differ greatly in average composition; but the former presents a generally pale ground, in which occur several very conspicuous dark seams, not much more than $\frac{1}{4}$ inch in width. That the earlier and more rapidly cooled portion is the more heterogeneous cannot, however, be ascribed to differentiation in place, for the banding does not stand in any evident relation to the surface of cooling. One dark basic seam does indeed form the actual margin, but others no less marked occur in the interior.

A good idea of the actual range of variety in the banded gabbros is given by the following chemical analyses by Mr J. H. Player[*] of bands occurring in close association with one another on Druim-an-Eidhne (p. 120).

[*] *Quart. Journ. Geol. Soc.*, vol. l., p. 653: 1894.

The third specimen is especially interesting. It is ultrabasic in the fashion, not of the peridotites, but of the eruptive iron-ore rocks described by Vogt from Norway and elsewhere. The base which increases rapidly as the silica falls off is not magnesia but iron-oxide. Hence we find that olivine is present only sporadically and in trifling amount, while iron-ores make up about one third of the rock. If it is to be regarded as a mixture of true magnetite and ilmenite, these are present in about equal proportions, a small quantity of pyrites being also indicated by the analysis. It is very noteworthy that both the augite and the felspar in this highly basic seam are identical with those of the ordinary gabbros. The felspar is a labradorite, while in one slide [5376] andesine and even oligoclase are recognised by their extinction-angles. Very remarkable is the absence of apatite.

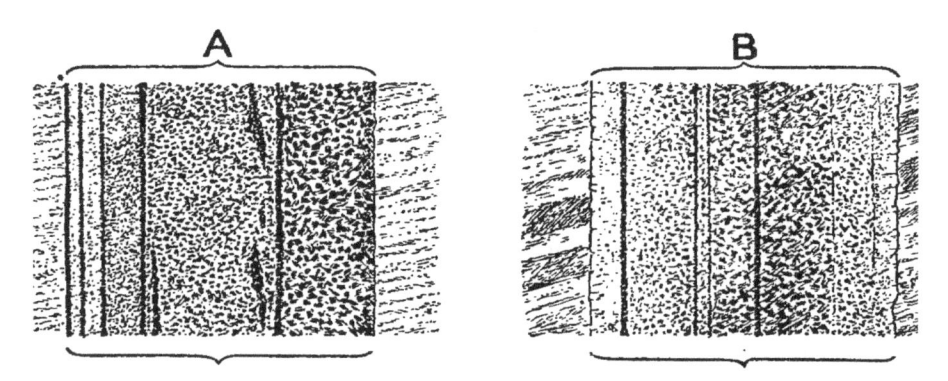

Fig. 23.—Dykes of banded gabbro cutting the banded peridotite group in glen south of Allt a' Chaoich, Loch Scavaig.
The bands contain different proportions of the constituent minerals, and narrow dark seams of very basic composition are especially conspicuous. There are also considerable differences in texture. In A the gabbro is coarse towards the right (eastern) side of the dyke, and becomes progressively finer towards the left. It is in the fine-textured part that the dark seams are most distinct and most regular. In B the rock is coarsest in the middle of the dyke, and becomes finer towards the sides, presenting evidently chilled margins to the peridotite.
These dykes bear nearly N.N.E.-S.S.W., cutting the banding of the peridotite at a high angle, and each has a width of about 1 ft 6 ins.

That the various bands crystallised simultaneously, and must therefore have existed side by side in the fluid state, is shown by the fashion in which their crystals interlock at the common surface of two contiguous bands. It also appears that flowing movement had in most places practically ceased prior to the beginning of crystallisation, for, as a rule, there is no parallel arrangement of the constituent crystals. To this statement there are only a few exceptions. One rock from Druim-an-Eidhne has a very decided fissile character, owing to parallelism of the felspar crystals, which here have a pronounced tabular habit (Plate XVIII., Fig. 6). Some-

	I.	II.	III.	A.
SiO_2	52·8	40·2	29·5	40·2
TiO_2	0·5	4·7	9·2	5·2
Al_2O_3	17·8	9·5	3·8	10·2
Fe_2O_3	1·2	9·7	17·8	10·2
FeO	4·8	12·2	18·2	12·1
FeS_2	..	0·4	0·4	0·2
MnO	..	0·4	0·3	0·2
MgO	4·8	8·0	8·7	6·9
CaO	12·9	13·1	10·0	11·4
Na_2O	3·0	0·8	0·2	1·5
K_2O	0·5	0·2	0·1	0·3
Ignition	1·2	0·5	1·0	1·1
	99·5	99·7	99·2	99·6
Specific gravity	2·91	3·36	3·87	3·43

I. [5373]. A light-coloured band mainly composed of labradorite. The other constituents are augite, uralitic hornblende, and magnetite.

II. [5377]. A dark band composed of augite, magnetite, and labradorite.

III. [5376]. A thin ultrabasic " schliere," mainly composed of augite and magnetite.

A. Calculated mixture of 45·9 parts of I. with 54·1 parts of III., for comparison with II.

thing similar occurs at the head of Loch Coruisk, but in general there is no special orientation noticeable. The several partial magmas seem to have been intruded while still completely molten and mobile, and their not mingling implies a high mutual surface-tension.

The mutual relations of the several rock-types associated together in the banded gabbros compel us to the conclusion that they were intruded simultaneously, and were derived from some common source, which may be pictured as a subterranean reservoir where the several fluid magmas existed together without commingling. If the distinct but closely associated magmas were the results of a " differentiation " of a common parent magma having more of the composition of a normal gabbro, the differentiating process was the result of causes which at present can be only a matter of speculation, and the question is not one to be discussed in this place. We may observe, however, that the governing conditions were probably of no very simple kind, for the process has evidently not followed always the same lines. The thin seam very rich in iron-ores analysed by Mr Player and described by Mr Teall appears to have had but little olivine; but in other similar seams from the same locality that mineral has been formed in abundance. It is represented mainly by pseudomorphs, sometimes serpentinous, sometimes "pilitic," and always containing much secondary magnetite.

It may be noticed that the variation indicated by the three analyses quoted is very closely of the "linear" type,* *i.e.* the composition of the second rock could be very nearly reproduced by a mixture in proper proportions of the first and third, as shown in column A above, and as illustrated graphically in one of Professor Vogt's papers.†

A striking feature in some parts of the Cuillins is the frequent occurrence of small *fragments or xenoliths of gabbro enclosed in gabbro of a somewhat different kind*. Sometimes the difference is not great, and the xenoliths are not seen distinctly except on a weathered face. Where, as sometimes happens, they are decidedly less durable than their matrix, they weather into little hollows, and, if numerous, give a curious pitted appearance to the surface of the rock. This is well seen at several places on the floor of Tairneilear and on the rocky platform just west of the mouth of that corrie. These xenolithic gabbros are no doubt to be attributed in general to the fact that the gabbro mass consists of numerous distinct intrusions, the later of which have often broken through the earlier. Possibly the phenomenon arises also in a rather different way. In numerous localities the xenoliths are found in the vicinity of enclosed patches of volcanic agglomerate, which contain abundant fragments of gabbro, derived, as we have pointed out above, from some older and wholly concealed mass of that rock. The agglomerates are greatly metamorphosed, and in some cases the actual boundaries of the patches are such as to suggest that portions have been incorporated in the gabbro magma. This points to a possible source of some of the xenoliths, but such an explanation cannot be extended to include all the occurrences. A third possibility, already suggested in the case of the peridotites, is that the xenoliths may have been brought up in the magma from a much lower level, being the result of local crystallisation in the magma-reservoir itself.

An instructive comparison may be made between the gabbros and the peridotites of the Cuillins, and some heads of such a comparison are set forth below in parallel columns. It will be observed that the peridotites are much more prone to variation than the gabbros, both in different intrusions and in the parts of a single intrusive body. The variations, however, follow very similar lines in the two groups of rocks, though with certain exceptions. Especially noteworthy is the difference between the extreme basic products of "concentration," chromium being the characteristic element in the ultrabasic and titanium in the basic rocks. This appears to be a general principle in the chemistry of igneous rock-magmas, and has been specially emphasised by Vogt.

In conclusion we shall briefly refer to the changes which the Skye gabbros have undergone in some places since they first became solid rocks. It will not be necessary to say much in this place relative to the *thermal metamorphism* of the rocks, often very marked, in the neighbourhood of the subsequently intruded granite.

* Harker, *Journ. of Geol.*, vol. viii., p. 391 : 1900.
† *Zeits. prakt. Geol.*, vol. ix., p. 186 : 1901.

Ultrabasic Group.	Basic Group.
(i.) Rocks composed of predominant olivine and generally augite as the two principal constituents, often with little or no felspar (anórthite);	(i.) Rocks composed of felspar (labradorite) and augite as the two principal constituents, with or without olivine;
variety characterised by a rhombic pyroxene not rare.	variety characterised by a rhombic pyroxene rare.
(ii.) The several intrusions differing widely in average composition.	(ii.) The several intrusions differing little in average composition.
(iii.) Banding generally prevalent and usually strongly marked;	(iii). Banding in part of the rocks and locally strongly marked;
bands of felspathic peridotite and troctolite alternating with others of picrite and peridotite very rich in olivine.	bands of more felspathic gabbro alternating with others of more augitic gabbro and olivine-gabbro.
(iv.) The more basic bands include seams rich in, or almost wholly composed of, spinels or iron-ores, highly chromiferous.	(iv.) The more basic bands include seams containing a large percentage of iron-ores, highly titaniferous.
(v.) A xenolithic character generally prevalent and often very conspicuous; xenoliths and matrix being sometimes varieties of one type, but frequently quite different types.	(v.) A xenolithic character locally prevalent, though not often very conspicuous; xenoliths and matrix being alike of gabbro, but of somewhat different varieties.
(vi.) The picrite and peridotite often traversed by coarser segregation-veins of troctolite.	(vi.) The gabbro often traversed by coarser segregation-veins of more felspathic gabbro.

When the effects are merely metamorphic (not also metasomatic) they present no peculiarity. The most frequent change observed in this connection is a partial or total uralitisation of the augite of the rock, such as is seen in the metamorphosed gabbros in other regions. The much more remarkable changes which have been set up where there has been actual interchange of substance between the gabbro and the granite magma will receive full attention in their proper place. It is not always possible, however, to be quite sure to what extent this latter condition has contributed to some of the transformations observed. The formation of biotite in the rocks is a case in point. On the western slope of Beinn na Cro, for example, which is one of the best places for studying thermal metamorphism in the gabbros, little flakes of bronzy mica are often conspicuous on a hand-specimen. In a thin slice this mineral shows the usual deep-brown colour, with intense pleochroism, and seems to have been developed mainly at the expense of augite (partly also of magnetite). Certain peculiarities of the felspars, however, and the occasional presence of a little interstitial quartz [8966] may be taken to indicate that there has been some small amount of impregnation of the gabbro by the granite magma, and it is not improbable that the formation of the mica also is due to something more than simple metamorphism.

The slow changes which affect igneous rocks independently of thermal and dynamic metamorphism, and apart also, as it seems, from atmospheric weathering, have left their mark in varying degree upon our gabbros. Here we may include the partial turbidity of much of the felspar, and here too the frequent passage of the augite into hornblende, which can by no means always be referred to any known "metamorphic" agent.

Concerning the *weathering* of the gabbro it is not possible to say much, for the reason that the rock is almost everywhere in a comparatively fresh condition. This is, of course, due to the scouring action of ice which has removed the superficial crust. The very few exceptions are of a kind to confirm the rule, for they are found in deep narrow gorges outside the actual mountain tract. The best instance is in the sides of Allt Coire na Banachdich below Eas Mòr, where the gabbro presents a very unusual appearance. Much of it is divided by plane joints into large blocks which, by the crumbling and scaling away of the surface, have taken on the form of giant spheroids. The rock is often so soft that it can be dug with a spade. The felspars remain when the other constituents have perished, and, breaking up, form a sand mingled with more or less of a rust-coloured clay, which represents the ferro-magnesian minerals of the gabbro. Another place where the gabbro is in a rotten condition is the gorge in which Allt a' Coire Ghreadaidh runs for nearly a mile of its lower course. Nothing of this kind is seen anywhere among the mountains and corries.

The other kind of decomposition which we distinguished in the basic lavas, viz. that connected with solfataric action, naturally finds no place in the gabbros, and no long list of alteration-products can be drawn up. Veins of chrysotile and of calcite are sometimes found, but they seem to be invariably connected with some degree of crushing and fracture of the rocks. Of recognisable new minerals the most frequent is perhaps greenish-yellow epidote, and this is sometimes found in good crystals. On Sgùrr Dearg, both on the S.W. ridge and on the south-eastern slope, epidote crystals covered with radiating fibres of natrolite occur in cavities in the gabbro. Solid veins of white prehnite, with embedded crystals of epidote next the rock, occur on Druim nan Ramh. Rarely on the southern slope of Sgùrr nan Gillean there are veins containing doubly-terminating quartz-crystals sprinkled with mammilations of prehnite, and the latter mineral is also recorded in the gabbro of Coire Labain and of the west side of Sgùrr nan Gillean, just below Sgùrr a' Bhàsteir.* Quartz-veins are found a little west of the

* See Heddle's *Mineralogy of Scotland.* pp. 65, 69, 104 : 1901.

124   *Effects of Crushing in Gabbros.*

summit of Sgùrr na Banachdich, but they seem to be in part connected with an enclosed patch of the basaltic lavas, and in the gabbro in general free silica is almost unknown.

The gabbro, at once a much more massive and a much stronger rock than the basalts, nevertheless shows sometimes *cataclastic effects* of an advanced kind. Such effects are confined, however, to the edge of the mass. They may be observed in specimens from various spots in Glen Sligachan and on Druim an Eidhne, and again from north of Garbh-bheinn and Belig, always near the boundary of the gabbro. As a rule the crushing has not been so directed as to set up a schistose structure, and often there is nothing in the appearance of a hand-specimen to indicate the crushing in its earlier stages. A more complete break-down of the rock, however, may be recognisable by an abnormally fine texture (though sometimes with uncrushed relics of the original rock), and in some cases by a dull aspect consequent upon chloritisation of the augitic constituent.

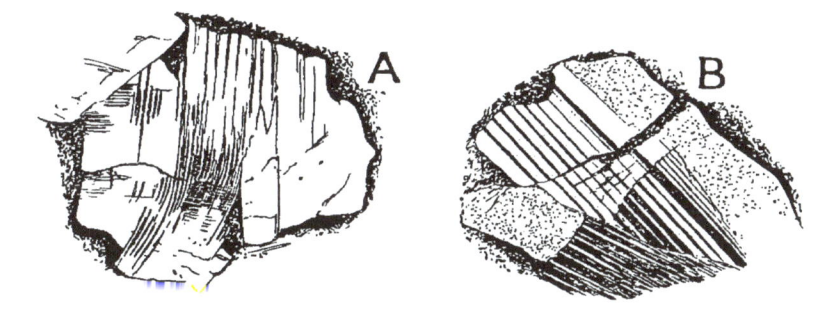

Fig. 24.—Secondary twin-lamellation, connected with strain, in the felspar of the gabbros : × 20, crossed nicols.

  A [2637]. Coire na Banachdich.
  B [5375]. Druim an Eidhne.

Thin slices of the more thoroughly crushed gabbros show various stages in the break-down of the original structure of the rock, culminating in what Törnebohm has styled " Mörtelstructur." The uncrushed remains of felspar and augite crystals are converted into round grains, embedded in a finely granular matrix. This may occur without any appearance of recrystallisation or of mineral change, the effects produced being purely mechanical [7116, 7120]. In other cases there is a partial uralitisation of the augite [7462], or that mineral may be almost wholly replaced by a green hornblende [2716]; but, as the specimens showing this come from the immediate neighbourhood of the granite, it may be an effect of thermal metamorphism.

Certain specimens examined, which have not been broken down in this way, exhibit strain-effects in the crystals of felspar, a peculiarity not found in connection with advanced cataclastic structures. Sometimes a crystal is bent, and where the curvature is sharpest there is a much closer twin-lamellation than elsewhere

(Fig. 24, A). Again, we may see a crystal in which some of the twin-lamellæ terminate abruptly against a crack (Fig. 24, B). Professor Judd* has given an interesting discussion of the secondary twin-lamellation of the felspars in the peridotites and gabbros of the Western Isles, and is disposed to attach great importance to it. Phenomena such as we have referred to are found occasionally in many of the Skye gabbros, but we have seen nothing to suggest that the twinning is *in general* other than an original character.

* *Quart. Journ. Geol. Soc.*, vol. xli., pp. 364-366 ; Pl. X., Fig. 1 : 1885.

CHAPTER IX.

Granites and Granophyres: Field-Relations.

Granite and granophyre cover in Skye an area which fully equals or exceeds that occupied by the gabbro. The principal development is found in the Red Hills, lying north-east and east of the Cuillins. This collective name for the granite hills seems to have been first used by Macculloch in 1816: it merely renders the Gaelic name Beinn Dearg, which is applied specifically to more than one hill near Glen Sligachan and again near Broadford.* The granite hills present much simpler and more rounded outlines than those composed of gabbro, and they are also lower, the granite itself never attaining the altitude of 2500 feet.

From Glen Sligachan a continuous tract of granite (including granophyre), six or seven miles across, extends north-eastward to the shore opposite Scalpay, with a prolongation into that island, and eastward to Glas-bheinn Bheag and Strath Beag. Here it joins for a short distance an otherwise isolated granite area, about three by two miles in extent, comprising the eastern Red Hills— Beinn na Caillich and its neighbours—which lie west of Broadford. Farther south, at Beinn an Dubhaich, occurs a separate mass of granite, and between these two are the Kilchrist granophyres, forming several smaller outcrops of a look in some respects peculiar. On the eastern side of the Blaven range granite is found, though not continuously, along a line from Strath Mòr to near the headland of Rudha Bàn, beyond Camasunary, these outcrops connecting themselves with the large mass first mentioned. Some intrusions on and near Creag Strollamus are probably related to, though not visibly continuous with, the neighbouring mass of the eastern Red Hills. On Scalpay, besides the area in the south-western corner of the island, which is evidently an extension of the large mass forming the main Red Hills of Skye, there is a sheet-like mass, or perhaps more than one, the outcrops of which encircle almost continuously the hill Mullach na Càrn at about 1000 feet altitude. Other occurrences have been mapped in Raasay by Mr Woodward, but these are not included in the scope of our detailed study.

Certain sheets of granophyre, large and small, intruded in the Mesozoic strata along a curved belt of country from Beinn Bhuidhe, near Broadford, to Suishnish, between Loch Slapin and Loch

* In the former neighbourhood there are also Meall Dearg and Ruadh Stac (Red Stack). Colour epithets are used in Gaelic with considerable laxity, but here the reddish tone is, in certain conditions of the weather, very marked.

Eishort, are reserved for special description. They have much in common with the rocks of the Red Hills, but seem to be of somewhat later date, and moreover exhibit certain peculiarities both geological and petrographical. We also postpone consideration of most of the minor intrusions—dykes and some irregular sheets—of granophyre and quartz-felsite; more particularly those which belong to a distinctly later epoch than the granite group, as opposed to those which are merely apophyses of the large intrusive bodies of the Red Hills.

As in the case of the gabbro, we have to distinguish here *two different habits* as regards the form and relations of the larger intrusive masses; viz. the sheet-like or laccolitic and the disruptive or boss-like. This was recognised by Macculloch in 1819, and again by Sir A. Geikie in 1858. The instances which those writers cite of the former kind of habit are taken only from the smaller intrusions in the Lias, where the sill form is sometimes displayed with considerable regularity. If we view the large mass forming the Red Hills with regard to its general form and position, neglecting irregularities of detail, we find that considerable portions of this too have the form of a thick sheet. The departures from regularity are, however, greater here than in the gabbro of the Cuillins. They seem to have some relation to the nature of the rocks with which the granite is in contact in different portions of its boundary.

We shall most clearly obtain an idea of the relations of this large mass of granite and granophyre by considering the form and character of its boundary in different parts. On the extreme west the line runs nearly north and south for two miles or more, close to the Sligachan River. The northern part of this boundary (against basaltic lavas) is concealed, but the remainder (against gabbro) is well seen, and seems to be everywhere nearly vertical. Farther south, on Druim an Eidhne, the junction is of a very different kind, the granite passing under the gabbro at a low angle. Where the volcanic agglomerate begins to intervene between the two plutonic rocks, the granite boundary is at an altitude of about 1000 feet; but it runs down eastward into Strath na Creitheach, underlying the much-expanded mass of agglomerate as the latter underlies the gabbro of Sgùrr an Eidhne. On the other side of the valley it ascends again, turning N.E. and N.N.E.; the upper surface of the granite here having an inclination not very different from the north-western slope of Blath-bheinn, as is shown by the occurrence of an inlier about ¾ mile long. For some distance along the flanks of Blath-bheinn the granite is in contact with gabbro, then a strip of the volcanic rocks again intervenes, as the boundary rises to over 1400 feet on the northerly ridge of Garbh-bheinn. Here begins the large agglomerate mass of Coire na Seilg and Coire Coinnich, and the granite sinks again, passing beneath this mass. It is quite clear that the sinuous southern boundary we are following represents the upper surface—not horizontal indeed but never very steeply inclined—of a mass which terminates upward (Fig. 25). Similarly, if we follow the northern boundary from Glen Sligachan towards Loch Ainort, we see that it represents the corresponding lower surface, the granite resting first on basaltic lavas and then on Torridon Sandstone. There are, however, considerable irregularities in this part of the boundary, partly connected perhaps with the dying out of the intrusion. Thus the basaltic lavas forming the summit ridge and much of the upper slopes of Glamaig are almost cut off, and must be in great part underlain, by a tongue of the granite. The boundary rises on the west side to near the main summit, drops by steps to about 1400 feet at the pass on the south side, rises again to the eastern summit, and drops sharply, with something like a vertical junction, along the north-eastern ridge. The tongue which runs along the north-western and northern faces dies out a little before reaching this ridge. The patch of basalt lavas, ½ mile across, to

FIG. 25.—View from Bealach a' Leitir, looking east and south-east. In the foreground is the south-easterly spur of Sgùrr nan Gillean, terminating in Sgùrr na h-Uamha; in the distance the Blaven range. Both these are of gabbro, while Strath na Creitheach and the low hills in the middle distance are of granite, underlying the gabbro. The junction is indicated by the dotted line on the slopes of Garbh-bheinn, Blathbheinn, and Druim an Eidhne.

the east of the Tormichaig valley is of the nature of an inlier beneath the granite.

Putting together what is seen at the southern and northern boundaries, we are able to picture this large mass of granite as presenting the general form of *a large irregular laccolite*, and having in the broadest sense a southerly dip. The varying altitudes and observed inclinations at the boundaries prove, however, that we must further conceive it as deformed, whether originally or owing to later movements, and that the deformation shows a considerable degree of correspondence with that of the gabbro laccolite. There is an elongated anticlinal dome extending from Marsco to Glamaig, and the Blaven syncline is also in part well marked, but merges northward in a broader one extending in the direction of Loch Ainort. As regards the extent of the laccolite, we can easily trace its dying out towards the south. It passes under the gabbro of the Blaven range, but emerges on the eastern side very much reduced in thickness. It is represented here only by the discontinuous and rather irregular series of strips which extend S. and S.S.W. from Glas Bheinn Mhòr to Camasunary, the actual dying out being seen above Rudha Bàn. It seems probable too that the laccolite has not extended very far northward of the present limits: indeed it shows signs of dying out in Glamaig, where it is already splitting up and behaving irregularly. Since neither upper nor under surface is exposed in the central part of the area, no estimate of the maximum thickness is possible; but it has probably exceeded 1500 feet, and possibly much more.

Considering the western half of the Red Hills as a whole, we see then that to the south the granite shows an upper surface, to the north an irregular under surface; but westward it terminates abruptly at a nearly straight and vertical boundary. Of this there is only one probable interpretation: the straight line, nearly

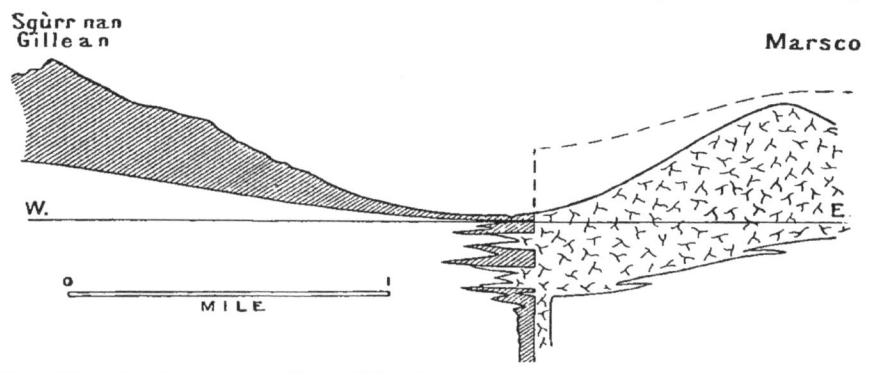

Fig. 26 —Section across Glen Sligachan from Sgùrr nan Gillean (gabbro) to Marsco (granite), to illustrate the supposed nature of the western boundary of the granite in this part.

coinciding with the course of the Sligachan River, must be supposed to mark the position of an important fissure of supply, through which the granite magma rose to spread laterally eastward. The vertical boundary may indeed be regarded as the western face of a large dyke, one of the feeders of the laccolite (see Fig. 26). Doubtless other feeders are concealed beneath the granite of the hills further east, and the situation of some at least can be conjectured with some probability. We have already noticed the long curving gabbro dykes, enveloped in the granite, which extend from Glen Sligachan to Coire na Seilg, as some of the feeders of the gabbro laccolite. The relations observed along this line suggest that the fissures which served for the uprise of the gabbro magma were at a later epoch utilised as channels for the magma of the acid rock (Fig. 27).

It is certain that the large mass of granite (with granophyre), the limits and relations of which have been partly sketched, was not the result of a single intrusion. It consists of distinct parts, usually having the general form of *quasi-horizontal sheets*, though in places with steeply inclined junctions and disruptive habit. Sometimes this composite structure of the granite mass is even apparent as a feature in the landscape. Looking across Strath na Creitheach from Druim an Eidhne to the slopes of Blath-bheinn, Clach Glas, and Garbh-bheinn, the granite is seen passing under the gabbro, the strongly contrasted colours of the two rocks making the junction very conspicuous. Now turning the eye to Ruadh Stac and Marsco, it can be seen that the granite composing these two hills is itself divided by a gently curved surface roughly parallel with the upper surface of the granite laccolite. The higher parts of the two hills consist of a rock which weathers with a different shape from that of the rock below, having a tendency to a rude columnar jointing, which in the prominent crag named Fiaclan Dearg is especially marked. The apparent relations are represented in the diagrammatic section (Fig. 27).

Again, in several places within the granite area we find the rock becoming a fine-textured quartz-felsite, or assuming a spherulitic

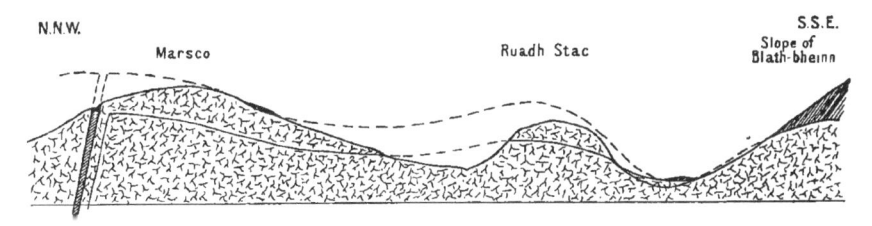

Fig. 27.—Section along a rather sinuous line through Marsco and Ruadh Stac, to illustrate the supposed manner of intrusion of the granite. Scale, 1½ inch to a mile.

and sometimes a fluxional structure, along a certain band. Such a band may be in sharp contact with normal granitoid rock, and clearly shows, not only that two distinct intrusions are here seen in juxtaposition, but that there was a sufficient interval of time between them for the later one to experience a relatively rapid chilling at its margin. Such a junction is seen a little to the east of the Glen Sligachan foot-path, where it crosses the watershed E. of Loch Dubh. Another thing which often seems to indicate the junction of distinct intrusions of granite is the inclusion of narrow strips of basaltic lavas, sometimes two or three occurring along the same line. These may, of course, be wholly enveloped by a single intrusion; but their arrangement, and the fact that the acid rock itself sometimes shows fine-textured modifications along the same lines, suggests that, in some cases at least, these relics of the volcanic group are really caught between two distinct intrusions.

We have not found that these various indications afford sufficient data for actually mapping out the several component parts of the large granite mass, and indeed the general uniformity of lithological characters prevailing over considerable areas discourages any such attempt. We are probably justified in stating that, while the granite mass is certainly built up of a number of distinct intrusions, it has not so high a degree of complexity of structure as is met with in some parts of the gabbro laccolite of the Cuillins. This is quite in accord with the general behaviour of the acid and basic magmas respectively, and so also is the greater irregularity of form and habit exhibited by the granite as compared with the gabbro.

Turning to the eastern portion of the main granite area, we find greater difficulty in deciphering the true relations, partly owing to the fact that in the Loch Ainort district the granite extends below sea-level. Where the boundary runs down to the sea, both at Maol na Gainmhich and at Dunan, the junction seems to be steeply inclined. The granite is in contact in the one place with Torridon Sandstone, in the other with quartzose grits belonging to the Jurassic. That part of the boundary, however, which runs N.-S., obliquely crossing the ridge of Glas Bheinn Bheag, shows an under-

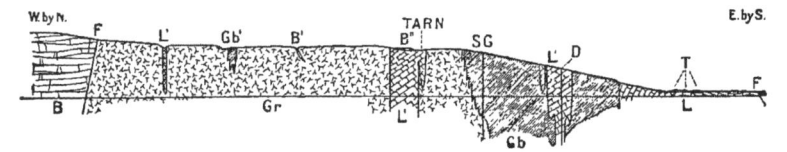

Fig. 28.—Section through Lochain Beinn na Caillich and towards Broadford, crossing the northern part of the granite boss of Beinn na Caillich and the southern part of the gabbro boss; scale, 2 inches to a mile.

F, F are faults, the easterly one bringing on the Lias (Pabbay Shales).
L, Cambrian Limestone (Balnakiel group); B, basaltic lavas; Gb, gabbro; Gr, granite.
L', B', Gb' are enclosed patches of limestone, basalt, and gabbro;
B'', an outlier of the basalt resting on an enclosed patch of limestone;
T, small outliers of Torridonian upon the limestone, with a thin sheet of granophyre intruded along the dividing "thrust-plane."
S G, dyke of spherulitic granophyre; D, dyke of basalt.

lying junction, apparently the upper surface of a sill-like mass. The grits here have a well-bedded and laminated character, dipping eastward at about 40°, and the intrusion beneath seems to have followed the bedding. In the lower part of Strath Beag the junction is concealed, and at the south end of Beinn na Cro it again has an abruptly transgressive character.

The granite mass which forms Beinn na Caillich and the other *eastern Red Hills* is almost isolated from the main area, and must be regarded as a distinct intrusion. It has very decidedly *the boss form*, and its unfaulted junctions, *e.g.* with the limestone and gabbro to the east, are nearly vertical. It owes part of its relief, however, to subsequent differential upheaval (Fig. 28). The north-western boundary, against the volcanic rocks and the underlying Torridonian, is a straight fault-line which can be traced for 2½ miles. The throw is greatest in the middle. North-eastward it dies out, against a small cross-fault, in the valley of Allt Fearna. About Creagan Dubha the metamorphosed state of the basaltic lavas, and the fact that they are penetrated by little tongues of granite, suggest that the present boundary is not very far from the original one; and the fault does not extend into Strath Beag. The southern, or at least the south-eastern, boundary of the boss is of a less simple kind; but here, too, the junction is probably not merely an intrusive contact. The bordering volcanic rocks are shattered by a number of faults with directions which tend to correspond roughly with that of the boundary, and some of these faults meet the boundary tangentially. The mapping certainly suggests that, while the southern limit of the granite (nearly a semi-circle in ground-plan) represents pretty nearly the original extent of the boss, there has been considerable differential movement along the line of junction, resulting in a relative elevation of the granite.

The *Beinn an Dubhaich granite*, extending 2¾ miles from E. to W., and ¾ mile from N. to S., is a typical example of the boss-like mode of occurrence. It is entirely surrounded by the Cambrian (Durness) limestones, and constitutes the core of an anticline (Fig. 30). The elevation along this axis belongs in part to an early time (pre-Liassic at least), but was repeated later, probably in connection with the intrusion of the granite. The mass is, from all appearances, a single one, but its boundary is in ground-plan highly irregular, and isolated patches of limestone, also of highly irregular shapes, are enclosed within the granite, especially in its marginal parts (Fig. 29). These enclosed patches range up to a quarter of a mile in extent. The limestone composing them, as well as that bordering the whole intrusion, is in a highly metamorphosed state. In consequence of differential weathering,* the limestone surface is depressed, sometimes three or four feet, below that of the granite; so that the actual contact-surface of the latter is exposed; and this is found to be *everywhere vertical* (Figs. 30 and 31). The appearances are, in short, identical with those described for the gabbro boss N.W. of Broadford, which is intrusive in the same group of limestones. There is an additional feature of interest in the presence of a number of basic dykes of pre-granitic age, traversing the limestone and abruptly cut off with it by the granite. Having regard to the strike and dip of the limestone and the courses of the dykes, it does not appear that the granite has occasioned any appreciable disturbance *in detail* of the rocks through which it breaks, or even in the patches of those rocks which it completely surrounds.

* The general lowering of the limestone surface by atmospheric weathering is partly a post-Glacial process. This is well illustrated at the "Stone" marked on the six-inch map in the Kilchrist Glebe. It is a large granite boulder standing on a two-feet pedestal of limestone, which it has protected from the general waste. In the central parts of Skye, at least, post-Glacial erosion of the solid rocks has been in general extremely slight (*Geol. Mag.*, 1899, pp. 485-491). The waste of the limestone by solvent action is an interesting exception. It is noteworthy that it is very similar in amount to that indicated by the pedestals of the well-known Norber erratics in Yorkshire.

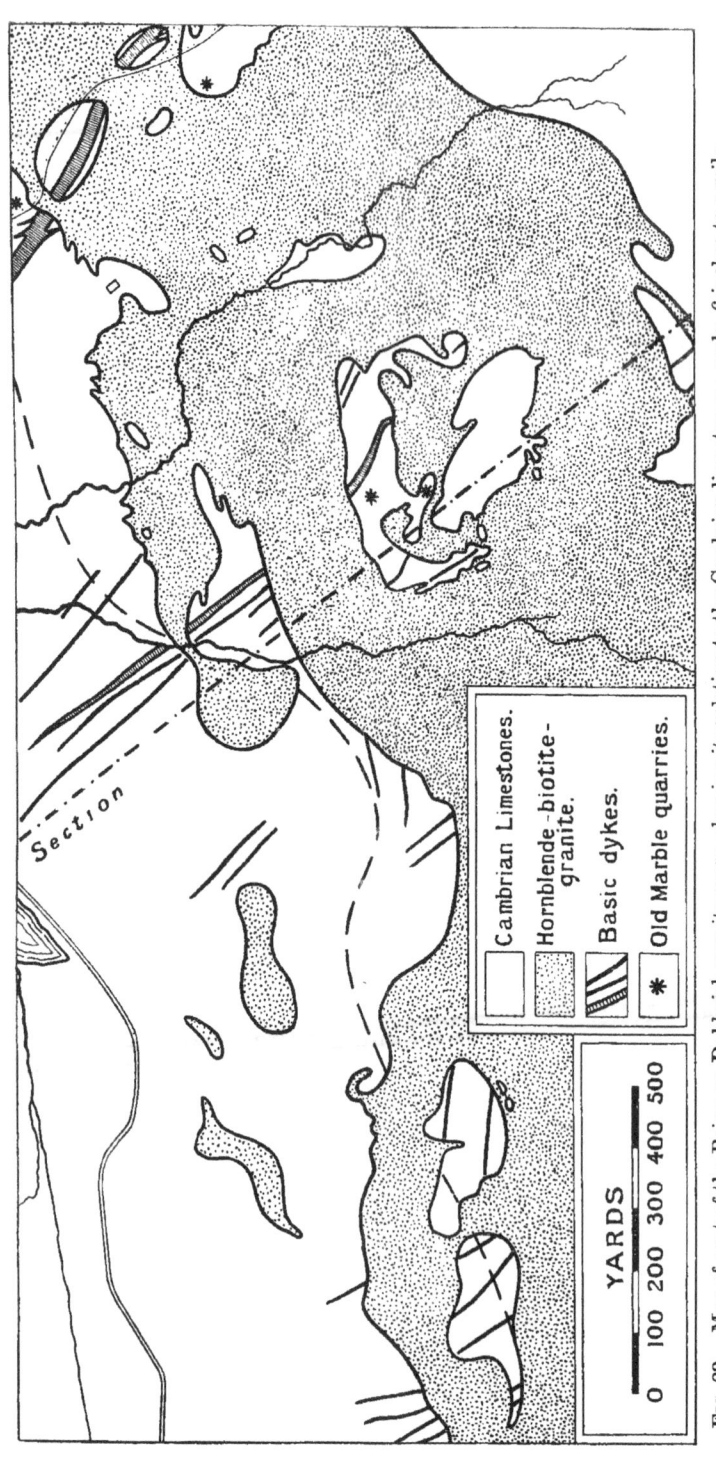

FIG. 29.—Map of part of the Beinn an Dubhaich granite mass, showing its relation to the Cambrian limestones: scale, 6 inches to a mile.

The area included lies to the south of the high-road and of Loch Kilchrist, the head of which is shown on the northern border of the map. The ground to the north of the high-road is covered by alluvium, concealing the junction of the Cambrian with the volcanic agglomerate of the Kilchrist vent. The limestones have been both dolomitised and metamorphosed, the metamorphism having to a great extent brought about de-dolomitisation, as described below. The broken line marks the division between the Balnakiel and Croissphuill groups, the former (lower) being the nearer to the granite axis, with an anticlinal arrangement.

Only a few of the numerous basic dykes are shown. Of those outside the main granite boundary, some are pre-granitic and cut off by the granite, others are post-granitic and stopped by the granite: the dykes in the enclosed patches of limestone all belong to the former category. No dykes intersect the granite.

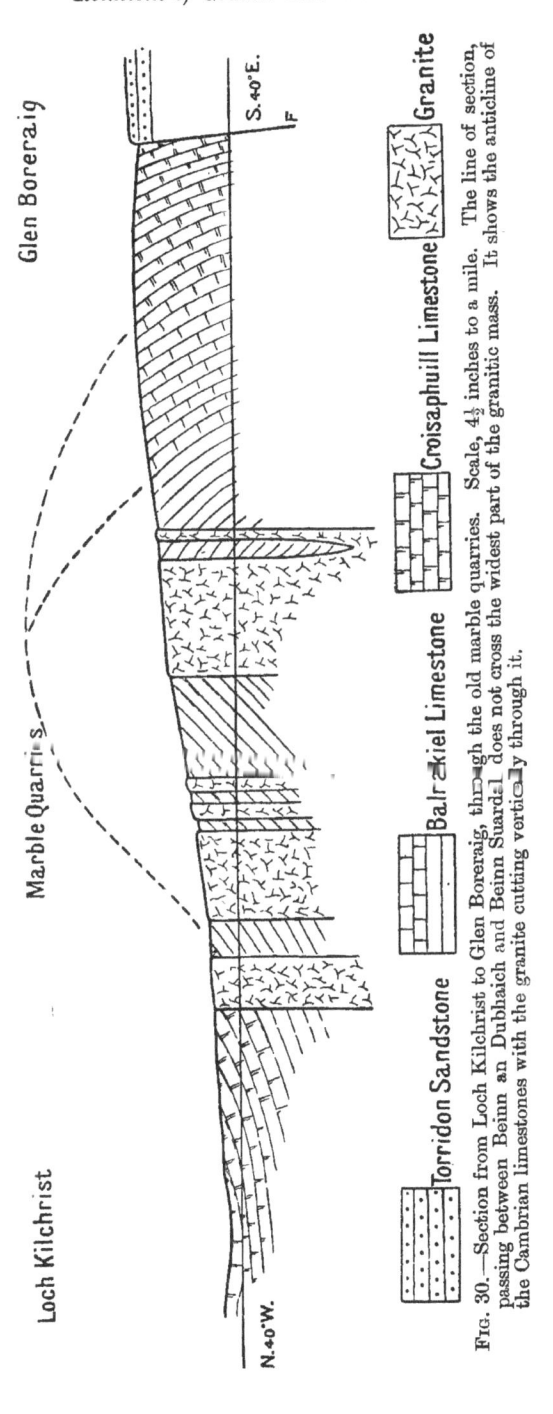

FIG. 30.—Section from Loch Kilchrist to Glen Boreraig, through the old marble quarries. Scale, 4½ inches to a mile. The line of section, passing between Beinn an Dubhaich and Beinn Suardal does not cross the widest part of the granitic mass. It shows the anticline of the Cambrian limestones with the granite cutting vertically through it.

This remarkable behaviour of the Beinn an Dubhaich granite presents, as we have already noticed in the corresponding case of the gabbro, a difficult problem in the physics of igneous intrusion. In one respect there is a difference between the two cases; for the dolomitised limestone was doubtless considerably denser than the granitic magma, and if we suppose the rock displaced by the granite to have been removed in the solid state we must therefore suppose it to have sunk through the molten magma. Nevertheless, making all due allowance for this difference in density, it is still not easy on this supposition to account for the complete absence of limestone xenoliths in the granite as now exposed. To suppose that the limestone has been to any important extent dissolved and incorporated in the acid magma raises an even greater difficulty. This would imply an enrichment of the granite in lime, which is quite inconsistent with the facts of the case. A specimen from the eastern end of the granite mass, in

Fig. 31.—Relations of granite and marble (metamorphosed Cambrian limestone) on the lower slopes of Beinn an Dubhaich. This figure represents a typical view of the junction of the two rocks, idealised only to the extent of omitting the heather and bracken which partly conceal the ground. A pre-granitic dolerite dyke is shown intersecting the marble and sharply cut off by the granite.

contact with the limestone, was found by Dr Pollard to contain only 0·47 per cent. of lime, *i.e.* not more, but less, than is found in the ordinary acid intrusions of the region. Even if we assume the acid magma to have been originally free from lime, it cannot have taken up more than $\frac{1}{212}$ of its own mass of that base, or $\frac{1}{85}$ of its own mass of dolomitic limestone; and in fact the figure 0·47 represents an unusually low percentage of lime for granitic rocks in general. It seems then that, whatever be the *rationale* of such intrusions as this, with abruptly transgressive relations but no concomitant disturbance at the junctions, the phenomena are not to be explained by any theory which involves appreciable incorporation of the country rock in the invading magma.

The granophyre associated with the large mass of volcanic agglomerate north-west of *Loch Kilchrist*, remarkable for the profusion of gabbro débris which it has enclosed and partially digested, has also an interesting mode of occurrence. There are five isolated areas, within and on the edge of the agglomerate. The two largest are on the eastern and western borders of the agglomerate mass, and form strips ¾ mile and ½ mile long respectively. The granophyre in these places has clearly been intruded along the wall of the old vent, between the agglomerate and the Cambrian limestones. Its boundary towards the limestone is a vertical surface; that towards the agglomerate has a more irregular form. The other three exposures, within the area of the old vent, occur in valleys, and the granophyre has every appearance of underlying the immediately adjacent agglomerate.* The most probable interpretation seems to be that which would make these outcrops portions of one irregular sheet, and the diagrammatic section already given is drawn on that hypothesis (Fig. 4, p. 16). What determined the intrusion of the magma in the form of a sheet at this particular horizon is a question not easily answered.

Of the remaining acid intrusions, all of small dimensions, which may be correlated with the granites as regards the epoch of their injection, little need be said in this place. That which forms the upper part of *Creag Strollamus* has a very irregular shape, showing in some places the sheet-like, in others the sharply transgressive kind of boundary. This is partly due to the fact that it is in contact in different places with Torridon Sandstone, basaltic lavas, and gabbro. Within the area occupied by the gabbro boss farther to the S.E. the distinct granophyre intrusions which occur are chiefly in the form of isolated short dykes, varying in width up to 30 yards, and having no common direction. An unusual mode of occurrence is seen at several places about a mile west of Broadford. Here, in an area of Cambrian limestones, occur a number of small outliers of Torridon Sandstone above the great thrust-plane, and granophyre is seen to have forced its way in the form of a thin sheet along the thrust-plane (Fig. 28). The gabbro, which also occurs in the immediate neighbourhood, has not done so. The same thing is seen on the S.E. slope of Creag Strollamus, towards Allt Fearna, where several small inliers of limestone occur in the surrounding Torridonian, and in more than one place granophyre has penetrated along the surface of junction. On the other side of Allt Fearna, where some rather large patches of limestone in the granite are intersected by the tributaries on the right side of the main stream, interesting relations are again seen. For a certain distance the intrusion seems to have been guided by the thrust-plane; but farther south the Torridonian had previously been stripped off (as is proved by relics of the lavas and agglomerate resting on limestone), and the sheet-like habit is at once lost.

A little east of the last locality an enclosed patch of the limestone occurs on the boundary between granite and gabbro. It is divided into a number of strips by vertical dyke-like tongues, which are offshoots from the two intrusive masses, and each of which consists in one half of its length of gabbro and in the other

* A sketch-map showing the several outcrops has been published in *Quart. Journ. Geol. Soc.*, vol. lii., Pl. XIII. : 1896.

half of granite. The limestone has first been penetrated by offshoots from the gabbro mass, and later, from the opposite side but along the same lines, by offshoots from the granite (*see* map, Fig. 20, p. 98).

Of the numerous enclosed patches of the volcanic group in the large granite tract of the Red Hills the only one requiring special notice in this place is that which forms the northern half of *Beinn na Cro*. Here a portion of the basaltic lavas more than a mile in length, previously penetrated by irregular sheets of gabbro, has become completely involved in the granite. In the northern part the granite distinctly underlies the enclosed mass, though with a very irregular surface of contact and numerous apophyses in the form of felsitic tongues and dykes passing obliquely up through the gabbro and basalt, as is clearly seen on the western slope. Farther south the granite breaks abruptly across, so as obliquely to truncate the enclosed patch; and it thus comes to form the summit (about 1790 feet) and the rest of the mountain (Fig. 32). At the southern end of the ridge, however, where the granite terminates at about 800 feet altitude, an outlying patch of lavas is seen resting on Liassic strata and dipping rather sharply to the south. This suggests that the abruptly transgressive behaviour of the granite seen just north of the summit is connected with the existence of a pre-granitic fault throwing the lavas down to the north.

Considering now the *character of the junctions* and the relations in detail of the granite to the rocks in contact with it, we see that the petrographical nature of the latter has had, as in the case of the gabbro intrusions, a very noteworthy influence upon the behaviour of the intruded magma. The junction with the dolomitic limestones of the Cambrian is always a clean-cut surface. No veins from the granite enter the contact-rock, nor are fragments of limestone enclosed by the margin of the intrusion. The junction with Torridon Sandstone, as seen especially about Creag Strollamus, is much more irregular on a small scale. Not infrequently it is impossible in a hand-specimen to draw any sharp line between the two rocks, which are here a fine granophyre and a rather close-grained quartzose grit. A slice [8053] shows that the intruded magma has insinuated itself for a short distance into the interstices between the sand-grains, and clastic grains of quartz are seen embedded in a delicate micropegmatite. In the Isle of Scalpay, and in various other localities, veins traversing the sandstone in the neighbourhood of the junction are visible in the field. This is the case especially in places where the granite sends out tapering sheets, which dovetail into the strata, a type of junction characteristic of the dying out of a large laccolitic body. The northward termination of the large granite mass, as displayed in the Isle of Scalpay, is represented in the accompanying section (Fig. 33). At its southerly boundary the granite again runs out into a number of rather irregular sheets, as is well seen on the western slope of the south ridge of Blath-bheinn, above Loch na Creitheach. Here the intrusive rock has picked up abundant clastic grains, and even

Section along Beinn na Cro.

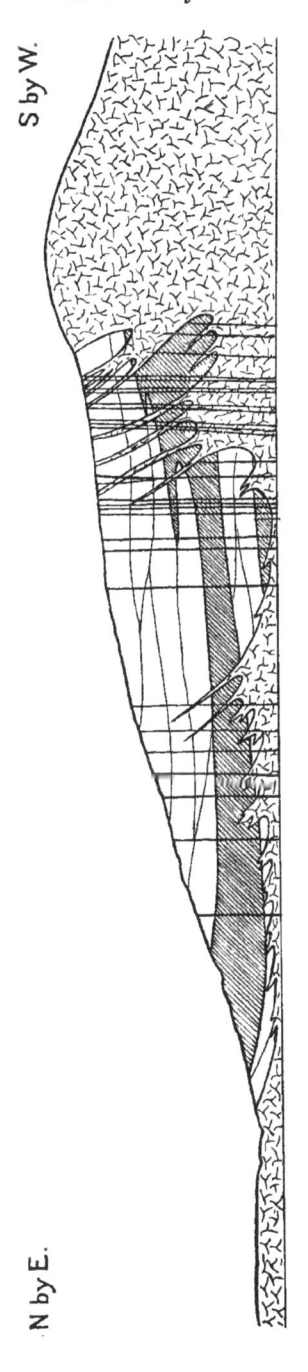

FIG. 32.—Section along Beinn na Cro. A patch of the basaltic lavas, already invaded by sheets of gabbro, has been enveloped in the granite of the Red Hills, which sends numerous offshoots in the form of tongues and dykes through the enclosed mass. The whole is intersected by later dykes of olivine-basalt. Scale, 4 inches to a mile.

small pebbles of quartz, from the Torridonian grits with which it is in contact; and the separation of the intrusive rock from the grit is by no means an easy task.

The junction of the granite with the more shaley portion of the Torridonian series is well displayed near Rudha Bàn, a headland on the coast of Loch Scavaig west of Camas Fhionnairidh. Here again we have what may be regarded as the final dying out of the large laccolite of the western Red Hills, and, as often happens in these circumstances, the intrusion takes on a rather irregular character, sending out numerous tongues and showing a very ragged boundary on the map. Essentially, however, it is a sheet, intruded here between the base of the basaltic lavas and the underlying shales, both of which are considerably metamorphosed. The latter are not much penetrated by offshoots from the granite, but their shattered fragments have been enclosed by the intrusive rock in extraordinary number, so that the granite is in places almost crowded with pieces of metamorphosed shales. The basaltic lavas above have not furnished so many xenoliths to the intrusion, but they have been traversed by a network of little veins which run out from the main mass.

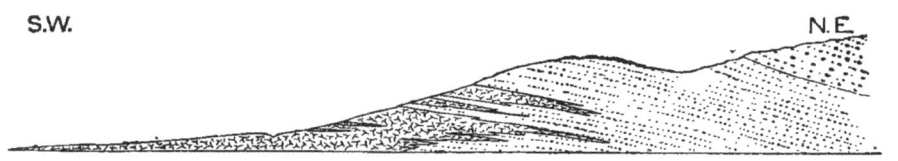

FIG. 33.— Section in the south-western part of Scalpay, from Corran a' Chinn Uachdaraich, showing the relation of the granite to the Torridonian strata. The former is the edge of the large mass building the Red Hills, which here terminates in a number of tapering sheets. Scale, 3 inches to a mile.

Veining on a minute scale is very characteristic of the basaltic lavas in the vicinity of the granite, and sometimes extends to very considerable distances from the contact, arguing a high degree of fluidity in the acid magma. The phenomenon is well seen about Creag Strollamus, Beinn na Cro, Glamaig, Belig, and elsewhere. It is very noteworthy that it affects the compact, not the amygdaloidal, varieties of the lavas, and it seems to have depended upon a certain fissuring of these rocks prior to the intrusion. The volcanic agglomerates and tuffs show veining less commonly and in a more irregular fashion: it is seen in Coire na Seilg.

There remain the junctions of the granite with the gabbro; and, as these afford the most obvious demonstration of the posteriority of the acid rock, and have also considerable interest in themselves, they demand a fuller notice.

Along the Sligachan River, where, as has been said, the junction is a vertical or highly inclined one, it seems to be usually of a simple type; but in places the granite sends out veins into the gabbro, as is well seen in the bed of the river N.W. of Loch

Dubh. The junction, as it rises from here to Druim an Eidhne, is concealed, and when it becomes clearly exposed, in the little pass between Meall Dearg and the ridge, the granite has assumed the laccolitic habit, passing clearly under the gabbro. Here it sends out a small tongue into the latter rock, which can be followed southward for about 100 yards. From this point a narrow strip of volcanic agglomerate is interposed; but the granite, or rather its felsitic modification, forces its way above this, and sends numerous apophyses in the form of dykes into the gabbro. These are seen at short intervals along the ridge, cutting alike the agglomerate, the main body of gabbro, and the irregular dyke-like intrusions of gabbro which we have pointed out as feeders of the main body. There are other dykes of the same type cutting the gabbro a little farther from the granite exposure and not visibly connected with it: they doubtless originate in the extension of the granite immediately beneath them.

These dykes of spherulitic and other acid rocks which intersect the gabbro of *Druim an Eidhne* present interesting but in no way abnormal characters; and we should not have thought it necessary to offer any evidence of their intrusive nature, had not a very different interpretation of them been put forth in a paper by Professor Judd.* That geologist regards them, not as dykes, but as portions of the granite enclosed and partially fused by the gabbro, which is in his view the later rock. Sir A. Geikie† has already given strong reasons for rejecting this idea, and has indeed conclusively proved that the supposed inclusions are dykes; but it will be convenient in this place to state briefly the evidence.

The outcrops of acid rocks in question, within the gabbro area, have the lineal form and parallel vertical boundaries characteristic of dykes, and of dykes alone. Owing to their more perishable nature they have given rise to trench-like depressions, which run nearly straight or with occasional deviations, after the fashion of dykes in general. These trenches maintain in each case a nearly uniform width of a few yards, and can be traced through the coarse gabbro for distances of $\frac{1}{4}$ or $\frac{1}{2}$ or even $\frac{3}{4}$ mile. In one or two cases they bifurcate. Their direction is that proper to the dykes of the district (N.N.W.–S.S.E.), and is not parallel to the boundary of either gabbro or granite. They are not parallel to the banding of the gabbro, so strongly marked in this place: they correspond roughly with it in strike, but not in dip, and often truncate the banding obliquely. All these facts are incompatible with the hypothesis of inclusions.

The floor of the trenches is in great part concealed by swampy ground, but there are sometimes considerable stretches in which the dyke-rock is perfectly bare, and always sufficiently frequent exposures to leave no doubt of its actual continuity. There is usually a strong fluxion-banding parallel to the walls. One or two of the dykes can be traced with visible continuity from the banded gabbro which they intersect, through the strip of volcanic

* *Quart. Journ. Geol. Soc.*, vol. xlix., pp. 175-195 : 1893.
† *Ibid.*, vol. l., pp. 212-229 : 1894.

agglomerate which next intervenes, to the edge of the main body of granite (*i.e.* its marginal modification). Precisely similar dykes cut the wide spread of volcanic agglomerate on the slope down to Loch na Creitheach. Moreover, the margin of the granite assumes in many places characters (such as the spherulitic and other structures) identical with those of the dykes.

Petrographically the dykes which cut the gabbro are perfectly normal igneous rocks, in no wise different from others in the district which intersect the volcanic rocks, and easily matched from other countries. This appears from Professor Judd's description no less than from our own examination. In particular, he has pointed out the close resemblance, extending to minute details, between the spherulites in these rocks and those in certain obsidians and rhyolites from America, which are indubitably normal igneous products. He has indeed likened these supposed inclusions of granite in gabbro to the inclusions of quartz-felsite in a nepheline-basalt at Ascherhübel in Saxony, but his description of the latter does not seem to shown any close resemblance between the two cases. The undoubted inclusions of granite so abundant in many of the basic dykes of Skye exhibit, as we shall see, very different characters. Mons. Lacroix, whose acquaintance with inclusions of all kinds is probably greater than that of any other petrologist, refers briefly to Professor Judd's description in his monograph, but states that he has seen nothing like it in any of the occurrences which he has studied.*

Druim an Eidhne is almost the only place where apophyses of any of the large acid intrusions take the form of typical dykes. It is to be observed that these spring from the *upper surface* of the laccolitic mass. The fringing out of the same at its *edge* takes the form of wedge-like tongues and tapering irregular sheets, as already noted near Rudha Bàn; and where offshoots are found in connection with a *vertical* or steeply inclined granite-contact, they form a plexus of irregular veins.

On the eastern side of Strath na Creitheach, although the laccolitic habit of the granite is still maintained, the rock does not throw off any vertical dykes. It is in most places divided from the gabbro by a narrow strip of basaltic lavas, and in several localities it sends out short tongues either into these rocks or into the gabbro. Several such tongues are seen in connection with the inlying patch of granite on the N.W. slope of Blath-bheinn; and one of them, cutting into the overlying gabbro, is distinctly visible from Loch an Athain. Another tongue, not continuous at the surface with the main body, crosses the much-broken northern ridge of Blath-beinn, giving rise to the principal break between that mountain and the peak known to climbers as Clach Glas. This col (altitude 2310 feet according to Dr Collie's measurements) is about 700 feet above the probable upper surface of the granite laccolite.

* *Les enclaves des roches volcaniques*, p. 654 : 1893.

The above observations afford indisputable evidence that the granite laccolite of the Western Red Hills is of later intrusion than the gabbro laccolite of the Cuillins. The posteriority of the granite boss of the eastern Red Hills to the neighbouring gabbro boss is equally clear. At many points along their common boundary, to the N.E. of Beinn na Caillich, the granite is seen penetrating the gabbro, and the latter is traversed in the neighbourhood of the contact by innumerable veins of the acid rock. In some places such veins form for a short distance a close network almost equal in bulk to the gabbro which forms the meshes, giving the effect of a breccia of gabbro in a matrix of granite. The veins are not confined to the immediate vicinity of the granite-contact; but they are most numerous there and near the dyke-like intrusions of granite already mentioned, which traverse both gabbro and limestone. These intrusions have rather peculiar characters. They are in the form of stout dykes which run only for short distances in comparison with their size, and then die out with singular abruptness. Closer inspection often shows that when one of these dykes comes to an end in gabbro (not in limestone), the country-rock beyond is traversed by very abundant little veins, which in a sense serve collectively to carry on the intrusion farther. A more curious phenomenon of the same order was observed in one or two places, where a dyke or rib of granite traversing the limestone is interrupted upon meeting a small tongue of gabbro, but continued nearly on the same line in the limestone beyond. The illusion that the granite has been cut by the gabbro is dispelled by a closer scrutiny, which shows that the acid rock has traversed the basic in the form of a plexus of very small veins. Indeed on examination we find that the granite magma has been able to penetrate the gabbro in threads of quite microscopic minuteness. The appearances recall in some respects the injection of gabbro by granite described by Professor Sollas* at Barnavave, Carlingford, but there are perhaps certain differences between the two cases. It appears from his description that the minute veins noticed by him are generally rectilinear, in one or two parallel sets, and he considers the gabbro to have been not only solid but fissured by contraction-joints before the intrusion of the granite. In Skye the veins form an irregularly reticulated plexus, and there are reasons for believing that no important interval of time elapsed between the solidification of the basic rock and the intrusion of the acid magma.

These phenomena in the Broadford district evince at least *a remarkable permeability of the gabbro by the granitic magma*, and this is no less apparent in the gabbro laccolite of the Cuillins. A striking feature in many parts of the mountain district is the occurrence of veins of granite, or usually granophyre, traversing the gabbro, in no visible connection with any larger body of acid rock. In many places, such as E. and S. of Loch na Creitheach and about the head of Loch Scavaig, the veins occur abundantly in

* *Trans. Roy. Irish Acad.*, vol. xxx., pp. 477-519, Pl. XXVI., XXVII.: 1894.

the lower part of the gabbro laccolite, where we have good reason for believing that granite exists not far below; but elsewhere they are absent in a like situation. The difference seems to be related to differences in the nature of the granite-junction below. On Druim an Eidhne, for instance, where the upper surface of the thick acid intrusion is (except for distinct dykes) a smooth one, and the granite passes into felsitic and spherulitic rocks towards its boundary, veins are not found in the gabbro. The other localities mentioned as remarkable for the profusion of veins are where the attenuated granite laccolite has become irregular in its behaviour, with numerous offshoots, and with no marginal modification.

Granophyre veins are found, however, in the mountains far above the base of the gabbro laccolite, and far above any presumable concealed body of acid rock. (*See* map, Fig. 58.) A good example of this occurs on the summit ridge of Sgùrr Dearg, near and to the south of the cairn, where the gabbro is so traversed by veins of granophyre as to present the appearance of a breccia. This must be nearly 3000 feet above the base of the gabbro laccolite, where, if anywhere, we should expect the westward extension of the granite from Druim an Eidhne to occur. If any nearer body of granite has been present, it can only have been a sheet intruded along the upper surface of the gabbro laccolite, now totally removed, and of such hypothetical intrusion we have no sort of evidence.* Other places where granophyre is seen traversing the gabbro of the mountains are the summit ridge of Sgùrr nan Eag and the slopes of Sgùrr a' Mhadaidh towards Coir' an Uaigneis.

The last point to be noted in the field-relations of the large acid intrusions relates to the presence or absence of noteworthy *marginal modifications* in texture and micro-structure towards the bounding surface. In some places the rock near the contact becomes fine-textured and "felsitic," sometimes compact, sometimes porphyritic, sometimes with visible spherulites, sometimes even with fluxion-banding like a rhyolite: in other places the rock maintains the character of a granite or a relatively coarse granophyre up to the actual contact. It is not difficult to see that these differences stand in relation to the varying habits of the intrusions which have been sufficiently distinguished above. Where the magma has been intruded strictly in the form of a sheet or laccolite regularly following bedding or other leading surfaces, as beneath the Jurassic grits of Glas Bheinn Bheag or the gabbro and agglomerate of Druim an Eidhne, there is constantly a marginal modification in the direction of finer texture and special structures. When the sheet-like habit breaks down or becomes very irregular, as in the Camasunary district, there is little or no modification of this kind. With quasi-vertical junctions, as in the bosses of Beinn an Dubhaich and the eastern Red Hills, there is no sign of textural or structural modification near the contact-surface. The Kilchrist granophyres are instructive in this connection. The

* About 700 yards E.S.E. of this spot begins the outlying patch of lavas forming the summit of Sgùrr Mhic Choinnich, which is not improbably the actual roof of the gabbro laccolite.

most easterly exposure on its eastern side, where it presents a smooth, nearly vertical face to the Cambrian limestones, is a coarse granophyre up to the actual contact: on its western side, where the junction seems to be of the underlying kind, though not very regular, little sheet-like apophyses entering the volcanic agglomerate, the rock becomes fine-textured, and contains in places beautiful stellate spherulites. The interior exposures, which we take to represent the upper surface of a sheet-like mass, also show felsitic and even rhyolitic modifications.

Junctions with and without fine-textured marginal modifications differ also as regards the apophyses which the intrusion sends out into the contiguous rocks. When these occur, they are in the former case dykes, in the latter case irregular veins. It is also to be remarked that thermal metamorphism of the adjacent rocks is in the former case often trifling in amount and extent, while in the latter case it may be intense and far-reaching.

The *metamorphism produced by the granites* in the basaltic lavas and in the gabbros has been described under the heads of those rocks. The metamorphism set up by the same cause in the various sedimentary rocks does not come strictly within the scope of our subject, and in general does not present any special features of interest. To this last statement, however, the metamorphism of the *Cambrian dolomitic limestones* makes an exception, and a summary account of this may properly find a place here. For valuable assistance in the examination of the specimens collected, and especially for the true identification of certain of the new-formed minerals, the writer is indebted to Mr Teall, who has found a close resemblance between the phenomena here and those observed at Ledbeg in Sutherland, where rocks of the same series are invaded by a large syenitic intrusion.

The Cambrian limestones, in great part dolomitic, which cover a considerable area in the Strath district were definitely proved to be of this age by Sir A. Geikie in 1887.* Since that time the mapping of Mr Clough and the examination of the fossils by Dr Peach† have enabled these rocks to be more precisely paralleled with the corresponding members of the Durness succession in Sutherland, and it is recognised that the rocks with which we are more particularly concerned are the equivalents of the Balnakiel and Croisaphuill groups. Where they are invaded by the gabbro N.W. of Broadford and by the granite round Beinn an Dubhaich, they become saccharoidal marbles; and in the latter area, not far from Kilchrist, they were formerly quarried. These Skye marbles were well known in the earlier part of the nineteenth century, and Macculloch‡ enumerates the several varieties then worked; but operations have been long abandoned, and probably the expense entailed by the short land-carriage would render the reopening of

---

* *Quart. Journ. Geol. Soc.*, vol. xliv., pp. 62-73 : 1888.
† *Summary of Progress* for 1898, pp. 54, 55.
‡ *Trans. Geol. Soc.*. vol. iii., pp. 101, etc. : 1816. *Description of the Western Islands of Scotland*, vol. i., pp. 418, 419 : 1819.

the old quarries unremunerative unless undertaken on a large scale. The largest quarries are on the slope of the hill to the south of Loch Kilchrist, one about 1000 yards south of the lake, and a lower one some 135 yards farther north.* A smaller one is situated a little west of the Boreraig foot-path and 500 yards south of the Glebe. This and the first-mentioned quarry yield some variety of mottled, veined, and serpentinous rocks, in addition to pure white marble. Another quarry lies just east of the footpath and by the southern angle of the Glebe fence. The rock here, like some others, though in appearance a fine-grained white marble, is in reality an aggregate of the pencatite type, consisting of calcite and brucite. A small quarry about 350 yards S.E. of the old ruined manse is in a white marble which, unlike the generality of the metamorphosed rocks, is still a dolomite-rock. Of the five quarries enumerated, the first three are in patches of limestone surrounded by the granite, and the other two are near the granite boundary, the last one, where the rock shows no very high grade of metamorphism, being situated near the attenuated termination of the intrusive mass.

The Cambrian limestones of Skye are almost free from detrital matter, and contain little original impurity other than silica of organic origin. This is in great part aggregated into distinct nodules and small patches of chert, or in some zones in spongeforms; but there is usually more or less silica in a disseminated form, as is shown by the accompanying chemical analyses made on material free from visible chert. Outside the areas affected by thermal metamorphism the limestones are usually, though not in every place, dolomitised, and there is abundant evidence that this is the result of metasomatic processes subsequent to the deposition of the rocks. While the limestones not thus altered usually have a compact fine-textured character, and are well bedded, the dolomitic rocks have lost their bedded aspect and acquired a crystalline saccharoid texture often similar in appearance to that of the true marbles within the areas of metamorphism. They have a specific gravity 2·84 to 2·86, and two specimens selected for analysis gave very closely the composition of true dolomite (I. and II.).

The metamorphosed equivalents of these rocks near the gabbro and granite are not dolomite-rocks, though some of them have some dolomite with the calcite: the magnesia that is present is contained in general in various new-formed silicates and other minerals. It results from the relative purity of the original rocks that they do not in general, like impure limestones and dolomites in many districts, become transformed to silicate-rocks, with total expulsion of the carbonic acid. They are converted to crystalline marbles with accessory silicate-minerals in greater or less amount, scattered through the rock or aggregated in various ways. These newformed minerals are distributed in a manner depending upon the

* These quarries are incorrectly placed on the Ordnance map, and the others are not given. All the principal openings are marked on the map given above (Fig. 29, p. 133).

K

	I.	II.	A.
Part insoluble in dilute hydrochloric acid	2·26	1·72	2·42
SiO_2	0·50		0·11
Al_2O_3, Fe_2O_3, FeO	0·45	0·34	0·62
MnO	0·22	0·19	0·24
MgO	21·19	20·81	20·25
CaO	30·50	30·53	30·05
CO_2	44·54	46·25	46·15
	99·66	99·84	99·84
Specific gravity	2·85	2·86	2·85

I. Dolomite-rock [8063], upper part of Balnakiel group (sponge-bearing zone), 600 yards north of Suardal Farm: anal. W. Pollard, *Summary of Progress* for 1898, p. 198. The analysis gives the molecular ratios:—

$CaO : MgO : CO_2 = 1·03 : 1 : 1·91$.

The slice shows merely a crystalline aggregate of dolomite with rare grains of calcite and a few little granules probably of diopside.

II. Dolomite-rock [8064], lower part of Balnakiel group (concentric ring zone), 625 yards N.W. of Loch Lonachan and just east of Boreraig footpath: anal. W. Pollard, *ibid.* The molecular ratios found are:—

$CaO : MgO : CO_2 = 1·05 : 1 : 2·02$.

Slice identical in appearance with the preceding.

A. Dolomite-rock [8130], Eilean Hoan, 2½ miles east of Durness, Sutherland, for comparison: anal. W. Pollard, *ibid.* Molecular ratios:—

$CaO : MgO : CO_2 \quad 1·06 : 1 : 2·07$.

---

degree of dissemination or the mode of concentration of the original silica which has contributed to the formation of most of them. They may be scattered in the form of granules, crystals, flakes, or fibrous patches, according to their nature, either uniformly or along certain bands following the stratification, in which case most of them (white mica excepted) are not conspicuous in the field. Where, however, the cherty matter has been concentrated in connection with sponge-bodies, chert-nodules, or particular seams of the rock, the new-formed silicate-minerals are richly present in certain parts of the marble, though very rarely to the exclusion of carbonates. At one place in the gabbro area the marbles include a bed of a white rock, with the general appearance of a quartzite but of specific gravity 3·09, which is found to consist wholly of diopside in little grains from $\frac{1}{20}$ inch downward [6781]. A similar rock occurs in contact with the granite at Camas Malaig [3205].

Some of the most striking appearances are found in connection with a remarkable structure peculiar to the lower half of the Balnakiel group in this district, the zone or sub-zone which is usually the one in immediate contact with the gabbro and granite, and in which the marble-quarries are situated. The structure consists of a system of numerous concentric rings or shells, building up a spheroidal body several inches or even a foot in diameter. These are most conspicuous on a weathered face of the metamorphosed rock, where some rings stand out more than the intervening parts, owing to their more siliceous composition, and are found to be made up chiefly of serpentine and other silicates. Although this structure is most prominent in the highly metamorphosed rocks, it is probably to be regarded as an original peculiarity further developed and accentuated by metamorphism. While not itself, so far as we can discover, an organic structure, it seems to stand in relation to organic bodies. Towards the top of the strata in question concentric shell structures with less perfect development constantly encircle sponge-forms, thus affording a transition to the upper Balnakiel limestone, characterised by sponges of similar form without the surrounding rings. It may be conjectured that the typical concentric shell structure has originated in connection with a sponge now destroyed, the silica of which has gone to enrich certain shells of the immediately surrounding rock. Some interest attaches to these curious bodies from the closeness with which they reproduce the micro-structures of the so-called Eozoön, a subject sufficiently dealt with by Professors King and Rowney.*

The succeeding zone or sub-zone, representing the upper part of the Balnakiel group of Durness and characterised in Skye by its abundance of sponges, only locally comes within the area of most intense metamorphism, but nevertheless shows a noteworthy formation of new minerals even at considerable distances from the granite. The metamorphism of the sponges is here the principal point of interest. The outer crust of each is replaced usually by a matted aggregate of tremolite fibres, mixed with granular calcite, giving a rather silky lustre on a hand-specimen [6736, 6739]. In the interior diopside has usually been formed instead of tremolite, and the granular aggregate of carbonates in which this is embedded is largely dolomite [6798].

The Croisaphuill limestone, characterised by the presence of small black cherts of irregular shape, is farther from the granite, but it too has been in some places considerably metamorphosed. The effects are usually not very evident in the field, but to this there are exceptions. One specimen, for example, shows a weathered face studded with minute light-coloured crystals, about

---

* *Quart. Journ. Geol. Soc.*, vol. xxii., pp. 185-218 : 1866. *Rep. Brit. Assoc.* for 1870, Sections p. 78 (abstract only). *An Old Chapter of the Geological Record*, pp. xvi., 11, 41, etc. : 1881.

$\frac{1}{30}$ inch long, which are found to be diopside [6745]. This mineral seems to be the commonest new-formed silicate in this group.

The metamorphosed dolomitic limestones as a whole afford a considerable number of new minerals, prominent among which are silicates containing lime and magnesia, and especially those rich in magnesia. Tremolite and diopside have already been mentioned. The former occurs usually in little needles, massed or felted together in patches, and is very common in the outer portion of the metamorphic aureole of Beinn an Dubhaich, especially in connection with sponge-forms. Diopside is very widely distributed, both in the less altered and the more altered rocks. It usually forms rather rounded crystal-grains of small size; but is sometimes large enough to be easily visible to the eye, and then often shows good crystal-forms. A rock about $\frac{1}{4}$ mile S.E. of Suardal contains nodular masses an inch or two in diameter composed wholly of this mineral, the individual crystals ranging up to $\frac{1}{3}$ inch in length [6738]. The diopside is always colourless in thin slices, and visible crystals are white with the lustre and general aspect of a felspar. Another interesting mineral is the magnesian olivine, forsterite, which appears to be very common, and has probably been more so, being now often replaced by serpentine. It has been identified by Mr Teall, and two examples analysed by Dr Pollard (see p. 149). In thin slices* it is often difficult to distinguish from diopside, occurring commonly in the form of rounded grains with the same general characters as the latter mineral. The forsterite is usually more rounded than the diopside, and when they occur together the less perfect cleavage is also a point of distinction [6739]. In some cases, however, the forsterite builds well-shaped crystals of characteristic form [6805]. Only exceptionally is it to be identified on a hand-specimen; but some examples show it projecting on a weathered face in the form of abundant little whitish tabular crystals, up to $\frac{1}{4}$ inch in diameter [6743].

Other minerals are of more local distribution. Little flakes of silvery white mica are scattered through some parts of the highly metamorphosed lower Balnakiel limestone of the granite area. They lie along certain bands, but have no parallel orientation [6744]. In one place there are nests about two inches in diameter consisting of a pale green talcose mineral in large flakes [6740]. At Camas Malaig, not far from the granite-contact, we find small nodular patches composed of idocrase and garnet [6782]. In one specimen only, at about 500 yards W.S.W. of Kilbride, have we observed small octahedra of a violet spinel [7083]. There is also an opaque sulphide, probably pyrrhotite, in the same rock.

The metamorphosed representatives of the Cambrian limestones include not only rocks composed of carbonates and new-formed silicates, but also in places others which consist essentially of

---

* See Harker, *Petrology for Students*, 3rd ed., Fig. 73 : 1902.

	I.	II.	A.	B.
SiO$_2$	42·6	41·5	42·2	41·16
Al$_2$O$_3$	1·2	0·9	0·8	1·02
FeO	1·1	1·3	0·5	2·00
MnO	...	...	...	0·26
MgO	51·2	55·6	57·0	54·86
CaO	0·6	0·3	0·3	0·26
Ignition	3·1	1·2	0·3	0·70
	99·8	100·8	101·1	100·26
Specific gravity	...	...	...	3·24

I. Forsterite, forming tabular crystals in pale grey marble (metamorphosed representative of Balnakiel group) [6743], ½ mile W. by N. of outlet of Loch Lonachan: anal. W. Pollard, *Summary of Progress* for 1900, p. 156. In this and the following analyses the iron was estimated as ferric oxide, but is calculated to ferrous. The molecular ratio, MgO : SiO$_2$ = 1·8 : 1.

II. Forsterite, forming rounded grains in banded serpentinous marble (lower part of Balnakiel group) [6783], near shore north of Camas Malaig, Torran: anal. W. Pollard, *ibid.* This mineral is the source of the serpentine in the rock. Molecular ratio, MgO : SiO$_2$ = 2·00 : 1.

A. Forsterite from marble of Ledbeg, Sutherland [3099]: anal. W. Pollard, *ibid.* Molecular ratio, MgO : SiO$_2$ = 2·02 : 1.

B. Forsterite, forming grains in the Glenelg Limestone [7923], rather more than ⅔ mile east of Sgiath Bheinn, Glenelg, Inverness-shire: anal. W. Pollard, *Quart. Journ. Geol. Soc.*, vol. lv., p. 379 : 1899. Traces of TiO$_2$ and F.

calcite and some hydrated magnesian mineral, the latter presumably formed subsequently at the expense of some product of thermal metamorphism. Of these rocks we may distinguish two types; the ophicalcites, composed of calcite and serpentine, and the predazzites and pencatites, composed of calcite and brucite.

The ophicalcite type is found in some parts of the lower Balnakiel limestone, where the rock is a rather coarsely saccharoid marble abundantly streaked and banded on a small scale with sulphur-yellow serpentine. The same thing is seen in the concentric-shell structures in these rocks, already mentioned. Good specimens can be obtained in the more southerly of the two small quarries by the Boreraig foot-path or at Camas Malaig near Torran [6804, 6783]. The serpentine has clearly been formed from grains of a silicate-mineral, portions of which often remain undestroyed. In many cases at least this parent-silicate is forsterite: whether diopside has also contributed is a question which we have not certainly decided.

The predazzite and pencatite type* is found in several localities. Some of the grey or mottled white and grey rocks in the area of extreme metamorphism next the granite belong here; but the purest example comes from the small quarry near the southern angle of the Glebe fence. The rock here is of fine texture and dull white colour, and has the specific gravity 2·574. A slice [7082] shows a calcite mosaic enclosing abundant grains of a colourless mineral of low refringence and rather high birefringence, which has been identified by Mr Teall as brucite.† Much of it shows a fibrous structure or sometimes a more confused arrangement, and it is doubtless pseudomorphic. In other cases the mineral shows a finely granular structure. In no instance are any relics preserved of the mineral which the brucite replaces, and the outlines are not characteristic, being always more or less rounded; but it may be supposed with much probability that the brucite comes from the hydration of periclase formed in the metamorphism of a magnesian limestone.

Mr Teall's researches on the marbles of Sutherland and Skye bring out a principle of great interest and doubtless of wide application, viz. the *de-dolomitisation* of dolomitic limestones by thermal metamorphism. In the Strath district, outside the metamorphic aureoles, both divisions of the Balnakiel group are found in general, though not everywhere, to be completely dolomitised. In the metamorphosed equivalents of these rocks, the carbonate is as a rule calcite, dolomite being usually absent, or present only in subordinate amount. This results from the fact that the new-formed minerals have taken up magnesia in preference to lime,‡ thus reducing the ratio of magnesia to lime in the residual carbonate or, in other words, converting a large part or the whole of the dolomite to calcite. Of the common minerals produced in the metamorphism of these rocks, the forsterite (with its derivative product serpentine) is purely magnesian, and its formation would necessarily set free a corresponding amount of calcite from the destruction of the double carbonate. The same is true of periclase and brucite. Tremolite, containing both bases but magnesia considerably in excess of lime, indicates a selective effect of the same kind but in a less degree. Diopside, if corresponding with Tschermak's formula, contains lime and magnesia in equal

---

* It is most in accordance with the original usage to employ the name pencatite for an aggregate of calcite and brucite in *equal molecular proportions*, i.e. with the percentage composition of 63·3 calcite to 36·7 brucite, reserving the name predazzite for varieties richer in calcite. The calculated specific gravity of typical pencatite should then be about 2·57, predazzite being denser.

† A specimen from Ledbeg, in Sutherland, isolated and analysed by Dr Pollard, gave very closely the formula MgH_2O_2: see *Summary of Progress of Geol. Sur.* for 1900, p. 155.

‡ We have found no simple lime-silicate. Heddle records wollastonite from "Coire Nuadh" [perhaps Coire Beithe] of Beinn na Caillich, *Mineralogy of Scotland*, vol. ii., p. 29 : 1901.

molecular proportions; but if there has been to any extent a subsequent alteration of this mineral to serpentine and calcite, de-dolomitisation has in this case been arrived at by two stages. It appears then that the calcite in the marbles is itself to be regarded as a new-formed mineral of metamorphism. That it has at least been recrystallised during the metamorphism might be inferred from its relation to the silicate-minerals as seen in thin slices.

It may be enquired whether de-dolomitisation is adequate to account completely for the comparative scarcity of dolomite in the highly metamorphosed rocks; and a full answer to this question would involve bulk-analyses of the marbles (carbonates, silicates, etc., together) to determine the molecular ratio of lime to magnesia. One such analysis has been made, and gives an affirmative answer to the question. The rock consists apparently of calcite, forsterite, and a colourless mica; and the partial analysis here quoted shows that the molecular ratio CaO : MgO = 1·08 : 1, agreeing with dolomite.

SiO_2	15·96
Al_2O_3	0·74
Fe_2O_3 (total iron)	0·70
MgO	21·43
CaO	32·17
Ignition	29·22
	100·22

Marble [6744], metamorphosed lower Balnakiel Limestone, ½ mile W.N.W. of outlet of Loch Lonachan: anal. W. Pollard, *Summary of Progress* for 1900, p. 157. This analysis gives the molecular ratio CaO : MgO = 1·08 : 1.

Another rock which may be recalled in this connection is that of the small quarry near the Glebe fence. As stated above, it is one of the predazzite-pencatite type, and since it is composed merely of calcite and brucite, its specific gravity is sufficient to determine roughly the proportions of the two minerals. The calculation shows that lime and magnesia must be present in about equal molecular proportions, as in dolomite. This rock seems then to be a typical pencatite.

CHAPTER X.

Granites and Granophyres: Petrography.

We proceed to describe in detail the acid rocks which build the large plutonic masses. Petrographically they vary from typical granites to varieties which Rosenbusch and others would designate granophyres. Sir A. Geikie, treating the large and small acid intrusions as a whole, has for convenience embraced them all under the general term granophyre. In our more detailed account it will conduce to clearness if we call the extensive masses which form the Red Hills granite, remembering, however, that in many places the rocks show some departure from the typical granitoid structure in the prevalence of micrographic intergrowths of felspar and quartz. The fine-textured spherulitic and other varieties, which in the Red Hills come in only in marginal modifications and apophyses, as well as the minor intrusions of granophyre and quartz-felsite of later date, which occur chiefly outside the tract of the Red Hills, will be reserved for description in a future chapter (XVI.).

The rocks of the Red Hills are of pale tint, usually yellowish on weathered faces. Little black lustrous crystals of augite or hornblende are usually visible. In many of the rocks these, with distinct crystals of felspar and irregular little grains of quartz, are embedded in a mass which has the rather dull confused appearance characteristic of fine micropegmatite. In the more granitoid rocks, on the other hand, all the principal elements are apparent to the eye, or with a lens, and sometimes little flakes of dark mica are seen in addition to hornblende.

The *chemical composition* of the average type of the rocks is fairly represented by two complete analyses made by Dr. Pollard and quoted in columns I. and II. below. The rocks analysed are hornblende-bearing granophyres, the first from the large continuous area of the main Red Hills, the second from an independent laccolitic or sill-like intrusion, more than a mile across, forming Beinn a' Chairn, to the north of Loch Eishort. The latter rock belongs to a group of minor intrusions to be described in a later chapter (XIII.), but is introduced in this place to show its close resemblance to the large mass. Partial analyses of other specimens, selected for special purposes, are given under III. and IV., and for comparison with the Skye rocks we reproduce published analyses of similar Tertiary intrusions from Ireland and one of the Carrock Fell rock, which may also be of Tertiary age though the evidence is inconclusive. Of the Mull and Arran granites no analyses have yet been published.

It may be remarked that the British Tertiary granites (and granophyric granites) fall into two sub-groups, a more and a less acid. In the first sub-group the silica-percentage is about 75 to 77. The ferro-magnesian element is characteristically biotite, and is present only sparingly. This sub-group includes the granites of St Kilda, the Mourne Mountains, and the main mass of Arran, but is represented in Skye only by the Beinn an Dubhaich intrusion. In the second sub-group the silica-percentage is 70 to 72. The ferro-magnesian minerals are hornblende and augite, and are more abundant than before. Also there is a stronger tendency to micrographic intergrowth of felspar and quartz, so that many of the

	I.	II.	III.	IV.	A.	B.	C.	D.
SiO_2	70·34	71·98	72·78	76·71	70·48	71·41	75·00	71·60
TiO_2	0·46	0·37	...	...	...	...	...	...
Al_2O_3	13·18	13·13	...	...	14·24	12·64	13·24	13·60
Fe_2O_3	2·65	1·33	...	...	3·72	...	2·52	2·40
FeO	2·24	1·64	...	...	...	4·76	...	not det.
MnO	0·19	0·14	...	...	...	...	...	...
MgO	0·40	0·56	...	...	0·40	0·63	...	0·21
CaO	1·24	1·15	...	0·47	1·48	1·80	0·69	2·30
BaO	trace	trace	...	...	...	...	...	...
Na_2O	3·61	2·98	4·08	...	3·66	3·03	3·07	5·55
Li_2O	trace	not found	not found	...	...	...	...	...
K_2O	4·90	4·93	5·18	...	4·26	5·47	4·33	3·53
H_2O {above 105°	0·76	1·38	...	... } 1·59	...	0·80	0·70
{at 105°	0·46	0·39	0·34	0·22 }				
P_2O_5	0·10	0·19	...	...	...	...	...	...
Cl	0·02	0·01	...	...	...	...	...	...
	100·55	100·18	...	...	99·83	99·74	99·65	99·89
Spec. grav.	2·66	2·63	2·492	2·609	2·593	2·632	2·595	2·670

I. Hornblende Granophyre [7124], Druim Eadar da Choire: anal. W. Pollard, *Summary of Progress* for 1899, p. 174. (The P_2O_5 and Cl here and the Cl in the next analysis have been inserted subsequently.)

II. Hornblende-Granophyre [7064], Beinn a' Chàirn, 3½ miles S. by W. of Broadford: anal. W. Pollard, *ibid.*, p. 173. Fluorine and sulphur sought but not found.

III. Riebeckite-Granophyre [8856], between Meall Dearg and Druim an Eidhne: anal. W. Pollard.

IV. Granite [8693] of Beinn an Dubhaich boss, in contact with limestone in Allt Cadha na Eglais: anal. W. Pollard.

A. Biotite-Granite, base of Slieve na Glogh, Carlingford; anal. S. Haughton, *Quart. Journ. Geol. Soc.*, vol. xii., p. 194: 1856.

B. Hornblende-Granite, Grange Irish, Carlingford: anal. S. Haughton, *ibid.*, p. 195.

C. Biotite-Granite, Slieve Corragh, Mourne Mountains: anal. S. Haughton, *ibid.*, p. 192.

D. Augite-Granophyre, Carrock Fell, Cumberland: anal. G. Barrow, *Quart. Journ. Geol. Soc.*, vol. li., p. 129: 1895.

rocks are most typical granophyres. Here we include almost all the Skye rocks, with those of Mull and Carlingford, and the granophyre (of doubtful age) of Carrock Fell. We have not had the opportunity of studying specimens from the Isle of Rum. The rocks of the two sub-groups seem to occur always in separate areas, and we are not able to say whether there is any constant relation between them as regards relative age.

The analyses show little that is out of the ordinary. It will be observed that soda and potash are about equally contained in these Skye rocks, when calculated to molecular proportions, one or other alkali slightly predominating. The molecular ratio $Na_2O : K_2O$ is, for the first three analyses

1·12, 0·92, 1·20.

The third rock, from Meall Dearg, is somewhat richer than the others in alkalies, and especially in soda; and this peculiarity shows itself in the formation of riebeckite as the ferro-magnesian element, while part of the felspar seems to be of the 'anorthoclase' type.

Some approximation to the percentage mineralogical composition of the rocks may be arrived at by comparison of the chemical and microscopical analyses. A rough calculation gives the results:—

	I.	II.
Quartz	27	29
Orthoclase	33 ⎱ 55	29 ⎱ 59
Oligoclase	22 ⎰	30 ⎰
Hornblende (with iron-ores)	17·5	11·5
Apatite	0·5	0·5
	100	100

For the Carlingford granites Haughton, using a somewhat different method of calculation, found:—

	A.	B.
Quartz	20·70	17·16
Felspars	66·37	67·18
Mica	12·76	...
Hornblende	...	15·40
	99·83	99·74

Without actual analyses of the constituent minerals such calculations cannot, of course, give more than rough approximations; but it appears that our rocks are richer in quartz and poorer in felspar than the Irish examples analysed.

A point of some interest as supplementing the ordinary chemical analyses relates to the nature and amount of the gaseous constituents contained in the rocks, chiefly if not wholly as inclusions in the crystallised minerals. Professor Tilden[*] found that two granites from Skye yielded respectively 1·6 and 2·8 times their

[*] *Proc. Roy. Soc.*, vol. lx., pp. 453-457 1897. *Chem. News*, vol. lxxv., pp. 169, 170 : 1897.

own volume of mixed gases. The percentage composition of these gases was found in one case to be:—

CO_2	23·60
CO	6·45
CH_4	3·02
N_2	5·13
H_2	61·68
	99·88

The important part played by hydrogen in this and other rocks and minerals investigated is a novel point. Spectroscopic examination failed to detect helium. The actual amount by weight of these gases in the rock is, of course, very small, being only about 0·04 and 0·07 per cent. in the two cases.

A large number of *specific gravity* determinations were made on the large acid intrusions. In some, as will be noticed later, the composition of the rock has been modified by absorption of gabbro or other basic material, and the density accordingly raised. Excluding these, we find for forty specimens of granites and relatively coarse granophyres from the large masses the mean value 2·59, the extreme figures being 2·51 and 2·65. Separating the rocks from different parts of the area, we obtain results as follows:—

Creag Strollamus district,	mean sp. grav.,	2·57
Beinn na Caillich district,	,, ,,	2·57
Beinn an Dubhaich,	,, ,,	2·59
E. and S. of Loch Ainort,	,, ,,	2·60
N. and W. of Loch Ainort,	,, ,,	2·64
E. of Blaven Range,	,, ,,	2·61
W. of Blaven range,	,, ,,	2·63

If these figures may be regarded as significant, they show that the rocks are somewhat denser (and presumably somewhat less acid) to the W. or S.W. than they are to the E. or N.E.

Grouping the specimens in another way, we find some apparent relation between the density of the rocks and their microstructure. For thoroughly granitoid examples the average specific gravity is found to be 2·61, but for typical granophyres 2·59, while the spherulitic modifications found locally on the margin of a mass and as apophyses give on the average only 2·53 or 2·54, resembling in their low density many of the minor acid intrusions of later date. Since all the rocks are holocrystalline, this would seem to indicate that the typically granitoid varieties are in general the richest in heavier minerals. It must be remembered, however, that the specific gravity of igneous rocks is considerably affected by secondary changes, and the differences indicated may be due, at least in part, to the varying freshness or alteration of the rocks.

The essential constituents of the Skye granites and granophyres are quartz, two felspars, and one or two minerals of the ferro-magnesian division. These latter include hornblende, augite, biotite, and exceptionally riebeckite. The common accessory minerals are magnetite, sphene, zircon, and apatite.

If we adopt the customary subdivision of the rocks according to the dominant ferro-magnesian element, we find that they fall under the heads hornblende-granite ("hornblende-granitite" of some authors, since there is often subordinate biotite) and augite-granite (often with hornblende in addition). We find further that the typically granitoid rocks mostly belong to the former category, while the latter is always characterised by more or less tendency to "granophyric," *i.e.* micrographic, structures, often taking the form of true micropegmatite. This constant association of micrographic structures with augite is not peculiar to Skye, but seems to embody some law of general application. The Carrock Fell rock is an example. Among the numerous acid intrusions of Caernarvonshire the typical granophyres always carry augite, to the exclusions of biotite; the ruder types of granophyre and the granite-porphyries contain the two minerals together; and the true granites have biotite alone. In Skye we find no biotite-granites (without hornblende), and original white mica never occurs. Petrographically, then, the majority of our rocks divide into hornblende-granites (with or usually without subordinate biotite) and augite-granophyres (very often with hornblende in addition), some hornblende-granophyres affording a connecting link between the two. Typical augite-granites are indeed found, as on parts of Marsco, but they are to be regarded as exceptional. Similarly a biotite-granophyre, though it is found in Am Fuar-choire and perhaps elsewhere, seems to be of comparatively rare occurrence.

Two felspars are constantly present, a plagioclase and an orthoclase. In many of the slides the latter seems, on a first impression, to predominate largely, but closer examination often reveals twin-lamellation in crystals which at a glance look like simple individuals. The difficulty of verifying this arises partly from the turbid aspect of many of the crystals, partly from their low extinction-angles reckoned from the twin-line. In symetrically-cut sections the angles are in a large number of cases not more than 3° or 4°. It is evident then that, besides the true monoclinic felspar, there is usually present a triclinic variety with very low extinction-angle. It must be an *oligoclase* of composition not very different from Ab_4An_1 or Ab_3An_1, which, according to Michel Lévy, give 1° and 5° respectively. In addition, many of the slides contain lamellated crystals with extinction-angles up to 16° or 18° in symmetrical sections. This third felspar is of a less acid variety, and its properties correspond with *oligoclase-andesine*, with a constitution represented approximately by Ab_5An_3.

The plagioclase felspars have formed before the orthoclase and quartz, and are idiomorphic, especially when enclosed by the orthoclase, as is sometimes the case. Carlsbad twinning is often seen in addition to the constant albite-lamellation, while pericline-lamellæ come in in some of the broader crystals. Sometimes, and especially in the micrographic rocks, polarised light reveals a zonary banding which indicates that a crystal is not homogenous in composition. The interior, for instance, may be a basic oligoclase or oligoclase-andesine with positive extinction-angle, this being followed by an intermediate zone of oligoclase with sensibly straight extinction, while the margin is of albite-oligoclase with negative extinction-angle. In other cases a narrow border of orthoclase occurs : this is found in granophyres rather than true granites.

The *orthoclase* in these rocks is more readily affected by weathering than the plagioclase felspars, and is always more or less turbid, often almost opaque in thin slices. The change is of the kind often described as "kaolinisation," though whether the finely divided secondary product is kaolinite or muscovite it is not possible to say. The crystals are allotriomorphic, and in the truly granitoid rocks tend to enclose quartz-grains as well as plagioclase and other minerals, while in the granophyric varieties the bulk of the orthoclase figures in the micrographic intergrowths. In other words, the orthoclase has crystallised slightly posterior to or simultaneously with the quartz.

In certain granophyres from Druim-an-Eidhne and Meall Dearg occurs a felspar which may be referred doubtfully to the *anorthoclase* or cryptoperthite group, the crystals being unfortunately not fresh enough for precise examination. Their shapes in sections are difficult to reconcile with the usual habits of either orthoclase or plagioclase, and compare rather with the peculiar felspar of the Norwegian rhomb-porphyries [2667, B]. Usually without evident twinning, they present nevertheless between crossed nicols a curious mottled appearance, little patches of irregular form extinguishing at a slightly different angle from the rest. This recalls the "felderweise mikroperthitische structur" often described in anorthoclase. It is significant that this felspar is found only in rocks otherwise exceptional in containing riebeckite, and, as the analysis shows, relatively rich in soda.

The *quartz* in these rocks occurs either in rather rounded irregular grains, which are often embraced by or enclosed in the orthoclase, or in micrographic intergrowth with that mineral. It contains in most cases numerous minute fluid-pores with bubbles, and in some rocks Zirkel* detected also cubes of salt (Glamaig).

The *augite* always occurs in roughly idiomorphic crystals, though not very sharply bounded by good faces. In some of the granophyric rocks it is found in two rather different habits, which may perhaps indicate two distinct generations; viz., in columnar crystals, averaging about $\frac{1}{30}$ inch in length, and in smaller and more slender crystals, forming groups enclosed in quartz or micropegmatite; *e.g.*, on Druim nan Cleochd [2668, 3198]. Twinning has not been observed. The augite is of a green, as distinguished from a brown, variety, but varies in thin slices from bright green to sensibly colourless. The extinction-angle $c\mathfrak{c}$ is about the same for all tints, viz. 39° to 42°. There is no perceptible pleochroism.

Very common is the conversion of the augite, whether green or

---

* *Zeits. deuts. geol. Ges.*, vol. xxiii., p. 89 : 1871.

colourless, to green hornblende. The latter is not fibrous, and differs in no respect from original hornblende in the same rocks. Partially altered crystals show the invariable crystallographic relation between the two minerals, as already noted in the gabbros. Other modes of alteration of the augite give rise to chlorite, limonite, less frequently epidote, and perhaps magnetite.

The original *hornblende* builds crystals which often show the prism and clinopinacoid faces and sometimes terminal planes. In some granophyric rocks there are two distinct habits similar to those remarked in the case of augite [2668]. These are not derivative after augite, though in some other rocks in the collection doubt may arise on this point. The hornblende, like the augite, is always untwinned.

The mineral is always deeply coloured in thin slices, and often in some brownish tone of green. In the truly granitoid rocks, where we should expect a green hornblende, it is often brown or greenish brown, four examples giving the following pleochroism-scheme:—

𝖆, light yellowish brown.

𝖇, deep brown (with very little tone of green) or greenish brown.

𝖈, deep brownish green (almost opaque) to deep brown (with only a slight tone of green).

In the granophyric rocks the hornblende is constantly green, sometimes of a bright tint very like that of the augite. The extinction-angle $c\mathfrak{c}$ is always about 16° to 18°.

The dark-blue soda-amphibole *riebeckite* is restricted, so far as our observations go, to Meall Dearg and the neighbouring part of Druim an Eidhne, where it was first detected by Mr Teall,[*] and the only other record of its occurrence in the Inner Hebrides is at Ailsa Craig.[†] It presents in our specimens crystals of two different habits side by side, a feature noticeable in various other riebeckite-bearing rocks. The larger crystals are sometimes partly idiomorphic, sometimes allotriomorphic and, it may be, of a very irregular shape, showing a ragged sponge-like appearance in slices; while the smaller ones are idiomorphic, having the prism-faces and sometimes the clinopinacoid, with ragged terminations (Fig. 34). The axis 𝖆 is very near to the vertical crystallographic axis, the inclination being seemingly 3° or 4°, though the intense absorption prevents any very precise measurement. The pleochroism is:—

𝖆 and 𝖇, deep indigo blue.

𝖈, greenish brown to brownish green.

In one or two slides from Marsco occur idiomorphic crystals, about $\frac{1}{40}$ inch in length, of a hornblende with a distinct blue-green tint, suggesting the presence of the riebeckite-molecule in small quantity.

[*] *Quart. Journ. Geol. Soc.*, vol. l., p. 219 : 1894.
[†] Teall, *Min. Mag.*, vol. ix., pp. 219-221 : 1891. Heddle, *Trans. Edin. Geol. Soc.*, vol. vii., pp. 265-267, Pl. XV., XVI. : 1897.

The *biotite* of the Skye granites occurs in flakes of a deep brown colour, and is probably a haughtonite. For vibrations parallel to the cleavage the absorption is strong, almost to opacity. The extinction is sufficiently oblique in some flakes to verify a lamellar twinning parallel to the basal plane. Decomposition gives rise to chlorite and sometimes epidote.

The opaque iron-ore of these rocks seems to be always *magnetite*, and the grains usually show more or less of the octahedral form.

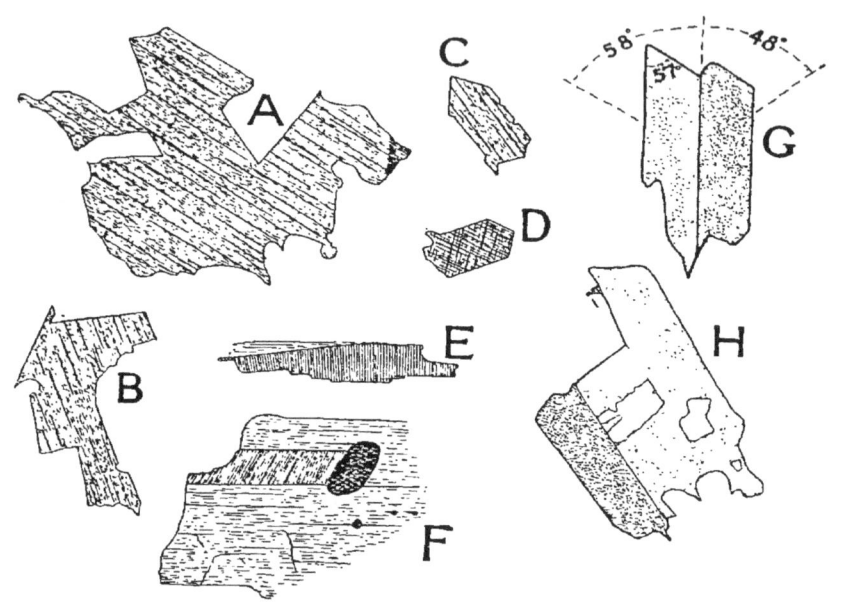

Fig. 34.—Some rarer minerals of the granophyres. A to D × 30, E to H × 100.

A to D are riebeckite crystals from the granophyre of Meall Dearg, illustrating the allotriomorphic habit of the larger and the idiomorphic shape of the smaller crystals [8856].

E and F show an unidentified brown mineral intergrown with green hornblende in a granophyre from Druim na Cleochd [3198].

G and H are twinned crystals of allanite(?) in the granophyre of Allt Fearna, near Broadford. In the former are shown the approximate positions of the axes of strongest absorption for the two individuals.

The mineral occurs only in quite subordinate quantity.* It is often intimately associated with the augite. The *sphene*, on the other hand, is associated with hornblende, and belongs characteristically to the granitoid as distinguished from the granophyric varieties. It is in imperfect crystals or rounded grains, with a faint brownish tint in thin slices. The riebeckite-granophyre contains

* In one place only, 50 yards S.E. of the old ruined Manse at Kilchrist, was found a lode of magnetic iron-ore. It cuts the granite vertically, bearing a little N. of W., and terminates at the junction of the granite with the Cambrian limestone.

flakes of what appears to be *ilmenite*, opaque or rarely translucent and then deep brown.

Most of the rocks contain *apatite*, though its distribution in any given rock is often rather local. It builds little prisms of the usual habit, which penetrate or are enclosed by other minerals; and frequently a number of minute needles are clustered together, usually enclosed in quartz. In certain places on Marsco, where the granite encloses portions of gabbro and is often modified in composition thereby, apatite is unusually abundant, and there occurs in rather stouter prisms with the regular hexagonal cross-section. The fact that in Skye apatite is more abundant in the granites than in the gabbros is not in accord with what is usually found on comparison of acid with basic rocks, but it is evident in the large collection of slices which we have examined, and is confirmed by Dr Pollard's analyses. Another point of interest is that the acid rocks were found to contain chlorine but no fluorine. Here the halogen elements can belong only to the apatite, and we see that our rocks do not bear out the rule which would assign the chlor-apatites to the basic and the fluor-apatites to the acid rocks. The Skye granites do not stand alone in this respect.*

Less frequent and less widely distributed in the granites is *zircon*, always in minute, well-shaped crystals. When enclosed in biotite, as is generally the case, it is always surrounded by the well-known "halo" of intense absorption and pleochroism.

In one slice, of a granophyre from Allt Fearna, near Broadford, there occur small twinned crystals of a mineral which we identify as *allanite* (see Fig. 34, G and H). It is of an intense brown colour with strong pleochroism. The strongest absorption gives a very deep red-brown colour, approaching opacity, while for vibrations in a direction perpendicular to this the colour is a deep brown of a greyer or greener tone. The mean refringence is high, and the extinction-angles from the the twin-line are wide; but the strong absorption precludes any accurate determination of these angles or of the birefringence. Another rock, a hornblende-granophyre from Druim nan Cleochd, also contains a strongly absorptive and pleochroic brown mineral, which is here intergrown with green hornblende (Fig. 34, E and F). The colours are like those of haughtonite, but the most intense absorption (practically opacity) is for transverse, not longtitudinal, vibrations. The extinction-angle is quite low, but cannot be determined with precision. There are no evident cleavage-traces, but a very marked striation making a high angle with the direction of elongation. These properties do not agree with those of any known amphibole mineral.

As regards *micro-structure*, the rocks which build the large intrusive masses of the Red Hills are, as has been said, sometimes granitoid, sometimes granophyric, with many varieties of micro-pegmatite. On the whole the latter predominate, and a strong tendency to graphic intergrowths of felspar and quartz may be

* In five granites from the eastern Highlands of Scotland Dr Mackie found that the percentage of chlorine amounted on the average to 0·054. *Trans. Edin. Geol. Soc.*, vol. vii., p. 54 : 1901.

regarded as the most striking petrographical feature of this assemblage of acid rocks. In the fine-textured marginal modifications, and in minor intrusions and apophyses of the large masses, this tendency is even more marked, and often assumes the form of spherulitic structures. It is clear, however, that no difference of an essential kind exists between "micropegmatite," "pseudo-spherulites," and some spherulites with fairly regular black cross, as developed in these rocks; and we may conveniently emphasise their essential identity by using the terms micrographic and cryptographic for the various types of intergrowth, according as they can or cannot be clearly resolved by the microscope. Graphic structures visible to the naked eye are not found.

The best examples of typical *granitoid* structure are afforded by the Beinn an Dubhaich boss, but such rocks occur also in many parts of the Red Hills tract, *e.g.* in Glen Sligachan. The quartz has tended to crystallise rather before than after the latest felspar (orthoclase), but often the two minerals have formed almost simultaneously. We include with the true granites those rocks in which a rude micrographic structure is locally developed, commonly of an irregular kind and on a relatively coarse scale.

As typical granophyres we include those rocks in which the chief bulk consists of a visibly *micrographic intergrowth of felspar and quartz* (micropegmatite). These, with connecting links between them and the true granites, predominate over a very large part of the Red Hills. Distinct crystals of felspar, and sometimes grains of quartz, enclosed in the micropegmatite give the rocks an aspect which may be described as porphyritic; but this must not be taken to imply that consolidation has been effected in two distinct stages under different conditions: the characters to be described militate against such a supposition.

In different specimens, and in different parts of one specimen, the micropegmatite differs in composition, in scale of magnitude and degree of regularity, in manner of arrangement and relation to phenocrysts, etc. The component minerals are usually orthoclase and quartz: less commonly oligoclase takes the place of the former, but the intergrowth is then not usually of a very delicate or regular kind (Pl. XIX., Fig. 1, A). The felspar is almost everywhere in greater quantity than the associated quartz, but the proportion between them evidently varies, even in different parts of an area with common orientation throughout. The felspar in such an area is continuous, enclosing very numerous detached elements of quartz, which behave optically as parts of a single crystal. The little elements of quartz are in the less minute intergrowths of rather irregular outline, or very often wedge-shaped, so as to show in a thin slice as little triangles similarly oriented. With increasing fineness of scale the intergrowth approximates more and more to a lamellar structure, giving a parallel-linear arrangement in sections.

A large proportion of the micropegmatite is disposed in relation to the felspar phenocrysts, forming a broad border round each crystal. The intergrowth constantly tends, in the neighbourhood

L

of a crystal, to assume a linear (probably a lamellar) arrangement at right angles to the faces of the crystal. It follows that, when most regularly developed, the border, as seen in a thin slice, consists of four portions, corresponding with the four sides of the rectangular section, adjacent portions being divided by a diagonal suture, as in a picture-frame. The intergrowth is most regular and most minute in contact with the phenocryst, while outwards the border usually passes by gradations into a coarser and less regular interstitial micropegmatite, or inosculates with contiguous borders belonging to other phenocrysts. Such borders surround crystals both of orthoclase and of oligoclase. In the former case it can often be verified that the felspar of the micropegmatite has the same orientation as the phenocryst, and is indeed an extension of it. This is probably not an occasional phenomenon but the general rule, though it is often obscured by the turbidity of the felspar. We have not observed a similar crystalline continuity in the case of oligoclase, and indeed the delicate intergrowth bordering the phenocrysts seems to be in general an orthoclase-micropegmatite. Oligoclase phenocrysts framed in such a border show a very narrow external shell of turbid felspar, which seems to be orthoclase, and the felspar of the border is probably continuous with this. Grains of quartz are sometimes surrounded by a zone of very irregular micropegmatite, the quartz of which is oriented like that of the grain, but this is a much less common occurrence (Plate XIX., Fig. 2).

We have observed nothing which affords any support to the view that these later outgrowths from phenocrysts belong to a time subsequent to the consolidation of the rock.* On the contrary, the phenomena become most intelligible on the supposition of no great break in time and no important discontinuity as regards physical conditions between the phenocryst stage and the micropegmatite stage of consolidation. It is possible indeed that no change of conditions is implied other than the progressive change in the composition of the residual magma which must result from the abstraction of the constituents of the felspar phenocrysts. We may conceive that the growing acidity of the residual fluid magma reaches a certain critical point, after which not pure felspar-substance but a minute intergrowth of felspar and quartz is deposited upon the faces of the crystals. It is not necessary to suppose, as Mr Teall has suggested,† that micropegmatite in general is of the nature of a eutectic mixture of felspar and quartz, which would require that the two constituents should always occur in certain constant proportions. So far as can be judged by eye, the proportion of quartz in the micropegmatite of our rocks seems to be smallest in that part of the border contiguous to the phenocryst, increasing slightly outwards and becoming largest in the irregular interstitial areas. It is these latter areas which we should rather expect to be of the nature of a eutectic mixture.

* *Cf.* Judd, *Quart. Journ. Geol. Soc.*, vol. xlv., pp. 175-186 : 1889.
† *British Petrography*, pp. 401, 402 : 1888. See also Anniversary Address in *Quart. Journ. Geol. Soc.*, vol. lvii., pp. lxxv, lxxvi.

Since the felspar phenocrysts doubtless acquired and maintained crystallographic outlines from a very early stage of their growth, a change such as we have imagined, from the deposition of felspar-substance to the deposition of micropegmatite, would result in a sharply bounded felspar crystal fringed by a micropegmatite border. But exceptionally the change seems to have come on in a less abrupt manner, for we sometimes find little patches of quartz in micrographic intergrowth in the interior of a felspar phenocryst. This is more frequent in the spherulitic marginal modifications of the rock than in the typical micrographic varieties. These spherulitic rocks afford evidence also on another point, viz. that the phenocrysts of the principal minerals were formed almost, if not quite, wholly after the intrusion of the magma, and are therefore not comparable with the phenocrysts of extruded lavas. This appears from the fact that the phenocrysts become smaller and of different habit towards the border of an intrusion which gives evidence of rapid chilling. The augite, for instance, on Glas Bheinn Bheag and Druim an Eidhne often assumes the form of small rods or needles, which sometimes share the radiate arrangement of the spherulites. This seems to indicate that this mineral crystallised subsequently to the intrusion of the magma, and the same must be true, *a fortiori*, of the felspars and quartz. It is noteworthy too that the phenocrysts in our granophyres are never broken.

The spherulitic or cryptographic structure is not found in the large intrusive masses of the Red Hills except along certain portions of the boundary, and in a few places along what appear to have been the margins of the distinct intrusions of which the large masses are made up. This modification is identical with what is the normal structure of many of the minor acid intrusions (dykes and sheets) in Skye, some few of which are indeed offshoots from the large masses under consideration, but most of which belong probably to a later epoch. We shall postpone the description of this type of structure until we come to consider these minor intrusions (Chap. XVI.).

While the fine-textured modifications of our rocks take for the most part the granophyric character, this is not everywhere the case, the dominant type in some places being a fine-grained rock with a *microgranitic structure*, usually with a *porphyritic* aspect due to the occurrence of conspicuous felspar crystals in the finer ground-mass. This is found in places, *e.g.* on some parts of Marsco, forming the border of one of the distinct intrusions of granite; and in such a case bears the same relation to the typical granitoid rock as the spherulitic and allied varieties do to the coarse granophyre. But there are also areas of porphyritic felsite contiguous with granite but probably representing separate intrusions, which have this character throughout. Such an area occurs on the border, and as it would appear at the base, of the main Red Hills mass at Meall a' Mhaoil and Meall Buidhe, to the north of Loch Ainort. Much of the rock has a dark and often bluish tint owing to secondary changes, to which these felsitic rocks are rather prone. A specimen, of specific gravity 2·66, has dull white crystals of orthoclase up to ⅛ inch in length. A slice [9571] shows in addition grains of augite, often of partly rounded form, and a felsitic ground-mass of ordinary appearance and rather fine texture. Another place where the porphyritic felsite modification may be studied is on Glamaig, but here the geology is complicated by other circumstances, and especially by the remarkable modification of the acid rocks in some parts by a profusion of basic xenoliths, a phenomenon which belongs to the next chapter. In most of the rocks of porphyritic habit the phenocrysts are of felspar only, but there are some with quartz in addition. A specimen from the foot-path on the N.W. side of the Moll River, and south of Meall a' Mhaoil, contains abundant crystals both of quartz and of orthoclase, up to $\frac{1}{10}$ inch in diameter. The ground-mass is of the "microfelsitic" type, and has a fluxion-structure in places [8970].

A very noticeable feature of the acid intrusive rocks of Skye, and indeed of the British Tertiary province generally, is the *drusy or miarolitic structure*. This is very widely found, but is especially characteristic of the common granophyres with micropegmatite, as distinguished from the granitoid rocks on the one hand and the spherulitic and felsitic modifications on the other. The dimensions of the little cavities vary from an inch downward, and they have highly irregular shapes owing to the crystals of the rock projecting into them. These crystals are quartz and felspars, occasionally also hornblende, and, where the vacant space has given them freedom of growth, they present perfect crystal-facets. We have not found in Skye druses so large as some of those in the granites of Arran and the Mourne Mountains, nor have we discovered in our druses any of the peculiar minerals which occur in those districts. It is well known that beryl, chrysoberyl, fluor, tourmaline, topaz, fayalite, etc., have been formed in the druses of the Mourne granite.* Their absence from the corresponding rocks in Skye may be ascribed to the want of certain essential conditions, the minerals in question being of species usually referred to the coöperation of special "mineralising agents." It is noteworthy that Dr Pollard found no fluorine in the rocks analysed.

Although the druses are a conspicuous feature in the rocks which contain them, they make up in reality but a small part of the whole volume. From specific gravity determinations of rocks, first in bulk and then in powder, it seems probable that the cavities do not often amount to so much as one two-hundredth of the total volume. In some cases the original druses have been reduced in size by the deposition of secondary minerals within them, usually quartz and epidote, or by a coating of ferric oxide.

The foregoing general description covers almost the whole of the granites, granophyres, etc., of the Red Hills, excluding only the spherulitic and other fine-textured margins and off-shoots to be described later. The special local variations, in composition and

* Mr Seymour has recently added cassiterite to the list,

in micro-structure, which remain to be noticed in this place are few and, as regards their distribution, insignificant.

As compared with the gabbros, and still more as compared with the peridotites, these acid rocks have a remarkably uniform composition. In the absence of many chemical analyses, this is sufficiently proved by the mineral constitution of the rocks. The most interesting of what may be regarded as aberrant varieties is the *riebeckite-granophyre* of Meall Dearg, already described by Mr Teall.* This rock consists chiefly of felspar and quartz in typical micrographic intergrowth, in which the crystals of the other constituent minerals are embedded. The crystals of felspar have in part the characters of "anorthoclase" [2667, B]. In addition to the riebeckite, there may be exceptionally a few grains of augite [8856]. Iron-ore is rather more plentiful than is usual in this group of rocks, and seems to be always ilmenite, in idiomorphic flakes closely associated with the riebeckite. Zircon is an occasional accessory. In the field the rock appears as an ordinary drusy granophyre, with a yellowish brown tint due to ferruginous staining. The riebeckite cannot be certainly distinguished from common hornblende on a hand-specimen, except by the irregular shape of the crystals. Two specimens of the rock gave specific gravities 2·512 and 2·492. Making some allowance on account of the drusy cavities, it is still evident that this variety, unusually rich in alkali-felspars, is notably less dense than the ordinary granophyres.

Another rare modification arises from the disappearance of quartz as an essential constituent, giving a rock which is petrographically a *syenite* according to the modern nomenclature.† Such a rock is exposed in isolated knolls below Creagan Dubha, to the north of Beinn Dearg Mhòr (of Strath), a locality where a considerable amount of crushing of the rocks has somewhat obscured their relations. It is mottled with dull greenish patches and veins, and was in fact mistaken at first for a volcanic agglomerate, but the peculiarity is due merely to brecciation. A specimen gave the specific gravity 2·66, which is rather higher than the specific gravities of the granites. A thin slice [6843] shows that it is essentially a felspar-hornblende rock. The felspar is principally orthoclase, but partly a finely striated oligoclase with nearly straight extinction. The hornblende is for the most part chloritised. Quartz is scarcely represented, except as narrow irregular veins traversing the felspar, and these seem to be secondary and connected with the brecciation. The locality of this rock would permit us to regard it as a marginal modification of the granite, but its mode of occurrence is not displayed, and it is in any case quite exceptional.

* *Quart. Journ. Geol. Soc.*, vol. l., p. 219 : 1894.
† Macculloch and other early writers, in applying the name syenite to this group of rocks as a whole, used it in its original sense for hornblendic granite (including granophyre). The identification of hornblende, before the introduction of the microscope into petrology, was necessarily uncertain in the finer textured rocks.

Any special peculiarity is quite as rare in the structural and textural as in the mineralogical and chemical characters of the rocks. A coarse *pegmatoid* structure (usually without graphic intergrowth) is found in two or three places where the granite is in intimate relation with earlier basic intrusions, viz. of gabbro on Marsco, and of a more peculiar rock on Sròn a' Bhealain, near Sligachan. The phenomena will be described in the following chapter. At the same places there is sometimes a rather vague flow-structure imparting a *gneissic* appearance to the rock. A rude gneissic structure of a different nature, due to crushing, is seen in Allt na Teangaidh, a branch of Allt Strollamus.

In some places the large bodies of granite and granophyre, whether of boss-like or of laccolitic habit, are traversed by pale fine-textured *aplitic veins*. These are of small width, often less than an inch. Though sharply cutting the normal rock, they have not the magnitude nor the straight course of dykes, and are not infrequently found ramifying. We may probably regard them as closely related to the granite itself, although distinctly later than its consolidation. They are of somewhat more acid composition, at least in respect of the proportion of the ferro-magnesian minerals which they contain. A specimen was sliced of a vein traversing the biotite-granite of Druim na Ruaige near its junction with Beinn Dearg Mheadhonach. This has the specific gravity of 2·59. Under the microscope it is seen to be of much finer grain than the granite and of somewhat different micro-structure. It contains biotite, but in less amount than the granite which it intersects [8708]. A good place for studying the fine-textured veins in the granite is the eastern part of the Beinn an Dubhaich mass. Here they sometimes reach a width of 3 or 4 inches, and narrower veins are abundant in places. At places in Coire na Laogh, on the north side of Marsco, where, as we shall see, the granite is crowded with partially digested débris of gabbro, aplitic veins traverse the dark modified rock as well as the normal type, and have the same pale appearance in both. This seems enough to prove that the veins are not merely excretions from the immediately contiguous granite, but distinct later injections, though doubtless from the same source.

The dark ovoid patches, representing relatively *basic secretions* from the magma, which are so common in the granites and granophyres of many regions, are not often met with in our rocks, and are never of large size. One place where they may be studied is at Am Fuar-choire, about 1½ mile S.E. of Sligachan. Here they are not more than an inch or two in diameter, always rounded in outline, and sharply defined. At the place where they were specially examined the rock itself is a biotite-granite with partial granophyric structure and of moderately coarse grain. The dark patches are of much finer texture, and they have also a different structure, the felspar being more generally idiomorphic and the quartz enwrapping it in micropœcilitic fashion. The ferro-magnesian element is much more plentiful than in the normal rock. It is completely chloritised, but there has probably been some hornblende in addition to the biotite.

PLATE VII.

FIG. 1.

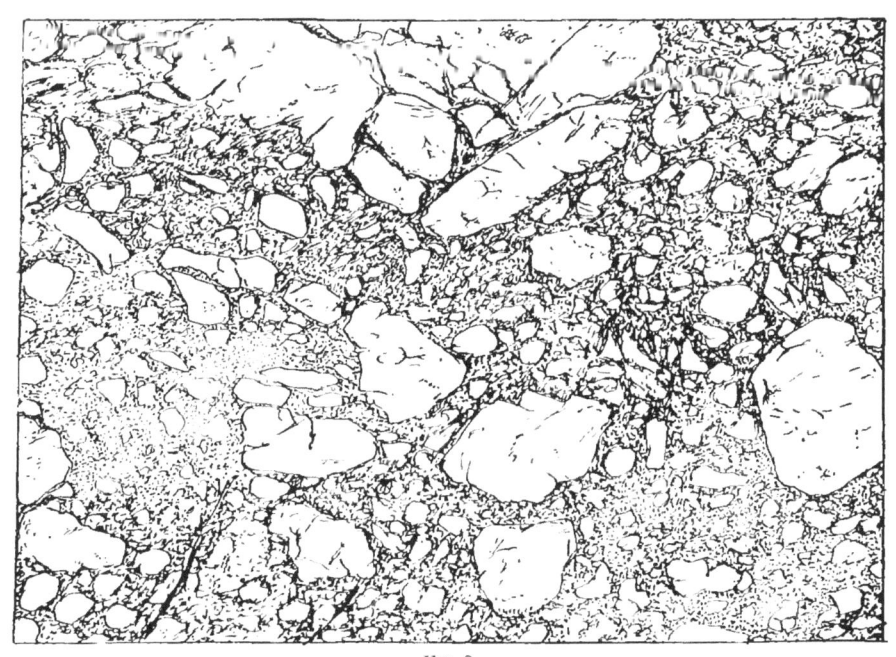

FIG. 2.

Crushed granite, from the shore between Allt Fearna and Strollamus Lodge, 2½ miles N.W. of Broadford. Natural size. The lower figure is from a typical specimen, while the upper one shows an earlier stage in the process of brecciation.

Such dark patches are to be distinguished from *xenoliths*. These, except in certain places where they occur in great profusion and with remarkable circumstances, are not very frequent. The exceptional occurrences will be described in the next chapter. Since the granite of the Red Hills, though a much less complex mass than the gabbro of the Cuillins, undoubtedly consists of a number of distinct intrusions, it may be expected that the later portions have sometimes caught up xenoliths of the earlier. This is occasionally to be verified. Possibly it escapes notice in other instances owing to the similarity between the enclosed and the enclosing rock. Such examples as we have noticed are inclusions of granite or relatively coarse granophyre in some finer-textured type, and they occur at no great distance from the junction of two distinct intrusive bodies. In two or three places in the valley of the Kinloch Ainort river (Abhuinn Ceann Loch Ainort) such xenoliths are abundant. They are never rounded or corroded.

The granites of Skye have not in general been invaded by later intrusive magmas of any considerable volume, and accordingly we do not find in them (apart from granite xenoliths enclosed in dykes) any indications of thermal metamorphism. Dynamic metamorphism, on the other hand, connected with subsequent crust-movements, has in numerous places left its impress on the rocks in *cataclastic phenomena* of various degrees and kinds. The granite is probably more often severely crushed than the gabbro, and certainly shows the results more frequently in the field; though the most marked effects still seem to be restricted chiefly to the vicinity of faulted boundaries. The most interesting and easily accessible locality is the shore about $2\frac{1}{2}$ miles N.W. of Broadford. Here much of the rock is so completely brecciated as to be easily mistaken at first for a volcanic agglomerate. The resemblance is sometimes enhanced by a partial chloritisation of the more finely ground material, imparting a darkened colour against which the pale larger fragments show out prominently. The true nature of the rock can be made out by examining places where the process of crushing is less advanced. It is often seen, as is shown in the lower figure of the accompanying plate, that the granite tends at first to break into lenticular fragments with a parallel arrangement; but the more completely crushed rock has no schistose structure (Plate VII.).

Besides this strip of coast-line and the neighbouring lower slopes of Creag Strollamus, there are other places where crushed granites simulate rather closely the volcanic agglomerates. The eastern slope of Beinn na Caillich, above Coirechatachan, is one such place. In Allt na Teangaidh, a branch of Allt Strollamus coming down from the col between Beinn na Caillich and Beinn Dearg Mhòr, the appearance of the crushed granite is rather different, a certain rude parallel structure imparting to it something of a gneissic aspect, as already remarked.

Thin slices of the rocks show various stages of the cataclastic process. In the earlier stages the fragments are angular, and it is still possible in places to see how they might be fitted together

[6835, 6837]. With the progress of crushing, and perhaps some degree of rolling, there is a rounding of the fragments and an increase in the amount of matrix [6840-6842]. The quartz shows strain-shadows between crossed nicols even before any considerable brecciation is set up, and in the earlier stages this character is constantly well marked [6834, 6835]: in the more thoroughly crushed rocks it is sometimes less evident. We have not observed in the granites any clear evidence of secondary twinning in the plagioclase felspar, such as we have noticed in the gabbros. This is perhaps explained by the fact that the oligoclase of the granites has naturally a closer twin-lamellation than the labradorite of the gabbros.

CHAPTER XI.

Invasion of Basic Rocks by the Granite-Magma.

In a comprehensive study of the varied suite of intrusive igneous rocks in Skye no feature is more remarkable than the frequent association of different rock-types in intimate and peculiar relations. This is shown in two ways, which, however, are often illustrated by the same occurrences, and are obviously so connected that any general consideration of the subject must take account of both together. We find firstly a strong tendency for different rock-types to be closely and regularly associated, so as to constitute what is in effect one composite rock-body; and secondly the frequent inclusion of partially digested débris (xenoliths) of one igneous rock in another. Such relations are found to exist in many instances between two rocks of widely diverse composition, such as gabbro and granite or basalt and granophyre, and there are also some curious cases in which more than two kinds of rock are involved. The phenomena have sufficient novelty to warrant more than a passing notice, and they will be described at some length and their bearings to some extent discussed. It appears from numerous scattered notices in the geological literature both of the Inner Hebrides and of the north-eastern counties of Ireland, as well as from an examination of specimens collected by the late Director-General in several of the islands, that the peculiar relations in question are in some degree characteristic of the Tertiary intrusions of the British province as a whole.

The probable significance of the phenomena will be pointed out as they are described, and such general considerations of a theoretical kind as are admissible in this memoir will be properly deferred to a later stage; but one remark may be made at the outset. There are good reasons, as will appear below, for believing that, when two different igneous rocks are *intimately and systematically associated*, whether as members of a composite intrusive body or as xenoliths and enclosing matrix, they are also closely related as regards source and origin; and further that, when such peculiarly intimate relations subsist between two igneous rocks of definitely intrusive habit, these have been separated by no great interval as regards the epochs of their intrusion. Petrographical phenomena to be described below can scarcely be explained except on the supposition that the first rock was still hot, and even in some cases its consolidation was not yet perfectly completed, when the second rock was intruded in juxtaposition with it. An essential distinction is thus to be drawn between the systematic and regular association of different rocks to form composite stocks, laccolites, sheets, or dykes and the merely fortuitous conjunctions, which also occur but are not usually attended by peculiarities of a petrographical kind. Equally must we recognise an essential distinction between the regular and abundant inclusions of one igneous rock, A, in another, B, repeated again and again through the country with the same remarkable circumstances, and the merely accidental inclusion of foreign rock-fragments (igneous or otherwise) which occur locally in these as in many other intrusive rocks.

In the large plutonic intrusions, which will be first noticed, the close association of basic and acid rocks does not assume the same regularity and symmetry as in the composite sills and dykes to be described in the next chapter. In several places, however, and especially on Marsco, gabbro and granite (including granophyre) are found with very remarkable mutual relations, the significance of which cannot be overlooked. Taking a broader view, the mere juxtaposition of the two rocks, recurring at a number of distinct centres, can scarcely be a coincidence without meaning. The great gabbro laccolite of the Cuillins has a great granite laccolite intruded beneath and partly into it; and the gabbro boss of Broadford has a granite boss intruded beside and partly through it. In the Carlingford district, in Arran, in Mull, in Ardnamurchan, in Rum, and so far away as in St. Kilda, occur other considerable masses of Tertiary gabbro, and in each of these places that rock has granite (including granophyre) for its intimate associate. Further, according to Sir Archibald Geikie, the sequence in time of the two rocks is everywhere the same, and the acid intrusion often intersects the basic one. The mutual relations of the two rocks have been described in the case of Carlingford by Professor Sollas,* whose account affords interesting material for comparison with some of the facts recorded below. Another district available for comparison, as regards the mutual relations of gabbro and granophyre, is Carrock Fell in Cumberland,† where, in default of direct geological evidence, the possible Tertiary age of the rocks is suggested by petrographical analogies.

We have first to describe some interesting phenomena which demonstrate that in certain places the gabbro has been partially fused in the vicinity of the invading granite magma, and to trace the effects which have resulted from reactions between the two rocks under these conditions.

Effects of this kind are to be observed on a small scale on the eastern and north-eastern borders of the eastern Red Hills, where

* *Trans. Roy. Ir. Acad.*, vol. xxx., pp. 477-512, Pl. XXVI., XXVII.: 1894. See also Prof. Busz on an occurrence in Ardnamurchan, *Geol. Mag.*, 1900, pp. 436-441.
† Harker, *Quart. Journ. Geol. Soc.*, vol. l., pp. 311-336, Pl. XVI., XVII.: 1894; vol. li., pp. 125-147, Pl. IV.: 1895.

we have already noticed a permeation of the basic rock by the acid. Microscopic examination shows clearly that this permeation has been attended, and doubtless facilitated, by a *local and partial refusion of the gabbro*. With the fused basic material has been mingled a small proportion of the acid magma, and the result has been, after consolidation, a rock of somewhat less basic composition than the normal gabbro, and differing from it in mineralogical constitution. Two specimens will suffice to illustrate this reaction. The first is from Creag Strollamus, and forms part of the gabbro close to the granite, which sends veins into it. It is a rather dark rock of fairly coarse texture, with some tendency to a separation in patches of the darker and lighter elements. A thin slice [8048] shows it to consist chiefly of green hornblende and felspar, with some brown mica, relics of augite, and a little magnetite in irregular grains. The hornblende is often fibrous, and both it and the mica are to be regarded as formed at the expense of augite, though not merely as pseudomorphs. The felspar is partly labradorite, with albite and carlsbad twinning, partly a variety giving low extinction-angles, probably andesine-oligoclase. The latter is in clear crystals, often untwinned, closely associated with fibrous hornblende or actinolite, and sometimes enclosing the same as a multitude of fine needles. The other specimen is a rock of rather finer texture from the slope east of Allt a' Choire, near Coirechatachan, and was cut to show fine veins of granite traversing the gabbro [8047]. The latter has been converted into an aggregate of green hornblende and felspar with little imperfect octahedra and granules of magnetite. Some of the felspar is labradorite, but most of it gives very low extinction-angles, and seems to be oligoclase. The granite-veins, of coarser texture than the modified gabbro, are not very sharply divided from it under the microscope. They consist of turbid felspar, both orthoclase and oligoclase, and quartz, with green hornblende and a little magnetite. The hornblende is perhaps a little more abundant than is usual in the granites, but not very noticeably so.

It seems beyond doubt that at junctions like these the gabbro has been in some measure enriched in silica and alkalies derived from the acid magma. This was apparently effected in the main by the fusion or solution of part of the labradorite by the acid magma and crystallisation therefrom of a more acid variety of plagioclase. In some cases part of the augitic constituent of the gabbro seems also to have passed into solution in the acid magma, giving rise on recrystallisation to hornblende or (in consequence of the accession of alkali) to biotite. Concurrently with the acidification of the gabbro there has been in some cases an evident modification of the acid rock in the opposite sense. Two examples of granophyre veins traversing and altering the gabbro give specific gravities 2·68 and 2·71, and are obviously of more basic nature than the main mass from which they are offshoots. This reciprocal modification of the granite or granophyre is, however, not always apparent, as we have seen in the case just described. If the reaction was quite local, the small amount of basic material taken up from the gabbro might be distributed by diffusion through a considerable volume of the acid magma. It is important to remark that in places where acid veins injected into the gabbro assume a fine texture, as if in consequence of rapid cooling, no perceptible effects of the kind in question are found. These reactions seem to have been dependent upon the injection of the acid magma into a mass of gabbro which was still hot.

Phenomena of the kind described, evincing reactions between granite and gabbro, are to be observed in many places along the outer borders of the large acid intrusions, where these are in contact with the earlier intrusions of gabbro. At these, which we may term *external*, junctions of the two rocks the effects are not on an extended scale or of a conspicuous kind. Reactions of a like kind, but of a more far-reaching scope and productive of much more striking peculiarities, have operated in certain localities at what may be distinguished as *internal* junctions; *i.e.* where portions of gabbro have been involved in the heart of a granite mass. The most remarkable relations are observed where continuous bodies of the earlier basic rock have thus been enveloped by the later acid magma; but we shall first describe the effects of the inclusion in the acid magma of a large amount of gabbro xenoliths.

The rocks which illustrate this type of intermixture most strikingly are the *xenolithic granophyres of Kilchrist*, in the broad strath leading up from Broadford towards Torran. These are crowded throughout with partially digested gabbro xenoliths. The mode of occurrence and probable geological relations of these rocks have already been discussed (*see* Fig. 4, above). They are in contact partly with the Cambrian limestones, chiefly with the agglomerate of the great volcanic vent. Nevertheless they contain no xenoliths of limestone; and fragments of metamorphosed basalt and grit which may be referred to the volcanic agglomerate are found only sparingly, chiefly in the fine-textured felsitic rock which in places forms the margin of the mass. The relics of gabbro, which are distributed in such profusion through the granophyre, are derived therefore from some unseen source. It is not impossible that a gabbro sheet underlies the granophyre, and has been disrupted by it; but this is entirely hypothetical, and there is nothing in the appearance of the gabbro débris to suggest their origin by the shattering of a solid sheet of rock. For reasons which will be discussed in connection with other xenolithic rocks in the district, we incline to the opinion that this gabbro has come directly from some primitive reservoir rather than from any intruded rock-body.

A description, illustrated by microscopical figures, of these rocks has already been published, and the following account is taken partly from that source.*

Compared with what may be called the normal granophyres of the neighbouring Red Hills, these rocks are darker and manifestly richer in the iron-bearing minerals. Examination shows, too, that they are decidedly denser: ten specimens gave specific gravities

* Harker, *Quart. Journ. Geol. Soc.*, vol. lii., pp. 320-328, Pl. XIII., XIV.: 1896.

ranging from 2·56 to 2·73, with a mean of 2·66, while twenty specimens of the normal granophyres of the district gave from 2·51 to 2·66, with a mean of 2·58. Closer inspection often reveals a mottled appearance, due to the dark minerals tending to cluster in vaguely defined patches, and in places these patches become more distinct and are seen to represent enclosed fragments of some basic rock. In other respects—for example, in the prevalence of the micrographic structure, in the drusy character of the more coarse-textured type, etc.—these rocks show a close correspondence with the normal granophyres of the district. It cannot, of course, be asserted that they agree precisely with the latter as regards the composition of the original magma, but it will be shown that the differences which now exist are certainly due, at least in the main, to the taking up and partial dissolution of gabbro material.

The xenoliths are, as a rule, less than an inch in diameter, though exceptionally larger. In a hand-specimen they are visible as dark blotches, often closely clustered together, with vague shadowy outlines which sufficiently indicate that the enclosed débris has suffered deeply from the caustic action of the magma. This becomes more evident in thin slices, where obvious xenoliths are not often recognisable as such, though unmistakably foreign material is universally distributed. Some constituents of the gabbro have suffered more or less complete fusion or solution in the acid magma; while other constituents, which resisted such action, have been set free, and now figure as xenocrysts, either intact or more or less perfectly transformed into other substances. At the same time the material absorbed has modified the composition of the magma, in the general sense of rendering it less acid, and this is of course expressed in the products of the final consolidation of the granophyre. In order to present in systematic form the observations made, it will be convenient to begin by enquiring what has befallen each of the chief constituents of the gabbro.

In these Kilchrist rocks, as in the similar ones to be described on Marsco, apatite needles are constantly present and rather abundant, though, as usual with this mineral, somewhat capriciously distributed. Doubtless any apatite contained in the gabbro would survive as such in the modified granophyre, but we know that the Skye gabbros are usually deficient or very poor in this mineral. It does not seem possible to distinguish apatite needles derived from the gabbro from those proper to the granophyre itself.

It is the augite that affords the most conclusive proof of the extraneous origin of the xenocrysts, and this is due to the characteristic basal striation of the gabbro-augite, a feature not found in the augite of the normal granophyres. In the recognisable enclosed fragments of gabbro [6704] the augite shows no change except a conversion to brownish-green, rather fibrous hornblende at the edge of the crystal, a transformation very common in the ordinary gabbros of the district. In the isolated xenocrysts the conversion to hornblende is usually far advanced, and in these rocks in general this mineral predominates over augite. It is yellowish to brownish-green or sometimes greenish-brown in colour, and of compact (as contrasted with fibrous) structure. Very often there is a core of unchanged augite with the basal striation that indicates its derivation from gabbro, and the traces of this structure are sometimes seen even when the conversion to hornblende has been complete. Failing this evidence, the derivation of the hornblende can often be inferred from the irregular shape of its crystals, or from its enclosing abundant shapeless grains of magnetite. On the other hand, there is usually some hornblende presenting the crystal outlines proper to that mineral, and this must certainly have crystallised out from the modified granophyre-magma. In some slides it is very plentiful. It does not differ materially in colour and pleochroism from the pseudomorphic hornblende. It may be remarked that, when the latter encloses a core of unchanged augite, the two minerals have the usual crystallographic relation, the b and c axes being common to both: in a clinopinacoidal section the extinction-angle of the augite is 39°, and of the hornblende 18°, on the same side of the vertical [2674]. In addition to the augite plainly derived from gabbro, several of the slides contain rather rounded grains of augite showing neither basal striation nor partial conversion to hornblende. These are to be regarded as crystallised directly from the granophyre magma. Two slides [2674, 6703] contain altered xenocrysts of rhombic pyroxene, a mineral which we have noted as an occasional constituent of the gabbros of the district. There is a partial conversion to hornblende at the margin, while the interior is usually serpentinised.

Occasionally pseudomorphs after olivine, apparently of "pilitic" amphibole, are seen enclosed in the relics of striated augite [6704], or isolated in the granophyre-matrix [6703].

Magnetite-grains of irregular shape are embedded in many of the augite-xenocrysts and the hornblende-pseudomorphs after them, and these do not differ from the grains in the original gabbro. Most of the abundant magnetite in the slices is, however, of a different kind, building perfect or imperfect octahedra. Though partly representing in substance iron-ore absorbed from gabbro-débris, it is evidently a new crystallisation from the modified granophyre-magma.

Distinct xenocrysts of gabbro-felspar are rare in the specimens sliced, but they are occasionally found, especially in the neighbourhood of actual gabbro-xenoliths. One suitably oriented crystal gave extinction-angles 35° and 36° in alternate lamellæ, and is presumably labradorite like the common felspar in the gabbros of the district. It has a marginal intergrowth of a more acid felspar, and, like the felspar-phenocrysts in all these granophyres, has served as nucleus for a growth of micropegmatite [6704]. It is clear that most of the felspar of the enclosed gabbro-fragments has been completely absorbed by the enveloping magma. The result is seen in a great preponderance of soda-lime- over potash- felspar in the rock as finally consolidated, compared with the normal granophyres of the district. This dominant felspar seems, however, to be chiefly oligoclase, with quite low extinction-angles.

Apart from the peculiarities described, the rocks here dealt with present a general similarity to the normal granophyres. There are, however, one or two special points worth noting. Several writers, in describing the phenomena of xenoliths of acid rocks in basalts and diabases, have remarked a tendency to the formation of hollow spaces, usually filled by later products. Indications of the same tendency are not wanting in the present converse case, though the circumstances are different. In one example are seen ring-like aggregates, about $\frac{1}{10}$ inch in diameter, of hornblende crystals, surrounding areas of clear quartz [6705]. Quartz is frequently seen moulded upon hornblende-crystals, and, in several slides, penetrated by actinolitic needles. Such patches of quartz are quite different from the quasi-porphyritic grains common in the granophyres, and they seem to be of late formation —not necessarily secondary in the usual sense. They probably occupy what have once been vacant spaces formed in connection with the destruction of xenoliths, and are quite distinct from ordinary druses. The latter are also found here just as in the normal granophyres, and are commonly filled by calcite and quartz [6707]. In places it can be seen that the calcite-crystals project into the quartz, which again indicates that some of the latter mineral belongs to a very late stage in the history of the rock.

In addition to the relics of gabbro in these granophyres there are occasional traces of inclusions of other rocks. In particular there are granular aggregates consisting largely of hornblende and magnetite and presenting angular outlines to the surrounding matrix [6709]. These, no doubt, represent small fragments of basalt in an advanced stage of dissolution, and are merely accidental xenoliths picked up from the volcanic agglomerate. They are of the same nature as the fragments enclosed in the felsitic rock already mentioned as forming the marginal part of the acid intrusion in certain places. These latter are much less altered from their original state, and often preserve sub-angular outlines.

We pass on to consider the more remarkable phenomena displayed on Marsco and about Glamaig, where the basic rocks involved in the acid intrusions are not merely detached small xenoliths from some subterranean source but large bodies of dyke-like and sheet-like form. Here the relations are of a very peculiar kind, being complicated by the intervention of a third rock in addition to the gabbro and the granophyre. Since this is unlike any type included in systematic classifications and nomenclatures, we shall for convenience refer to it under the provisional name "*marscoite*." This is done merely to avoid repeated periphrases, and it is not intended to establish a new rock-type: the rock indeed is certainly a hybrid one, and therefore not entitled to systematic rank or formal designation. In this place it is sufficient to state that it is a conspicuously porphyritic rock, with large crystals of labradorite, and, though of generally basic composition, contains quartz, usually in visible grains. On Marsco gabbro, marscoite, and the dominant acid rocks are associated in a peculiarly intimate fashion; while in the neighbourhood of Glamaig the marscoite is again found associated with granophyre, the gabbro being here scarcely represented. We shall describe the rocks of these two areas in turn, noting in each case first the relations of the rocks as seen in the field and then the more interesting petrographical details. These lead to results which have in some respects more than a local interest.

At the north-western base of *Marsco* the tourist-track up Glen Sligachan crosses a boggy slope, which is conspicuous at a distance as a bright green delta-like area, and is due to a mass of red sand or loam washed down from a deep gully in the hillside (Plate VIII.). On examining the gully, it is seen that this material is derived from a gabbro-like rock which, unlike most of the Skye gabbros, is deeply decayed, and by its decomposition has determined the line of the gully. The rock has been affected by spheroidal weathering, with exfoliation, and the large spheroids themselves are sometimes decayed to the core; so that what looks at first sight like solid gabbro may be seen traversed by numerous rabbit-burrows. This strip of basic rock is usually less than 50 yards wide, though considerably expanded at the lower end, where it is covered by the delta of sand. It runs eastward, with some departures from the straight course, for nearly ¾ mile (*see* sketch-map, Fig. 36); and the way in which it crosses ridge and hollow without deviation, as well as the nature of the boundaries when visible, shows that it is a large dyke-like body with a small inclination to the vertical (Fig. 35). While the greater part of it consists of gabbro (including gabbro partly acidified by impregnation), the northern border is of the rock which we have styled marscoite. On both sides the strip of basic rocks has been attacked by the acid magma and mutual changes have been produced. The acid rocks on the south and north sides seem to belong to distinct intrusions, for the one is granitoid or coarsely granophyric, while the other is fine-textured and porphyritic.

Since an examination of the exposures in this gully illustrates several points of interest in the behaviour of the four rocks involved, we give a transverse section across it in the accompanying figure (35). Beginning on the south side, we find little indication of any abnormality in the acid rock at A. It is a pale granite, often coarsely granophyric, and the exposures give very little evidence of modification due to the absorption of basic material. The actual boundary against the gabbro, where such evidence might be more confidently expected, is not easily examined. The gabbro, however, is very decidedly affected in the fashion already described elsewhere. Even so far away as in the crags overlooking the burn there is a notable degree of acidification, the specific gravity at B being only 2·84. The gabbro in the burn at C and that with spheroidal structure in the slope C D are not very different from the normal type, and have a specific gravity 2·91. Between D and E the rock shows no evidence of acidification; but here it begins to assume

PLATE VIII.

Marsco, from the North-west.

something of a pophyritic aspect by the occurrence of prominent glassy-looking crystals of labradorite. These become more conspicuous, while the rock otherwise becomes progessively finer in grain. There is thus a general resemblance in appearance to the marscoite of other parts of the hill; but the quartz-grains are so far wanting, and even at F, where the porphyritic structure is well pronounced, the rock is thoroughly basic in composition, its specific gravity here being 2·98. Before reaching G, however, quartz-grains have appeared in considerable abundance, and the specific gravity has fallen to 2·86. The rock which forms what must be regarded as the border of the basic strip is a characteristic marscoite. Between this and the porphyritic felsite at H no sharp boundary can be drawn. There is an intermediate zone, a few feet in width, of a hybrid rock resulting from the intermixture of the marscoite

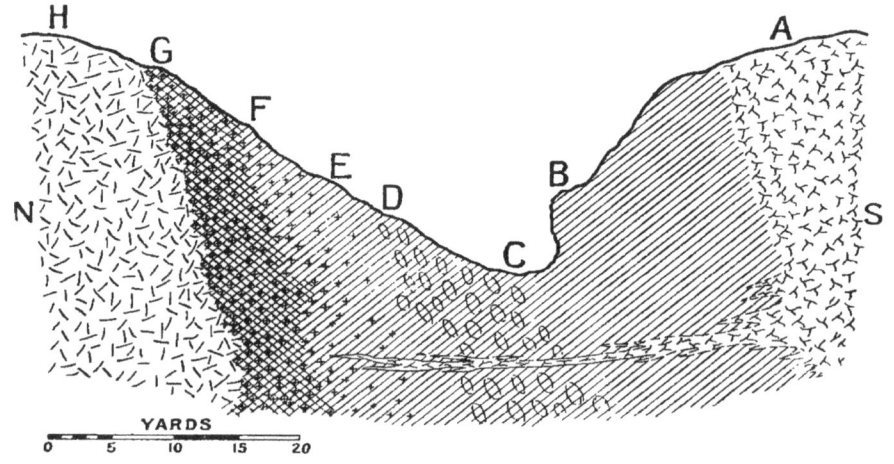

FIG. 35.—Section across the deep gully on the N.W. slope of Marsco. Explanation in the text. K is granite of pegmatoid and gneissic structure veining the gabbro as exposed in the bed of the stream a little lower down. Its connection with the granite to the south is only conjectural.

and the felsite. The rock of this zone is of grey colour, with a rather fine-grained ground enclosing porphyritic felspars and quartz-grains. Its heterogeneous origin is manifest to the eye in a curiously patchy appearance, darker and lighter portions being in some places rather sharply separated and in other places shading into one another. The darker and ligher patches, which may be well displayed in a hand-specimen, represent the marscoite and the felsite respectively; but, even where they are most distinct, it is certain that the one has been partly acidified and the other partly basified. Admixture has thus taken place both by bodily intermingling and by diffusion, and it can scarcely be doubted that the two rocks represented were in a partially fluid state at the same time. The relations between the marscoite and the felsite on the north side of the gully thus differ in some respects from those between the gabbro and the granite on the south side.

Following the strip of basic rock eastward from the head of the gully, we find that the marscoite on the northern border is not to be traced continuously. After disappearing, however, it reappears near the eastern end of the strip, being here at some little distance from the edge of the gabbro and wholly enveloped in the acid rock, as shown in the sketch-map (Fig. 36). This is enough to show, what is elsewhere sufficiently evident, that the marscoite is not merely a modification *in situ* of the gabbro, but represents a distinct act of intrusion. We shall see that this rock is everywhere younger than the gabbro, but older than the acid rocks. The only place where it has been observed clearly to graduate into the gabbro is in the gully already described, and there we must suppose that the marscoite was intruded along the edge of the gabbro while that rock was still in a fluid condition. In other places the two have been divided by a more decided, though probably only a short, interval. In the eastern portion of the gabbro strip the relations of this rock to the granite are well seen. The acid rock sends numerous veins into the gabbro, as well as impregnating it on a minute scale. Moreover the rock bordering the gabbro on its south side is for some distance rich in xenoliths and xenocrysts derived from the gabbro and in process of dissolution. It is here rather a granophyre than a granite, but evidently richer than is normal in the ferro-magnesian elements.

A little farther south is another but smaller strip of basic rock, running S.S.E. along the west side of Coire nan Laogh. Its eastern side is a dyke-like strip of marscoite, up to 50 feet in width; and in contact with this on its west side is gabbro, which, however, is of irregular width, and does not extend to the northern extremity of the strip. This illustrates a point which is elsewhere noticeable on Marsco, viz. that, except in the gully first noticed, the gabbro has been more readily attacked by the acid magma than the marscoite; so that, where the latter rock intervenes, it has to some extent protected the former. Another small enclosed strip of basic rock occurs further west, near the precipice named Fiaclan Dearg. This is for the most part of gabbro, much modified by the acid magma and having in places a rather ill-defined boundary. Northward, however, a dyke-like strip of marscoite comes on on the western or lower side of the gabbro, and continues beyond it, as shown in the sketch-map (Fig. 36). The boundary of the marscoite is sharply marked, and without close examination it might pass for a dyke cutting the granite.

The largest of the enclosed strips of gabbro is that which takes a curved course, more than $1\frac{1}{2}$ mile in length, to the east of the summit, and may be traced as far as the burn in Coire na Seilg. Here again the acid rocks to the north and south are different, the one being fine-textured and porphyritic, the other coarse and granophyric to granitoid in structure. This seems to indicate that the basic rock has not been enveloped by a single acid intrusion but caught between two distinct intrusions. The

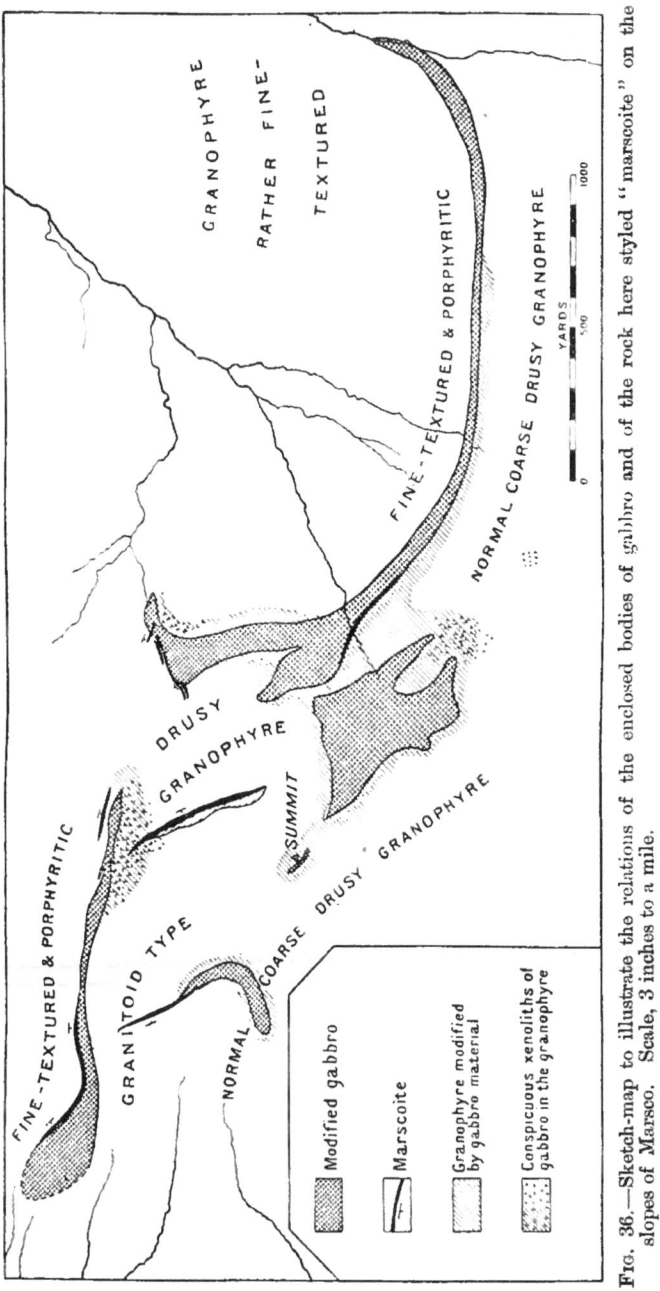

FIG. 36.—Sketch-map to illustrate the relations of the enclosed bodies of gabbro and of the rock here styled "marscoite" on the slopes of Marsco. Scale, 3 inches to a mile.

northern part of the strip is irregularly expanded, and terminates northward at a burn which runs down to Allt Mam a' Phobuill, the gabbro being bordered here by a dyke-like strip of marscoite. Following the strip of gabbro where it turns south-eastward, we find marscoite again on the south-western border; but this dies out after about 300 yards, leaving the gabbro in contact with the drusy coarse granophyre, which assumes a dark colour near the junction. This relation continues eastward, as the gabbro strip, with a width usually of 30 or 40 yards, runs up to Druim Eadar da Choire and over to Coire na Seilg. Throughout this stretch the coarse granophyre to the south is manifestly modified by basic material taken up from the gabbro, but the porphyritic felsite to the north shows little sign of such modification. The rock which, for the purpose of describing the field-relations, we are calling gabbro, is in this part very different from a normal gabbro, and increasingly so eastward. It has here become so impregnated with the acid magma as to approach petrographically rather to a granite, and a specimen from the ridge of Druim Eadar da Choire gives a specific gravity only 2·75. Here, as in the locality first described, the rock is in great part decomposed to a reddish sand, and the spheroidal weathering formerly noted also reappears at several places on the line of this long strip.

These long narrow strips of gabbro seem to have had, prior to the invasion of the acid magma, the general nature of large dykes intersecting rocks of which no trace is now to be seen. We have alluded to them in a former chapter as probably representing some of the feeders of the large gabbro laccolite of the Cuillins. This latter has, in this immediate neighbourhood, been removed by erosion; but a relic of it seems to be represented by another patch of gabbro situated on the main ridge of Marsco itself, to the south-east of the summit (Figs. 27 and 36), and having evidently the sheet-like, not the dyke-like, habit. There is no rock of the marscoite type in this place. The gabbro has very evidently been attacked and partially corroded by the acid magma, and for some distance below it on all sides the coarse drusy granophyre is enriched in the darker and more basic elements, isolated xenoliths of gabbro in an advanced stage of dissolution being detected in places for at least 500 yards farther along the south-east ridge. This outlying sheet of modified gabbro on the summit-ridge of Marsco may with much probability be taken to represent the base of the great laccolite. Prolonged for about a mile southward it would just miss the top of the lower granite hill Ruadh Stac (see Fig. 27), and it is worthy of note that on the eastern shoulder of this hill the granite contains abundant little half-digested xenoliths of gabbro. On the north-western slope of Ruadh Stac a small patch of gabbro has been mapped, which by its low specific gravity (2·82) gives evidence of a certain degree of acidification, and others, not more closely examined, occur at two or three places in the granite of this part of the district.

Summarily, the chief igneous rocks of Marsco fall under three heads, the gabbro, the marscoite, and the acid rocks; and these were intruded in order as named. The gabbro was the earliest, and existed in the form of large dyke-like bodies, doubtless more continuous than at present and of greater and more constant width. The marscoite was intruded along the border of the gabbro in numerous places, and this also had the dyke-habit. Further, it is not improbable that the acid rocks were also intruded in the first place after the fashion of dykes, following still the old channels; but the overwhelming volume of the acid magma which was eventually forced up has obliterated the evidence on this point, and further has left only much corroded relics of the older basic rocks. The nature of the mutual reactions which have taken place among the several rocks indicates that they were intruded in somewhat rapid succession, and even in certain places that one was not completely solidified before it was invaded by another. Finally, if the several rocks were forced up along the same channels, with only brief intervals of time, we may infer that they were very closely connected in origin. Further light is thrown on some of these considerations by the petrographical study of the rocks.

Taking these peculiar rocks of Marsco in order, we shall note first the petrographical evidence of the *impregnation and internal fusion of the gabbro by the acid magma*. A good example of an early stage of the process comes from the south-eastern ridge of the hill, at about 600 yards from the summit-cairn. It is a dark crystalline rock very like many examples of the medium-grained normal gabbros of the Cuillins. The only suggestive feature on the hand-specimen is the presence of a few flakes of brown mica, a mineral rarely if ever found in our gabbros save in connection with reactions between them and other igneous rocks. The specific gravity is 2·92. A thin slice [8965] shows nevertheless some noteworthy points. The felspar is a labradorite, giving extinction-angles up to 30° in sections perpendicular to the albite-lamellæ. Except that it is unusually clear, a common incident of thermal metamorphism, it resembles the felspar of the normal gabbros. The pale augite is also quite normal, but has been converted in small part into a light-green hornblende. There are also the usual irregular grains of opaque iron-ore, and little hexagonal prisms of apatite are locally present. There are, however, other constituents not proper to the gabbros; viz. some interstitial quartz, little crystals of brown hornblende, and flakes of deep-brown mica, the last chiefly surrounding the iron-ore grains. The brown silicate-minerals are partly idiomorphic, but in places their relation to the quartz is such as to prove that they belong to the same stage as that mineral. It cannot be doubted that these three are the results of reactions consequent upon a certain permeation of the gabbro by the acid magma.

Rocks similar to that just described occur at other spots on the ridge and in the gully on the north-west face of the hill. The next specimen, taken from the last-named place, illustrates a further stage of modification of the gabbro. To the eye it looks very like the preceding, though perhaps a little richer in the felspathic constituent. A slice (Pl. XX., Fig. 1) shows some points of difference. Apatite is rather plentiful—a characteristic of these Marsco gabbros as compared with the generality of those in the district. Some of the original augite, very pale brown in colour, still remains, but the plates seem to be breaking up, and most of the augite in the slide is in pale greenish grains similar to those in the acid rocks. The brown hornblende and brown mica are more abundant than before, and so too is the interstitial quartz, which has become quite an important constituent. Further, the felspars show a considerable difference. Some large crystals indeed remain, with all the characters of the ordinary felspar, though clarified, but most of the felspar is in smaller crystals evidently of new formation. They are in the main oligoclase-andesine, but they are strongly zoned, and the outermost zones are of a thoroughly acid variety. The magnetite is in small crystal-grains, and its relation to the new-formed augite proves that it is recrystallised.

The extreme result of the invasion of the gabbro by the acid magma is well illustrated by the eastern part of the longest enclosed strip, where it crosses Druim Eadar da Choire. It is pretty sharply distinguished from the granophyre on either side of it, especially by its deeply weathered condition, which causes a marked dip in the ridge and a deep gully on each slope. Its geological relations, and its continuity with undoubted gabbro to the west, prove clearly that it represents an enclosed strip of that rock; but, taken by itself, there is nothing in its petrographical characters that would suggest referring it to the gabbro family, and it corresponds in composition much more nearly with a granite. Like these hybrid rocks in general, it does not fall under any normal rock type. Mineralogically, it has too little quartz for a granite and too much of the ferro-magnesian minerals for a quartz-syenite, while the nature of the felspathic elements separates it from the quartz-diorites. A fresh specimen is a medium-grained crystalline rock of specific gravity 2·75. It has a mottled black and white aspect suggestive in itself of admixture. A slice [7133] shows that the dominant coloured mineral is a green hornblende, but much of this is clearly derived from a pale augite, kernels of which still remain. Brown mica occurs in subordinate amount, partly intergrown with the augite. There are grains of magnetite and a few little prisms of apatite, while a more unexpected constituent is zircon in small pyramids and prisms. The felspar is mostly an oligoclase with very low extinction-angles; but there is also orthoclase, which shows some degree of zonary banding between crossed nicols. There is no micrographic structure here, the quartz being simply the latest product of crystallisation.

Such rocks as the specimen just described illustrate in a striking way the extent to which interchange of material may be carried between an enclosed strip of gabbro and an enveloping granitic magma without notably impairing the individuality of the former as a rock-body with well-defined boundaries. The same thing is constantly observable as between xenoliths and their matrix, even when viewed microscopically. Such facts go far to negative the assumption made by some petrologists that the viscosity of rock-magmas must be a serious check upon diffusion. In the case of our rocks it is clear that diffusion proceeded with great freedom when intermixture by flowing was not possible, and when dense inclusions were not able to sink in a lighter medium. A rock comparable in acidity and in density with that last described might be made by fusing together about one part of gabbro with two of granite, but it is not likely that the actual composition of the rock can be represented in this crude fashion. There has been free diffusion, and, as we shall see in the case of the xenolithic granophyres to be described next, the several constituents of the rocks involved did not diffuse with equal facility. If in the laboratory we fuse together two rocks of known composition in known proportions, we can calculate the composition of the resulting product; but the conditions which make this possible—viz., the isolation of the materials in a crucible and the reduction to a homogenous condition of everything within that circumscribed space—are conditions not realised in nature. The processes which have operated in the cases of the Kilchrist and Marsco rocks were of a less simple kind, mere admixture being supplemented by diffusion. The resulting hybrid rocks in such a case are thus only in a general sense intermediate in composition between the two parent rocks, and may be abnormal in comparison with any ordinary igneous rocks formed from a single magma. In other words, the series consisting of two extreme rock-types and the various hybrid rocks which they have generated will not in general be a "linear" series as regards chemical composition.

We proceed to notice the *modification experienced by the granophyre* near the gabbro strips of Marsco in consequence of the *incorporation of basic material* in its substance. As seen in the field, the rocks vary from the normal drusy granophyre of the district [8967], or in places a granitoid variety, to an extremely dark type, obviously much enriched in the ferro-magnesian minerals. Specimens but little modified show evident xenoliths in the form of little patches, rarely an inch in diameter, not very sharply defined against their matrix. These little patches are evidently richer in hornblende and other dark minerals than the surrounding matrix, and the felspar in them usually appears dead-white instead of the yellowish tint common in the granophyres. The indications of xenoliths are often less apparent in specimens of the darker, more modified rocks, but there is still a certain mottled aspect due to ill-defined patches of darker and lighter tints, respectively richer and poorer in the dark constituents.

In the thin slices prepared from various examples it is found that none of the principal constituents of the gabbro can be recognised as surviving: the xenoliths, though preserving sufficient individuality to indicate their approximate outlines, are represented entirely, or almost entirely, by new-formed minerals. The change is not a mere metamorphic one, but one of substance, for the new minerals include alkali-felspars and quartz. The xenoliths are in fact pseudomorphed by a relatively basic granophyre, and there must have been both addition and subtraction of material.

The only original mineral of the gabbro which has possibly survived is the apatite, with perhaps some part of the iron-ore. Apatite is constantly found in the rocks, and sometimes rather abundantly; but to what extent it is derived from destroyed gabbro it is not easy to decide. In some part, however, the apatite in these rocks must have belonged to the gabbro. One specimen sliced [7554] shows dark patches about $\frac{1}{2}$ inch in diameter enclosed, without a very sharp boundary, in rock with the characters of a normal granite. These patches are not only much richer in hornblende, relatively to felspars and quartz, than the matrix, but contain also abundant apatite and magnetite, which are wanting outside the patches.

As regards the ferro-magnesian minerals, it is very noticeable that augite, which is usually well represented and often predominant among the normal granophyres of the district, is here subordinate or entirely absent. Green hornblende is constantly the dominant mineral of this group, both within the altered xenoliths and in the interspaces between them, and it is sometimes accompanied by brown biotite (Plate XX., Fig. 3). Much of the hornblende is idiomorphic, though without good crystal-forms, and it has clearly crystallised as such from fusion. In addition there may be patchy aggregates of hornblende, and perhaps biotite, with finely granular magnetite, which seem to replace augite [8694]; and indeed the gradual conversion of augite to green hornblende with magnetite granules can sometimes be observed in various stages [7550]. The hornblende thus arises in two distinct ways, and the same is true of the magnetite. Indeed this latter mineral is perhaps of three kinds, for in addition to little octahedra evidently crystallised from the basified granophyre magma and clusters of granules formed at the expense of augite, there are sometimes larger irregular grains which may be derived almost intact from the gabbro.

Both plagioclase and orthoclase are always present, but the former predominates, at least in those rocks which are much modified from the normal granophyre type. It is oligoclase; but occasionally there are also a few crystals which give higher extinction-angles, and seem to be andesine. Quartz is always well represented, though usually in notably less amount than in the normal granophyres. It builds irregular grains or enters into micrographic intergrowths, the structure of the rocks (granitoid or more commonly granophyric) presenting in this respect no peculiarity.

It is interesting to enquire what proportion of gabbro substance has actually been taken up by the acid magma. The crowded dark patches seen in some of the rocks give, no doubt, an exaggerated impression of the amount of foreign material present, for these patches have not the composition of gabbro. They have been permeated by the acid magma, and the basic material abstracted from them may have been diffused through a considerably larger volume than that of the visibly xenolithic rock. A specimen [8694] from the south-east ridge of Marsco was examined by Dr Pollard, who found it to contain 64·72 per cent. of silica and 2·98 per cent. of lime. This was an average example of the dark basified granophyres. We may compare it with a mixture of 23·5 per cent of gabbro and 76·5 of granophyre, taking the figures for these from analyses already given :—

	Silica.	Lime.	Sp. grav.
Gabbro - - -	46·39	15·29	2·85
Granophyre - - -	70·34	1·24	2·66
Calculated mixture -	64·71	4·54	2·70
Dark granophyre (found)	64·72	2·98	2·73

The discrepancy here as regards lime can scarcely be accounted for by the variable composition of the gabbro and granophyre of the district, and we must suppose that the different constituents (such as silica and lime) diffuse through the magma in different degrees. We may, however, conclude that the acid magma has in some places taken up something like one-third of its mass of material derived from the gabbro. Some of these dark basified granophyres, indeed, cannot be much less basic than the extreme results of acidification in those rocks which are, from the point of view of their geological relations, included above as acidified gabbros.

A remark should be made concerning the drusy structure of the modified granophyres of Marsco. This structure, of very general occurrence in most parts of the Red Hills, is especially well displayed on Marsco ; and in those granophyres which enclose evident xenoliths, or preserve the outlines of destroyed xenoliths, the druses often seem to stand in relation to the xenoliths. It may be supposed that the druses in this case have been rather of the nature of gas- and steam- cavities, and that the solid or quasi-solid fragments distributed through the magma have served as starting-points for the growth of bubbles. The association of druses of various kinds, usually of small size, with xenoliths is a very general phenomenon, as appears clearly in the literature of the subject.

Before leaving the acid rocks of Marsco, it should be remarked that in several places pegmatoid veins and streaks traverse the gabbro or the marscoite for a short distance from the junction with the granophyre. These are well seen in the gabbro about 750 or 800 yards east of the summit, and again at the base of the gabbro-sheet in a little ravine running down towards Coire nan Bruadaran. At both these places large crystals of bronzy-looking mica are conspicuous. Pegmatite-veins with a marked gneissic banding intersect the gabbro of the gully on the north-west slope. All these rocks are of very coarse texture, the individual crystals of quartz, orthoclase, and oligoclase, which make up the bulk of the veins, ranging up to an inch in diameter, and the flakes of brown mica being sometimes nearly as large. Lustrous black crystals of hornblende, brown and strongly pleochroic in a thin slice, are of smaller dimensions, and have good crystal-forms, with the customary habit. A few prisms of apatite are also present [8052]. There is little or no approach to graphic intergrowth in these pegmatite veins. Another feature is that they do not, like the granophyre itself, take up any appreciable amount of extraneous material.

Lastly we have to notice the characters of the peculiar rock which we have for convenience named *marscoite*. We have seen that it holds an intermediate place, as regards epoch of intrusion as well as in actual situation, between the gabbro and the granite. It is intermediate between them also to some extent in composition, but no analysis has been made of it.

The usual type is a dark finely crystalline rock, enclosing glassy-looking crystals of finely striated felspar, $\frac{1}{4}$ to $\frac{1}{2}$ inch long. Small grains of quartz are visible in places. There also occur, more sparingly and less uniformly distributed, dull white xenocrysts of felspar, contrasting with the fresh phenocrysts, and exceptionally little aggregates of felspar crystals and quartz which may be regarded as partially digested xenoliths. An average specimen of the rock gave the specific gravity 2·82. In a slice [7858] the felspar phenocrysts are quite clear. They have a markedly tabular habit parallel to the brachypinacoid, with a breadth of sometimes less than $\frac{1}{50}$ inch, and there is a certain degree of rounding of the angles. These crystals are of medium labradorite (extinction-angle 38°), with carlsbad, albite, and pericline twinning. The quartz-grains, which occur plentifully, are about $\frac{1}{20}$ inch in diameter. They show in various stages the rounding and corrosion and the border of granular augite, or usually hornblende, which indicate their extraneous origin. The derived felspars, partly orthoclase, are also somewhat corroded and otherwise altered by the basic magma in which they have been enveloped.

The general mass of the rock consists chiefly of greenish brown hornblende and felspar. The hornblende is partly in crystal-grains, partly in elongated narrow prisms enclosing granular magnetite. In the latter form it seems to be derived from augite, some of which mineral still remains, and the process of conversion is seen in some places in the slice (Pl. XXI., Fig 2). Besides the finely granular magnetite, there are little octahedra, doubtless crystallised from fusion. The felspar is partly in little striated prisms, partly in rather shapeless grains, some untwinned. Oligoclase is certainly present, in addition to a more basic plagioclase, and some of the grains may be of orthoclase. Further there is a certain amount of quartz in clear interstitial grains. A striking feature of the rock is the immense number of minute needles of apatite which it contains.

It appears from this description that the marscoite represents a basic magma which has taken up granitic material, and, by the partial absorption of this, become in some measure acidified. The quartz and acid felspars have not been derived directly from the contiguous acid rocks, or at least this cannot be the general explanation of their presence; but it is none the less noticeable in some occurrences that these quasi-foreign elements become more abundant on the side neighbouring the acid rock. A like peculiarity will be observed below in the marscoite of the Glamaig neighbourhood. The section in the deep gully (Fig. 35) exemplifies this fact. A specimen from this place, but taken towards the gabbro, shows on the other hand the transition from marscoite to gabbro which we have already pointed out. It is notably denser than the ordinary marscoite, having a specific gravity 2·94. A slice [7859] shows that quartz-grains occur more sparingly than before, and are more corroded, having always a relatively broad border composed of augite-grains with some hornblende. Of the two coloured silicates the pale yellowish brown augite is in this slice the dominant one, though the greenish-brown hornblende also occurs. They build larger crystal-grains than before, and the same is true of the felspar, which shows albite and carlsbad, and rarely pericline, twinning. From its extinction-angles it seems to be an acid labradorite or andesine-labradorite. Interstitial grains of quartz are still found, though in somewhat less amount than before. In other respects, including the great profusion of fine apatite-needles, this slide resembles the other. The close resemblance between the labradorite phenocrysts in the marscoite and the crystals of the same mineral in the gabbro suggests a like origin for both; but further light is thrown upon this question by the phenomena, which we next proceed to describe, in the neighbourhood of Glamaig.

The peculiar rocks now to be discussed are exposed on *Glamaig* itself; in the burn, named Allt Daraich, to the south-west, which drains Coire na Sgairde; and at the termination of the ridge Druim na Ruaige on the opposite side of the corrie. This ridge is a spur from Beinn Dearg Mheadhonach, and consists of the ordinary granite, often granophyric, which forms so much of the Red Hills. At its northern end, however, the smooth flowing outline of the ridge is broken by a wart-like excrescence named Sròn a' Bhealain, which is a prominent object in the view from Sligachan. The prominence is caused by a sheet-like mass of marscoite, 200 to 250 feet thick, with a northerly dip of about 20°, which covers the northern face of the ridge and rises into a knoll nearly 1500 feet above sea-level (Fig. 37). The base of the sheet is invaded by the underlying coarse granophyre, which sends little tongues obliquely into the marscoite; and the sheet itself is seen to be two-fold, with a parting along which the acid magma has found access. Both in this parting and below the base of the sheet the acid rock is crowded with partially digested xenoliths of the marscoite, usually from half an inch to two or three inches in diameter and of ovoid shape. These dark spots in a lighter matrix give the rock a very striking appearance, and we shall speak of it for convenience as the "spotted granophyre" (see Fig. 41, below). In places the little dark patches become merged in their matrix, so that their outlines are almost or quite obliterated, and we have merely a very dark partly basified granophyre, representing the admixture of marscoite with the normal acid rock.

Farther north, in the bed of Allt Daraich, we find some relics of marscoite and a considerable quantity of the spotted and dark granophyres, the whole probably representing the prolongation of the Sròn a' Bhealain sheet (see Fig. 38). Coming to Glamaig itself, we cross two sheets of marscoite on the ascent from Bealach na Sgairde to the summit. Each of these in turn, for some distance separates the granophyre of the lower part of Marsco from the overlying basaltic lavas, the boundary between granophyre and basalt ascending by steps, each of which corresponds with a sheet of marscoite. These sheets, however, continue as sills in the basalt, and may also be traced for some distance in the granophyre, by which they have been attacked and corroded. These relations are illustrated in Figures 38 and 39. Another sheet of marscoite is seen for 300 or 400 yards on the west slope of the hill, in this case at the lower boundary of the granophyre against the basalts. In all cases the granophyre near its junction with the marscoite has taken up abundant débris of that rock, and

FIG. 37.—Outlines of Glamaig and Beinn Dearg, seen from the road a mile north of Sligachan. The broken north face of Glamaig, on the extreme left, consists largely of metamorphosed basaltic lavas. Beinn Dearg illustrates the characteristic rounded outlines of the granite hills, while, in strong contrast with this, the abrupt knoll of Sròn a' Bhealain is seen towards the right of the sketch.

when a sheet of marscoite comes to an end in the granophyre, its course can still be traced for some distance by a band of xenolithic and basified rocks.

The interpretation of these relations is, to a certain point, sufficiently evident. The marscoite, apart from subsequent modifications due to the acid magma, represents a distinct rock, which was intruded in the form of sills at several horizons in the basaltic lavas. An invasion of acid magma, of much greater volume, has followed, and this has at first found its easiest channel along the surfaces of the sills of marscoite. Where guided by these, it has often kept for some distance to one horizon, but elsewhere it has broken across irregularly. On the south-western slope of Glamaig, as shown on the map and in Fig. 39, it has broken across by successive steps from one sill to another. This irregularity of behaviour was doubtless facilitated by the destructive action which the acid magma exercised upon the basic sills, disintegrating and partially dissolving their substance. Such action was most effective when the acid magma had access to both the upper and

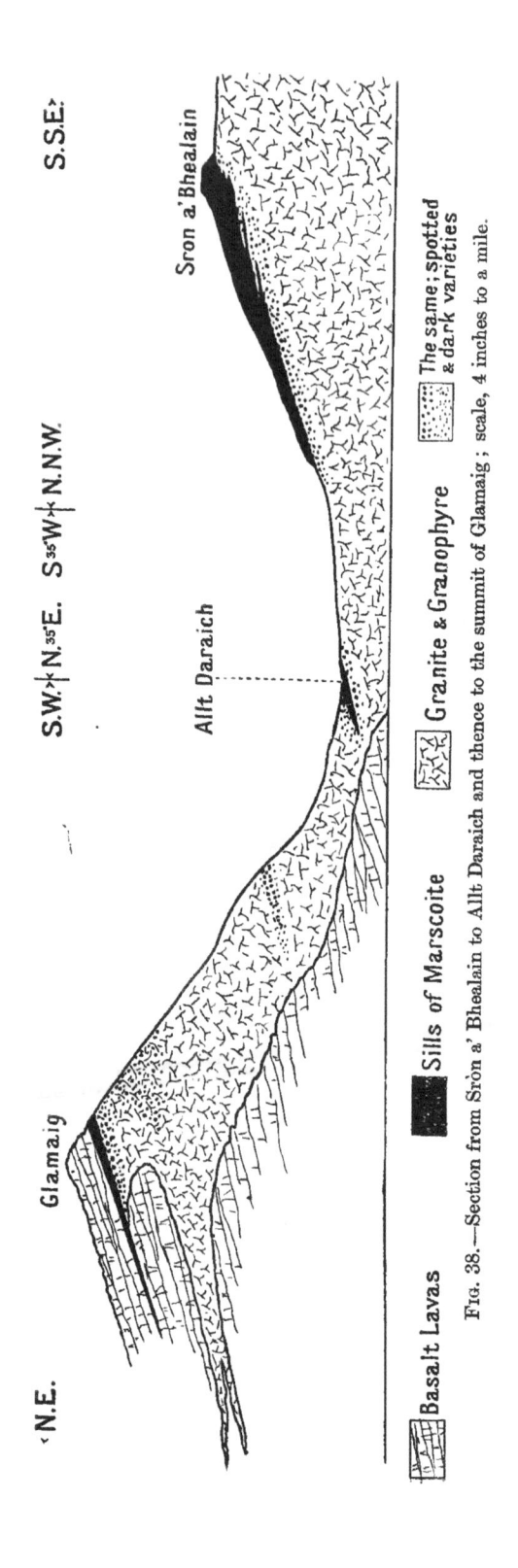

FIG. 38.—Section from Srón a' Bhealain to Allt Daraich and thence to the summit of Glamaig; scale, 4 inches to a mile.

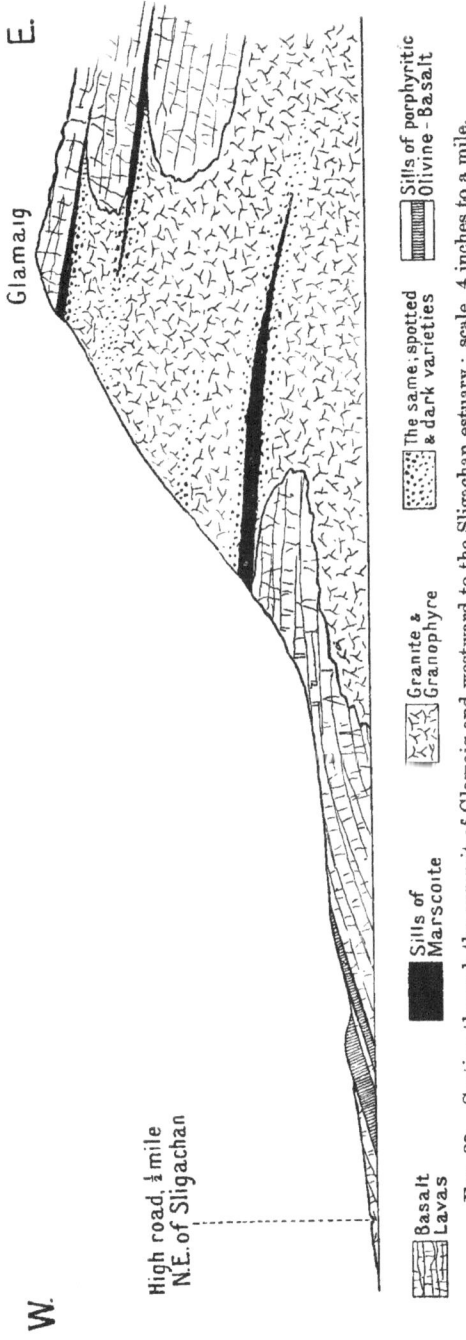

FIG. 39.—Section through the summit of Glamaig and westward to the Sligachan estuary; scale, ¼ inches to a mile.

the lower surfaces of a marscoite sill, and so a sill, once enveloped by the granophyre, soon comes to an end, at least as a continuous body. The sill of Sròn a' Bhealain, which has probably been completely enveloped, owes its preservation to its exceptional thickness. We proceed to discuss the petrographical characters of the various associated rock-types.

The *marscoite* of these sill-formed intrusions is in all essentials closely comparable with that which forms the dyke-like bodies on Marsco. It is on the whole more modified in the sense of acidification, but it varies in this respect in the several sheets and in different parts of the same sheet. There are abundant phenocrysts of labradorite, usually fresh and glassy-looking, up to ½ inch or more in length. Very abundant also are the rounded quartz-grains, always with a border of imperfect crystals and grains of green hornblende, or of augite in process of transformation to hornblende. These hornblende-crystals often project for a short distance into the quartz-grain, proving that the marginal portion of the latter is of new formation. The rocks also enclose occasional xenocrysts of orthoclase, turbid and altered, and exceptionally groups of these, with some quartz, which may perhaps be regarded as little xenoliths of granite in an advanced stage of dissolution.

In the ground-mass the relative proportions of brownish-green hornblende and pale augite vary considerably; but, since some part of the hornblende is certainly pseudomorphic after augite, this difference is perhaps not significant. The felspar, in little imperfect prisms or in irregular crystal-grains, is mostly of a striated variety with low extinction-angles, but some is untwinned. Apparently the dominant kind is near oligoclase or oligoclase-andesine in composition, but orthoclase sometimes occurs in addition. There is a variable and sometimes considerable amount of interstitial quartz. Magnetite and little needles of apatite occur abundantly.

The marscoite, as stated, shows a certain range of composition; and this is most easily studied in the thick sheet of Sròn a' Bhealain. Two specimens from the upper part of the sheet (as exposed) gave specific gravities 2·80 and 2·81, and two from the lower part 2·73 and 2·74. Comparison of thin slices [7546, 7547, 7549] shows that the latter rocks are decidedly more acid than the former, being richer in enclosed quartz-grains and in interstitial quartz. It appears then that, although the derived acid material in the marscoite cannot be ascribed, at least in the main, to the contiguous acid rock, this sheet does grow more acid towards its junction with the granophyre. A comparison between the marscoites of Marsco and those of the neighbourhood of Glamaig is suggestive in the same connection. The latter, which are much more intimately invaded by the granophyre, are also as a whole decidedly more acid, the variety which prevails in the Marsco occurrences being found here only in the interior of the thick sheet of Sròn a' Bhealain. The fact that even in this case the rock contains not only interstitial quartz, but quartz-grains and xenocrysts of acid felspars, shows, nevertheless, that the marscoite had, in the main, acquired its peculiar characters prior to its intrusion.

We conclude then that the marscoite as intruded represented an originally basic magma modified by the inclusion of granitic material, relics of which still remain as xenocrysts. This process, while prior to the intrusion, was probably posterior to the epoch of the labradorite phenocrysts : it is at least difficult to conceive these crystallising from the partially acidified magma, and they never enclose any of the derived elements. If some portion of the magma had been intruded prior to the absorption of granitic material which converted it to marscoite, it would presumably have given rise to ordinary basic rocks containing phenocrysts of labradorite. It is not improbable that such intrusions are actually represented in the neighbourhood. On the moorland near the west base of Glamaig two or three sills occur in the basalts, coming down to the high-road about ½ mile N.E. of Sligachan (see Fig. 39). We shall see later that the innumerable basic sills of the plateau country, which are of later age than the plutonic intrusions, never approach so near to the granite, and we are thus led to separate these Sligachan sills from the great group and to refer them to an earlier epoch. They are also separated petrographically from the plateau sills by the occurrence in them of abundant large phenocrysts of labradorite, like those in the marscoite. They are thoroughly basic rocks, with a considerable amount of olivine represented by pseudomorphs. Being found in such close proximity to the marscoite sheets of Glamaig, and unknown elsewhere, these porphyritic sills may not improbably represent an early intrusion of that basic magma which was subsequently converted to marscoite by taking up acid material.

Another point worthy of notice is the possible significance of the large crystals of labradorite in the marscoite. At one place on Marsco we remarked an unusually intimate association of gabbro and marscoite, with no sharp division between them, and we pointed out in that connection the resemblance between the labradorite crystals in the two rocks which there graduate into one another. Gabbro is not represented by distinct intrusions among the rocks of Glamaig; but in one place it is found in the form of irregular patches enveloped in the marscoite. This occurrence is in the bed of Allt Daraich, and the relations at this place are shown in Fig. 40. The locality is at a considerable distance from the main area of gabbro ; but it is noteworthy, and perhaps significant, that a small patch of that rock is intruded among the lavas to the west of Glamaig in actual contact with the largest of the porphyritic basalt sills mentioned in the preceding paragraph. The gabbro enclosed in the marscoite of Allt Daraich is seen at a point about 150 yards below the infall of Allt Bealach na Sgairde. The largest patch, in so far as it is exposed, is about 20 feet across and of very irregular outline. It is intimately penetrated by tongues and veins of the surrounding marscoite, and there are detached portions of gabbro in the latter, one large enough to be shown in the accompanying ground-plan.

Two small patches of gabbro lower down in the stream have probably also been enclosed in the marscoite, though they are now surrounded by dark basified granophyre of the spotted or xenolithic kind. The gabbro contains no quartz, and is of quite normal characters, though, like the Marsco gabbros, somewhat richer in apatite than is usual in rocks of this family in Skye. The point to which we would direct special attention is that in the marscoite surrounding the gabbro patches the labradorite phenocrysts show a tendency to aggregate in clusters. So marked is this tendency in places that, on the smooth channel of the burn, little areas, a few inches across, crowded with crystals, appear sharply defined against the neighbouring rock, which contains the crystals only sparingly. It is impossible on the ground to draw any absolute distinction between these portions rich in crystals of labradorite and undoubted xenoliths detached from the neighbouring large patch of gabbro; and the conclusion seems to be forced upon us that the labradorite crystals in the marscoite are derived from the gabbro.

If this last conclusion is to be applied to the marscoites of Marsco

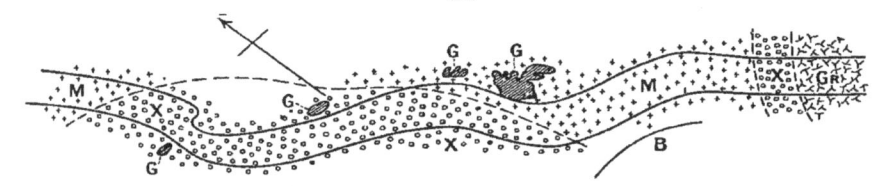

Fig. 40.—Ground-plan of part of Allt Daraich, near Sligachan.

GR. Coarse granophyre or granophyric granite of normal type.
M. Marscoite.
X. Xenolithic ("spotted") granophyre.
G. Gabbro, enclosed patches.
B. Amygdaloidal basalt (lava).

and Glamaig as a whole, it is not, however, to be supposed that the labradorite crystals in these rocks have in general come from the disintegration of solid gabbro. Rather should we suppose that, after the intrusion of the gabbros of the Cuillins, crystallisation began under intratelluric conditions in an unexhausted portion of the gabbro-magma, and labradorite was formed, a subsequent modification of the residual magma due to the addition of granitic material giving rise to the marscoite. If in places intratelluric crystallisation had already proceeded so far as to form actual gabbro, clots or patches of this might be caught up in the marscoite and so intruded with it; but this seems to have been exceptional.

We have still to describe the modification in the granophyre of Glamaig due to the inclusion of marscoite xenoliths in the magma. Everywhere in the vicinity of the marscoite sills effects of this kind are shown in various stages in the acid rocks. The only exception is presented by certain pegmatite veins and strings which traverse the lower portion of the Sròn a' Bhealain sheet. These, like the similar occurrences on Marsco, show occasionally a banded or gneissic structure. They are very coarse-grained, consisting essentially of crystals of orthoclase, sometimes two or three inches long, enclosing quartz crystals up to $\frac{3}{4}$ inch in diameter. There is no graphic structure on a large scale, but a thin slice shows a delicate micropegmatite fringe surrounding each crystal of quartz, the quartz and felspar of this fringe being continuous with the adjacent crystals of those minerals, respectively. These veins have never taken up basic material.

The *granophyres with partially digested xenoliths of marscoite* are well seen beneath the sheet of the latter rock on Sròn a' Bhealain, and occupy a considerable area on the south-western slopes of Glamaig, but they are perhaps most easily studied in the little patches exposed in the bed of Allt Daraich some 200 yards below

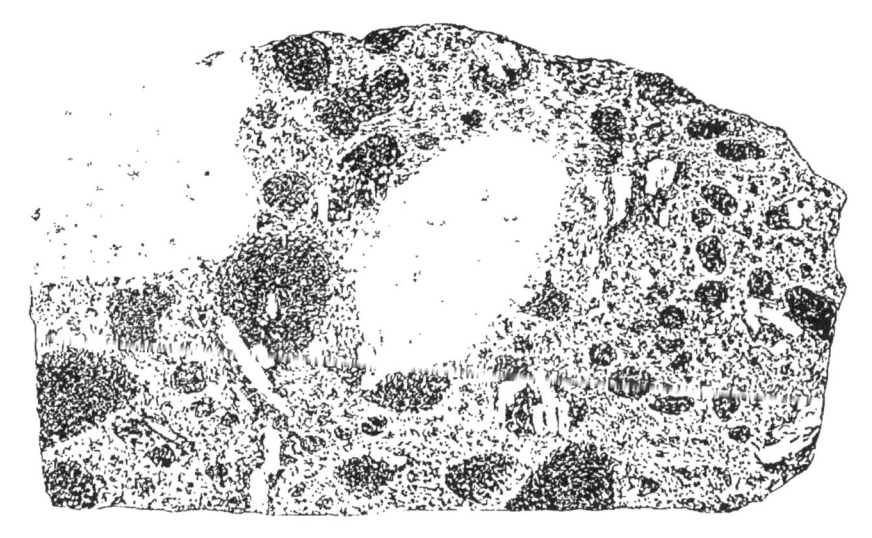

Fig. 41.—Granophyre crowded with xenoliths of marscoite and the débris of these, including released crystals of labradorite; specimen drawn of the natural size; from Allt Daraich, near Sligachan.

the infall of Allt Bealach na Sgàirde. There, with progressive destruction of the enclosed débris, every stage is exhibited down to a dark, almost homogeneous basified granophyre in which the outlines of the xenoliths are lost.

The most usual type is a rock presenting crowded dark patches or spots, of ovoid shape and usually less than an inch in diameter, in a lighter grey matrix (Fig. 41). The phenocrysts of labradorite seem to have resisted the caustic action of the acid magma more successfully than the rest of the marscoite, for they are sometimes seen, with angles but little rounded, projecting from the dark spots into the surrounding matrix. Occasionally they are found quite detached; and this also happens, though it is less easily verified in hand-specimens, with the corroded quartz-grains and sporadic xenocrysts of turbid alkali-felspar. These minerals, which were xenocrysts in the basic rock, thus became what may be styled xenocrysts of the second order, i.e. twice derived, in the granophyre. An average specimen of the spotted rock gave the specific gravity 2·76, while a part of one of the dark spots, separated from the matrix, gave 2·806.

In thin slices [7551, etc.] the xenoliths of marscoite in these rocks resemble generally the marscoite of the sills. They have, however, a larger proportion of quartz and alkali-felspar in the ground-mass, or at least they are comparable in this respect with the most acid portions of the marscoite sills in immediate proximity to the granophyre. This is doubtless due to injection of the xenoliths by the granophyre magma. It is worthy of note that here, as in the sills, the quartz and alkali-felspar do not assume the form of micropegmatite. There is, as before, an abundance of brownish-green hornblende, often partly idiomorphic, octahedra of magnetite, and little needles of apatite (Plate XXI., Fig. 1). One peculiarity is that the large crystals of labradorite are often cracked and shattered, as if by the heat of the granophyre magma. The paler matrix in which the dark xenoliths are enclosed requires no detailed description, being merely a granophyre richer in hornblende and magnetite than the normal kind.

A transition from the distinctly spotted rocks to the uniformly dark granophyres is illustrated by specimens exhibiting a rather indistinct mottling on a small scale [7548]. This appearance is due to the breaking up of the ovoid xenoliths preparatory to their final dissolution. In a thin slice the darker parts are marked out by the abundance of hornblende and magnetite which they contain. Augite is scarcely found except in rings surrounding xenocrysts of quartz or minute xenoliths of orthoclase and quartz, which are still recognisable. A flake or two of biotite is also present. As regards the felspar and quartz of the ground-mass, there is no appreciable distinction between the darker and the lighter patches of the rock, both alike being now characterised by micropegmatite. Apatite-needles occur in both parts, but are both stouter and more numerous in the darker portions of the slice.

From such rocks as this there is a gradation (often in a very short space) to those in which no heterogeneity is apparent to the eye, and in which the microscope shows that the component elements are uniformly distributed [7550]. They are simply granophyres unduly rich in hornblende, magnetite, and apatite. Part of the last-named mineral seems to have been derived directly from the marscoite, but no other simple xenocrysts of this kind are to be detected. The large crystals of labradorite, already shattered, have broken up as soon as they became isolated in the acid magma, and have been dissolved like the rest. The quartz-grains and crystals of turbid orthoclase, which were found as xenocrysts in the marscoite, remain undestroyed in these dark granophyres as xenocrysts of the second order. We may suppose that minerals proper to acid rocks found themselves in something like chemical equilibrium when again enclosed in an acid magma. The quartz-grains, however, have lost their border of augite or hornblende, and the orthoclase xenocrysts show certain interesting peculiarities. These, when enveloped in the basic magma, had sometimes undergone an incipient breaking up by minute fissures following the cleavages—an effect often noticed by Lacroix and other writers on xenocrysts—; and this rectangular system of fine fissures, not so pronounced as to impair the continuity of the crystal, has subsequently been occupied by newly formed quartz supplied from the granophyre magma.

Phenomena in any close degree comparable with those described about Sròn a' Bhealain and Glamaig have been observed in one other locality only—viz., on the north-eastern slope of Meall a Mhaoil, to the north of Loch Ainort. Here a narrow strip of basaltic lavas is enclosed in the granite, running steeply down towards the coast in an E.S.E. direction. On the southern edge of it a strip or sheet of a basic intrusive rock is interposed between the basalt and the granite, the last-named rock penetrating both the others in the form of small tongues and veins. The basic intrusion is of a rock somewhat similar to that of Sròn a' Bhealain, though of rather coarser grain. It might be matched more closely in the deep gully on Marsco. It has the same porphyritic crystals of labradorite as the typical marscoites, and like them is evidently a basic rock partially acidified; but the slice examined shows no recognisable xenocrysts, the quartz present being wholly of interstitial occurrence. The ferro-magnesian mineral is exclusively hornblende [8980]. The rather fine-grained granophyre in contact with this rock is seen to be in places enriched in hornblende and magnetite, and to enclose little dark patches which must be interpreted as destroyed xenoliths of the marscoite [8981]. This Meall a' Mhaoil occurrence thus reproduces in most essential particulars the peculiar phenomena described near Glamaig, but only on a small scale and with fewer complications.

It is to be observed that the Glamaig rocks are petrographically of more peculiar characters than those described in the earlier parts of this chapter. At Kilchrist and on Marsco hybrid rocks have been produced from gabbro and granite, and they are, as we have shown, essentially abnormal in chemical and mineralogical composition. On Glamaig, however, the intermingling has taken place between marscoite and granite, the former itself a hybrid rock of peculiar composition, and the results are correspondingly complicated. We have here to deal, in short, with hybridism of a second order. On Marsco effects of this kind are to be verified only exceptionally (for instance, between G and H in Fig. 35), the marscoite there not having entered, as a rule, into important reactions with the acid magma.

CHAPTER XII.

Composite Sills and Dykes: General Features.

In the preceding chapter we have seen how in certain places the granite (including granophyre) of the Red Hills enters into remarkable relations with the gabbro (on Marsco) and with sills of a peculiar hybrid basic rock (on Glamaig). We have next to describe somewhat analogous phenomena exhibited in minor intrusions outside the mountain tract. These intrusions take the form partly of composite dykes, partly of composite sheets, which from their regularity and parallelism with the bedding may be termed sills. Some of the composite dykes stand in close relation to the composite sills, and have doubtless been their feeders.

The frequency of multiple basic dykes and sills in Skye shows the strong tendency for later intrusions of the basic magmas to follow channels already selected by earlier intrusions. The tendency to be thus guided is, however, much stronger where an acid magma has been intruded in the neighbourhood of earlier basic dykes and sills. Even the granite bosses show this disposition occasionally. The Beinn an Dubhaich granite, intruded through Cambrian limestones, as we have already remarked, truncates a number of pre-granitic basic dykes. In one or two places about Torran the granite has sent out irregular tongues along these earlier dykes. Such a tongue always clings closely to the side of its dyke, and sends veins into it, but never into the limestone. The acid magma has evidently been guided by these dykes, just as it has been by the marscoite sills on Glamaig. The destructive action of the acid magma on these dykes is much less than in the case of the Glamaig sills, but it is still to be perceived; and it is probable that the facility with which an acid intrusion finds its way along a basic dyke or sheet results in general from a certain amount of reaction between the acid magma and the surface of the basic rock. It is noteworthy that, although the acid magma has sometimes insinuated itself along the side of a single basic dyke or sill, it has more frequently selected the surface of junction of two contiguous dykes or sills. The composite intrusions which include acid members are, as a rule, not merely double but triple or multiple. Moreover, where such a composite dyke or sill includes an acid member with two or more basic ones, the acid rock seldom, if ever, occupies an outside position.

For purposes of description it will be convenient to distinguish among composite intrusions, whether dykes or sills, two main types, *symmetrical* and *unsymmetrical*. The symmetrical type has usually a central member consisting of one kind of rock, flanked on either side by marginal portions consisting of another kind of rock: it may be represented by XYX. More rarely three kinds of rock enter into the complex, the arrangement being then represented by XYZYX. In the other type no such bilateral symmetry exists, and we have such arrangements as XXXYX, XYXYXY, XYZXX, etc.

Since composite dykes and sills, consisting of basic and acid rocks in intimate association, seem to be a characteristic feature of the British Tertiary province, it will be useful to collect here the scattered records of their occurrence. The only examples of which detailed descriptions have yet been published are certain composite dykes in Arran and in County Down, but brief references are numerous in the literature of the region.

Little is to be gleaned from the writings of the earliest observers. Jameson[*] seems to have partially appreciated the nature of the Cir Mhòr dyke in Arran, and gives a fairly clear account of the "stratified veins" at Tormore in the same island; but the complex dykes incidentally noticed by Macculloch[†] in Skye seem to be merely accidental conjunctions. One of the first clear references comes from the Mourne district in Ireland, where in 1835 Patrickson[‡] recorded at Glasdrummon Port a porphyritic acid dyke bounded by two "hornblende" dykes in parallel contact. In 1840 Necker,[§] in cataloguing a number of dykes on the the Arran coast, remarked that each consists in general of a single kind of rock, but noted two exceptions to this rule. One is a "dyke composée" at the foot of "Kidvoe," consisting of pitchstone in the centre, flanked by "argilolite" on both sides, and further flanked by "trap" also on both sides: the other is an assemblage of alternating dykes of greenstone and "porphyre argilolitique," six members in all. Here we have examples of the two types distinguished above, the symmetrical and the unsymmetrical. "Kidvoe" is evidently Cir Mhòr, disguised by transliteration and accidental error, and the dyke in question is that which was briefly described in the following year by Ramsay.[‖] Bryce[¶] observed in 1859 that almost all the dykes of Arran are simple, but "a few, of which the most remarkable are those of Tormore, are composed of parallel bands of different substances." Subsequently[**] he added something to Ramsay's account of the Cir Mhòr occurrence, and both these

---

[*] *Mineralogy of the Scottish Isles*, vol. i., pp. 81, 102-105 : 1800.

[†] *Trans. Geol. Soc.*, vol. iii., Pl. IV., Fig. 2 : 1816. *Description of the Western Islands*, Pl. XVIII., Fig. 1 : 1819.

[‡] "A Descriptive List of the Dykes appearing on the Shore which skirts the Mourne Mountains . . .," *Journ. Geol. Soc. Dubl.*, vol. i. : 1835.

[§] "Documents sur les Dykes de Trap d'une partie de l'Ile d'Arran," *Edin. Phil. Trans.*, vol. xiv., pp. 677-698, Pl. XXIII. : 1840.

[‖] *The Geology of the Island of Arran from Original Survey*, p. 26 : 1841.

[¶] *Geology of Clydesdale and Arran*, pp. 81, 82 : 1859. *Cf.* Zirkel, *Zeits. deuts. geol. Ges.*, vol. xxiii., p. 41, Pl. II., Fig. 6 : 1871 ; and Allport, *Geol. Mag.*, 1872, pp. 5, 541.

[**] *The Geology of Arran and the other Clyde Islands*, p. 164 : 1872.

Arran localities have since been fully described in an important paper by Professor Judd.*

In Ireland composite dykes have been mapped by the Geological Survey and mentioned in the published Memoirs, Professor Hull † noting in particular one at Murphy's Point, County Down, which consists of a 35-ft dyke of greyish " felstone-porphyry " flanked by two 8-ft dykes of basalt. Professor Cole‡ has since given a description of Patrickson's dyke, already mentioned, and has entered into some interesting speculations relative to the interpretation of its phenomena.

The first clear notice of the composite sills of Skye is found in Sir A. Geikie's memoir on " The History of Volcanic Action during the Tertiary Period in the British Isles," published in 1888,§ though the intrusions at Carn Dearg, Suishnish, had attracted notice earlier, as mentioned below (Chap. XXII.). That such sills are not confined to this island seems probable from certain observations of what may prove to be similar cases in Ardnamurchan‖ and Arran,¶ but no detailed account of any of these occurrences has yet appeared.** Sir A. Geikie has, however, furnished some additional information, as regards both dykes and sills of composite habit in Skye, in his later writings.††

A few composite dykes are known on the mainland of Scotland. The Eskdale dyke takes on this character at Wat Carrick, a compact, more or less vitreous rock forming a band 16 to 18 feet broad between two 8-ft bands of dolerite.‡‡ Other dykes of the symmetrical triple kind have been recorded by Mr Symes §§ in the district south of Oban.

Records of composite dykes in extra-British areas are not numerous. The district which presents most analogy in this respect with Skye is undoubtedly the north-western part of the Thüringer Wald. Composite dykes seem to have been observed

* " On Composite Dykes in Arran," *Quart. Journ. Geol. Soc.*, vol. xlix., pp. 536-565, Pl. XIX. : 1893.
† *Explanatory Memoir to accompany Sheets 60, 61, and Part of 71 of the Maps of the Geological Survey of Ireland*, p. 39 : 1881.
‡ " On Derived Crystals in the Basaltic Andesite of Glasdrummon Port, Co. Down," *Sci. Trans. Roy. Dubl. Soc.* (2), vol. v., pp. 239-245, Pl. XXVI. : 1894.
§ *Edin. Phil. Trans.*, vol. xxxv., pp. 21-184 : 1888. See p. 174.
‖ Judd, *Quart. Journ. Geol. Soc*, vol. xxx., p. 271, footnote : 1874.
¶ Corstorphine, *Tscherm. Min. Petr. Mitth.* (N.S.), vol. xiv., pp. 18-23, 29, 30 : 1895. See also Boué, *Essai géologique sur l'Ecosse*, p. 296, Pl. IV., Fig. 20 ; 1820. Delesse, *Ann. des mines* (5), vol. xiii., pp. 349, 350 : 1858.
** Since this was written, the occurrence of composite sills in Arran has been more definitely announced, and some account has also been published of an interesting example in southern Bute, which differs from others in having the basic rock in the middle with acid borders above and below. See *Mem. Geol. Sur. Scot., The Geology of North Arran, etc.*, pp. 98, 99 (W. Gunn) and 114-117 (A. Harker) : 1903.
†† *Quart. Journ. Geol. Soc.*, vol. lii., pp. 393-395 : 1896. *Ancient Volcanoes of Great Britain*, vol, ii., pp. 162, 163, 433, 434 : 1897. See also brief notes in *Ann. Rep. Geol. Sur.* for 1896, pp. 73, 74.
‡‡ Geikie, *Proc. Roy. Phys. Soc. Edin.*, vol. v., pp. 219-253, Pl. V., VI. : 1880. *Ancient Volcanoes of Great Britain*, vol. ii., p. 137.
§§ *Summary of Progress of Geol. Sur.* for 1898, p. 154.

there by J. L. Heim* as early as the end of the eighteenth century, and they have been described in some detail by Senft,† Pringsheim,‡ Weiss,§ and Bücking.∥ All these are of the symmetrical type, usually triple (XYX), sometimes quintuple (XYZYX), and they compare closely with the British examples. The unsymmetrical type (*e.g.* XYXYXY) is, however, also met with in the Thüringer Wald, and has been described by Loretz ¶ and others. Weiss** has remarked among other examples a dyke showing alternations of quartz-porphyry (silica-percentage 69) and porphyry (60), *i.e.*, an association of an acid and an intermediate rock, for which we have found no precise parallel in our own country. On the whole these Thüringian composite dykes, probably of pre-Permian age, show a remarkable correspondence with the Tertiary examples in Skye. The sills are wanting in the foreign area, but this is sufficiently explained by the intrusions there occurring in a tract of granite and gneiss. It cannot be doubted that in the two groups of intrusions here compared, in different areas and of different ages, some factor was operative which in most groups of basic and acid intrusions has been absent.

In the foregoing citations we have expressly excluded all cases in which heterogeneity in a dyke is *manifestly* due to differentiation subsequent to injection, since this explanation is certainly inadmissible for the composite dykes of Skye. On this point a few remarks are necessary. Professor Judd, in an instructive paper on composite dykes already referred to, distinguishes between those in which a differentiation has gone on in the material that has filled the dyke and those in which there has been injection of different materials into the same fissure. What is here premised of dykes may be extended also to sills and, in a general sense, to larger and more massive intrusions. Although the distinction seems to be logically an absolute one, it is, however, probably less fundamental than it appears. Professor Judd indeed recognises that there are cases which seem to constitute a link between the two classes, and this becomes much more evident when we turn from the dykes to the large bosses. The leading characteristics of composite intrusions are common to both classes: such are, in dykes and sills, the bilateral symmetry of the arrangement, the disposition of the most acid member at the centre and the most basic at the sides, and probably we may add the indications of what Iddings has called "consanguinity" among the different associated rock-types. Moreover the criterion which naturally suggests itself for discriminating the two classes, viz. the contrast of a gradual transition in the one case with abrupt boundaries in the other, sometimes breaks down in practice.

* *Geologische Beschreibung des Thüringer Waldebürgs*, part 2, section 1, p. 138, footnote, etc. : 1798.
† *Zeits. deuts. geol. Ges.*, vol. x., pp. 305-355, Pl. IX., X. : 1858.
‡ *Ibid.*, vol. xxxii., pp. 111-182, Pl. X., XI. : 1880.
§ *Ibid.*, vol. xxxiii., pp. 483-489 : 1881.
∥ *Jahrb. k. preuss. geol. Landesanst.* for 1887, pp. 119-139, Pl. V. : 1888.
¶ *Ibid.*, pp. 100-118.
** *Ibid.* for 1883, pp. 213-237, Pl. XX. : 1884.

With this understanding, it may be said that the composite dykes and sills of Skye fall under the second of the two heads, the phenomena being the result of successive injections of different rock-magmas into one channel. Many single dykes in Skye exhibit variations due to differentiation in place, but these variations have in any given case a very limited range, and present no unusual features.

It results from the strong tendency of the acid intrusions to be guided by pre-existing basic ones that the area of distribution for the composite (basic with acid) dykes and sills is nearly coextensive with that for the acid dykes and sills in general. The acid sills are more restricted in range than the acid dykes, and the composite sills show a like restriction as compared with the composite dykes. We shall notice first the composite dykes of unsymmetrical type, since these exhibit the least peculiarity of habit, and have nothing abnormal in their petrographical characters.

In many instances the association of acid with basic dykes is only of a loose kind. This is well seen in the Strathaird peninsula, and especially in a group of acid dykes on the slopes of Ben Meabost, about 1000 yards west of the summit. Here we find one acid dyke running alone; another, after running alone for some distance, impinges obliquely upon a basic dyke, to which it clings thenceforward; another runs throughout in contact with a basic dyke, thus constituting a double composite dyke; and still another has insinuated itself between two contiguous basic dykes, so as to form a triple composite dyke of symmetrical type. East of Elgol there are other examples showing how a felsite dyke may run independently until it meets a basic dyke, to which it then adheres. One of the same group, about 800 yards east of the School, runs by itself throughout its course, and is obliquely cut by a number of basic dykes. This is instructive as illustrating the fact that, while the acid dykes have taken advantage, as described, of any pre-existing basic dykes in their neighbourhood, they are themselves earlier than the majority of basic dykes in the district.

Double composite dykes, consisting of one basic and one acid member, occur in numerous localities, intersecting the Jurassic strata, the basaltic group, or the gabbro. Examples may be seen east of Camas Fhionnairidh; south-east of Sgùrr nan Each (striking N.N.E.); north-east of Vikisgill Burn, which drains into Loch Harport; and on Glas Eilean, opposite Harrabol, Broadford. Unsymmetrical multiple dykes including one or more acid members are also found quite frequently in certain parts of the area, and some of these will be mentioned later in connection with the common multiple basic dykes. Good examples occur in the Allt Daraich gorge near Sligachan and in Allt Airidh Meall Beathaig, a tributary of the Varragill River. As already intimated, an acid member almost always occurs between two basic ones; and, when evidence of their relative age is obtainable, the acid rock is always found to be newer than its immediate neighbours, though not necessarily newer than all the basic members of the complex. Another point is worthy of note. The basic members of a multiple dyke often show chilled edges against one another, which may be taken to imply a certain lapse of time between successive intrusions: in the acid members of composite dykes, on the other hand, we often find no such evidence of chilling at the edges; which suggests that the acid intrusion in such a case may have followed its neighbours after no long interval of time. In like manner, we may sometimes see that in a merely double composite dyke the acid member shows clear indications of chilling on the side towards the country-rock, but not at its junction with the associated basic member. A good example, intersecting the gabbro, crosses Allt Dearg Beag about 1000 yards below the Basteir ravine.

A very common case among composite dykes is that in which an acid member has forced its way between the two members of a double basic dyke, thus forming a symmetrical triple dyke. A fine group of these, with the normal direction, occurs along a belt extending from near Drynoch to Coire na Creiche, a distance of about 3¼ miles. Several triple composite dykes of this group are well exposed on the moorland west of Beinn Bhreac, in Coire Gaisteach, and in Allt Coir' a' Mhadaidh. A smaller group traverses the gabbro in Allt nan Clach an Geala, east of Sgùrr nan Gillean, and one example is seen on Bealach na Beiste, between Garbh-bheinn and Belig. The general type of these is a central member of granophyre flanked by two of basalt or dolerite. There are no peculiarities of a petrographical kind, and it is evident that the bilateral symmetry is only an accident, resulting from the propensity of the acid magma to insinuate itself between two contiguous basic dykes.* Indeed in some of the composite dykes belonging to the group first mentioned this symmetry is lost, owing to the granophyre magma having been intruded into a multiple basic dyke instead of a merely double one. The two straight reaches of Allt Grillan follow multiple dykes of this kind, consisting of several basic and one acid member.

The intrusions which we shall now more particularly consider, and which will be described in detail in the succeeding chapter, are *triple composite sills and dykes* in which the *bilateral symmetry* is to be regarded as an essential feature, and they are characterised by peculiar petrographical phenomena indicative of remarkable *mutual reactions* between the two associated rock-types. The very distinctive characters common to these intrusions as a whole leave no doubt that they belong to one natural group, referable to a definite epoch and affecting a certain restricted area. They in no case intersect, but are clearly intersected by, such simple dykes as they encounter belonging to the phase of minor intrusions. The first manifestation of this phase was, as we shall see later, the

* *Cf.* Sir A. Geikie's remarks on an example described by him at Market Stance, Broadford, *Quart. Journ. Geol. Soc.*, vol. lii., p. 394: 1896; and *Ancient Volcanoes of Great Britain*, vol. ii., p. 163: 1897.

injection of a great group of basic sills; but the basic members of the composite sills differ petrographically from the great group, and have certainly emanated from a different focus of eruption. We have not found direct field-evidence to determine whether they are older or younger, but other considerations indicate that they are older. The acid members of the composite sills differ in no respect from the granophyres of the Red Hills, which, as we have seen, locally enter into peculiarly intimate relations with the remarkable basic rock designated marscoite. The basic members in certain respects resemble the marscoite, and the relations to be described are in like manner analogous to those already noticed in the neighbourhood of Glamaig. These peculiar relations, whatever their interpretation, must depend upon a very nice adjustment of conditions, which was not likely to be realised at more than one epoch in the sequence of events in our area*. We might then regard the intrusion of these composite sills and dykes as the closing event of the plutonic phase of activity or the opening event of the succeeding phase of minor intrusions. For reasons to be given later we prefer to regard the epoch as marking accurately the transition from the one phase to the other (*see* below, Chap. XXV.).

We shall for clearness refer to these peculiar composite sills as the *Cnoc Càrnach type,* and we shall include with them, as undoubtedly belonging to the same natural group, certain composite dykes of like constitution. The composite sills of this type in Skye, where some twenty have been mapped, show a well-defined distribution (*see* sketch-map, Fig. 58, p. 273). They occur, with one exception, in or near the Lias, and are best developed in the country south of Broadford. Beginning not far from Suishnish Point, between Lochs Slapin and Eishort, a discontinuous belt of sills may be traced from the moorland between Carn Dearg and Beinn Bhuidhe north-eastward by Beinn a' Mheadhoin and Beinn a' Chàirn to Cnoc Càrnach and northward to Braigh Skulamus, reappearing after an interval to the north-west, on the west shore of Broadford Bay. The semicircle thus traced out has a diameter of about seven miles, and its distance from the large granite intrusions varies from a mile to 2½ miles. Ten miles to the W.N.W. we find the composite sill of Allt an' t-Sithean, near the head of Loch Sligachan. This interesting intrusion, only a mile from the peculiar sills of Glamaig, differs from the rest in being situated in the basaltic lavas, and at a considerable distance above the base of the group. The gap between Rudh' an Eireannaich, near Broadford, and Allt an' t-Sithean, near Sligachan, is completed by that portion of Scalpay† which falls within the belt of country indicated. At Camas na Geadaig, on the north-west coast of that

* It is possible, however, from phenomena observed in the Isle of Arran, that conditions in some respects comparable recurred locally at a much later epoch, that of the pitchstones.
† The sills at Suishnish Point in Raasay do not seem to belong to this group, their relations, as described by Sir A. Geikie, being of a different kind. *Quart. Journ. Geol. Soc.*, vol. lii., pp. 394, 395 : 1896.

island, a perfectly typical composite sill is well seen in the Torridon Sandstone, and one or two others, either less perfect or less clearly exhibited, might be noted in other parts of Scalpay.

The composite sills in the Lias occur at various horizons, and sometimes at more than one horizon in the same place. This is seen on and to the east of Cnoc Càrnach (Fig. 42). Again, the broad sheets of granophyre which form Beinn a' Mheadhoin and Beinn a' Chàirn have apparently been continuous, but are now divided by a wedge-like strip brought up between two faults. In this, much broken by smaller faults, is seen a much lower sill, intruded in the Triassic conglomerate and even beneath it, in contact with the underlying Torridonian. Owing to their position, and to the synclinal disposition of the strata, the large sill of Beinn a' Mheadhoin and Beinn a' Chàirn and that near Carn Dearg lie nearly flat, and their upper portions have been removed by erosion. Nevertheless the existing thickness must exceed 150 feet in the one case and 200 feet in the other. These two most southerly sills are the thickest. The former can be traced (disregarding the break referred to) for about a mile and a half, and the latter for a mile. The longest sill is that which forms the ridge of Cnoc Càrnach and can be followed northward to beyond Braigh Skulamus, a distance of two miles.

The typical constitution of these sills is, as already stated, triple. The middle and chief portion is of granophyre or other acid rock, while above and below it are sheets of a more basic rock, which for the present we may name basalt. The latter are usually much inferior in thickness to the middle part, not often exceeding six or eight feet in the largest sills and one or two feet in the smallest. These relations are well illustrated by examples easily accessible from Broadford; *e.g.* on the shore at Rudh' an Eireannaich and on the rough track leading to Heast, at Braigh Skulamus and for about ¾ mile beyond. The posteriority of the acid intrusion to the basic is often clearly demonstrated by the metamorphism of the basalt at the junction and by the inclusion in the granophyre of abundant xenoliths of the basalt, which are also metamorphosed and rounded by corrosion. Further, as Sir A. Geikie has remarked, the granophyre often sends out numerous veins into the basalt, ranging in width from about an inch down to very minute dimensions. These are well seen as a fine network on an exposed dip-slope of the upper basalt, as, for instance, on the west side of Cnoc Càrnach. As seen in the field, the junction between the acid and the basic rock is usually quite sharp, however irregular it may be as a result of the acid magma corroding the basalt. Sometimes, however, there is, so far as the eye can judge, a transition, rapid but not abrupt, from the one rock to the other. That this is due to some sort of mingling of the two rocks, not to differentiation in place, is certain; for, tracing the junction along for a few yards, we may find the gradual passage giving place to the more usual sharply defined contact.

The symmetrical sandwich-like constitution of these triple composite sills is explicable *a priori* in two ways. The acid magma

may have forced a passage along the surface of junction of two contiguous basic sills, as has undoubtedly happened in the case of many composite dykes; or it may conceivably have found a plane of weakness along the middle of a single basic sill, and thus split it into two. It seems possible that both cases are represented. The circumstances observed in some instances, and especially the local interposition of an inconstant basic sheet in the heart of the granophyre, seem to point to a pre-existing double or triple or even quadruple basic sill invaded by the acid magma. In other instances it will be shown that a single basic sill has been thus invaded while its interior part was still imperfectly consolidated, or at least still hot, and ready to be corroded by the acid magma. In such a case there may be so much intermingling of the two rocks as to give the general effect of a gradual transition, as described below for the sill of Rudh' an Eireannaich. We shall see that the intermingling which is there so strikingly demonstrated has operated also in varying degree in the other composite sills of the group, and there can be little doubt that the second alternative suggested is the one generally applicable.

We have next to notice the variations exhibited by some of these composite sills from what may be regarded as the ideal type,

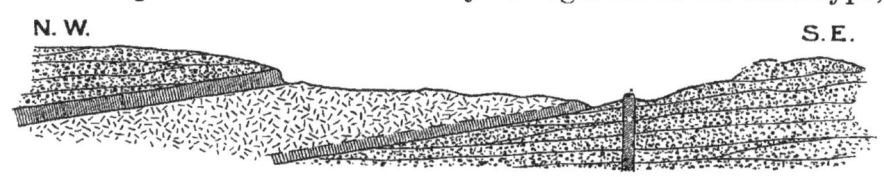

N. W.   S. E.

FIG. 43.—Section of triple composite sill intruded in the coarse pebbly felspathic sandstones of the Torridonian (Applecross Grits) on the southern shore of Camas na Geadaig, in the N.W. of Scalpay. The middle and principal member of the sill is a spherulitic granophyre; above is basalt, 4 ft thick, with a sharp junction; below is basalt, 2 ft thick, with the appearance of a more gradual transition. The junctions show reactions between the basic and acid rocks of the kind described below.

and first as regards their regularity and persistence. With respect to sills in general, in this district and doubtless in others, it may be remarked that the uniformity of their thickness and the accuracy with which they follow a given bedding-plane depend partly upon the " country " rock and partly upon the nature of the magma injected. In Skye the sills always run most regularly in the basalt lavas and the Jurassic shales. In the bedded sandstones of the Lias they are less regular, and in the limestones the sill form is usually lost altogether. In the Durness Limestones and Torridon Sandstone, rocks usually without any good bedded structure, we find as a rule no sills. Further, the basic magmas, besides taking the sill form more readily than the acid and extending in that form for greater distances, also maintain their course with greater regularity. These general rules are illustrated by the behaviour of the triple sills. It can clearly be seen in several cases that the acid rock, though thicker, is less extensive than the basic. If the acid magma was not in great quantity, it merely formed a lenticular mass in the midst of the basalt, which is found to continue after the granophyre has died out. This is well illustrated at Allt an' t-Sithean, near Sligachan (Fig. 44). If, on the other hand, the basalt failed while the granophyre was still in some force, the latter seems to have been reluctant to leave the former, and has swollen so as to present a blunt laccolitic termination instead of the usual acutely tapering form. This is well shown by a branch of the Beinn a' Chàirn mass, on the east side towards Heast. The same mass on its west side, near Allt na Pairte, illustrates another effect. The granophyre has reached the limit of the guiding basalt while still in such force as to be driven farther: it has then broken across the strata until it reached the Lower Lias limestone, and there entirely lost the sill habit.

Any want of correspondence with the bedding of the contiguous rocks is connected in these composite sills, as in the ordinary basic sills of the district, with imperfect development of the bedding-planes themselves as divisional planes. The example at Camas Geadaig in Scalpay, where the country rock is a coarse Torridon Sandstone, is an illustration of this. It preserves very well the regular sheet form, but does not follow the stratification of the sandstone (Fig. 43).

The most common departure from the typical bilateral symmetry in these composite sills, and one to be observed more frequently in certain dykes of like habit, is an irregularity in appearance only. This is the absence, for some distance, of one or other (rarely both) of the flanking basalts, and it arises merely from the granophyre magma having totally destroyed the continuity of the basalt. Such breaks frequently occur for a short distance, the former presence of the basalt being attested by abundant xenoliths of it in the marginal part of the granophyre. These xenoliths, however, are themselves evidently in various stages of dissolution, and are sometimes represented merely by obscure débris in a matrix modified by the absorption of basalt material. It is easy to believe that in some circumstances all trace of the xenoliths may have disappeared and their substance been distributed through the general body of the granophyre. The flanking basalt sheets are never wanting in the smaller composite sills, but only in those in which the acid rock attains a very considerable volume.

Another, but rarer, departure from the regular type consists in the interpolation of relics of an additional basic sheet in the interior of the granophyre. A basalt in this position, invaded on both sides by the corroding acid magma, would doubtless be readily destroyed, and the relics of this kind that we have observed are of a very fragmentary sort. Only two instances are to be cited from our area, and, since they seem to illustrate two different cases, we may mention them more particularly. One example is presented by the large composite sill of Carn Dearg, near Suishnish. As now exposed, this is of the nature of an outlier, in that its present extent of nearly a square mile is determined in every direction by the progress of erosion, which has also removed all the upper portion (*see* Fig. 45, p. 211). Round the greater part of the circumference there is seen merely a single sheet of basalt, usually 6 to 10 feet thick, forming the base of the much thicker granophyre; but at places on the south side we find relics of two other basic sills enveloped in the lower part of the granophyre mass. They differ petrographically from the type of basalt which forms the lower sheet and is found in these peculiar composite sills elsewhere; and it is probable that their inclusion here is only an accidental circumstance. We may suppose that in this case a triple or perhaps quadruple basic sill was invaded by an overwhelming volume of acid magma, and that only the lowest basic member (and probably the highest one, now removed by erosion) had a genetic relationship with the acid rock.

In the Carn Dearg occurrence the departure from the usual arrangement is of an unsymmetrical order, but in the other case to be noted the regular symmetry is preserved, and the explanation is of a different kind. This is the quintuple composite sill of Allt an' t-Sithean, near Sligachan (Fig. 44). Its shape is that

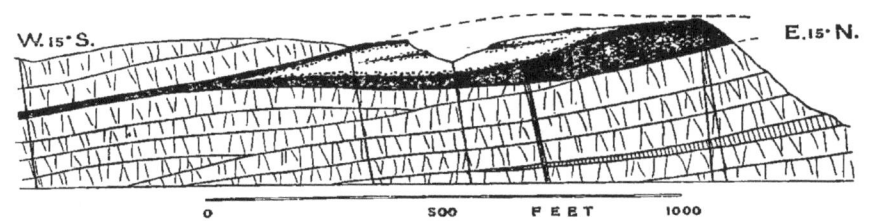

Fig. 44.—Section across Allt an 't-Sithean and through Cnoc an 't-Sithean, about 1¼ mile N.N.W. of Sligachan, to show the relations of the basalt (black) and granophyre (white) in the quintuple composite laccolite. The intrusion occurs in the basaltic lava group, and one of the ordinary dolerite sills is shown lower down. The triple composite dyke which has probably fed the laccolite does not appear in this section, but some later basic dykes of simple habit are shown, and these in some cases have failed to penetrate the thick mass.

of a laccolite rather than a sill, owing to the lenticular form assumed by the granophyre portion, which is traceable for only 400 or 500 yards along the strike. The maximum thickness of the whole is perhaps 150 feet, the greater part of which is granophyre; but, in addition to the upper and lower basalts, a thin sheet is seen in the middle of the granophyre, running for 300 yards or more. It is greatly metamorphosed and corroded into xenoliths, and it dies out in every direction before the granophyre.

One of the most remarkable features of these peculiar symmetrical composite sills has yet to be mentioned, and a full account of it will be deferred to the next chapter. Not only does the later rock, the granophyre or other acid type, carry xenoliths of the earlier basic one, but the earlier rock also encloses at least xenocrysts from the later. These are seen as crystals of alkali-felspars and grains of quartz scattered through the basalt, especially near its junction with the acid rock. Moreover, while the granophyre has locally been rendered less acid by incorporating in its magma dissolved débris of basalt, the basic rock has been modified in the opposite sense, and usually to a greater degree, by absorbing acid material. Indeed much of the rock which we have for convenience been styling basalt has petrographically no right to that title, being much more acid than any normal basalt. That the derived acid material, whether displayed as xenocrysts or absorbed, comes in great part from the contiguous acid rock will be made sufficiently clear in the sequel. The crystals of alkali-felspars and grains of quartz in the " basalt," like the basic xenoliths in the granophyre, become progressively more abundant towards the basalt-granophyre junction; and it is often evident, even when the dividing line is sharply defined, that the basic rock becomes more acid and the acid rock more basic towards the contact of the two. Only in certain extreme cases does the sharp division fail, and the two rocks appear to graduate into one another without any interruption.

At several places within the curved belt of country which includes the symmetrical composite sills of the Cnoc Càrnach type there occur *triple composite dykes* with like symmetrical constitution, consisting of the same pair of rocks with the same remarkable mutual reactions. The association of the dykes with the sills is of so close a kind as to leave little or no doubt that the former are, or have been, continuous with the latter, and have served as feeders to them. Immediately south of Loch na Starsaich, a tarn lying to the north of Heast, a triple composite dyke can be followed for about 400 yards in an E.N.E.–W.S.W. direction, with a maximum width of over 100 feet. Westward it ends abruptly before reaching the neighbouring tarn Loch an Eilean; but eastward it can be followed to within a very short distance of a composite sill which is exposed just east of Loch na Starsaich. Just below the outlet of Loch an Eilean a similar dyke is seen, with the same bearing, and this is visibly continuous with a composite sill exposed for some 400 yards immediately south of the tarn. Another, seen 250 yards east of Loch na Starsaich, is continuous with the Cnoc Càrnach sill. In all these dykes granophyre is the predominant rock. The first one is flanked on both sides by basalt, but not continuously, the basic rock being represented in most places only by xenoliths in the marginal part of the granophyre. The second and third dykes have a border of basalt on the north side but not on the south. This imperfection is probably attributable to the caustic action of the acid magma on the basalt, which has in general been decidedly more energetic in the dykes than in the sills. Regarding the dykes as marking the channels which fed the sills, this difference may be ascribed to difference of temperature, the magma losing heat continually as it penetrated first through and then along the strata.

In other cases we find large dykes which are in visible continuity with the composite sills, but which are simply granophyre dykes without encasing basalt, at least on the side which is exposed. In the light of what has just been said it seems probable that here too pre-existing basalt dykes have been entirely devoured by the granophyre magma to which they served as guides. On the west flank of Cnoc Càrnach the granophyre of the composite sill which builds the ridge is succeeded by its upper basalt, running nearly N.–S. and dipping to the west. About 200 yards west of Loch a' Mhullaich, however, the boundary suddenly takes a turn to the W.S.W. and becomes vertical, the basalt disappearing. This continues for more than 200 yards, the vertical nature of the wall of granophyre being further proved by its crossing undisturbed a fault which causes a considerable displacement in the Liassic strata. Then the boundary turns again, and the basalt reappears with the same low dip as before. Here erosion seems to have brought to light the position of a portion of the channel which fed the granophyre sill and probably also the basalt sill which preceded it. A precisely similar thing is seen on the northern edge of the Carn Dearg composite sill, just west of Loch Fada (Fig. 45).

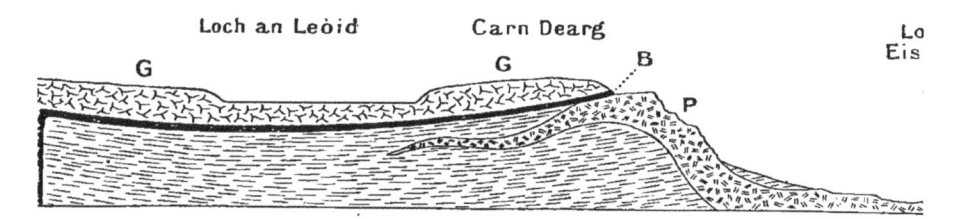

FIG. 45.—Section across the composite sill of Carn Dearg, near Suishnish. Scale, 6 inches to a mile. G, granophyre of sill; B, lower basalt member; D, supposed dyke-feeder of sill; P, later independent intrusion of rock varying from olivine-gabbro to picrite (see Chap. XXII.).

In every case, where composite sills are found, there is a dyke of the kind under discussion at no great distance. The Allt an' t-Sithean sill, for example, is situated far from the others and, as remarked, among the basaltic lavas. No dyke which can represent its feeder is seen in visible continuity with it, but 300 or 400 yards to the north and pointing towards the sill there is a handsome triple composite dyke some fifty yards wide and with the typical characteristics. All these remarkable dykes are wide but short, and obey no evident rule as regards direction, in several instances running almost at right angles to the generality of dykes in the district. They consist typically of a wide granophyre dyke in the centre flanked by two narrower borders of basic composition. More frequently than in the sills this symmetrical disposition is disguised or lost by the destruction of one or both of the basic margins; but the other kind of departure from the ideal type, viz. the interpolation of additional basic members in the midst of the granophyre, is not found in the dykes. This may be due to the same cause, the more intense corrosive action of the acid magma. In all cases where the flanking basic members are preserved they are found to be much corroded at their contact with the granophyre, to which they 'have furnished material in the form of xenoliths, etc. This clearly distinguishes these triple composite dykes associated with the sills from the others already referred to, in which the triple symmetry may be regarded as accidental. Of one of these latter, at Market Stance, Broadford, Sir A. Geikie* has remarked that "the several parts of the dyke are as distinctly marked off from each other as they could have been had they been injected at widely separated intervals of volcanic activity."

The petrographical characters of the composite dykes associated with the Cnoc Càrnach group resemble those of the sills themselves, and the same curious phenomena of admixture are to be seen. These will be discussed in the following chapter. In this place, however, we shall briefly notice certain other intrusions which may be distinguished as *imperfectly symmetrical composite*

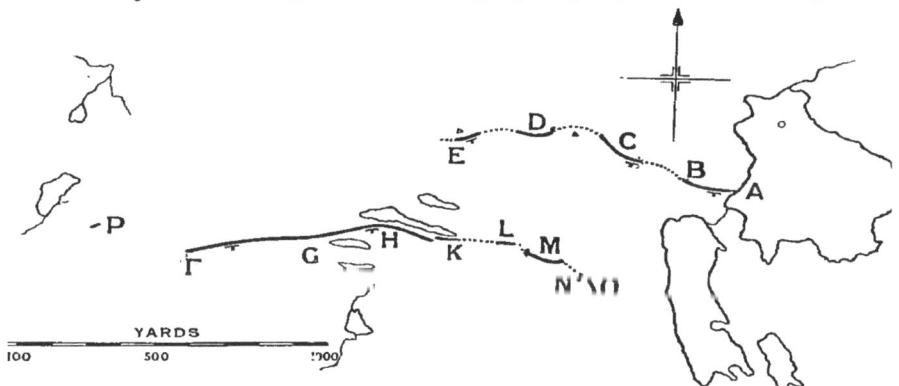

FIG. 46.—Sketch-map of a small area in the interior of the Isle of Scalpay: explanation in the text.

dykes. These are not connected with sills, but constitute independent intrusive bodies. In certain parts of their course they present a composite structure with the regular triple symmetry, but elsewhere they are imperfect owing to the defect of the acid, or less commonly of the basic member. Since it appears doubtful on a first consideration whether these dykes should be assigned to the essentially symmetrical or to the unsymmetrical type, it may be profitable to examine them more particularly. They are best exhibited in the district, consisting of Torridonian grits and studded by numerous tarns, in the centre of the Isle of Scalpay.

Here the dykes are of moderate width, with a general E.–W. direction and a more or less pronounced hade to the south. The component rocks are a spherulitic granophyre and a basalt, of which the latter is the more persistent. It is of uniform aspect

* *Quart. Journ. Geol. Soc.*, vol. lii., p. 394 : 1896.

on a fresh fracture, but a weathered face shows numerous rusty sub-angular patches in basso-relievo, indicating xenoliths of a not very different rock. There are also scattered porphyritic crystals of felspar. Two of the dykes are shown on the small map (Fig. 46). It will be seen that they are remarkable for their sinuous course and also for frequent interruptions of continuity, *i.e.* as regards the outcrop at the surface.

The first, at its eastern end, at Loch an Leòid, has for some distance, A B, the typical arrangement, viz. a granophyre dyke flanked on each side by a narrower dyke of basalt. Farther west there are interruptions of continuity, and the granophyre is not seen again; but the unmistakable xenolithic basalt reappears in three detached exposures, C, D, E. The second dyke is seen continuously exposed for 800 yards, from F to K, with only one slight interruption, where it is displaced about 15 yards northward; and throughout this extent it has the typical constitution. At H the granophyre is 10 feet wide, the northern basalt 2 feet, and the southern one 1 foot. At G an additional basaltic member is added at the northern edge. This is non-xenolithic, about 10 inches wide, and sharply divided from its neighbour: it is probably a later intrusion. East of the continuous exposure two detached portions, L and M, show the triple symmetry as before, the granophyre being 7½ feet wide and each of the basalts 1 foot; but beyond this we find only some small isolated outcrops of the basalt alone, at N, and of the granophyre alone, at O. Westward a single small outcrop of the characteristic xenolithic basalt was observed at P: this may belong to one or other of the two dykes. Another dyke of the same group, nearly on the line of the second one, crosses the northern end of Loch a' Mhuillin, just outside the eastern border of the small sketch-map. On the east side of the tarn it has the typical triple constitution; on the west side the acid rock is not present as a distinct member, but is represented by a network of veins traversing the basalt.

These dykes may be taken as representatives of a number of others, specially well exhibited in the central and eastern parts of Scalpay, and their phenomena are very instructive for comparison with those of the typical composite dykes with triple symmetry throughout. The fact that incompleteness of constitution is found associated with a sinuous line of outcrop and frequent breaches of continuity is doubtless significant. In dykes in general these two latter features, and especially the last, seem constantly to indicate the upward dying out of the intrusions, the present surface of the ground passing near the upward limit of the dykes, in one place below and in another place above that limit. In these composite dykes it appears that the acid member was liable to die out before the basic, in the vertical as well as in the horizontal direction. In the first dyke noticed the complete triple portion is exposed at about 600 feet above sea-level, and the portions consisting of basalt alone at about 800 to 1000 feet. The second dyke does not illustrate the point in the same way, for the complete portion, from F to M, runs at an altitude of between

900 and 1000 feet, while the separate outcrops of basalt and granophyre at N and O are from 50 to 100 feet lower. As will be shown in a later chapter, however, the flow of molten magma in a dyke-fissure is not necessarily directly upward, but may take a direction considerably inclined to the vertical and even in places approaching the horizontal. These imperfect composite dykes occur on the verge of the area affected by the typical composite intrusions of the symmetrical kind, and incline downward in the direction of that area. We may further suppose that when the intruded acid magma reached a point where it was nearly spent, its temperature had become considerably lowered; and accordingly these dykes do not present, at least to inspection in the field, any clear signs of reaction between the basic and acid members.

The tendency of an acid magma to be guided by a pre-existing basic dyke or sill is, as we have seen, a very general principle among all the rocks of our area. This tendency is, however, greatest in the case of the granophyres belonging to the Cnoc Càrnach group where they have encountered the xenocryst-bearing basalts of the same group. In this case we may even find a granophyre sheet sending out an offshoot along a basalt dyke. An instance of this exceptional phenomenon is seen on the north side of Beinn a' Chàirn, about 500 yards N.W. of the summit. Here for some distance the lower basalt of the large composite sill has been destroyed; but there is a basalt dyke of the type in question, which has probably served as feeder for this and the neighbouring smaller sills at a lower horizon, the acid magma, however, having in this case risen through some other channel. The dyke terminates at the base of the thick granophyre sheet of Beinn a' Chàirn, and this has given off a tapering tongue which follows for a short distance the edge of the basalt dyke.

CHAPTER XIII.

COMPOSITE SILLS AND DYKES: DETAILED DESCRIPTION.

Having considered the general characteristics of the peculiar composite intrusions with symmetrical habit, and obtained some partial conception of their geological relations and their significance as members of the great suite of Tertiary igneous rocks of the Skye centre, we have next to describe the characters of the rocks which constitute these intrusive bodies. These include primarily some of thoroughly acid and others of thoroughly basic composition, but the petrographical interest attaches chiefly to the remarkable reactions which these closely associated rocks have exercised upon one another. These reactions have resulted, in varying degree, in a certain acidification of the basic rocks and a correlative basification of the acid rocks; but such a rough characterisation expresses only in a general way the modifications of the bulk-composition of the respective rocks, the actual phenomena being of a complex kind. The extreme result of intermingling, however effected, has been in certain cases the production locally of rocks of mean acidity, but normal intermediate rock-types do not occur. The peculiar mutual relations of the basic and acid members will be best illustrated by describing the distinct occurrences severally, and only a few preliminary remarks on the petrography of the acid and basic members will be necessary.

In all but one case—the composite sill of Rudh' an Eireannaich, to be described later—the normal acid rocks fall under one general head. The common type is a granophyre of an ordinary kind and with a chemical composition not differing in any essential from that of the large plutonic masses of the Red Hills. This appears from an analysis already given in Chapter X. and here reproduced (column I.). The rock selected for analysis is a granophyre of a spherulitic type, and, in addition to phenocrysts of felspar and quartz, contains green hornblende, both as little crystals and as slender rods. Such rocks, except that augite sometimes takes the place of hornblende, constitute the acid members of these composite sills and dykes in general. There are variations in micro-structure, the spherulitic arrangement becoming in some cases more pronounced and regular, or in other cases the granophyric giving place to a merely granular structure. Such variations are found in the ordinary minor acid intrusions of the district, and do not necessarily import any special conditions; but it is possibly not without significance that in the composite intrusions a change from a granophyric to a microgranitic structure is often associated with a modification of the acid rock by the inclusion of basic material.

The basic rocks studied present wider variation, but this is due to the difficulty in many cases of finding a specimen which can with confidence be regarded as representing the normal rock. We have already seen that in these composite intrusions the acid member is always in considerably greater volume than the basic,

	I.	A.
SiO_2	71·98	70·34
TiO_2	0·37	0·46
Al_2O_3	13·13	13·18
Fe_2O_3	1·33	2·65
FeO	1·64	2·24
MnO	0·14	0·19
MgO	0·56	0·40
CaO	1·15	1·24
BaO	trace	trace
Na_2O	2·98	3·61
Li_2O	not found	trace
K_2O	4·93	4·90
H_2O {above 105°	1·38	0·76
{at 105°	0·39	0·46
P_2O_5	0·19	0·10
Cl	0·01	0·02
	100·18	100·55
Specific gravity	2·63	2·66

I. Hornblende-Granophyre [7064], Beinn a Chuirn, 3½ miles S. by W. of Broadford: anal. W. Pollard, *Summary of Progress* for 1899, p. 173. (The Cl here and the P_2O_5 and Cl in the next analysis have been inserted subsequently. Fluorine and sulphur sought but not found.)

A. Hornblende-Granophyre [7124], Druim Eadar da Choire: anal. W. Pollard, *ibid.*, p. 174. This is from part of the great plutonic mass of the Red Hills, and is quoted here to show its substantial identity with the preceding.

and it has resulted from this that the basic rocks are liable to be much more radically modified in composition than the acid, and are often completely disguised. Those of them which have not suffered in this way have, however, in general well-marked characteristics common to them as a group. They are basalts or fine-grained dolerites, of thoroughly basic composition but without olivine. The structure is usually the micro-ophitic, though "granulitic" varieties, in Professor Judd's sense of the word, are not wanting. They resemble in these respects the commonest type of basic sills in Skye, which, as we shall see later, are found in extraordinary profusion in the north-western portion of the island, far from any acid rocks. They differ, however, from those in that they are generally porphyritic, enclosing conspicuous felspar crystals, which probably have not always the same significance. In some cases, as we shall see, the inclusion of felspar crystals is one feature of the special modification of the basic sills in contact with the accompanying acid rocks. More usually the felspars must have been introduced with the basic magma itself, but even in this case there are circumstances which prove that some of the crystals are not normal constituents formed from the magma. In these respects the phenomena recall those of the marscoite of Glamaig and other places, as described in Chapter XI., but there are differences of degree, if not of kind. The peculiarities of the marscoite resulted from processes effected prior to intrusion, and only in a less degree from reactions with an acid magma after intrusion; in the rocks now under consideration the reverse was the case. We shall employ the name "basalt" for these rocks notwithstanding the abnormal characters which they so frequently exhibit.

We shall briefly describe the several composite intrusions of this group in order from south to north. This order will have the advantage of introducing us by degrees to the more peculiar effects of mutual reactions between the associated rock-types. We refer here to special modifications affecting the constitution of both the rocks involved. Of mere bodily destruction of the earlier basic by the later acid intrusion the southerly occurrences present more striking instances than the northerly, owing to their larger size and to the greater preponderance of the acid over the basic rock in respect of volume.

The first of the composite sills to be noticed is that of *Carn Dearg, near Suishnish Point*, with its small outlier forming the summit of Beinn Bhuidhe. Apart from the picrite below, which gives rise to a prominent feature on the sea-ward slope, but is probably an entirely independent and later intrusion, this occurrence presents some degree of complexity as regards field-relations. The granophyre which is the principal member not only has a thinner basic sill below (besides probably one above, now removed by erosion), but also encloses relics of others enveloped in its interior. It appears that a multiple basic sill was here invaded by an overwhelming volume of acid magma, which separated the several members and in great part corroded and destroyed them. There are nevertheless indications that the lowest basalt sill holds a more intimate relationship with the granophyre than the other basic members do, and is of later age, having preceded the acid intrusion by a brief interval only.

The granophyre shows, except at its base, no noteworthy peculiarity [3188]. The underlying basic member is a porphyritic basalt or fine-textured dolerite, without olivine. It has a micro-ophitic structure, and, without the porphyritic elements, would be identical with a common type among the ordinary basic sills of the "great group" to be described in a later chapter. The porphyritic crystals are felspars, and are of two kinds. Some are labradorite, and are quite clean and fresh; the others give lower extinction-angles, and are crowded in the interior with glass-inclusions, presumably of secondary origin [7072]. The latter are doubtless in some sense xenocrysts. Another feature found here, as in many of the basic sills of this group, is the occurrence of little patches which appear to be microscopic druses. They consist of quartz with good crystal-faces and crystalline calcite filling in the interspaces. This rock, with a specific gravity 2·86, is from a place beyond the direct modifying influence of the acid intrusion. At its junction with the overlying granophyre the basalt is obviously much corroded, and xenoliths of it occur plentifully in the acid rock. These xenoliths [7068] differ from the basalt in place chiefly in the presence of a certain amount of interstitial quartz, which must be ascribed to an impregnation by the acid magma. The acid rock contiguous with the xenoliths is very noticeably modified: it not only loses its granophyric structure, as is very generally the case in these circumstances, but is rendered decidedly less acid in composition. The ferro-magnesian element (now chloritised) is in greater abundance, and in some places the basification is such that a quartz grain has been surrounded by a green corrosion-border.

The discontinuous relics of basic sheets involved in the body of the granophyre show some variety. One is a basalt of specific gravity 2·83 with small porphyritic felspars. Besides the microscopic druses already noticed, it has a few small round vesicles, sometimes filled with a felsitic-looking substance which may represent the granophyre magma. In other respects there is no peculiarity [7073]. Another sheet is represented by specimens of a porphyritic dolerite of sp. gr. 2·89 and a rather coarser example of sp. gr. 2·92, which are quite normal in their characters, though metamorphism has given rise to a considerable amount of green and brownish-green hornblende [7074, 7075]. In these rocks there has been, at least in general, no transfusion of the acid magma causing acidification.

A specimen [3210] among the older collections of the Geological Survey, labelled as from a sill beneath the granophyre of Carn Dearg, is probably from a distinct intrusion, but we have not identified the locality. It is a quartz-dolerite with interstitial micropegmatite. Although such rocks occur in some other regions as normal products of magmatic differentiation and crystallisation, its presence here as a unique occurrence is probably significant. If it is to be regarded as a hybrid rock, it most likely represents the result of admixture prior to intrusion.

The *Beinn a' Chairn* mass consists, in its present eroded state, merely of a thick sheet of hornblende-granophyre with a few feet of basalt at the base. The former rock sends veins into the latter, and encloses near the junction abundant xenoliths of it; while the basic rock is much corroded by the acid, and, as at Carn Dearg, is in some parts of the boundary totally destroyed. The granophyre, away from the junction, is the quite normal acid rock of which we have given a chemical analysis above. The underlying basalt is a dark fine-grained rock of specific gravity 2·90 to 2·91, free from olivine, and with micro-ophitic structure, like the corresponding rock at Carn Dearg. The scattered porphyritic felspars, however, present points of difference. They are of labradorite, the more acid variety being apparently rare or wanting; but these labradorite crystals are much fissured, as if by heat, and contain the round glass-inclusions elsewhere found to characterise xenocrysts (Fig. 47, C).

The contact-phenomena are more remarkable than in the former case, the xenoliths of basalt in the granophyre being more highly modified. They contain quartz not only interstitially and in the usual microscopic druses, but also as rounded grains with the characteristic green corrosion-border (Fig. 47, H, K). They also enclose very turbid crystals of acid felspars, oligoclase with some orthoclase (Fig. 47, F). Since the xenoliths have undoubtedly been detached in the first place from the immediately adjacent basalt sheet, in which no such abundant quartz-grains and alkali-felspars occur, these elements can only have been introduced into the xenoliths from the surrounding acid magma in which they did and do occur. This implies that the xenoliths have been in an effectively fluid state within the fluid acid magma, without mingling freely with it and losing their identity. Similar phenomena have been described, and a like interpretation given, by Professor Grenville Cole* in the case of a composite triple dyke at Glasdrummon Port, County Down; and some of the junctions of marscoite with granophyre described above present somewhat analagous phenomena. The fusion of the basalt offers no difficulty, and indeed it is by no means certain that these xenoliths were completely consolidated when the acid magma picked them up; the remarkable feature is that the xenoliths, though often partially rounded, still preserve a sharp boundary against their matrix. When they were sufficiently fluid to permit not only molecular diffusion but the bodily entrance of foreign crystals, it might have been expected that they would become completely merged in their surrounding.

The acid rock near the junction, at least where it encloses basalt xenoliths, is very sensibly modified. In most places it becomes a quartz-porphyry instead of a granophyre, and its felspar phenocrysts assume rather rounded outlines. The ferro-magnesian mineral here is a pale green augite, though in the altered xenoliths it is hornblende [7066, 7067]. The conditions which have governed the formation of one or other of these minerals might furnish an inquiry of some interest, but unfortunately both are often replaced by chlorite, and in that form frequently indistinguishable. A noteworthy point is the occasional occurrence of an augite crystal showing the basal striation suggestive of derivation from gabbro.

We may notice in passing the composite triple dyke immediately south of *Loch na Starsaich*. Here the principal rock is not a granophyre but a microgranitic quartz-felsite. The phenocrysts are pale augite, quartz, and felspars, which include an oligoclase-

* *Sci. Trans. Roy. Dubl. Soc.* (2), vol. v., pp. 239-248; 1894.

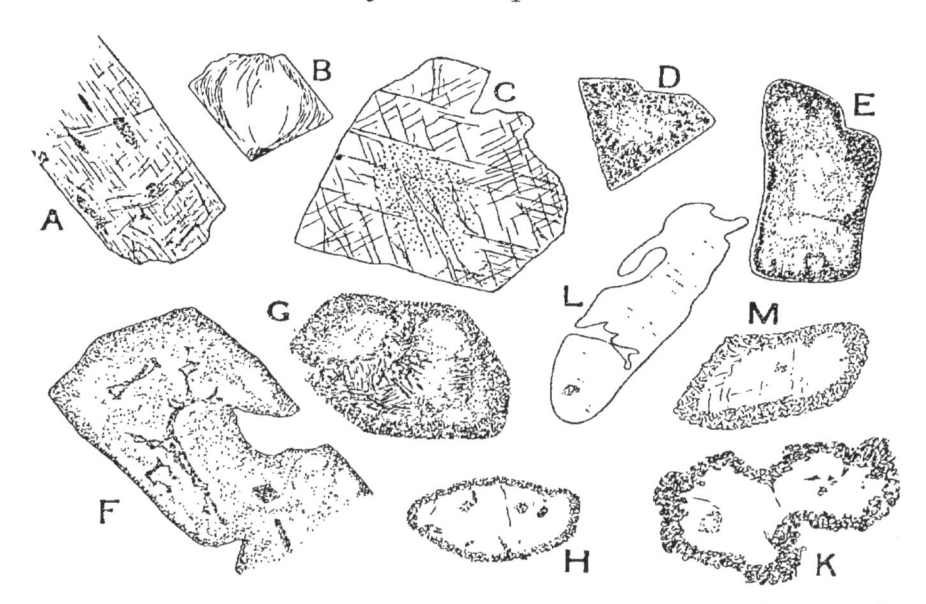

Fig. 47.—Altered phenocrysts and xenocrysts in the basalt of the composite sills; × ca. 10.

A [6735]. Labradorite phenocryst in upper basalt of Cnoc Càrnach; the cleavage cracks opened probably by heat due to the succeeding acid intrusion.

B [6735]. Labradorite phenocryst in the same rock; showing peripheral fissures with a tendency to concentric arrangement.

C [7071]. Labradorite phenocryst in lower basalt of Beinn a' Chairn; showing opening of cleavage cracks and glass-inclusions, probably of secondary origin, in interior of crystal.

D [6735]. Orthoclase xenocryst in upper basalt of Cnoc Càrnach; turbid owing to secondary glass-inclusions.

E [6732]. Oligoclase xenocryst in lower basalt of Creag Bhriste; showing similar turbidity and also rounding of the angles by magmatic corrosion.

F [7069]. Oligoclase xenocryst in basalt xenolith enclosed in acid rock of Beinn a' Chairn; showing a more advanced stage of corrosion, affecting the interior as well as the border of the crystal.

G [6735]. Oligoclase xenocryst in upper basalt of Cnoc Càrnach; showing a very advanced stage of corrosion, with formation of new felspar microlites in the interior of the crystal.

H [7069]. Quartz xenocryst in basalt xenolith at Beinn a' Chairn; rounded, and with border of granular augite (now decayed).

K [7066]. Quartz xenocryst in basalt xenolith at same place; showing more advanced corrosion and a deeper border composed of larger granules.

L [6733]. Quartz xenocryst in acidified basalt xenolith at Creag Bhriste; showing more advanced corrosion, but the augite border has been resorbed with increasing acidification of the matrix.

M [6731]. Xenocryst of alkali-felspar in lower basalt of Rudh' an Eireannaich; showing the margin honeycombed by secondary inclusions.

andesine; and all have rounded outlines [3214]. As usual in these dykes, the flanking basalts are in great part destroyed by the acid magma, and are represented in many places only by xenoliths in the felsite.

The composite sill forming the main ridge of *Cnoc Càrnach* has the symmetrical triple arrangement, with both upper and lower basalts preserved in most places. Only where the granophyre swells out to its thickest in Cnoc Càrnach itself is the lower basalt entirely destroyed for about 500 yards. The chief member is a hornblende-granophyre with rather rounded phenocrysts of quartz, orthoclase, and oligoclase up to about $\frac{1}{10}$ inch. Green hornblende, magnetite, and apatite are seen, the rest of the rock being of micropegmatite [3189]. The basic members are dark rocks with scattered porphyritic felspars, resembling in general characters the corresponding rocks of Carn Dearg and Beinn a' Chairn. A thin slice of the upper basalt [6735] bears out the resemblance, except that the ophitic development of the augite is no longer seen. There are phenocrysts of labradorite, well shaped and quite clear, though fissured (Fig. 47, A, B); but also occasional corroded xenocrysts of quartz and felspar, the former with the usual corrosion-border and the latter (oligoclase and orthoclase) crowded in their marginal parts with secondary inclusions and sometimes deeply corroded (Fig. 47, D, G). Since the basalt, in this specimen, has been in no wise modified by the granophyre which it overlies, these xenocrysts must certainly have been brought up in the basalt magma itself. It is clear that in the basic rocks of this group we have in different cases acid xenocrysts, acquired perhaps from the same ultimate source, but at two different stages. Sometimes, as in the present case, they have been enclosed by the basic magma before its intrusion: sometimes, as in some xenoliths already described, they have entered the basic rock (fused at the time) after the intrusion of both it and the acid rock, which in this case directly furnished the xenocrysts. In the latter case there is evidently no reason why xenocrysts derived in these two different ways should not coexist; and we have already found ground for this supposition in the parallel instance of the marscoite of Sròn a' Bhealain, etc. The identical characters presented by the two sets of xenocrysts and their resemblance, except for corrosion-effects, to the phenocrysts of the granophyre, are among the facts which go to establish a common origin and peculiarly intimate relationship for the basic and acid rocks associated in these composite intrusions.

In the *lower composite sill of Cnoc Càrnach*, which passes just east of Loch a' Mhullaich, the acid member, an ordinary hornblende-granophyre, is of moderate thickness throughout, and the basalt is never wanting either above or below. This is the case also with the remaining sills northward of this, which never attain the great thickness of the more southerly examples.

The composite sill upon which the *Heast road* runs for nearly a mile, from Aodann Clach to Braigh Skulamus, presents new points of interest. The acid member is, near its junction with the lower basic one, a quartz-porphyry enclosing in most places numerous altered xenoliths. These, as at Beinn a' Chaìrn, not only have insterstitial quartz introduced into their ground-mass, but enclose quartz-grains similar to those in the surrounding quartz-porphyry [6733]. Xenoliths are much less frequent at the upper junction, and it appears that the overlying basalt has, at least in the places examined, been less energetically attacked than the underlying. This is true not only as regards bodily destruction, but also as regards impregnation, as is seen on comparing specimens of the two. The upper basalt is a dark rock of specific gravity 2·89, and a thin slice [6734] shows no indication of modification to be ascribed to the acid intrusion. There are, however, in addition to clear phenocrysts of labradorite an occasional grain of quartz with its corrosion-border of granular augite and crystals of oligoclase and orthoclase full of secondary glass-inclusions. These are evidently xenocrysts picked up prior to the intrusion of the basalt. The lower "basalt" is very different. It is a dull-grey rock showing to the eye rather numerous grains of quartz, as well as scattered felspars of dead-white colour. The specific gravity is only 2·69. A thin slice shows that xenocrysts are present in abundance, and also that the general mass of the rock has been considerably modified in the sense of acidification [6732]. The felspar xenocrysts, including both orthoclase and oligoclase, are as usual crowded with secondary glass-cavities except in their central parts (Fig. 47, E), and the quartz-grains are rounded and have a corrosion-border of granular augite, now replaced by calcite and chlorite. This last feature, so characteristic of foreign quartz-grains in a basic rock, is not seen in the altered xenoliths, where acidification has proceeded farther, and the quartz was more nearly in chemical equilibrium with its environment. The normal micro-structure of the basalt ground-mass is, as invariably observed in like circumstances, quite lost, and a noteworthy proportion of interstitial quartz is present, apart from the microscopic druses of quartz and calcite which we have remarked in other examples. It is evident then that at the locality studied, viz. Creag Bhriste, not only the basalt xenoliths, but in somewhat less degree the basalt in place beneath, has been acidified by the later magma intruded in juxtaposition with it. This we have already observed in the case of Bheinn a' Chaìrn; but in the present instance the modification of the underlying basalt has gone farther, for the rock has not only been impregnated with the acid magma, but has also, like the xenoliths, had xenocrysts of quartz and alkali-felspars introduced into it at the same time. This can scarcely be doubted on comparing the lower with the upper basalt, where such xenocrysts are much fewer; and the proof would be complete if we could assume, what is probably the case, that the upper and lower basalts represent not a double sill but a single one, which, while still scarcely consolidated in its interior, was eviscerated by the acid intrusion. We have hitherto left this question open; but facts to be detailed below, especially the phenomena at Rudh' an Eireannaich, show that in some at least of our composite sills the supposition here made is the only one admissible.

We may conveniently distinguish the two orders of acid xenocrysts already recognised in our basic rocks by using the term *antecedent* for those acquired prior to the intrusion, and *consequent* for those forced upon the rock posterior to its intrusion; and a like distinction may be made in respect of the partial acidification of the general mass of this rock. In the marscoite described in a former chapter the peculiarities observed were mainly of the antecedent order, though at some of the junctions consequent effects of the same general kind were to be verified. In the upper basalt at Creag Bhriste, and in the other rocks described which have not been directly affected by the subsequent intrusions of granophyre, we have only antecedent xenocrysts sparsely distributed and no demonstrable acidification of the ground-mass. In the xenoliths described at Carn Dearg we had consequent acidification of the ground-mass only, and in those at Beinn a Chàirn consequent xenocrysts in addition. In the lower basalt at Creag Bhriste, and still more in the xenoliths, we have consequent acidification in an advanced degree with consequent xenocrysts in abundance, and these prevent the verification of any like effects of an antecedent order. As already remarked, the mutual relations of the two rocktypes involved become more complicated as we proceed northward, and we shall see that they are most complicated of all in the Rudh' an Eireannaich occurrence. Comparing the several composite sills with one another, we may conclude that the variable factor determining these petrographical peculiarities was the interval between the intrusions of the basic and acid members. On the other hand, the chief variable factor determining the bodily destruction of the basalt by the acid magma was the relative volume of the latter, allowing in the case of the dykes for prolonged flow.

The xenoliths of basic in acid rock at Creag Bhriste introduce us to a further complication in the curious mutual relations of these rocks [6733]. Here the ground-mass has undergone a notably greater degree of acidification than in the basalt sill below. Interstitial quartz is abundant, and the felspar, judged by its extinction-angles, seems to be andesine rather than labradorite. Concurrently with these changes the ophitic structure is, as usual, lost, and the ferro-magnesian mineral becomes idiomorphic. Its forms point to hornblende, but it is completely chloritised. The xenoliths enclose the usual xenocrysts derived from the acid rock, their abundance showing that they are mainly of the consequent kind. It is evident that, by the time that the acidification of the ground-mass was completed to the degree observed, these xenocrysts must have found themselves in a medium not differing greatly from an acid rockmagma. It is to be expected therefore that corrosive action upon the xenocrysts had ceased before this point was reached, and it is conceivable even that an opposite tendency had been set up. These suppositions are borne out by the facts. The numerous quartzgrains have been eaten into highly irregular shapes, but they have no corrosion-border of granular augite (Fig. 47, L). Either this has never been formed or, what is much more probable, it has been absorbed at a later stage of the progressive acidification. The xenocrysts of alkali-felspars have rounded outlines and are crowded throughout most of their extent with the usual secondary inclusions, but each has a narrow border of similar felspar substance which is quite clear. This border is sharply defined against the turbid mass of the crystal, but rather ragged in places against the surrounding matrix; and we interpret it as a new growth added at a late stage, when the xenolith had become sufficiently rich in silica and alkalies to secrete alkali-felspars.

Another feature of these xenoliths of greatly modified basalt is that they enclose smaller basalt xenoliths which have undergone no such modification. These xenoliths within xenoliths do not exceed a fraction of an inch in length, and have the shape of fragments, though somewhat rounded at the angles. They are of rather fine texture, and have been partly metamorphosed, either by the basalt which caught them up or subsequently by the acid intrusion, the chief new mineral product being brown mica. These little chips cannot be derived from the country rock, which is Jurassic shales. They probably represent the marginal part of the basalt sill itself, as rather rapidly consolidated in contact with the shales, subsequently broken up, and enclosed in the still fluid basalt magma. Whatever their origin, they were clearly solid when caught up by the basalt of the sill, and have not been fused either then or since. The fact that they have not, like the basalt enclosing them, been permeated by the acid magma, enforces this conclusion. If the enclosing basalt, now itself in the form of xenoliths, had been fused by the heat of the acid magma, the little chips would have been fused and permeated in common with it. This is one among other considerations which go to show that, where the basalt of the sills (and of the xenoliths) has been thus permeated and acidified, it is merely because, in those places, it had not yet completely consolidated when the acid magma invaded it.

This last conclusion accords with other features which indicate that, where these peculiar phenomena are found in triple composite sills, the acid member has not been thrust in between the two members of a double basic sill, but has found its way along the middle of a single basic sill, the central zone of which was still in a partially fluid or potentially fluid condition. Quite apart from the petrographical evidence this alternative is inherently the more probable. Double basic sills are indeed frequent in some parts of Skye, but not in this district; and the hypothesis that a number of double sills have been intruded in this belt of country at various horizons, the two members being in each case of nearly equal thickness, and not more than two being intruded in any instance, is an unnatural one.

That the symmetrical triple arrangement is due to the evisceration of a basic sill by a slightly later intrusion of acid magma along the same channel admits of no reasonable doubt in the case of the composite sill next to be discussed, that of *Rudh' an*

Eireannaich, forming the western horn of Broadford Bay. This is not only the most easily accessible of the group, but also in some respects the most remarkable. The intimate association of the two component rock-types is here exhibited in its most extreme phase, the effect being that of a gradual transition from one type to the other affecting almost the whole thickness. In other words, the interval between the two intrusions was in this case the briefest of all, and the basic sill must have been still practically fluid throughout almost the whole of its thickness when the acid magma was intruded into it. There is another respect in which this composite sill differs from the others. The acid member is not in this case a granophyre or quartz-porphry, but a felsite of a less common type, poorer in silica but richer in alkalies.

As approached from Broadford the sill is first seen in a small cliff, some 20 feet high, a little before the headland is reached, and the upper surface of the sill itself forms the top of the cliff for a short distance (Fig. 48). It is more conveniently studied a little

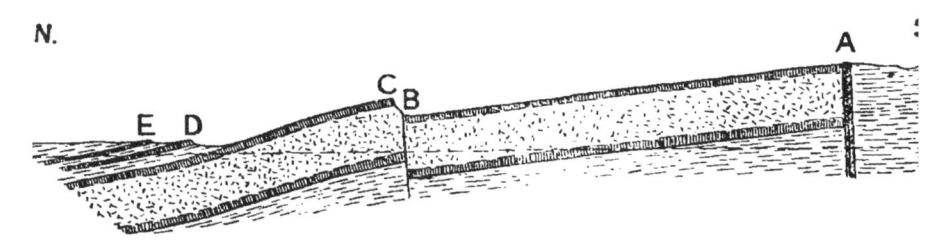

Fig. 48.—Section of composite sill in the Lias at Rudh' an Eireannaich, Broadford Bay.
 A, a fault; its fissure occupied by a double basalt dyke.
 B, a small fault.
 C, escarpment running out to sea eastward, and forming the actual headland.
 D and E, thin sills, 1½ ft and 1 ft respectively, referred to below.

farther north, beyond a small fault, where it forms a small escarpment running out eastward into the sea (C in the section). Here again the upper surface is exposed as a dip-slope, but its inclination soon carries it out of sight. The total thickness of the sill is 14½ feet. Of this we may reckon perhaps 2 feet to the upper basalt and about 2½ feet to the lower, leaving nearly 10¼ feet for the middle member. These measurements, however, have no accurate meaning, for divisional lines of any true significance can scarcely be said to exist between the several members. In the field an observer will readily set down the rock forming the summit and that forming the base as basalts and the middle part as a felsitic rock, but the dark colour of the one passes so insensibly into the light grey of the other that no precise separation is possible. Microscopic evidence only serves to confirm this conclusion, and specific gravity determinations (in default of chemical analyses) give a general indication of the gradual nature of the transition (*see* Fig. 49). To speak more accurately, there are a few inches of rock at the top and a similar thickness near the bottom which may be taken as representing the original basalt as intruded, these being presumably the portions which had become effectively solid before the more acid magma was forced in. In the middle part of the felsite there is a thickness of about 3 feet in which no appreciable variation of composition is to be detected, though we cannot safely assume that even this represents accurately the felsite magma. All the rest is to be regarded as hybrid rock of variable composition, due to the admixture in different proportions of the basaltic and felsitic magmas, both

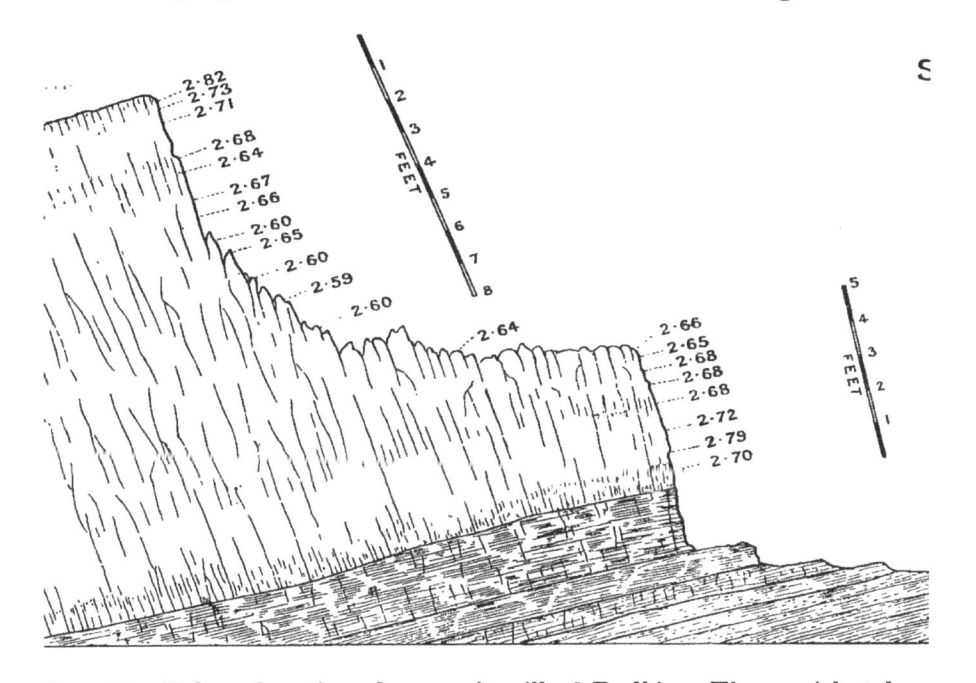

Fig. 49.—Enlarged section of composite sill of Rudh' an Eireannaich, taken at the low escarpment on the shore, the eastward continuation of C in the preceding figure.
The numbers indicate the specific gravities of specimens from different parts of the section.

effectively fluid at the same time. The specific gravities given in Fig. 49 show that the varieties are regularly arranged, the rock becoming denser by degrees, both upward and downward, from the felsite to the basalt. The variation is more gradual towards the felsite, which was presumably the more fluid of the two magmas, and becomes more rapid towards the basalt. The exposed upper surface of basalt forming the roof of the sill is fine-textured, and has a rough, wrinkled, and broken aspect. The lower surface is not so well exhibited, and is less regular, but in places it shows a narrow selvage of quite compact texture. The middle portion of the sill has a well marked rudely columnar jointing, and the joints often pass upward and downward into the basalt, indicating that the whole thickness has cooled in common.

The basalt, taken where it is not perceptibly affected by the later intrusion of felsite, is a dark fine-grained rock of specific gravity 2·79 to 2·82 in several specimens. It encloses little felspars, usually not more than $\frac{1}{8}$ inch in length; and, as usual in these rocks, we can distinguish among them dull white crystals of squarish shape and fresh glassy-looking crystals of more slender tabular habit. The former are xenocrysts of alkali-felspar, belonging of course to the "antecedent" category, while the latter are the labradorite phenocrysts indigenous in the rock. Thin slices show that the basalt differs in no essential respect from those of the other composite sills, the abundant augite having in this case the "granulitic" habit. Only in the xenocrysts do we find a difference. These are all of alkali-felspar, with the usual corrosion-effects (Fig. 47, M), quartz-grains being wholly wanting. This is to be correlated with the absence of quartz-phenocrysts in the felsite; and we have here a strong confirmation of what we have already inferred, that the antecedent as well as the consequent xenocrysts in the basalts of these composite sills have been derived in each case from the immediately associated acid rock.

The felsite is, in the purest specimens, a dull, compact-looking rock of pale grey to bluish white colour, with a specific gravity 2·59 or 2·60. There are dull white felspar crystals up to $\frac{1}{4}$ inch or more in diameter, and a little pyrites is sometimes seen. The rock is not so fresh as the basalt, and thin slices are obscured by secondary calcite [6727, etc.]. The felspar phenocrysts are so much altered that their true nature is not easily made out. Some of them show fine twin-striation, with the nearly straight extinction of oligoclase. Others show no definite twinning except on the Carlsbad law, but there is often a patchy appearance suggestive of a cryptoperthitic intergrowth. Associated in clusters with the felspar are yellowish pseudomorphs which probably represent augite, and a little of this mineral is seen in some of the slides. There are also occasional small cubes of pyrites and prisms of apatite. The ground-mass is composed essentially of little felspar crystals giving imperfect rectangular sections ·004 to ·007 inch in length. They may be either simple or twinned, but all give nearly straight extinction. There is usually a certain amount of interstitial quartz, but this is wanting or almost wanting in the freshest specimens, and is perhaps wholly of secondary origin. The rock, then, consists essentially of alkali-felspars, or felspars rich in alkalies, with little or no quartz. It probably falls into the ceratophyre division, though on this point chemical evidence is to be desired, and it approaches in many respects the bostonite type. We shall have to notice certain rocks of somewhat similar characters among the minor acid intrusions of simple habit, where again they are of exceptional occurrence.

The hybrid rocks produced by admixture of the basalt and felsite exhibit, as we have said, a wide range of variation, with fairly regular gradation. Specimens taken at about a foot from the top of the whole sill are dark grey rocks with specific gravity 2·74 to 2·72. To the eye they are very like the normal basalt, though less dark in colour. The xenocrysts are rather larger, ranging up to ¼ inch in diameter. They are also more numerous, preponderating very decidedly over the labradorite phenocrysts, and we must suppose them to be in part of "consequent" derivation. In thin slices the ground-mass has at first glance a sufficient resemblance to that of the normal basalt, except that the augite, now mostly decayed, has evidently been less abundant. On further examination we find that the little felspars, which are the principal element, are not, as before, labradorite. They give much lower extinction-angles, and may be set down as in the main oligoclase-andesine or one of the more basic kinds of oligoclase. We see then that this rock is of anomalous composition, being clearly much richer in silica and soda than any true basalt. A specimen from a corresponding situation near the base of the sill shows closely similar characters, the diminution in the amount of augite (here better preserved) and the relatively acid nature of the felspars of the ground-mass being well shown. Small flakes of brown mica are sparingly distributed, their formation being connected doubtless with an accession of potash to the basalt. There are little sharply defined patches of fine texture, doubtless xenoliths of the first consolidated basalt at the actual base.

Somewhat farther from the base—between 3 and 4 feet—where the specific gravity has fallen to 2·70 or less, the rock has little of the appearance of a basalt, either in hand-specimens or under the microscope. The colour has become paler, the general mass duller of aspect, and the visible crystals of felspar perhaps rather more abundant. Among these latter the glassy-looking labradorites are no longer to be recognised. A thin slice [6729] shows that they still occur, but they are corroded and turbid like the alkali-felspars. It appears that the phenocrysts proper to the basalt, as well as those proper to the felsite, reacted with the hybrid magma of intermediate composition. The little felspars of the ground-mass probably include both oligoclase and orthoclase: they give sensibly straight extinction, and twinning is with difficulty detected. There is quartz present, but it is not possible to decide to what extent it is of secondary origin. The augite granules have been replaced by calcite, etc., but this mineral has certainly not been very abundant. Little granules of magnetite are fairly plentiful, and there are larger grains and crystals of pyrites, visible in the hand-specimens. Rock comparable with this also occupies a corresponding position relative to the other (upper) surface of the sill.

We see that rocks which stand midway, in a general petrographical sense, between the basalt and the felsite are reached at 2 or 3 feet from the contacts. The transition from these to the felsite of the middle part of the sill is less rapid. The magnetite granules and augite of the ground-mass gradually disappear. The enclosed crystals of labradorite are quickly lost, and it appears that crystals of a basic felspar in an alkaline felspathic magma are more energetically attacked than crystals of alkali-felspar in a basic magma. As we pass to rocks more nearly approximating to the normal felsite, the enclosed crystals of alkali-felspar must be regarded as phenocrysts rather than xenocrysts. They show less rounding of their angles, and begin to occur in clusters. They are still very turbid, but this is due now to chemical decomposition, apparently the production of finely disseminated white mica. The coming in of the scattered augite phenocrysts, or of pseudo-morphs representing them, completes the transition to the felsite as described above.

The steady gradation indicated by the specific gravities shown in Fig. 49 shows few irregularities. The most considerable exception to the rule is only in appearance an irregularity. The rock of intermediate composition and specific gravity 2·70, which occurs at the actual base in this section, belongs in reality to a separate thin sill. This becomes evident a short distance away, where a bed of calcareous sandstone intervenes between this thin sill and the main one above. It is probable, however, that the small lower sill is not in origin quite independent of the other, and the same may be predicated of two other thin sills at horizons a little above the main one, shown at D and E in the section in Fig. 48. These show in the field no bilateral symmetry or other evident complexity of structure; but closer examination reveals some anomalous characters which are highly suggestive. Specimens from the uppermost sill (E), which is only one foot thick, show a dark close-grained rock enclosing little felspars about $\frac{1}{8}$ inch in length. Of these some are fresh and of tabular habit, while others are dull and of squarer shape, corresponding respectively with the phenocrysts of labradorite and xenocrysts of alkali-felspar described in the marginal parts of the composite sill. Moreover the rock of this thin sill is itself heterogeneous, though without regular arrangement so far as we have observed. Two specimens, taken only a short distance apart and certainly belonging to a single intrusive body, give specific gravities 2·83 and 2·72.

A comparison of these two specimens in thin slices gives interesting results. Both contain xenocrysts of the kind observed in the larger sill, chiefly of striated oligoclase and always showing an advanced stage of corrosion (*see* Plate XXI., Fig. 4). Apart from these, the former specimen [9370] consists of little crystals of labradorite, ·03 to ·06 inch long, granules of augite, and abundant brown glass. A higher magnification shows that this glass is crowded with very slender felspar fibres, and encloses numerous little rods of magnetite. This rock then may fairly be regarded as the partially vitreous representative of that which forms the marginal zones of the neighbouring composite sill. The other specimen [9371] is somewhat richer in brown glass of the same characters as before; but this is not sufficient to account for its much lower density, and examination shows that it is of decidedly less basic composition than the former rock. Augite granules are no longer present, and the little felspars give low extinction-angles, most of them apparently being near oligoclase in composition. It seems then that this is the glassy representative, not of the unmixed basalt, but of one of the hybrid varieties met with in the composite sill.

The largely vitreous nature of these rocks must be attributed to the small dimensions of the intruded body and the consequent rapid cooling of the magma. This, on reflection, is a point of considerable interest; for we are forced to the conclusion that in this case the admixture of which we have such clear evidence was already effected when the magma was intruded into its present situation, and forthwith began to cool: in other words, that the partial intermingling of the basaltic and felsitic magmas took place either in the channel of uprise or in some deeper-seated reservoir. The absence of any symmetrical arrangement of the different varieties of rock in the sill points to the same conclusion. The conception of a local magma-basin or reservoir, in which the basalt- and felsite- magmas have coexisted in a fluid state, has already been foreshadowed by the unfailing occurrence of "antecedent" xenocrysts in the composite sills of this group. A like hypothesis seems to be necessitated by the peculiar characters of the marscoite as described in a former chapter; and we shall be brought to contemplate it again, on a larger scale, in discussing the xenocrysts in the basic dykes of this region. We do not picture all the composite sills of the group under discussion as derived from a single reservoir. Their distribution rather suggests that they belong to a number of distinct centres, at each of which the parent magmas underwent a like series of processes; and the unique nature of the felsite of Rudh' an Eireannaich decidedly supports this view.

If in these symmetrical composite sills the basic and acid magmas have risen through the same fissures and spread along the same bedding-planes, the one closely following the other, it is difficult to resist the conviction that they not only came from a common reservoir, but were intimately related in origin. They may have been, in Brögger's phrase, complementary products of differentiation, and a certain rough proportion between the two rocks in the several occurrences is consistent with this hypothesis. The proportion is not a strict one, for in the largest composite sills the acid rock greatly outweighs the basic; but it is nevertheless very noticeable that the thicker basic sheets are always associated with the thicker acid ones and the thinner with the thinner. The proportion would doubtless become more evident, and might perhaps be precisely realised, if we could restore those portions of the basic sills which have been destroyed by the acid magma and absorbed into it.

The several composite sills of this group, taken in order from Suishnish to Broadford, illustrate, as we have pointed out, successive advances in the intimacy of relationship and the degree of intermingling of the associated rock-types. In this view, the small subsidiary sills at Rudh' an Eireannaich present almost the extreme type. The actual final term of the series, which may perhaps be represented in small sills and dykes not specially examined, would be a complete admixture resulting in a homogeneous rock of medium acidity. It is to be expected that a rock resulting from such complete admixture, even if all xenocrysts were entirely absorbed, would still present petrographical peculiarities distinguishing it from, e.g., a normal andesite.

On this last point it is proper to make some remarks of a general kind, which will apply not only to the composite sills and dykes, but to the mixed rocks already described in Chapter XI. and to other instances to be noticed later. We consider that all these *hybrid rocks are essentially abnormal in composition*, and do not find any place in a classificatory system of normal igneous rocks. The processes, whatever be their nature, by which basic, intermediate, and acid rocks of ordinary types are evolved or differentiated from a common stock-magma are processes of a complex and subtle kind, and are not reversible by so crude a means as the mixture of two different rock-types. A rock of mean silica-percentage produced by the mixture of an acid with a basic rock will not have the chemical or mineralogical composition of any normal intermediate rock-type. For this reason it would be misleading to apply to such a mixed rock the name of any recognised normal type or family, such as tonalite, quartz-diorite, dacite, andesite, and the like; and we have accordingly spoken of such rocks as partially acidified gabbros, dolerites, and basalts or partially basified granites, granophyres, and felsites. For one rock, which appeared in numerous occurrences with the same peculiar characters, we have used a special name (marscoite); but this was done solely for convenience of description, and in general the variability of the rocks is such that no definite types can be profitably recognised.

That an abnormal chemical composition is to be expected in a hybrid rock follows from general considerations, and a brief statement of the argument will be sufficient in this place.* The general laws which control the variation in composition of igneous rocks, though in the present state of knowledge empirical, are sufficiently well known. The variations in particular natural series of rocks have been studied, and are conveniently expressed in graphic form by a diagram in which abscissæ represent the silica-percentages of the several members of the series and ordinates the corresponding percentages of the other oxides. For igneous rocks in general the variations in composition have of course a wider range, but certain broad principles still hold. The magnesia, for instance, falls off as the silica increases; but it does not fall off at a steady rate: it diminishes first rather rapidly and afterward slowly. Its variation may thus be illustrated diagrammatically by a curve which is concave upward (Fig. 50). Lime behaves differently, and its curve of variation will be convex upward (Fig. 51). It is easy to deduce that a mixture of a basic and an acid rock will in general be richer in magnesia and poorer

* For a fuller discussion of this part of the question, see Harker, Igneous Rock-Series and Mixed Igneous Rocks, *Journ. of Geol.*, vol. viii., pp. 389-399 : 1900.

in lime than a normal igneous rock of like silica-percentage. If such differences, viz. a relative excess in some constituents and deficiency in others, pass certain limits, they must affect the mineralogical constitution of the resulting rock: thus an undue richness in magnesia and poverty in lime may determine the formation of a hornblende instead of an augite. Such considerations seem to throw some light on some of the peculiarities of the rocks described above.

The application of the above argument must, however, be limited by what is in some measure a countervailing consideration. We have so far regarded admixture as a simple process, and tacitly assumed that a hybrid rock derived from the two normal types A and B can be represented, in respect of chemical composition, by such a formula as $mA + nB$, where m and n are the propor-

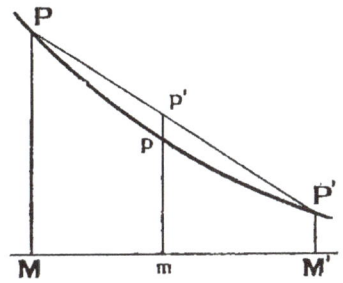

FIG. 50.—Ideal curve of variation of magnesia, PpP^1. Here PM and P^1M^1 represent the percentages of magnesia in a basic and an acid rock; p^1m, that in a hybrid rock formed by the admixture of the two; and pm, that in a normal rock having the same silica-percentage as the hybrid. The latter has thus an excess of magnesia.

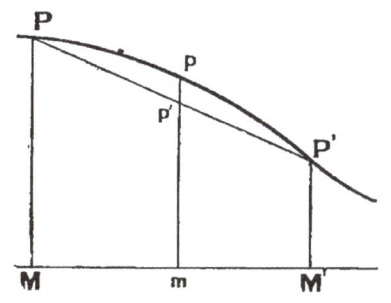

FIG. 51.—Ideal curve of variation of lime. The diagram is lettered to correspond with the preceding, lime being understood instead of magnesia. It is seen that the hybrid rock has a deficiency of lime as compared with the natural rock of the same silica-percentage.

tions in which the two parent rocks are mingled. In fact, however, this is not the case, the process of admixture being complicated by diffusion. We have seen in Chapter XI. that the composition of the granophyre modified by gabbro débris on Marsco does not correspond with a simple formula of the kind suggested; and both in that chapter and the present one we have seen abundant evidence that diffusion has proceeded more or less freely, even in some cases where the sharp boundary between the two rocks involved has not been obliterated. If, as is generally supposed, the origin of diverse rock-types among normal igneous rocks is in great part dependent upon diffusion, this consideration may go to modify in some degree the argument advanced above concerning the necessarily abnormal composition of hybrid rocks; but it is at most a mitigating factor.

Of the triple composite sills not yet particularly described, only one calls for any special notice. We may remark that the intimacy of association between the different members, which reached a climax in the basalt-felsite sill of Rudh' an Eireannaich, is displayed in a high, though less extreme, degree in the other northerly examples, which have the more usual basalt-granophyre combination. At Camas na Geadaig in Scalpay the central acid member is sharply delimited against the upper basalt, but seems, to the eye at least, to shade insensibly into the lower one. At *Allt an 't-Sithean*, near Sligachan, the boundaries are in most places fairly distinct, though of highly irregular form, but this has not prevented a remarkable degree of intermingling between the two rocks. This occurrence deserves some brief notice. It differs from most of the others in its decidedly laccolitic development, the granophyre forming a lenticular mass in the interior of a basalt sill (*see* section, Fig. 44). This is susceptible of simple explanation. The basalt sill, prior to the intrusion of the granophyre, was swollen in this place to an unusual thickness, and its interior portion was here partly fluid when in other places the sill was consolidated throughout. Here the acid magma consequently found easy access, and entered into reactions with the imperfectly consolidated basalt. There was here, however, some peculiarity in the conditions attending the consolidation of the basalt, which enabled the process to begin in the central zone as well as at the margins, and an inconstant sheet of the rock, usually not more than 3 feet thick, was thus enclosed in the heart of the granophyre, which found its way both above and below. It is certain that some part of this middle basalt was actually solid when the acid magma came in; for, although most of the deeply corroded sheet is in a greatly modified state, a part is quite normal. It is a dark grey crystalline basalt of specific gravity 2·85, enclosing only scattered xenocrysts, which clearly are of the "antecedent" kind never absent from this type of rock. As might be anticipated, its texture is not so fine as in other basalts of this group.

Such portions of the upper and lower basalts as can be considered normal rocks do not differ, except by their finer texture, from the specimen just noticed. The normal granophyre is a beautiful spherulitic rock, but in most places deeply weathered. It does not contain quartz phenocrysts of any visible size, and this explains the general absence (to the eye at least) of quartz-grains among the xenocrysts, whether antecedent or consequent, in the basalts. On the line of our section there is not much basic rock of normal character seen in the valley of Allt an 't-Sithean itself, the rock which does duty as basalt being mostly acidified in greater or less degree. An average example of the lower "basalt" at this place has a specific gravity only 2·63. It is of rather light grey colour, and contains fairly abundant dull white felspars, $\frac{1}{8}$ to $\frac{1}{4}$ inch, some of which are probably "consequent" xenocrysts. It encloses little patches, either angular or rounded, of finer texture and evidently of more normal basic composition, and in these the felspars are smaller and less numerous. They are presumably pieces of the first-consolidated marginal zone of the basalt, subsequently broken up, and xenoliths of this kind are very common in this sill. The "granophyre" near all its contacts with the "basalt" encloses very numerous partially digested xenoliths of that rock, which have the appearance of being much acidified. In the same places the acid rock itself is considerably modified in the opposite sense, and, as usual in such cases, has lost its spherulitic structure.

As we have remarked, the boundary between "basalt" and "granophyre," though highly irregular, is in general not obliterated. There has, however, been free diffusion across the boundary in both directions, and it is not difficult to select specimens from the "basalt" side of the line which are evidently more acid than some specimens from the "granophyre" side. In the absence of chemical tests, this is sufficiently proved by specific gravity determinations. Thus a specimen of quite pale grey colour representing the middle "basalt" in a greatly modified condition gives only 2·577, while a neighbouring "granophyre" (containing, however, some small xenoliths) gives 2·656.

In conclusion we may notice briefly the large composite dyke, probably connected with this sill, which is exposed not far to the north. It has a maximum width of nearly 150 feet, and, excepting a narrow border on each side, is of granophyre. It contains felspars with rounded angles and little round grains of quartz. All these are the nuclei of spherulites, and other spherulites make up the rest of the rock. It is conspicuously drusy; but, as usual, the sum total of the vacant spaces which go to produce this appearance is in reality quite small. Specific gravity determinations taken on a specimen, first in bulk and then in powder, differ by less than ·01, and the druses certainly make up less than one part in 200 of the total volume. A fresher rock, with no lining of secondary products in the druses, would give a rather higher proportion.

The much shrunken width of the bordering basalts is in agreement with what is elsewhere observed in the dykes of this group, as compared with the sills. Equally to be anticipated is the greatly modified character of such basalt as remains, no part of which has escaped being impregnated by the acid magma. A specimen selected to represent the least altered rock has a specific gravity only 2·59, and contains conspicuous xenocrysts of felspar. This rock is definitely divided from the granophyre, but in other places it is not possible to draw any sharp line. Both the "basalt" and the edge of the granophyre adjoining it enclose abundant xenoliths of a dark fine-textured rock, up to 2 or 3 inches in length in some places. These never contain xenocrysts, or indeed any visible crystals, and they often show but little rounding of their angles. They are probably derived from the basalt lavas which the dyke intersects.

CHAPTER XIV.

Basic Sills: The Great Group.

Among the intrusive rocks occurring outside the mountain district, by far the most important are those which form the very numerous sills of generally basic composition (dolerite, basalt, etc.) intercalated among the basaltic lavas and subjacent strata.

The intrusive nature of the sheets of "trap" intercalated among the Secondary strata in the northern part of Skye was clearly recognised by Macculloch. So long ago as 1819 he illustrated by admirable diagrams,* which have often been reproduced, how these sheets, while preserving for long distances a close parallelism with the bedding and a very uniform thickness, sometimes break abruptly across to a new horizon, or divide into two or three thinner sheets separated by sedimentary beds; how in places the sheets thicken out, and irregularly cut out and truncate the strata, portions of which, bent and broken, have become entangled in the igneous rock; and how veins or small offshoots are sometimes given off from the sheets, traversing the overlying as well as the underlying strata. It is remarkable that, notwithstanding these decisive proofs of intrusion, the sheets of basic rock continued to be generally regarded as true lava-flows and therefore of the same Oolitic age as the strata with which they are associated. Even after the true age of the great series of basalts above had been determined by botanical evidence, eminent geologists held that in this district of Trotternish occur volcanic rocks of two distinct ages, Jurassic and Tertiary.

The intrusive nature and Tertiary age of the basic sills in the Jurassic are now generally conceded, and indeed admit of no dispute. What geologists have not yet fully recognised is that such sills occur in enormous profusion, and attain individually and collectively a great thickness, among the overlying bedded lavas; that throughout the basaltic plateaux, which make up two-thirds of the area of Skye, these intrusive sills determine almost all the salient features, and indeed are the cause of the plateau form itself (*see* Fig. 79, below). The proofs of the intrusive habit of a basic sill are, in the nature of the case, less obvious when it occurs among basalts than when it is intercalated in a group of shales and sandstones, but upon examination the evidence is equally convincing. Notwithstanding the surprisingly regular disposition of the sills along defined horizons in the series, occasional transgressions are to be verified; and, what is an even more striking proof of intrusion, the sills are observed here and there to intersect some

* *Description of the Western Islands of Scotland*, vol. iii., Pl. XVII.

of the earlier basic dykes. Petrographically the resemblance of the sills in the basalt group to those among the Jurassic strata is as evident as their difference from the undoubted lava-flows among which they occur; while a study of their micro-structure shows that they have almost invariably something of that ophitic character which is much less common in the lavas. The existence of numerous intrusive sills in the basaltic group having once been recognised, it is found that they have, as a group, definite characteristics, which enable us to identify and map them with perfect confidence even when, as is usually the case, the field-observations afford no ocular demonstration of their intrusive nature.

It is not to be understood that all the sill-formed basic intrusions in Skye belong to a single group referable to one epoch. We shall indeed make some remarks in the next chapter on certain smaller groups of sills, in addition to those, closely associated with acid rocks, which we have already described; and it is also worthy of mention in passing that some of the basic dykes occasionally assume for some distance the habit of sills. We are at present concerned, however, with the vast majority of basic sills in the island, which do in fact constitute one natural group of intrusions, and will be spoken of for the sake of clearness as the "*great group of basic sills*" or of dolerite sills. It is these rocks that play so important a part in the constitution of the basaltic plateaux, besides occurring in force, as noted above, in the underlying Jurassic strata as exposed along some portions of the coast.

The *epoch of intrusion* of these sills is quite determinate. They are later than any volcanic or plutonic rocks in the island, but earlier than the great majority of the minor intrusions. Their injection constitutes therefore the earliest episode of the last of the three phases of igneous activity which we have pointed out as recognisable in our area. The intrusion of so many distinct sills, often individually of great volume, was a process which doubtless occupied a prolonged lapse of time. If we could assign to this group any of the basic sills which, near Suishnish and elsewhere, are closely associated with acid intrusions, it would appear that the earliest of the great group of sills were, at certain points, overlapped in time by the latest of the intrusions belonging to the granite and granophyre group of the Red Hills. We have described, however, remarkable circumstances characterising the basic members of the composite sills, which lead us to infer for them a common origin with the acid rocks with which they are associated. We therefore separate them from the rocks now under consideration, and refer them to a somewhat earlier date. Considering the composite intrusions as a peculiar group belonging to the interval between the plutonic phase and that of the minor intrusions, we must regard the latter phase as beginning with the intrusion of the great group of sills.

As regards the *distribution in space* of the sills, it is in the first place very noticeable that in Skye they are developed in greatest force, both individually and as a group, in the northern part of the island. Over all the plateau country, lying to the north and west of the central mountains, the sills form every prominent feature; but, approaching nearer to the gabbro and granite of the mountain tract itself, we find that they thin out and finally disappear (Fig. 52). This is certainly not due to the dying out of the group as a whole, for beyond the mountain tract the sills reappear in the Strathaird peninsula and elsewhere. They never attain, however, to the south and east of the mountains the massive dimensions which they display in the northern and western parts of the island, but become rarer as well as smaller, and do not extend into the south-eastern part of Skye. It is not easy to assign exactly the limits in this direction of the area affected by the sills; partly because the lava-group, in which the sills are elsewhere principally developed, has here been removed by erosion; partly because other groups of sills come in, which cannot always be readily separated in the field from the great group. A comparison of the Jurassic series of Strath with that of Trotternish, as regards the occurrence of intercalated basic sills, is, however, sufficiently conclusive, and the greatly diminished thickness as well as the increasing rarity of the occurrences leaves no doubt as to the dying out of the group.

It is clear from the distribution thus indicated that the sills have no close connection with the plutonic focus of central Skye. So far as our information goes, they are probably related to some quite distinct focus, either in the north of the island or beyond its limits. We might place it conjecturally in the neighbourhood of the Shiant Isles, 12 to 14 miles north of Skye, where Professor Judd[*] and Sir A. Geikie[†] have described what appears to be a single sill 500 feet thick.

The failure of the sills in the neighbourhood of the mountains is beyond doubt due to the obstacle presented to their spread by the ring of metamorphosed basalt lavas. The sill-magma, which easily found a way along the divisional planes of the lava-flows outside the metamorphosed belt, was arrested when it encountered the tougher and more stubborn rocks, devoid of apparent bedding, which fringe the plutonic intrusions; and sills are accordingly absent in this belt, as well as in the gabbro and granite themselves. This, of course, would be sufficient to prove the posteriority of the sills to the plutonic intrusions, even were no other evidence available. The total absence of the sill rocks among the patches of basalt entangled in the gabbro and granite is equally significant. The belt of metamorphosed basalts free from sills has usually a width of nearly a mile from the main boundary of the gabbro or granite (see Fig. 52).

With reference to the *thickness* of the individual sills, we have observed none in Skye comparable in magnitude with that mentioned above in the Shiant Isles, supposing the 500 feet there seen to belong really to a single sill. Many of the sills in the northern and north-western parts of Skye, however, attain a thickness of 100 feet, and there are some which exceed 200 feet. Still

[*] *Quart. Journ. Geol. Soc.*, vol. xxxiv., pp. 676, 677 : 1878.
[†] *Ibid.*, vol. lii., pp. 373, 375 : 1896.

238   *Distribution of Great Group of Sills.*

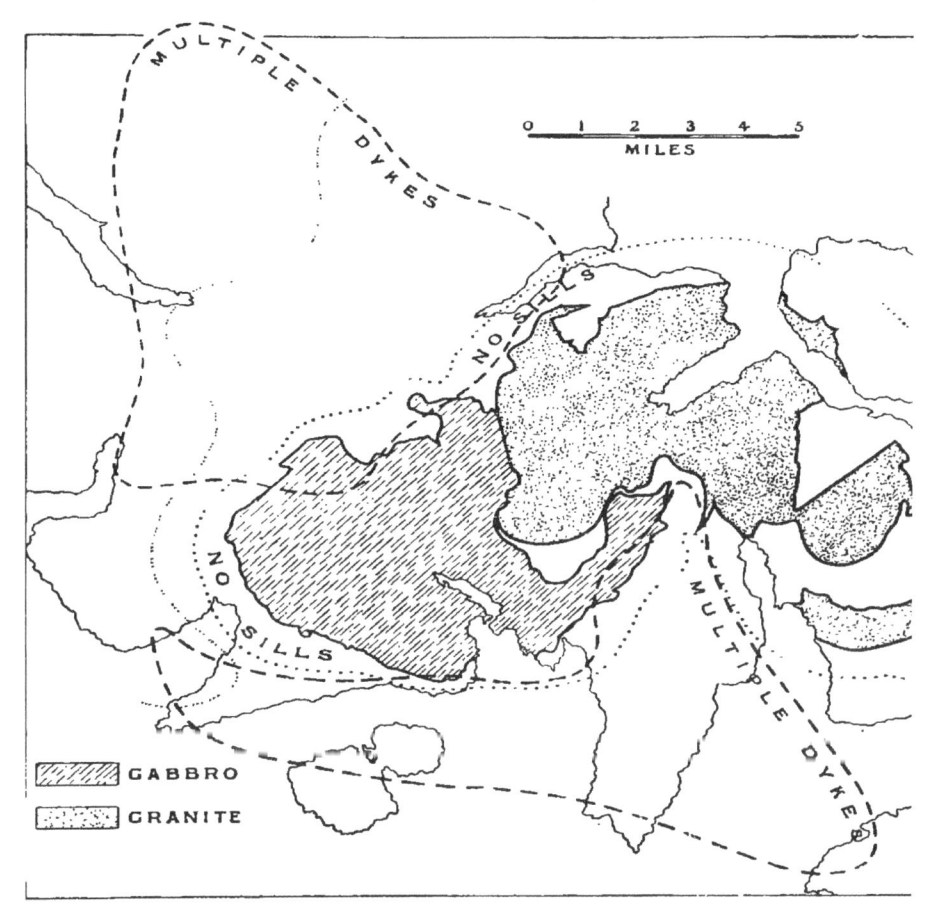

Fig. 52.—Sketch-map illustrating the distribution of the basic sills, and also of the multiple basic dykes, in relation to the large plutonic intrusions. Scale, ¼ inch to a mile.

(*a*) The heavy dotted line indicates the area (embracing the plutonic intrusions with a narrow surrounding belt) which is free from sills belonging to the great group. The lighter dotted line marks the limit (in this part the eastern limit) of multiple sills. This depends partly upon the general attenuation of the group in this direction, but partly also upon the progress of erosion, since the multiple sills are developed chiefly in the upper portion of the lava group.

(*b*) The heavy broken line indicates the distribution of the principal multiple basic dykes. They are found within an elongated oval tract, about eleven miles long, centring in the great gabbro laccolite and having its long axis in the general direction of the dykes themselves. This oval tract, however, is divided into two detached areas by the plutonic masses. It is not improbable that better exposures might enable us to join these two areas on the west side of the Cuillins, but on the east side the granite has offered an impenetrable resistance (see Chap. XVII.).

greater thicknesses of sill-rocks are found where two or more large sills come together without any intervening "country" rock. This is, among the basaltic plateaux, a very frequent occurrence, and in this way arise what we shall style for convenience *double, triple, and multiple sills*. The thickest multiple sill verified in the area mapped is that with fine columnar jointing which forms Preshal More, near Talisker : here the total thickness shown is about 500 feet.

The accompanying section (Fig. 53) will illustrate the important part which the sills play in the structure of the basaltic moorlands. It is taken in a north-easterly direction from the high-road a little west of Inver Meadale farm-house, near Struan, and traverses Monadh Meadale, one of the hills to the north-east of Loch Harport. Here a total thickness of about 2000 feet is distributed approximately as follows :—

Feet.		Feet.
325	Four-fold sill	
	Lavas	55
200	Four-fold sill	
	(Lavas to S.E.)	—
35	Sill	
	Lavas	50
115	Double sill	
	Lavas	65
140	Double sill	
	Lavas	65
165	Double sill	
	Lavas	60
55	Sill	
	Lavas	100
40	Sill	
	Lavas	120
30	Sill	
	Lavas	105
50	Sill	
	Lavas	175
50	Sill	

Twenty sills, 1,205 ft.   795 ft, Lavas.

It is seen that the sills become more numerous as we ascend in the succession, and collectively make up three-fifths of the whole thickness. Of the upper half of the section the sills make about five-sixths, of the lower half about three-eighths. It is also seen in the section that the tendency of the sills to run together as double or multiple sills becomes more pronounced as we pass upward, and this too seems to be very generally true throughout the basalt tract. A section taken farther northward, *e.g.* at the Quiraing, would probably bring out even more strikingly the importance of the intrusive sills intercalated among the basaltic lavas, but our detailed survey has not extended into that part of the island.

The *persistence and regularity* of the sills are very remarkable. Whether in the basaltic lavas or in the Jurassic strata, they may often be traced for long distances, maintaining accurately a defined horizon. Among the basalts it is not uncommon to find two sills which have been separated coming together; but this is susceptible of two alternative explanations: one of the sills may have broken obliquely across the basalt lavas intervening, or a lava-flow dividing the two sills may have died out. Since the several flows of lava are as a rule not distinguishable, except in so far as they are separated by sills, no simple criterion is available; but the latter alternative is probably the usual explanation, and the indications go to show that the individual sills have in general a much greater lateral extension than the individual lava-flows.

We shall have to point out in another chapter that the basic dykes of our area do not traverse different kinds of rock with equal facility, but exhibit very marked preferences. In the nature of the case a sill does not usually, like a dyke, encounter different country rocks in its progress; but when such a case occurs we find the same reluctance to enter certain kinds of rock. Thus the sills have not without difficulty penetrated a mass of volcanic agglomerate lying in their path, and may sometimes be seen to die out rapidly in such a mass. A good illustration of this is seen at the southwestern corner of Camas Bàn, near Portree (*see* Fig. 6, p. 23). We have already seen that the sills are completely stopped, not only by the peridotites, gabbros, and granites, but also by the basaltic lavas metamorphosed in the vicinity of those rocks.

As regards the manner of intrusion of the sills, it cannot be doubted that they were fed through dyke-fissures. The difficulty of identifying with certainty any of the dykes representing these feeders is one to which it is not necessary to attach much importance. Apart from an ocular demonstration of the continuity of a sill with its dyke-feeder, which could only be expected as a rare accident, there seems to be no means of discriminating the feeders of the sills from the feeders of the basalt lava-flows. It may be therefore that some of the basic dykes, earlier than the majority of those in the area, belong to the great group of sills. It is probable, however, that the fissures through which rose the material to form these sills are for the most part situated in that portion of Skye lying to the north of the ground as yet surveyed in detail. That basic sills may spread laterally to great distances from their source is evident from their extent as actually seen in Skye, and is still more clear in areas where the confusing element of a great number of sills is not present. The Great Whin Sill of Teesdale, for example, can be traced over an extent of 80 or 90 miles; and, if its origin be at Cauldron Snout, the magma must have forced its way laterally for a distance of at least 70 miles.

We shall have to notice later that the more massive sills have presented an obstacle to the passage of dykes subsequently injected. This would lead us to anticipate that *the higher sills of the great group were in general those earlier intruded*. That this was the case appears from several circumstances, and especially from the fact that multiple sills become more frequent towards the upper part of the group. A dyke-fissure propagated upward would often be arrested at the lower surface of a sill, and the magma forced up through the fissure would then spread laterally, forming a new sill immediately below the earlier one. In this way the new sill would at most have to traverse the dyke-feeder or feeders of the earlier sill, a much easier matter than penetrating the sill itself. It is also probable that a given fissure has often served for more than one intrusion, so that the feeders would sometimes be multiple dykes.

The basic sills of this great group, presenting a very general community of petrographical characters, show also considerable uniformity as regards habit and appearance in the field. In thickness there is great variation, the single sills ranging from a few inches to 200 feet or more. Apart from this, the chief difference observable among the sills in the field depends upon the degree of development of columnar jointing in the rocks. This character may be wholly wanting, or may occur with varying development and regularity. Where it is absent, the sills, and especially those of moderately large dimensions, very often show a certain platy or rudely laminated structure parallel to the upper and lower surfaces and most marked in the neighbourhood of those surfaces. This is often found also in association with the columnar jointing. It imparts a certain quality of fissility to the sill, but is not related to anything in the intimate structure of the rock, and must be regarded as an effect of contraction.

Conspicuous *columnar jointing* in the sills seems to have a well-defined geographical distribution in the island. It is very prevalent and often very perfectly developed in the north, but gives place, as we pass southward towards the central tract, to a rude division into blocks, frequently showing the quasi-horizontal platy structure already mentioned. When most clearly marked, the columns are as a rule at right angles, or nearly so, to the surfaces of the sills, and therefore make only a small angle with the vertical, depending on the dip of the sills themselves. Irregularities are, however, found in some places (Plate IX.). The columns extend from top to bottom of even the thickest sills, though they may be broken at intervals by cross-joints.

Some of the finest examples of columnar jointing are seen in the two hills named on the Ordnance map Preshal More and Preshal Beg,* near Talisker. They are two outliers of the same multiple sill, which is columnar throughout. The most regular development is seen in the lowest member, which forms the steep sides of each hill. As seen on the south-east side of Preshal Beg, this is from 70 or 80 to 100 feet thick, the columns often ranging unbroken through this distance. They are perpendicular to the surfaces of the sill, and at the west end, where the sill itself is rather sharply tilted up, the columns are inclined so as to preserve their approximate perpendicularity. On the north side, however, their inclination is less according to rule. The cross-section of any column is an irregular polygon of from 4 to 7 sides, with

* They have attracted the notice of several of the earlier writers, the name appearing under various disguises: Briis-mhawl (Pennant), Breeze-hill (Jameson), and Brishmeal (Macculloch).

diameter usually between 1 and 2 feet; and the same form and dimensions are preserved throughout the length of the column. Resting upon this regularly jointed sill, and forming the upper part of the bold hill, are two or more other sills, in which the columns are smaller and less perfectly formed, and tend to form rather divergent bunches. These upper sills have a thickness (left after erosion) of 180 to 200 feet, the thickness of the whole multiple sill being not less than 275 feet. Preshal More shows a like arrangement (Fig. 54), and here, in the precipitous northern face of the hill, the total thickness of columnar rock shown is scarcely less than 500 feet. There are in places irregularities in the disposition of the columns, which are sometimes curved (Plate IX.). The arrangement shown in these hills, of a lower sheet with very regular columns overlain by one or more sheets with a more confused prismatic structure, seems to be not uncommon in other parts of the Inner Hebrides, Fingal's Cave in Staffa being a well-known example.

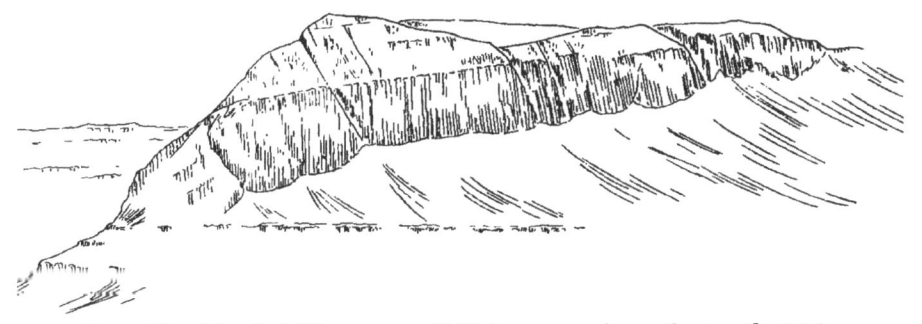

Fig. 54.—Preshal More, near Talisker, seen from the south-west.

Perhaps the most striking exhibitions of columnar jointing in Skye, however, are to be seen on the east coast. As we proceed northward, the first example is met with at Rudha Buidhe, between Loch Sligachan and Portree Harbour (Plate X.). Beyond Portree, the thick sills intruded in the Jurassic strata display, as exposed in the sea-cliffs, a highly developed and very regular columnar structure, which reaches its climax in the Kilt Rock* and along the coast of Loch Staffin.†

Very striking are the *magnetic phenomena* connected with the sill-rocks.‡ In the moorland country these rocks, as we have remarked, usually form all the salient features. In the neighbourhood of any prominent ridge or knoll, which stands out above the surrounding ground, the compass shows a very sensible deflection from the normal magnetic meridian. Projecting knobs of rock are

---

* See sketch by Sir A. Geikie, *Quart. Journ. Geol. Soc.*, vol. lii., p. 374: 1896.
† The name Staffin, like that of the island Staffa (from the Norse *stav*, staff) is doubtless in allusion to this feature.
‡ Harker, Magnetic Disturbances in the Isle of Skye, *Proc. Camb. Phil. Soc.*, vol. x., pp. 268-278, Pl. XI., XII.: 1900.

Part of the northern face of Preshal More, near Talisker,
showing curvature of columns.

Columnar sill of dolerite forming the cliff at Rudha Buidhe, near Braes.

found to be places of violent magnetic disturbance, particular points in the rock attracting either the north or the south pole of the needle, and giving evidence of strong permanent magnetism distributed in an irregular fashion, as already noticed in the gabbro of the mountains. Again, areas sometimes hundreds of yards in extent often show disturbances of a lower order, but still easily verified with the pocket-compass. Such an area embraces one or more centres of violent local disturbance, and the effects become gradually less noticeable with increasing distance. There appear to be evident relations between the two orders of phenomena, and it is possible that much more wide-spread but feebler disturbances, only to be detected by a systematic magnetic survey, may also be connected with permanent rock-magnetism. The localisation of the more strongly marked phenomena in exposed summits and ridges decidedly suggests atmospheric electricity as the cause of the magnetisation.

The *metamorphism produced by the sills* in older rocks adjacent to them is never comparable in degree and extent with the effects set up in the neighbourhood of the gabbro and granite masses. The basaltic lavas in contact with the sills of the plateaux often show no perceptible change from this cause. Even in the Jurassic rocks invaded by the thick sills of the Trotternish coast, as Sir A. Geikie* has noted, the alteration "seldom goes beyond a mere induration of the strata for a few yards, often only for a few inches from the surface of junction." In their being attended as a rule by little or no conspicuous thermal metamorphism the sills resemble the ordinary dykes of the district.

Of reciprocal modification of a mineralogical kind in the sills themselves at their contact with sedimentary rocks we have not found any indication. Bryce† recorded dipyre as occurring in a thick sill on the shore of Loch Staffin. This sill is intruded among Jurassic strata, partly calcareous, and forms the base of the well-known Loch Staffin section.

One place only calls for special notice as illustrating an advanced degree of metamorphism produced by the basic sills. This is in the Isle of Soay, where the relations of the rocks have been studied and specimens collected by Mr Clough. The country-rock here is a coarse-grained grit of Torridonian age, consisting of quartz with a considerable amount of alkali-felspars, these latter being turbid and iron-stained [9984]. At certain localities the grit has been in great part vitrified in contact with basic sills, which are in no case more than 10 feet thick. A series of specimens has been examined from a little bay near the extreme south point of the island [9981–9983]. In its most altered condition the rock has the black vitreous appearance of a pitchstone, but in this as a matrix are enclosed little pale spots which represent undestroyed grains of quartz. Mr Clough found the specific gravities of two specimens to be 2·42 and 2·47. Thin slices present under the microscope a

* *Quart. Journ. Geol. Soc.*, vol. lii., p. 376 : 1896 ; and *Ancient Volcanoes of Great Britain*, vol. ii., p. 310 : 1897.
† *Quart. Journ. Geol. Soc.*, vol. xxix., p. 328 : 1873.

Q

very beautiful appearance. In one variety relics of quartz-grains are preserved in a matrix consisting principally of colourless glass. The grains are evidently corroded, and a large part of the quartz of the grit, with the whole of the felspar and iron-oxide, has been fused to make the matrix. This latter is a clear colourless glass crowded with little crystals (see Pl. XXI., Fig. 3). Three minerals are to be recognised among these crystals. First there is magnetite in sharp octahedra, usually not more than ·0005 inch in diameter. Secondly, and of later formation than the magnetite, which it sometimes encloses, is cordierite, in well-shaped crystals averaging about ·001 inch. These are perfectly clear and colourless. They have the crystal habit usual in this mode of occurrence,* giving rectangular and hexagonal sections, but we have not detected polysynthetic twinning. The third mineral builds slender rods with a fibrous structure longitudinally, and has a faint greenish-yellow tint. It seems to be pleochroic, and the extinction, when it can be verified, is nearly parallel to the length of the rods. The mineral is perhaps ægirine.

In another specimen [9981] the same three minerals occur in the colourless glass, magnetite being specially abundant, but there are in addition little rods of clear new-built felspar. These seem to be connected in a very intimate manner with the corrosion of the quartz-grains, being densely massed in embayments of these. This slice shows the junction with the dolerite sill. Approaching this, the cordierite-crystals disappear, while the pale-tinted fibrous rods become very plentiful. They are here of stouter shape than before, and their pleochroism and low extinction-angle can be verified, but it is not certain whether they belong to an amphibole or a soda-pyroxene. Towards the dolerite the glassy matrix encloses felspars from that rock and little grains of augite resembling, except in their granular form, that of the dolerite. The quartz-grains are not found in this part. Immediately contiguous to the dolerite, the glassy matrix assumes a brown colour. It seems that there has been a certain degree of commingling between the dolerite magma and the fused grit. This is evident at the actual junction, and even in other places the formation of cordierite seems to imply an accession of magnesia. The dolerite itself, beyond the narrow zone characterised by brown glass, is, however, of quite normal character. In another specimen sliced [9983] the relations are more complicated, the actual junction between the vitrified grit and the dolerite being of highly irregular form. The matrix enclosing the relics of quartz-grains is here pale brown and turbid, and is found to depolarise, being apparently in great part felspathic. There has evidently been considerable later

---

*The forms present are the prism, brachypinacoid, and basal, and the habit is such as to simulate very closely a hexagonal prism. The vertical length is not much greater than the transverse diameter. For such microscopic cordierite crystals see especially Prohaska, *Sitz. Wien Akad., math.-naturw. Classe*, vol. xcii., pp. 20-32 : 1885 ; and Zirkel, *Neu. Jahrb.*, 1891, vol. i., pp. 109-112 ; also, for figures, Hussak, *Sitz. Wien Akad., math.-naturw. Classe*, vol. lxxxvii., pp. 332-360 : 1883.

decomposition, the yellowish-green rods, abundant in places, being quite destroyed. Cordierite is not recognised here.

It is by no means certain that the sills which produce these very striking changes in the Torridonian grits belong to what we have styled the "great group." Of the basic sills of Soay in general, which are rather numerous though individually of no great magnitude, it appears that some at least are to be referred to a much later epoch. Mr Clough has observed three clear instances of the vitrification of grits in Soay, besides others in which the effects seem to be obscured by subsequent alteration. Some of these are in connection, not with basic, but with ultrabasic sills, which belong to a very late stage, and will be discussed in a later chapter. The vitrification is only locally produced in the case of any given sill.

We pass on to the *petrographical characters* of the great group of sills. They appear in the field as dark rocks usually of moderately fine texture, but evidently crystalline : only exceptionally, in some of the thinner sills, do we find a compact appearance comparable with what is seen in the basalt lavas. The rocks are typically non-porphyritic, and in general not amygdaloidal, though in some cases amygdules occur sparingly. There is as a rule little appearance of decomposition, excepting a rusty surface due to oxidation. The specific gravity is high. Forty examples gave figures varying from 2·82 to 3·07, with a mean of 2·94. It is clear that the rocks are all of basic composition, and are not varied, as in the volcanic group, by sub-basic types.

A striking characteristic of the basic sills as compared with the basic lavas is their much fresher condition. This is partly connected with the general absence of any vesicular structure. When scattered amygdules are present, they consist of calcite or other secondary products, rarely chloritic. Veins of decomposition-products are decidedly rare. In the thick sill which forms the cliff at Rudha Buidhe, between Portree and the Braes, there are irregular veins and knots of yellowish crystalline calcite. This has in part a brecciated structure with clear radiating growths surrounding dull patches, and in the interspaces there is a little chalcedony, also with radiate structure [9256].

The very small amygdules, which occur sparingly in some of the sills, are of regular spherical form. Where scattered amygdules of larger size are present, they have a rather more irregular shape, but still, as a rule, without systematic elongation in any particular direction. This is a point of contrast with the basaltic lavas and also with many of the basic dykes of the region. The infrequency of a conspicuous amygdaloidal structure is a character not only of the great group of sills but also in varying degree of other groups of sill-formed intrusions in our area. Mr Clough notes that in some of the sills in the Isle of Soay amygdules are more abundant near the top than near the bottom, but they always decrease in size close to the margins, as is also the case in the dykes.

To illustrate the *chemical composition* of the sills of the great group two complete analyses have been made by Dr Pollard (I.,

II.). We have not for comparison with these any other published analyses of rocks from the British Tertiary suite, which are definitely stated to be from sills, and can be assumed to belong to the "great group." It is highly probable, however, that the "trap" rocks from Fingal's Cave and the Giant's Causeway, analysed many years ago by Streng, are to be placed here, and we accordingly quote the figures for these in columns A and B.

It is to be noticed that, while these rocks have about the same silica-percentage as the gabbros, they differ widely in other respects. The sills are poorer in alumina and lime, and richer in iron and alkalies. Two minor constituents also show significant differences: the sills have an exceptionally high percentage of titanic acid, and, unlike the gabbros, they contain phosphoric acid to an amount such as is usual in basic igneous rocks in other regions.

In the photographs of the arc-spectra of these two rocks kindly communicated by Sir J. Norman Lockyer the lines corresponding with Ti, Cr, Va, and Sr are all very clearly shown, those for

	I.	II.	A.	B.
SiO_2	46·13	45·24	47·80	52·13
TiO_2	3·60	2·26	not det.	not det.
Al_2O_3	17·07	15·63	14·80	14·87
Cr_2O_3	trace	trace	..	..
V_2O_3	0·03	..	..	..
Fe_2O_3	6·61	5·56	not det.	not det.
FeO	8·20	7·19	13·08	11·40
NiO, CoO	..	trace	..	..
MnO	0·28	0·23	0·09	0·32
MgO	4·38	7·88	6·81	6·46
CaO	7·15	9·38	12·89	10·56
Na_2O	3·58	2·01	2·48	2·60
K_2O	1·19	0·72	0·86	0·69
H_2O { above 105°	1·71	2·21	} 1·41	1·19
{ at 105° C.	0·59	1·12		
CO_2	..	0·49	..	..
P_2O_5	0·09	0·20	not det.	not det.
	100·61	100·06	100·25	100·22
Specific gravity,	2·91	2·85	(2·957)	(2·878)

I. Olivine-dolerite [8057], sill 500 yards N. of tarn, Broc-bheinn, about 4 miles W.N.W. of Sligachan: anal. W. Pollard, *Summary of Progress Geol. Sur.* for 1899, p. 173. Vanadium and strontium were detected spectroscopically by Sir J. Norman Lockyer in this and the next rock.

II. Olivine-dolerite [7854], sill forming summit of Ben Lee, N.W. of Loch Sligachan: anal. W. Pollard, *ibid.*, p. 174.

A. "Trap" [? dolerite sill], Fingal's Cave, Staffa: anal. A. Streng, *Pogg. Ann.*, vol. xc., p. 114; 1853. (Specific gravity by von Dechen, on another specimen.)

B. "Trap" [? dolerite sill], Giant's Causeway, Antrim: anal. A. Streng, *ibid.* (Specific gravity by von Leonhard, on another specimen.)

titanium and strontium being especially prominent in I. and that for chromium in II.*

The *constituent minerals* of the rocks are not many: felspar, augite, olivine, iron-ore, and apatite. The felspar is in general a labradorite, but, judged by extinction-angles in thin slices, often a rather basic variety of labradorite; and sometimes, as in the Ben Lee sill of Analysis II., it is a bytownite. The crystals in rocks of average texture are about $\frac{1}{50}$ inch long, but there is considerable difference in this respect in different sills. They show the usual tabular habit parallel to the brachypinacoid, giving rectangular sections, which in the finer-textured rocks are of slender form. Carlsbad and albite twinning are constantly found. Sections parallel to the twin-lamellæ often show a more rounded outline, and between crossed nicols a zonary banding.

The augite has invariably crystallised after the felspar. It is light brown to nearly colourless in thin slices. In some sills, such as the great one in the Jurassic at Steinscholl, there is a purple tinge with distinct pleochroism [5336]. The mineral is usually quite fresh. If it shows any alteration, this is of the serpentinous, not the chloritic, kind, and the augite is probably of a non-aluminous variety.

The great majority of the rocks contain olivine, which is certainly much more general here than in some other groups of basic rocks in Skye. Sometimes it shows crystal outlines with the usual habit, but more often it has a rounded shape. In most of the rocks it is quite fresh: if altered, it gives rise sometimes to green or yellow serpentine, sometimes to a light yellowish or reddish brown mineral with mica-like cleavage, which seems to be of the iddingsite class.

Magnetite, or at least an iron-ore with octahedral form, is constantly present, and sometimes abundant, *e.g.* in the Brocbheinn sill of analysis I. Only exceptionally does it form irregular grains, which may then be moulded upon the felspar crystals. The only remaining mineral is apatite, which is generally distributed in small quantity.

The *micro-structure* is almost as uniform as the mineralogical constitution, the great majority of these sill-rocks being typically ophitic. This structure is not only much more general, but also as a rule much better developed than in the basic lavas, and it is common to find the augite building plates sufficiently large to enclose numerous felspar crystals.† The structure is found on

---

*Since the above was written, Dr Pollard has made actual estimations of chromium and vanadium in some of the Skye rocks (*Summary of Progress, Geol. Sur.* for 1902, pp. 60, 61). The figures are here reproduced:—

		Cr_2O_3	V_2O
[8185]	Olivine-Basalt lava (p. 31),	0·04	0·04
[8043]	Olivine-Gabbro (p. 103, I.),	0·03	0·03
[8194]	Olivine-Gabbro (p. 103, II.),	0·02	0·02
[8057]	Olivine-Dolerite, sill (p. 248, I.),	trace	0·03
[8062]	Dolerite, inclined sheet (Ch. XXI.),	0·01	0·06

† The olivine-dolerite, probably a sill, from Portree figured in Teall's *British Petrography*, pl. X., fig. 2, is a good example.

various scales, but is most marked in the finer-textured varieties. A micro-ophitic dolerite of this kind forms, *e.g.*, the lower columnar sill of Preshal Beg [9249], where the interlocking augite-plates are about $\frac{1}{20}$ inch in diameter, and each encloses many little felspars about $\frac{1}{300}$ inch long. The ophitic structure is, however, not universal. The "granulitic" type is found in some of the rocks, *e.g.* in that from Broc-bheinn analysed above, although neighbouring sills are ophitic. We consider, with Professor Judd, that the "granulitic" structure is a result of movement in the mass prolonged to a late stage in the consolidation : it does not import any difference in the nature of the rock.

The rocks composing the sills of the great group are then for the most part *olivine-dolerites*. Where olivine fails, as in the Preshal Beg rock mentioned above and the Slat Bheinn rock to be described below, this character does not connect itself with any other essential differences, and we are not disposed to regard it as of primary classificatory value. Little difference is observable among the several sills of the group, excepting that the smaller ones, especially when they occur among the Jurassic strata, are of somewhat finer texture, and might be denominated basalts rather than dolerites.

The sills are in general non-porphyritic, presenting an even-grained appearance without any evident crystals of conspicuous dimensions. There are, however, exceptions to this rule, and these are in some parts of the area not uncommon. Here felspar phenocrysts occur, often $\frac{1}{2}$ inch or 1 inch in length. They are never closely set, and in most cases are scattered so sparingly through the rock that they scarcely attain to the rank of normal porphyritic elements, but suggest rather some special conditions attending the intrusion of these particular sill-rocks. Good examples of these *sporadically porphyritic or quasi-porphyritic* rocks are the great columnar sills of Preshal Beg and Preshal More and the strong sills forming the higher parts of Biod Mòr near Loch Eynort. As an occurrence more easily accessible may be mentioned the sill which forms the hills of Dùn Merkadale and Cnòc Simid, near Carbost.

Typically *porphyritic* rocks are decidedly rare. We exclude here certain special sills of composite habit, which differ entirely from the ordinary sills of the great group, and will be described separately. As an example of a sill rich in porphyritic elements we take one which forms a strong escarpment on the steep slope overlooking Loch Harport, beyond the mouth of Meadale Burn. This shows abundant felspars, besides little grains of olivine, in a close-textured matrix. The felspars are of irregular shapes, and in a slice [9806] they are seen to be, not single crystals, but aggregates, which further include here and there a little patch of augite, unlike the ophitic augite of the matrix. This "glomeroporphyritic" structure—to adopt a term of Professor Judd—suggests that here also these enclosed elements have not the status of true porphyritically developed crystals. The felspars, ranging up to about $\frac{1}{8}$ inch in length, have rather broad twin-lamellæ, and enclose round glass- or stone-cavities of rather large size, concentrated in the interior of the crystals. The rock is rich in round grains of olivine. The ground is micro-ophitic, the felspars being very minute and of slender shape.

It may be inquired whether any law is apparent in the vertical distribution of different petrographical varieties among the sills of the great group, but on this point our observations are very inconclusive. If a sequence of increasing basicity held among the successively intruded magmas, we should expect to find the higher sills somewhat less basic in composition than the lower; and this would also imply that the denser magmas were intruded at lower levels. It is very doubtful, however, whether any such law should be expected in this group of rocks, which, as we have seen, is not one of the groups connected with the Skye focus of eruption; and such observations as have been made do not appear to fall under any defined principle. We may take as an example the sills exposed on Biod Mòr, near Loch Eynort. Specimens of the sill-rocks taken on the western slope of this hill, at intervals of about 100 feet in altitude, give the following results: in descending order :—

Fine-grained, black, with rather sparse glassy felspars to $\frac{1}{2}$ inch, ... sp. gr.		2·96
Fine-grained, dark grey, felspars more sparse, ..	,,	2·92
Dark grey, with platy fracture, ...	,,	2·92
Felspars more abundant than before, but much smaller,	,,	2·85
Very fine-grained, with rare scattered felspars to $\frac{1}{4}$ inch,	,,	2·83
With only a few small felspar phenocrysts, ..	,,	2·90
Very fine-grained, black, ...	,,	2·83
Very fine-grained, black, ...	,,	2·82
With abundant slender felspars, up to $\frac{1}{8}$ inch, and scattered round amygdules, ...	,,	2·85
With a tendency to spheroidal weathering, ..	,,	2·91

Here no law is apparent in the arrangement of more and less dense rocks. The occurrence of scattered felspar crystals of relatively large size in the higher sills is, however, a feature noticed in numerous localities, and is possibly of significance.

One feature occasionally observable in the basic sills remains to be noticed, viz. the *inclusion of foreign rock-débris (xenoliths)*, or of isolated crystals (xenocrysts) coming from the disintegration of these. These foreign elements are found only infrequently and sporadically. Some of them are doubtless of accidental nature, picked up from the rocks traversed by the sills, *e.g.* fragments of basaltic lava. Most of the derived material, however, has probably a somewhat different significance, and is not derived from rocks visibly traversed by the sills. The most common xenoliths are of gabbro, and, as has been remarked above, the sills now under consideration nowhere come into contact with the gabbro actually exposed at the surface. A like remark applies to the granite xenoliths which are of rarer occurrence. These foreign elements are probably derived from a considerable depth, and may have the same source as the gabbro and granite fragments in the volcanic agglomerates, from which we have already been compelled to infer the existence of an older suite of plutonic rocks nowhere brought to light by erosion.

The petrographical characters of xenoliths will be considered more particularly in treating of the basic dykes, where they are of much more frequent occurrence. In this place it will be sufficient to notice a single case, the only one within our knowledge in which the derived elements are found in such profusion as to set their mark on the appearance of the rock as seen on the ground. The locality is in the northern part of the Strathaird peninsula, and the sill forms the flat top of Slat Bheinn or An Dà Bheinn, a hill built essentially of the basaltic lavas.* In the neighbourhood of the little tarn marked on the map the rock shows abundant crystals of felspar, $\frac{1}{8}$ to $\frac{1}{4}$ inch long, scattered through the dark grey finegrained ground. There are also many enclosed pieces of gabbro, and it is easy to see, even in hand-specimens, that the felspar crystals are not normal porphyritic elements of the rock, but arise from the breaking up of the gabbro xenoliths. Some xenolithic dykes on the slopes of Slat Bheinn perhaps represent the channels by which the sill was supplied, but their actual connection with it has not been demonstrated. Four slices were made of the sill-rock with its inclusions [7466-7469]. The rock itself is a rather finetextured ophitic dolerite with no special peculiarities. The felspar xenocrysts show little sign of change except the production of granular epidote, which is sometimes so plentiful as to impart a yellow colour to the crystals in hand-specimens. The derived augite, from the gabbro, when preserved, is more or less obscured by secondary magnetite dust, and in general the mineral has been totally destroyed, being represented only by clotted patches of ferruginous matter and presumably by some part of the augite of the dolerite. The undoubted gabbro xenoliths often show but little sign of any caustic action of the magma upon them giving rise to chemical reactions; and this might be expected from the resemblance in composition between the enclosed and enclosing rocks. It is different with certain small xenoliths, usually an inch or less in diameter, which seem to represent granite, and are completely transformed. Towards the junction with one of these the dolerite becomes rather richer in augite, and there is some uralitisation. Then, on the border of the xenolith, comes a zone, up to $\frac{1}{10}$ inch wide, of light green pleochroic chlorite with fan-like groupings. This encloses little crystals of epidote and occasionally what looks like a bastite pseudomorph after a rhombic pyroxene. The interior of the xenolith is recrystallised as an irregular mosaic, or shows a tendency to a radiate arrangement extending inward from the periphery. It is of clear felspar, usually, without twinning, and some quartz, and these enclose needles of actinolite and little crystals of pale epidote.

* The rock carrying the xenoliths was at first grouped tentatively with the lavas (*Ann. Rep. Geol. Sur.* for 1896, p. 73, and Sir A. Geikie's *Ancient Volcanoes of Great Britain*, vol. ii., p. 269; 1897). Closer examination, both geological and petrographical, proves it to be a sill.

It is remarkable that the sills rarely enclose recognisable fragments even of the lavas among which they are intruded. Among the few instances observed may be mentioned one in Allt na Coille, above Drynoch, and another in a burn crossed by the Portree road about $3\frac{1}{2}$ miles from Sligachan. It is possible, however, that in some other cases the true nature of enclosed pieces of basaltic lava is disguised by the metamorphism which they have undergone. Occasionally we find in the sills sharply defined patches with an amygdaloidal structure which is wanting in the surrounding rock. Good examples of this are seen in the Varragill River near where it is crossed by the Portree-Sligachan road.

CHAPTER XV.

Basic Sills: Minor Groups.

While the great majority of the basic sills of Skye are clearly referable to one natural group, the intrusion of which belonged to a defined epoch in the sequence of eruptions, there are in numerous parts of the area examined sills, or sometimes less regular intrusive sheets, which are to be separated from those described in the preceding chapter. They seem to be in general younger than the great group, and they certainly belong to more than one distinct set; but our information concerning their occurrence and their petrographical characters would have to be considerably enlarged to warrant any attempt at discriminating the several groups in a systematic way. The following treatment is therefore confessedly incomplete, and the inclusion in this chapter of rocks by no means contemporaneous involves some departure from chronological order. Some of these minor groups of sills are developed more especially in the south-eastern part of the island; and the basic lavas, which are elsewhere the principal home of the sill-formed intrusions, are there absent. With the question of recognising distinct minor groups of sills is also connected in some degree that of the precise limit in a south-easterly direction of the great group itself.

We find then that to the east and south of the mountain district of Skye basic sills, or sheets of basic rock having more or less of the habit of sills, are not of infrequent occurrence. They are, however, far less abundant here than to the north and west of the mountains; nor do they individually attain a thickness comparable with what is seen in the great group of sills. Moreover, they do not always adhere with such strictness to a definite bedding-plane; but this is doubtless due mainly to the nature of the country rock in which they are intruded. Mr Clough has supplied the following notes on the basic sills and sheets in the area surveyed by him:—

"Basaltic sills which keep tolerably well to the bedding are common in the Secondary rocks, but not elsewhere. In the Torridonian rocks there are occasional sheets inclined at rather low angles to the horizon, but these do not generally keep along the bedding: most usually, indeed, they incline in an opposite direction. Thus in Abhuinn Lusa, nearly half a mile above the bridge, there is a sheet of olivine-dolerite which dips S.E., though the Applecross Grits in which the sheet occurs are dipping N.W. Olivine-dolerite sheets which incline S.E. or S. occur also in a tributary of Abhuinn Lusa about half a mile N.N.W. of Loch an Ime, and in a burn about a mile slightly N. of E. of Kinloch.

"In one locality nearly half a mile N.N.E. of Tarskavaig Point a dolerite dyke sends off various thin sheets into Torridonian shales and grits. They keep nearly along the bedding, but they are only about eight inches thick, and do not extend far.

"Basaltic sheets have intruded along some of the Post-Cambrian thrusts. A sheet between four and ten feet thick is seen every here and there along the Moine thrust from near Loch an Uamh almost to Meall Buidhe,—a distance of nearly four miles. About 300 yards W.S.W. of Meall Buidhe a thin sheet, about a foot and a half thick, is seen in the same thrust-line. Sheets are also seen in other thrusts on the S. side of Sgùrr na h-Iolaire, and about a third of a mile N.E. of Gillean.

"Most of the basaltic sheets and sills are earlier than the dykes with which they are seen in contact, and appear to be often thrown by faults. For instance, a little E. and S.E. of Cnoc Càrnach (S.S.E. of Broadford) a series of sills in the Secondary rocks are repeatedly displaced by faults which strike between N.N.W. and W.N.W. There are, however, various sheets which are not crushed or displaced by the faults which strike across them. For instance, a N.N.E. sheet on the coast about a quarter of a mile N. of Tarskavaig Point comes up to a N. and S. fault, and runs along it for a short distance, but is not crushed or thrown by it: the sheet is older than a close series of N.N.W. dykes, which cut it distinctly. Again, in the bay E.N.E. of Rudha Chàrn nan Cearc there are thin sheets which cut a series of E. and W. crushes: these sheets are, however, probably of later age than most of the sheets, and they cut some N.W. dykes."

That the sill-habit should be maintained with less regularity among the coarser and more massive strata of the Torridonian than among Jurassic shales, and should often be wholly lost in the former, might be anticipated, and seems to be generally true. It is well seen along the northern coast of Scalpay, where a number of basic sheets, from 2 to 5 feet thick, occur in the coarse pebbly Applecross Grits. They have as a rule a north-westerly dip, agreeing roughly with that of the stratified rocks, but the angle of dip is sometimes different, and in places the sheets are seen cutting obliquely across the strata.

That typical sill-formed intrusions are of earlier date than most of the dykes, and in general earlier than the chief epoch of Tertiary faulting, is also an observation of general application. Indeed it might be inferred on mechanical grounds that regular sills of any important extent would not readily be formed after the country rocks had been disturbed and broken.

Petrographically the smaller basic sills and sheets of the south-eastern part of Skye offer much greater variety than those belonging to the great group as typically developed in the north and west. Some, especially in the Broadford and Strathaird districts, seem to have a composition similar to that of the great group, to which they are probably to be attached. Their closer texture may be attributed to the smaller size of the sills. Others, however, present types which are not to be matched in the north-western parts of the island, and must be referred to distinct groups. Although these have not been studied exhaustively, some of them deserve passing notice. A peculiar sill of a spherulitic basalt at Camas Daraich, Point of Sleat, will be described in Chapter XIX., and a group characterised by abundance of olivine and the presence of picotite will be included with the later ultrabasic rocks in Chapter XXII. One thick sill occurring at the base of the Mesozoic rocks in the southern part of Sleat may be mentioned here. It is an ophitic olivine-dolerite with abundant porphyritic crystals of labradorite. Olivine is also abundant, and seems to belong to two distinct generations [7365]. The rock has a specific gravity 2·96. It resembles certain dykes, also rich in phenocrysts, which are found in the neighbourhood, and will be noticed in their place (Chapter XVIII.).

It is, however, in another part of Skye that we find the most interesting of the basic sills not referable to the "great group." These we shall for clearness call the *Roineval type*. They are *composite double sills or laccolites*, the limited extent and swollen shape of some examples meriting rather the latter description; and they are composed, not of a basic and an acid rock, but *of two basic rocks* of different kinds. We shall show that, in some cases at least, the two rocks have been in a more or less fluid condition at the same time, and have to some extent intermingled during or after their intrusion; but, the petrographical difference between the two rock-types involved being much less here than in the Cnoc Càrnach group of intrusions, their mutual reactions are of a less remarkable kind. The distribution of the double sills in question, at least in that part of Skye surveyed, is very restricted. They have been mapped in three localities, and the separate intrusions known are not more than eight or nine in number. Their precise age has not been fixed with certainty. They are younger than the sills of the great group, and not improbably belong to a much later epoch, perhaps that of the trachy-andesite dykes to be described in Chapter XXIII. All the intrusions occur among the basaltic lavas.

The first locality to be noticed is Druim na Crìche, a flat ridge 2 miles N.E. of Roineval and 5 miles S.S.W. of Portree. The basalts here dip to the south-west, and the outcrops of the several sills in question form in general strong features divided by peaty flats. They are five in number, four being of composite structure, while the fifth (at its outcrop at least) consists of one rock only. This last, since the missing member is the stronger rock, does not make any marked feature. The apparent relations are shown in the accompanying section (Fig. 55). The rock which occasions the prominence of four of the sills is an olivine-dolerite crowded with large porphyritic felspars of fresh glassy appearance. In each case this constitutes the upper member, and usually much exceeds the other in volume. In the highest or most south-westerly intrusion the porphyritic dolerite itself seems to be doubled, so that the whole sill is really triple. The other rock which constitutes the lower member, or in one instance (the second from the bottom) apparently occurs alone, is, when fresh, a black compact-looking rock without phenocrysts. In most places it is much weathered, assuming a dull yellowish-brown colour and a fissile structure parallel to the surfaces of the sill, which gives it a platy fracture. As this rock will be referred to frequently, and belongs to a peculiar type, we shall find it necessary to give it a provisional name. It will be spoken of as "mugearite," a name adopted from that of Mugeary, the crofter village lying at a short distance north. The thick peat which covers most of this tract renders it difficult to ascertain the extent of the intrusions in the direction of strike. Towards the south-east they disappear in a short distance, but this may be owing to a concealed fault. Having regard to the variations in thickness shown in the visible outcrops, it seems probable that they have something of the laccolitic habit, with no great lateral extension. It is also to be noticed that the relative thickness of the two members varies, even in one double sill, and one or other of the two may thin away. It is not improbable that the sill which appears to be a simple one has in reality the same constitution as the others, the porphyritic dolerite dying out before reaching the actual outcrop. This latter rock is on the whole very decidedly the predominant one, and attains in places a thickness of fully 100 feet.

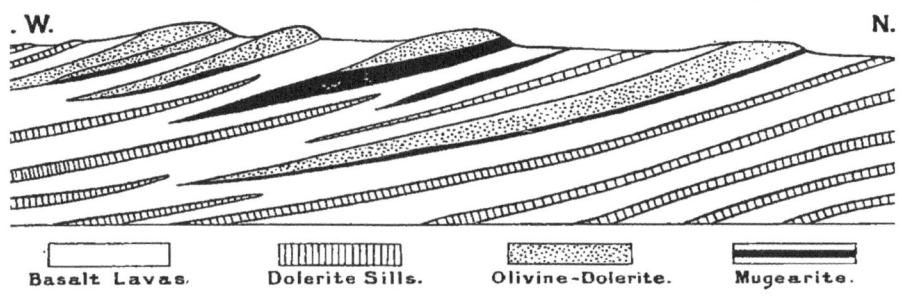

Fig. 55.—Section through Druim na Criche, about 5 miles S.S.W. of Portree and 5½ miles N.W. of Sligachan; showing composite double sills or laccolites of the Roineval type. Scale : 6 inches to a mile. The prolongation below the surface is partly conjectural.

The second locality is Roineval itself, a bold moorland hill, 1440 feet in altitude, situated some 2 miles N. of Drynoch and about 5¼ miles N.W. by W. of Sligachan. Even from a distance its ontline is seen to be decidedly more rugged than that of the neighbouring hills, and examination shows that the summit is made by a thick sheet of porphyritic dolerite similar to those mentioned above. At least 150 feet of this rock are exposed, and the thickness may have been greater before erosion. Below and in contact with this rock is a sheet of mugearite about 9 feet thick. This can be traced along the base of the summit-escarpment round more than half the circumference of the hill (see Map, Fig. 56), but its thickness varies somewhat, and on the north-eastern side it is wanting. The whole has a dip of about 9° to W.S.W. At a lower horizon another sill of the porphyritic dolerite, about 40 feet thick, is exposed on the southern slope, but does not continue round the hill. Just below is another sill of mugearite, which makes some

258   *Roineval Type of Composite Double Sills.*

spread on the western slope of Roineval, as shown on the map and in the section (Fig. 57). The two members of this lower pair do not actually come together here, but they do so a short distance farther east, forming a double sill exposed as an outlier to the south-east of the main hill (Fig. 56). Excepting the porphyritic dolerite of the summit, the original shape of which cannot be ascertained, the Roineval intrusions seem to have more of the typical sill habit than those of the former locality.

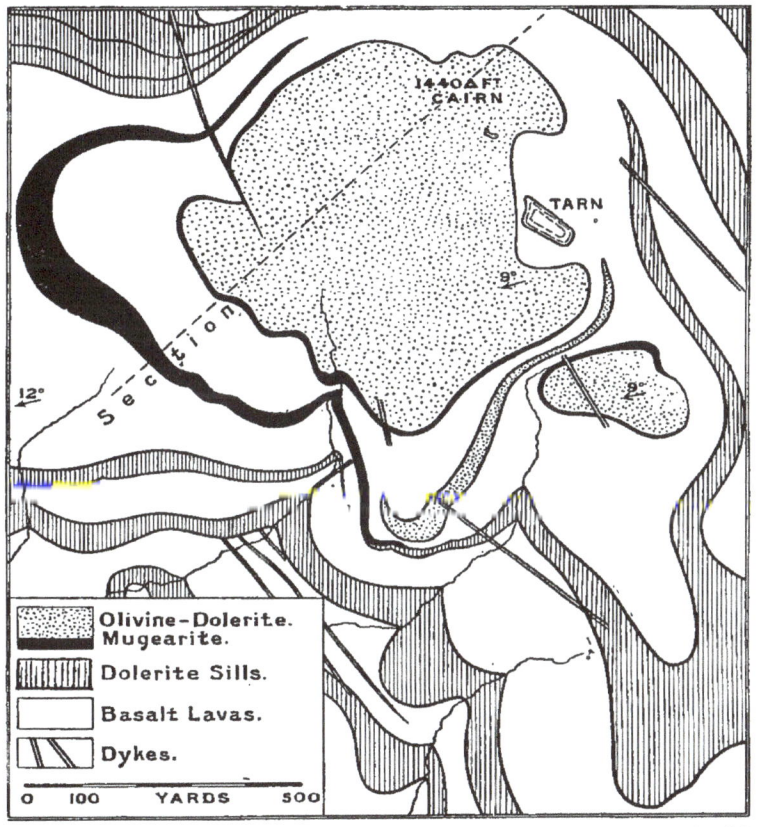

FIG. 56.—Geological map of Roineval, showing the composite double sills. Scale: 4½ inches to a mile.

When we examine the surfaces of junction of the two associated rocks in the several occurrences, some interesting points are observed. At Druim na Criche, in the few places where the actual contact is exposed, it shows a perfectly sharp boundary with no appearance of intermingling. No positive evidence bearing on the relative age of the two rocks is there obtainable, though the infraposition of the mugearite in every instance seems to indicate that it is the younger. In the summit escarpment of Roineval there are abundant exposures of the junction of the two rocks, and these suffice to show that the relations differ in certain respects from those at the former locality. The mugearite, at one or two places on the south side, sends little tongues 3 or 4 inches wide a short way into the overlying rock, and is clearly the younger of the two. Further, the junction between the two rocks does not always present a perfectly sharp line, and the mugearite close to the junction encloses porphyritic felspars derived from the porphyritic dolerite above. These are found, in diminishing numbers, to distances of 4 or 6 inches from the line which we take to mark the actual division. Turning to the lower double sill, as exposed in the outlier to the south-east, we find that here the mugearite contains scattered felspars throughout its whole thickness of 6 or 8 feet. They are identical with the felspars in the porphyritic dolerite, and have undoubtedly been derived from the immediately overlying rock subsequently to the intrusion. In proof of this we find that farther west, where the mugearite sill has parted company with its associate, it contains no porphyritic felspars. The crystals seen in the mugearite have, then, sunk into it while it was in a fluid

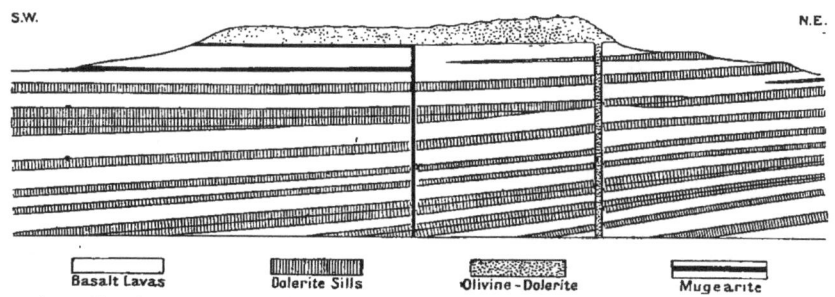

FIG. 57.—Section through Roineval, showing the double sill at the summit and the lower mugearite sill; also conjectural relation of the sills to dyke-feeders. Scale : 4½ inches to a mile.

state; and what we have seen in the sills of the Cnoc Càrnach group (Chapter XIII.) suggests that at that time the matrix of the porphyritic dolerite may also have been partially fluid. The two rocks involved being in the present case not very different in composition,* the tendency to interchange by diffusion would doubtless be much less than in the basalt-granophyre sills.

Roineval affords better opportunities than Druim na Crìche of investigating the field-relations of the rocks, and here we find certain dykes which not improbably mark the channels of supply of the sills. One large dyke is a prominent object on the east side of the hill, about 200 yards E. of the principal tarn (see Map, Fig. 56). It is porphyritic olivine dolerite closely resembling that of the sills. At several places too there are dykes of a close-textured, brown-

* The comparison is between the mugearite and the *groundmass* of the porphyritic dolerite, which would differ much less than the bulk-analyses given below.

stained rock with strongly fissile structure parallel to the walls, and these may perhaps represent the feeders of the mugearites. They resemble equally in their general appearance the trachytic dykes of the Drynoch group, to be described later (Chapter XXIII.), but they are not sufficiently well preserved for detailed examination. The Drynoch dykes have many points in common with the mugearites, and we are inclined to refer these latter to the same epoch, which is certainly a very late one. It is in any case important to observe that the dykes on Roineval intersect all the ordinary dolerite sills. At one or two places in the Drynoch neighbourhood there are double dykes, one member being a highly fissile close-textured rock and the other a porphyritic olivine-dolerite or basalt, not unlike the Roineval type but of finer texture. The dykes on Roineval itself are, however, simple ones.

The third locality where a sill comparable with those of Roineval has been studied is more than six miles distant. Two miles from Talisker in the direction N. 15° W., and 600 yards N.N.E. of the tarn named Loch Dubh, is an abrupt isolated hill crowned by a ruined fort or Dùn.* This hill is made by an outlier of a strong sill about 100 feet thick. To the S.W. and S. of the hill the main outcrop of the sill is seen running along the lower slopes of Beinn an Dubh-lochain, overlooking Huisgill. Towards the N.W. it dies out rapidly, but in the opposite direction it can be traced for a considerable distance. The best section is offered by the Dùn hill. Here the upper part is composed of porphyritic dolerite, in appearance like that of Roineval and Druim na Crìche. From the summit to about half-way down the large felspar crystals are as abundant as in the former occurrences; but lower down, without any dividing line, they become sparser, and increasingly so downward. At the actual base they are almost or quite wanting. The lower part of the sill, in which the felspars occur at the most sparingly, resembles in the field the mugearite of the other localities. It is generally in a fresher condition, but shows the characteristic fissile structure.

That part of the main outcrop which is nearest to the outlier seems to have a like constitution, but it is not well exposed. Following the sill south-eastward and southward, we find the porphyritic felspars still richly abundant in the upper part and rare at the base, until we reach the corrie drained by the burn which comes down eastward from Beinn an Dubh-lochain. Here the sill is for some space lost under the peat. When it emerges beyond this place (Buile na h-Airidh), it contains only scattered felspars, and these become still rarer southward. The dark matrix also assumes a very fine-textured, compact character, with a splintery fracture. We have not been able to trace the sill far beyond this place.

We see that not only do these double sills recall in a general way some of the characteristic features of the composite triple

* The situation is thus particularised because on the Ordnance maps, down to the date of writing, the hill and Dùn are incorrectly placed. They are 400 yards N.N.E. of the position marked on the maps.

sills of the Heast and Broadford tract, but they also show, when the several occurrences are compared, a somewhat similar range of variety as regards the intimacy of association of the two rock-types involved. On Druim na Crìche there is a sharp junction between the two rocks, and no sensible modification of either towards their contact. In the upper double sill of Roineval the sharp line of demarcation is softened to some extent, and phenocrysts from the upper and earlier rock have penetrated the lower one for a few inches. In the lower double sill at the same locality the phenocrysts have sunk, though only in small numbers, through the whole thickness of the lower and younger member. They have not, however, been carried far in a lateral direction. At the Dùn hill, although it cannot be doubted that the sill represents two successive intrusions, intermingling has obliterated the boundary between them, and the porphyritic felspars pass down, in diminishing numbers, practically to the base of the whole sill. Separating in imagination the two members which thus merge into one another, we may explain the scarcity of the phenocrysts throughout the thickness of the sill south of Buile na h-Airidh by supposing that the upper member dies out at or near this place. In the last exposure, some 65 or 70 feet thick, on the north side of the concealed ground the large felspars are abundant throughout the greater part of the section. On the other side they have become scarce throughout the whole thickness, and what appears to be the same sill on the opposite side of Huisgill, ¼ mile to the east, contains no phenocrysts. The scattered crystals seen in the prolongation of the lower member beyond the limits of the upper may have been carried forward with it from the place farther north where they were received; but it is also possible that they are "antecedent" xenocrysts taken in prior to the intrusion.

We have tacitly assumed that the sill at the Dùn hill belongs to the same group of intrusions as the double sills of Roineval and Druim na Crìche, its upper and lower portions representing respectively the two distinct members in those other localities. We do not, however, imply petrographical identity, but merely, or primarily, equivalence from the genetic point of view. The rocks present, as we shall see, a considerable range of variety.

We proceed to describe the petrographical characters of the two rock-types which constitute the double sills of the Roineval group. They have been judged worthy of chemical examination, and Dr Pollard has accordingly made the two full analyses quoted below. Both have a silica-percentage of about 50. Compared with the basic sills of the great group, or with other basic rocks of our area, both show a decided poverty in magnesia and lime and a relative richness in the two alkalies. In these respects the mugearite represents a greater departure than the porphyritic dolerite from the common standard.

The two rock-types have mineralogical characters which would serve to link them together even apart from their intimate association in the field. Olivine occurs in some quantity in both the specimens analysed; in the first with labradorite and augite; in the second, in more unusual association, with felspars rich in alkalies and only subordinate augite. Both rock-types, moreover, present varieties (not analysed) in which the place of olivine is taken partly or wholly by another and unknown mineral.

This problematical mineral seems to be the same in the two rocks. It is first detected in the thin slices, and has the general appearance of a brown mica. It usually builds idiomorphic crystals with rectangular sections, but sometimes also irregular plates into which the little felspar crystals project. It also occurs in a few places in confused aggregates, which rather suggest that it may have originated in part from the alteration of olivine or some other mineral; but these possible pseudomorphs are in no case so evident as to permit of a decisive conclusion on this point. The little flakes, in which the mineral most commonly occurs, are about $\frac{1}{100}$ inch long. There is a strong cleavage parallel to that pair of faces which is most developed, and occasionally some indication of a second weak cleavage making an oblique angle with the first. The absorption-colours are light brown, with strong pleochroism. The interference tints are not so high as in the mica group, and the extinction-angles, measured from the strong cleavage-traces, are much higher. About 22° is a common angle, but the measurements range up to about 32°. The mineral is therefore monoclinic or triclinic; and the fact that a number of flakes in which the cleavage is particularly well marked give straight extinction rather suggests monoclinic symmetry. In all cases tested that axis of vibration nearer to the cleavage-traces was found to correspond with the lower index of refraction and the stronger absorption.

The characters here recorded do not agree with those of any common rock-forming mineral. There are points of resemblance to iddingsite, but that mineral, according to Lawson, has rhombic symmetry.[*] Our mineral also recalls in some respects some of the ill-characterised alteration-products of olivine observed in Skye and elsewhere, such as the "ferrite" of Heddle.[†] But, as we have stated, the brown micaceous-looking mineral in the rocks now in question is only doubtfully and exceptionally, if ever, a secondary product, presenting in general all the appearance of a primary constituent.

The *porphyritic olivine-dolerite* is a remarkably handsome rock full of large crystals of labradorite, $\frac{1}{2}$ inch to 1 inch in length, set in a dark, finely crystalline ground-mass. Specimens from the several occurrences are identical in general appearance, and show very close resemblance when studied, but there are certain differences to be noted. The Roineval rocks are perhaps slightly less basic than those of Druim na Crìche, while the corresponding rock from the Talisker neighbourhood is decidedly more basic.

[*] *Bull. Dept. Geol. Univ. Calif.*, vol. i., p. 33; 1893.
[†] *Min. Mag.*, vol. v., p. 29; 1882.

	I.	II.	A.	III.
SiO_2	50·33	49·24	49·25	46·423
TiO_2	1·81	1·84	1·41	not det.
Al_2O_3	19·97	15·84	16·97	14·010
Cr_2O_3	trace	trace	..	..
Fe_2O_3	2·81	6·09	15·21	5·027
FeO	6·23	7·18	not det.	9·022
NiO, CoO	trace	trace	..	..
MnO	0·17	0·29	trace	not det.
MgO	3·24	3·02	ca. 3·00	3·820
CaO	8·03	5·26	7·17	8·104
BaO	0·06	0·09	..	..
SrO	trace	trace	..	..
Na_2O	4·30	5·21	4·91	3·820
K_2O	1·19	2·10	2·01	2·000
H_2O { above 105°	0·99	1·61	ca. 0·30	7·222
H_2O { at 105° C.	0·87	1·08		
P_2O_5	0·17	1·47	0·76	not det.
F	not sought	0·18	..	..
S	not found	0·03	..	..
	100·17	100·46*	ca. 100·99	99·448
Specific gravity,	2·81	2·79	..	..

I. [9250]. Porphyritic Olivine-Dolerite, upper member of a composite double sill or laccolite, Druim na Crìche, 5 miles S.S.W. of Portree: anal. W. Pollard. Both this and the following rock contain chromium, vanadium, and strontium, as determined spectroscopically by Sir J. Norman Lockyer.

II. [8732]. Mugearite, lower member of the same composite intrusion, viz., the middle one of the five mentioned in the text: anal. W. Pollard. The fluorine may be somewhat overestimated. * The total is 100·53, less 0·07 (for oxygen-equivalent of fluorine).

A. Essexite, Dignäs, near Gran, Norway: anal. A Damm and L. Schmelck, cit. Brögger, *Quart. Journ. Geol. Soc.*, vol. l., p. 19; 1894.

III. "Dolerite," sill near summit of approach to Quiraing: anal. M. F. Heddle, *Min. Mag.*, vol. v, p. 8; 1882.

This last has a specific gravity 2·87 to 2·88, while the rocks from the former localities, which we take as the regular type, give only 2·78 to 2·82 in the different intrusions. Dr Pollard's analysis (I.) shows that the type is somewhat less basic than the ordinary dolerite sills of the region. The composition is not markedly peculiar, but we may note a certain tendency towards those special characters which become more accentuated in the associated mugearite, in particular the low magnesia and high alkalies. A rough calculation of the mineralogical constitution gives about 77 per cent. of labradorite, 11 of augite, and 12 of olivine, magnetite, and apatite.

The most conspicuous feature of the rock is the abundance of large and usually well-shaped felspar-phenocrysts. It is remarkable that, in each occurrence, these seem to be of two distinct kinds; one perfectly clear and colourless, the other, though still quite fresh, having a yellow tinge. The latter are commonly larger than the former. We have not been able to verify any other difference, or to discern any significance in the occurrence of the two kinds. Carlsbad and albite twinning are evident to the eye, and thin slices show pericline-lamellation capriciously distributed in some of the crystals. The inclusions are scattered glass-cavities, with occasionally a scrap of augite, a crystal-grain of magnetite, or a little patch of the ground-mass. In places too the small elements of the ground-mass project slightly into the border of the phenocryst, showing that this has continued or resumed its growth to a certain extent at a late stage of the consolidation. This feature is most strongly marked in the Talisker sill, and it is evident in polarised light that the border is of slightly different composition from the rest of the crystal. The extinction-angles of the porphyritic felspars point to a medium labradorite of composition near $Ab_3 An_4$ or $Ab_5 An_6$.

The ground-mass consists of felspar, augite, olivine or its pseudomorphs, magnetite, and rather abundant needles of apatite, besides a variable amount of the brown micaceous-looking mineral described above. This occurs in different specimens apparently in inverse proportion to the olivine, as if the two minerals played the same rôle in the rock. The small felspars, averaging about $\frac{1}{100}$ inch in length, are not very well shaped, having crystallised at a late stage. Most of the crystals show carlsbad and albite twinning, with extinction-angles up to 32° in symmetrical sections; and they are therefore labradorite, probably of a rather more acid variety than the phenocrysts. The augite, of a very pale tint in the slices, is usually idiomorphic towards the felspar, and sometimes towards the iron-ore. Olivine is only exceptionally found in a fresh state, but is plentifully represented by green or greenish brown serpentinous pseudomorphs. Magnetite in more or less perfect octahedra is sometimes quite abundant, and apatite is constantly present in slender rods, often enclosed in the felspars.

The above description of the typical rocks will serve also with little modification for the denser variety at the Dùn hill, near Talisker. This shows a rather larger proportion of olivine and magnetite, especially the former. On the other hand, the augite (here in little interstitial patches [9807] or in ophitic plates [9809]) is not very plentiful, and the little felspars, instead of being of a more basic variety, seem from their extinction-angles to be more acid. These points indicate a certain assimilation in composition to the associated mugearite, and are probably to be attributed to some degree of admixture by diffusion between the two magmas.

The *mugearite* of Druim na Criche, in its freshest state, is a dark, finely crystalline rock, without phenocrysts, and might pass in hand-specimens for an ordinary basalt. Its mode of weathering is, however, sufficient to distinguish it in the field from all other sill-rocks in our area; and the exposed outcrops, with their dull yellowish brown tint and highly fissile character, look much more like the trachyte dykes of Drynoch, to be described in a later chapter. The specimen analysed has the specific gravity 2·79, while others gave 2·77 and 2·75. These lower figures are doubtless connected with partial weathering, and a specimen selected for its fresh appearance gave 2·82. The chemical analysis (II. above) shows a composition quite removed from those of most other rocks in our area, and not reducible to any of the more widely distributed rock-types. The special features, as compared with average rocks of like silica-percentage, are the low magnesia and lime and the high alkalies, including potash as well as soda. Chemically the rock falls most nearly into the essexite family, though its petrographical characters do not assimilate it closely to any example hitherto described. We cite for comparison (in column A) the analysis of an essexite (the more acid variety) from the Gran district in Norway. This was first given by Brögger under the name "olivine-gabbro-diabase," and has since been included by the same writer* among the olivine-monzonites, with which it has evident affinities. The rather high amount of phosphoric acid in the mugearite is also a characteristic of the Norwegian and some other essexites. The only important point distinguishing our rock from the true essexites is its lower proportion of lime. This has given rise to a peculiar mineralogical constitution, and seems therefore to justify us in regarding the mugearite as a distinct type.

The chief mineralogical pecularities of mugearite, which result from its unusual chemical composition and go to characterise it as a special rock-type, are two. Firstly, the felspar is not labradorite but oligoclase, with subordinate orthoclase; and, secondly, the ordinary bisilicate minerals are very poorly represented, augite being typically quite subordinate to olivine (or its equivalent the brown mineral already described) and iron-ore. Among minor points of interest may be noted the unusual richness in apatite. The percentage mineral composition of the rock analysed must be approximately as follows:—

Oligoclase,	$57\frac{1}{2}$
Orthoclase,	$12\frac{1}{2}$
Olivine, iron-ore, and augite,	$26\frac{1}{2}$
Apatite,	$3\frac{1}{2}$
	100

Felspars of species rich in alkalies thus make up about 70 per cent. of the rock. They appear in thin slices as a crowd of little elongated sections, averaging about ·005 inch in length, with parallel or subparallel arrangement at any given point, the microstructure being consequently of the trachytic type. Most of the

* *Eruptivgesteine des Kristianiagebietes*, part II., p. 50; 1895.

little crystals show albite-twinning, often with repetition. They give nearly straight extinction, and must belong to oligoclase. The untwinned crystals are doubtless to be identified as orthoclase, for the amount of potash in the rock is much too great to be contained in a felspar of the oligoclase type. On this understanding the composition of the oligoclase may be reckoned as nearly $Ab_7 An_2$, which agrees with the approximately straight extinction observed.

Of the other constituents, the olivine forms little well-shaped crystals or rounded grains, usually about $\frac{1}{100}$ inch in diameter The mineral is commonly fresh. The augite, sensibly colourless in thin slices, has the ophitic habit; but it is present in such small quantity that the several minute pieces belonging to one ophitic plate are only perceived to have that relation by their polarisation. The magnetite is in minute octahedra, and there is often in addition a certain amount of limonite of secondary origin. The apatite is in very slender needles. The analysis of the rock proves that it is a fluor-apatite, contrasting with the chlor-apatite of our acid rocks, and making an exception to the general rule. The mugearite sometimes contains a few microscopic amygdules of spherical shape, occupied by analcime [9252]. It will be observed that the textural and structural characters of the rock remove it from the essexite type as represented by the known (plutonic) examples.

Regarding the rock selected for analysis as the type of mugearite, we may note as the only important variety at Druim na Crìche that in which the place of olivine is taken by the unknown brown mineral [9251]. The mugearite of Roineval has the same general characters as the type rock, but seems to be more highly felspathic. A specimen from the higher of the two intrusions is entirely free from augite, and is judged (though doubtfully) to have a larger proportion of potash-felspar than the rock taken as type. Olivine is absent in this slice [8190], the brown mineral occurring instead, and with forms that forbid us to regard it as pseudomorphic. This specimen gives a specific gravity only 2·62, and, even allowing for weathering, it must be very decidedly less dense than the type of Druim na Crìche. It may be mentioned that on the south side of the summit-escarpment it contains fusiform amygdules of chalcedony, 2 or 3 inches long. A specimen of the lower sheet contains very little augite. Here again olivine is wanting, but there are instead, and probably replacing it, abundant elongated crystals or pseudomorphs of a deep-brown mineral, apparently of the iddingsite kind. This substance, or one very like it, is also found occasionally in the Druim na Crìche rocks. It is clearly quite distinct from the brown mineral already described above, which occurs in small amount in the same slide. The colour is deeper, the pleochroism much feebler, and the extinction sensibly straight. In other specimens unaltered olivine occurs with its usual characters.

Turning now to the third locality, we have to notice in Huisgill, near Talisker, a *more basic variety of mugearite*. This is sufficiently evident from its high specific gravity, ranging from 2·91 to 2·96 in four examples selected, but we shall see nevertheless that the rocks bear the unmistakable stamp of consanguinity with the typical mugearite. For characteristic examples we must examine the southerly prolongation of the sill beyond its interruption by the peaty flat of Buile na h-Airidh. Here, as has been shown, the overlying porphyritic dolerite has died out, and its modifying influence on the lower member which persists is scarcely noticeable, except by the occurrence of a few scattered phenocrysts (here more properly xenocrysts), which become rarer southward. There is indeed no longer any essential difference between the upper and lower portions of the sill as displayed in this place [9810, 9811]. The rocks are fresher than in the other localities, and also of decidedly finer texture, presenting to the eye a very compact appearance, sometimes lustrous enough to suggest the presence of a glassy base.

Thin slices show that the relatively basic nature and high density of the rocks are connected chiefly with the abundance of magnetite, which in this respect is of next importance to the felspar. It is sometimes present as innumerable minute granules, in addition to the usual little octahedra. Olivine is abundant in fairly well shaped little crystals with a pronounced elongation parallel to the a-axis. There is often a relatively large glass-cavity in the centre, and in the most fine-textured rocks the olivine sometimes builds mere skeletons. The peculiar brown mineral formerly described is sometimes present [9811]. Augite occurs in very small interstitial granules, but not usually in any abundance. The little felspars, which make the principal constituent, are closely packed, giving something of the trachytic structure. They have in general quite low extinction-angles, and often the sensibly straight extinction of an oligoclase. We have not been able to decide whether orthoclase is also present. In some cases there occurs a certain amount of interstitial glass, colourless but charged with magnetite dust. In a later chapter (XIX.) we shall have to notice a rock of much more vitreous nature, which probably has affinities with those here described. These basic mugearites, like the typical rocks of Druim na Crìche, contain a few microscopic amygdules of analcime.

A chemical analysis of this variety would be of interest. From what has been said, we may infer that it has the same low magnesia and lime, with high alkalies, as the typical mugearite, but is poorer in silica and richer in iron.

We have stated that farther north, where the equivalent of this rock underlies the porphyritic olivine-dolerite, there has been an intermingling of the two magmas; but, owing to the want of sufficient exposures, it is not easy to study the phenomena in detail. Specimens from the lower part of the Dùn hill, where the large porphyritic crystals occur only very sparingly, are dark, finely crystalline rocks of specific gravity 2·95 to 2·96. A thin slice not containing any large phenocryst shows, however, a certain micro-porphyritic structure [9808]. There are abundant little crystals of labradorite about ·02 to ·05 inch long, but the chief element of the ground-mass in most places consists of smaller felspars which, from their low extinction-angles, seem to be near oligoclase and oligoclase-andesine. An appearance of coarser and finer texture in different places depends on the preponderance of one or other of the two kinds of felspar, and rather suggests an imperfect mixture of two different magmas. Where the small labradorite crystals are only thinly distributed, there is a trachytic structure and a general resemblance to the typical mugearite. Augite is represented only by minute interstitial granules, but magnetite is abundant, and there is a considerable amount of olivine.

Comparing the several intrusions in the localities which we have considered, we find that, where there is noteworthy variation, the two associated rocks seem to vary together, although the variation has a much greater range in the mugearite than in the porphyritic olivine-dolerite. The specific gravities of the rocks, as shown below, bear out this remark:—

	Upper Member.	Lower Member.
Roineval, higher double sill,	2·775	2·62
Do., lower double sill,	2·80	2·82
Druim na Crìche, highest double sill,	2·82	—
Do., second from top,	2·79	2·77
Do., third from top,	2·81	2·79
Dùn Hill, near Talisker,	2·88	2·96

If we are to regard the two associated rocks as, in Brögger's phrase, "complementary" products of differentiation, this joint variation seems to imply that such differentiation was a process effected separately for each double intrusion. The greater range of variation in the mugearite, as compared with the porphyritic olivine-dolerite, connects itself with the fact that the former is usually much inferior in bulk to the latter. At Druim na Crìche, where the disparity is not very marked, the mugearite is least variable; while on Roineval, where the mugearite forms only thin sheets beneath the massive porphyritic dolerite, the greatest range of variation is found.

The specific gravities given above suggest another point, which may be of significance, but would require further testing. The denser rocks seem to have been intruded at the lower levels. The Roineval sills are much higher up in the basalt group than those of Druim na Crìche, and the occurrence near Talisker is probably, though not demonstrably, lower.

In leaving these remarkable double sills we may remark that, although composite intrusions of this kind have been discovered only in the three localities mentioned above, it is not impossible that separate intrusions of one or other of the two rocks may be found, whether as dykes or sills, in other parts of Skye. Certain dykes, apparently by no means common, will be mentioned in their proper place, which have the general composition of mugearites, and approximate in some measure to the type described above. The porphyritic olivine-dolerite, being a less strongly characterised type, is naturally less easy to identify elsewhere.*

One sill-rock worthy of notice in this place is that analysed by Heddle from the Quiraing. We have not had the opportunity of examining any specimen of this, but a rough calculation shows that the dominant felspar must be a basic oligoclase, while orthoclase must also be present. The chemical composition alone, as quoted in Column III. above, seems sufficient to remove this rock from the "great group" of sills, and to assimilate it in some respects to the rocks of the Roineval group of intrusions. The occurrence of a glassy selvage is a point of interest, and one which we have in no case met with among the sills of the great group.

Certain *porphyritic basalt sills in the Isle of Soay* deserve special mention. This island is built of Torridonian grit, a rock which, as we have remarked, does not in most places contain intrusions with regular sill habit. Here, however, there are numerous intrusions in the form of sheets approximating more or less closely to the regularity of typical sills, and it appears further that some rocks which elsewhere take the form of dykes occur with the stratiform habit in the Torridonian of Soay. This is certainly true of the younger peridotite group to be described later (Chapter XXI.), and it seems to be so also of some of the minor basic intrusions. Without asserting that the great group of sills is quite unrepresented in Soay, we are thus led to refer some at least of the sheet-like intrusions there observed to some later epoch. This is especially the case with the conspicuously porphyritic rocks now to be noticed. It is worthy of remark that, in addition to the sills or sheets, dykes of similar petrographical type are found in the district.

The rocks show large glassy-looking felspars closely set in a dark finely crystalline ground. They resemble in general appearance the olivine-dolerite of the composite sills on Roineval and elsewhere; but they are of less basic composition and devoid of olivine. An interesting point is the varying size and frequency of the porphyritic felspars in different parts of a sill. In the interior they attain very large dimensions; Mr Clough records masses of felspar as much as 8 inches long and 4 in width. "These felspar crystals, however, never occur near the chilled margins. They are largest and most abundant in the centre of a sill, and gradually diminish in size and abundance as the chilled margins

* Conspicuously porphyritic sills with the same general characters have since been found in Canna, where on the higher ground they become the prevalent type. Two or three occur also in Eigg. Mugearite has also been recognised in these two islands; while in the western part of Rum it occurs as a number of sheets with a total thickness of about 500 feet. These observations make it very doubtful whether the rocks now described are to be sharply separated from the "great group" of sills, and referred to a different epoch.

are approached. They are usually quite small at about 9 or 10 inches from the margins, and not visible at 5 or 6 inches. I have noticed this phenomenon so often, that I am driven to conclude that the crystals in these cases have been developed in the sill, and are not importations ready made." (C.T.C.) That the phenocrysts in intrusive rocks, as distinguished from lavas, have in many cases not been brought up in the magma, as supposed by Rosenbusch, but formed *in situ* after the intrusion, is a thesis which has been maintained by several petrologists,[*] and Mr Clough's observations seem to be conclusive on this point as regards the sills in question. It is to be observed that, not only the size of the phenocrysts, but their relative abundance decreases from the centre to the margin of the sill, so that the interior is more felspathic, and doubtless somewhat less basic in composition, than the marginal portions. This comes out clearly from some of Mr Clough's determinations of specific gravity:—

(i.) Sill ½ mile S.E. of Doire Chaol:
    Interior (felspars up to 1 inch and more), .   2·72
    Margin (non-porphyritic),   .   .   .   2·75
(ii.) Sheet at Leac nan Faoileann:
    Interior (felspars up to 1 inch and more), .   2·76
    Margin (non-porphyritic),   .   .   .   2·79

The porphyritic felspars are labradorite with albite and carlsbad twinning. The ground-mass, in the only specimen sliced, is an ordinary basalt or fine-textured dolerite without olivine. This example, from the interior of a sill on the east coast of Soay, has a specific gravity 2·78.

[*] Zirkel, *Lehrbuch der Petrographie*, 2nd ed., vol. i., p. 737; 1893: Whitman Cross, 14th *Ann. Rep. U.S. Geol. Sur.*, p. 231; 1895: Pirsson, *Amer. Journ. Sci.* (4), vol. vii., pp. 271–280; 1899. See also Crosby, *Amer. Geol.*, vol. xxv., p. 299; 1900.

CHAPTER XVI.

MINOR ACID INTRUSIONS.

Under the head of the *minor acid intrusions* we include for the purpose of petrographical description in common various dykes, sills, and sheets, of small or quite moderate dimensions; of which some are offshoots, or presumed offshoots, of the granite of the Red Hills, while others belong to the second principal epoch of acid intrusions in Skye, when no large bodies of rock were formed. The former are in part visibly apophyses of abyssal rock-masses, while the latter are of typical hypabyssal habit; and the fact that the two are often indistinguishable in specimens has an evident bearing upon the question, what factors go to determine the micro-structure of igneous rocks. It is clear that no important difference of pressure can be postulated for the consolidation of the granite of Strath na Creitheach on the one hand and the spherulitic dykes of Druim an Eidhne, which are its apophyses, on the other hand.* Differences there would doubtless be in temperature and rate of cooling, and also more flowing movement within the narrow fissures than in the main body of magma. To discuss this general question, however, would be outside our present province.

Similarity of petrographical characters is a sufficient reason for describing the two groups of minor acid intrusions together; but there is a further reason in the practical difficulty in some cases of separating the later from the earlier group. The only important group of rocks which can be assigned with certainty to the interval between the two chief epochs of acid intrusions is the great group of basic sills; and it follows that where these are not present there is no absolute criterion for discriminating the minor acid intrusions of the later epoch from those of the earlier which are not visibly offshoots from the granite. The failure of the basic sills, with this consequent ambiguity, affects us principally in the mountain district. Beyond the mountains and a narrow sub-montane belt there is no difficulty, as a rule, in applying the simple criterion, and it is found that the minor acid intrusions there belong in general to the second group, which has a much wider distribution than the first. It is to be observed, however, that the break between the earlier and later groups is not an absolute one. A few acid rocks were intruded during the interval between the two principal epochs, and these entered

---

* It may be remembered also that the marginal part of the large body has in places the same character as the dykes.

into relations with basic intrusions to form the peculiar composite sills and dykes already described at length. The acid intrusions of the second group also sometimes form part of composite dykes, but without the peculiar relations referred to between the basic and acid members, so that they are to be included with the rest in this place. A few acid dykes again, mostly pitchstones and devitrified pitchstones, are to be referred to a time probably long posterior to the second principal epoch here recognised, and these will be described in a later chapter.

We have already considered the field-relations of those minor intrusions, chiefly dykes, which are in visible continuity with the granite and granophyre masses of the Red Hills. It is highly probable that we ought to include with these, as belonging to same epoch, many of the acid dykes within and just outside the Red Hills district which have no such direct connection with the plutonic masses, unless it be a subterranean connection. This may be true of some dykes which intersect the plutonic rocks themselves, for, as we have seen, the granite consists of a number of distinct intrusions. There are, for instance, spherulitic dykes cutting the granite in a few localities which are identical in characters with the Druim an Eidhne apophyses.

Probably some of the acid dykes in the same district, and certainly most of those outside it, are to be referred to the second chief epoch of acid intrusions which we have specified; and to these dykes we may add the sheets and irregular sills which are of less frequent occurrence. The area of distribution of these rocks is a fairly large one, but quite sharply defined; extending in every direction round the Red Hills, but to varying distances of one to eight miles from them. This extension is greatest towards N.W. and S.E., a circumstance observable in other groups of minor intrusions in Skye, and doubtless related in some way to the dominant direction of the dykes in the region, with which it agrees very closely. As is shown in the sketch-map (Fig. 58), the area in question embraces all the acid igneous rocks of Tertiary age in Skye. The earlier groups of acid rocks (and also the pitchstones, etc., which came later) were limited to smaller areas lying within this large irregular oval. The intrusions pertaining to this group represent then the maximum extension of igneous activity in Skye as regards acid rocks. Next to the granites, they constitute by far the most important group of acid rocks in our region; and when we speak of the group of minor acid intrusions or the epoch of the minor acid intrusions, without qualification, it is this group or this epoch that will be intended.

The larger of the minor acid intrusions are usually of irregular shape, and have partly transgressive relations towards the stratified or other rocks among which they have been intruded. They partake more or less of the nature of sheets, but rarely, if ever, behave as perfect sills for any great distance. In this they contrast strongly with the minor basic intrusions. A good example is the mass of granophyre, intruded mainly in the Lias, to the east of the Broadford River. This has in great part the form of a sheet, but it passes obliquely from one horizon in the Lias to another, and in places is more sharply transgressive. Where it enters the Cambrian Limestones, it at once assumes a

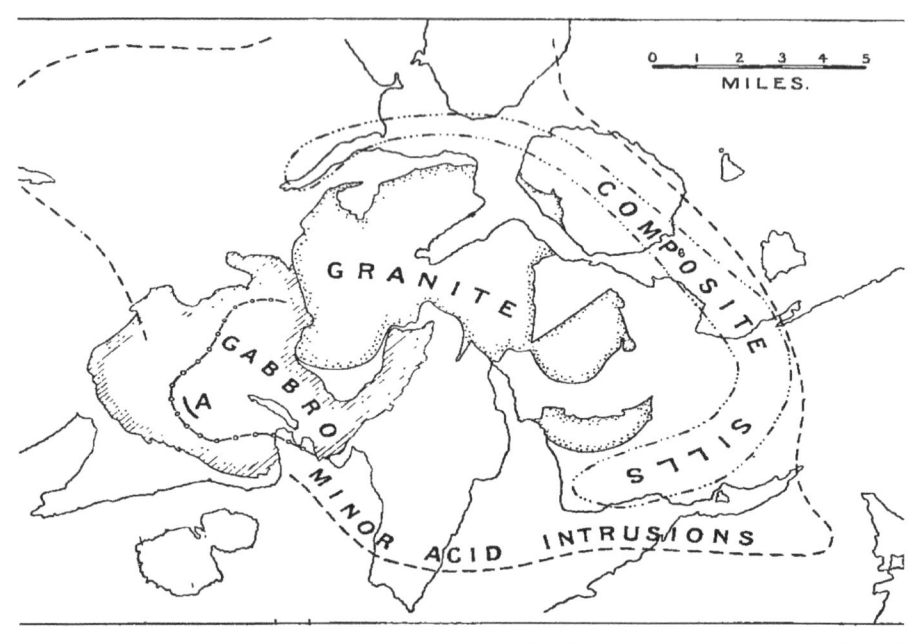

Fig. 58.—Sketch-map illustrating the distribution of certain groups of acid intrusions in relation to the granite of the Red Hills. Scale, ¼ inch to a mile.

(*a.*) The line (of small circles connected by dashes) in the gabbro area indicates the western limit of granite and granophyre veins, in so far at least as they are locally abundant and noticeable, in the gabbro of the Cuillins. It may probably be taken as showing, with rough approximation, the concealed extension of the granite beneath the gabbro laccolite.

(*b.*) The roughly semicircular belt, enclosed by a line of dots and dashes, marks the distribution of the peculiar composite (basic and acid) intrusions of the symmetrical kind, which we have distinguished as the Cnoc Càrnach type.

(*c.*) The heavy broken line indicates the area of distribution of the minor acid intrusions in general. It is an irregular oval, about 24 miles long, centring in the granite of the Red Hills, and having its long axis in a direction nearly agreeing with that of the dykes.

(*d.*) The short heavy line at A marks the position of the peculiar felsite of the Alaisdair Stone-shoot.

frankly transgressive attitude, with vertical junctions, and runs out in the form of narrow tongues or curving dykes, recalling the behaviour of the granite of Beinn an Dubhaich in the same country rock. This occurrence is probably to be referred to the epoch of the minor intrusions rather than to that of the granite, but there is no decisive evidence on this point.

Further north we have a group of granophyre intrusions in the Lias of the broad hill named Beinn Bhuidhe, N.W. of Broadford Bay. These, where best exhibited along the coast, have clearly the form of sills, although they show some irregularity of habit. They are referable to the principal epoch of minor acid intrusions, and in one place, near some ruined huts, they enter into rather peculiar relations with certain basic sills of earlier intrusion.

Mullach na Càrn, the highest hill on the isle of Scalpay, is nearly encircled by the outcrop of a rather large sheet of granophyre. This shows a higher degree of regularity than might be expected, considering that the country rock is coarse-textured Torridonian sandstone. It is probable, however, that this sheet

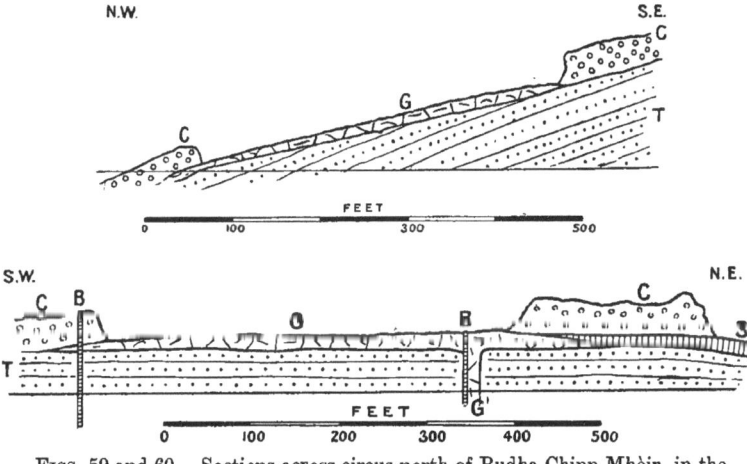

FIGS. 59 and 60.—Sections across circus north of Rudha Chinn Mhòir, in the N.W. of Scalpay.

T, Torridonian sandstone; C, Triassic conglomerate; G, granophyre sill; G', granophyre dyke; S, basalt sill; B, B, basalt dykes.

belongs to the epoch of the granite, and has been connected with the large body of that rock which crosses over into Scalpay, and approaches within ¾ mile of the sheet. A like supposition cannot be applied to a smaller sheet or sill of granophyre in the north-western part of the same island. It is exposed over a nearly circular area, 120 to 150 yards in diameter, forming the floor of a curious circus on the northern slope of the hill Rudha Chinn Mhòir. It is surrounded by a wall of Triassic conglomerate, and was evidently intruded along the junction of that formation with the underlying Torridonian, as shown in Figs. 59 and 60. The sill cannot extend far beyond the limits of the circus, and on the coast only 100 yards to the N.E. a basalt sill is seen occupying a like position at the horizon of the unconformity.

The granophyre sill seems to have been fed by a dyke (G' in Fig. 60), but the exposures are not sufficient to put this beyond question.

Several intrusions of granophyre, mostly of the nature of short stout dykes but with rather irregular habit, occur on the N.W. side of Loch Sligachan, besides a sheet exposed by the road-side on the opposite side of the loch. These are intruded in the basaltic lavas. The composite sill and dyke of Allt an t-Sithean in the same neighbourhood have already been described, as well as the similar composite intrusions in the Lias near and to the south of Broadford. The felsite intrusions on the slope of Sgùrr Thuilm have also been noticed (Chapter V.) as possibly connected with the rhyolitic lavas. A remarkable intrusion in the gabbro at the head of Coire Labain and in the "Alaisdair Stone-shoot" will be more particularly noticed in the petrographical part of this chapter.

The ordinary dykes referable to the principal period of minor acid intrusions need not be enumerated individually. Though always greatly inferior in number to the basic dykes, they occur with some frequency in the country to the north of the Cuillins, the most westerly being three on Braigh Coille na Droighniche, overlooking Loch Harport, and two in the Vikisgill valley. In numerous instances the acid dykes are in contact with, and then usually flanked by, basic dykes. Examples of this may be seen in Allt Airidh Meall Beathaig, a tributary of the Varragill River; in Allt Daraich, near Sligachan; and especially a group occurring in the belt of ground running from Coire na Creiche to near Drynoch. Several acid or sub-acid dykes occur in the Strathaird peninsula, and some of these also are members of composite dykes. Dykes, and occasionally sheets, of felsite and granophyre are found at numerous places on and near the borders of the granitic tract.

Concerning the tract of stratified rocks farther south-east, Mr Clough writes as follows:—"No granophyre or felsite intrusions of Tertiary age have been seen N.E. of a line connecting Skulamus and Loch na Dal, nor S.W. of Sgiath-bheinn an Uird. They are most numerous near Ben Suardal, Skulamus, and Heast. Near these localities their mode of occurrence is varied. The larger intrusions may perhaps be regarded as laccolites, but none continue far on one stratigraphical horizon. The acid intrusions certainly keep to the bedding less usually than the basic sills. Only four or five intrusions belonging to this class have been seen on the S.E. side of Loch Eishort. These are all in the form of dykes which strike N.W. or N.N.W., about parallel to the basaltic dykes near them. The broadest of the granophyre dykes on this side of the loch is seen on the shore about a mile E N.E. of Rudha Dubh Ard, where it forms part of a composite dyke. It is ten or twelve yards wide, and has been traced about three quarters of a mile S.S.E. Another thinner dyke, again part of a composite dyke, occurs on the Rudha Dubh Ard itself. On the E. side of Monadh Morsaig there is a granophyre dyke varying in width between four and ten feet. On the W. side of Mullach an Achaidh Mhòir, near Drumfearn, there is a dyke about one foot thick. The dyke that occurs farthest S.E. is in Allt Duisdale, about three quarters of a mile W.N.W. of the bridge."

It is in accordance with the general behaviour of basic and acid magmas in our region, to which we have repeatedly alluded, that the acid dykes and sheets show less perfect regularity in their field-relations than the corresponding bodies of basic composition. The dykes show a certain degree of order in their direction, the prevalent bearing being about N.W. or N.N.W., as in the basic dykes of the region, but with more frequent departures from the general rule. It is noteworthy that, though belonging to a local group, connected with the special focus of central Skye, the dykes are governed as regards direction by the same rules as the dykes of regional distribution. In those of the basic dykes which are most intimately connected with the local focus of activity we shall find a different law prevailing (Chapter XXI.). The intrusive sheets of acid rocks, even where they preserve the sill habit with considerable persistence, sometimes show irregularities on a small scale at their surfaces of contact, and may send off little tongues along the bedding of the contiguous strata. A good example is seen in a low cliff a little west of Rudh' an Eireannaich, near Broadford.* In the basic sills any such irregularity is of rare occurrence; and equally so in an acid sill which has been guided by an earlier basic one, even where, as we have sometimes observed, it has totally destroyed its guide. Many of the ordinary minor acid intrusions give evidence of relatively rapid cooling at their edges, either by a finer texture or by spherulites of diminishing size, as in the sill near Broadford mentioned above.

We proceed to consider the *petrographical characters* of the rocks. With a few exceptions, to be noted below, they are of thoroughly acid composition. Although no chemical analyses have been made, the microscopic examination leads us to believe that these minor intrusions are as a whole somewhat more acid than the large masses of the Red Hills: they seem at least to be poorer in the ferro-magnesian minerals. The low specific gravity of most of the rocks points to the same conclusion: ten examples gave a mean of 2·54, as compared with 2·59 for the granites, etc. Those dykes which are visibly off-shoots from the granite intrusions show the same difference, at least when they are spherulitic or otherwise fine-textured. We shall confine our attention in the first place to the truly acid members of the group, reserving certain aberrant types for subsequent consideration.

The *constituent minerals* of the rocks may be dismissed briefly. They are quartz, orthoclase, and oligoclase, with in most cases some ferro-magnesian mineral and one of the iron-ore group, but

* This was noticed by Sir A. Geikie, *Quart. Journ. Geol. Soc.*, vol. xiv., pl. I., fig. 8; 1858.

these latter always in quite subordinate amount. The ferromagnesian mineral is, in different cases, augite, hornblende, or biotite, the first-named being the most usual. In some instances the hornblende is secondary after augite, but primary hornblende is also found. The augite shows in thin slices the very pale green tint which is customary for this mineral in acid rocks, but it is often replaced by chloritic alteration-products of a deeper green colour. The hornblende is brown or, when of secondary origin, green. Many of the rocks show no ferro-magnesian mineral except little chloritic and limonitic patches, and even these may occur only sparingly. The iron-ore minerals met with in different examples are magnetite and pyrites. The former is the more common, but the latter is found in a considerable number of cases, with all the appearance of a primary mineral. It seems to be specially characteristic of the spherulitic types, and it is possibly connected, as Professor Judd has suggested, with some kind of solfataric action.* The pyrites forms little cubes, usually fresh but sometimes partially converted to hæmatite.

The rocks present much more variation in *microstructure* than in mineralogical constitution. The more typical varieties met with range themselves for the most part in two parallel lines, the microgranitic (quartz-porphyries, etc.) and the micrographic (granophyres of many kinds), though these are connected by numerous intermediate links. On the whole, the tendency to micrographic intergrowths, which we observed in the acid rocks of the large plutonic masses, is at least as strongly marked in these minor intrusions of like composition, and often attains in the latter a more typical development.

The rocks which fall under the former of the two divisions thus recognised do not require any lengthy description, and it will be sufficient to select a few illustrative examples. The evident porphyritic crystals are felspars, up to $\frac{1}{8}$ or sometimes $\frac{1}{4}$ inch in length, and quartz, usually of rather smaller dimensions. The dominant felspar is orthoclase, and shows the customary crystal habit: the quartz is in bipyramidal crystals, and contains glass-inclusions. Ferro-magnesian minerals are never abundant, and there is at most a small amount of magnetite, or in some cases pyrite. The ground-mass, of various scales of texture but generally quite fine, usually resolves into a granular aggregate of felspar and quartz. In the finer-textured varieties the felspar, especially if it predominates very decidedly, may assume idiomorphic habit, forming narrow crystals. In some of the rocks there has doubtless been a glassy base, which is now devitrified or in great part decomposed.

A variety with relatively large and conspicuous dihexahedra of quartz is of somewhat exceptional occurrence. Examples occur

* In the Druim an Eidhne rocks, to be more particularly described below, iron sulphide occurs not only in visible crystals, but also in a finely disseminated form, as Dr Cullis has proved by blowpipe tests (*Quart. Journ. Geol. Soc.*, vol. xlix., p. 190 ; 1893).

S

in the form of small dykes near the northern base of Glamaig, above the village of Sconser. In most of the rocks the more evident phenocrysts are of felspar. The ferro-magnesian element, never very abundant, may be either a pale augite or a brown mica. The ground-mass has in general a microgranitic structure, and varies in size of grain, a fine texture being the most usual.

A well-characterised quartz-felsite forms two or three irregular sheet-formed intrusions on the northern face of Creag Strollamus, in the Broadford district. It contains very abundant pinkish crystals of orthoclase, about $\frac{1}{8}$ inch across, and smaller crystals of quartz, in a compact light grey ground. Two specimens of identical appearance showed some differences in thin slices. In one from 500 yards N. by E. of the summit of the hill [9572] the ground-mass, though fine-textured, is easily resolved. Besides the phenocrysts, it encloses little patches of micropegmatite, abruptly bounded and perhaps of the nature of xenoliths. In the second specimen [8969], taken about 70 yards farther N.W., the ground-mass is similar to the other, though a little finer. Some one or more ferro-magnesian minerals have been fairly represented, but are now totally destroyed: the shapes suggest both augite and biotite. There are a few little cubes of pyrites. The specific gravity of this rock is 2·57. A rock with pink crystals of felspar, very like the preceding and of specific gravity 2·53, is seen on the eastern slope of Belig, about 500 yards N.W. by N. of Loch na Sguabaidh. Similar rocks are found elsewhere, not only in occurrences which we assign to the group of minor acid intrusions proper, but also, on Glamaig and in other places, where they are probably to be regarded as special modifications of the granitic intrusions of the Red Hills.

Rocks with characters which suggest the former presence of a large amount of glass in the ground-mass are found in the form of small intrusive sheets and dykes on Glamaig and in various parts of the Red Hills. They usually intersect the granite or granophyre, but this is the only datum for their age, and they are included in this place only for convenience. Here we may note an interesting rock, a specimen of which was kindly furnished by Professor Judd, who drew our attention to its occurrence in the screes on the western slope of Marsco. It has not been found in place. It has a dark ground-mass of dull aspect and bluish tint, in which are set abundant reddish-yellow crystals of orthoclase, about $\frac{1}{8}$ inch long and sometimes aggregated in groups, with smaller pyramidal crystals of quartz. A thin slice [9285] shows that the dark colour of the ground-mass is due to a crowd of minute rods, not more than ·001 inch long, probably of augite. They show only a very faint colour under the microscope, and, being contained within the thickness of the slice, do not lend themselves to polariscopic examination. They show little parallel arrangement except where they lie tangentially to the porphyritic crystals. The base in which these rods are set is colourless and of low refractive index, and in natural light might be taken for a glass, but it is doubtful whether any truly vitreous matter remains. The bulk of it at least depolarises, having nearly the birefringence of an alkali-felspar. The specific gravity of the rock is 2·63, and it may not improbably be a devitrified pitchstone.

Comparable in some respects with the preceding is a dyke which intersects the gabbro just W. of the Sligachan River, near the outfall of Allt Coire Riabhach. It is 2 feet wide, and has margins about 3 inches wide showing strong flow-structure. The central portion, of specific gravity 2·63, shows scattered crystals of white orthoclase up to $\frac{1}{10}$ inch long in a dull compact ground-mass of dark bluish-grey colour. The slice [8976] reveals also scattered crystals of some ferro-magnesian mineral, now destroyed. The ground-mass is crowded with little dark rods having at each spot a parallel arrangement, often with a second set grown at right angles to the first. The colourless matrix in which these minute rods are embedded has probably been vitreous, but is too obscure to permit of a definite pronouncement. The marginal modification of the dyke, specific gravity 2·60, with marked fluxion-structure, is paler, with narrow bands of lighter and darker tints, and encloses scattered felspars as before. Under the microscope [8977] it has in natural light all the appearance of a glassy rock, clouded with minute limonite specks and having little patches and streaks of the same. Between crossed nicols, however, the ground breaks up into an irregular mosaic of little birefringent areas, the whole being very similar to what is seen in the devitrified pitchstones to be described in a later chapter.

Rocks showing a sinuous flow-structure, and presenting a "microfelsitic" texture which may probably be attributed to devitrification, are met with in numerous localities, either making up the whole width of a small dyke or forming the marginal part of a dyke or of a larger and less regular intrusive body. Examples may be seen on Ben Meabost, in the Strathaird district; near the coast $\frac{3}{4}$ mile S. of Camasunary; at one or two places in Scalpay; and near An-t-Sithean, Broadford.

Some rocks containing only isolated and scattered spherulitic growths form a connecting link between the two main divisions which we have distinguished. They are found at numerous localities in the belt of country bordering the Red Hills, and occur not only in Skye but occasionally also in the smaller islands to the north-east. Here belongs a quartz-porphyry dyke to the north of Mullach na Càrn in Scalpay. It is a nearly white rock with orthoclase phenocrysts up to $\frac{1}{10}$ inch and smaller crystals of quartz. There has been a little augite, now destroyed. The fine-textured ground-mass is in general of micro-granitic structure, but each quartz crystal (not felspar) is surrounded by a spherulitic border [9376]. Here too we may probably place a felsitic dyke, part of a double dyke, intersecting the gabbro of Guillamon on the east coast of that islet. Quartz-crystals $\frac{1}{20}$ inch in diameter, with glass-inclusions, are enclosed in a ground-mass which is much obscured by secondary changes; but numerous isolated spherulites are still recognisable as such, although their original structure is almost obliterated [9378]. A few rocks of this kind show what we may term rhyolitic characters, and to this extent resemble the spherulitic dykes of Druim an Eidhne to be described below. We may cite especially a 2-ft dyke, parallel to a larger dyke, exposed about 400 yards N.N.W. of Scalpay House. It is a dull grey rock with a well marked laminated structure parallel to the bounding walls, and with altered spherulites showing as lighter spots about $\frac{1}{50}$ inch in diameter. A thin slice shows it to consist largely of bundles of parallel felspar rods and interstitial granules of quartz, but the latter mineral seems to be in part secondary. The spherulites are nearly opaque, and no longer show any structure: each is surrounded by a rusty border.

We come now to that division of the acid rocks in which the whole, or almost the whole, of the ground-mass is affected by special structures, which are usually of the *spherulitic* kind. In using this term we desire to make no distinction between spherulites which exhibit a regular black cross between crossed nicols and those which Rosenbusch has distinguished as "pseudospherulites." The differences between these appear to be differences of degree rather than of kind, the essential characteristic of all being fine graphic intergrowths of alkali-felspar and quartz. From this statement we except certain complex spherulites to be separately noticed, and even these may probably be regarded as the final term of the series, connected with the others by unbroken gradations.

The transition from a visibly micrographic to a cryptographic intergrowth is well illustrated in some of the separate minor intrusions, but even better in the marginal modifications of coarser granophyres which occur in some places on the borders of the large intrusive bodies of the Red Hills. The chief features of such transition may be briefly summarised. The more regular micrographic structures in the granophyres in general always tend to arrange themselves about centres, either with or without a small phenocryst to serve as nucleus, and this tendency is more marked in proportion to the fineness of the intergrowth. With increasing fineness of texture, a radiate arrangement about the centre becomes more apparent, the distinct areas in a thin slice, within which the felspar and quartz severally show crystalline continuity, being disposed increasingly in the form of sectors of a circle. These sectors become narrower and more numerous, while the minute elements which compose them assume a more linear form and a more regular radiate grouping. A point is reached at which the several elements of the aggregate cease to be resolvable in a thin slice, and the structure may be styled cryptographic. Beyond this point, a spherulite, examined between crossed nicols, merely shows evidence of a radiate fibrous structure, the dark brushes approximating more or less to the ideal black cross with arms parallel to the principal planes of the nicols. Such a spherulite has the appearance of being built entirely of radiating fibres of felspar, and there can be little doubt that quartz really plays a less important part here than in the coarser micrographic intergrowths.

In spherulites of moderate diameter, say $\frac{1}{4}$ inch, there is often a marked difference between the central and peripheral portions; the former being finely cryptographic, with well marked radiate structure, while the latter is visibly micrographic, with an increasingly rude type of intergrowth, and may merge insensibly into a merely granular aggregate which forms the interspaces between the spherulites (Plate XIX., Fig. 1, B). The transition which we have described is thus illustrated in the different parts of a single spherulite. The peripheral portion of the spherulite appears also to be decidedly richer in quartz than the interior.

These facts perhaps throw some light on the mode of origin and growth of the structure. The spherulite began, as we may conceive, with a radiate growth of felspar fibres, preferably attached to some solid body as a nucleus. The surrounding magma at this stage had a composition equivalent to that of a mixture of alkali-felspar with a smaller proportion of quartz. As the felspar fibres grew by extending outward, the abstraction of this constituent tended to make the magma more acid, which was only partially counteracted by the liberation of free silica. This was set free at the places where the felspar was growing, and entered into an intimate intergrowth with that mineral. It seems to have been, not the spherulite, but the residual magma, that tended towards a determinate composition; and, if we suppose it to have solidified *en bloc* when this was reached, the said composition is represented by the interspaces between the spherulites, which have commonly a microgranitic structure. On this view, the substance of the interspaces would be comparable, under certain limitations, with a eutectic mixture (*see* Plate XXII., Fig. 1).

There are, however, some spherulitic structures into which quartz does not enter at all, and in these the radiating felspar elements become distinct and take form individually. This is seen exceptionally and on a small scale in certain spherulitic groupings which have been embedded in glass; and it is displayed in a remarkable manner in cases where large spherulites have been developed at places where vapour was disengaged from the magma, and a cavernous structure has resulted. To illustrate the former case we take an interesting micro-spherulitic rock which is found as a small dyke, 8 inches or a foot across, cutting the granite on the ascent of Druim an Eidhne from Strath na Creitheach, a little to the left of the tourist-track.* It is a rather dark greenish grey rock, of specific gravity 2·56, with very evident flow-lines, sometimes curving, and full of minute darker spots. In a thin slice these are found to be spherulites, from $\frac{1}{200}$ to $\frac{1}{100}$ inch in diameter, and of two kinds. The majority are of a common type, ovoid in shape with well marked outline, and giving the characteristic black cross in polarised light. In certain bands there occur, instead of these, skeleton spherulites consisting merely of a stellate arrangement of little felspar rods, not mere fibres. These rods occupy only a part of the space within the spherulite, the rest being filled by substance like that in the interspaces between the spherulites. This interstitial

* This dyke was not detected during the survey. For the information and for a specimen of the rock we are indebted to Mr A. K. Coomára-Swámy.

ground, quite small in amount in comparison with the crowded spherulites, has probably been glassy or partly glassy; but, if so, is now devitrified. It recalls in some respects the devitrified pitchstones of Coire-chatachan, etc., to be described later.

The common type of spherulitic granophyre, in which the greater part of the mass is made up of regular cryptographic spherulites, is so frequently represented among our minor acid intrusions that there is no need to enumerate particular occurrences. As good and well preserved examples, easy of access, we may mention the rather irregular sills in the Lias which are exposed on the coast west of Broadford Bay. One is found in a little cliff west of the composite sill of Rudh' an Eireannaich, and another some 800 or 900 yards farther N.W. Here the spherulites are very evident in hand-specimens. In thin slices it is seen that they do not graduate into the granular interspaces, but are rather sharply bounded, and preserve the fine radiate fibrous appearance to the actual boundary. Between crossed nicols they show well defined dark sectors or brushes, which correspond approximately, but not always exactly, with the principal planes of the nicols. In addition to small scattered felspar phenocrysts, there are others of quartz. These are either well formed crystals or grains with rounded outlines, and they seem to have the latter form especially when they serve as the nuclei of spherulites. An interesting feature is the occurrence of micropegmatite phenocrysts, having the outlines of felspar crystals but full of quartz in micrographic intergrowth. They are always surrounded by a spherulitic growth in the form of radiating bunches of fibres starting from numerous points on the boundary of the phenocryst. Scattered through the rock, in spherulites and interspaces alike, are slender rods, usually less than $\frac{1}{20}$ inch in length, of some ferro-magnesian silicate, probably augite, now destroyed. These are not uncommon in other rocks of this group, and they sometimes share in the radiate arrangement of the spherulites, but in the specimens here noticed the rods have no definite orientation.

We have failed to establish any criterion of a petrographical kind to discriminate between those spherulitic dykes and sheets which are to be regarded as subterranean offshoots of the large masses of the Red Hills and those referable to the later epoch of independent minor intrusions. Again, there are some occurrences which perhaps belong to a different epoch (between the other two), viz. that to which we have relegated the composite intrusions of the Cnoc Càrnach group. It is at least possible that some portion of the acid magma of that epoch took lines of its own, and formed independent intrusive bodies which, in the absence of the guiding basalt, would be of somewhat irregular habit. Such may perhaps be the origin of the group of intrusions seen on the north-west side of Loch Sligachan, just east of the composite sill of Allt an 't-Sithean. A specimen from here shows turbid felspars about $\frac{1}{10}$ inch in diameter, with rounded angles, and corroded quartz-grains in a spherulitic ground-mass. There is a close resemblance to the granophyres of Allt an 't-Sithean and of the neighbouring com-

PLATE XI

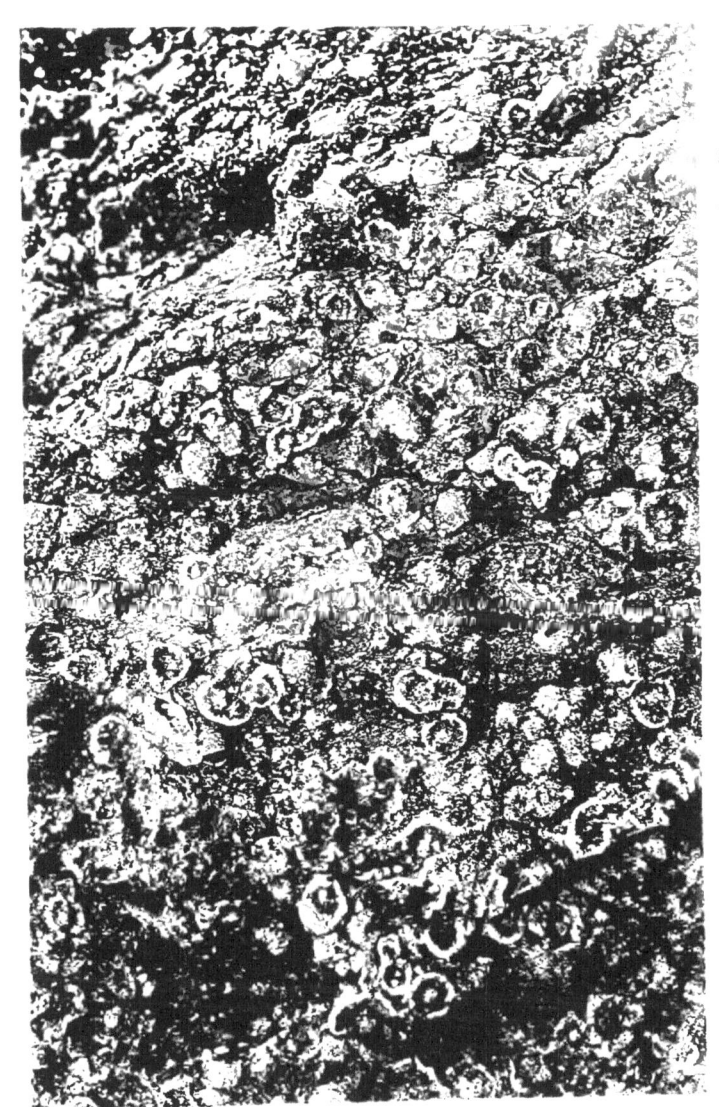

Weathered surface of acid dyke, Druim an Eidhne, showing crowded spherulites.

posite dyke, though the spherulites here have a more evidently micrographic structure [3197].

We have next to notice a remarkable group of dykes which, in their petrographical characters, show decided *rhyolitic* affinities. This is the more interesting, since these dykes belong to the plutonic phase of intrusion, and are visibly apophyses of the granite. We may conveniently speak of them as the *Druim an Eidhne type*, the most characteristic examples being met with on the ridge of that name. Here, as already stated in Chapter IX., the dykes are seen to be offshoots from the granite mass of Strath na Creitheach, etc., which itself at some places along its margin assumes very similar petrographical characters; and they may be traced for some distance through the adjacent rocks, viz. the volcanic agglomerate and the banded gabbros. A few other dykes within the granitic area, in Strath na Creitheach and elsewhere, resemble the typical examples more or less closely. They intersect the granite; but, since the granite itself undoubtedly represents several distinct intrusions, this fact does not preclude our attaching these dykes provisionally to the Druim an Eidhne group.

The field-relations of the acid dykes of Druim an Eidhne have been sufficiently set forth in the former chapter. Our petrographical examination of the rocks does not add much to the account already given by Professor Judd,[*] although our reading of the phenomena leads to very different conclusions as regards the origin of the rocks. It is to be remarked, however, that the dykes are not all of one type. In addition to the rocks to be described more particularly, there are others which are simple quartz-felsites, presenting no special features of interest and not calling for further notice. These have the same mode of occurrence as the others.

The rhyolitic dykes of Druim an Eidhne have in natural exposures a yellowish brown colour due to atmospheric action, and considerable excavation is sometimes needed to arrive at the unaltered rock. This shows a bluish grey ground of very compact texture, enclosing quartz-grains, small crystals of felspar, and pyrites. The characteristic features of the rock are, however, more apparent upon a weathered surface: they are especially an abundant development of large spherulites and a strongly-marked fluxion-banding— both characters, as Professor Judd remarks, belonging to rhyolitic rather than granitic rocks. The spherulites weather out in strong relief, and are easily detached (Plate XI.). They range in diameter up to about 2½ inches (6 centimetres[†]), and, even to the

---

[*] *Quart. Journ. Geol. Soc.*, vol. xlix., pp. 182–191, pl. II., III.; 1893.

[†] The 60 centimetres of Prof. Judd's paper is a clerical error, corrected in the author's separate copies. The only spherulites of this larger size (2 feet) recorded in Britain occur in some of the Lower Palæozoic intrusions oi the Lleyn district of Cærnarvonshire; but at Silver Cliff in Colorado Whitman Cross has remarked spherulites as much as 10 feet in diameter. The Welsh rocks mentioned present many analogies with the dykes of Druim an Eidhne: see Miss Raisin, *Quart. Journ. Geol. Soc.*, vol. xlv., pp. 247–269; 1889: and Harker, *The Bala Volcanic Series of Caernarvonshire*, Chap. III.; 1889.

naked eye, often give evidence of a complex structure. The flow-structure, which is most developed at the sides or the dykes, is also rendered very conspicuous by weathering, certain narrow bands, usually about ten or twelve in the width of an inch, standing out prominently above the intervening bands (Plate XII.). In some places the fluxion is indicated by an allignment of small spherulites, as in many rhyolitic lavas and in the "rodded" spherulitic dykes to be described in a later chapter. The flow has been naturally parallel to the walls of the dykes; but, with increasing distance from the edge, it often becomes sinuous or even sharply reflexed at acute angles. This is partly due to the interference occasioned by large spherulites round which the flow-lines wind, or between which they thread their way. The phenomena certainly go to show that these spherulites were already in existence while flowing movement was still in progress, and cannot be attributed to devitrification at a later stage. A remarkable feature in some cases is the appearance of *discontinuity* in the flow. We may explain it by supposing that a small portion of the rock, having as nucleus a group of spherulites or phenocrysts but otherwise in a pasty condition, behaved in some degree as a solid inclusion, and was rolled over in the differential flowing movement of the enveloping mass. This peculiarity is seen on a small as well as on a larger scale (*see* Fig. 61).

The microscopical characters of the rocks have been carefully described by Professor Judd in the paper already cited. Porphyritic elements, though generally distributed, are not very abundant. They consist mainly of small crystals of quartz, containing relatively large glass-inclusions and patches of the ground-mass, orthoclase and oligoclase, and iron ores, both pyrites and magnetite. A ferromagnesian mineral has also been sparingly present, and seems to have been a green augite; but it is replaced by pseudomorphs of some chloritic substance charged with ferric oxide. Occasionally there is a pseudomorph which may represent biotite. Very characteristic of this group of rocks is the occurrence of phenocrysts of micropegmatite or, to use Professor Iddings' term, "granophyre groups," a feature well known in rhyolitic lavas in various districts.* Professor Judd, following out his view, already discussed, that these rocks are not dykes but fused inclusions of granite in the gabbro, regards the micropegmatite phenocrysts as undestroyed relics; but we find nothing to indicate that they are of exceptional origin. That they may have been formed at a distinctly earlier stage than the ground-mass and under somewhat different conditions may be granted; and it is seen that, like the ordinary phenocrysts, they have served as nuclei for subsequent spherulitic growths (Plate XX., Fig. 2; and Fig. 61 in text). On Professor Judd's view they should be either angular fragments or

* Iddings, *7th Ann. Rep. U.S. Geol. Sur.*, pp. 274-276, pl. XV.; 1888 (Obsidian Cliff, Yellowstone Park): *Monogr. XX. U.S. Geol. Sur.*, p. 375, pl. V., fig. 2; 1893 (Eureka district, Nevada): Reed, *Quart. Journ. Geol. Soc.*, vol. li., p. 162, pl. VI., figs. 3-5; 1895 (Fishguard, Pembrokeshire).

PLATE XII.

Weathered surface of acid dyke, Druim an Eidhne, showing tortuous flow-structure.

rounded by corrosion or fusion, whereas they often present the outlines proper to felspar crystals.

The spherulites, which are the most interesting feature of the rocks, range from microscopic dimensions to the large size already remarked, and they exhibit much variety of structure. The small ones are of a simple type, showing merely a radiate-fibrous arrangement of the felspar which is their principal element. They give an imperfect "black cross" effect between crossed nicols. They are often collected in groups, though without coalescing;

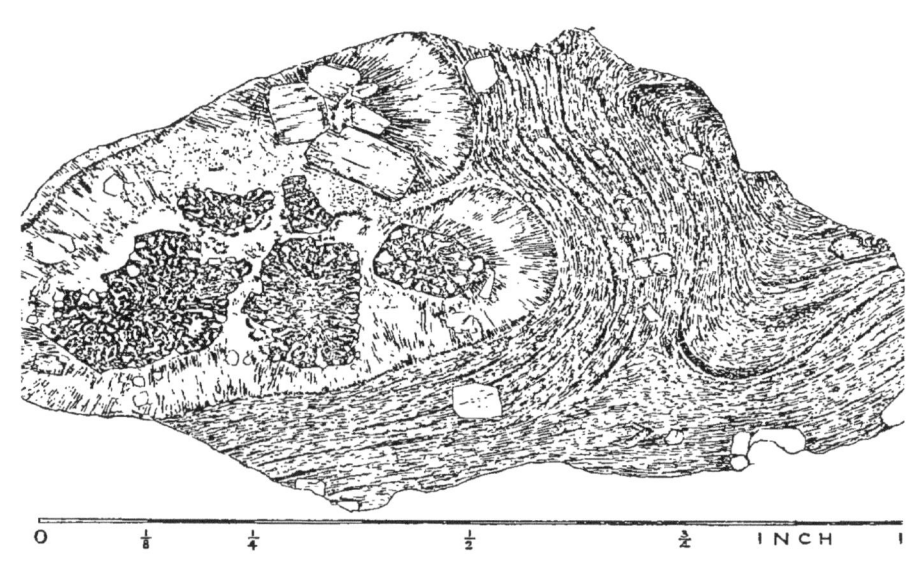

FIG. 61 [8971]. Thin slice from one of the rhyolitic dykes, apophyses from the granite, intersecting the gabbro of Druim an Eidhne; magnified four diameters.

To the left are seen a number of coalescing spherulites. These have grown in one place round a group of felspar crystals, in other places round micropegmatite phenocrysts, which have in part the outlines of felspar crystals but are crowded with inclusions of quartz in micrographic intergrowth.

The general mass of the rock has a strongly marked flow-structure, and in the right-hand half of the figure the fluxion-lines are seen to diverge in a fashion which indicates discontinuous flowing movement in the mass.

and not infrequently they are enclosed in the larger spherulitic growths, which we may infer to be of somewhat later formation. The larger spherulites are of complex structure, the radiate arrangement of the delicate constituent felspar-fibres being modified in various ways. In some cases there seems to be repeated bifurcation of the fibres at acute angles, giving the fox's brush structure figured by Professor Judd (*l.c.* Plate III., Figs. 8 and 9). In other cases subsidiary centres of radiation have been established at certain points, which have become the apices of conical bundles of fibres disposed in accordance with the general radiation from the primary centre (Plate XXII., Fig. 3). The fibres of the large spherulites may be interrupted by enclosed phenocrysts or small spherulites. The interstices between the felspar fibres are now occupied by quartz, but it is probable, as Professor Judd suggests, that they were once in great part vacant, and that these structures were then identical in all essentials with the much better preserved examples which have been described by Whitman Cross and Iddings from Colorado and the Yellowstone Park. He has even found in the large spherulites of Druim an Eidhne minute crystals which appear to be fayalite, as well as some indications suggesting the former presence of little aggregates of tridymite scales. The close resemblance to the American examples, extending to these interesting details, is further enhanced by the occurrence in some of our rocks of bodies which have apparently been lithophyses, and preserve something of the delicate concentric shell structure described by Iddings at Obsidian Cliff (Judd, *l.c.*, Plate II., Fig. 5).

If, while a portion of one of the large plumose spherulites is being viewed between crossed nicols, a mica-plate be interposed with its axes approximately at 45° to the fibres, it is observed that the polarisation-tints are raised in some parts and depressed in others in the same bundle of fibres. This presumably indicates that the axis of optical elasticity most nearly parallel to the length of the fibres is the mean axis, and that the crystallographic direction of elongation of these felspar-fibres is the vertical or *c*-axis. The same arrangement has been noticed by Iddings[*] in the Obsidian Cliff rocks. In our spherulitic acid rocks in general the spherulites are of the ordinary "negative" kind, the felspar fibres being elongated parallel to the *a*-axis, with which the greatest axis of optical elasticity makes only a small angle.

That the marginal portion of a large body of granite and the apophyses from it may in certain circumstances assume all the mineralogical and structural characters of rhyolites, including such special peculiarities as large composite spherulites and lithophyses, is, as we have remarked above, a fact of more than local interest. It certainly goes to show that the petrographical differences between plutonic and volcanic rocks as commonly developed are referable much more to differences of temperature and rate of cooling than to differences of pressure at the epoch of consolidation. It must be borne in mind that the rocks which build the Red Hills represent a number of distinct intrusions, which may have covered collectively a very considerable lapse of time, and we are led to refer the acid rocks of Druim an Eidhne to a rather late epoch of this time, when the neighbouring gabbro had long become cool. The relations between the two rocks here present the strongest contrast to what we have described on Marsco, where we believe the intru-

[*] *Bull. Phil. Soc. Washington*, vol. xi., p. 457 ; 1891. See also Cross, *ibid.*, p. 427 (Silver Cliff, Colorado).

sions of gabbro and granite to have been separated by only a short interval.

So far, the rocks treated in this chapter have been of thoroughly acid types. We have now, in conclusion, to notice certain examples which are most properly included in this place, although they are of *sub-acid composition*, being highly felspathic and comparable rather with *quartzless porphyries and trachytes* than with quartz-felsites and granophyres. The rocks consist indeed essentially of alkali-felspars, with at most a small amount of interstitial quartz and in some cases a ferro-magnesian mineral. They differ petrographically from the trachytic dykes of the Broadford and Sleat districts, to be described in a later chapter. Further the scanty evidence available would lead us to refer them to a very early epoch of the phase of minor intrusions, while the Broadford and Sleat trachytes belong to one of the closing episodes. For these reasons, we regard the rocks in question, at least provisionally, as aberrant members of the group treated in the present chapter, representing a special line of development from the main stock of the minor acid intrusions. Their areal distribution is in accord with this view, for the several dyke-formed, and sometimes sill-formed, intrusions in which these rocks appear are situated in general on the fringe of the area which we have marked out (Fig. 58) as that affected by the minor acid intrusions. It may also be remarked that, like these acid rocks and unlike the later trachytic dykes, the rocks now to be described often occur in close association with basic intrusions. The association is not usually of the regular and systematic kind ; but this also is found in one instance in a rock which may possibly be attached to to this sub-group, viz. the felsitic or bostonitic rock already described as forming part of the triple composite sill of Rudh' an Eireannaich, near Broadford. If, however, following the argument set forth in a former chapter, we refer the peculiar symmetrical composite sills and dykes to a distinct group of somewhat earlier date, then the Rudh' an Eireannaich felsite bears the same relation to the acid members of that group as the rocks now in question bear to the principal group of minor acid intrusions.

The first occurrence to be noticed, in the heart of the Cuillins, is in some respects unique. The rock forms two or more irregular dyke-like bodies of considerable magnitude intersecting the gabbro of the main range about the head of Coire Labain. Between the highest summit of the Cuillins and its nearest neighbour less than 100 yards to the N.E., known to climbers as Sgùrr Alaisdair and Sgùrr Tearlach respectively, is a deep notch, from which the great talus called the *Alaisdair Stoneshoot* streams down some 1200 or 1300 feet to the floor of Coire Labain. The break in the ridge is caused by a strip, here about 50 feet wide, of a more perishable rock traversing the gabbro. At this place it is, in its freshest state, a dark grey, finely crystalline rock, in general appearance not unlike many of the dolerite dykes of the district, but containing amygdules of quartz sometimes ½ inch or even 1 inch in length. More usually it has a pale colour consequent upon weathering, and in this state contributes largely to the talus mentioned. The strip of pale rock can be followed south-eastward along the ridge joining Sgùrr Tearlach to Sgùrr Dubh-na-dabheinn for some 250 yards, dying out near the pass. It can be traced for about the same distance in the opposite direction, turning rather more westward and ramifying before it dies out. A similar strip is seen just above the screes farther north, and runs nearly northward along the western face of Sgùrr Mhic Choinnich for 400 yards to the Coire Labain pass, where it is considerably expanded. This too ramifies, and also sends small veins into the gabbro and encloses xenoliths of that rock. The situation of the intrusions is indicated in a generalised way at A on the sketch-map, Fig. 58. The amygdaloidal variety of the rock has been met with only near the head of the great stone-shoot. The common variety elsewhere, always with the pale tint due to weathering, is of somewhat less fine texture, and the little green crystals of altered augite are often visible.

A thin slice [8717] of the prevalent type shows rectangular sections of felspar about $\frac{1}{30}$ inch long as the principal constituent. This is largely orthoclase, but striated oligoclase is also present. Pale greenish pseudomorphs of hornblende after augite, about $\frac{1}{50}$ inch in length, are fairly abundant, and as a prominent secondary constituent there is pale yellowish pleochroic epidote, partly replacing crystals of oligoclase. A certain amount of quartz is present, but this too is probably of secondary origin. A specimen of the fresher and finer-textured variety, with quartz-amygdules, from the head of the great stone-shoot, gives the specific gravity 2·68. Under the microscope it shows a different structure [8718]. A microporphyritic character, which was scarcely evident in the former specimen, is here well developed. The phenocrysts include orthoclase, oligoclase, and fresh colourless augite in crystals from ·01 to ·05 inch in length. These occur closely clustered, with a few small octahedra of magnetite, in a finely granular groundmass, which must be chiefly of orthoclase. The quartz which occurs here is certainly a secondary product.

In its geological relations as well as in its petrographical characters this rock stands alone. It is not seen to cut anything younger than the gabbro, and the only rocks which cut it belong to a late epoch. Its precise age is therefore not certainly fixed, but we attach it rather to the principal group of minor acid intrusions than to the granites.

Several dykes of the kind considered here—*i.e.* composed largely of alkali-felspars with little or no quartz—are seen in the neighbourhood of Allt a' Mhaim, on the north-west side of the Cuillins, near the foot-path from Sligachan to Glen Brittle. They are of more than one type. One is a dull reddish rock, of fine texture but evidently crystalline, which may be termed a biotite-bearing orthophyre. The felspar phenocrysts, which are not closely set, are of orthoclase with less frequent oligoclase, and are about $\frac{1}{8}$ inch long. There are scattered flakes of brown mica, sometimes enclosed in the felspars, some iron-ore, and a few grains of sphene. The ground-mass is composed of little felspars giving rather stout rectangular sections, and these are mostly if not wholly orthoclase.

A neighbouring dyke differs from the preceding in having hornblende instead of biotite, and also in having a trachytic instead of an orthophyric structure in its ground-mass. The rock is of light colour with white felspar phenocrysts, exceptionally as much as $\frac{1}{4}$ inch long, and lustrous black hornblendes $\frac{1}{8}$ to $\frac{1}{4}$ inch. A thin slice [9257] shows that the felspar is a plagioclase: the hornblende is brown, and the crystals, often twinned, have their outlines rounded by magmatic corrosion. Magnetite crystals and rather stout little prisms of apatite are present. The ground-mass consists of little interlacing felspars, only about ·005 inch long, with minute granules of magnetite. This rock, with a specific gravity 2·63, is probably somewhat less acid than the preceding. Both dykes, as well as others in the vicinity, are associated in the field with basic dykes and run in contact with them, but not consistently.

A dyke seen on the lower slopes of Beinn Réidh-beag, near the north-west coast of Scalpay, resembles the former of the Allt a' Mhaim dykes in its orthophyric structure, but the latter one in the nature of its ferro-magnesian element, and it may be named hornblendic orthophyre. It is stained to a brick-red colour very like that of the Torridonian sandstone which it intersects, and might easily be passed over except for the occurrence in it of green crystals of hornblende up to $\frac{1}{4}$ inch in length. Its specific gravity is 2·66. In a thin slice [9379] the hornblende shows as idiomorphic crystals, sometimes twinned, with a colour varying from brown to green, the latter owing to alteration. The rest of the rock consists of stout little felspar crystals, about ·01 inch long, with a very little interstitial quartz. This dyke is only half a mile distant from the fringe of the large granite mass, but it is more probably to be referred to the minor intrusions than to the plutonic phase.

Some of the felsite dykes of the Strathaird peninsula belong to this place. We have already remarked that, like the Allt a' Mhaim dykes which they resemble petrographically, they sometimes run for a certain distance in contact with basic dykes. A specimen from about 250 yards S.E. of Elgol is a pale grey, fine-textured rock enclosing rather abundant felspar phenocrysts, often clustered in "glomeroporphyritic" groups up to $\frac{1}{2}$ inch in diameter. They are considerably altered, some being opaque and white, others nearly black. In a thin slice [7485] these felspars show characters very suggestive of cryptoperthite. There are rare flakes of decayed biotite, and the ground-mass consists of little rectangular felspars, about ·01 inch long, with sensibly straight extinction, and some interstitial quartz. Rocks of this kind approximate in some respects to the bostonite (or bostonite-porphyry) type. The resemblance to the original bostonites is closer, as regards micro-structure and the absence of ferro-magnesian minerals, in certain of our dykes which consist entirely of a plexus of little crystals of alkali-felspar. One rock of this kind [2675], among the older collections of the Geological Survey, is labelled "Glen Brittle House," but we have not succeeded in discovering it in that locality. This specimen gives the low specific gravity 2·51. It is of fine texture, the little felspar crystals being only ·005 to ·01 inch in length.

CHAPTER XVII.

BASIC DYKES: FIELD RELATIONS.

Every geologist who has written of Skye, or of others of the Inner Hebrides, has remarked upon the prominent part played by dykes in the igneous geology of the region. By far the greatest number of them are composed of basic rocks—diabase, dolerite, basalt. They are by no means all of one age, or approximately so: on the contrary, numerous successive episodes in the history of Tertiary igneous activity in the region have been characterised by the intrusions of a vast number of dykes. Nor have they all fulfilled the same functions. We have already stated that some of them occupy the fissures through which the lavas were poured forth; while others, of later age, may perhaps stand in a like relationship to the intruded sills. We shall see that others again, and these doubtless a majority of the whole, did not, so far as we can ascertain, fulfil any such office, but are to be regarded as complete and self-contained intrusive bodies. These are younger than lavas or sills, and belong to more than one distinct epoch.

A complete investigation of the dykes would include the separation of them into distinct groups, the arranging of these in chronological sequence, and the petrographical description of each group. We have not been able to obtain the requisite data for such a complete account, and it may be doubted whether such data are attainable. The imperfect results which represent the very partial success of our attempts in. this direction will be given below; but in the present chapter we shall make some general remarks upon the basic dykes of Skye as a whole, and more especially upon the characters which they exhibit in the field. These remarks are prompted by observations made during our detailed survey, which embraced only a part of the island; but from what has been written by other geologists, and in particular from the general account given by Sir A. Geikie,* it cannot be doubted that the results are applicable, not only to the whole of Skye, but to a much wider region.

The most striking features of the dykes as a whole are undoubtedly their astonishing number and their general community of direction. These and some other points appear clearly on the geological map, but we shall proceed to consider them more fully. And first it is very noticeable that the dykes are by no means equally numerous in different parts of the country. A

---

* *Trans. Roy. Soc. Edin.*, vol. xxxv., pp. 29-74; 1888: *Ancient Volcanoes of Great Britain*, vol. ii., chapters xxxiv., xxxv.; 1897.

small part of this inequality is no doubt only apparent, and results merely from the fact that over considerable areas the rocks are totally concealed by peat; but this affords no adequate explanation of the differences actually observed. For instance, the hills composed of granite and of Torridon Sandstone afford everywhere abundant exposures, but they often contain much fewer dykes than other areas adjacent.

A glance at the map is sufficient to show that *the frequency of the dykes* in different places depends very largely upon *the nature of the country rock.*

A striking illustration of this appears on comparing the basalt country and the gabbro of the Cuillins on the one hand with the granite tract on the other. While a square mile of the former often contains as many as a hundred dykes, an equal area of the latter shows on the average only five or six at most. This point calls for some remark as regards its bearing on the relative ages of the various intrusions. As Sir A. Geikie has long ago pointed out, there are dykes obviously older than the granite, being clearly cut off or enclosed and highly metamorphosed by it; while others again are later, and cut the granite. ✦ But the fact that the great majority of the dykes which approach the granite do not intersect it, must not be taken as implying that most of the dykes are pre-granitic. The reverse is certainly the case; and the dykes in general do not cut the granite, only because they experienced a difficulty in penetrating it. This is abundantly proved. We see, for example, that where the granite becomes a sheet of no great thickness the dykes do cut it, and where apophyses run out from the main body the dykes cut these freely. Further, in places where very numerous dykes approach close to the granite without entering it, as on the south side of the Beinn an Dubhaich mass, the great majority of them are not metamorphosed. These must be newer than the granite, although they stop short against it.

The fact that the gabbro in certain places in the Cuillin tract is, in contrast to the neighbouring parts, relatively free from dykes is explained by the presence of granite underlying it. This is well seen on Druim an Eidhne and in Coire Riabhach, where for about three-quarters of a mile from the granite boundary the gabbro contains almost no dykes, excepting those sent out by the granite itself. The Blaven range affords another good illustration, having far more dykes on its eastern than on its western side. This is doubtless due to the fact that the granite sheet, thick in Strath na Creitheach, thins out rapidly eastward. It also thins out southward, and so, as we approach Camasunary, we find the dykes appearing in force in the valley.

The resistance offered by the granite to the passage of the dykes cannot arise from its hardness and toughness, for in these respects it is inferior to the gabbro. Possibly chemical as well as physical considerations enter into the question. The freedom with which dykes, often of very small width, cut through the massive gabbro is a striking phenomenon. They are not noticeably fewer on the summits of the Cuillins than in the adjacent valleys, although they must have traversed between 2000 and 3000 feet of gabbro. To this, however, there seems to be a limit; for when we turn from the gabbro laccolite of the Cuillins to the gabbro boss to the north-west of Broadford, we find the latter almost entirely free from dykes, excepting only those of acid composition clearly belonging to the adjacent granite. Similarly the granite of the eastern Red Hills, apparently of the nature of a boss, is cut by very few dykes, and the undoubted boss of Beinn an Dubhaich by none.

The basalt lavas, as we have said, are freely traversed by dykes, and the same is true of the sills intercalated among the lavas, so

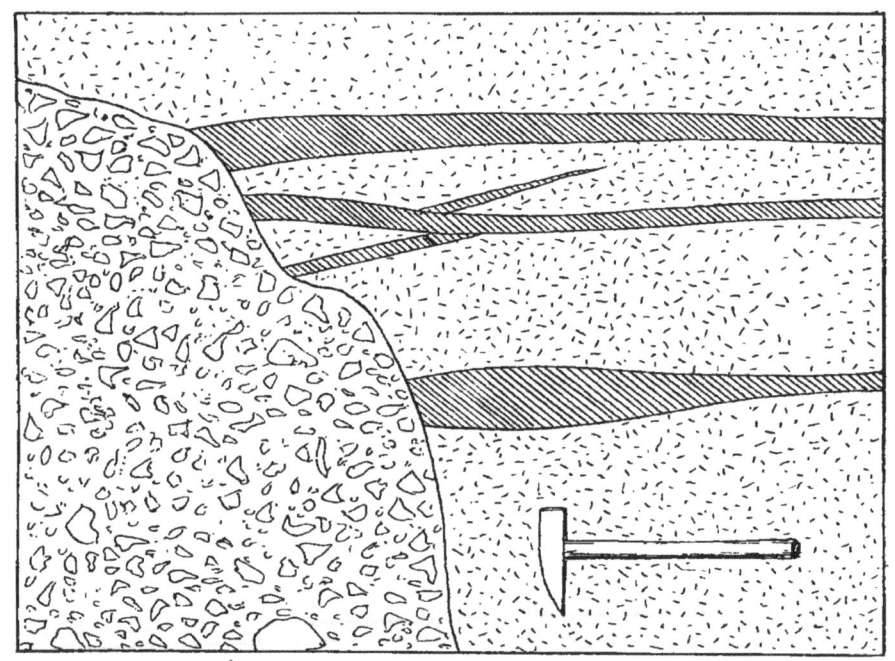

Fig. 62.—Ground-plan of a small area in the lower part of Tairneilear, showing dykes terminating abruptly against volcanic agglomerate.

long as they are of small or moderate thickness. We find, however, that those parts of the moorland hills which consist largely of thick sills have often very few dykes. Doubtless some of the dykes seen on the lower ground represent the feeders of the sill-like intrusions themselves, and naturally terminate in their own individual sills; but the general explanation must be that the thick sills offered an almost impenetrable barrier to the passage of dykes intruded later.

Another rock which is not often cut by basic dykes is the volcanic agglomerate. This is very remarkably illustrated in the lower part of Tairneilear, where dykes traversing the gabbro are

T

seen to end abruptly against the boundary of one of the patches of agglomerate enclosed in the gabbro (Fig. 62). It is noticeable that each dyke becomes slightly swollen towards its termination.

Turning to the sedimentary rocks, we find, as might be anticipated, that the Cambrian limestones are easily cut by the dykes, which occur in these rocks in the Strath district with great profusion. The Torridon Sandstone, which is here overthrust so as to rest on the limestones, affords a strong contrast in this respect; and near the junction of the two formations it is seen that while basalt dykes occur in the limestone often at average intervals of ten yards or less, a very small fraction of the number have penetrated the overlying sandstone. Leaving out the Sleat district, where over a large area the Torridonian is the sole country-rock, the only places where the sandstone contains abundant dykes are the isle of Soay, with a small area along the coast at the south-eastern base of Garsbheinn, and some parts of the isle of Scalpay. An apparent difficulty is suggested by the consideration that the Cambrian limestones of Strath, which are often crowded with dykes, presumably rest on Torridon Sandstone in its proper position beneath; through this the basalt dykes, or the basalt of the dykes in some form, must have found a way. The Torridon Sandstone again underlies probably the whole of the Cuillins. We must admit that the dykes were able to traverse the sandstone when no other course was open to them; and that the sandstone in the Strath district is comparatively free from dykes, only because the limestone in the immediate neighbourhood offered an easier passage.* It is important to note, as we shall show hereafter, that the molten magma has often travelled along the dyke-fissures in directions very considerably inclined to the vertical and sometimes nearly horizontal. (See Chap. XXIII.)

A rock remarkably impenetrable to dykes is the coarse Triassic conglomerate. At Eilean Leac na Gainimh, on the N.W. coast of Scalpay, a 12 ft dolerite dyke traversing the Torridonian stops abruptly at the base of this conglomerate.

Dykes are usually very numerous in the Jurassic strata. Macculloch[†] noted their remarkable abundance on the east side of the Strathaird peninsula, where, he says, without much exaggeration, " they in some places nearly equal, when collectively measured, the stratified rock through which they pass." Notwithstanding his statement to the contrary, they are equally abundant on the west side of the peninsula. It seems certain that in places

---

* The implied assumption that the Torridonian was stripped from Ben Suardal, etc., in pre-Tertiary times is a justifiable one. In the Torran neighbourhood we see that it had been removed, not only from the summit, but from both flanks of the anticline before the deposition of the Lias. For some distance north of Strath Suardal too the sandstone must have been stripped away in pre-Tertiary times, for in several of the patches enclosed in the Beinn na Caillich granite the basaltic lavas are seen resting on Cambrian limestones.

† *Trans. Geol. Soc.*, vol. iv., p. 171; 1817: *Description of the Western Islands of Scotland*, vol. i., pp. 395-398; pl. XVI., fig. 1; 1819.

a considerable proportion of them fail to penetrate the outliers of basaltic lavas (with sills) which rest on the Jurassic strata of Strathaird.

If we confine our attention to a single country-rock, we find that the dykes are not always uniformly distributed throughout its area, but sometimes show a certain tendency to congregate in particular belts of country. Mr Clough notes this in the Torridonian tract which forms the greater part of Sleat. "As we pass from Kyleakin to the Point of Sleat, along a line oblique to the general direction of the dykes, they gradually become more abundant; but there are certain spaces in which they are fewer than on either side. For about three miles S.W. from Kyleakin we do not usually find more than three or four in the breadth of a mile; near Kinloch there are more than twice as many in the same breadth; in a tract which comes to the Sound of Skye between Knock Bay and Camas Baravaig they are again less numerous; but S.W. of this they appear again in great force. On the S.W. side of a line connecting Ob Gauscavaig and Tormore they are too numerous to be all shown on the one-inch map." In the basaltic tract, the only more extensive area of uniform geological constitution, the irregularities in the frequency of the dykes seem to have something of the same peculiarity; but here the principle, if it be one, is obscured by a more important factor, viz. the obstruction offered to dykes by the massive sills. There are thus more dykes in the valleys than on the plateaux. Moreover there are considerable stretches of country almost wholly concealed by peat. The principal area of granite presents a distribution of dykes more nearly comparable with that found in the Torridonian tract of Sleat. If a line be drawn in a direction N.W. by N.—S.E. by S., from Glamaig to Torran, it is seen that in the granite to the north-east of this dykes are very rare, their scarcity being emphasized by the occurrence of numerous dykes in the patch of basaltic lavas and gabbro forming the northern part of Beinn na Cro. To the south-west of the same line, between it and a parallel line near Allt na Measarroch (N.E. of Marsco), lies a belt which includes most of the dykes of the granite tract: about Beinn Dearg (of Sligachan) it contains as many as thirty dykes in a breadth of two miles. Still further to the south-west, on Marsco, Ruadh Stac, and the slopes beyond Strath na Creitheach, dykes again become comparatively rare. We must remember, however, that, in consequence of the different geological relations of the granite in different parts of the area, its vertical thickness must present great variations, and this may, as already remarked, have an important influence on the frequency of the dykes.

In this connection we may notice the distinction drawn by Sir A. Geikie* between the "Solitary" and the "Gregarious" types of dykes. His instances of the former are drawn from outlying parts of the Tertiary igneous province, *e.g.* the Cleveland dyke, and the Skye dykes undoubtedly tend to occur in sets; but we find

* *Trans. Roy. Soc. Edin.*, vol. xxxv., p. 33; 1888: *Ancient Volcanoes of Great Britain*, vol. ii., p. 122; 1897.

also single dykes, usually of rather large size, occurring alone. A good example is the diabase dyke, more than 50 feet wide, which makes a prominent feature on the eastern face of Beinn na Caillich as seen from Broadford (*see* Fig. 5, p. 17). It bears W.N.W. and can be traced for only a short distance. There are also some which, though occurring among other dykes, may be far from any other of their own kind. Such are the coarse diabase or gabbro-like dykes, not belonging to the gabbros proper, which are found in a few places.

More striking than their gregarious habit is the tendency of the dykes to occur in actual juxtaposition, without any intervening strip of country-rock. Two or more dykes, sometimes ten or twelve, can often be traced running in actual contact with one another for considerable distances. In this way arise what may be styled double, triple, and *multiple dykes*, a peculiarity already noticed in the basic sills. The several members of such an assemblage constitute in some respects a geological unit: for example they are necessarily mapped in most cases as one dyke, to which the epithet "multiple" may be attached to mark its true nature. They may die out successively, producing the effect of the multiple dyke thinning away, or they may part company, giving a fallacious appearance of bifurcation or branching. A good example of a multiple dyke is seen near Kilchrist, to the south-east of the loch. Here, abutting upon the road from Broadford to Torran, is a prominent ridge formed by what appears to be a large dyke more than 100 feet wide traversing the Cambrian limestones. Following it for a short distance from the road, we find it dividing, so as to enclose a strip of limestone some 400 feet long and 30 or 40 feet wide. This strip is not enveloped by a single large dyke, but caught between two distinct dykes; and a closer scrutiny of the road-side section reveals that we have to do not with one large dyke but with at least six contiguous dykes. They are recognisable as distinct intrusions by petrographical differences and in some cases chilled margins.

Multiple dykes are not confined to any one part of Skye, but there are certain parts of the island, very rich in dykes, where this mode of occurrence is exceedingly prevalent. This is the case in the basaltic country to the north-west of the mountains, between Loch Sligachan and Glen Eynort or between Glen Varragill and Loch Harport; and again throughout the Straithaird peninsula, to the south-east of the mountains (*see* Fig. 52, p. 238). There are even places where the dykes which run singly are a minority. In the granitic tract multiple dykes are very rarely met with. One is seen on Druim Eadar da Choire, having a total width of $23\frac{1}{2}$ feet and consisting of nine members, as follows, from S. to N. :—(i.) with strong prismatic jointing, $\frac{1}{2}$ ft; (ii.) massive, with a few amygdules, 2 ft; (iii.) highly amygdaloidal and much decomposed, $\frac{1}{2}$ ft; (iv.) like ii., 6 ft; (v.) with spheroidal structure, 3 ft; (vi.) like iii., $\frac{1}{2}$ ft; (vii.) with large irregular crystals of augite, up to 1 inch, and grains of olivine, 6 ft; (viii.) like iii., $\frac{1}{2}$ ft; (ix) with spheroidal structure and containing large felspar phenocrysts, $4\frac{1}{2}$ ft.

The several components of a multiple dyke are certainly not always referable to the same group of intrusions. This appears both from petrographical considerations and from direct evidence— such as the chilling of one member against another—which proves a certain time-interval between the separate intrusions. Chilled edges are, however, less frequently seen in the area of principal distribution of multiple dykes than in outlying districts, where occurrences are rarer and the multiple character perhaps a more fortuitous circumstance. Rarely, if ever, can we verify that one member cuts a transverse dyke, while others are cut by it. Mr Clough notes that at one place in the Sleat district, "half a mile N.N.E. of Rudha Chàrn nan Cearc, a N.N.W. coarse dolerite dyke is crossed by some E.—W. calcite strings, while a later fine-grained dyke runs with the coarse dyke and cuts through some of the strings."

In most of the multiple dykes the several members, while differing in histological and structural characters and perhaps to some extent in composition, are all of basic rocks; but in other cases acid rocks are associated with the basic. An example easily accessible is seen on the shore N.E. of Corry Lodge, Broadford. It is a multiple dyke 26 ft in width, half of which is occupied by a single member consisting of granophyre. This has on one side a single basalt dyke 1 ft wide, and on the other a group of basalt dykes with a total width of 12 ft. The granophyre cuts obliquely across one of the latter, proving that it is of later intrusion. Dykes consisting of several members which differ considerably in composition may conveniently be termed *composite multiple dykes*. As an example showing more complexity, we may take one near the coast 1100 yards S.S.E. of Camasunary, well seen just below the escarpment formed by the basaltic lavas of Strathaird. This shows, in order: compact felsite with sinuous flow-structure, 8 ft; basalt, 2 ft; felsite as before, 11 ft; basalt, 7 ft; felsite, 4 ft; basalt, 1 ft; felsite, with a tongue of basalt cutting into it, 4 ft; porphyritic felsite, 1 ft; basalt, 2 ft; compact felsite, 17 ft; basalt, $\frac{1}{2}$ ft; compact felsite, 18 ft; in all twelve members in a width of 75 ft. This is perhaps not the full width, for after 20 ft of concealed rocks we come next to a porphyritic dolerite, and other dykes follow without any interval. We have had occasion in a former chapter to allude to composite multiple dykes consisting, like these, of basic and acid members. They were there introduced in connection with certain triple composite dykes of symmetrical habit presenting remarkable petrographical phenomena at the junctions of the component members. The commoner kinds of composite dykes have no systematic symmetry of habit (though this may come in locally and by accident), and do not show any sensible effects of reaction between basic and acid rocks. They have a somewhat wider distribution than the special type, and are of later date, being constantly found to intersect the ordinary basic sills. After what has been said before, there is no need to mention more examples in this place.

The splitting of one dyke by a parallel dyke distinctly later and independent is very exceptional.* There are, however, in certain dykes, of more or less basic composition throughout, appearances suggestive of the splitting and *evisceration* of a partially consolidated dyke by a slightly later injection of a magma sufficiently different to be distinguishable. The result is a triple arrangement with bilateral symmetry, comparable in this respect with that described in the peculiar composite dykes and sills of the former chapter, where it has originated in the same way. The dykes now under notice, however, are basic throughout, though they exhibit variations between their central and marginal parts so great as to bespeak considerable differences in chemical and mineralogical composition. This is illustrated by the following specific gravity determinations :—

Dyke (18 ft), in Cambrian limestone, on shore at mouth of stream immediately north of Sgeir Mhòr, Torran—

Central porphyritic band	2·86,
Non-porphyritic part, 1 ft from edge ...	3·02.

Porphyritic dyke (3 ft), in Cambrian limestone, about 1000 yards N.N.E. of summit of Beinn Suardal—

Central porphyritic band	2·85,
Marginal non-porphyritic band	2·80.

Dyke (1 ft), in Lias, on shore 150 yards N.W. of Rudh' an Eirreannaich, Broadford—

Centre	2·80,
Margin (including fine selvage)	2·74.

Dyke like the preceding, at same locality—

Centre	2·82,
Marginal part (not actual selvage) ...	2·78.

Dyke cutting gabbro in valley of Allt Aigeinn, 600 yards E. of summit of Garbh-bheinn—

Central part	3·00,
Marginal part	2·66.

In these cases, and others which might be cited, there is a symmetrical disposition of the variations, the two marginal portions of the dyke resembling one another and differing from the interior portion. There is no such sharp line of demarcation as would exist had the marginal and central portions been intruded at quite different epochs. It is not possible, however, to account for the variation by "differentiation in situ" after the intrusion. This appears from the magnitude of the differences observed, especially in the last example. It would be difficult also on such a hypothesis

* See, *e.g.*, Macculloch, *Description of the Western Islands of Scotland*, vol. iii., pl. XVIII., fig. 1; 1819.

to explain the fact that in the first two cases instanced the distribution of the porphyritic elements is involved; or again that, except in the first case, the marginal portion of a dyke is apparently less basic than the interior. We must therefore suppose, either that the magma as intruded consisted of distinct and different portions, which did not mix freely; or that there was a first intrusion, represented by the margins of the dyke, and, before that had consolidated in the interior part, a second intrusion, now represented by the central band of the dyke. The phenomena of some other dykes* seem to indicate that the former alternative is a possibility; but the circumstances of the cases here noticed, and especially the symmetrical arrangement, accord better with the latter explanation.

Considering now the *directions of the dykes*, we may glance first over the wider area, including a large part of Scotland and the northern parts of Ireland and England, in which dykes which are either known or reasonably supposed to be of Tertiary age are met with. Sir A. Geikie has given a map indicating the distribution and bearings of these dykes.† From this it appears that in the west and south of Scotland, including the islands, and the north of Ireland the general direction varies between N.W.—S.E. and N.N.W.—S.S.E., changing in the north of England to W.N.W.—E.S.E. In the Midland Valley of Scotland and the Southern Highlands the general bearing seems to be W. by S.—E. by N., becoming more W.S.W.—E.N.E. as we approach the Grampians.‡ These latter departures from the more usual direction of trend might with some straining be interpreted as a tendency towards a roughly radial arrangement; but the change takes place rather abruptly, and is more suggestive of a second distinct system of dykes. At the same time it is noteworthy that those dykes which differ markedly in bearing from the majority occur in an extensive tract of Palæozoic and older rocks, so that their Tertiary age cannot, in the nature of the case, be established by direct proof. If we

---

* One instance is a dyke of porphyritic basalt near Port na Long in the southern part of Sleat, noticed below. This contains a number of bands alternately rich and poor in phenocrysts. The following note by Mr Clough illustrates what seems to be a phenomenon of the same kind: "The weathered horizontal section across a dyke [7373] rather less than a mile W.S.W. of the top of Cnoc an Sgùmain, near Armadale, shows a close alternation of paler and darker parts, often about an inch thick, parallel to the sides. The darker parts are also finer grained, and project somewhat. It is not clear that the sides of the bands are chilled, and perhaps the finer bands have been injected before the earlier rock was thoroughly cooled. In the thin slice of the same rock are many little patches of fine grained dolerite, and these perhaps represent a phase of consolidation of the magma rather than something quite foreign to the dyke."

† *Trans. Roy. Soc. Edin.*, vol. xxxv., pl. I.; 1888.

‡ The camptonite dykes of the Orkneys, conjectured by Dr Flett to be of Tertiary age, also have this latter direction: see Flett, *Trans. Roy. Soc. Edin.*, vol. xxxix., p. 870; 1900. So far as any direct evidence goes, however, these may be Palæozoic intrusions.

exclude them, we may say that the British Tertiary dykes have a very general bearing between north-west and north-north-west.

In Skye this general direction is maintained with remarkable persistence, and is common to dykes belonging to different petrographical groups and different epochs of intrusion. In and about the Cuillins only do we find, in addition to the dykes having the normal trend, other sets which depart widely and systematically from it; viz. one set with a roughly radiate disposition and another conjugate set at right angles to the former. Excluding these from present consideration, we may say that the vast majority of the Skye dykes have directions between N.W. and N.N.W. Locally there are variations extending to N. by W. or nearly N. on the one hand and to N.W. by W. on the other, the change coming on gradually. Taking seventy localities pretty evenly distributed over the whole area, we find the average bearing to be about N. 37° W. In some places we find, in addition to dykes having the normal direction, others which run N.—S., N.E.—S.W., or E.—W. These are few in number and obviously exceptions. In some cases their direction has been determined by pre-existing faults. In the Lias about Broadford, for instance, there are a number of N.—S. dykes occupying small fault-lines. In the Sleat district Mr Clough has found dykes occasionally following lines of crushing as well as of faulting. Thus several N.N.E. dykes following crush-lines were noticed on the shore W.S.W. of Ramasgaig.

If we examine the variations from the average direction seen in dykes which still fall within the normal limits, we see very evident indications of some law governing those variations. These limited departures from the average seem to be disposed in relation to the great plutonic intrusions, or no doubt more accurately to crust movements closely connected with those intrusions. We may express this roughly by saying that there is a certain tendency for the dykes to radiate from the central mountain district (Fig. 63). A large proportion of the dykes do point more or less accurately towards the mountains, but this is partly owing to the fact that the general trend of the whole island is approximately in the normal direction of the dykes. Where the radial arrangement would involve a departure of more than 20°, or at most 25°, from the average bearing for the whole region, it is not found, but the tendency in question becomes merely a modifying factor, within those limits, of the general law. Thus, over a considerable area to the north-west of the Cuillins and round Loch Harport the bearing of the dykes is quite normal; south-west of there it is somewhat more westerly; north-eastward it becomes steadily more northerly. But, although near and to the north of Loch Sligachan it is only a few degrees W. of N., it never deviates so far as due N. On the south-east side of the Cuillins we find in and near the Strathaird peninsula a similar tendency in the dykes to point towards the mountains. At the extremity of the peninsula the bearing is N.N.W., but passing northward we find it change gradually until to the east of Belig it has become N. 60° W.

Directions of Basic Dykes.

In the tract to the south-west and south of Broadford the dykes tend to point towards the granite boss of the eastern Red Hills and to be at right angles to the curved anticlinal axis which runs from Broadford to Torran and includes the other granite boss of Beinn an Dubhaich. Thus, about Kilchrist and Beinn Suardal the bearing is N.W. by W., but south and south-west from there it changes gradually to N.N.W. on the north and south sides of Beinn an Dubhaich. Farther west, however, about Kilbride and Torran the dykes have a much more westerly trend, as if belonging

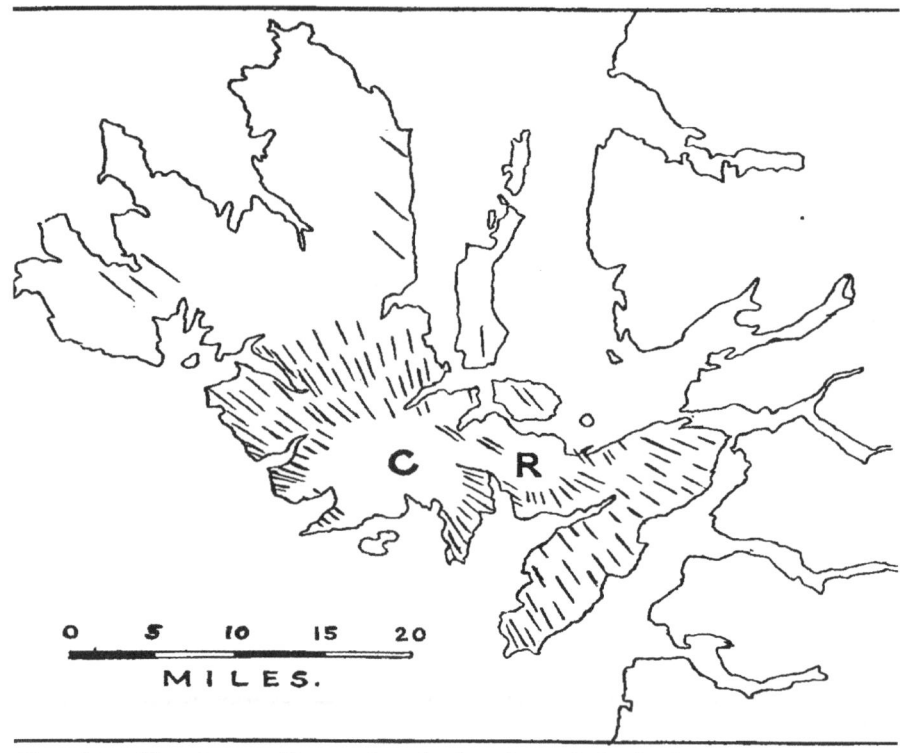

FIG. 63.—Sketch-map illustrating the bearings of the basic dykes in different parts of Skye. The letters C and R mark the situations of the Cuillins and the Red Hills respectively.

to the former system connected with the Cuillin centre. In the tract extending from Kyleakin to the Point of Sleat the tendency to a radiate arrangement is equally marked, though spread over a greater extent, in accordance with the greater distance from the central mountain district. In the middle of this tract the bearing is quite normal; towards the north-east it is much more westerly; and towards the south-west it changes gradually to something like N.N.W.

The direction of the dykes seems then to depend upon two factors. Causes of primary importance have impressed an approximate parallelism upon the dykes throughout a large region of which Skye is only a small part: the normal direction in Skye does not differ much from N. 37° W. Variations from this direction stand in relation to causes of secondary or local importance, which find their expression in a partial radiate arrangement with reference to certain centres of disturbance (*see* below, Chapter XXV.).

A characteristic feature of the dykes is their general *rectilinearity*. Writing more especially of the Sleat district, Mr Clough says :— "The directions of most of the dykes are tolerably straight and parallel. Dykes which bend sharply and run out of their usual direction for considerable distances are not common. In a few places, however, we do see dykes which twist when they come to lines of pre-existing crush or fault. Instances of this are seen on the N. side of Camas a' Mhuilt (Isle Ornsay), where a dyke, coming from the S.E., suddenly twists and runs slightly S. of W. along a crush line; and again about a quarter of a mile N.N.E. of Geur Rudha, where a dyke, coming from the N.W., runs slightly S. of E. along a fault. In the latter locality the width of the dyke when running with the fault is only half the usual breadth: the fault-breccia is hardened by, and certainly older than, the dyke.

"In a few places dykes make conspicuous changes of direction, though we do not know that the changed path is a line of fault. Perhaps it is merely a thin joint line. Several instances of this kind occur a little E. of Ob Lusa: in the most marked instance a N.W. dyke several yards wide suddenly bends and runs N.E. for perhaps 20 yards: in the N.E. part the width is in places hardly a foot.

"It is occasionally found that a dyke comes suddenly to a blunt end, but that at a little distance from this end, either in a N.E. or S.W. direction, a dyke of a similar character suddenly appears and runs in a direction parallel to that of the old dyke. A marked instance of this kind was noticed on or near the coast rather more than a third of a mile E.N.E of Rudha Dubh Ard, near Ord, where a peculiar dyke with xenocrysts of quartz [6134] appears to be shifted laterally, the S.E. portion towards the N E., in four different places, though the dyke is never seen in a crushed state: the amount of the apparent displacement in these four places together is nearly 100 yards."

Displacements of the same kind but amounting only to a few feet may be seen in numerous places in the Lias on the shores of Broadford Bay, as shown in the accompanying ground-plans. Sometimes the dyke is cut off abruptly (Fig. 64); sometimes it runs out into a number of tapering veins, which may or may not be directed towards the detached continuation of the dyke (Figs. 65 and 66); sometimes an actual continuity is preserved between the several portions by means of a narrow connecting string of dyke-rock. The same neighbourhood affords examples of a whole set of dykes bent aside for a short distance into a new direction,

Widths of Basic Dykes. 303

without any ostensible reason in the form of faults or joints (Fig. 67). In the Cowal district of Argyllshire Mr Clough* has noticed similar sharp diversions occasioned by lines of crush in the country-rock, earlier than the dykes affected. In the case here considered such crushing, if it occurs, affects only the concealed strata below the Lias.

Apart from such abrupt changes, the dykes usually hold their course very steadily; but there seems to be some difference in this respect when they occur in different country-rocks. In the Lias shales departures from rectilinearity, though not usually to any great degree, are frequent. In the Cambrian limestones the dykes are straighter, though in a few places near Torran some curiously curved examples occur. The straightness of the dykes which intersect the basaltic country is generally very striking. The same is usually true in the gabbro, except in the case of some small dykes and veins, which are also apt to have abnormal directions; but in the granite irregularities on a small scale are more frequent. A curved or zig-zag course is not seldom found in connection with variations in width and interruptions of continuity in outcrop, peculiarities which may be taken to indicate the dying out of a dyke in the upward direction.

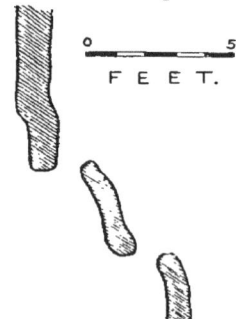

FIG. 64.—Ground-plan on shore west of Broadford Bay; to show the abrupt breaking off and lateral shifting of a dyke.

In *width* the basic dykes vary from a few inches to over 100 feet, not reckoning the greater widths attained by the grouping of several to form a "multiple dyke." The widest single dykes are those which occur remote from any others of their own kind. Dykes of one kind in the same neighbourhood and in the same country-rock do not vary very greatly in width; but dykes of presumably the same group in different places and in different rocks may show considerable variations. The numerous dykes which intersect the Liassic shales on the shores of Broadford Bay are as a rule not very large ones. Excluding on the one hand very narrow and rather irregular intrusions, which may be called veins rather than dykes, and on the other hand a very few large

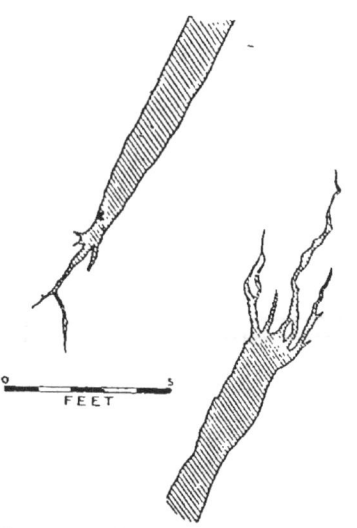

FIG. 65.—Ground-plan on shore west of Broadford Bay; to show lateral shifting of a dyke, the two portions of which run out into veins.

* *Geology of Cowal* (*Mem. Geol. Sur. Scot.*), p. 144; 1897.

multiple dykes, we find from about forty examples a mean width of 4 ft. In the crofts of Harrabol a large double dyke may be followed for about 300 yards, the two members of which are 70 and 30 feet wide, respectively; and at Rudha na Sgianadin, a headland about two miles north-west of Broadford, there is a 100 feet triple composite dyke, consisting of a central member of granophyre and two of dolerite.

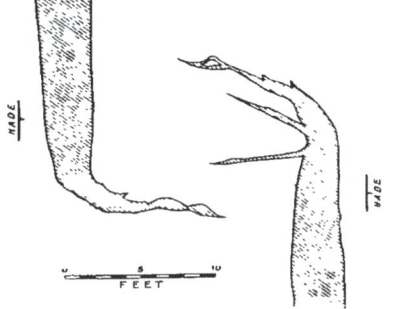

The dykes in the Cambrian limestones are as a rule rather larger than those in the Lias shales. The largest, ranging up to as much as 50 ft in width, belong to the pre-granitic set, and are of thoroughly basic rocks. For the rest, a large number of those about Kilchrist, Torran, etc., range from 4 to 10 ft in width, but there are many smaller. On Beinn Suardal, where they are very numerous and close, Mr Clough notes that they are also comparatively narrow. In the Sleat district, mainly of Torridonian strata, he found them generally wider. They there average 5 to 10 ft: dykes 30 or 40 ft wide are not common. A coarse diabase dyke about ¼ mile west of Tormore is in places 120 ft wide, but does not maintain this size.

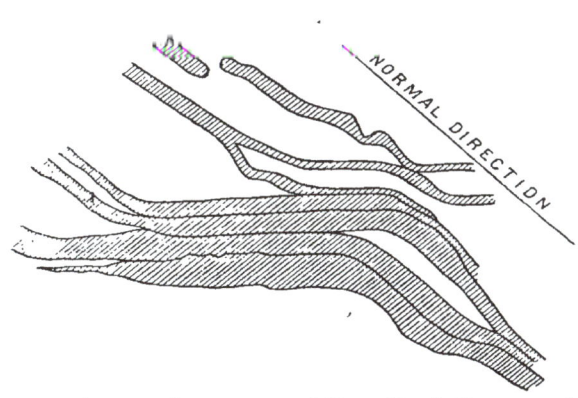

FIG. 66. — Ground-plan on shore west of Broadford Bay; to show lateral shifting of a dyke with veins tending to connect the two detached portions.

FIG. 67.—Ground-plan on shore west of Broadford Bay; to show a number of associated dykes sharply deviated for a short distance.

The dykes which cut the granite vary from 1 ft to 20 ft in width: measurements of thirty-five examples gave an average of 6 ft. The only very large one is the solitary coarse diabase dyke already noticed on the flanks of Beinn na Caillich, with a width of over 50 ft. The much more numerous dykes intersecting the basaltic plateaux probably average 4 or 5 ft in width or less. This does not include the multiple dykes, which often exceed 50 feet. As before, the single dykes which reach the greatest size are those of "solitary" type, of coarse texture and thoroughly basic composition. One on the south-west slope of Broc-bheinn, and about 1¼ mile north-east of Drynoch Lodge, is locally 150 feet wide. The dykes cutting the gabbro of the Cuillins are on the whole fairly comparable in magnitude with those of the basalt country; but there are in places very numerous narrow dykes, sometimes running in unusual directions or changing their course abruptly.

Although the majority of the dykes do not depart very noticeably from the vertical attitude, there are very many which do show a marked *hade*. If this is seen in one, it is usually seen in numerous others in the same neighbourhood. In many parts of the basaltic country in particular both simple and multiple dykes show a more or less marked inclination, the moorland hills north of the Cuillins and between Sligachan and Portree affording abundant instances. The hade is especially noticeable where the weathering away of a dyke, or of the less durable members of a multiple dyke, has given rise to a little ravine. Allt Daraich, near Sligachan, is a good illustration.

The hade is not a mere accident, but must have some real significance. This is manifest from the fact that it has always the same direction. With scarcely an exception among the large number of cases observed, the inclination is downward towards the N.E., or at least towards some point in that quadrant (according to the varying direction of strike of the dykes). Now we have already seen that the prevalent dip of the basalt plateaux is towards the west or some point south of west. The observed hade of the dykes is, then, in a general sense, such as would result if they had been originally vertical, and had been tilted in common with the rocks which they intersect. If such a suggestion could be established, it would be of very great help in classifying the dykes; for the regional disturbance to which the inclination of the plateaux is due belongs to a fairly determinate epoch, and we might thus discriminate between those dykes of earlier epochs and those of later. Unfortunately we have not found it possible to use this apparently simple criterion in the manner suggested. A large proportion of our observations relate to multiple dykes, and it cannot be doubted that a later intrusion would tend to follow the guidance of an earlier one, even when that involved some departure from the vertical direction. Even the simple dykes we cannot assume to have been always vertical when intruded, for what is presumably the primary law might conceivably be modified by the condition of crustal strain at the epoch of the intrusion. Such a modifying factor is certainly suggested in the case of the special sets of dykes peculiar to the Cuillins and not included in the present discussion, as well as in the imperfectly symmetrical composite dykes of Scalpay described on pp. 212-214. Further, we are not at liberty to suppose that when a country is broken into blocks and these tilted at an angle to the horizon, vertical dykes are necessarily tilted through a like angle: we must allow for possible deformation of the individual blocks themselves. These reasons sufficiently explain why we have failed to discover any evident connection between the hade of the dykes and their age.

The *longitudinal extent* of the individual dykes is a point on which it is not easy to obtain very precise information. On the moors the rocks are often obscured or wholly concealed by peat, and even on the bare mountains dykes are lost by passing under the screes. In some other tracts, such as that occupied by the Cambrian limestones, where the rocks are fairly well exposed, the number and closeness of dykes of similar lithological characters often makes it impossible to identify an individual dyke along its extent, unless it can be followed uninterruptedly, foot by foot. Perhaps the granite offers the best ground for such an examination, the ground being often quite bare over considerable areas, and the dykes usually not too numerous. A given dyke, six to ten feet wide, cutting the granite can in several instances be traced for a mile or a mile and a half. The dying out of the dykes in general is often connected with a change in the country-rock. On the slopes of the basalt plateaux the ending of a dyke against one of the thick intrusive sills is of course a dying out in the upward direction, and does not imply the termination of the dyke laterally. It is by no means a rule that the broadest dykes are also the longest: the solitary dykes of coarse diabase, for instance, are usually less than a quarter of a mile in length.

In a very few cases we have observed what may be an interruption of continuity, *i.e.* two closely similar portions occurring on the same line but divided by an interval, the appearances suggesting that the two may be parts of one dyke, continuous at a greater depth. Such a thing may often occur without detection, or at least without the possibility of proof. It may be considered in connection with the interruptions by lateral displacement already described, and is probably always associated with the dying out of the dyke upward, as already remarked in the imperfect triple composite dykes of Scalpay.*

The visible termination of a dyke is not uncommon where exposures are plentiful, *e.g.* in the bare glaciated corries of the Cuillins or on a rocky shore. It does not always take place in the same way. Sometimes the dyke ends rather abruptly; more frequently it tapers to a point, though it may be rather suddenly; very often it branches, and ends in a number of irregular veins. A 50-feet dolerite dyke crosses the south-easterly ridge of Marsco, in a saddle near the figures 2112 on the six-inch map, and is quickly lost; but on the same line a little to the S.W. occurs a number of narrow parallel veins of basalt, about thirty in all, divided by narrow

* *Cf.* Sir A. Geikie, *Trans. Roy. Soc. Edin.*, vol. xxxv., pp. 52-55; 1888: and *Ancient Volcanoes of Great Britain*, vol. ii., pp. 147-150; 1897.

strips of the country-rock, the total width being about six feet. In this case the continuity, if it exists, cannot be traced. Almost all cases of bifurcation and branching of dykes which we have seen have been in connection with dying out. Other irregularities, such as changes of direction, width, and shade, often occur near the terminations of dykes.

Some of the more obvious petrographical characters of the basic dykes as seen in the field will be more conveniently noticed here than under the heads of the several groups.

One such point is the occurrence of *amygdules*, which are not uncommon in certain types of dykes, chiefly those consisting of the finer-textured rocks. It is to be noted, as compared with the amygdules in the lavas, that those in the dykes are usually considerably smaller and also more regularly spherical, only occasionally showing any very noticeable elongation in the direction of flow. As a rule, too, they occupy collectively a much smaller proportion of the total volume. Mr Clough has remarked an exceptional case. "In a basaltic dyke, about three feet thick, a little above the road in Allt Bealach na Coise (S.W. of Isle Ornsay), the central half is extremely full of amygdules. Perhaps they constitute half the mass of the rock. Many of these amygdules are notably different from those in most of the basaltic dykes, being of very irregular shape and repeatedly branched, and sometimes as much as three or four inches long." The same observer remarks that dykes with amygdules elongated parallel to the walls are decidedly more common in the Isle of Soay than in other parts of our area.

Sir Archibald Geikie[*] has drawn attention to some of these points, and has further remarked what is a very characteristic feature of the amygdules, viz. that they are not uniformly distributed through the width of the dyke. Very often they are absent from the marginal parts and clustered chiefly along a central band ; or there may be narrow bands containing amygdules on both sides of the central one. The largest amygdules occur towards the centre of the dyke.

The amygdules are seldom empty. Their contents are usually such as may be regarded as alteration-products of the minerals conposing the dyke, and there is more variety here than in the amygdules of the basaltic lavas.

Many of the dykes have features indicative of *flowing movement*. The most obvious are the orientation of the felspar phenocrysts in porphyritic dykes, the elongation of amygdules in a common direction (which, as just remarked, is not very often seen), and various kinds of banding depending on the distribution of phenocrysts, amygdules, xenoliths, etc. Mr Clough writes: "In all portions of the basic dykes the phenocrysts usually have their long axes in planes parallel to the adjacent side. A clear instance of

[*] *Trans. Roy. Soc. Edin.*, vol. xxxv., p. 38 ; 1888 : *Ancient Volcanoes of Great Britain*, vol. ii., pp. 129, 130 ; 1897.

this parallelism is seen at the N.E. side of a broad dyke on the coast S.S.E. of Tarskavaig Free Church: in one place the side bends at an angle of about 45° and the long axes of the felspar phenocrysts change direction also, so as to keep parallel to the side. At the side of another dyke about a quarter of a mile N.E. of Ardnameacan, there are a great number of thin tabular crystals, hardly $\frac{1}{100}$ inch thick, of felspar, and nearly all these have their broad sides parallel to the sides of the dyke. Within the basic dykes it is also commonly found that there are certain bands approximately parallel to the dyke side which contain amygdules and phenocrysts in special abundance. The amygdules in the bands nearest the side are of much smaller dimensions than those farther off. The phenocrysts, on the other hand, are often quite as large close to the side as in the middle. A well-marked alternation of bands, some crowded with and others almost destitute of felspar phenocrysts, is found in a few cases." In some of the finer-textured rocks a microscopic examination sometimes shows a partial parallelism of the little elongated felspars of the rock which is an indication of flowing movement prolonged to a somewhat later stage.

Very many of the basic dykes, and more especially those of small or moderate breadth, show some degree of *marginal modification* in texture, structure, etc., in consequence of the more rapid cooling of the edge as compared with the interior parts of the dyke. Even in dykes of moderate dimensions, however, this is by no means universal, and it is easy to understand that the chilling depends upon a number of variable factors ; the distance from the source of the intruded magma, prolonged flow of molten matter through the dyke-fissure, the specific thermal conductivity of the rock bounding the dyke, its temperature prior to the intrusion, etc.

The extreme result of rapid chilling, viz. a vitreous selvage, is not a common phenomenon ; the petrographical characters of these selvages of basalt-glass will be discussed in a separate chapter. Much more often we find merely a progressive change of texture, in the sense of its becoming finer, towards the edge of the dyke, and perhaps a change also in micro-structure ; sometimes the appearance of a small amount of interstitial glassy matter in the margin of the dyke. Again the marginal parts of a dyke may differ from the interior in the absence of amygdules or of porphyritic crystals, or in other ways as already intimated.

The smallest dykes, less than a foot in width, often show a uniform fine texture throughout, indicative, as we must suppose, of a relatively rapid cooling of the whole. This is especially well seen in many of the small dykes cutting the gabbro ; and in this case the dyke seems to be firmly welded on to the gabbro in contact with it, so that it does not break away from it under the hammer.

Apart from modifications of a marginal kind, the rock of a dyke is commonly uniform throughout. Anything in the nature of *segregation-veins* is found only very exceptionally. A few cases have been observed, the segregations being in the form of irregular streaks, elongated but discontinuous, of coarser texture and lighter colour than the general body of the dyke. This difference is due to a higher proportion of the felpathic relatively to the ferromagnesian constituents. In an example from the northern ridge of Beinn Suardal the dyke-rock gave the specific gravity 2·92, the veins only 2·67.

To be distinguished from these inconstant and irregular "segregation-veins" are the true veins or narrow strings occasionally seen in a dyke, which clearly cut the general mass of the dyke, so that they must be regarded as distinct and later injections. The phenomenon is not a common one. Mr Clough has noted one or two cases. "In a broad dolerite dyke with felspar phenocrysts, about a third of a mile slightly N. of E. of the head of Loch Ghlinne (in one-inch map 61), there are many thin strings, from a quarter to one inch thick, which keep parallel to the sides. These strings also contain felspar phenocrysts, but their margins are distinctly chilled. In a basaltic dyke rather more than half a mile N.W. of the head of Loch Eishort a number of finer strings, about an inch thick, were observed, which had no special joints confined to themselves."

Very many of the basic dykes are traversed by *joints*, which are evidently of the nature of shrinkage-joints, due to the contraction of the rock in cooling. By far the most common type of regular jointing is the columnar or prismatic, the rock being broken into rude, or sometimes into rather regular, columns perpendicular to the walls of the dyke. The joints are best developed at the margins, but in small dykes they extend through the whole width. Columnar jointing with any approach to regular arrangement is usually confined to dykes consisting of fine-textured rocks, and the joints may then occur rather closely, so that the individual columns are sometimes not more than an inch in diameter. They may be less, especially in very compact selvages; and the thin glassy crust found at the extreme margin of some dykes may, as Professors Judd and Cole have shown, exhibit columnar jointing on a microscopic scale.

More rarely the dykes have a platy structure due to plane joints parallel to the bounding walls. This feature, exceptional in the basic dykes, is found more frequently in some other groups in the district. In some instances it is connected with a flow-structure in the dyke-rock.

In Skye, as in most other regions, it is found that the dykes do not, as a rule, produce any very noteworthy *metamorphism in the rocks which they traverse*. Conspicuous exceptions to this rule are few: they are found where the dykes occur in great profusion, and the country-rock is one specially susceptible to thermal metamorphism. The most interesting case observed is on the east shore of Camas Fhionnairidh, an inlet of Loch Scavaig, at about 700 or 800 yards from Camasunary farm-house. Here a

v

large number of dykes occur in close succession, and the earthy limestones of the Lias, exposed on the shore, are highly altered. They contain large aggregates of lime-bearing silicate-minerals, including good crystals of diopside of considerable dimensions, forming nodular masses.*

Although any important metamorphism in the sense of the production of new minerals is only exceptionally found in the rocks bordering our basic dykes, minor alterations, such as the production of platy jointing in shales, the marmorisation of limestones, and especially the decoloration (by partial deoxidation) of red sandstones, are observed much more widely. On these points Mr Clough has furnished the following notes. The case of the Ord limestones is interesting in connection with what has been said above of the Strath marbles, near the plutonic intrusions, but no close examination of the rocks has been made.

"The contact-metamorphism in the neighbourhood of the dykes is not usually great. About a quarter of a mile W.S.W. of the N. end of Loch an Iasgaich a band of shale in the Kinloch Torridonian series is crossed by close joints, not more than $\frac{1}{8}$ inch apart, for rather more than a foot off the side of a thin dyke. The joints hade steeply N.E. parallel to the side of the dyke: they do not extend into some pebbly grits which are equally near the side.

"The reddish colour of the Torridonian arkoses and grits is generally converted into a dirty grey. This red colour is largely due to clastic grains of felspar, and in the altered beds these grains are of a grey colour. The change of colour extends eight or nine yards off the sides of some of the dykes, and is seen well on the coast N. of Tarskavaig Point, and between Ob Gauscavaig and Inver Aulavaig.

"The reddish colour in the Tarskavaig Moine schists, which have been stained with an Indian red colour near the conglomerate at the base of the Secondary rocks, is also changed into grey near a large intrusive sill near the base of the conglomerate. The felspar pebbles in the schistose grits are generally of a red colour, but near the sill they all become dirty grey. The quartz veins in the same schists become crossed by many thin short cracks or joints running in different directions. Some of the veins have also a peculiar pale amethystine colour. The foliation planes of the schists also lose their lustre to a large extent in the neighbourhood of intrusions, so that it is difficult to distinguish the phyllites from Torridonian shales. This is particularly noticeable in Gillean Burn, and on the N. side of this burn near the E. boundary of the schists.

"The greenish epidotic grits at the base of the Torridonian system are often changed into black or dark grey rocks for several feet off dykes. The change is seen near basaltic dykes in the following places:—in a burn 250 yards N.N.E. of the foot of Allt

* Heddle records the occurrence of idocrase at the junction of a dyke with a calcareous rock, $1\frac{1}{2}$ mile from Broadford, on the road to Kilbride. *Mineralogy of Scotland*, vol. ii., p. 53; 1901.

Doire Daraich; near the foot of Allt Thuill; two-thirds of a mile W.S.W. of the foot of this burn; and about 700 yards W.S.W. of Rudha Guail.

"The green chloritic schists in the Lewisian gneiss series are also often rendered dark grey or black and hardened near dykes. This is seen rather more than half a mile S.W. of Cnoc a' Chaise Mòr, on the shore S. of Kilmore Church, and in the bay N.W. of Bogha Charslice.

"The limestone veins which penetrate the Torridonian rocks near the Secondary conglomerate about two-thirds of a mile N.N.E. of Tarskavaig Point are rendered saccharoid near some dykes. One specimen of the altered limestone gave a specific gravity of 2·68.

"In the burn about 1500 yards slightly S. of W. of Ord a dyke goes through Cambrian limestones belonging to the Ghrudaidh and Eilean Dubh divisions, and alters them considerably for a breadth of about four feet. The Ghrudaidh limestone loses its leaden colour and granular aspect and becomes a white compact rock with black streaks. A specimen of the unaltered rock gave a specific gravity of 2·825, while an altered specimen taken on the same strike and about two feet and a half off the dyke has a specific gravity of only 2·709. The change in the Eilean Dubh limestone is less marked, as this limestone is of a creamy colour when unaltered. The colour of the altered rock becomes, however, a purer white and is varied with greenish strings composed of some soft substance. A specimen of the unaltered limestone has a specific gravity of 2·83, while one of the altered limestone on the same strike gave the figure 2·64.

"Much of the limestone near Ben Suardal is too much altered by granitic intrusions to allow a special alteration near the dykes to be discerned. We often see, however, a prominent set of nearly vertical joints parallel to the dykes. Such joints are conspicuous in the limestone scars a little N. of the top of Ben Suardal, and as seen from the road in Strath Suardal they might be mistaken for bedding. Similar joints, sometimes three or four in the breadth of a yard, are well seen a little N.W. of Loch Lonachan." (C. T. C.) In some localities near Torran, again, where dykes are especially numerous, they have perhaps given rise to some further change in Cambrian limestones already metamorphosed by the granite; but this, in the nature of the case, is very difficult to verify.

Some of the dykes have produced certain metamorphic effects, small in degree and in extent, in the amygdaloidal basalts; but this is usually a mere induration without any evident production of definite new minerals. For example, some hundred yards beyond Carbost Pier a dyke stands up in prominent relief on the rocky shore of Loch Harport. Adhering to each face of it is a band a few inches wide of amygdaloidal basalt which is hard enough to behave under erosion as if it were part of the dyke. A thin slice, however, does not reveal any characteristic mineral of thermal metamorphism [9805].

In the gabbro, the granite, and the basic sills again we have found little indication of any change due to the dykes which traverse them. The sills, and also earlier basic dykes cut by later ones, not infrequently exhibit a certain development of epidote, which is perhaps to be ascribed to this cause. Thus Mr Clough has noted, about 250 yards N.E. of the summit of Ben Suardal, near Broadford, an irregular sheet of coarse dolerite with enclosed xenoliths of granophyre, both the sheet and its xenoliths showing epidotisation.

Most of the basic dykes are in a very fairly fresh condition, even so susceptible a mineral as olivine showing in the majority of cases but little indication of chemical change. This is probably due less to the comparatively late geological date of the intrusions than to the scouring effect of ice, which has removed very generally those superficial portions of the rocks which had been decomposed by pre-Glacial weathering. Nevertheless, there are abundant instances of dykes exhibiting the effects of *atmospheric decomposition,* and Mr Clough's observations prove that some part of this is post-Glacial. Writing of the south-eastern part of the island, surveyed by him, he says:—

"There is evidence that some dykes which are now in a very soft and readily disintegrated condition have during the Glacial period formed ridges. If the boulder-clay at their sides could be cleared away, these dykes would appear as ridges projecting more or less conspicuously over the surrounding rocks, but it is evident that in their present soft condition they could not long continue as ridges. It is still less likely that in the boulder-clay period rocks in such a condition could resist the strong denuding influences at work. Consequently the decomposition of these rocks must be held to be comparatively recent—at all events post-boulder-clay. The evidence referred to was observed in sections at the sides of new roads in the following places:—about 150 yards N.E. of Loch Gauscavaig, nearly half a mile slightly S. of E. of Tarskavaig Free Church, and rather more than a third of a mile E.S.E. of Tormore (near Armadale). In the first locality the junction between the boulder-clay and the N.E. side of the dyke is vertical for at least three feet. In all the sections there are indications of a thin deposit lying over the boulder-clay and composed in the main of portions of disintegrated dyke rock. In the second locality a similar deposit, four or five feet thick, appears to occur *in situ* below a portion of the boulder-clay. The boulder-clays in all the localities are of the common stiff stony character."

The progress of chemical decomposition in a dyke has in most cases been directed by the joint-fissures which traverse the rock. In certain types of dykes there has resulted from this a division of the rock into rude spheroids, a few inches in diameter, with sound interior and decomposed exfoliating crust. On the other hand, there are cases in which decomposition seems to have affected most readily the rock in the interspaces between an irregular system of joints. Some of Mr Clough's observations in the Sleat district fall apparently under this head. He says:—" Some of the decomposed dolerite dykes contain thin cross-jointed strings of sounder hard rock, varying in width from two to six inches. The strings have no general direction nor chilled margins, and in sections at right angles to the dyke direction they sometimes form a polygonal network, the meshes in which are filled with more decomposed rock. On the roadside two-thirds of a mile S. of Dun Scaich (near Tokavaig) some of the meshes are three or four feet long: many of the strings have median sutures and remind us of the 'sheaths' in tachylyte, to be described in another place (p. 336). They sometimes pass gradually into the decomposed rock, and we could not discern by microscopic examination that the constituents of the two rocks differed in character. About 700 yards S.W. of Ob Gauscavaig an olivine-dolerite dyke which weathers into huge irregular blocks, and is for the most part in a very soft decomposed condition, contains a few scattered strings of harder rock which seem also composed of olivine-dolerite. The strings have no general direction nor chilled margins, and they are perhaps allied in character to those in the dyke near Dun Scaich."

The behaviour of the dykes as contributing to the details of superficial relief of the country is, of course, determined by the joint effects of chemical and mechanical destruction, or more accurately by their differential effects as between the dykes and the country-rock. According as a dyke is more or less durable than the encasing rocks, it tends to form a prominent *feature* or ridge on the one hand or a *trench* or depression on the other.

On the floor of any of the glaciated corries of the Cuillins the gabbro and the dykes which intersect it, both in a perfectly fresh state, make up together a single smooth surface. There has been no differential weathering, because there has been no appreciable weathering at all since the glaciation. On the slopes above, the dykes often occasion gulleys, and on the mountain-ridges they sometimes give rise to deep notches. The weathering of the dyke in the latter case is not in general connected with any considerable chemical decomposition, but results from splintering by frost. The dykes, and notably the multiple dykes which cut the basaltic lavas and intercalated sills, are very often marked by trenches and gulleys, sometimes deep ravines, and the courses of the streams have very frequently been determined by the dykes. On the other hand, the dykes so numerous in the limestone district stand out in relief, often forming very regular walls two or three feet high. The same thing is seen in a less marked degree in the granite area, and sometimes in the Liassic strata, *e.g.* in some parts of the coast sections. Concerning the older rocks of the Sleat district, Mr Clough writes as follows:—

" Most of the dykes are easy to trace by their features. In the Torridonian and Moine rocks only a few dykes make scars or ridges: most of them make either little trench-like hollows which often cross contour lines for considerable distances, or else smooth narrow terraces which keep nearly parallel to the contour lines and are bounded on the high side by a cliff of the country-rock. A great many of the burns in the district run along dykes, and have worn deep narrow channels—some almost impassible—along them. The dykes which form hollows and terraces have no doubt been more readily decomposed and denuded than the country-rocks at their sides. In some of the soft granulitic and chloritic rocks belonging to the Lewisian gneiss series on the S.E. side of the Moine thrust the dykes make scars or ridges much more frequently than in the harder rocks, whether these be Torridonian or Moine rocks or hard mylonitised gneisses. This is very well shown by comparing the dyke features in the area between the head branches of Allt a' Charn-aird with those made by the same set of dykes a little further N.W., where they pass through mylonitised gneiss and Torridonian rocks."

CHAPTER XVIII.

Basic Dykes: General Petrography.

Our petrographical account of the basic dykes of Skye will be based on the examination of hand-specimens (including determinations of specific gravity) and microscopical preparations. Knowledge of the chemical composition of the dykes is limited at present to four analyses: one (of a tachlytic selvage) quoted from Dr Heddle; another made for this memoir by Dr Pollard; and two by Mr T. Baker, communicated by Professor Lebour. Possibly more data from the chemical side might assist materially in classifying the rocks and ultimately in establishing their mutual relations to one another and to other basic intrusions in the form of sills and sheets.

The chief difficulty in the way of dividing the basic dykes into distinct groups belonging to different epochs arises from the fact that certain petrographical types, and these among the commonest, have recurred at more than one epoch. It is easy to show, for instance, that certain dykes are cut off by the granite, while others cut that rock; but some of the former are indistinguishable lithologically from some of the latter in the field, and offer no certain criteria for discrimination even on a microscopic examination. Hence in places not near the granite, and where no other sufficient test is applicable, it is often impossible to separate pre-granitic from post-granitic dykes. Such difficulties arise especially in the case of the non-porphyritic dolerites, rocks which are extremely common and widely distributed. The presence or absence of olivine, except in certain types where the mineral is very abundant, does not seem to be a character of much diagnostic value: many of the rocks hover on the line between "olivine-bearing" and "olivine-free."

The principal criteria for determining the relative ages of the dykes are their direct relations to one another where they come into juxtaposition, their relations to other igneous rocks of Tertiary age in the neighbourhood, and their relation to faults and other tectonic features of the district where they occur. Owing to the very general parallelism of direction of dykes of all ages in the country, actual intersections of one dyke by another are by no means often seen.* When two or more different dykes run side by side, so as to constitute what we have called a double or a multiple dyke, the nature of the contacts will sometimes afford a

---
* Certain groups of dykes in the Cuillin district must be excepted from this statement for reasons already explained.

clue to the relative ages of the several members; but such indications, from chilled margins, etc., are not always free from ambiguity.

The principal igneous intrusions, other than dykes, which serve as standards of reference, and afford where they occur a relative scale of time, are:—

       (i.) the gabbros,
      (ii.) the granites,
     (iii.) the basic sills of the great group,
     (iv.) the "inclined sheets" of basic rocks, intersecting the gabbro of the Cuillins, to be described in Chapter XXI.

Of these the third have the most extended distribution. It is to be remarked, however, that there are no dykes referable to the brief interval between the gabbros and the granites, and none are certainly known (with the probable exception of certain composite dykes) intervening between the granites and the great group of sills. Practically, therefore, the first three standard groups mentioned only enable us (where they are represented) to distinguish the dykes belonging to the volcanic phase of activity from those belonging to the phase of minor intrusions. To the former category belong the dyke-feeders of the fissure-eruptions; to the latter (apart from possible feeders of the basic sills) belong the majority of the dykes of the region, in general constituting independent intrusive bodies. Of these latter, the greater part are older than the inclined sheets included under (iv.), but some are younger.

The value of the four sets of intrusions just enumerated for our present purpose lies in the fact that the members of each set constitute a natural group belonging to one epoch. It is nevertheless necessary to remember that the members of such a group are not in the strict sense contemporaneous with another. Thus the fact that a given dyke is seen to cut one or more of the basic sills is not in itself sufficient to prove that the dyke is younger than the sill-epoch: it may be the feeder of a somewhat later sill at a higher level. A like remark applies to the inclined sheets, and also to the basic lavas.

One of the strongest reasons for considering the majority of the dykes younger than the basic sills is derived from the relation of these various intrusions to faults. It appears that the faults of Tertiary age in the island constantly affect the sills. On the other hand, few of the dykes are displaced or crushed by faults, and some of them have followed pre-existing fault-planes. In so far as the faulting can be referred to a definite epoch, this reasoning applies to dykes even at a distance from any basic sills. Allowance must of course be made for the fact that a small fault with nearly vertical displacement would occasion but little visible disturbance of a nearly vertical dyke.

Different Epochs of Basic Dykes. 317

In the basaltic country the general uniformity of lithological characters among the lavas, and also among the sills, makes faulting often difficult to verify. In the Broadford district and in Sleat, where the stratified formations afford well-marked geological horizons, the case is different. Mr Clough writes :—" Most of the faults in the district appear to be older than the dykes; but the directions of many of them are not noticeably different from the general direction of the dykes, and so the existence of these has not tended to divert the dykes out of their ordinary paths. Many of the N.W. and N.N.W. dykes occur along faults which effect considerable displacements in the rocks at their sides. This is particularly noticeable along the junctions of the Secondary and Torridonian rocks, and of the Applecross and Kinloch divisions of these latter rocks. But both near these junctions and elsewhere it is quite rare to find dykes which are themselves crushed or faulted. It is perhaps desirable to mention a few exceptional instances. Rather more than three-quarters of a mile N.E. of Kinloch a N.E. fault breaks through a N.W. dyke and displaces it slightly: in the line of fault there is in one place another uncrushed dyke. About a mile slightly W. of N. of Kinloch a dyke running slightly W. of N. is partly crushed in a line parallel to its sides: the dyke is in a line of fault with considerable displacement, and in view of its somewhat unusual direction it appears probable that prior to the intrusion of the dyke there was a crush-band along this line of which the dyke took advantage. On the coast rather more than a quarter of a mile N.E. of Armadale Castle a N.N.W. dyke is much crushed and slickensided along various lines, some of which are nearly horizontal."

As already stated, we have not found that the hade of the dykes gives any trustworthy information as to whether they are older or younger than the tilting of the plateaux. The earliest dykes—those at least which were contemporaneous with the lavas—have presumably shared in the tilting; but the fact that some dykes with marked hade are certainly later than some which are vertical shows that some other factor has to be reckoned with.

In so far as the dykes can be divided into natural groups with distinctive petrographical characters, such that the members of the same group can be referred confidently to the same epoch, we are justified in collating the evidence derived from different members of such a group to deduce the relative age of the group as a whole. If, for instance, certain dykes in one place are demonstrably later than the basic sills, and other dykes of the same group in another place demonstrably earlier than the " inclined sheets," we may infer that the group belongs to some part of the interval between the epoch of the basic sills and the epoch of the inclined sheets. The application of such reasoning is, however, limited in important cases by the impracticability of discriminating petrographically groups which belong to different epochs.

Although, for reasons sufficiently set forth, we cannot in our petrographical description of the basic dykes follow a chronological order, we may conveniently take first those which belong demonstrably to an early epoch. To this end we put together all the dykes which are clearly seen to be cut off by the granite intrusions; a considerable number of these have been examined, more especially in the district between Broadford and Torran. Dykes of the same general type are found in many other places, and some of these doubtless belong to the same epoch; but others are clearly younger, and we accordingly confine ourselves here to the area specified, *i.e.* the neighbourhood of the eastern Red Hills and especially of Beinn an Dubhaich.

These *pre-granitic basic dykes* are decidedly less regular in their behaviour than the generality of the Skye dykes. They depart more frequently from the normal direction, and they never seem to be very persistent, often dying out in a short distance or leaping aside to resume a parallel course on another line. A noticeable hade from the vertical is much commoner here than in other groups of dykes. The width is usually small, though in some instances it reaches 20 feet or even 50 feet, but not for any great distance. Chilled edges seem to be characteristic of this set of dykes, though by no means confined to them: an amygdaloidal character, on the other hand, is rare.

Petrographically almost all these earlier dykes examined fall under one general head, though with variations in coarseness or fineness of texture, which are related to the size of the dyke and sometimes also to the distance of the specimen from the cooling surface. The rocks may be named diabase, dolerite, or basalt according to texture, but the micro-structure is usually the same for all, viz. the ophitic or occasionally the sub-ophitic. Although we have no chemical analyses, it is evident that the rocks are of thoroughly basic composition. The specific gravity is usually more than 3, ten specimens giving a mean of 3·03. These, however, include some which have been more or less metamorphosed by the granite, a process involving a slight increase of density in cases where it has been tested. There are certain dykes of less basic composition than the rest and with lower specific gravity. Some of these are apparently normal, but others have been modified by taking up xenolithic material, in a manner to be described in a later chapter.

The ordinary varieties consist of labradorite, augite, and magnetite, with a little apatite but not olivine. The labradorite varies somewhat in composition, and the crystals have sometimes zonary banding, but the dominant kind gives extinction-angles up to about 35° in symmetrically cut sections. The light brown ophitic augite is probably rich in iron, for it gives rise to clotted patches of magnetite when it becomes chloritised. Only in the coarsest variety of rock is a partial diallagic structure found [7061]. Original magnetite is usually rather abundant in these rocks, and we may perhaps infer that they are rich in iron-oxides, but not in magnesia.

The *metamorphism of the early basic dykes* by the granite is well observed round the Beinn an Dubhaich mass. Interesting examples of this change may be seen near Kilchrist Old Manse,* near the Marble Quarries, beside Allt an Inbhire, and at other places. The metamorphism is specially well marked where portions of the dykes have become detached and enveloped in the granite: this may be seen near the shore south of Torran, as noticed by Sir A. Geikie,† and at one or two spots in the valley of Allt Leth Slighe.

The general character of the transformation is much like what has been described in the basic lavas, and a summary account will therefore be sufficient. The most conspicuous change is seen in the augite, which is converted usually into hornblende. This mineral is often in patchy, rather fibrous aggregates, but passes finally into crystal-grains and plates, the yellowish-green colour at the same time becoming deeper and browner. Some part of the hornblende must come from chloritic alteration-products of the augite, for it is sometimes found in little veins traversing the felspars.‡ In the vicinity of the magnetite grains brown mica often takes the place of the hornblende. The felspar of the rock is not in general recrystallised, but it is partly freed from its inclusions, and so appears clearer and fresher. Whether the opaque iron-ore is to any extent recrystallised it is not easy to decide, but the little granules seem in some cases to have drawn together into more compact grains. In hand-specimens these metamorphosed dykes are dark, dense, crystalline rocks. Three specimens gave specific gravities 3·02, 3·05, 3·08. An exceptional specimen from a 50-ft dyke on the south side of the granite, east of Allt an Inbhire, gave a specific gravity 2·85; but this has evidently had its composition considerably modified (prior to metamorphism) by taking up foreign material: it encloses numerous grains of quartz. It shows, however, the same changes as the other examples. In addition, it has small amygdules, once doubtless lined with a chloritic mineral and filled with calcite. They now consist of granular pale-green hornblende with a patch of recrystallised calcite in the centre [7060].

As might be anticipated, no changes comparable in degree with those just described are found where the basic dykes have been invaded by the later intrusions of small volume—dykes, sills, and sheets. The only noticeable change which seems probably due to the metamorphic effect of these minor intrusions is a partial epidotisation of earlier basic dykes intersected by them. Epidote is a mineral well known as a product of thermal metamorphism, especially in the less advanced stages, though of course it may also originate in quite different circumstances. Mr Clough has noted in several places a production of epidote in basic dykes and sills where they are intersected by later intrusions, and regarded it as

* The locality most easily found is a little S.W. of the footpath to Boreraig, where it is crossed by a wall, south of the Glebe. Here a large dyke intersecting the limestone is cut off and metamorphosed by the granite. Specimens taken at 9 or 10 feet and at 2 feet from the granite show different grades of metamorphism.

† *Quart. Journ. Geol. Soc.*, vol. lii., p. 382; 1896.

‡ See Harker, *Petrology for Students*, 3rd ed., fig. 74; 1902.

a metamorphic effect. He has not found it in the Tertiary dykes to the east, south-east, or south of the Broadford and Beinn Suardal area.

We notice next the *solitary dykes of coarse diabase*, which occur only in small number, but are widely distributed. By the epithet " solitary " we mean to express that they occur singly, or sometimes in couples, but never in numerous groups like most of the other types. They attain considerable dimensions, the greatest width being usually more than 50 feet, but this is not maintained, and the dykes themselves are rarely traceable for more than 400 or 500 yards. Their place in the sequence of intrusions in Skye has not been ascertained very precisely ; but they are later than the great group of basic sills, and in one or two cases have been observed to cut finer-textured dykes of dolerite. They belong therefore to the phase of minor intrusions, and have no close connection with the gabbro, for which they might easily be mistaken in hand-specimens.

Since these dykes are few, and usually make conspicuous features, it is worth enumerating the principal examples. Several have already been mentioned on account of their large size. Whether any occur in the north-western portion of the island, our survey does not enable us to say. The most northerly examples observed are two, about 50 ft and 24 ft wide respectively, on Meall na Gainmhich, about 6 miles S.S.E. of Portree, or 4½ miles N.W. of Sligachan. The largest one recorded is on the south-western slopes of Broc-bheinn, about 1¼ mile N.E. of Drynoch Lodge : this is 150 foot wide where it crosses the upper part of Allt na Coille, but dwindles in a south-easterly direction. A dyke of this set, 45 feet wide, is seen in Bealach na Beinne Brice, 2½ miles W.S.W. of Sligachan. Farther south two occur near together on Meall a' Mhaim. They are perhaps 30 or 40 feet wide, and one of them is seen very conspicuously at the large cairn at the head of Bealach a' Mhaim, the pass between Sligachan and Glen Brittle. Some 1200 yards W. of the summit of Meall a' Mhaim occurs another, 75 feet in width, remarkable for enclosing abundant xenoliths of gabbro up to as much as a foot in length. Another crosses Allt Dearg Beag near the northern boundary of the gabbro : this forms part of a multiple dyke. On the other side of the mountains a large dyke makes a prominent feature crossing the southerly ridge of Blath-bheinn at about 1100 feet altitude. Another is seen near the little tarn on Slat-bheinn, Strathaird : its greatest width is about 50 feet. Two dykes, 30 or 40 feet wide, a little east of Loch Coire Uaigneich, south-east of Blath-bheinn, are perhaps to be referred here, as well as a 60-ft dyke, perhaps the continuation of one of these, farther S.E.; but they have not been subjected to microscopic examination. There remain the conspicuous 50-ft dyke on the east face of Beinn na Caillach, and the 70-ft dyke at Harrabol. The latter is part of a double dyke, the other member, 30 ft wide, being of an intermediate rock of specific gravity 2·75. To these may perhaps be added one or two recorded by Mr Clough in the Sleat district, notably a dyke seen ¼ mile W. of Tormore, near the Point of Sleat, which is in places 120 feet across. We have not seen any specimen of this.

The rocks forming these large solitary dykes are of coarse texture and to the eye scarcely distinguishable from some of the gabbros. They usually contain olivine, but not as a constituent easily visible on the hand-specimens. Two examples gave specific gravities 3·02 and 3·08, while the Blath-bheinn dyke, which is free from olivine, gave 2·92. This last has been sliced [7477], with two from the tract north of the Cuillins, both containing abundant olivine [7555, 7556].

The olivine may be either fresh or converted to green serpentine and magnetite. Both original magnetite and ilmenite are found, the latter in characteristic skeleton crystals, and the Blath-bheinn rock has also little cubes of pyrites, passing into hæmatite. The felspars contain rounded glass- and other inclusions, sometimes of comparatively large dimensions, collected in the central part of the crystal. They constantly show zonary banding between crossed nicols, and that in a much more marked degree than is occasionally seen in the gabbros. Extinction-angles for the central and chief portion of a crystal range in symmetrically cut sections up to 45°, indicating the most basic variety of labradorite. Carlsbad, albite, and pericline twinning are constantly found. The augite is moulded upon the idiomorphic crystals of felspar. It is of light brown colour in thin slices, with perhaps a rather deeper tint than is customary in the gabbros. It shows good prismatic cleavage, but no basal striation or diallagic structure. The rocks have thus under the microscope diagnostic characters which enable us to differentiate them from the gabbros, notwithstanding a strong general resemblance in some respects and a nearly identical appearance to the unaided eye. In the field these dykes are easily distinguished from most others, not only by their large size and coarse texture, but by their making more or less prominent features in relief against the country rock.

The remaining *non-porphyritic basic dykes* of Skye, excepting only some in the Cuillins to be referred to in a later chapter, we have not succeeded in dividing into natural groups referable to defined epochs. This is unfortunate, since they include the majority of the dykes seen in most parts of the island. The rocks present, as a rule, little that is remarkable, and do not call for any full description. The porphyritic dykes will be described subsequently.

We give below chemical analyses of two dykes which probably belong here, although their precise ages cannot be ascertained, since they are seen to cut the Torridonian only. The second, with 46·68 per cent. of silica and 16·69 per cent. of iron-oxides, belongs to a type which is very abundant and widely distributed. The rocks as a whole seem to be of decidedly basic character, though perhaps less so than the earlier dykes. Forty examples gave specific gravities ranging from 2·80 to 3·06; but most were nearer to the lower limit than to the upper, and the mean value was only 2·86. Only about half of these dykes were proved to intersect the gabbro, the granite, or the basic sills of the great group; and it is probable that some of the others belong to the pre-granitic set.

	I.	II.
SiO_2	48·30	46·68
Al_2O_3	20·06	18·89
Fe_2O_3	1·29	8·74
FeO	10·15	7·95
MgO	5·21	5·36
CaO	10·10	10·00
Na_2O } K_2O	2·80	1·96
Ignition	2·00	0·40
	99·91	99·98
Specific gravity	..	2·90

I. Dolerite or basalt, dyke (passing into a sheet) on coast opposite Sgeir na Iasgaich, near Ob Allt an Daraich, 2½ miles W. by S. of Kyleakin: anal. T. Baker. Specimen not seen: this and the following rock were collected by Prof. G. A. Lebour, who has kindly communicated the analyses.

II. Dolerite, dyke at point E. of mouth of Allt na Nighinn, 2 miles W. of Kyleakin [8951]: anal. T. Baker. The chief constituents are a rather acid labradorite in striated crystals about $\frac{1}{17}$-inch long and a light brown augite in imperfect crystals, either mineral in places idiomorphic towards the other. There are pseudomorphs after olivine and little octahedra of magnetite: also a subordinate later felspar, not closely lamellated but with concentric zonary structure. The shapeless patches of this later felspar enclose very numerous needles of apatite (phosphoric acid not determined in the analysis). See Plate XXII., Fig. 2.

Here, as in some other cases, the presence or absence of olivine does not seem to us a character of primary classificatory value, since it does not evidently correlate itself with other points of difference. The innumerable non-porphyritic basic dykes of our area, other than those separately treated, fall conveniently under two heads according to their relative coarseness or fineness of texture. The ophitic structure prevails in the coarser rocks and the granulitic in the finer, and other differences may also be recognised between the two sets, though not always without exceptions.

The more coarse-textured dykes may be termed *dolerites and diabases.* Some contain olivine, while others, in most respects similar, do not. When that mineral is present, it forms as a rule rounded grains, often replaced by green or greenish yellow or brown serpentine and other secondary substances. Magnetite occurs in varying amount in little octahedra and granules. Any evidently titaniferous iron-ore seems to be rare, but chemical tests would be necessary to decide this question. Needles of apatite are often detected, but have a capricious distribution. The felspar is labradorite: it shows in slices the usual rectangular shapes with carlsbad and albite twinning and in some of the most coarse-textured rocks some pericline-lamellæ in addition. The augite, crystallised subsequently to the felspar, is light brown in section without any special peculiarity. It is doubtless of an aluminous variety, and is often partially replaced by a chloritic mineral, sometimes with radiate-fibrous arrangement. It has invariably an

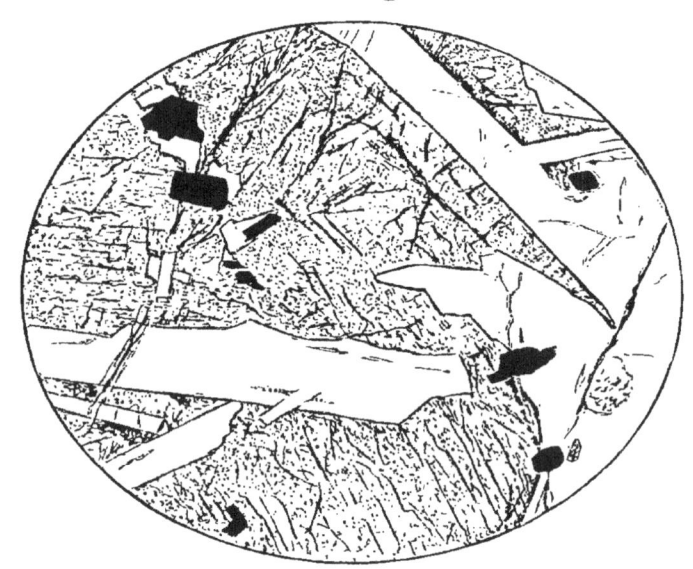

Fig. 68.—[5421] × 30. Diabase or coarse dolerite, dyke ½ mile E.S.E. of summit of Ben Aslak and 2 miles S.W. of Kylerhea. Typical ophitic structure. The felspar crystals in this and numerous similar rocks show between crossed nicols a strong zonary banding, which does not disappear with the albite-lamellation, and is therefore due to the marginal portion being of different composition from the interior.

ophitic or sub-ophitic habit, though the individual crystal-plates are not often of such size as completely to enclose the felspar (Fig. 68). Rocks with these characters have a quite general distribution, and are found cutting the basalts of the plateaux, the gabbro of the Cuillins, and the stratified rocks of the south-eastern part of the island.

The finer-textured rocks we shall term *basalts*. These again may or may not contain olivine. Some of high specific gravity (about 3) and doubtless thoroughly basic composition are devoid of that mineral: these rocks are very rich in augite. Magnetite occurs as before. The felspars are smaller and of narrower shape ("lath"-shape) in section, but all except the smallest show twin-striation. They are found to be labradorite whenever they can be tested. The augite, of quite pale tint in the slices, is in granules wedged in among the felspars or, if more abundant, aggregated in patches, and the varieties of micro-structure met with depend chiefly upon the amount and habit of the augitic constituent. One special type, seen in some rocks rich in augite [7131, 8191], exhibits the structure already noticed under the name "ocellar" as occurring in some of the basalt lavas (*see* Plate XVII., Fig. 3, C), viz. a tendency of the augite to build imperfect prisms, or at least elongated elements, with a confused sheaf-like or partially radiate arrangement about certain points.

These basalt dykes differ from the augite-andesite dykes to be described in a later chapter in that they have as a rule no glassy base. Only exceptionally do we find any indication of a base, and then only in connection with a marginal modification of the rock. A small proportion only of the dykes have an extremely thin tachylytic edge, as we shall notice in the following chapter. Small scattered amygdules are occasionally found.

The basalt dykes have the same wide distribution as the dolerites, and, like them, belong undoubtedly to more than one epoch of injection. Some of them are among the latest intrusions of the Cuillins. In some parts of the gabbro mountains we find very numerous little dykes, or rather veins, of very compact-looking basalt, often only two or three inches wide. They sometimes have an irregular course, curving or bending abruptly aside, and in places ramifying, a peculiarity distinguishing them from other dyke-rocks in our area.

We pass on to the *porphyritic basic dykes*. Those basic dykes which exhibit conspicuous porphyritic elements seem referable, in most cases where evidence is available, to a rather late stage in the history of igneous activity in the region. An exception to this rule we have already noticed in the peculiar rocks, often containing quartz-grains, which sustain such remarkable relations towards associated acid intrusions. Apart from these, no noticeably porphyritic dykes have been observed which are clearly referable to an early stage. Both the basic lavas and the basic sills are, as has been remarked, in general non-porphyritic, and porphyritic dykes are not to be expected as common among their feeders. Of the dykes now to be described, some intersect the granite, and others cut minor intrusions themselves younger than the granites and in some cases of quite late age. Several distinct groups are to be recognised, but the data do not enable us to arrange them in chronological order.

Very noticeable are certain porphyritic dykes rich in olivine which traverse the granite in various parts of the Red Hills. They are from 2 to 15 feet in width, and vary in direction between N.W.–S.E. and W.N.W.–E.S.E. The conspicuous minerals in hand-specimens are rectangular felspars and golden yellow olivine, less frequently lustrous black augite. The felspars range up to ¼ inch in diameter and the olivines to about ⅛ inch, while the texture of the general mass of the rock shows some variation. Dykes of this kind are seen on Glamaig and the Beinn Dearg ridge near Glen Sligachan, on the slopes of Glas-bheinn Mhòr and Beinn na Cro, and on the western slope of Beinn Dearg Mhòr of Strath; and they may conveniently be styled the *Beinn Dearg type*. They occur scarcely, if at all, outside the granitic tract. Within that area they are the most usual type; though other dykes are also found, consisting of a rather dense and dark non-porphyritic rock, with a tendency to spheroidal weathering.

These olivine-bearing dykes of the Red Hills are of thoroughly basic composition. Seven specimens gave specific gravities from 2·86 to 2·96, with a mean 2·90. One example has been completely analysed by Dr Pollard, whose results are given in the accompanying table. The figures differ very notably from those for the more widely distributed types given above. In particular,

SiO_2	44·01
TiO_2	1·66
Al_2O_3	12·69
Cr_2O_3	trace
Fe_2O_3	3·62
FeO	8·75
NiO & CoO	trace
MnO	0·21
MgO	12·86
CaO	10·57
Na_2O	1·68
K_2O	0·49
H_2O { above 105°	2·73
{ at 105°	0·89
CO_2	trace
P_2O_5	0·17
S	0·11
	100·44
Specific gravity	2·95

Porphyritic Olivine-Dolerite [7862], dyke cutting granite, Ciche na Beinne Deirge: anal. W. Pollard, *Summary of Progress* for 1899, p. 174. See Plate XXII., fig. 4.

the richness in magnesia, the comparative poverty in alumina, and the low silica-percentage are significant points. The Beinn Dearg dykes, again, have no close resemblance to the sills of the great group, being decidedly poorer in alumina and alkalies and richer in magnesia. Since these dykes are undoubtedly a *local* group, connected with the special focus of central Skye, we might perhaps more reasonably compare them with the gabbros; but they differ

W

quite as decidedly from these, being much poorer in alumina and richer in iron and magnesia, as well as poorer in silica. In short, the Beinn Dearg type of dykes represents a highly specialised derivative from the hypothetical common stock. If there exists in the district a "complementary" product of the same differentiation, it must be represented by thoroughly acid rocks very poor in ferro-magnesian minerals. (See below, p. 427.)

The porphyritic felspars are of a rather basic labradorite (with extinction-angles up to 40° in symmetrical sections), and show carlsbad and albite twinning. Their inclusions are mainly of glass. The olivine-grains, with but little approach to crystal-outline, are fresh or only slightly serpentinised, and occur in abundance. When augite figures among the phenocrysts, it is a variety very pale in thin slices, differing from that of the ground-mass. The opaque iron-ore is either in little octahedra or in more shapeless grains. The felspar of the ground-mass, in little striated prisms, the larger ones showing carlsbad as well as albite twinning, is labradorite of a less basic kind than the phenocrysts (extinction-angles up to 30°). The augite is light brown with more or less of a purplish tone and sensible pleochroism. It seems probable that part of the titanic acid has gone into this mineral, the iron-ore being chiefly magnetite. Apatite needles are sporadically distributed.

In micro-structure these rocks show some differences. There are porphyritic olivine-basalts, with a ground-mass composed of small felspar prisms and granules of augite and magnetite. There are porphyritic olivine-dolerites, in which the augite of the ground-mass varies from a partly idiomorphic to a sub-ophitic habit (Plate XXII., Fig. 4). Here, in addition to the rectangular striated felspars of the ground, there are some of later crystallisation and shapeless habit, with strong zonary banding and no close twin-lamellations. Finally, there are ophitic olivine-dolerites, in which the porphyritic felspars are wanting: these, too, show the subordinate shapeless and zoned felspars in addition to the dominant set.

A very numerous set of porphyritic dykes is found in the Strath district, especially round Beinn Suardal, and may be distinguished as the *Suardal type*. Felspars are usually the only evident phenocrysts: if olivine occurs it is in smaller grains than in the Beinn Dearg dykes. A striking feature is the great frequency of enclosed xenoliths, usually of gabbro or granite, and of xenocrysts derived from the disintegration of these. In most of the dykes something of this nature may be noticed; and exceptionally, as in a dyke to the west of Allt an 't-Suidhe near Loch Kilchrist, gabbro débris makes up locally quite half the bulk of the rock [6718]. The dyke just mentioned, traversing the volcanic agglomerate, bears about N.N.E., and has a width of 50 feet: most of the dykes of this group, however, are only a very few feet wide, and the common direction is N.W.–S.E.

Twelve examples of the Beinn Suardal porphyritic dykes, free from xenoliths, gave specific gravities from 2·74 to 2·95, with a mean of 2·86. Their mineralogical composition, too, evinces a very considerable range of variation. This is certainly due in great part to the magma having often absorbed a considerable amount of material from foreign sources, and become modified in consequence. For this reason a summary notice of the petrography of the dykes will be sufficient: the phenomena of the xenoliths will be treated in another chapter (XX.).

The porphyritic felspars proper to the rocks are labradorite, containing glass-cavities. Augite phenocrysts are never abundant, and olivine may or may not occur. There is always plenty of magnetite, in small granules or minute octahedra. The usual ground-mass consists mainly of little felspars, in imperfect prisms and bundles, with augite in granules and sometimes in imperfectly-built crystals (Pl. XXII., Fig. 5). Other constituents, such as biotite, seem to be connected always with reactions between the basaltic magma and material of foreign origin. The felspars of the ground-mass are usually labradorite. Sometimes they are of a less basic kind, and the rock becomes rather an andesite than a basalt; but this modification, observed in association with enclosed granite débris, finds an explanation in the consideration already set forth.

To the Suardal group we may probably attach many of the dykes of porphyritic basalt found at numerous localities throughout the district of Sleat. Mr Clough has supplied some field-notes on these rocks, but they have not been examined more closely. The specific gravities of ten examples ranged from 2·78 to 2·94, with a mean of 2·85. The rocks contain conspicuous porphyritic felspars, and in some cases porphyritic augites: sometimes also they carry xenoliths of gabbro, etc. In the Moine Schists at Inver Dalavil, on the west coast of Sleat, occurs a dyke in which the porphyritic felspars are sometimes as much as 3 inches long, rivalling those near Tobermory in Mull. These felspars gave the specific gravity 2·69, indicating labradorite. Another of Mr Clough's observations relates to the unequal distribution of the felspar phenocrysts in a dyke. One of this group on the west side of Port na Long, near the Point of Sleat, shows bands roughly parallel to the walls of the dyke, some very rich in porphyritic felspars, others almost free from them. The edges of the several bands show no sign of chilling against one another, and the cross-joints in the dyke pass uninterruptedly through; so that the whole appears to belong to a single intrusion.

These porphyritic basalt dykes of Sleat have the normal direction. It is not possible to prove that they are of precisely the same age as the Suardal dykes which they resemble, but Mr Clough's observations would make us refer them, like the others, to a somewhat late epoch. They cut the ordinary basic sills of the district, as well as the granophyres and some of the non-porphyritic basic dykes. On the other hand, they are cut by some non-porphyritic dykes of thoroughly basic composition.

Other porphyritic dykes in the Sleat district present types quite different from the preceding. One from the neighbourhood of Kylerhea has phenocrysts of augite and olivine, the latter replaced by serpentine and carbonates, but not of felspar. The augite is pale in a thin slice, with a faint purplish tint towards the border of the crystal, and shows in polarised light a well-marked and regular "hour-glass structure" [5419].

A group of porphyritic dykes intersecting the Torridon Sandstone on the shores of the Sound of Soay presents rather peculiar features. In hand-specimens the rocks show fresh glassy-looking felspars, with tabular habit and from $\frac{1}{4}$ to $\frac{1}{2}$ inch in length, set in a fine-textured matrix of a rather light grey colour. A slice [8714] shows these porphyritic felspars to be labradorite, with carlsbad, albite, and pericline twinning, the lamellæ being rather unevenly distributed. Some of the crystals contain large inclusions generally resembling the ground-mass. Associated with the porphyritic felspars are imperfect crystals of magnetite and certain light green serpentinous pseudomorphs very suggestive of a rhombic pyroxene destroyed. Other light green patches, consisting mainly of fibrous hornblende, have the shape of olivine. The ground-mass consists of small felspar crystals, granular augite in quite subordinate amount, and rather abundant magnetite. The small felspars show narrow rectangular sections, often only once twinned, and constantly give nearly straight extinction. They must therefore be oligoclase, perhaps even with some orthoclase. In the inclusions within the porphyritic felspars the small felspars do not, so far as can be judged, give the very low extinction-angles. The abnormal composition of the specimen examined might be explicable on the supposition that the magma has been to some extent acidified after the crystallisation of the porphyritic elements. We are reminded in some respects of the dykes elsewhere to be described which have demonstrably been modified in this way by taking up granitic material. No undestroyed relics of an acid rock, however, were observed in the case now in question. The several dykes belonging to this group, so far as they have been examined, show no difference of an essential kind. A conspicuous dyke, 12 feet wide, just E. of Ulfhart Point, has a less fine texture than the specimen described above, but the felspars of the ground-mass, though of larger size, give the same nearly straight extinction as before. If we reject the supposition, for which no direct evidence can be adduced, that these rocks have been modified by absorption of extraneous matter, we may compare them with other dykes to be noticed at the end of this chapter as approximating in composition to the mugearite type. The nature of the dominant felspar and the subordination of augite to magnetite and olivine are significant in this connection, but the phenocrysts of labradorite make an important difference.

A different type is represented by numerous dykes of small width in the neighbourhood of Drynoch and Meadale, to the N.E. of Loch Harport. These are olivine-bearing rocks of finer texture than the Beinn Dearg type and having phenocrysts of felspar only. An example at the sharp bend of the high-road about 6¼ miles from Sligachan gave the specific gravity 2·80. A slice [8715] shows that olivine occurs in small grains which are fairly abundant, some fresh, but others replaced by green serpentine. The porphyritic felspars, ¼ inch long or more, are fresh and glassy-looking: they are only scattered through the fine-textured matrix. This is chiefly of little striated felspar prisms, with a strong tendency to fluxional arrangement, while light brown augite occurs in ophitic plates and rather plentiful magnetite in small octahedra and granules. These rocks recall in some respects the porphyritic olivine-dolerite of the Roineval type of double sills (p. 262).

Here we may notice a conspicuous dyke seen on Roineval, east of the summit, and already alluded to as possibly one of the feeders of the peculiar double sills or laccolites there exhibited. It has a maximum width of 35 feet, with the normal direction. The rock shows a finely crystalline dark grey ground, enclosing very numerous fresh felspars about ⅛ inch long and little grains of olivine, and is a porphyritic olivine-dolerite with "granulitic" structure. In a thin slice [8188] the felspar phenocrysts show carlsbad, albite, and pericline twinning, and the extinction-angles (up to 34° in symmetrically cut sections) indicate labradorite, but not of a very basic variety. They contain round inclusions of relatively large size, and these are chiefly confined to the interior portion of each crystal, which often shows definite crystallographic outlines more perfect than those of the crystal itself. This indeed is often moulded upon the augite-granules of the ground-mass, and there can be no doubt that the broad margin of the crystal represents a later growth of the phenocrysts continued during the crystallisation of the ground-mass (Plate XX., Fig. 4). We have observed a similar appearance in the phenocrysts of some other dykes, and Professor Judd* has described it as a phenomenon of frequent occurrence. The olivine of the rock, in grains about $\frac{1}{20}$ inch in diameter, is perfectly fresh. The ground-mass consists of granules of pale yellowish-brown augite, little striated felspars giving elongated sections, and small crystals of magnetite.

The next type to be noticed among these basic dykes may also be termed *porphyritic olivine-dolerite*. It does not seem to be very widely distributed, but within the areas where it occurs is numerously represented. The rocks are of thoroughly basic composition. Five examples gave specific gravities ranging from 2·84 to 2·93, with a mean of 2·88. The special feature as regards structure is the association of abundant porphyritic elements with an ophitic ground. These dykes may be called for distinction the *Gheal Gillean type*.

A number of dykes of this kind occur in the neighbourhood of Camasunary. Some larger ones, up to as much as 50 feet in width, are seen near the foot-path from there to Strathaird, and another

* *Quart. Journ. Geol. Soc.*, vol. xlv., pp. 175-186, pl. VII. ; 1889.

large one about 400 yards N.E. of Kirkibost House. Their direction is the normal one, varying from N.W.–S.E. to N.N.W.–S.S.E. Specimens of these large dykes have quite a coarsely crystalline appearance, owing to the abundance of porphyritic crystals. These are of felspar, often from ¼ to ½ inch in length. Thin slices show that they are a somewhat basic labradorite. They have carlsbad, albite, and pericline twinning, and contain numerous rounded glass-inclusions, usually collected towards the centre of the crystal. These crystals are set in a matrix consisting mainly of augite and felspar with the ophitic relation. This felspar is quite subordinate in amount to the augite. It forms numerous little striated crystals, from $\frac{1}{20}$ inch to as little as $\frac{1}{160}$ inch in length in different specimens. Olivine is represented by pseudomorphs in yellowish-brown serpentine and pilitic amphibole, and there are ragged grains of black iron-ore.

Dykes of rock comparable in many respects with the above occur about Tarskavaig, in the Sleat peninsula, where Mr Clough describes them as a common type. The porphyritic crystals are so crowded together in some specimens examined as almost to hide the ground-mass, giving the rock the general aspect of a gabbro. Three specimens sliced showed a close similarity to one another. Olivine is more plentiful than in the dykes of Gheal Gillean, etc., and is better preserved. It seems to occur sometimes in two generations [7367]. The porphyritic felspars, which make up more than half the rock, are of a thoroughly basic kind: some appear from their optical properties to be anorthite. The felspar of the ground-mass, not a very abundant constituent, is a medium labradorite. These dykes are evidently of the same general type as those near Strathaird and Camasunary. They have the N.N.W. direction, and if prolonged on that line would pass near Strathaird. Mr Clough found similar dykes to be common farther south, towards the southern point of Sleat [7366]. In several instances they cut porphyritic basalt dykes of more ordinary types, and this might perhaps lead us to assign this group to a rather late epoch. It is not clear, however, that all the dykes of this general type belong to one group. Some of them bear a very close resemblance to the large sill which runs at the base of the Mesozoic strata in the neighbourhood, but no direct evidence of any connection has been observed.

Among dykes of *porphyritic dolerite without olivine*, but still of basic composition, we may notice a group intersecting the Torridonian strata in the Isle of Scalpay. A specimen selected from a dyke about 400 yards N.W. by N. of Scalpay House is a grey, finely but evidently crystalline rock, enclosing porphyritic felspars up to ½ inch in length. Its specific gravity is 2·904. In a slice [9372] the porphyritic crystals are seen to be labradorite, with carlsbad and albite twinning. The felspars of the general groundmass, judged by their extinction-angles, are of a somewhat more acid variety. The light brown augite is in irregular grains wedged in between the felspars, but the two minerals seem to have crystallised simultaneously, and in places they are associated in a rudely micrographic intergrowth. Magnetite is abundant, and there are also occasional patches of pyrites, which are very evident on the hand-specimen. This is the character of the general mass of the rock; but enclosed in it are numerous little patches of a different kind, which appear in the slice as well-defined circular areas up to about $\frac{1}{8}$ inch in diameter. These are almost wholly of felspar, which is partly lamellated, with very low extinction-angles, partly untwinned. Magnetite occurs very sparingly and in minute crystals; while augite is absent, and its place taken very inadequately by a few slender needles of pale green actinolitic hornblende and small flakes of brown mica, the latter grown round the magnetite (see Plate XXV., Fig. 1). There is sometimes a little interstitial quartz. It is clear that these small round patches are of very decidedly more acid composition than the enclosing rock. They have not the characters which we look for in xenoliths; and their small and fairly uniform size, their equable distribution, and their spherical form lead us to regard them as vesicles which at a late stage, when the rock was far advanced towards complete consolidation, became occupied by the residual and relatively acid portion of the magma. A similar phenomenon has been recorded in andesitic rocks from more than one British locality,[*] and we shall have to notice it later among the andesitic dykes of Skye (See pp. 399-401.)

A very distinct type among our basic dykes, and one of very restricted occurrence, differs from the rest in the nature of the felspathic constituents and in other respects which lead us to attach it provisionally to the *mugearites* described in Chapter XV. The best example is a well-known dyke at Am Bile, about $1\frac{1}{4}$ mile E.N.E. of Portree, to which we shall have to refer in the following chapter. It has a glassy selvage, an analysis of which is quoted below (p. 338, II.). The interior of the dyke is not necessarily identical in composition with the selvage, but there is no reason to suppose that it differs in any very essential way. The silica-percentage is somewhat higher than in the ordinary basic dykes, while the lime and especially the magnesia are lower, and the alkalies higher, including a notable proportion of potash. All these points connect the rock with the mugearites.

The peculiar mineralogical composition of the rock bears out the comparison. The dominant constituent is striated oligoclase in imperfectly shaped crystals from $\frac{1}{20}$ inch downward. Another felspar, in shapeless grains of later crystallisation, is untwinned, and must doubtless be referred to orthoclase. The coarser texture of the rock, as compared with the mugearites of Roineval and Druim na Criche, enables the felspars to be identified more easily; and it is seen that the orthoclase is here rather more abundant, as might be expected from the relative proportions of the alkalies in the analysis. It makes up probably about one-fifth of the total

[*] See, *e.g.*, Teall, *Geol. Mag.*, 1889, pp. 481-483, pl. XIV.

felspar and more than one-eighth of the whole rock. Besides the interstitial grains mentioned, there are a few orthoclase phenocrysts, or perhaps xenocrysts, of larger size, with much-corroded border and abundant glass-inclusions. Augite plays only a subordinate part in this rock; but there has been an abundance of olivine, now represented by pseudomorphs of serpentine stained to a deep red-brown colour. Little octahedra of magnetite are fairly plentiful, and little slender needles of apatite are exceedingly numerous [9373]. The finer-textured rock towards the edge of the dyke (not the glassy selvage) shows a micro-structure more closely comparable with that of the typical mugearites. The felspars are of the same acid varieties as before, but the ferromagnesian silicates are too completely destroyed to be identified. The magnetite and apatite occur abundantly, as before [9374]. There is also an occasional corroded orthoclase, as much as $\frac{1}{10}$ inch in diameter, quite honeycombed with glass-inclusions, and the same thing is seen in the actual glassy selvage of the rock [9375].

We shall notice in the next chapter certain small dykes seen S. of Loch Ashik, near Broadford, and at one or two places in the district of Sleat, which probably approach mugearite in compostion; but these, being thoroughly glassy rocks, do not lend themselves to a petrographical comparison.

CHAPTER XIX.

Basic Dykes: Tachylytic Selvages.

In this chapter we shall give some account of the selvages of black glass which occasionally border the basic dykes of our area. With the dykes we shall include such intrusive sheets or sills as have come under our notice, in which like phenomena are observed. Some exceptional cases will be noticed, in which the vitreous character affects more or less the whole width or thickness of the intrusion, instead of being confined to narrow marginal zones. Further, while treating of the truly glassy form locally assumed by the basic magmas, we shall describe also those modifications in which there has been a considerable development of crystallitic growth, usually with spherulitic arrangement, some of the rocks embraced here being such as are sometimes styled "variolites."

From one or two incidental references in Macculloch's work it seems probable that he had observed instances of tachylytic selvages in Skye. The true nature of this vitreous substance was, however, first recognised by Necker,* who found it as a crust two or three inches thick on a basic dyke in the "Beal valley" to the north of Portree. It had previously been observed here by Murchison, who regarded it as a pitchstone: Necker discovered that it is denser and more fusible than the rocks properly ranged under this title, and considered it as bearing the same relation to the basic rocks that true pitchstone does to the acid. In 1882 Dr Heddle† noticed a tachylyte forming a half-inch crust at the lower surface of a basic sheet (presumably an intrusive sill) on the Quiraing, and he proved by chemical analyses its practical identity in composition with the rock which it borders. In the following year Professors Judd and Cole‡ gave a full description of the "Beal" rock with some others in the Western Isles; and subsequently the latter author,§ in a supplementary paper, did the same for the Quiraing occurrence.

So far as our observation has extended, tachylytic selvages to the ordinary basic dykes are of rare occurrence in the basaltic portion of the island. A thin film of glassy material resembling coal in appearance coats the surface of some of the smaller basalt dykes on Meall Odhar Beag and Ben Lee, to the north-west of

---
* *Edin. New Phil. Journ.*, vol. xxix., p. 75; 1840.
† *Min. Mag.*, vol. v., p. 8; 1882.
‡ *Quart. Journ. Geol. Soc.*, vol. xxxix., pp. 444-464, pl. XIII., XIV.; 1883.
§ *Ibid.*, vol. xliv., pp. 300-307, pl. XI.; 1888.

Loch Sligachan, and a few other occurrences have been noted. Any approach to a vitreous selvage is very exceptional also in the mountains. Macculloch[*] found on Gars-bheinn a loose fragment showing the transition of basalt into "a fine black pitchstone," presumably from a dyke cutting the gabbro or the metamorphosed lavas. A small basalt dyke with selvages of tachylyte, $\frac{1}{10}$ inch thick, intersects the strip of gabbro enveloped in the granite of Marsco, as seen in the gully on the north-west face. A few other small dykes with glassy edges have been observed cutting the gabbros and peridotites of the Cuillins in An Garbh-choire and elsewhere.

When tachylytic selvages occur, they are usually very thin: excepting the examples at the "Beal" and the Quiraing, we know none in the north-western and central parts of the island exceeding $\frac{1}{10}$ inch. It may be remarked generally that evidences of decided chilling are less frequently met with in the parts of Skye where the country rocks are igneous than in the parts farther south-east, where sedimentary strata prevail. Possibly the temperature of the "country" rocks at the time when the dykes were injected is in part answerable for this difference; but there are doubtless other factors which would influence the rate of cooling of a dyke, more especially the specific thermal conductivity of the rock forming the walls. Professor Kendall[†] has pointed out the influence of this on the formation of tachylytic margins to basalt dykes in Mull: a selvage which has a thickness of $\frac{1}{4}$ inch in contact with a sheet of compact basalt is reduced to a mere film when the dyke passes through a highly vesicular sheet. A similar change is seen in some of our Skye dykes which have glassy selvages.

In the Sleat district Mr Clough has found that selvages of black tachylyte are not uncommon, but most of them are extremely thin, perhaps not more than $\frac{1}{20}$ inch.[‡] In certain instances, which are worth particularising, he has observed a more considerable development of the basalt-glass, or even a small dyke wholly composed of it. At the head of a small burn $\frac{1}{3}$ mile south of Loch Ashik, near Broadford, tachylyte forms the whole of two narrow dykes, six or eight inches across, running E.–W., within a broader dyke of ophitic dolerite with N.N.W. bearing. It is crowded with quasi-spherulitic growths, which are much larger in the interior of a dyke than at the margins. On the N.W. side of Allt Evan, $\frac{2}{3}$ mile N.E. of Kinloch, is a dyke of spherulitic

---

[*] *Description of the Western Islands of Scotland*, vol. i., p. 402; 1819.

[†] *Geol. Mag.* 1898, p. 555.

[‡] Examples are noted at the following places: three or four dykes to the N.E. of Ob Allt an Daraich, between Broadford and Kyleakin; Rudha Guail, to the N.E. of Isle Ornsay; two dykes at $\frac{1}{2}$ mile and $\frac{1}{4}$ mile S.W. of Rudha Guail; 300 yards N. of Camas Daraich, near Tarskavaig; two dykes at $\frac{1}{4}$ mile and $\frac{1}{4}$ mile S.W. of Ob Gauscavaig, in the same neighbourhood; 150 yards E.S.E. of Armadale pier; $\frac{2}{3}$ mile E.S.E. of Sgùrr na Leth-bheinn, near the Point of Sleat. All these are either in Torridon Sandstone or in Moine Schists.

tachylyte a foot thick, with specific gravity of 2·80. Some of the spherulites in it are as large as boys' marbles. Where the bridle-road crosses Allt Thuill, to the N.E. of Loch na Dal, near Isle Ornsay, the later of two north-westerly dykes in the burn shows a glassy modification. On the north side of the road the dyke is three or four feet wide, and has tachylytic selvages from 1 to 3 inches thick, besides a few thin streaks and patches more in the interior. On the south side of the road the dyke is reduced to 12-18 inches in width, and here the whole, or nearly the whole, has a resinous lustre, with a specific gravity of 2·81. It is perhaps significant that several of these thicker bands of tachylyte are found in connection with dykes intersecting earlier intrusions of basalt or dolerite, doubtless better conductors of heat than such rocks as the Torridon Sandstone. A like remark applies to the sheet at Rudh' an Iasgaich, described below. We shall, however, show reason for believing that the tendency to assume the vitreous form in these rocks is primarily dependent upon some peculiarity in their composition as compared with the ordinary basic intrusions of the region.

We have stated that tachylyte selvages are sometimes found on the basic sills and sheets of intrusive habit, as well as on the dykes. In some cases, as in a sheet of spherulitic basalt at Camas Daraich near the Point of Sleat, the glass is little more than a skin on the surface; in other cases, as in Heddle's instance at the Quiraing, it forms a rather more considerable crust. Mr Clough has observed two cases presenting features of interest to be further described. One is to the west and north-west of Knock, where the tachylyte and the compact rock immediately next to it are seen in unusually extensive exposures, some perhaps 100 yards long and nearly as broad. The other is on the west coast of Sleat, about half-way between Rudh' an Iasgaich and Rudha Chàrn nan Cearc, where glassy selvages up to 3 inches in thickness occur on the margins of a thin basalt sheet, which runs rather irregularly along the interior of a thicker sill of dolerite intruded at the base of the Mesozoic strata. The relations have been described and figured by Sir A. Geikie.* Other sheets with selvages of tachylyte were observed at the S.W. side of Loch Doir' an Eich, farther to the N.W., and at Ard Thurinish near the southern extremity of Sleat.

In their mode of occurrence and customary thickness the tachylytic selvages in Skye resemble those in others of the Western Isles. In Mull, for example, in nearly fifty examples catalogued by Prof. Kendall, the thickness is not often more than $\frac{1}{8}$ to $\frac{1}{4}$ inch, and the greatest thickness recorded is $2\frac{1}{4}$ inches, at Glen Aros. At Loch Scridain, however, in the same island, Prof. Heddle † has described a dyke bordered by tachylyte which in certain local expansions reaches a thickness of 6 or 7 inches, and even 22 inches.

If we examine in the field a dyke which has tachylyte selvages,

* *Quart. Journ. Geol. Soc.*, vol. lii., pp. 179, 180, fig. 23 ; 1896.
† *Trans. Geol. Soc. Glasg.*, vol. x., pp. 80-95 ; 1895.

we find as a rule that the rock becomes very compact as the margin is approached, and takes on a resinous lustre like that of some pitchstones. This change is a gradual one; but the final change to the thin crust of true tachylyte, black and lustrous as polished jet, comes on rather suddenly. It is in the basalt-pitchstone rather than the true tachylyte or basalt-obsidian that some of the special structures often occur, such as relatively large spherulites conspicuous to the eye. The glassy edge is often finely fissured, the delicate cracks running perpendicularly to the boundary surface, and the compact pitchy-looking rock may also be divided sometimes in a remarkable manner. Of the Allt Thuill dyke, Mr Clough notes that in the selvages there are " closely fitting perlitic forms, some of which are more than an inch in length in one direction parallel to the side of the dyke, and not much less in breadth in the same plane. The tachylyte also contains spherulites, bodies of a spherical or oval shape, and spherulitic rods like those in the trachyte dykes, to be described later." Some of his more

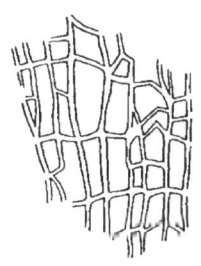

Fig. 69.—Sheaths and cores on surface of a basaltic sheet, rather more than ⅓ mile S.W. of Cnoc a' Chàise Mòr, near Knock. Scale, ¼ of natural size. (C. T. C.)

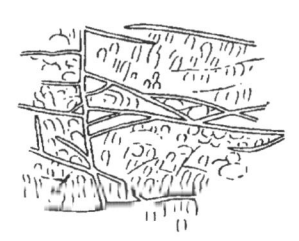

Fig. 70. — Sheaths and cores, the latter with perlitic forms, on surface of a basaltic sheet, same locality as the preceding. Scale, $\frac{1}{10}$ of natural size. (C. T. C.)

interesting observations relate to the sills or sheets with tachylytic selvages already mentioned. The first of the two cases described in the following note shows features analogous with the curious reticulated structure in the Eskdale dyke, Dumfriesshire, as detailed by Sir A. Geikie.[*]

" In some of the extensive exposures of the sheets near Knock we see a rectangular pattern formed by more or less straight-running bands which project on the weathered face and have median sutures (Figs. 69 and 70). These bands have not now a glassy aspect, and their sides often weather with a rusty colour. Neighbouring bands make different angles with one another and enclose spaces which are filled in with a black glassy tachylyte with small perlitic forms. These bands are perhaps of the same character as the 'sheaths' of the Eskdale pitchstone dyke, and

[*] *Proc. Roy. Phys. Soc. Edin.*, vol. v., pp. 242, 243, plate V.; 1880: *Trans. Roy. Soc. Edin.*, vol. xxxv., p. 41; 1888: *Ancient Volcanoes of Great Britain*, vol. ii., pp. 133, 134; 1897.

the tachylyte interspaces may be compared with the 'cores' of the same dyke. Some of the 'sheaths' end bluntly, or diverge into two branches, each of which ends bluntly, within a 'core.' In some parts the 'sheaths' which run in one direction are much closer together than those which cross them, but the directions of the closer set are liable to vary rather rapidly. A little below the tachylyte there are often close joints or divisional lines which remind us of the joints to be mentioned near Rudh' an Iasgaich. Some of them are connected by other shorter joints which make considerable angles with them.

" In the thin sheet mentioned near Rudh' an Iasgaich the tachylyte at the surface is in some places as much as three inches thick and crowded with perlitic forms. The parts next below the tachylyte are intersected by many close joints, often hardly half an inch apart, some of which are nearly at right angles to the adjoining tachylyte surface, while others make a slight angle with it. These joints are very varied in direction and often curved. Their general effect gives the appearance of a number of rather ill-defined oval forms, from eight to eighteen inches in length, and separated from one another by spaces which are often about the same breadth as themselves: these oval forms are crossed, near their long axes, by joints which are nearly parallel to them, and also near the sides by other joints which become more curved and more nearly parallel to the sides as the sides are approached. The spaces between the forms are also crossed by a multitude of joints which keep as a rule nearly parallel to the side of the oval form which is nearest them. These joints become gradually less prominent and numerous as they proceed toward the interior of the sheet, and about a foot off the surface they are hardly noticeable. Similar joints also occur near the under surface of the sheet." (C. T. Clough.)

One dyke which is worthy of notice on account of its historic interest is that which has already been mentioned as the "Beal" dyke. The name does not appear in this form on the maps of the Ordnance Survey, but Am Bile is marked on the six-inch map, and not far from this place is the dyke which we identify as that noticed by earlier writers. It is immediately west of the little inlet named Port a' Bhata, about $1\frac{1}{4}$ mile E.N.E. of Portree, and is reached by a steep road leading down from the farm of Torvaig, which is marked on the one-inch map. At this place a recess in the basalt cliffs is occupied by Jurassic rocks, and the dyke traverses these in a generally N.W.–S.E. direction. It has a maximum width of about 6 feet. The south-westerly face is well exposed, and shows a crust of tachylyte varying in thickness up to about an inch. The actual surface shows everywhere a delicate linear marking which we interpret as a flow-structure, and the direction of this varies considerably and rapidly. Thus towards the landward (N.W.) end of the exposure it dips S.E. at about 50°; farther seaward it becomes vertical, and then dips in the opposite direction; while still farther it becomes sensibly horizontal. These changes are observed in a distance of about 30 yards. It is one among other cases which seem to show that the flow of a rock-magma in a dyke-fissure is by no means always in the vertical direction. Illustrations of this are much more frequent among the intermediate than among the basic dykes of our area, and we shall return to the subject in a later chapter (XXIII.).

Passing from the characters of the tachylytes as seen in the field to a closer examination of the rocks themselves, we consider first their *chemical composition*. We reproduce in the accompanying table the analyses of two examples from Skye, and, for comparison,

	I.	II.	A.	B.	C.	D.
SiO_2	45·613	52·59	53·03	55·40	56·05	53·63
Al_2O_3	14·423	17·33	20·09	13·24	17·13	15·93
Fe_2O_3	4·927	11·14	9·43	5·48	10·30	20·00
FeO	9·411	not det.	not det.	5·64	not det.	not det.
MnO	0·153	0·66	not det.	0·80	trace	trace
MgO	4·000	2·62	2·63	1·57	1·52	0·78
CaO	8·098	6·47	6·05	7·07	6·66	7·88
Na_2O	4·186	4·24	4·52	2·01	3·29	4·48
K_2O	2·397	2·40	1·27	1·64	0·98	0·50
H_2O	6·830	3·27 (ign.)	2·64 (ign.)	7·20	3·50 (ign.)	0·56 (ign.)
	100·090	100·72	99·66	100·05	99·53	103·76
Spec. grav.	2·68	2·72	2·83	..	2·714	2·99

I. Quiraing; anal. M. F. Heddle, *Min. Mag.*, vol. v., p. 8; 1882.
II. " Beal"; anal. Hodgkinson, *Quart. Journ. Geol. Soc.*, vol. xxxix., p. 455 : 1883. Traces of barium and copper.
A. Ardtun, Mull; anal. G. A. J. Cole, *Quart. Journ. Geol. Soc.*, vol. xlv., p. 303, 1889.
B. Slievenalargy, Co. Down; anal. S. Haughton, *Journ. Roy. Geol. Soc. Irel.*, vol. iv., p. 231 : 1877.
C. Lamlash, Arran; anal. Delesse, *Ann. des mines* (5), vol. xiii., p. 369 : 1858.
D. Carrock Fell, Cumberland; anal. R. H. Adie, *Quart. Journ. Geol. Soc.*, vol. xlv., p. 298; 1889. Traces of titanic acid. The high total of this analysis is unsatisfactory, even with allowance for part of the iron being in the ferrous state.

of four other British representatives. Of these four, the first three, and possibly the last also, belong to the Tertiary suite of intrusions.

Although the six rocks show a considerable range of silica-percentage, they are evidently, as a group, somewhat more acid than the ordinary basalt and dolerite dykes and sills of the region. Another and equally noticeable point is the low proportion of magnesia, while in most cases the alkalies are decidedly high for basic rocks. The dyke of "the Beal" or Am Bile we have already referred to in the preceding chapter, and have attached to the peculiar type named mugearite. We have also noticed (pp. 263-269) the Quiraing rock, and have pointed out in its analysis peculiarities of the same kind though less marked in degree. It is probable that in other occurrences in Skye, in which there is an unusually amount of basic glass, there is something of the same peculiarity of composition. In default of chemical data, this is sometimes indicated by the nature of the enclosed crystallitic elements, *e.g.* by the development of oligoclase microlites rather than labradorite. In certain cases it cannot be doubted that, if the conditions of consolidation had been such as to produce a crystalline aggregate instead of a glass, the dominant constituents would be felspars of comparatively acid kinds, while the more basic elements would be represented principally by magnetite and sometimes olivine. It appears that magmas having this kind of composition assume the vitreous form more freely than ordinary basalt-magmas.

In the literature of the subject we find that the basic glasses (excluding those altered by subsequent hydration) have often been divided into tachylytes and hyalomelanes, and that the most typical examples of the latter are generally characterised by rather high silica and alkalies and constantly low magnesia. This distinction seems to correspond in a general way with that suggested by a study of our rocks, and a chemical investigation might perhaps enable us to carry it out. One distinctive character claimed for the hyalomelanes is their greater resistance to solution by acids; and it is noteworthy that such rocks as those of "the Beal," Gribun, and Lamlash are only slightly soluble.* This test has, however, been discredited by Rosenbusch and others; and we are content here to indicate what seems to be a real distinction without desiring to revive a rather ill-defined terminology.

Some interest attaches to the *specific gravity* of the tachylytes. Professors Judd and Cole have remarked that "the basalt-glass of the Western Isles of Scotland appears to be generally distinguished by its very high specific gravity." As regards the vitreous modification of the ordinary basalt dykes, our observations are quite in accord with this statement. Seven fresh examples from Skye gave the figures 2·76 to 2·92, with average 2·84. The somewhat less basic tachylytes, however, with less magnesia and more alkalies in proportion to lime, are often less dense, and for the most part have specific gravities between 2·65 and 2·75, though sometimes up to 2·80. These, as we have remarked, include the most considerable developments of basic glass known in Skye. It should be remembered that the specific gravity is considerably affected by secondary changes. We have selected the freshest material obtainable for our determinations, but in some cases of tachylytes of low density from other areas there is no definite information concerning the state of preservation of the rocks.

Taking the specific gravities of the tachylytes of the Western Isles as a whole, and comparing with their chemical analyses, we obtain results which at first sight appear rather discordant. In the following list we collect from various sources the particulars for all those cases for which we have chemical data, arranging them in order of specific gravity, and adding for comparison the tachylyte from Carrock Fell, Cumberland. Judging merely by these figures, it appears that the specific gravity bears no close relation

* Judd and Cole, *Quart. Journ. Geol. Soc.*, vol. xxxix., p. 452; 1883.

to the silica-percentage, within the limits 45 to 55. The three specimens richest in iron are also the three densest, and the order of the three follows the same rule, but the rest of the list shows no such correspondence. The examples richer in water are without exception the lighter, the comparison of the first and last on the

	Specific gravity.	Silica.	Total Iron (as metal).	Water.
Quiraing, Skye	2·68	45·61	10·77	6·83
Lamlash, Arran	2·714	55·20	7·70	3·50 (ign.)
Beal, Skye	2·72	52·59	7·80	3·27 (ign.)
Gribun, Mull	2·82	50·51	10·05	..
Brodick, Arran	2·83	53·96	..	..
Ardtun, Mull	2·83	53·03	6·60	2·64 (ign.)
Screpidale, Raasay	2·84	46·68	10·80	..
Sorne, Mull	2·89	47·46	12·47	..
Carrock Fell, Cumberland	2·99	53·63	14·00	0·56 (ign.)

list being especially striking;[*] and this is probably a point of importance. There is another essential circumstance, which does not appear in the chemical analyses. These rocks, although conveniently spoken of as basalt-glasses, often contain a considerable proportion of individualised minerals and aggregations in the form of spherulitic, crystallitic, and globulitic growths; and the relative amount of these in the glassy matrix may affect the specific gravity of the rock to an important degree, apart from differences in total chemical composition.

A curious anomaly appears, however, in at least one case, on comparing the specific gravity of a tachylyte selvage with that of the interior of the same dyke. In a dyke on Lamlash, Arran, Delesse[†] found for the interior 2·649 and for the selvage 2·714. In the same dyke the late Mr Thomas Davies[‡] found 2·67 for the interior and 2·72, 2·74, 2·78 for successive zones of the selvage, the last being the extreme edge. On the assumption that the chemical composition is the same throughout, this seems to be inconsistent with the general principle that substances are denser in the crystalline than in the vitreous form. This principle is abundantly verified by experiments, including those of Delesse himself. In a carefully conducted experiment by Barus[§] a diabase of specific gravity 3·0178 gave after fusion a glass of specific gravity 2·717; showing therefore a decrease of 9 per cent. in density or an increase of 11 per cent. in volume.

The French observer noticed the discrepancy, but considered it easily explicable by the fact that the tachylyte contains more silica and a little less water than the basalt. Professors Judd and Cole,[||]

---

[*] Of the Slievenalargy and Ballymacilreiny tachylytes, the one very rich and the other very poor in water, the specific gravities are unfortunately not recorded.

[†] *Ann. des mines* (5), vol. xiii., p. 369; 1858.
[‡] *Quart. Journ. Geol. Soc.*, vol. xxxix., p. 449; 1883.
[§] *Amer. Journ. Sci.* (3), vol. xlii., pp. 498, 499; 1891.
[||] *Quart. Journ. Geol. Soc.*, vol. xxxix., pp. 449, 453 : 1883.

with apparent justice, regard this explanation as inadequate, the observed differences falling within the limits of error. The more important figures in Delesse's analyses are:—

	Dyke.	Selvage.
SiO_2	55·20	56·05,
Fe_2O_3 (including FeO)	11·00	10·30,
Ignition	3·85	3·50;

in which it will be seen that the differences in silica and iron, if significant at all, ought to tell in the direction of a *lower* density for the glassy selvage. The difference in water shown is very small: if real, it probably indicates that the basalt of the central part of the dyke has suffered somewhat from secondary alteration. There may possibly be a difference in the relative proportions of ferric and ferrous iron, not separated in the analyses.

To ascertain whether basic rocks do really make an exception to the general rule would require careful analyses of the dykes and their selvages to prove identity of composition. It is unfortunate that in the only pair of analyses of this kind which we possess from Skye, those of the Quiraing occurrence, the specific gravity of the interior is not recorded. We are able to show, however, that the Lamlash dyke is by no means unique in having a vitreous selvage of higher density than itself. The "Beal dyke" gave the following results with the hydrostatic balance:—

[9373].	Centre of dyke,	2·645,
[9374].	Part next selvage,	2·678,
[9375].	Glassy selvage,	2·686.

In this case, however, the difference may not be very significant for the interior of the dyke at least is not in a fresh condition It may be remarked that, while secondary alteration probably reduces in most cases the density of crystalline rocks, this is not always the case. In the first of the three rocks mentioned next below there is a certain amount of pyrites formed, which tells in the opposite direction to vitiate the comparison. Professor Sollas has kindly determined for us by his diffusion-column the specific gravities of the glassy skins of some of our basalt dykes, and we here compare these with the results found by the hydrostatic balance for the interior or for the whole specimen:—

[8845].	Dyke on N.W. face of Marsco—	
	Part next to selvage (altered)	2·90,
	Glassy selvage,	2·80.
[8846].	Dyke on Meall Odhar Beag—	
	Whole specimen,	2·86,
	Glassy selvage,	2·91.
[8847].	Dyke N.W. of Ben Lee—	
	Whole specimen,	2·84,
	Glassy selvage,	2·94,

x

In the last two, which are fresh rocks, the glassy selvage is very decidedly denser than a specimen representing the full width of the narrow dyke: a comparison of selvage with interior would of course show a slightly greater difference of the same kind. It is possible that there may be some real difference in chemical composition between the central and the marginal parts; and if such difference exists, and has been set up as a result of differentiation in place, it probably takes the form of a certain concentration of iron-oxides in the margin, which would account for the higher density of that part.

In describing the *micro-structure* of the rocks we shall endeavour to distinguish the *true basalt-tachylytes* from those of more peculiar composition, approximating in varying degree to the mugearite type. We shall begin with the former, which, as a rule, are found only as thin skins on the surfaces of a dyke or sheet.

In the first place a few words are called for relative to the occurrence of a vitreous "base" in the general mass of some of our basalt dykes and sheets. We have already remarked that any notable amount of glass in the body of an intrusion is of rare occurrence. In some instances, however, the marginal part developes an abundant glassy base, without assuming the character of a tachylyte, and interesting micro-structures are found. We select to illustrate this an intrusive sheet or sill in the Torridonian grits of the Isle of Soay, ¼ mile W. by N. of An Dubh-sgeire. The marginal part of this is a dark rock of generally doleritic aspect, and of specific gravity 2·80, enclosing very numerous dull black spots of round or ovoid shape up to 1 inch or more in diameter. These spots, very conspicuous on a cut face, are scarcely to be detected on an ordinary fracture, but stand out prominently on the weathered surface. A thin slice [9987] shows that they represent vesicles, into which the residual magma has forced its way at a late stage in the consolidation. We shall have to notice this circumstance as specially characteristic of the augite-andesite dykes, but this rock is of thoroughly basic composition. A brown residual "base" is abundantly present. In the interstices of the labradorite crystals and (decomposed) augite grains it is a true glass; but in the larger and more defined patches which represent the vesicles it is mostly found to depolarise. Here a large part is made up of little spherulitic growths of the kind that we shall have to notice so frequently in the tachylytes and variolites. Owing to the oblique extinction of the felspar elements, which constitute most of their substance, these spherulites do not show the "black cross" effect; but the radiate structure is evident, and is rendered more so by the arrangement of numerous slender dark rods, representing probably destroyed augite.

Coming now to those basalt dykes which have glassy selvages, we notice as an invariable characteristic that the marginal part of such a dyke has a strongly banded structure parallel to the bounding wall. A transverse section will often show as many as six or eight narrow bands, averaging perhaps $\frac{1}{30}$ inch in width; the outermost of which is the actual tachylyte, while the others show a great variety of micro-structure, into which true glass enters in some proportion. The outermost band is that which in a hand-specimen is conspicuous for its jet-like colour and lustre, while the others have a more subdued aspect—pitchy, resinous, or quite dull.

The actual tachylyte is extremely dark, becoming transparent only in very thin slices or finely crushed splinters. It shows then a deep brown colour, usually a reddish or yellowish brown, but sometimes with an olive tone. It is not always homogeneous, but often shows minute opaque spots or scarcely resolvable aggregates of dust of the kind termed "cumulites." There are as a rule no distinct crystallites, but an occasional small phenocryst, usually of felspar, may be enclosed here as well as in the other bands. Scattered microscopic amygdules, either spherical or ovoid, occur in some cases.

The succeeding bands have not usually the opacity of the true tachylyte, but show various depths of brown coloration, and also differ in the nature of their structures. Crystalline or crystallitic matter enters in various ways, and its proportion relative to the glassy base does not always decrease progressively outwards. The several bands are fairly well defined, but the sharpest division is usually that which separates the penultimate one from the border of true tachylyte. The principal varieties of micro-structure depend upon the presence of different spherulitic growths and of crystallites, and upon the extent to which these encroach upon the glassy base.

The spherulites are usually from $\frac{1}{100}$ to $\frac{1}{40}$ inch in diameter, though both smaller and larger examples have been found. They may be isolated in a glassy matrix or closely packed to make up the whole of a particular band. In the former case they are sharply bounded, with a spherical or ovoid outline, a ragged or irregularly stellate form being rarely found; in the latter case they show polygonal boundaries, due to mutual interference. Sometimes again spherulites in a glassy matrix coalesce in rows parallel to the wall of the dyke. The spherulites are always paler than the glass, and when best developed show a strong yellowish brown colour in thin slices. The centre of each spherulite is of a deeper brown colour, which fades gradually into a paler tint towards the periphery. There can be little doubt that the colour of the spherulites results mainly from an admixture of glass in the interstices of the felspar fibres which constitute the essential element of the structure. The proportion of glass varies in different cases, and is higher in the centre than at the periphery. The appearance between crossed nicols agrees with this. In some cases spherulites of dark colour are sensibly isotropic, but the more ordinary examples depolarise very decidedly. This is most pronounced in the paler spherulites, and especially so in the pale peripheral zone, where the birefringence approximates to that of a felspar. Some indication of radiate structure may or may not be perceptible in natural light, but it is seen with the aid of crossed nicols, whenever the depolarisation is sufficiently strong. The dark brushes, having more or less roughly the "black cross" arrangement, are most distinct in the outer portion of each spherulite. As a rule there is a certain irregularly tufted appearance, as if the fine fibres were grouped in sub-parallel bundles, the bundles rather than the individual fibres having the radiate disposition.

In exceptional cases there are features which are not easily explained by our simple conception of these spherulites as aggregates of felspar fibres with interstitial brown glass. A specimen from Ben Lee, near Sligachan, consists in one band of closely packed spherulites about $\frac{1}{50}$ inch in diameter, which, though strongly depolarising, are of a deep colour (Fig. 71, E). Each spherulite is built up of several distinct tufts or irregular sectors, of which some are deep brown, while others have a grey or fawn colour. They are quite strongly pleochroic, the brown portions showing a stronger absorption for vibrations in the direction of the radius and the grey portions for vibrations in the transverse direction. Almost identical phenomena have been described by Prof. Grenville Cole[*] in a tachylyte from Ardtun in Mull. In our rock the pleochroism is stronger in the brown parts than in the grey, and certain of the latter which have a rather browner tone than the rest behave like the brown parts as regards the direction of stronger absorption. Prof. Cole suggests that the phenomena may be due to the presence of fibres of some pleochroic mineral, perhaps an alkali-bearing pyroxene, as an element in the spherulitic aggregate. This is possible, though it is not easy to specify any known mineral which is likely to occur and possesses the required quality of pleochroism. An alternative explanation might perhaps be based on the fact that colourless anisotropic crystals may acquire pleochroism when stained.[†] It is to be remarked, however, that the brown and grey parts of the spherulites differ also in respect of optical orientation. In the former the fibres have the "positive" character, i.e. the axis of optical elasticity most nearly parallel to the length of the fibre is the least axis. The grey sectors are "negative," but those of a browner grey tint which resemble the brown parts in the quality of their pleochroism resemble them also in being positive. In all cases, then, the least axis of optical elasticity corresponds with the stronger absorption. These facts perhaps point to the presence of actual pleochroic fibres mingled with the felspar, and apparently to the presence of two different pleochroic minerals, one in the brown sectors and the other in the grey.

As probably distinct from spherulites, we may mention the occurrence in some cases of dark spherical spots, often coalescing into botryoidal aggregates, which show no apparent structure and have no reaction upon polarised light. These are perhaps of a "concretionary" rather than a spherulitic nature.

[*] *Quart. Journ. Geol. Soc.*, vol. xliv., p. 302, pl. XI., fig. 2 ; 1888.
[†] Weinschenk, *Zeits. anorg. Chem.*, vol. xii., p. 377 ; 1896.

Apart from the felspar fibres of the spherulites and the globulitic separation of iron-oxide in the glass, distinct crystallites are not very characteristic of the rocks under discussion. When present, they are of the usual minerals—felspar, olivine, and probably augite, this last generally decomposed. Fibrous terminations, sheaf-like groupings, skeletal forms, and other characteristic habits are found; but we can rarely see any indication of crystallites, other than the fibres of felspar, entering into the radiate arrangement of the spherulites.

After the foregoing general description a few examples will suffice to exhibit the kind of variety met with among these rocks. A simple case is illustrated by a small dyke on the north-west face of Marsco. The hand-specimen is a very compact-looking basalt showing rare crystals of augite and labradorite and rather numerous patches of iron pyrites. At about $1\frac{1}{2}$ inch from the edge the rock begins to assume a dull pitchy lustre, and this becomes gradually brighter, but the final change to the true tachylyte selvage is, as usual, rather an abrupt one. A thin slice [8845] shows the compact basalt of the interior to consist of minute prisms of felspar, granules of augite, and skeleton growths of magnetite, with only a small amount of glassy base. In the pitchstone-like portion this last is in much greater quantity: the little felspars are still very abundant, but the augite granules become scarcer. Then the felspars also disappear, and the rock becomes a deep yellowish-brown glass, crowded with minute shadowy objects difficult to resolve. There are, however, dark globulites of iron-oxide, collected into nebulous patches ("cumulites"), within which are darker spots caused by a condensation of the same.

A $2\frac{1}{2}$-inch dyke from Meall Odhar Beag, near Sligachan, appears very compact throughout, though with only dull lustre in the interior. The actual selvages are of black glass with fine fissures, which show as curved perlitic cracks on the contact-surface. A slice [8846] shows rare crystals of felspar and green augite, about $\frac{1}{100}$ inch long, distributed through the dyke. The general mass shows marked banding throughout. The central part consists of narrow bands alternately lighter and darker, an appearance dependent on the smaller or larger proportion of glassy base. Crystallites are in this case very abundant and of more than one kind, the most conspicuous being skeletons of felspar, often with forked extremities (Plate XXIII., Fig. 1, B). The darker bands are almost opaque except for these crystallites. At about $\frac{3}{10}$ inch from the edge of the dyke this almost opaque portion gives place to a light brown band irregularly fissured and composed of closely packed spherulites about $\frac{1}{100}$ inch in diameter. This is succeeded by a narrow band containing small oval spherulites isolated in a glassy ground. The latter is opaque in a thin slice, and the same is true of the selvage, $\frac{1}{10}$ inch wide, of actual tachylyte which follows.

From N.W. of the summit of Ben Lee, in the same neighbourhood, comes another $2\frac{1}{2}$-inch dyke or vein, which in a hand-specimen closely resembles the preceding. In thin slices it shows a banded structure throughout, the successive bands exhibiting considerable variety of character, as shown in the accompanying figure (Fig. 71).

About half a mile E.S.E. of Loch Mhic Charmichael, in the Sleat peninsula, a thin basalt sill (specific gravity of the interior 2·82) passes at the edge into a black glass. In a thin slice [6854] this shows a deep brown colour, with only vague indications of crystallites. A little farther from the edge the rock, still in the main glassy, is crowded with fine felspar fibres and with minute rods of magnetite disposed in two sets to build a rectangular grating.

A rock collected by Mr Clough at Camas Daraich, near the Point of Sleat, is of interest as possibly throwing light on the minute structures of some of these semi-vitreous basalts, here presented on a larger scale. The rock is seen near the middle of the little bay as an irregular sheet one or two feet thick running nearly

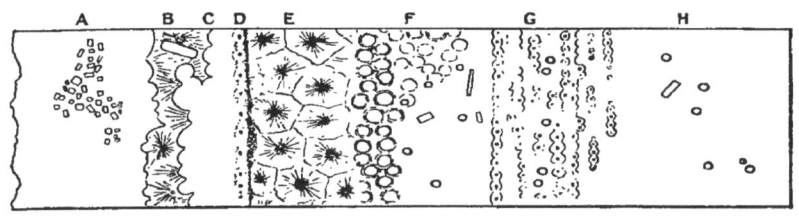

FIG. 71.—Margin of small basalt dyke, N.W. of Ben Lee, near Sligachan; × 10. This figure is merely diagrammatic.

A. Interior of dyke, very dark in the slice, but crowded with minute felspar microlites and enclosing locally groups of little felspar crystals.
B. Narrow spherulitic band, birefringent but without any good "black cross."
C. Dark spherical bodies of concretionary nature, without action on polarised light.
D. Single band of small spherulites like G, and narrow seam of black glass.
E. Pleochroic spherulites, described in text, p. 344.
F. Band full of obscure spherical bodies giving no reaction between crossed nicols.
G. Minute spherulites, coalescing into bands.
H. Black glass forming actual edge of dyke.

horizontally through a series of contorted granulitic grits.* It is a thoroughly basic rock, of specific gravity 2·92, and consists almost wholly of spherules, often as much as $2\frac{1}{2}$ or 3 inches in diameter. They are usually so closely packed as to leave little or no interstitial space, and consequently assume polyhedral outlines. In hand-specimens the rock is dark grey or almost black, with the peculiar sheen due to innumerable slender fibres, which are seen to have a radial arrangement about the centres of the individual spherules. Thin slices [7845, etc.] show that these fibres are of felspar, probably labradorite, and that they form the bulk of the

* For a fuller description of the rock see Clough and Harker, *Trans. Edin. Geol. Soc.*, vol. vii., pp. 381-389, pl. XXIII; 1899.

rock. The other minerals are olivine, in crystals $\frac{1}{500}$ to $\frac{1}{200}$ inch in diameter; augite, in granules and patches of about the same size; and magnetite in octahedra and granules still smaller (Pl. XXIII., Fig. 2, A). The olivine often builds good crystals, bounded by the forms m (110), k (021), and b (010); but the augite has a subophitic arrangement. This, the prevalent, type of the rock has very little residual base. A blacker and more lustrous specimen, however, taken nearer to the surface of the sill, is seen in the slice [7846] to contain an abundance of brown glass. Here the divergent fibres of felspar are more slender, and the augite and magnetite specks smaller, while the olivine takes the form of little skeleton crystallites. These are elongated parallel to the a-axis of crystallography, and are hemimorphic with reference to the b-axis. They have forked terminations, and are often little more than shells occupied in the interior by glass (Pl. XXIII., Fig. 2, B). At the actual surface of the sill there is a thin tachylytic selvage, perhaps $\frac{1}{20}$ inch in thickness. The special interest of this sill is that it presents on a relatively large scale, and in an unusually fresh state, that type of spherulitic structure, often called variolitic, which is associated with basaltic rocks. In most "variolites" which have been described the structure is on a much more minute scale, and is obscured in varying degree by subsequent chemical changes.

There remain to be noticed the *less basic tachylytes*, not corresponding in composition with normal basalts, and in some cases resembling in this respect the type which we have named mugearite. Here we no longer find the strong tendency of the glass to concentrate as a thin purely vitreous band at the actual margin, nor again the rapid variation in successive narrow bands differing in micro-structure. Typically we find a considerable proportion of glass throughout what may be a rather broad border, measuring several inches, with only gradual change in microstructure in this distance. The glass itself is commonly paler than in the true basaltic tachylytes, and is sometimes quite colourless in thin slices. Judged by the specimens that we have examined, there seems to be much less tendency to microspherulitic structures. On the other hand, there may be a much greater development of crystallitic growths, sometimes assuming complex groupings which have the general effect of spherulites of relatively large dimensions. These characteristics are not set forth as absolute, and examples are found in this group of tachylytes which reproduce in some measure special features already described in the former group.

The dyke of Am Bile or "the Beal" is an illustration of the last remark. The passage from the crystalline interior to the vitreous edge of the dyke, though not abrupt, is rapid, and is completed within a distance of 2 or 3 inches. The glass itself, though not nearly opaque, is of a yellowish to reddish brown colour. The mainly glassy part, though without marked parallel banding, exhibits some variety of structure. It is partly spherulitic, but the spherulites, excepting their darker centres, scarcely differ from the surrounding glass in colour, so that their outlines are usually invisible in natural light. These outlines are often irregularly toothed. The spherulites are about $\frac{1}{20}$ inch in diameter, have an evident radiate structure, and depolarise. In both spherulites and matrix there are numerous little round spots of dark brown with a narrow paler border, which have no action on polarised light. Professors Judd and Cole have remarked in this tachylyte felspar crystals deeply honeycombed with glass-inclusions.[*] These are of clear orthoclase or sanidine. They occur also in the interior of the dyke, and are perhaps xenocrysts. The glass also encloses crystals of oligoclase, which are not corroded, and both felspars have served as nuclei for spherulitic growths.

This rock, belonging in virtue of its chemical composition to the present group rather than to the former, is in petrographical characters intermediate between the two.

The next dyke to be noticed occurs at Allt Thuill, in the Sleat district, and has already been referred to as showing an unusual thickness of vitreous or semi-vitreous rock. The central portion, without noticeable lustre, contains only a small proportion of interstitial glass. There are little narrow rods of augite, from $\frac{1}{50}$ inch downward, often hollow or with brush-like extremities; narrow twinned crystals of oligoclase, about the same size or less; minute crystals of magnetite and needles of apatite, and perhaps a little orthoclase [5429]. The vitreous margin of the dyke appears very dark in thin slices [5428, 8851]. This, however, is not due to any colour in the glass itself, but to a dense charge of finely divided magnetite in a perfectly colourless glassy base. There are abundant crystallites in addition to this, including augites with brush-like terminations, just like those noticed above, and felspar rods of more minute size. This highly vitreous marginal portion of the dyke passes gradually into the more crystalline interior without any noticeable banding.

A dyke to the south of Loch Ashik, near Broadford, is in great part vitreous throughout its width of six inches or more. The interior and principal portion has a pitchy lustre, while the selvages are of black glass, extending inward for an inch, or even in places two inches, though interrupted by narrow bands of duller aspect. Throughout there are bodies which look like large spherulites, rather shadowy in appearance except where accentuated by weathering. In the interior they range up to $\frac{1}{2}$ inch in diameter, and are rather closely packed; towards the edge of the dyke they diminish to less than $\frac{1}{20}$ inch, and are isolated in the matrix. Slices of the interior portion show a peculiar structure, the most prominent feature being innumerable dark rods set in a clear colourless matrix. Parallel rods are closely ranged in groups, which interlace at various angles; and it is a roughly radiate arrangement of the groups, not of the individual rods, that imparts the quasi-spherulitic structure. The interspaces between

[*] *Quart. Journ. Geol. Soc.*, vol. xxxix., pp. 459, pl. XIII., figs. 3, 5 ; 1883.

the spherical bodies have a constitution not very dissimilar, but here the rods are shorter and have a less regular arrangement. The colourless base is isotropic and clearly glassy. Towards the centre of each "spherulite," where it is in rather greater force relatively to the dark rods, it develops numerous little felspar microlites, occasionally with radiate grouping, and there may be a group of small felspar crystals with octahedra of magnetite at the actual centre. The felspar always gives sensibly straight extinction, and is presumably oligoclase. The dark rods which are so prominent a feature of the rock are not easily identified in all cases. In some places they seem to be opaque, and have irregularly serrate edges suggesting a string of octahedra of magnetite (Plate XXIII., Fig. 1, A). In other places they are transparent, with the strong birefringence and high extinction-angles of augite. These latter are less abundant.

The dark glassy selvage shows a curious patchy structure in thin slices [8848, etc.]. Portions are transparent, with a light brown colour, and encloses only scattered opaque globulites. The other and principal portions are dark, and present convex botryoidal boundaries to the paler patches, as if the pigment had been concentrated by a concretionary process. Here, but not in the pale portion, the abundant dark rods may sometimes be detected, and we may infer that these were formed after the concentration of the pigment.

The heterogeneous patchy nature of this selvage is illustrated by some specific gravity determinations kindly made for us by Professor Sollas with his diffusion-column. The greater part of the finely crushed powder gave from 2·74 to 2·85; but there was a heavier portion which gave 2·91, and a much lighter portion which gave 2·54. The less completely vitreous interior of the dyke gave, on a hand-specimen, the specific gravity 2·72. Under the microscope the greater part of the powder is translucent only in places; the denser part (sp. gr. 2·91) is almost all opaque; and the lighter part (sp. gr. 2·54) is translucent to transparent, with a greyish or greenish brown colour. Those minute chips which are not opaque show nevertheless occasional perfectly opaque spots, due presumably to a separation of magnetite.

The last example to be noticed is a dyke one foot wide from about ¾ mile N.E. of Kinloch. It has a black velvety appearance throughout, and is manifestly rich in glass. There are numerous well-defined bodies resembling spherulites, ¼ to ½ inch in diameter, scarcely visible on a fresh fracture, but very evident on a weathered surface. In thin slices [8850, etc.] these resemble in general character the "spherulites" in the preceding rock, having only a rude approach to the radiate structure. Here, however, the rods are of augite, often barred across at short intervals by magnetite (Plate XXIV., Fig. 1, A). They are embedded in a colourless glass, which, however, assumes a pale brownish tint in the peripheral zone of each "spherulite." The interspaces do not differ essentially from the "spherulites" themselves. The latter have the character described throughout the greater part of their mass, but towards the centre of each little crystallites of felspar begin to develop in the colourless glass. At the centre the interstitial glass is reduced to a minimum, and the essential constituents are interlacing crystallites of felspar, augite, and magnetite. The felspar is mainly oligoclase, but there are some broader and more shapeless elements which are probably orthoclase (Plate XXIV., Fig. 1, B).

We may suppose with some probability that the colourless interstitial glass in these rocks has approximately the composition of an oligoclase, perhaps with some admixture of potash-felspar; the iron as well as the magnesia being entirely contained in the crystallitic elements, a feature never found in the normal basalt tachylytes. The apparent absence of olivine and, in the last rock, the presence of abundant augite, suggest, however, that the composition differs from the mugearite type by a higher content of silica and lime.

There are some dykes in the south-eastern part of Skye which closely resemble the one last described in many respects, but are wholly crystalline. One occurs at Lòn Buidhe, near Heast. A thin slice [5771] shows grouped rods of augite set in a clear colourless matrix, and has much the same appearance as the preceding; but polarised light shows that the clear interstitial substance is here oligoclase. This felspar has a radiate arrangement about centres, building distinct spherulites about $\frac{1}{4}$ inch in diameter, and we may even observe a brownish tint in the peripheral zone of each spherulite, as in the former case. Such rocks have decided affinities with those to be described as trachyandesites (Chap. XXIII.), and such evidence as we have concerning the age of the less basic tachylytes would permit of their being assigned to the same late epoch.

CHAPTER XX.

Basic Dykes : Xenoliths.

An account of the basic dykes of Skye would not be complete without some notice of the *foreign or derived material* which, in the form of distinct rock fragments (*xenoliths*) or isolated crystals (*xenocrysts*), is found enclosed in so many of the dykes. This peculiarity is observable, in different degrees, in other groups of intrusive rocks described in this memoir. We have seen that in certain circumstances the granite becomes crowded with partially digested débris of gabbro. The composite intrusions, dykes and sills, consisting of associated basic and acid rocks, exhibit more remarkable phenomena of the same order. The ordinary basic sills of the plateaux seem to be very poor in xenoliths; but in the inclined basic sheets, to be described later, which intersect the gabbro mountains, and in the basic dykes throughout much of the area surveyed, derived material, usually débris of plutonic rocks, occurs with remarkable frequency.

We may divide xenoliths in general into two classes, those which are merely *accidental* and those which are *cognate* with the enclosing rock.* The former are such as may be enclosed in almost any igneous rock, and represent merely fragments picked up by the magma from the "country" rocks which it has traversed. Under the latter head we include those cases in which there is a genetic relationship between the enclosed and the enclosing rocks, and here the xenoliths have probably a deeper significance. The facility with which the various Tertiary intrusive rocks of Skye have enclosed relics of one another seems to be a characteristic of the whole series. In many cases the dissolution of the enclosed foreign débris has materially modified the composition of the enveloping magma, and so of the resulting solid rock. We proceed to describe a few selected examples illustrative of the phenomena.

The most remarkable instance of *accidental xenoliths* is afforded by a dyke which crosses the long southerly ridge of Blath-bheinn at about 1300 feet altitude. It is a conspicuous object, having a width of about 27 feet, and presenting at a glance the appearance of a quartz conglomerate. Pebbles and fragments of white quartz and quartzite, sub-angular or rounded, up to several inches in diameter, are crowded together in a greenish-grey diabasic-looking matrix. The dyke is one of those already referred to as repre-

* *Cf.* Harker, *Journ. of Geol.*, vol. viii., p. 394 : 1900.

senting some of the feeders of the gabbro lacolite : traced northwestward it is found to be continuous with the gabbro, which itself at this place encloses pebbles of quartz.* Similar xenoliths are found in abundance in irregular sheet-like intrusions of granophyre close to this place and on the slope farther south.

The purely accidental nature of these xenoliths, consisting of vein-quartz and quartzite, is of course obvious.† But, even if they had been of some igneous rock, their narrow restriction to one locality and the fact that at that locality they are found in three different kinds of intrusive rocks would be sufficient to prove that no close genetic relationship can exist in this case between the xenoliths and their enclosing matrix. In this case the probable source of the foreign material can be pointed out in the near vicinity. The Triassic conglomerate, as seen in some steep crags overlooking the foot-path to Strathaird,‡ is locally composed of quartz-pebbles ; and although some of the quartz-fragments enclosed in the dyke are of larger size and more angular shape, it is probable that better exposures might enable us to match these too from the conglomerate in place. The subjacent Torridonian grits also contain abundant small pebbles of quartz, which are doubtless the chief source of the xenoliths in the granophyre sheets, and may have contributed also to those in the dyke.

Thin slices of the conglomeratic dyke show numerous points of interest [7478, 7479]. The enclosed quartz-pebbles exhibit strain-shadows in polarised light, and are often traversed by fine fissures. These are probably mechanical effects of the heating, and from the same cause the quartz has been broken up into fragments, the smaller débris being distributed through the general matrix. Reactions have taken place at the contact of the quartz with the enveloping magma. As seen in the slices, the boundary of a pebble is often interrupted by gulf-like inlets, occupied mainly by felspar in narrow crystals or elongated fibres. Very often curved fibres of felspar are crowded together in divergent or imperfectly radiate aggregates, recalling the structure of some variolitic rocks ; but, if we may judge by the nearly straight extinction of the fibres, the felspar is here of an acid species (Pl. XXIV., Fig. 4). From these inlets narrow veins, also consisting essentially of little needles and fibres of felspar, penetrate the quartz of the pebble. The outer boundary of the pebble often shows a border with a similar development of fine felspar needles, but these are here associated with abundant pyroxene: a like border often surrounds the fragments resulting from the breaking up of the pebbles.

The matrix in which the pebbles are set is a rock of a peculiar kind, representing an originally basic magma greatly modified by absorption of silica. It does not appear that silica has crystallised

---

* The spot is just 500 yards east of the most easterly point of Loch na Creitheach.
† The dyke locally contains a few xenoliths of granite, which are of different significance, and fall under the "cognate" category.
‡ The branch passing east of An t-Sròn, now generally disused.

out, as such, from the magma; the abundant quartz found being rather mechanically derived from the xenoliths; but the actual products of crystallisation none the less bespeak an abnormal composition for the magma. They are, in order of relative importance, felspar, enstatite, and augite. There is no olivine and little or no iron-ore. The felspar is in rather irregular striated crystals, referable by their extinction-angles to andesine. The rhombic pyroxene is in idiomorphic crystals, usually $\frac{1}{50}$ to $\frac{1}{20}$ inch in length, almost always converted to green pleochroic bastite. The colour of this latter indicates a certain content of iron, but where the original mineral is preserved it shows the pale tint of enstatite. This is especially in the neighbourhood of the quartz, and possibly the rhombic pyroxene was not all of the same composition. The augite is in shapeless grains, very pale in the thin slices.

Assuming the magma to have had originally the composition of a dolerite, as the field-evidence indicates, it is manifest that it has been greatly modified by absorbing silica from the enclosed xenoliths. It is also noteworthy that the rock has not the relatively coarse texture and the characteristic micro-structure of a dolerite. Doubtless the inclusion of so large a quantity of foreign material, derived from cold rocks, caused a relatively rapid cooling of the magma.

Among the dykes met with in our survey instances are rare in which accidental xenoliths play so prominent a part as in the case just described. Two dykes traversing the coarse pebbly sandstones of the Torridonian (Applecross group) of the Isle of Scalpay may be mentioned. One occurs on the western slope of Mullach na Càrn, and is a large dyke containing abundant xenoliths near one edge only; the other, to the north of Bealach Bàn, also shows a somewhat uneven distribution of the included material. In both cases pebble-like inclusions of quartz and quartzite are accompanied by pieces of granite, presumably derived from a deep-seated source, so that both accidental and cognate xenoliths seem to be represented. Mr Woodward has remarked a dyke carrying abundant pebbles at Rudha nan Leac on the east coast of Raasay, where it intersects the red sandstone of the Trias.

The remarks made in a former chapter concerning the necessarily abnormal composition of mixed or hybrid igneous rocks apply with greater force to such cases as these, where a molten rock-magma has enclosed, and in part dissolved, extraneous material of non-igneous origin. The resulting rock, even excluding any undissolved relics of the xenoliths, must have a chemical, and consequently a mineralogical, composition unlike those of any rock resulting from the crystallisation of a pure rock-magma.*

The *cognate xenoliths and xenocrysts* in our basic dykes come mainly from two rocks, gabbro and granite: other types, such as troctolite, are more rarely represented. It is of the first importance

* The special case of a magma which has dissolved quartz of extraneous origin is considered in the paper already cited : see *Journ. of Geol.*, vol. viii., pp. 395, 396, and fig. 3 ; 1900.

to notice that, on the one hand, they are always of rocks familiar among the Tertiary intrusions of the region; on the other hand, the situation and proved age of the dykes are often such that the xenoliths cannot be derived from any known mass of the said rocks in the vicinity. This independence of the country rocks is to be regarded as a characteristic of cognate xenoliths. As regards distribution, it may be remarked that the phenomenon is not confined to any one type of dykes, but it is specially frequent in certain of the groups which we are able to distinguish by their petrographical characters and their relative ages. It is very common in some of the later groups, but comparatively rare in the earlier. This is quite in accord with what has been stated above; for the pre-granitic dykes are doubtless in most cases feeders of the lavas, and the immediately post-granitic dykes possibly feeders of the sills; and we have already seen that the lavas do not carry xenoliths and the normal basic sills do so but rarely.

The enclosed foreign material has often suffered considerable alteration in consequence of its inclusion in a molten magma. Despite this, distinct xenoliths, even when of quite minute dimensions, are as a rule easily recognised; and even detached crystals, if not totally destroyed, are not so much disguised as to obscure their true nature. On the other hand, there may be some difficulty in recognising xenocrysts as such in the absence of characteristic alteration. The changes experienced arise from two causes, viz. from the mere heating of the crystals, which give rise to effects mostly of a mechanical kind, and from chemical reactions between the crystals and the enveloping fluid magma. Changes of the latter kind, which are the more unmistakable, are not always developed. They seem to depend generally upon the existence of a considerable difference in composition between the enclosing rock and that which has furnished the derived material.* Where débris from an acid rock has been enclosed in a basic magma, some minerals (the ferro-magnesian constituents in particular) are often totally destroyed, and the rest (excepting certain accessories, such as zircon and apatite) have constantly suffered more or less from the caustic action of the magma. A similar remark applies to basic material involved in an acid magma. But where the débris of a basic rock has been enclosed in a basic magma such chemical reactions are by no means universal. In particular, gabbro-felspar in a basalt or dolerite dyke may show little or no sign of caustic action. There seems to have been in such a case something like chemical equilibrium between the crystals and the environing medium. Evidence may still be forthcoming—from the form of the crystals and the nature of their minute inclusions, from their unequal distribution in the dyke or their association with actual gabbro xenoliths—sufficient to indicate their true origin. The source of the foreign elements enclosed in the dykes will be more

* This principle, in one form or another, has been recognised by more than one writer: see, *e.g.*, Zirkel, *Lehrbuch der Petrographie*, 2nd ed., vol. i., p. 599; 1893.

appropriately considered after a description of some illustrative examples.

Good instances of *gabbro xenoliths* are afforded by the porphyritic basalt dykes about Suardal and in other parts of the Strath. Especially noteworthy is a 50-ft dyke a little S.W. of the fork of Allt an 't-Suidhe, to the N.W. of Loch Kilchrist, where gabbro débris makes up in places about half the bulk of the rock. The locality is not far from the exposures of the Kilchrist granophyre with abundant xenoliths of gabbro. This dyke intersects the volcanic agglomerate, but most of the other Suardal dykes occur in the Cambrian limestones. A numerous group of dolerite dykes rich in gabbro xenoliths may be examined to the north-east of Camasunary, viz. in the rocks of the Abhuinn nan Leac valley and in the basaltic lavas of the slopes above, rising to An Dà Bheinn or Slat Bheinn.

The appearances observed in thin slices of these rocks, or of some of them, may be described briefly. The felspars of the xenoliths are sometimes partially rounded where they have been in contact with the molten magma; more frequently they show no such change, though they may be fissured or partly shattered. They may show evidently secondary inclusions just within the border of the crystal (Pl. XXV., Fig. 2, A), and the very turbid appearance seen in some cases is possibly attributable to more numerous and minute inclusions of like origin; but neither of these phenomena is so general as to be considered a distinctive criterion. Not infrequently there has been some addition of new felspar-substance, forming a border continuous with the xenocryst. Often none of these changes can be verified. The augite, like the felspar, may show rounding and bands of secondary inclusions [7483]. It is more readily affected by chemical changes than the felspar. At the junction of the two minerals in a xenolith there has sometimes been a mutual reaction, giving rise to prisms of brown hornblende and granular aggregates of magnetite, set in a matrix of new-formed augite, new felspar (partly in continuity with the old), and a little quartz [6712]. In detached xenocrysts the augite does not long survive. It gives rise presumably to new augite, which forms part of the enclosing rock, but also to granular magnetite with sometimes a little brown mica. Patches rich in these latter minerals may remain to indicate vaguely the site of vanished augite xenocrysts [6718]. It is difficult to decide whether the magnetite of the gabbro ever escapes destruction. When apatite has been present, it is left unchanged after the disintegration of the containing xenolith [6712].

As illustrating the phenomena of *granite xenoliths* in basic dykes, we may take first those so frequently encountered in the porphyritic basalt dykes which have been distinguished above as the Suardal type. As already stated, granite débris occurs locally in considerable abundance, and by its partial dissolution has sometimes modified in some degree the composition of the basalt-magma; but on the whole it is the earlier stages of alteration of the xenoliths that are best exemplified in the specimens studied from these dykes. Pieces of granite two or three inches in diameter occur, and the manner of their disintegration is clearly exhibited. It is partly a mechanical breaking up, consequent upon the different coefficients of expansion of the several minerals and upon shattering by heat of the individual crystals. But in every case there is a certain amount of corrosion by the enveloping magma, which finds its way even into very minute fissures and co-operates with the purely mechanical process; and there are also reactions between the different component minerals of the granite itself.

The ferro-magnesian element of the granite is the most readily affected, and biotite in particular is almost always destroyed at the outset. In some cases it seems to have been fused in the interior of the xenolith; but in general the material, or much of it, seems to have been removed by some leaching-out process. Even when a flake of biotite has been embedded in a felspar crystal, it is quite destroyed and represented only by some finely granular magnetite, this being arranged in fine lines in a way which indicates that the process was effected along the cleavage-planes. Such a vanished biotite-flake may be surrounded by a clear ring of apparently new-built felspar continuous with the surrounding crystal but differing slightly from it in optical properties [6715]. Except when its place is marked in this way, the biotite of the granite is totally lost, and only partially represented by clotted granular magnetite or brown limonite not in the form of the original mineral. Sometimes a little granular augite is associated with the iron-oxide: less frequently some new-built brown mica.

The quartz of the xenoliths sometimes shows no change other than the formation of fine cracks. These occasionally tend to run parallel to the boundary of the grain (Pl. XXV., Fig. 2, B), but very often they have been determined by rows of fluid-pores in the quartz, which have perhaps burst the crystal by the expansion of the contained fluid. In this case the cracks often show some degree of parallelism in each grain. Occasionally, along the border of a detached grain or along a crack, the quartz has become a rather finely granular aggregate with a clear interstitial substance which is isotropic and is probably hyaline silica [6716].

The felspars (orthoclase and oligoclase) of the granite are, in this early stage of alteration of the xenoliths, more easily attacked than the quartz. This is especially the case where felspar has been in contact with a ferro-magnesian mineral in the granite. Here is formed, round the site of the latter mineral, a patch of new-built felspar with some admixture of iron-ore and perhaps new-built biotite. The new felspar is in small imperfect crystals or in fibres aggregated in fan-shaped bundles [6751]. The felspar of the granite is only vaguely outlined against such a patch, but the quartz presents a sharp edge to it. Often again there is an alteration along the border of the felspar crystals of the xenolith at their contact with one another or with quartz. This takes the form of a zone of rather fine-textured new-built felspathic material. If it is orthoclase, it tends to a granular structure; if oligoclase, it forms an aggregate of little imperfect twinned crystals, which near the original oligoclase of the xenolith may assume a regular orientation with it. In their interior the felspars of the xenolith, at least until they become isolated from it, show little change in many examples; but some exhibit the peculiar shagreen appearance which Bäckström* styles *gekörnelt* or granulated.

An excellent place for studying the more advanced dissolution of granite xenoliths in basalt is found close to Broadford, on the west shore of the bay. The locality is about 250 yards beyond the pier, and nearly north-east of Corry Lodge. Here two dykes (among others) are exposed at low tide, running out into the water in a S.S.E. direction. Both contain abundant débris of granite, and in the second (*i.e.* the more north-easterly one) large patches of that rock are locally present in various stages of breaking up and dissolution. The xenoliths, however, have not been uniformly distributed through the dykes, and this enables us by comparison of specimens to demonstrate the reciprocal modification of the basic magma consequent upon incorporation of the acid material.

A specimen of the first dyke, taken as free as possible from extraneous material, is a dark grey, finely but evidently crystalline rock, of specific gravity 3·03 and clearly of basic composition. It has no phenocrysts nor xenocrysts. A slice [6719] shows it to be a normal sub-ophitic dolerite composed of labradorite, augite, and magnetite (Plate XXV., Fig. 3, A). The little felspars are about $\frac{1}{40}$ inch long. A specimen was selected for comparison which showed numerous xenocrysts, both quartz-grains and dull white felspars. Here the matrix is of a much lighter grey colour and of finer texture. A slice [6720] shows the quartz-grains to be partially rounded and bordered by a ring rich in granular augite, due to reaction between the grain and the enveloping magma; a familiar feature in other districts where quartz-grains may have been enclosed in basic rocks (Plate XXV., Fig. 3, B). The felspar xenocrysts, which are chiefly of oligoclase, are extremely turbid, excepting a clear patch in the interior of each crystal. The felspars of the matrix are of more slender shape than in the normal dolerite and not more than $\frac{1}{160}$ inch long, while their nearly straight extinction proves them to be oligoclase, perhaps with some orthoclase. The augite also is smaller, and is in granules, and magnetite is less abundant. Finally there is a certain amount of quartz, in small interstitial patches, with all the appearance of an original constituent.

These two specimens, taken only a short distance apart, are undoubtedly parts of one dyke, and the abnormal characters of the second one are due to the modification of the basic magma by absorption of granitic material. The acidification shows itself

* *Bihang til k. svenska Vet.-Akad. Handl.*, vol. xvi., pl. II., figs. 7–9; 1890.

especially in the formation of a relatively acid felspar and the presence of some excess of silica crystallised as quartz. The finer texture and rather different micro-structure of the modified rock as compared with the normal type are also interesting. We might refer them with some plausibility to the more rapid chilling consequent upon the inclusion of so much solid rock-débris. The contrast between the two specimens implies that no important diffusion has operated in the dyke during or after the corrosion and absorption of the granite débris. It may be taken as indicating that, although the xenoliths were brought up by the basic magma from some unknown depth, they did not begin to be dissolved to any considerable extent until after the intrusion of the dyke. A certain degree of super-heating in the magma, consequent upon relief of pressure, may have been the determining factor. The reciprocal action then proceeded energetically, and probably rapidly, for it must have been checked as cooling went on.

The second dyke shows phenomena closely comparable with those described above, but it is richer in granitic material, and no part of it that is exposed can be taken to represent the normal rock. A specimen was taken, however, from the portion poorest in quartz and other xenocrysts, and this gave the specific gravity 2·84. It is an evidently crystalline dolerite, generally resembling the normal type of the former dyke. A thin slice [6721] shows that the little felspar crystals are labradorite, up to $\frac{1}{20}$ inch in length: the pale brown augite has the sub-ophitic habit, and there are irregular grains of magnetite. Four specimens taken from near granite xenoliths, and themselves containing abundant xenocrysts, were sliced for comparison [6722–6725]. The hand-specimens show a lighter colour and a finer texture than the preceding specimen, and one gave the low specific gravity 2·73. The quartz-grains in these slices show always more or less rounding and corrosion, and have the usual border of granular augite, sometimes decayed and represented by carbonates, etc. The derived felspars, both orthoclase and oligoclase, are very turbid throughout, or have only a clear patch in the centre. Sometimes there is in the interior of a crystal an incipient new formation of granular felspar, which is quite clear. The ferro-magnesian minerals of the granite are always totally destroyed. The matrix in which the derived elements are enclosed is like that described in the other dyke. The felspar is oligoclase, or at least gives sensibly straight extinction, and is in slender prisms usually not more than $\frac{1}{100}$ inch long. The augite occurs in granules. There is in every case a certain amount of interstitial quartz. Another feature shown in some of the slices is the occurrence of small druses, with idiomorphic quartz projecting into the cavity, which has subsequently been occupied by calcite. We have pointed out the same peculiarity in the basic members of the composite sills of Cnoc Càrnach, etc. (p. 218.)

Sufficient examples have been given of the occurrence of foreign elements in noteworthy amount in the basic dykes. *Sporadic xenocrysts*, and to a less extent xenoliths, have, however, a much wider distribution in the Tertiary dykes than has been indicated by these particular occurrences. We do not refer to merely accidental inclusions of the country rock, which sometimes occur here as in other dykes, but call for no special remark. Nor need we do more than mention another not uncommon feature, viz. the inclusion of little fragments of rock of similar composition to the enclosing matrix but of finer texture. These probably represent a portion of the dyke-magma rather rapidly consolidated at an early stage of the intrusion, in contact with the wall of the dyke, and torn away by a later up-rush of the molten magma. We are concerned more especially with the inclusion in basic dykes of foreign material for which the known rocks in the neighbourhood do not afford any possible source.

Certain occurrences are perhaps to be explained by the supposition that an earlier dyke has been totally destroyed, excepting fragmentary relics, by a later one of a different kind, illustrating thus what may be regarded as an extreme case of a composite dyke. For instance, one of Mr Clough's specimens [7364] is described as forming a band in a compound dyke and containing rows of pale-red weathering spots up to 2 or 3 inches. This is from two-thirds of a mile N.N.E. of the west end of Ard Thurinish, in the southern part of Sleat. The rock is a fine-textured ophitic dolerite of specific gravity 2·87. The spots are xenoliths of a spherulitic granophyre, containing little patches of brown ferruginous substance with radiate structure, probably representing the ferro-magnesian mineral of the granophyre.

No such explanation is applicable to the gabbro-felspars and granitic quartz and felspars, which occur usually as isolated xenocrysts but occasionally grouped so that they may be called small xenoliths. They are found sparingly but not infrequently in basic dykes, not only in the mountain district and in Strath but in Sleat, the rock mentioned in the preceding paragraph being an example. Rarely in the outlying portions of the area does the enclosed débris occur in such quantity and of such a kind as to modify the composition of the enclosing rock in the fashion already described, but this is sometimes seen. One of Mr Clough's specimens, from Loch Doir' an Eich, about two miles S.E. of Ord, carries quartz-grains in unusual abundance. It has no doubt come from a basic magma, but has been considerably acidified. The little felspars are found to be oligoclase, and there is some interstitial quartz [6853]. The specific gravity of the rock is only 2·75, and it compares closely in all respects with the occurrences described above near Corry Lodge, Broadford.

In addition to detached xenocrysts, actual xenoliths of both gabbro and granite are recorded by Mr Clough from localities in the southern part of Sleat, ten or twelve miles from any considerable outcrop of like rocks. Thus in the Tarskavaig neighbourhood several of the basic dykes about Camas Daraich and the coast north-eastward are described as very full of gabbro inclusions. A more remarkable case occurs about a mile east of another Camas Daraich near the Point of Sleat. Here a dyke on the shore, besides porphyritic crystals, contains numerous large pieces of felspar, one measuring 18 by 9 inches and another 2 feet in length and 3 inches in breadth. They are of specific gravity 2·70, and give an extinction-angle of 5° in basal cleavage-flakes, agreeing with acid labradorite, Ab_1An_1. Some of the large pieces are single crystals, but others are complex; and we are probably to regard them as xenoliths of anorthosite, a varietal form of gabbro. Dykes enclosing gabbro are found also near Tormore and Gillean. "A dolerite dyke on the coast rather less than two-thirds of a mile W.S.W. of Gillean is unusually full of gabbro inclusions, or pieces of felspar which seem of the same kind as the felspar in the gabbro inclusions. Many of the inclusions are four or six inches long, and for a breadth of six or eight feet they take up as much space as the including rock. A specimen of one of the felspar lumps has the specific gravity of 2·68.

"The inclusions in a dolerite dyke [6135] on the coast rather more than a quarter of a mile S.S.W. of Rudha Dubh Ard, near Ord, vary greatly in abundance in different parts. Near high-water mark a breadth of two or three feet on the W. side of the dyke is nearly without inclusions, but the other part is crowded with them. Between this place and about sixty yards south of it no inclusions were noticed; farther on to the S.W., for more than 100 yards, the inclusions nearly equalled the dyke-rock in bulk. Some of the inclusions are three or four inches long and one or two broad. The longer axes are rudely parallel to the sides of the dyke. There are some inclusions, an inch or more in breadth, which seem entirely composed of quartz like that in the granophyre inclusions, but the rock from which they have been derived must have been unusually coarse in grain." (C. T. Clough.) Numerous inclusions of granite or granophyre were noticed by Mr Clough in a dyke a mile north-east of the mouth of Gillean Burn, near Tarskavaig, and in another farther south, on the coast N.W. of Loch Nigheann Fhionnlaidh. Another example is a coarse dolerite dyke on the west side of Ardvasar.

In the country to the west and north of the Cuillins the basic dykes less frequently contain foreign inclusions of an easily recognisable kind, but evident xenoliths of gabbro do sometimes occur at considerable distances from the plutonic intrusions of the Cuillins. One locality is the coast immediately west of Fiskavaig. One of the dykes here contains abundant pieces of gabbro, some with a diameter of three or four inches, although the place is nearly nine miles from that rock as exposed *in situ*. Detached crystals which seem to be of foreign origin are of more frequent occurrence, and some of these are of minerals belonging to acid rocks. We have already mentioned the orthoclase enclosed, in a greatly corroded state, in a basic dyke at Am Bile, to the north of Portree; notwithstanding the occurrence of orthoclase as a normal constituent of the same rock, these are probably to be ranked as xenocrysts. (*See* p. 348.)

The characters of the sporadic xenocrysts do not call for very full description, being closely similar to those already detailed above and, we may add, to those of other occurrences which have been described by many petrologists.* The felspars, when they have suffered any appreciable change, have not always behaved in the same fashion. Sometimes there is a formation of fissures following the two cleavages and incipient fusion along these fissures, which, carried farther, would break up the crystal into minute fragments. More commonly in the examples studied the crystal is not disintegrated. A certain amount of fusion or corrosive action on the edges has produced a partially rounded outline, and this reaction with the basic magma is especially noticeable in the case of the alkali-felspars. The most common change observable in the felspar xenocrysts is, however, the production of secondary glass- and other inclusions. Not infrequently these occur along a zone just within the border of the crystal. They follow the shape of this, however it may have been modified by rounding (*cf.* Pl. XXV., Fig. 2, A). In the case of a xenolith or group of crystals the zone of secondary inclusions is found only along that border of a crystal which is in contact with the enclosing matrix. It results probably from the fusion of primary inclusions in the felspar, but there has apparently been an enlargement occasioned by a reaction between this fused matter and the surrounding felspar-substance. Very often the felspar xenocrysts are extremely turbid throughout, or perhaps with the exception of a clear patch in the centre, and it seems probable that this appearance is due to a multitude of minute secondary inclusions. Outside the nearly opaque xenocryst there may be a clear border of new-formed felspar, in continuity with the old. This is frequently to be observed. When the augite of the enclosing rock has the granular habit or an idiomorphic tendency, it can sometimes be seen that the clear felspar-border is moulded upon the little grains of augite, proving its later growth. The derived quartz-grains in the dykes constantly show rounded contours, and are invariably surrounded by a ring or shell of granular augite.

The source of these xenocrysts is evidently a question of some difficulty. Even in dykes situated near the gabbro and granite intrusions the derived elements cannot always be attributed to the source which seems most obvious. Thus, a dyke a little to the south of the Beinn an Dubhaich granite contains abundant derived grains of granitic quartz [7060]; but the dyke is metamorphosed by the granite, and must therefore be older. That an earlier suite of plutonic rocks, both gabbro and granite, exists, or has existed, concealed from view beneath the mountain district we know from the

* The literature of xenoliths and xenocrysts is very extensive. The most exhaustive treatment of the subject is to be found in Lacroix's memoir *Les enclaves des roches volcaniques*, Macon, 1893.

evidence of the volcanic agglomerates, and this is a possible source of some of the foreign débris in our basic dykes; but, if we are to extend this explanation to dykes carrying xenocrysts throughout the island, we must postulate a much wider extension of these concealed rocks than is indicated by any other line of evidence.

The question must be considered in connection with various records, scattered through the literature of the British Tertiary intrusions, which suggest that the phenomena to be explained have a very wide distribution. Besides descriptions of evident xenocrysts, such, for instance, as the occurrences noticed by Dr Corstorphine in the southern part of Arran,* we find in the accounts of not a few "porphyritic" basalts, etc., observations which suggest that the enclosed felspar crystals may be in some sense not normal constituents of the rocks in which they occur. For instance, Mr Holland,† describing the large felspars in a basalt near Tobermory, Mull, remarks that they frequently exhibit schillerisation. Even so far away as the North of England Tertiary, or probably Tertiary, dykes exhibit some peculiarities in porphyritically enclosed felspars. That the crystals have not usually been corroded or otherwise evidently altered by the magma‡ does not, as we have seen, preclude the possibility of a derivative origin The Tynemouth dyke, with so much as 58·30 per cent. of silica, encloses felspars which were proved by analysis to be anorthite.§ They are unevenly distributed in the dyke, and occur usually in aggregates; the component crystals being irregularly bounded in the interior of an aggregate, but externally presenting good faces, which Mr Teall ascribes to a later addition. He suggests that these aggregates were formed under plutonic conditions, and were broken up and carried away by movements which took place after this consolidation had progressed to a certain extent.∥ Comparable in some respects with this is the peculiarity which Professor Judd has termed the "glomeroporphyritic structure," as exemplified in the ophitic dolerite (doubtless an intrusive sill) of Fair Head, in Antrim.¶ The rock encloses little patches, from $\frac{1}{10}$ to $\frac{1}{3}$ inch in diameter, consisting of anorthite and olivine with the mutual relations of a plutonic rock (troctolite). Professor Judd detected no clear indication of change where these patches are in contact with the enclosing matrix, but he remarks that the felspar crystals are much fissured, and contain a large number of secondary inclusions.

These troctolite-patches, in that they are foreign as regards

---

* *Tscherm. Min. Petr. Mitth.* (N.S.), vol. xiv., pp. 443-452, pl. X.; 1895.
† *Min. Mag.*, vol. viii., p. 155; 1888.
‡ Lacroix describes and figures a felspar xenocryst from the Cleveland dyke at Great Ayton, which shows the characteristic breaking up by fusion along cleavage-cracks (*Les enclaves des roches volcaniques*, pp. 653, 654, pl. II., fig. 1). Since, however, the dyke at this locality has probably traversed the Great Whin Sill, this xenocryst may be of the accidental kind.
§ Teall, *Quart. Journ. Geol. Soc.*, vol. xl., pp. 234, 235, pl. XIII; 1884.
∥ *British Petrography*, p. 141: 1888.
¶ *Quart. Journ. Geol. Soc.*, vol. xlii., p. 71, pl. VII., fig. 3; 1886.

composition to the rock in which they occur, may perhaps without impropriety be called xenoliths. Whether the anorthite-crystals in the Tynemouth dyke, as explained by Mr Teall, are to be styled xenocrysts, seems to be merely a question of terminology. In this view the sharp distinction between phenocrysts and cognate xenocrysts breaks down genetically as well as diagnostically, the difference becoming one of degree rather than of kind. Phenocrysts in a dyke are probably the results of crystallisation in the dyke-magma prior to its intrusion,* under "intratelluric," but not in the general case plutonic, conditions. We can, however, easily concede the possibility of such crystallisation taking place in some cases in a deep-seated magma-reservoir, where truly plutonic conditions obtained; and crystals so formed must be expected to possess characters (*e.g.* schiller-structures) proper to a plutonic origin. If we conceive such crystallisation in the magma-reservoir to proceed undisturbed, perhaps locally, until continuous portions are consolidated, there is no difficulty in supposing the rocks so formed to be subsequently broken up and portions of them involved in the magma as forced upwards to supply dykes. On such lines as these we may perhaps seek an explanation of the xenocrysts of gabbro-felspar and xenoliths of gabbro in our basic dykes; and it is clear that such an explanation, if admitted, will account for a distribution of xenocrysts coextensive with that of the dykes themselves.† Crystallisation in the deep-seated magma-basin, being supposed slow and progressive, would afford a reason for the prevalence of these quasi-foreign elements in the later rather than the earlier dykes of the series.

To apply this explanation to the granitic xenocrysts and xenoliths in the basic dykes as well as to those of gabbro, we must postulate the coexistence of acid and basic magmas in the supposed deep-seated reservoir and the beginning of crystallisation in both. To such a hypothesis we have already been led by the phenomena of the associated basic and acid intrusions of the region. If we conceive crystals to be formed in an overlying acid magma and to sink into an underlying basic one, we find a possible clue to some of the peculiar features described above, and one which may be worth pursuing both in this region and in others.‡

* To this statement we must admit some exceptions, as pointed out in another place (p. 270).

† The phenomena in question are not confined to the strictly British portion of the large "petrographic province." See, *e.g.*, Bréon, *Notes pour servir à l'étude de la géologie de l'Islande* . . . ., Paris, 1884.

‡ *Cf.* Harker, The Lamprophyres of the North of England, *Geol. Mag.*, 1892, pp. 199-206, and On Porphyritic Quartz in Basic Igneous Rocks, *ibid.*, pp. 485-488.

Special Minor Intrusions of the Cuillins.

CHAPTER XXI.

Basic Dykes and Sheets of the Cuillins.

The minor basic intrusions to be described in the present chapter are those peculiar to the Cuillin district; in which district must be included the Blaven range as well as the Cuillins proper. In other words, we have to deal with certain groups of intrusions which have a distribution limited by the boundary of the great gabbro laccolite, or extending only a little beyond it. Some of these have the form of dykes and others of inclined sheets. Both are very numerous, and contribute in a very important degree to the physical features of the gabbro mountain-district. We shall consider the dykes and the sheets in turn, this being generally the chronological order of their intrusion.

In discussing the direction of the basic dykes of Skye in general, we expressly excluded from our remarks those of the Cuillin district, as in part following other laws special to themselves. We proceed to set forth these laws, in so far as we are able to discover them. What are here styled laws are of course empirical, and are merely a convenient summing up of observations in the field: nevertheless, as serving to connect the bearings of the dykes with local crust movements centring in the heart of the gabbro tract, they probably do embody some real principles in the mechanics of dyke-intrusions, which further knowledge of this somewhat obscure subject may be expected to elucidate.

In the first place it is to be remarked that a vast number of dykes in the gabbro tract have approximately a radiate arrangement with reference to the centre of the tract. We shall style these the *radial set* of dykes. A tendency to radiation about the mountain tract was pointed out in the bearings of the Skye dykes in general. There, however, it was only a tendency, being a secondary influence modifying the operation of the primary law of parallelism, and producing deviations from the normal direction which did not exceed a moderate limit. In the gabbro area of the Cuillins radiation becomes (for this set of dykes) the primary law, and sweeps round the whole circle, excepting only the north-eastern quarter, where the granite interposes and these dykes are wanting. At the same time it is interesting to note that the law of parallelism comes in here as a secondary modifying influence; for in places where the radiate arrangement would impose a direction not very different from the normal direction for Skye (say N. 37° W.), there seems to be a tendency for the dykes to be attracted towards this latter direction.

Secondly there are many dykes which follow directions nearly at right angles to the radial dykes at their locality, as if forming a set in some sense conjugate with the other. These will be distinguished as the *tangential set*. They are subordinate to the radial set, and are not found everywhere; but in some places, *e.g.* the upper part of Coir' a' Ghreadaidh, they become extremely numerous. They seem to be constantly earlier than the radial dykes, and are often seen to be cut by them. As a rule, they are most developed towards the periphery of the gabbro laccolite, and some dykes outside this limit are probably to be referred to the same set.

Further, there is a very great number of dykes within the gabbro tract which have what may be regarded as the normal direction for the dykes of the island, and these may conveniently be called the *normal set*. This is not meant to imply that they constitute a single natural group referable to one epoch, for such is not the case. In those parts of the gabbro tract where the radial and tangential dykes make considerable angles with the direction common to the region (*e.g.* if one set runs E.–W. and the other N.–S.), the normal set comes out distinctly. In other circumstances it is apt to be confused with one of the other sets, unless some evidence as to relative ages can be obtained.

The sequence of the several sets of minor intrusions peculiar to the Cuillin district is apparently as follows:

(i.) the tangential set of dykes;
(ii.) the radial set, or the majority of these;
(iii.) the inclined sheets, to be described below;
(iv.) a radial set of ultrabasic dykes, to be described in the following chapter.

In this scheme no place is assigned to the normal set of dykes, for the reason that they belong to various epochs. Some are earlier than any of these local sets of intrusions; others cut not only the tangential and radial dykes but the inclined sheets also; none, however, cut the ultrabasic dykes, which are thus the latest of all the igneous rocks of the Cuillins.

The fact that the several local sets of minor intrusions peculiar to the Cuillin district fall into a fairly definite chronological order may be taken to indicate that each set constitutes a distinct natural group belonging to a certain defined epoch. If we regard them all as related to crust-movements which originated beneath the centre of the gabbro laccolite, we must connect the several groups with different stages of those movements, when the varying condition of strain set up in the rocks of the area favoured the formation of fissures in different directions. The number of intersections actually observed among the groups (i), (ii), and (iii) is, however, not large, and the sequence deduced perhaps needs further confirmation and possibly correction.

The general account of the field-relations of the basic dykes of

Skye contained in a former chapter is in many respects applicable to the special groups of dykes under notice; so that a few remarks on this subject will be sufficient. Both tangential and radial dykes are of quite moderate width, never rivalling the imposing dimensions attained by several of the basic dykes in other parts of the island. They may often be traced for long distances with practically straight courses and uniform width, though in some places towards the centre of the tract the smaller ones tend to become rather sinuous and otherwise irregular. A noticeable hade is not uncommon, more particularly towards the peripheral part of the gabbro tract and a little beyond it; and the hade, when it occurs, is evidently not determined by the same law which operated in the dykes away from the mountain-tract. It is found especially in the tangential set of dykes, and there the direction of inclination is outward from the centre of the tract. Multiple dykes are very rare in the radial set, and have not been observed in the tangential, although the individual dykes sometimes occur at very short intervals. This is perhaps due in part to the fact that each set of dykes belongs to a single epoch. It is partly attributable to the nature of the country-rock, but not wholly so; for in what we have called the normal set in the gabbro mountains multiple dykes are in some parts not infrequent.

It is not necessary to enter upon any full petrographical account of the dykes of the Cuillins, since this would be in great part a repetition of what has already been written. It is to be remarked, however, that these dykes are, so far as our observations go, all of thoroughly basic composition, the less basic types found in some other parts of Skye being unrepresented. The specific gravity of the rocks varies from 2·88 to 3·00, being often near the higher limit. The common types are non-porphyritic dolerites and basalts, of medium to fine texture, the smallest dykes having a very compact aspect.

The *inclined basic sheets* demand fuller notice. This very remarkable set of intrusions consists, in brief, of a vast number of roughly parallel sheets of basic rock intersecting the gabbro mountains in almost all parts, and having a general inward dip at moderate angles. We shall style them intrusive sheets, not sills, since it is convenient to reserve the latter term for that particular type of sheet-formed intrusion which follows the surfaces of bedding of stratified rocks. This latter type has been sufficiently illustrated by the sills of the basalt-plateaux, the thin lava-flows acting for this purpose as bedded rocks. The intrusive sheets cutting the massive gabbros obviously have their direction and inclination determined by quite other factors.

That the two great sets of sheet-formed intrusions are quite distinct in origin is sufficiently apparent from their distribution. The sills proper, attaining their maximum development in a distant part of the island, die out in the belt of metamorphosed lavas which fringes the gabbro of the Cuillins, and nowhere enter the latter rock. The inclined sheets, on the other hand, are strictly confined to the gabbro mountains, and their peculiar disposition, in whatever way it may be explained, points to a connection with some focus of eruption situated beneath the gabbro laccolite. Further, the considerations detailed above enable us to assign them to a late epoch in the history of igneous action in Skye, certainly much later than the epoch of the great sills.

The inclined sheets, though, as stated, found only in the gabbro mountains, are not limited to the gabbro itself. They intersect also the numerous patches of volcanic rocks enclosed in the gabbro mass and, in places, the basalt, shales, and granite which underlie it. They also intersect, as we have said, numerous dykes which themselves cut the gabbro. It is evident therefore that, whatever the

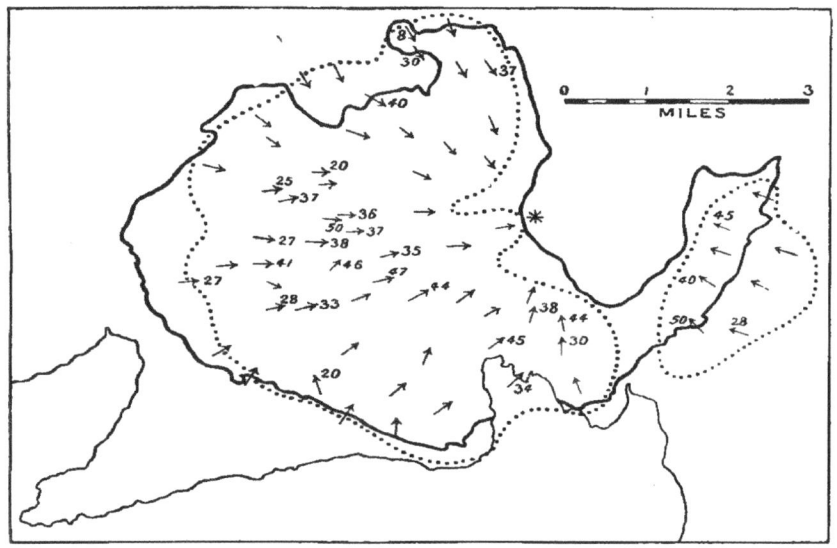

Fig. 72.—Sketch-map to illustrate the distribution and inclination of the inclined basic sheets of the Cuillins. The strong line marks the outline of the gabbro area: the dotted lines enclose the areas within which the inclined sheets are found, and the arrows (with figures) indicate the dips of the sheets.

relation of the inclined sheets to the plutonic rock may be, they are quite distinct from it, and belong to a time long posterior to its intrusion.

The distribution of the inclined sheets is roughly indicated on the accompanying sketch-map (Fig. 72), and it is at once evident that it is closely related to, though not coincident with, the limits of the gabbro itself. The limit of the sheets lies within that of the gabbro to the west, but beyond it to the east. Closer examination, with reference to a contoured map, makes it clear that there is a vertical as well as an areal distribution. Within a certain area, roughly that of the gabbro outcrop and perhaps corresponding pretty closely with the original extension of the gabbro laccolite, the sheets are present *everywhere above a certain imaginary surface*. It is in many places not very different from a horizontal plane at an altitude of about 1000 feet. From this, however, it makes some noteworthy departures corresponding in a general way with the deformed base of the gabbro laccolite itself, as illustrated in the accompanying longitudinal section across the mountains (Fig. 73). Over the greater part of the area the lower part of the gabbro is almost or quite free from sheets. This is well seen on the western border, where this gabbro practically without inclined sheets amounts to about 1000 feet vertically, and makes a strip about a mile wide on the map. Traced southward and eastward, the lower limit of the sheets approximates more and more to the lower surface of the gabbro, and in the southward direction reaches it a little beyond Coire Labain. In the interior valleys of Sligachan and Camasunary, with their main branches, and on the shores of Loch Coruisk, there is only a small thickness of gabbro free from inclined sheets; although it makes a considerable spread, owing to the fact that the form of the ground corresponds nearly with the

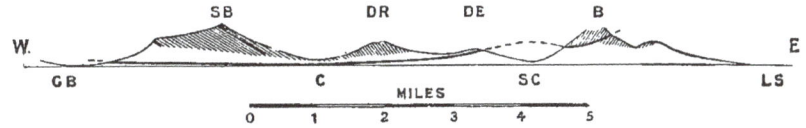

FIG. 73.—Section across the gabbro area to show the vertical distribution of the inclined sheets. The strong line shows the base of the gabbro laccolite; the short lines represent the inclined sheets, and are drawn at approximately the true inclinations. The letters refer to localities, as follows: GB, Glen Brittle; SB, Sgùrr na Banachdich; C, Coruisk; DR, Druim nan Ramh; DE, Druim an Eidhne; SC, Strath na Creitheach; B, Blath-bheinn; LS, Loch Slapin.

base of the gabbro not far below. It is particularly to be remarked that similar strips of gabbro without sheets, nearly half a mile in width, run along Glen Sligachan and Druim an Eidhne respectively, although the one rises only a few hundred feet above sea-level and the other is above the thousand-foot contour-line. This illustrates the way in which the lower limit of the sheets follows the shape of the base of the gabbro. Along the southern border the inclined sheets come down to the base of the gabbro; and along the south-eastern border, *i.e.* on the outward slopes of the Blaven range, they come down considerably below the gabbro, intersecting the strips of basaltic lavas and Jurassic strata and the irregular sheets of granite which together form the slopes.

The inclination of the intrusive sheets is with a very marked regularity inwards: in other words, as shown by the arrows in the figure, they *dip towards a certain point in the interior* of the district, approximately beneath the granite hill Meall Dearg, marked by an asterisk. The angle of dip varies. On the ridges both of the Cuillins and of the Blaven range it is usually about 35° to 40° from the horizontal, and similar or somewhat higher angles are observed on the slopes of the Cuillins towards Coruisk, the dip sometimes rising to as much as 50°. On the outward slopes of the Cuillins, on the other hand, the inclination is gentler, the dips falling to 20° or even as low as 10° in places. There seems indeed to be a general rule that the inclined sheets become steeper towards the interior of the district.

At any given locality the sheets preserve their parallelism with a remarkable degree of regularity, rarely touching or cutting one another, although, in the higher parts of the mountains especially, they occur at very short intervals. Nor do they often, like the sills in the lava group, run in contact with one another, though such instances of double and triple sheets are not unknown. The individual sheets attain no great magnitude, the great majority being not more than two or three feet thick, and many less than a foot. They are visibly continuous for very long distances, and run as a rule with great regularity. Only occasionally is a sheet found to be interrupted and displaced in a fashion already noticed in the case of the dykes; either with or without visible connection of the parts by strings and veins, but at least with a tendency to such connection (Fig. 74). The general regularity of

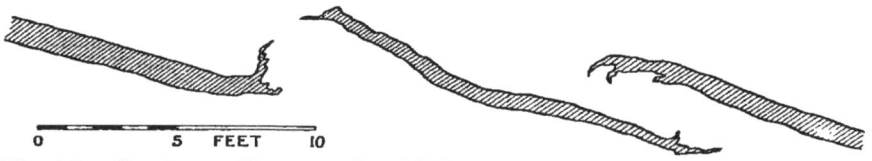

Fig. 74.—Section to illustrate the shifting of an inclined basic sheet, cutting the gabbro, near the outfall of Allt a' Chaoich, Loch Scavaig.

behaviour of the sheets in such a country-rock as gabbro is very striking.

Since there is almost conclusive evidence that the sheets die out downwards, we must suppose that they have been fed by dyke-fissures, and the only dykes which can be pointed out as probably marking the positions of these fissures are some of those with radiate disposition. In a few instances dykes of this set have been observed turning abruptly into sheets. It is true that in the great majority of cases which we have noticed during the mapping the radial dykes are cut by the sheets, but exceptions are found in which the reverse relation occurs. Even if the inclined sheets invariably cut the radial dykes, it might still be that the latter were, as a group, contemporaneous with, and the feeders of, the sheets; for it may be with these sheets, as with the sills of the plateaux, that the higher were intruded before the lower. It is more probable that some of the radial dykes hold this relation, while others are of somewhat earlier age, and are independent intrusions.

To illustrate the *chemical composition* of the inclined sheets a complete analysis has been made by Dr Pollard. Side by side with it we reproduce for comparison the analyses of two other basic rocks of the district. It is to be noticed that, despite the intimate association of the inclined sheets with the gabbro laccolite, there is no close resemblance between them as regards chemical composition. The characteristic high alumina-percentage of the gabbro, and its low titanic acid, iron-oxides, alkalies, and phosphoric acid, find no parallel in the inclined sheets. These late intrusions show more general resemblance to the basic sills of the plateau country; but this has probably no special significance, the sheets being undoubtedly a local group connected with the Cuillin centre. In the arc-spectrum taken by Sir J. Norman Lockyer the lines of chromium and vanadium are conspicuously shown.

	I.	A.	B.
SiO_2	47·64	47·28	45·24
TiO_2	1·27	0·28	2·26
Al_2O_3	14·15	21·09	15·63
Cr_2O_3	0·01	. .	trace
V_2O_3	0·06	0·02	. .
Fe_2O_3	5·18	3·52	5·56
FeO	7·96	3·91	7·19
NiO, CoO	trace	. .	trace
MnO	0·33	0·15	0·23
MgO	7·38	8·06	7·82
CaO	11·71	13·42	9·38
Na_2O	2·38	1·52	2·01
K_2O	0·71	0·29	0·72
H_2O { above 105°	1·44	0·53	2·21
{ at 105°C	0·19	0·13	1·12
P_2O_5	0·09	trace	0·20
S	0·03	. .	CO_2 0·49
	100·53	100·22	100·06
Specific gravity	3·01	2·90	2·85

I. [8062]. Dolerite, inclined sheet intersecting the gabbro, 100 yards S. of Loch a' Bhàsteir, near Sgùrr nan Gillean: anal. W. Pollard. Barium sought but not found.

A. [8194]. Olivine-Gabbro, Coir' a' Mhadaidh: anal. W. Pollard; repeated for comparison.

B. [7854]. Olivine-Dolerite, sill in basaltic lavas, summit of Ben Lee, near Loch Sligachan: anal. W. Pollard; repeated for comparison.

Petrographically the inclined sheets, while constantly of basic composition, present some range of variety. The most usual type is a *moderately fine-textured dolerite, without olivine.* Such rocks are widely distributed throughout the gabbro mountains, and may be studied in the Sgùrr nan Gillean group and many other places. In hand-specimens they are dark grey, evidently crystalline rocks, without porphyritic elements. In thin slices they are seen to have a typical ophitic to sub-ophitic structure. The felspars present narrow rectangular sections, about $\frac{1}{50}$ inch long, with albite twinning: when a little broader, they show carlsbad twinning in addition. Their extinction-angles indicate labradorite. The augite, very pale brown in the slices, enwraps and sometimes encloses the felspars. It is usually fresh, but in places has given rise to patches of a green chloritic material with confused scaly structure. Opaque iron-ore is abundant in grains and sometimes in skeleton-shapes: it is in the main magnetite, though ilmenite can also be identified. In addition there may be a little pyrites, visible as brass-yellow specks on a hand-specimen. Olivine is not found in this common type, and apatite is only sparingly present. An amygdaloidal structure is rare here and in the inclined sheets generally.

Slight variations from this type occur in some examples. In one or two slices there are, in addition to the dominant felspar with its "lath-shaped" sections, scattered crystals, larger and broader, with no good outlines. These are untwinned, and sometimes show a slight zonary banding between crossed nicols. They are clearly of somewhat late crystallisation, being moulded on the augite, which in these places is partially idiomorphic [8061]. More exceptionally these shapeless zoned felspars become an important constituent [7472], as in some varieties of the basic dykes.

Another variety arises from the presence of relatively large felspars, $\frac{1}{8}$ inch or more in diameter, which give the rock something of a porphyritic appearance. The sporadic occurrence of these felspars often suggests that they may be derived elements (xenocrysts of Sollas) from the gabbro, and this suspicion is confirmed by microscopic examination. The crystals are sometimes curiously fissured, and contain little round inclusions with a peculiar disposition (often following pericline lamellæ) which may be of secondary origin [7471]. These scattered felspars are found in several cases in sheets which enclose abundant débris (xenoliths) of gabbro, e.g. on Sgùrr a Bhàsteir [7855], in Lota Corrie, and at several places on Druim nan Ramh; a circumstance which strengthens the supposition that they are of foreign origin.

Distinct from the preceding are the truly porphyritic rocks which are found, sometimes numerously, in certain parts of the mountains. The prevalent type in Coir' a' Chruidh, to the east of Gars-bheinn, is a *porphyritic dolerite*, without olivine [8710]. It has a compact dark grey ground, through which are scattered abundant small felspars and rarer black specks of augite. Thin slices show these felspars to be labradorite with carlsbad and albite twinning and some degree of zonary banding. They are clear, and contain large inclusions of the ground-mass. Sometimes they are aggregated, together with some augite, to form "glomero-porphyritic" groups. The ground-mass is of little felspar laths with subordinate augite, but abundant magnetite in minute crystals and granules. The specific gravity of a specimen from Coir' a' Chruidh is 2·907.

A common type on Gars-bheinn and its neighbour to the north, Sgùrr a' Choire Bheag (not named on the Ordnance map), has porphyritic felspars up to nearly ¼ inch in diameter with more or less rounded outlines. These are sometimes so numerous as to make up quite half of the rock [8711]. They are labradorite, with carlsbad, albite, and rarely pericline twinning, and contain round glass-inclusions. The ground-mass is rather fine-textured, and has the granulitic structure as a rule, consisting of little felspars, abundant augite, and some small crystal-grains of magnetite.

On Sgùrr Thuilm occur numerous sheets of a *porphyritic olivine-dolerite* [7856], not observed elsewhere. It is a dark grey, finely crystalline rock, showing abundant small felspars, usually less than ⅛ inch in length, with partially rounded shape. These in a thin slice are seen to contain irregular inclusions like altered glass-cavities. They have the usual carlsbad and albite twinning, and also very evident zonary banding between crossed nicols. The ground-mass is of the granulitic kind, and consists mainly of small lath-shaped felspars and light brown granules of augite. In addition to the slender felspars with albite twinning, ranging up to about $\frac{1}{50}$ inch in length, there are a few more shapeless crystals, zoned but not twinned, forming a later generation. Magnetite granules are fairly plentiful, and olivine is represented by green or yellow-green strongly pleochroic pseudomorphs, with straight extinction referred to a marked set of cleavage-traces, comparable with the mineral already noticed in the basaltic lavas and gabbros.

The prevalent type is, as we have stated, that of a dolerite without olivine. There are, however, in several parts of the mountains sheets of *olivine-dolerite* of a decidedly more basic type, in which that mineral is present in some abundance. Such sheets do not occur in great number, but they are often very prominent, owing to their superior durability and to the rusty weathered surface which they present. A strong sheet of this kind, with conspicuous felspars (not porphyritic) from ⅛ to ¼ inch in diameter, forms the two summits of Blath-bheinn. This is of coarse texture, resembling a gabbro in general appearance [8712]. Another red-weathering sheet is seen at the summit of Sgùrr Dearg, forming the perilous slope towards the east. This is, like the other, a dark rock with a tendency to spheroidal weathering, but it is not of such coarse texture [8836]. It has a specific gravity 2·96. Several small sheets, comparable in some respects with that of Blath-bheinn summit, crop out on the western face of Sgùrr na Stri [8713], and others might be enumerated from other localities.

The felspar of these rocks is of varieties more basic than labradorite. In the Sgùrr na Stri sheets it is bytownite, in the other examples mentioned anorthite. It always shows a strong zonary banding between crossed nicols, but this is only near the border of the crystal; our specification applies to the interior and principal portion. There is carlsbad and albite twinning, and in the coarser-textured rocks pericline also. Glass-inclusions are sometimes conspicuous by their relatively large size. Olivine is represented by abundant pseudomorphs of green serpentine, sometimes with pilitic hornblende. Magnetite occurs in various forms, and occasionally a few needles of apatite. The augite is of a pale brown colour in thin slices, with evident zonary growth, the central part being paler than the margin. In the Sgùrr Dearg sheet it has the ophitic habit, but the coarser rocks have a structure approximating more to the hypidiomorphic.

In the strong ledges which these sheets rich in olivine build, and usually too in the rusty colour which they assume on exposed faces, we find a resemblance to the peridotites to be described in the following chapter. Although the apparent similarity is dispelled by closer examination, we have seen that these sheets are still decidedly more basic than the majority. Regarding them as a distinct sub-group, we also find indications that they are of somewhat later intrusion than the general assemblage of inclined sheets. So far as has been observed, they intersect all other intrusions which they encounter, and are intersected by none, which cannot be predicated of the inclined sheets as a whole. It is therefore possible that these few sheets may be intermediate in age, as well as in composition, between the ordinary dolerite sheets and the succeeding ultrabasic intrusions.

The inclined sheets of basic rocks not infrequently carry *xenoliths*, though rarely in such quantity as is observed in certain groups of the basic dykes of the island. Instances occur on Sgùrr a' Bhàsteir, on Bidein Druim nan Ramh and the neighbouring part of the ridge, in Lota Corrie, Coir' a' Mhadaidh, and other parts of the Cuillins. The "Inaccessible Pinnacle" of Sgùrr Dearg rests on a sheet exceptionally full of xenoliths. In certain sheets also there are, as remarked above, quasi-porphyritic crystals of felspar which seem to be of foreign derivation. The phenomena are very similar to those already described in the dykes. In the present case, however, the enclosed débris is apparently always of gabbro, and may therefore have been picked up from the rocks which the sheets traverse. The xenoliths are often clustered together about particular places along the outcrop of the sheet in which they occur, and they are sometimes very unequally distributed in the width or thickness of the sheet, a circumstance also observed in some of the dykes. This is well seen in an inclined sheet, 6 feet thick, which crosses the southerly ridge of Sgùrr an Eidhne at about 1240 feet altitude. The sheet consists of two bands, the underlying one full of gabbro xenoliths, the overlying one quite free from them. There is, however, no sharp division between the two portions, and it cannot be doubted that the whole represents a single intrusion. The magma as intruded must have consisted of two portions, one with and the other without xenoliths, and the two portions have been drawn out into the sheet form without mingling except at their actual junction with one another.

z

CHAPTER XXII.

Later Peridotites.

In this chapter we have to describe certain ultrabasic rocks, and rocks bordering on the ultrabasic in composition, which are younger than the laccolitic bodies of plutonic peridotites described in Chapter VI. Some, at least, of them are very much younger, and are among the latest intrusions in Skye. The age of others cannot be determined with the same precision. We have indeed to recognise more than one group, and, since the differences are petrographical as well as geological, separate descriptions are necessary.

We take first the most numerous and striking group of later ultrabasic rocks, the *peridotite dykes of the Cuillins and of the Strathaird peninsula*. In the mountains these dykes are not uniformly distributed, but are found within the crescentic area indicated in Fig. 75, and are most abundant about the middle of that area. The most northerly example occurs about ¾ mile north of the summit of Sgùrr nan Gillean, upon the east side of the deep ravine which drains the corrie Am Basteir. Its bearing is a little E. of N. Another is seen not far to the west, in the burn which comes down from the east side of Meall Odhar. This has in places a curved course, but its general direction is towards N.N.W. Two others, bearing something W. of N.W., occur on Sgùrr Thuilm and in the upper part of Coir' a' Ghreadaidh, one of these crossing the main ridge close to the deep notch between Sgùrr a' Mhadaidh and Sgùrr a' Ghreadaidh. One on the slope below An Diallaid bears about W.N.W., and two or three on Sgùrr nan Gobhar W. by N. Some eight or nine dykes of this group are met with in a distance of about ¾ mile on Sgùrr na Banachdich and Sgùrr Dearg, this being the part of the range in which they are most frequent. Here their direction is about W.–E. Farther south the dykes become rarer, and their direction swings round still further. Two on Sgùrr nan Eag strike almost due S., and two on the west slope of Gars-bheinn a little E. of S. After this the dykes of this group are apparently wanting for a considerable interval, though peridotite dykes belonging to the earlier epoch are found entangled in the gabbro, as already noticed. Then, nearly four miles away, at Ben Cleat in the peninsula of Strathaird, three other dykes of precisely similar characters are seen, two near the top of that hill and one in the dip between it and the neighbouring Ben Meabost. These run in a S.S.E. direction.

From the varying strike of all the dykes, as stated, it is evident they have a regular *radiate disposition* about a centre in the interior of the gabbro area. The group as developed does not, however, comprise a complete circle but a little more than a semicircle; and this is situated towards the south-west, the quarter in which the peridotite laccolites were intruded at a much earlier epoch.

The ultrabasic dykes of the Cuillins cut all other rocks which they encounter, including the inclined basic sheets, and are therefore the youngest rocks in the mountain district. There can be no

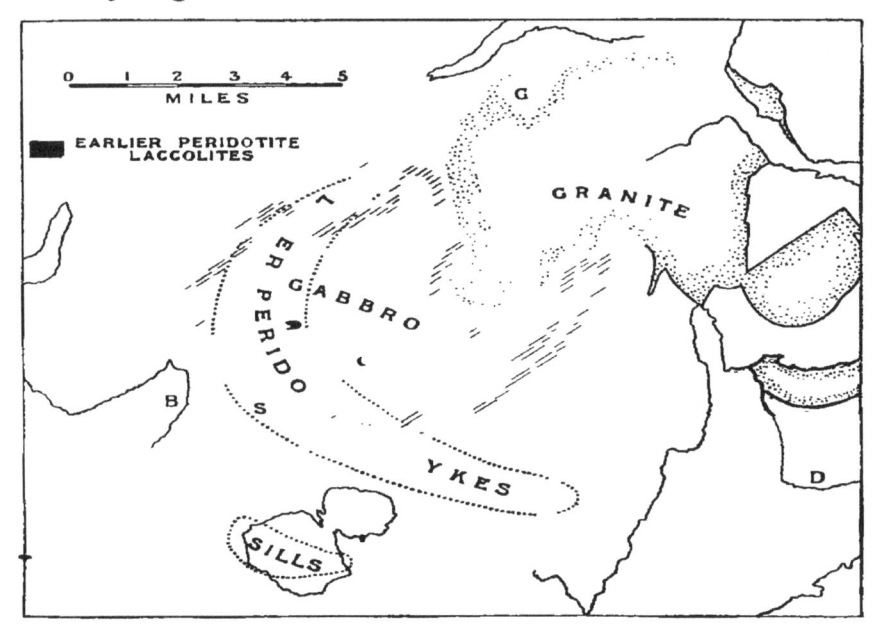

Fig. 75.—Sketch-Map to illustrate the distribution of the peridotites, older and younger. Scale, ¼ inch to a mile.

The older plutonic laccolites of the south-western Cuillins (with one in the Isle of Soay) are marked in black.

The large crescentic area enclosed by a dotted boundary embraces the younger peridotite dykes of the Cuillins and the Strathaird peninsula. The only peridotite dykes outside this area are a group on the coast of Loch Brittle at B, but peridotite sills occur in Soay as indicated. The boss of An Sgùman is situated at the point marked S, and the intrusions of Glamaig and Carn Dearg at G and D, on the prolongations of the two horns of the crescent.

reasonable doubt that the Ben Cleat dykes, in Strathaird, belong to the same well marked natural group, though direct evidence tells us only that they cut the basic sills of the great group, and are not themselves cut by any other dykes.

These dykes have very distinctive characters in the field, as well as petrographical peculiarities. Their direction, as we have seen, varies in different localities, in accordance with their radiate grouping about a centre. It is often noticeable, however, that they do not hold straight courses, being much more liable to irregularity in this respect than the basic dykes of the region. They often occur associated in twos and threes, and then may sometimes intersect one another (Sgùrr nan Gobhar) or run side by side in contact for a certain distance (An Diallaid). A dyke about 15 feet wide, conspicuous in the upper part of Coir' a' Ghreadaidh, is split along the middle by a parallel dyke, one foot in width, of similar type; and the latter has chilled selvages, indicating that, while the dykes of this group belong in a general sense to one epoch, they were not all strictly contemporaneous. These ultrabasic dykes range up to 30 or 40 feet in width, and most of them are wider than the generality of basic dykes; while they are further conspicuous from the fact that they always stand out in relief, as being more durable than the gabbro. Another feature whch catches the eye is the rusty weathered surface, which characterises these dykes in common with the older peridotites of the district.* Among other irregularities of behaviour, the dykes of this group pass in one or two instances into inclined sheets. This is seen on the summit ridges of Sgùrr na Banachdich and Sgùrr Dearg. In the latter case the sheet is seen to cut other peridotite dykes, which is sufficient to separate it sharply from the group of inclined basic sheets already described, with which it agrees in dip.

To the dykes of the Cuillins we must add, as appertaining with tolerable certainty to the same group of intrusions, certain *peridotite sills* intercalated among the Torridonian strata in the Isle of Soay. Specimens have been examined from four such sills, mapped by Mr Clough. The only direct evidence of the age of these intrusions is that they cut such other rocks as they encounter; but the close petrographical resemblance which they present to the Skye dykes leaves little doubt of their belonging to the same epoch. We have already seen that Soay contains an outlying member of the older group of plutonic peridotites. The sills seem to be somewhat irregular in their behaviour, and may enclose portions of the Torridonian grit partially vitrified in the manner already described in the basic sills of the same island [9985].

It is probable that peridotite dykes of late age are to be found at other centres of igneous activity in the Western Isles. In Rum Professor Judd, though not explicitly recognising two distinct epochs of ultrabasic intrusions, points out that the rocks of this family are not all of one age. He figures† a vein of peridotite intersecting and shifting one of olivine-gabbro, which itself cuts an olivine-rock (dunite). He apparently regards the later peridotite as of the nature of a "segregation" or "contemporaneous" vein, but its petrographical nature (as a porphyritic dunite) suggests a

---

* The name Sgùrr Dearg (Red Peak) is probably derived from the red-weathering dykes which are prominent objects on the slopes of the mountain; and Coireachan Ruadha, where the older peridotites give a similar effect, has presumably received its name from the same circumstance.

† *Quart. Journ. Geol. Soc.*, vol. xli., p. 359; 1885.

different view. We shall see that porphyritic dunite is a type represented among the later peridotite dykes of Skye.*

Petrographically our dykes and sills present several features of interest. They resemble in many respects the earlier peridotites of plutonic habit already described, but they differ from those just as the dolerite dykes differ from the gabbros, having distinctive characters which we may describe summarily as those of hypabyssal rocks. The hypabyssal representatives of the peridotites in general have received hitherto but little notice from petrographers, and the literature of the subject furnishes only scanty information concerning them. Classificatory schemes, such as that of Rosenbusch, make no provision for these rocks, and they have received as yet no collective name, the few which have been recorded having been included with their abyssal equivalents under the name peridotite, here adopted under protest. Although the differences between abyssal and hypabyssal types among the ultrabasic rocks are less conspicuous than among those of acid, intermediate, and basic composition, they are nevertheless sufficiently noteworthy and significant.

The dykes and sills consist of dense crystalline rocks usually of dark colour, with the great hardness and toughness already remarked in the plutonic peridotites. The dykes almost constantly enclose xenoliths up to three or four inches in diameter, but these may be very unevenly distributed, across the width as well as along the length of a dyke ; and in other respects also there may be very marked variations from place to place in a given dyke. The xenoliths, giving rise sometimes to projections, sometimes to depressions, on a weathered face, help to increase the characteristic roughness of the iron-stained surface.

The constituent minerals are the same as those of the rocks forming the earlier laccolites, but without the " schiller " structures and other peculiarities characteristic of deep-seated intrusions. The olivine only quite exceptionally contains the inclusions described on pp. 68, 69, and then only imperfectly developed, the dendritic growths of magnetite being too on a very minute scale [9233]. The augite is never diallagic, but shows only the ordinary prismatic cleavage, with a very pale brown colour in thin slices. The felspar seems to be always near anorthite in composition: it has albite twin-lamellation and, in the larger crystal-plates, occasional lamellæ answering to the pericline law. The mineral which plays the part of an iron-ore, forming little octahedral crystals, is probably always chromiferous. In the thinnest parts of the slices it becomes translucent or transparent, with a deep coffee-brown colour, and it may be conveniently spoken of as picotite.

These dyke-rocks exhibit a range of petrographical variety corresponding generally with that presented by the earlier plutonic

* Since this was written, the survey of Rum has shown that dykes of this group are only sparingly represented there. Two intersect the Torridon Sandstone of the south of the island, to the east of Papadil.

peridotites. The rare enstatite-anorthite type (norite), however, has not been met with here, and the olivine-anorthite-rock (troctolite) does not build separate dykes, though it is very common in the form of xenoliths. As seen in hand-specimens the dyke-rocks differ from those of the older laccolites in their generally finer texture and in the frequent coming in of the porphyritic structure. Where this latter is found, the phenocrysts are of olivine and sometimes augite.

One of the most beautiful rocks is that of a dyke crossing the ridge of Sgùrr na Banachdich not far north of the chief summit. It may be termed a porphyritic dunite, and exhibits abundant yellowish green crystals of olivine, $\frac{1}{4}$ to $\frac{1}{2}$ inch long, in a darker ground of medium grain. The microscope shows that the groundmass also consists essentially of olivine in a granular aggregate, enclosing little octahedra of picotite [8838]. A tendency to parallel orientation of the crystals in this dyke gives rise to a rough platy fracture. A specific gravity determination gave 3·065, but the density of the specimen has been somewhat lowered by serpentinisation.

As in the older peridotite group, so in these later dykes and sills the pure olivine-rock is not the prevalent type. Several of the rocks are augite-peridotites, consisting of olivine (predominant) and augite, with the usual picotite and only a very small proportion of felspar. The prominent dyke on the N.E. slope of An Diallaid, in Coir' a' Ghreadaidh, is a good example [9244]. In others, of the same general constitution, there is again a porphyritic development of olivine. Examples of this occur on Sgùrr Dearg and Ben Cleat [8716, 9245]. In some instances, while relatively large olivine crystals are seen in the hand-specimen and a thin slice shows that the finer grained portion of the rock consists largely of the same mineral, the separation into two distinct generations is somewhat obscured by the occurrence in addition of crystals or crystal-grains of intermediate size. This is the case in one of the sheets intruded in the Torridonian of Soay. It is a handsome rock of dark green colour with a specific gravity 3·16, and evidently consists mainly of olivine, partly in crystals up to $\frac{1}{4}$ inch in length. A thin slice [9979] shows that olivine, in larger and smaller elements, is the dominant constituent, but there are also a fair amount of pale brown augite and some anorthite, in addition to the usual picotite crystals. This rock, which may be styled a porphyritic peridotite, has a certain parallel orientation of its crystals which gives rise to a decided fissility, as in the porphyritic dunite of Sgùrr na Banachdich.

By the coming in of some felspar (anorthite) as an essential constituent, with some diminution in the proportion of olivine, we have a transition from peridotites in the narrower sense to picrites. This is illustrated, *e.g.*, in the dyke of Allt an Uchd Bhuidhe, N.E. of Meall Odhar, on the northern border of the Cuillins [9240]. Good examples of picrite dykes are found in Sgùrr Dearg and again between Ben Cleat and Ben Meabost in Strathaird [7480]. This latter picrite has a specific gravity 3·02. All these peridotites and picrites are rocks of medium to rather fine grain. They have suffered more serpentinous alteration than the plutonic peridotites, but some of these are still in a remarkably fresh state.

One rock, differing somewhat from all the rest, requires more particular notice. It forms a small dyke already mentioned as running along the middle of a larger one in the upper part of Coir' a' Ghreadaidh. The large dyke is a peridotite approaching picrite in composition, and offers no peculiarity [9241]. It is a prominent object, coming down from the northern end of Sgùrr a' Ghreadaidh, crossing the floor of the corrie, and running up to the ridge of Sgùrr Thuilm. The small dyke, resembling the larger in containing abundant xenoliths of troctolite, *etc.*, is of much finer texture, and microscopic examination shows at once that it is of less basic nature. Its central portion [9242] has indeed the appearance of a basalt or fine olivine-dolerite rather than a picrite. Felspar is abundant, in narrow rectangular sections about $\frac{1}{40}$ inch long, and it is apparently not true anorthite. The augite forms sub-ophitic grains, as in many doleritic rocks. Olivine, however, is very abundant, and the presence of picotite also affords a link with the ultrabasic rocks. Towards the margin of the dyke the rock becomes finer [9243], the felspars sinking to about $\frac{1}{100}$ inch in length, and the augite granules becoming very minute. At the same time olivine becomes comparatively scarce, though octahedra of picotite are still present, and there is also abundant magnetite in a finely granular form. Still nearer to the edge of the dyke the rock is very compact, with felspars only $\frac{1}{500}$ inch long. Here olivine is plentiful again, though represented by serpentinous pseudomorphs. These have the form of perfect crystals, $\frac{1}{1000}$ to $\frac{1}{500}$ inch in diameter, often hollow. The actual selvage of the dyke is a narrow crust of brown glass. If other dykes of this type exist in the Cuillins, they have not been distinguished in the course of our survey from ordinary basalt dykes, and this rather peculiar rock seems therefore to be the only representative of the very latest magma intruded in the Cuillin district. It partakes of the characteristics both of basic and of ultrabasic rocks, and has noteworthy points in common with some intrusive sheets in the Sleat district to be described below (Ben Aslak type). It is probable, however, that rocks on the borderland between basic and ultrabasic have been intruded at more than one epoch, some preceding the later peridotites.

Another interesting type is presented by a sill mapped by Mr Clough in the Isle of Soay, about $\frac{1}{4}$ mile S. by E. of Leac nan Faoileann. It is a dark, dense rock of specific gravity 3·14, showing very abundant fresh olivines in a fine-textured ground. These porphyritic olivines are about $\frac{1}{4}$ inch in length and have crystal outlines. In a thin slice [9980] it is seen that the mineral occurs also in a second generation, forming more or less rounded grains about $\frac{1}{200}$ inch in diameter. Octahedra of picotite are also present in two different sizes, and doubtless of two generations. The ground-mass consists mainly of innumerable slender rods of felspar with interstitial augite, the felspars having at any one spot a parallel or slightly divergent arrangement, as in many so-called variolites. This disposition of the felspars is not a flow-structure, for the direction of the rods often abuts upon the porphyritic olivines: the rods are indeed arranged in sub-parallel or sheaf-like fashion to form bundles, which lie in various directions and partly interlace with one another (Plate XXVI., Fig. 1). The rock is mineralogically a picrite, its special features being the porphyritic development of olivine, which it shares with other members of this group, and the quasi-variolitic structure of the ground-mass, which we have not elsewhere observed in decidedly ultrabasic rocks, though something similar is found in the Ben Aslak type of intrusions, to be noticed below.

We have next to notice an isolated occurrence of ultrabasic rock of plutonic habit, the *picrite boss of An Sgùman*, forming the hill of that name on the south-western border of the Cuillins. It thus occupies about the middle of the crescentic area within which the dykes already described are developed, and with this group of dykes we connect it, notwithstanding its different mode of occurrence. The mass is 1000 yards long from N. to S., with a curiously irregular shape in ground-plan. Its relations along its boundary seem to be everywhere of the abruptly transgressive kind, the junction-surface being approximately vertical. The rocks through which it cuts are the metamorphosed basalt lavas and, at its northern end, the gabbro; and it is thus clear that this intrusion cannot belong to the earlier peridotite group. The boss runs out into rather pointed terminations both north and south, while it sends out from near its northern end straight dykes towards the east and west. These dykes closely resemble those of the radiate group already described, and they have the proper direction. A group of similar dykes is seen again to the west, on the coast close to the mouth of Allt Coire Labain, the intervening ground being covered by peat. The evidence, though not conclusive, is decidedly in favour of referring this boss-formed intrusion to the same epoch as the radiate dykes. A rock of plutonic habit belonging to so late an epoch in the sequence of intrusions is, however, anomalous, and the *direct* evidence of its age only proves that it is later than the marginal part of the gabbro of the Cuillins.

The picrite of the An Sgùman boss is a dark crystalline rock of specific gravity 3·10, of somewhat coarser texture than the dykes and resembling more closely the prevalent type in the earlier laccolites. The rusty weathered surface is usually pitted, owing to the xenolithic structure which affects most of the mass; but this is not always very pronounced, since xenoliths and matrix are of very similar nature. A noteworthy point of difference from the laccolites, and doubtless connected with the different mode of occurrence, is the absence of any banded structure. A thin slice shows the component minerals to be opaque iron-ore, olivine, augite, and felspar, crystallised in order as named (Plate XXV., Fig. 4, A). The iron-ore, in little octahedra, has not been tested for the presence of chromium. The abundant olivine, in crystal-grains $\frac{1}{20}$ to $\frac{1}{10}$ inch in diameter, contains flat cavities with dendritic inclusions of magnetite of the familiar kind, and these are of unusually large dimensions, being ·002 to ·005 inch in length (Plate XXV., Fig. 4, B). The augite, of a faint green tint in thin section, is perhaps a chrome-diopside. It has neither the diallagic structure nor the basal striation (salite-structure), but contains bands of dark inclusions. The felspar is anorthite, in shapeless plates with carlsbad, albite, and rarely pericline twinning. As minor accessories there are a few scraps of brown hornblende and red-brown mica associated with the augite.

In addition to the ordinary xenolithic structure, which it shares with most of our peridotites, the An Sgùman boss contains in places along its margin xenoliths of a different kind, belonging not to the "cognate" but to the "accidental" denomination. They are pieces of the immediately contiguous amygdaloidal basalts, but in so advanced a stage of dissolution that everything but the amygdules themselves has been totally destroyed, these remaining in a metamorphosed state but still capable of identification [8724]. The phenomena are strictly comparable with those already described in the gabbro of the neighbouring part of the Cuillins, and must be taken as proving that this picrite, like the gabbro, has locally and to a very limited extent dissolved and incorporated portions of the contiguous basaltic lavas. (*Cf.* pp. 96, 97.)

Two other isolated intrusions, forming irregularly shaped masses, remain to be noticed. One of these is situated immediately below *Carn Dearg*, near Suishnish Point, between Lochs Slapin and Eishort. The epoch of its intrusion is doubtful. It occurs among Liassic strata just below a triple composite sill already noticed in Chapters XII. and XIII., and its behaviour certainly suggests that it is younger than the sill, which seems to have barred its upward passage. We may conclude that the intrusion belongs to some epoch during the phase of minor intrusions, but its relation to the later peridotite dykes of the Cuillins remains problematical.

References have been made to this locality, and diagrammatic sections drawn, by more than one author.* The hill, with the immediately adjacent country inland, is formed by a thick sill of granophyre underlain by a thinner one of basalt, the whole constituting, as stated, one of the peculiar composite intrusions in the Lias already described at length. Immediately beneath the basalt on the southern or seaward face of Carn Dearg appears the

---

* Macculloch, *Description of the Western Islands of Scotland*, vol. i., p. 384, and vol. iii., pl. xiv., fig. 5; 1819: Geikie, *Quart. Journ. Geol. Soc.*, vol. xiv., p. 17, and pl. i., fig. 4; 1857: Zirkel, *Zeits. deuts. geol. Ges.*, vol. xxiii., p. 83, and pl. iv., fig. 13; 1871: Geikie, *Trans. Roy. Soc. Edin.*, vol. xxxv., pp. 59, 60, fig. 14; 1888. In the earlier papers cited the hill is called Carn Nathrach.

picrite, a dark crystalline rock forming a broad rib in the face of the cliff. It runs down nearly vertically in a S.S.E. direction, and disappears under the waters of the sea-loch. Previous writers, differing on other points, have regarded this rib-like mass as passing into the basalt sill above, which was supposed to be a sheet-like expansion of it. The detailed mapping has led to a different conclusion (see Fig. 45), and shown that the picrite mass is quite independent of the other intrusions. The basalt, very different in composition and texture from the picrite, has probably come from a dyke forming part of the northern boundary of the composite sill, just west of Loch Fada, a dyke which served also at a slightly later time for the uprise of the granophyre magma. The picrite mass viewed from the south might be considered as of the nature of a dyke, though of an irregular kind, the width of the outcrop increasing upward. But on closer examination it is found to pass at the top into an irregular sheet, which, at first touching the overlying basalt, soon breaks away from it, and quickly dies out. This is clearly seen on the western slope of the hill (see Fig. 45, p. 211).

The rock, which we have termed picrite, is in reality of rather variable nature, ranging from a typical picrite to a variety approaching olivine-gabbro. The specific gravity is 2·98 to 3·01 in different specimens. Mr Baker analysed a portion comparatively poor in olivine, which yielded 43·86 per cent. of silica and 16·64 of magnesia (I.). This is petrographically an ophitic olivine-gabbro [8953]. The prevalent type is apparently a picrite very like those of the Cuillin laccolites, but without xenoliths. In thin slices of this olivine is seen to make up about one half of the bulk [7076, 7077]. The mineral has the dendritic magnetite inclusions already noticed in the plutonic rocks. Augite is abundant, showing in the slices a very faint yellowish tint and an

	I.	II.
SiO_2	43·86	44·06
Al_2O_3	10·63	12·16
Fe_2O_3	0·74	4·85
FeO	10·15	5·48
MgO	16·64	18·21
CaO	6·68	9·80
Na_2O } K_2O }	*	0·98
Ignition	1·51	3·80
	..	99·34
Specific gravity	3·00	..

I. Olivine-gabbro, verging on picrite [8953], below Carn Dearg, near Suishnish Point: anal. T. Baker. (*The alkalies are omitted, as requiring redetermination.)

II. Olivine-dolerite, verging on picrite [8952], Aodann Clach, Heast Road, about 2 miles S.E. of Broadford: anal. T. Baker.

incipient "schiller" structure. Felspar occurs interstitially in quite subordinate quantity, and the other constituents are a few grains of magnetite and ragged flakes of reddish brown mica. In the specimens sliced the rock shows considerable breccciation on a small scale.

It is probable, however, that the transitions observed at Carn Dearg from picrite to olivine-gabbro and olivine-diabase do not express completely the range of variation in this intrusion. There is reason to believe that the mass extends northward beneath the composite sill which forms the hill, and is continuous with the rock which emerges near Loch Fada and extends for some distance towards Allt Leth Slighe, as mapped by Mr Barrow and Mr Wedd. A sliced specimen from this supposed northward extension, between Glen Boreraig and Allt Leth Slighe, is a well characterised gabbro without olivine [10,078], and in the same neighbourhood this graduates into diabasic varieties. If the continuity through Carn Dearg can be assumed, there is thus a rather remarkable difference between the southern and northern parts of a single intrusive body.

The other isolated intrusion occurs a little west of the summit of *Glamaig*, near Sligachan. Like the Suishnish mass it is in one place like an irregular dyke and in another like an irregular sheet. It is not seen to cut any rock other than the basaltic lavas, and there is therefore no direct evidence as to its precise age. We may connect it conjecturally with the somewhat similar intrusion at Carn Dearg, near Suishnish. Like this it is rather variable in petrographical characters, but part of the mass consists of true peridotite. A slice of this [9254] shows what is essentially an olivine-augite rock, with only an occasional small patch of felspar, and with octahedra and grains of picotite. This rock is in great part transformed to serpentine, colourless, yellow, or light brown in the slice, with the usual copious separation of magnetite dust in strings and patches.

Finally we shall notice certain irregular sills or *intrusive sheets rich in olivine* occurring in the south-eastern part of Skye. Mr Clough has observed such rocks near Drochaid Lusa, $3\frac{1}{2}$ miles E.N.E. of Broadford, and near Kinloch, Allt Thuill, and Ben Aslak, all in the central part of the Sleat district. We may conveniently refer to these sheets as the *Ben Aslak type*. They are found in Torridonian strata far to the east of the true peridotites; but they have some of the features of ultrabasic rocks, and may perhaps be regarded as occupying an intermediate place between the basalts and the hypabyssal picrites. The data are insufficient to fix the epoch of intrusion of these sheets.

The rock of the Ben Aslak type of intrusion has rather peculiar characters. In hand-specimens it is seen to be crowded with crystal-grains of yellowish-green olivine, about $\frac{1}{5}$ inch long, set in a dark ground-mass of finely crystalline or microcrystalline texture. A fresh specimen from about a mile E. by N. of Kinloch gave the specific gravity 3·00. Thin slices show the rocks to consist of olivine to the extent of from one third to fully one half [8852-8854], the crystals sometimes showing good faces with the usual habit, but more frequently having a rounded shape. In a finer-textured variety of the rock there are in addition little granules of olivine about $\frac{1}{300}$ to $\frac{1}{100}$ inch in diameter, apparently of a later generation; but this point is not quite clear, and in one case at least a hand-specimen shows the conspicuous olivines becoming smaller towards the edge of the sheet. In decayed specimens from near Drochaid Lusa the olivine is replaced by pseudomorphs of carbonates [5077, 5078].

A prominent constituent in all the specimens is picotite, which is constantly the earliest product of crystallisation, and forms well shaped octahedra, occasionally as much as $\frac{1}{30}$ inch in diameter, though usually smaller. As a rule it is quite transparent in the slices, with the usual deep brown colour, but its appearance varies to a scarcely perceptible translucency in some cases. Apatite is not found. The felspar is in idiomorphic crystals, tabular parallel to the brachypinacoid, so as to give elongated rectangular sections. They range up to about $\frac{1}{50}$ inch in length, but in the finer-textured variety of the rock are smaller and of more slender shape. They show at any given point an approximate parallelism, consequent upon their tendency to lie tangentially to the olivine-grains or to be squeezed in between two grains of that mineral. The sections show twin-striation and some degree of zonary banding, but the felspar is evidently in the main anorthite, the extinction-angles in symmetrically cut sections ranging up to about 55°. The augite, which has been the latest mineral to crystallise, is very pale in thin slices, but always brown rather than green. In the less fine-textured rocks it enwraps and encloses the felspars in typical ophitic fashion, but in other slides it shows a more peculiar habit. Here it is still ophitic, in the sense that it forms patches moulded upon and enveloping the felspars; but each such patch consists of a number of elongated rods or plates, in contact with one another, with a sub-parallel or slightly divergent arrangement.

A rock petrographically referable to this group has been analysed by Mr Baker, and we are permitted to give the results here (column II. above). In a thin slice it shows very numerous little octahedral crystals, some of which have the translucency and strong brown colour of picotite. Olivine is very abundant, and the other constituents are anorthite and ophitic pale brown augite. We have no information as regards the mode of occurrence and geological relations of this rock, which was collected by Professor Lebour. It will be noticed that in chemical composition it compares rather closely with the specimen analysed from Carn Dearg.

It seems probable from Mr Clough's observations that sheets of the Ben Aslak type are not confined to the few localities from which specimens have been collected; and, further, that there are dykes of similar rock, very rich in olivine. One of these latter, with specific gravity 3·07, was noted near Isle Ornsay, about ⅓ mile W.S.W. of the pier. In this connection too may be mentioned a dyke of picrite, or of rock between picrite and olivine-dolerite, seen about a mile to the south-east of Drochaid Lusa. It is very near to one of the sills just described, but Mr Clough found no direct evidence of their connection. The rock consists of opaque octahedra (? magnetite), abundant grains of olivine up to ⅛ inch in length, pale yellowish brown augite in irregular grains, and felspar giving the extinction-angles of labradorite. The last is partly in roughly rectangular crystals with albite-lamellation, partly in more shapeless grains with less frequent twin-lamellæ but strong zonary banding — a feature common in many of the doleritic rocks [5076].

The collections of the Geological Survey from the Inner Hebrides contain a few other rocks lying on the border-line between the basic and the ultrabasic. There may perhaps be a distinct group of sills in the Jurassic intermediate in character between olivine-dolerite and picrite and graduating into both; but our information is not sufficient to lay down the relations of such occurrences to the great group of basic sills and to other groups of intrusions; and, so far as our knowledge goes, such rocks seem to belong less to Skye than to some of the neighbouring islands. It is perhaps more likely that in the thicker members of the great group of sills itself there may sometimes have been differentiation of the magma after intrusion, which in extreme cases was carried so far as to produce rocks almost or quite of ultrabasic composition. Professor Judd* found that the great sill, 500 feet thick, in the Shiant Isles, 12 miles N. of Skye, is in part of ordinary basic rock but in part of picrite and even peridotite; and Sir A. Geikie† has suggested that this is to be explained by differentiation under the action of gravity. A sill-rock from north of Meall Daimh in the Isle of Raasay, of specific gravity 2·92, is very rich in olivine, and in composition verges upon picrite. Like similar rocks from the Shiant Isles, it is characterised by a purplish brown augite with distinct pleochroism and an imperfect "hour-glass" structure [6774]. An augite with these characters is well known in some nepheline-dolerites and teschenites, and some of the sills outside Skye seem to have affinities with these rocks. Nepheline has been recorded by Heddle‡ in the great sill of the Shiant Isles, and at least one sill of an analcime-diabase approaching teschenite occurs in the south of Arran.§

* *Quart. Journ. Geol. Soc.*, vol. xli., pp. 393, 394 ; 1885.
† *Ancient Volcanoes of Great Britain*, vol. ii., pp. 307-310 ; 1897.
‡ *Mineralogy of Scotland*, vol. ii., p. 46 ; 1901.
§ Corstorphine, *Tsch. Min. Petr. Mitth.* (N.S.), vol. xiv., p. 464 ; 1895.

Trachyte and Trachy-Andesite Dykes.

CHAPTER XXIII.

Trachyte and Trachy-Andesite Dykes.

The present chapter and the succeeding one will be devoted to an account of the trachytes, andesites, and pitchstones (with some rocks probably devitrified and otherwise altered pitchstones) which are found in the form of dykes, usually of no great size, at numerous localities in our area. Although our detailed survey has not embraced the whole of Skye, it may be taken as probable that these rocks belong especially to the south-eastern portion of the island. The principal known exception to this statement is made by a separate group of trachyte dykes in the Drynoch neighbourhood. We assign all the rocks, on such evidence as is obtainable, to some of the very latest stages of igneous activity in the region. Their relation in point of age to the latest intrusions of the Cuillins cannot be determined, but they seem to be the youngest rocks in their own area at least. Another reason for discussing together these various rocks, of which the extreme types differ widely, is that they seem to be genetically connected. More accurately, some of the andesites stand in close relation with the trachytes, and are linked with them by transitional varieties, while other andesites are apparently intimately related to the pitchstones. Trachytes, trachy-andesites, andesites, and pitchstones will be described in order in this and the next following chapters.

We notice first a group of *trachyte dykes* found in the district to the N.N.W. of the Cuillins, and especially on the moorlands about the head of Loch Harport. They occur indeed from near the upper part of Glen Brittle to Glen Vidigill at least, the ground farther to the N.N.W. not having been surveyed. The area of distribution, so far as it has been proved, is an oval with a long axis of about 6½ miles, following as usual the direction of the bearing of the dykes themselves. Drynoch is situated near the centre of the oval, and we may conveniently refer to these dykes as the *Drynoch group* (see Fig. 76).

Within this area trachytic dykes are fairly numerous, though always outnumbered by those of basic composition. They are mostly of moderate width, the largest being about 15 feet across, and they follow courses which, while in the main straight and parallel, show some deviations and curvature on a small scale. They usually form salient features, and the larger ones are very conspicuous objects: a good example is the prominent dyke which comes down to the high-road near the bridge north of Drynoch

Lodge. The most striking feature of these dykes in the field is a very pronounced fissile structure, brought out especially by weathering, and giving the rock the appearance of a shale. In the narrower dykes this structure runs parallel with the walls, but in the wider ones, and especially in their interior, it is often sinuous and irregular. It depends upon a flow-structure in the rocks.

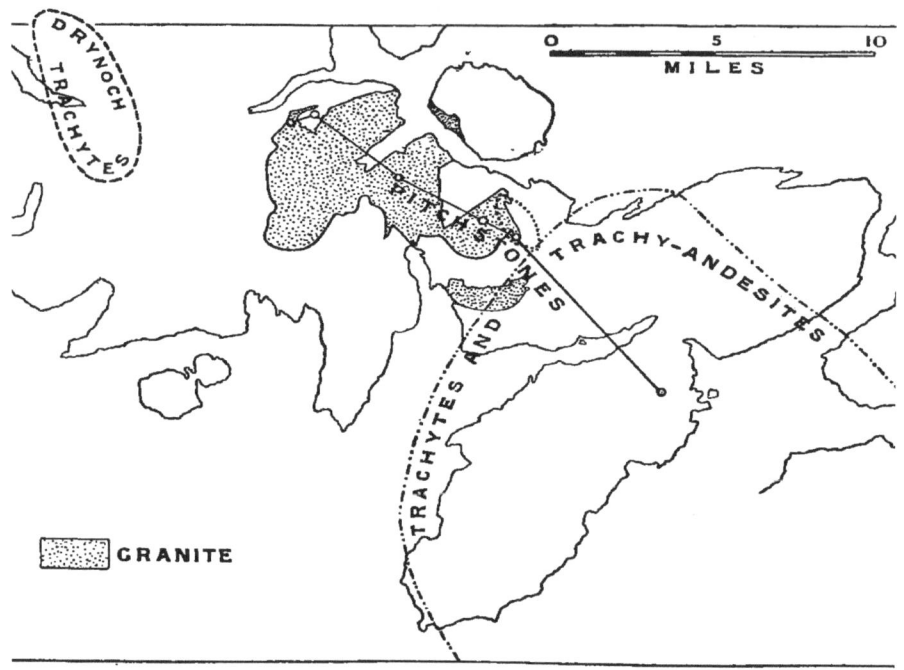

FIG. 76.—Sketch-Map to show the distribution of some trachytic and other dykes.
 (a.) The broken line encloses the oval area of distribution of the Drynoch group of trachytes.
 (b.) The line made up of dots and dashes marks the limits of distribution in Skye of the trachytic and allied dykes of Sleat and the Broadford district.
 (c.) The small circles connected by straight lines indicate the known localities of acid pitchstone dykes.
 (d.) The small oval enclosed by the dotted line shows the area affected by the Coirechatachan type of dykes, probably altered pitchstones. It falls in the middle of the narrow strip of country including the occurrences under (c).

Although, as remarked, these trachytic dykes stand out in relief from the basaltic lavas which they intersect, they have almost always suffered very considerably from atmospheric weathering, and it is difficult to procure specimens which can be regarded as representing the fresh rock. The best example found is one of the dykes in the burn by the old crofts of Satran, near Drynoch. The least altered portions of the rock are in the form of nodular masses, analogous to the spheroids in many basic rocks, but having a flat shape in accordance with the fissile structure already noticed. The freshest specimens have a very dark grey colour, but average examples are pale and often show a rusty staining connected with the platy fracture. The rocks are of close texture and dull aspect, and are non-porphyritic. A fresh example gave the specific gravity 2·72, but the usual figures are lower—2·66, 2·64, or even 2·62—the density being notably lowered by weathering.

Under the microscope these trachytes are seen to consist essentially of closely packed little felspar crystals, usually $\frac{1}{200}$ inch or less in length, giving narrow sections with well marked parallel arrangement due to flow. They give sensibly straight extinction. Doubtless both orthoclase and oligoclase are represented, but it is not easy to judge the relative proportions of the two. That the potash-felspar is abundant, if not actually predominant, appears from the low density of the rocks, taking into account the considerable amount of heavier substances present, and the name trachyte may probably be used without impropriety. When freshest, the rocks are found to contain minute granules of augite, though always in subordinate quantity [9812]. In other slides minute clotted patches of ferruginous matter, perhaps limonite, may represent destroyed augite. Little octahedra of magnetite are always present and in quantity more than equal to the ferro-magnesian element. There are sometimes a few scattered small flakes of biotite, more or less affected by resorption, as is usual in trachytes [7857]. Although the rocks are never conspicuously porphyritic, there may be a few small felspar crystals of an earlier generation, from $\frac{1}{40}$ to $\frac{1}{20}$ inch in diameter, consisting of orthoclase and less commonly oligoclase. These trachytes differ from the "mugearites" described in Chapter XV. chiefly in the absence of olivine, and there is possibly a relation between the two groups.

We pass on to describe an interesting group of dykes which have been carefully studied in the field by Mr Clough. In the course of mapping the rocks have been provisionally designated trachytes, and we shall retain this name for them as a group, although some of them have affinities also with the andesitic family as commonly understood. In Skye these dykes occur chiefly in the Sleat district, being found at intervals from the line of the Kylerhea high-road to within about a mile of the Point of Sleat, though in much less number than the basic dykes. They are more abundant than usual in the neighbourhood of Kinloch: in Allt Cùl Airidh Lagain, a little below the road, three or four are found in a length of 70 or 80 yards, while another occurs rather more than two-thirds of a mile above the road. There are also a number of dykes of this group about Heast and Ben Suardal, but they do not extend farther N.W. than Broadford. Mr Clough, who has supplied this information, has found similar dykes on the other side of the Sound of Sleat and far up Loch Hourn; and he has also recorded them in the Cowal district of Argyllshire.* It thus appears (*see* sketch-map, Fig. 76) that the group as a whole belongs less to Skye than to the mainland of Scotland, where it has a wide distribution. The late age of all these dykes seems to be established by the fact that, while they have been observed in a number of cases to intersect basic dykes, the converse relation has been noticed in only a single instance. For convenience of reference we shall speak of these rocks as the *Broadford and Sleat group*

The dykes are mostly of small or moderate width, and have the same N.W. or N.N.W. bearing as the basic dykes of the district. They are usually quite fine-textured or compact rocks, with or without scattered glassy-looking felspars about ¼ inch long, and showing no other mineral to the eye except an occasional small scale of brown mica. The ground-mass has a grey colour, which may become brown by weathering. Little calcite amygdules are very often seen. The most interesting feature of the dykes as seen in the field is the spherulitic or quasi-spherulitic structure which they very generally exhibit in their marginal portions. On this subject Mr Clough has supplied the following notes. It should be premised that what appears to the eye a pronounced spherulitic structure, and is so termed here, is usually resolved under the microscope into a rather imperfect or rudimentary type of radiate growth.

"The marginal portions of the granophyre, felsite, acid pitchstone, and trachyte dykes often contain conspicuous spherulitic structures, and so also do the corresponding parts of a few of the basaltic dykes. The spherulitic portions of these dykes display many characters in common, and these may be described together.

"Spherulitic bodies are as a rule confined to the portions of the dykes which are within eight or nine inches of the sides. They are sometimes isolated and approximately spherical in shape, but more usually they form rudely spherical or polygonal bodies which are in such close conjunction, or union, at their ends that they form structures resembling *rods or strings of beads*. The average diameters of the isolated spherulites and the greatest breadths of the spherulitic rods are found to be much the same in any dyke so long as we confine our attention to one thin layer of rock which is parallel to the sides, but in layers at different distances the dimensions vary greatly. Six or eight inches off the side the coalesced spherulites are often the size of a pea, but in layers nearer the sides they are less, and within an inch or two of the side they are perhaps less than mustard seeds, and the rod-like bodies appear almost like threads. On surfaces parallel to the dyke-side the rods are generally in close juxtaposition, so that the whole surface is covered with them. On such surfaces they are generally straight and parallel, but on larger surfaces slight alterations, and sometimes

* See Geikie, *Ancient Volcanoes of Great Britain*, vol, ii., p. 139; 1897: Clough in *Geology of Cowal, (Mem. Geol. Sur. Scot.)* pp. 166-171; 1897.

sharp twists of direction, are observed, all the rods appearing to bend at the same axial planes of folding.

"The rods on one surface parallel to the dyke-side are not necessarily parallel to the rods on the adjoining surfaces nearer to or further off the side. They are, it is supposed, generally parallel, but several instances have been noticed in which the directions of the rods on one surface differ from those on a closely adjoining surface by as much as 30° or 40°. This is well seen in a trachyte dyke that crosses Allt Réidh Ghlais nearly 400 yards below the road.

"In the spherulitic portions of many of the dykes amygdules of a greatly elongated form occur. They are sometimes an inch or two long, though their diameters are not more than $\frac{1}{40}$ inch. It has been noticed in a good many places that the long axes of the amygdules are parallel to the spherulitic rods in the same portions of the dyke, and in no case have they been seen to be different. It seems probable therefore that the rods are parallel to a direction of flow of the molten magma in which they were formed. To that supposition objection may perhaps be made on the ground that, as already stated, the directions of the rods on closely adjoining surfaces are not always the same. It seems quite possible, however, that the flow movements were of a much more complicated order than would at first seem probable, and that the direction of flow in one part, at a certain distance from the side, may have been different from the direction a little further from the side. Let us suppose, for instance, that in a certain layer near and parallel to the dyke-side the direction of flow immediately preceding the period of consolidation of that layer was in a certain direction: that layer is consolidated and the direction of the latest flow is fixed and still discernible: after this consolidation a short period of time may elapse before another layer parallel to but a little further off the side consolidates, and in this period the direction of flow has possibly altered so as to be no longer parallel to the former direction.

"Whether, however, the spherulitic rods are indications of directions of flow or not it seems desirable to observe their directions in various localities. They are not often vertical. They are apparently more often horizontal than vertical. Most commonly they are diagonal, and perhaps on the average about half way between horizontal and vertical. When diagonal, and the dykes are striking in their usual N.W. or N.N.W. direction, the lower ends of the rods are in some localities the N.W. ends, and in others the S.E. We cannot say that the former case is more frequent than the latter.

"It seems possible that the materials of some dykes have travelled for great distances in a direction not very far from horizontal from some source of comparatively limited extent near one end of the dyke outcrop. On this supposition we can understand how dykes may retain uniform characters for long distances, and it seems unnecessary to postulate a deep-seated source lying almost vertically below the whole extent of their outcrop.

" Perhaps the simplest way to show the directions of the rods is to draw a rectangle to represent the exposure of the dyke in which the rods are observed. The two long sides of the figure represent horizontal lines and the side on the observer's left hand represents the N.W. side of the exposure. Lines are then drawn to represent the rods (see Fig. 77). In the list accompanying the figure the localities and lithological varieties of the dykes to which the diagrams in the figure refer are stated, and the cases in which the amygdules are known to be elongated parallel to the rods are indicated. The diagrams marked by '*a*' refer to the dyke situated furthest N.E.; the diagram marked by '*b*' refers to the dyke coming next to this on the S.W. side, and so on. In case of exposures which belong perhaps to one dyke at different parts of its course the diagram referring to the exposure furthest N.W. is given first, and it is joined by a bracket to the diagrams referring to the other exposures.*

" Some dykes which show no spherulites yet contain conspicuously elongated amygdules. In the marginal portions the directions of elongation always lie in planes which are approximately parallel to the adjacent side, but in different localities they are inclined at different angles to the horizon, just as the amygdules in the spherulitic dykes are.

"In the trachyte dyke in Allt Réidh Ghlais the spherulitic rods are not all so close together as usual. Sometimes two adjacent rods gradually diverge, but after running a certain distance and bending about a little they come together again. In the spaces between two rods we cannot always be sure that there are any spherulitic forms, but in other places there are obscure forms, and some of these are arranged in lines which are almost at right angles to the enclosing rods.

"In some of the dykes with elongated amygdules and spherulitic rods there are also phenocrysts of felspar, but these phenocrysts sometimes have their long axes at a considerable angle to the rods and amygdules. This is well seen in the pitchstone dyke of Allt Duisdale, in which there are a number of phenocrysts of sanidine, and in the trachyte dyke in Allt Cùl Airidh Lagain nearly three-quarters of a mile above the road. In the latter dyke the amygdules have a decided tendency to bend round the sides of the phenocrysts.

" As already stated, the amygdules in the interiors of most of the dykes are generally larger than those at the sides. In most of the trachyte dykes those in the interior are also much less elongate than those at the sides. In the basaltic dykes elongate amygdules are rare in all parts. Perhaps in these dykes it was unusual for there to be any further flow movement in the molten magma after the amygdules were formed.

"In the interiors of some of the trachyte dykes the forms of the amygdules indicate directions of flow which make considerable

* The diagrams given in the figure are only a part of those drawn in the field.

392   *Rodded Structure in Dykes.*

angles with the sides. In a thin vertical dyke, four or five feet thick, in Ob Lusa, in a steep exposure crossing the dyke almost at right angles, the amygdules near the centre give nearly circular sections. A little way on either side of the centre they give oval

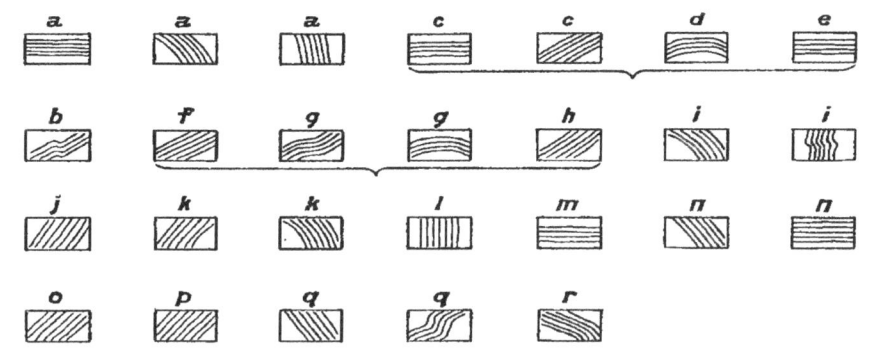

FIG. 77.—Diagram to show the varying inclination of the "rodding" in the dykes of the Broadford and Sleat districts. Explanation in the text. *Del.* C. T. C.

a. Trachyte. Allt Mòr, about two miles S.E. of Drochaid Lusa. In amygdules also.
b. Trachyte. Burn about a mile W. of the top of An Sgulan, Kinloch.
c. Trachyte. Allt Cùl Airidh Lagain, nearly three-quarters of a mile above the road.
d. Trachyte. Allt Réidhe Ghlais, nearly three-quarters of a mile above the road. In amygdules also.
e. Trachyte. Rather more than half a mile S.E. of Broadford Bridge.
f. Trachyte. Allt Cùl Airidh Lagain. Nearly a third of a mile below the road. In amygdules also.
g. Trachyte. Allt à Choin, about 200 yards slightly E. of N. of Kinloch. In amygdules also.
h. Trachyte. Near the foot of Allt Lochan Sgeir, near Kinloch. In amygdules also.
i. Felsite. Burn E. of Cnoc na Cubhaige, Broadford.
j. Felsite. Burn about half a mile slightly E. of S. of Cnoc na Cubhaige.
k. Trachyte. About two-thirds of a mile E.N.E. of Ben Suardal.
l. Trachyte. Coast, about 200 yards E.N.E. of Ardnameacan, Loch na Dal. In amygdules also.
m. Acid Pitchstone. Allt Duisdale, nearly 1500 yards above the road. In amygdules also.
n. Dyke of doubtful character, with oligoclase, hornblende, and biotite [6855]. Rather more than half a mile S. of Cnoc a' Chàise Mor, Knock. In amygdules also.
o. Basaltic : S.G. 2.87. Rudha Dubh Ard, near Ord.
p. Basaltic. Coast about 330 yards N.E. of Inver Aulavaig.
q. Trachyte. Coast, nearly half a mile S.S.E. of Ostaig House. In amygdules also.
r. Trachyte. Nearly a mile E.S.E. of Meall Buidhe (S.W. of Armadale). In amygdules also.

sections, and these become more elongated the further from the centre they are. The long axes of the sections incline downward from the centre towards the side and become steeper the neare they are to the side. Close to the side they are parallel to it and approximately vertical.

"In a dyke in Allt Cùl Airidh Lagain, also, rather less than a third of a mile below the road, vertical exposures across the central part of the dyke show that the long axes of the sections of the amygdules incline downward from the centre towards either side, and become steeper as the sides are approached.

"In dykes in Allt a' Choin, about a quarter of a mile N.N.E. and 300 yards slightly E. of N. of Kinloch, the long axes of the sections of the amygdules in the interior parts have a tendency to dip N.E. In the dyke in Allt Réidh Ghlais the long axes seen in a section at right angles to the strike of the dyke are in one place near the centre nearly horizontal: in other places only a few inches off the S.W. side they dip S.W." (C. T. Clough.)

Evidences of the inclined or even horizontal direction of flow in dykes, as described by Mr Clough, have not often been observed in the country farther west and north, for the reason that the types of dykes most favourable for such observations are there wanting. An exception must be made, however, for the Coirechatachan group of dykes, which often show the beaded lines or rods described above, and always with a considerable inclination to the vertical. It is to be noticed too that the inclination of the rodding varies in some instances rapidly as we pass along the dyke (Fig. 78). This has

FIG. 78.—Dyke with "rodded" structure, near the river and foot-path, E. of Coire-chatachan, near Broadford. The figure shows the southerly face of the dyke as exposed, with the rodding, the inclination of which to the horizon changes in a length of five yards from 8° to 52°.

already been remarked in the well-known "Beal dyke," near Portree, where the structure is exhibited in the tachylytic selvage of a basic dyke allied to the mugearite type (p. 337).

Petrographically the trachytes and trachy-andesites of Sleat and the Broadford district, as represented by Mr Clough's specimens, show some range of variety. Most of them, however, fall under one fairly marked type. These are rocks of specific gravity 2·59 to 2·64, sometimes with a few scattered felspar phenocrysts. When these occur they are either sanidine or more commonly a plagioclase felspar: in one case a crystal with albite-lamellation gave extinction-angles 24° and 28° from the twin-line, indicating some variety more basic than andesine. The general mass of the rock always consists essentially of a plexus of little felspar crystals with other minerals in smaller quantity. The characteristic ferromagnesian silicate is brown biotite, which in the form of very numerous minute flakes is constantly found in all the fresher rocks.

In some other cases greenish and yellowish ferruginous pseudomorphs with finely granular magnetite may represent biotite; though more probably vanished hornblende, since these and fresh biotite sometimes occur together and are of somewhat different habits. Minute octahedra and skeletons of magnetite are constantly found and often very numerous; while another constant constituent is apatite, which is relatively abundant in very fine needles. Exceptionally there is a small amount of interstitial quartz.

The felspars which make up the bulk of the rock are partly orthoclase, partly oligoclase. This can be directly verified in the less fine-textured rocks, and in the others may be inferred from the low density of the rocks—assuming, what seems to be true with few exceptions, that there is no glassy residue. The crystals vary in length, in different examples, from about $\frac{1}{50}$ to $\frac{1}{200}$ inch or less. When of relatively large size, they have an elongated rectangular shape, the monoclinic felspar in simple crystals or carlsbad twins, and the triclinic showing both carlsbad and albite twinning. When the crystals are smaller, they are of very slender shape, and the distinctive characters are lost. There is constantly a tendency to grouping in sub-parallel bundles and in fan-like and sheaf-like forms, and this is more pronounced in proportion as the texture of the rock is finer (Plate XXVII., Fig. 1). These imperfectly radiating structures compare rather with the "variolitic" structures of some andesitic and basaltic rocks than with the true spherulites of acid rocks. They closely resemble, for instance, what is seen in certain narrow dykes and veins of variolitic andesite on Carrock Fell, Cumberland.*

These remarks apply more particularly to the interior portion of a dyke: at the edge the micro-structure may present some modification, with a closer approximation to a true spherulitic structure.

Some dykes belonging to this group, more especially in the Broadford neighbourhood, differ from the preceding in being more decidedly of orthoclastic composition, and these have an ordinary trachytic structure with little or no tendency to radiate growths. A good example is a dyke from rather more than ½ mile N.N.E. of the summit or Ben Suardal [9569]. It is a fine-grained cream-coloured rock studded with little brown dots, and shows a certain parallel structure parallel to the walls of the dyke, an arrangement shared by the few small porphyritic felspars. The specific gravity of the somewhat weathered rock is only 2·50. A thin slice is seen to consist essentially of a plexus of minute felspars of rod-like appearance in section, doubtless mostly if not wholly orthoclase. The brown dots referred to are little patches of limonite, mostly shapeless but in places apparently pseudomorphs after biotite.

On the other hand, we find, among dykes which we are not able to separate as a whole from the same group, rocks of decidedly andesitic character. This is shown by oligoclase, or some variety

* Harker, *Geol. Mag.*, 1894, pp. 551-553.

near oligoclase, becoming the dominant or the sole felspathic element, while augite appears usually instead of biotite, and magnetite becomes more abundant. With these differences there is of course an increased density. Such rocks may or may not show spherulitic structures and "rodding" on the edge of the dyke. A typical example of these occurrences, which mineralogically approach augite-andesites, is a dyke from rather more than $\frac{1}{5}$ mile S.W. of the summit of Ben Suardal. It is a close-grained grey rock with little scattered black specks of augite, and has the specific gravity 2·75. In a slice [6748] the augite is nearly colourless, building scattered imperfect crystals which sometimes show an hour-glass structure between crossed nicols. Magnetite is quite abundant in irregular crystal-grains of early separation. The bulk of the rock consists of little imperfect prisms of felspar, apparently oligoclase, sometimes grouped in bundles. A similar rock, of specific gravity 2·72, forms a dyke $\frac{1}{4}$ mile S. by W. of Suardal Farm [9574], and other dykes probably of like nature are found in the district.

Although glassy varieties are exceptional among dykes referable to this group, they are not wholly wanting. Here probably we may place a rock collected by Mr Clough in the Isle of Soay [9988]. It represents the vitreous portion of a spherulitic dyke 1 foot in width, and is a dark rock of specific gravity 2·50, with resinous lustre. It is apparently a pitchstone corresponding in composition with an andesite or a trachy-andesite. In a thin slice it shows a much deeper brown colour than is seen in the acid pitchstones, though not so deep as in the tachylytes. Different depths of colour are related to secondary changes, as is proved by their distribution with reference to a system of curved perlitic cracks. In the glassy matrix there are certain paler spots, $\frac{1}{50}$ to $\frac{1}{20}$ inch in diameter, of the nature of spherulites. These depolarise feebly, and show a rough radiate disposition, but without distinct fibrous structure.

The last-mentioned occurrence is quite outside the area of distribution which we have laid down above for the trachy-andesite dykes of Skye, and it is possible that we have to do here with a distinct group or sub-group. We have already seen some indication of this in the minor ultrabasic intrusions, with the further point of resemblance that the Soay occurrences assume the sill instead of the dyke form. Another of Mr Clough's specimens from Soay, taken from a two-inch sheet exposed on the south coast of the island, is a trachyte, but of a type somewhat different from those of Broadford, etc. It is a dull grey, compact-looking rock, enclosing grouped phenocrysts of orthoclase and some oligoclase, with a few pseudomorphs perhaps representing augite. The ground-mass is composed essentially of little felspar microlites, with sensibly straight extinction, showing no tendency to radiate arrangement.

It is unfortunate that we have no chemical analyses of any of the above rocks, which might throw light upon their nature and affinities. We quote, however, the analysis (A) of one of the trachyte dykes of the Cowal district, which may be taken as very similar to some of the Broadford and Sleat group; also that of the well-known vitreous rock of the Sgùrr of Eigg (B), which will be referred to later.

	A.	B.
SiO_2	56·4	65·81
Al_2O_3	19·0	14·01
Fe_2O_3	3·5	4·43
FeO	4·8	not det.
MgO	1·5	0·89
CaO	2·6	2·01
Na_2O	4 5	4·15
K_2O	5·0	6·08
Ignition	2·6	2·70
	99·9	100·08
Specific gravity	2·48	[2·42]

A. Trachyte, dyke, Dunans, near head of Glendaruel, Argyllshire [3452]: anal. J. H. Player, Geikie's *Ancient Volcanoes of Great Britain*, vol. ii., p. 139; 1897: also *Geology of Cowal* (*Mem Geol. Sur. Scot.*), p. 170; 1897.

B. Subacid Pitchstone, Sgùrr of Eigg: anal. Barker North, *Quart Journ. Geol. Soc.*, vol. xlvi., p. 379: 1890. [Specific gravity taken from another specimen.]

Among the most interesting of the more aberrant types found within the area of distribution of the Sleat trachytes, and presumably to be attached to that group, are certain rocks which seem to have close affinities with the ceratophyres of certain authors. One such rock is noted by Mr Clough as forming perhaps the broadest and most conspicuous dyke of this group. It comes to the coast nearly a mile N.N.E. of Tarskavaig Point. "It is perhaps ten yards wide, and in a S.E. direction makes an almost continuous ridge for about a mile: soon after this it ceases to be traceable in its old line, but about forty yards N.E. of the apparent end another dyke of similar character appears and is traceable for more than a mile in a S.S.E. direction, crossing Gillean Burn in three different places. The two dykes in the burn between half a mile and two thirds of a mile slightly W. of N. of the top of Cnoc an Sgùmain near Armadale, are perhaps continuations of this."—(C. T. C.)

A specimen taken to the west of Loch Gauscavaig is a fresh rock of specific gravity 2·61, with little glassy-looking porphyritic felspars up to $\frac{1}{8}$ inch in length. In a thin slice [7370] these felspars seem at first sight to be simple crystals and carlsbad twins; but there are little patches in them which show a close twin-lamellation with very low extinction-angles, and elsewhere there are vague indications of a like intergrowth on a more minute scale. It seems probable therefore that we have to deal here with crystals of micro perthite and cryptoperthite (anorthoclase of some authors). These felspars occur only rather sparingly, and more rarely there is phenocryst of light brown augite $\frac{1}{20}$ inch long. The general mass of the rock (Plate XXVI., Fig. 2) is of medium texture or, in comparison with the trachytes, coarse. It consists mainly of rectangular felspars, up to about $\frac{1}{30}$ inch in length and of rather stout build. Most of them are not to be distinguished from sanidine, in simple crystals or carlsbad twins; but in places there are obscure indications of a very minute twin-lamellation, and it is probable that these felspars are of the same nature as the phenocrysts. There are rather abundant imperfect crystals and grains of augite, up to $\frac{1}{50}$ inch, and a little magnetite, which is moulded on the felspar crystals.

The dykes, mentioned above, to the north of Cnoc an Sgùmain, in a branch of the Glen Meadhonach river, are also of peculiar nature. The more north-westerly of the two is in its interior a rather finely crystalline rock of specific gravity 2·60, having something of the dark look of a dolerite. It encloses little glassy-looking felspars of stout build, to over $\frac{1}{8}$ inch in diameter. In a thin slice [6851] these are seen to be a good deal fissured, and to contain inclusions of the ground-mass. They show in places the fibrous look, the rather patchy extinction, and the vague appearance of very fine lamellation which suggest cryptoperthite. Some smaller crystals of augite and a few magnetite grains also belong to the earlier stage of crystallisation, and there is the abundance of minute needles of apatite which we have noted as one of the characteristics of the Sleat trachytes. The ground-mass is mainly an aggregate of roughly rectangular but interlacing crystals of felspar; but has a peculiar appearance owing to very abundant little rods and needles of augite, partly decomposed, the smaller ones arranged in parallel groups or in sheaf-like bundles (Plate XXVI., Fig. 3). Many of the felspars of the ground-mass show fine twin-lamellation, but often this is visible only in portions of the crystals.

This dyke takes on a much finer texture at its margin. A specimen taken an inch or two from the edge gave the specific gravity 2·57. In a thin slice [6850] the ground-mass is much obscured by alteration, but it seems probable that a glassy base is or has been present, and crowded delicate fibres of felspar are discernible in places. The specimen is a dull grey compact rock with the usual scattered fresh felspars. The other dyke at the same locality has a selvage of black, more or less vitreous, rock 2 inches thick. It has a pitchy lustre, encloses yellowish felspar phenocrysts up to $\frac{1}{4}$ inch in length, and gave a specific gravity 2·55 to 2·57. In a thin slice [6849] the felspars show no conspicuous twin-lamellation, but have, as before, in places a faintly defined striated appearance suggestive of a microperthitic intergrowth. Both these and an occasional augite crystal enclose patches of the ground-mass. There are in addition numerous microlites of felspar and augite and a few granules of magnetite. The ground-mass consists of a brown glass crowded with densely packed bundles of slender felspar fibres. Towards the margin these bundles take on a general parallelism and become more separated from the glass, which appears in yellowish strings or streaks. This rock resembles in many respects those of the Sgùrr of Eigg and Hysgeir, though it is perhaps somewhat more basic in composition. There is considerable similarity between the porphyritic felspars of the several rocks.* An analysis of the Sgùrr of Eigg rock is quoted above (B).

One dyke bearing a certain resemblance to the above has been met with far outside the area of distribution of the trachytes. It occurs on the slope between Druim an Eidhne and Loch na Creitheach, about 350 yards W.N.W. of the northern end of the lake. The rock shows a fine-textured grey ground, enclosing dull porphyritic felspars up to ½ inch in length. These have rounded outlines and, excepting a narrow border, are dark, as if from numerous inclusions. Excepting for the shape of the felspars, the rock resembles to the eye the Norwegian rhomb-porphyries. Its specific gravity is 2·71. A thin slice [7486] shows that these felspars are usually grouped together in aggregates. They are evidently corroded, and often show a line of secondary inclusions a little within the curved outline. Some show the fine lamellation and nearly straight extinction of oligoclase, and this felspar is seen in places in evident microperthitic intergrowth with orthoclase. Other crystals, without clearly visible lamellation, have something of the appearance of cryptoperthite. The other elements of the earlier crystallisation are apatite, magnetite, and augite, preceding the felspar in order as named. In one place the augite is seen in micrographic intergrowth with the felspar. The ground-mass is of small felspar prisms, with sensibly straight extinction and no evident twinning, granules of augite, and some minute crystals of magnetite.

It is possible that this dyke, remote from the others, belongs to a different and much earlier epoch, and is to be regarded, together with certain dykes near Elgol and elsewhere already described (on pp. 288–290), as a specialised derivative from the magma which gave rise to the chief group of minor acid intrusions in Skye.

* Judd, *Quart. Journ. Geol. Soc.*, vol. xlvi., p. 380; 1890: Harker, *ibid.*, vol. lii., p. 372; 1896.

CHAPTER XXIV

AUGITE-ANDESITE AND PITCHSTONE DYKES.

We proceed to give a brief account of some of the *andesite dykes* of Skye. Rocks with the characters of typical augite-andesites form dykes, usually of small size,* in the neighbourhood of Broadford and in numerous parts of the Sleat district. These localities fall within the range of the Broadford and Sleat group of dykes described above, and these, as we have seen, are in great part intermediate between trachytes and andesites, while some are frankly andesitic. It is possible that the rocks now to be noticed are likewise related genetically to the trachytes and trachy-andesites: but, showing no trachytic affinities in their petrographical characters, they will be severed from the preceding group as probably distinct, and we shall show that they stand in close relation to another group of rocks to be described, viz. the acid pitchstones.

Our augite-andesite dykes show some variety of characters, and, though we have no chemical data, it is evident from the microscopical examination and from specific gravity determinations that they differ among themselves in chemical composition. These differences are in great measure connected with the existence in some varieties of a considerable amount of glassy base, the rocks in which glassy matter is abundant being more acid than those which contain little or none. The point has been emphasised by Professor Judd† in his account of the "younger augite-andesites" of the Western Isles, among which doubtless our rocks are to be included.

As an example of the most crystalline type we take a specimen from a dyke ⅔ mile W.S.W. of Sgòrach Breac, or about 1½ mile E. of Ord, in Sleat. It is a dark grey close-grained rock, with only a few small phenocrysts and some small round spots which look like amygdules. Its specific gravity 2·80 shows that, for an andesite, it is of relatively basic composition. In a slice [6858] it is seen to consist of little striated crystals of labradorite, abundant granules of augite, and small imperfect octahedra of magnetite. An interesting feature of the slice is the occurrence of circular areas up to

---

* The only large dyke observed which probably belongs here is one 30 feet wide running in contact with a coarse 70-ft diabase dyke in the Harrabol crofts. The rock is rather fine-textured and has the specific gravity 2·75, but has not been examined microscopically.

† *Quart. Journ. Geol. Soc.*, vol. xlvi., pp. 371-382, pl. XV.; 1890.

about $\frac{1}{10}$ inch in diameter, round which the little felspar prisms are arranged tangentially. They clearly represent vesicles. They are occupied sometimes by chalcedonic quartz and other secondary products, sometimes by a fine-textured rock-substance consisting of small interlacing prisms of oligoclase, altered microlites of augite, and interstitial matter which is probably devitrified glass. In some cases the centre of the vesicle is occupied by quartz and the rest by the fine-textured and devitrified material.

We have here an instance of a phenomenon which seems to be not uncommon in this group of rocks throughout Britain. Vesicles in the rock have been filled, or partly filled, at a late stage in the consolidation, by an oozing in of the residual fluid magma. This is doubtless of more acid composition than the bulk of the rock. It has usually consolidated mainly or wholly as a glass, which, however, may have been subsequently devitrified. Mr Teall[*] has remarked the peculiarity in the andesitic dyke of Tynemouth. Professor Judd[†] has recorded it in a rock of specific gravity 2·89, apparently a basic andesite, occurring on Ben Hiant, Ardnamurchan, and regarded by that author as a lava-flow but by Sir A. Geikie as an intrusive sill. Professor Sollas[‡] has noticed the same thing in an augite-andesite dyke at Barnesmore in Donegal.

Those andesites which contain a moderate amount of glassy base exhibit usually the "hyalopilitic" structure of Rosenbusch, and have often a fine texture. A good example is from a dyke at Glas Eilean, Broadford [9442]. It has a compact ground-mass with the light grey colour which the rocks of this type invariably show, due partly to weathering. There are numerous rectangular crystals of fresh striated felspar, often with markedly tabular habit; and in the slice these give extinction-angles up to 34° in symmetrically cut sections, indicating a moderately acid labradorite. The only distinct element of the ground-mass is felspar in minute "lath-shaped" sections, but there have apparently been little augite granules as well as interstitial glass, both now destroyed. A dyke 1050 yards E.N.E. of the summit of Ben Suardal is identical in characters with the preceding, except that it is of rather finer texture and more altered. Its specific gravity is 2·68 [9573].

A different type, much richer in glass, is represented by a dyke on the shore of Loch Eishort, W. of Boreraig [3201]. It is a fresh rock of nearly black colour with glassy-looking felspars up to nearly $\frac{1}{4}$ inch long. In the slice these are seen to contain large inclusions of the ground-mass: there are also smaller porphyritic felspars, which are clear. The light brown augite also belongs in part to an early date of consolidation, and is then idiomorphic. In addition there are imperfect crystals of magnetite. The dominant felspar is andesine or andesine-labradorite. The abundant ground-mass is essentially of a pale glass crowded with little

---

[*] *Geol. Mag.*, 1889, pp. 481-483, pl. XIV.
[†] *Quart. Journ. Geol. Soc.*, vol. xlvi., p. 378; 1890.
[‡] *Sci. Proc. Roy. Dubl. Soc.* (2), vol. viii., p. 93; 1893.

rectangular gratings composed of two systems of black rods crossing, with minute felspar fibres, and what seems to represent destroyed augite (Plate XXVI., Fig. 4).

Another type corresponds with the "tholeiite" of Rosenbusch, with characteristic "intersertal" structure. Here the proportion of glassy base may vary between wide limits, even in different parts of one dyke. A good example is a dyke between Rudha Guail and Loch na Dal, on the coast N.E. of Isle Ornsay. This becomes richer in glass towards the margin, and has a thin tachylytic selvage. One slice of this dyke [5423] shows rectangular felspars about $\frac{1}{30}$ inch long, augite in granules and little subophitic patches, little crystals of magnetite, and abundant needles of apatite; but in addition interstitial patches of glass crowded with microlites of felspar and augite. A slice [5424] of a more glassy portion is similar in all essentials, except that the patches of interstitial base are much more abundant. Some of these patches are of circular form, with the felspar "laths" arranged tangentially about them. These doubtless represent vesicles occupied by the residual base of the rock (Plate XXVII., Fig. 2).

The extreme glassy type of andesite is illustrated by a dull grey rock of specific gravity 2·75 from a dyke in Broadford Bay [9441]. This is evidently considerably altered from its original state, but seems to have been of the nature of an andesite pitchstone. There are no phenocrysts, but only a much altered base full of slender felspar fibres and little dark rods, with partial parallel and rectangular grouping, which probably represent destroyed microlites of augite.

Rocks in any way comparable with the above seem to be at least very rare in Skye outside the area which has been indicated; but certain rocks from Druim an Eidhne may be mentioned here as probably devitrified andesitic pitchstones. The best example was found as a dyke, a foot in width, intersecting the gabbro on the highest point of the ridge named. It is a grey, compact, and rather splintery rock of specific gravity 2·79, with a strongly-marked fine banding, caused by lines and little spots of dark greenish-grey upon a lighter ground. The little spots, as seen on the hand-specimen, suggest spherulites. In a thin slice [8702] the appearance in natural light is precisely that of a pitchstone. The only porphyritic elements are rare crystals of brown hornblende and felspar of small size. The general mass of the rock shows a multitude of minute crystallites, varying in size and arrangement. In some bands these are preserved intact, and appear as a crowd of minute rods of pale green colour, probably augite. More usually the crystallites are replaced by chloritic or ferruginous matter. The larger ones occur in groups with a stellate arrangement, surrounded by a clear space. These clear spaces, with the general base in which the crystallitic growths are set, appear colourless and structureless in natural light. Polarised light, however, shows a finely crystalline and evidently felspathic mass with confused interlacing structure. It is probably a devitrified glassy base, but concerning devitrification in rocks of this kind of composition there is very little information available.

A point to which we have already alluded is the relation subsisting between the augite-andesites and pitchstones in the same area. Not only do the andesitic dykes contain in many cases a variable amount of glassy base, and come to be represented in some instances by practically vitreous rocks, still of intermediate acidity; but there seems to be a somewhat intimate relationship between the andesites and true pitchstones of acid composition. This is better illustrated in some other parts of the British province—e.g. in Arran—than in Skye, but a few words on the subject will not be out of place.

Professor Judd,* in a paper already cited, has remarked on the tendency in these "younger augite-andesites" for the glassy to become separated from the crystalline portion. The point is an interesting one as perhaps throwing light upon one kind of differentiation—viz., that effected by the separation, or partial separation, of the crystals already formed at a given stage from the residual fluid magma.† The composition of the residual magma thus separated would depend upon the stage of consolidation at which the process was effected: it might be sub-acid or thoroughly acid. Again we may recognise different degrees of separation, depending upon circumstances, as follows: (*i.*) a patchy arrangement on a small scale of the glassy base in the augite-andesites, such as is often seen in slices, and the oozing of the magma into vesicles as noted above; (*ii.*) kernels and patches of larger size, composed of relatively acid glass, embedded in an andesitic dyke; (*iii.*) composite dykes of augite-andesite and pitchstone, such as those of Cir Mhòr and Tormore in Arran‡; and (*iv.*) separate dykes of augite-andesite and pitchstone associated in the same area.

The second of these four cases is illustrated by one example from Skye cited by Professor Judd. It is from Bealach a' Mhaìm and presumably from a dyke, though the mode of occurrence is not recorded. The dyke-rock itself is stated to have a specific gravity 2·89, and must therefore be of considerably basic composition. The glass which occurs locally as patches in the midst of it yielded the analysis here quoted in column I.: its relatively acid nature, and especially its high content of alkalies, are very remarkable. For comparison we have the Eskdale dyke, in Dumfriesshire, described by Sir A. Geikie, with enclosed glassy portions of which analyses are quoted under B and C. It is interesting to refer also to the Armathwaite dyke, described by Mr Teall, an augite-andesite closely like some of those of the Western Isles and doubtless belonging to the same group. It illustrates how the interstitial base of such a rock, which yields 58 per cent. of silica in bulk-

---

* *Quart. Journ. Geol. Soc.*, vol. xlvi., p. 379; 1890.
† Compare also Judd in *Geol. Mag.*, 1888, pp. 1-11.
‡ Judd, *Quart. Journ. Geol. Soc.*, vol. xlix., 536-564; 1893.

analysis, may be comparable in composition with some acid pitchstones (*see* column C).

	I.	A.	B.	C.
SiO$_2$	61·80	58·67	65·49	70·76
Al$_2$O$_3$	14·91	14·37	14·66	10·93
Fe$_2$O$_3$	8·27	1·64	. .	3·59
FeO	not det.	6·94	5·44	not det.
MnO	not det.	trace	. .	. .
MgO	0·27	4·65	1·57	4·21
CaO	3·33	7·39	3·73	3·29
Na$_2$O	6·50	3·01	not det.	} 7·22
K$_2$O	5·19	1·42	not det.	} by diff.
Ignition	0·87	2·02	not det.	. .
	101·14	100·11	. .	100·00
Specific gravity	2·63	2·7	. .	. .

I. Glass in "labradorite-andesite" (? dyke), Bealach a Mhaim between Sligachan and Glen Brittle: mean of duplicate analyses by S. Parrish and H. J. Taylor, *Quart. Journ. Geol. Soc.* vol. xlvi., p. 364; 1890.

A. Glassy portion of the Eskdale dyke, near Eskdalemuir Manse Dumfriesshire: anal. J. G. Grant-Wilson, *Proc. Roy. Phys. Soc Edin.*, vol. v., p. 253; 1880.

B. Isolated kernels of black glass dispersed through the same rock anal. J. G. Grant-Wilson, *ibid.*, p. 254.

C. Insoluble residue of Armathwaite dyke, Cumberland, amounting to 35·57 per cent. of the rock, and representing approximately the insterstitial base: anal. W. F. K. Stock, *Quart. Journ Geol. Soc.*, vol. xl., p. 225; 1884.

We have next to describe the *acid pitchstones* of our area Pitchstone is a rock of comparatively rare occurrence in Skye; but in virtue of its very distinctive appearance it attracts the eye wherever it is found, and it was recorded by some of the earliest explorers of the island. As the observed occurrences are few, and exemplify more than one variety of the rock, we shall notice them severally. They are all situated nearly on one line running N.W.-S.E.; and with one exception they are within or closely on the border of the granite area (*see* Fig. 76, p. 387). They form, in every case examined, dykes of quite small width, and in some cases no the whole width of the dyke has the character of a typical pitch stone. In more than one instance the dyke itself is concealed beneath the great screes of the Red Hills, and only loose fragment have been found.

Two or three pitchstone dykes occur on Glamaig. Jameson found here fragments of yellowish and green pitchstone, but was not able to discover their source. Macculloch[†] noted fragments c

---

* *Mineralogy of the Scottish Isles*, vol. ii., p. 90; 1800.
† *Descr. West. Isl. Scot.*, vol. i., p. 401; 1819.

two varieties, one black with a few glassy felspars enclosed, the other olive-green with a structure (spherulitic) which he remarked as a novel peculiarity. Von Oeynhausen and von Dechen * found a dyke 2 or 3 feet wide of dark green spherulitic pitchstone, apparently on the north face of the eastern peak of Glamaig, at $\frac{3}{4}$ of the height of the hill, besides loose fragments of the black variety. Zirkel† uses nearly the same language as the authors just quoted, but it is not clear whether he refers to the same dyke.

At least two pitchstone dykes intersect the granite of Glamaig, and these are the most northerly and the most westerly of which we have found any evidence in Skye. One at about 1300 feet altitude, or about half-way up, on the western slope is not that of von Oeynhausen and von Dechen, but may possibly be the same that was recorded by Zirkel. It bears N.W. by N., and has a width of about 2 feet, but seems to be a double dyke, consisting of two members each about a foot wide. The purely glassy portion is of a dark greenish grey colour, and has a specific gravity 2·31. It encloses only rare crystals of felspar up to $\frac{1}{8}$ inch in length, but more frequently little spherulites. These are usually only $\frac{1}{10}$ to $\frac{1}{20}$ inch in diameter, but some, especially in the dull devitrified portion of the dyke, reach a diameter of an inch. The glass is pale yellow in a thin slice [8733] and mostly free from any crystallitic growths; but in certain narrow bands ($\frac{1}{10}$ inch wide), parallel to the dyke, there are little rod-like bodies with a tendency to star-like groupings reminiscent of the well known Arran pitchstones. They seem to be of augite or hornblende, but are too minute to exhibit their optical properties clearly. The little felspar crystals, which are scattered very sparingly through the rock, are simple or once twinned: occasionally they form the nuclei of spherulites. The small spherulites are paler in slices than the glassy matrix, but have a well defined border of deeper tint, a light yellowish brown: sometimes there are two or even three concentric rings of this nature. The spherulites have an elliptic section, being elongated in the direction of flow, *i.e.* parallel to the walls of the dyke. The black cross which they show between crossed nicols is not a very regular one, and it is clear that it arises not from a radiate structure but from a concentric-shell arrangement, like that seen in many oolitic limestones (Plate XX., Fig. 5). The birefringence is comparable with that of an alkali-felspar. By using a mica-plate we find that the spherulites are of the "positive" kind (*i.e.* the least axis of optical elasticity is in the radial direction), and we may conceive this effect as resulting from "negative" felspar-fibres arranged tangentially.

There is more than one dyke of this type on Glamaig, for fragments of a rock closely resembling that just described occur in the screes some 600 feet higher up. Macculloch's black porphyritic pitchstone belongs probably to still another dyke concealed by the screes. We have not found it on Glamaig itself, but boulders of it

* *Karsten's Archiv für Mineralogie*, vol. i., p. 85, pl. III., fig. 2 ; 1829.
† *Zeits. deuts. geol. Ges.*, vol xxiii., p. 89 ; 1871.

occur in the drift of the district on the line of the other Glamaig boulders. It is a black rock with pitchy lustre, enclosing fresh felspars up to ¼ inch in length, and having, like most of these pitchstones, a certain fissile character. A specimen from the drift near Drynoch Lodge gave the specific gravity 2·37. A specimen of the well known rock of the Sgùrr of Eigg, selected for its resemblance to these boulders, gave 2·42. The resemblance, however, seems to be a superficial one only. The felspars in our rock are wholly of a monoclinic species, with carlsbad twins. The other porphyritic elements are green augite crystals and some small octahedra of magnetite. The ground-mass has a yellowish colour, with evident flow-structure. It encloses little rods, from ·005 inch downward, of faint green colour and presumably of hornblende or augite; the smaller ones are gathered into stellate groupings, each surrounded by a clear space. Much more minute crystallitic growths disseminated through the colourless glassy base impart the yellowish tint and slight turbidity which are noticeable with a low magnification,

The next locality for pitchstone is on the eastern slope of Glas Bheinn Mhòr. Loose fragments are found beside the Strath Mòr foot-path, in some of the scree-deltas thrown out by the small streams which intersect the slope. Our attention was called to these fragments by Sir A. Geikie; but, though their source is probably in the immediate neighbourhood, we have not succeeded in detecting it, and it is probably concealed under the screes. The rock has a dark olive-brown glassy ground-mass enclosing closely-set crystals of felspar up to ¼ inch long. Its specific gravity is 2·44. Thin slices show that, besides felspars, both oligoclase and sanidine, green augite and magnetite figure among the phenocrysts, and these several minerals are grouped in aggregates. Some felspar crystals are so honeycombed with inclusions of the ground-mass that they consist to the extent of fully one-half of glass. A more unusual feature is the occurrence of quartz micrographically intergrown in felspar phenocrysts and of radiating fringes of micropegmatite bordering groups of crystals. The glassy ground-mass has a yellowish cloudy appearance, due to an immense number of very minute crystallitic elements visible only with a high magnifying power. They are partly globulites, partly short rods. Perlitic fissures are sometimes seen surrounding the phenocrysts (Plate XXIV., Fig. 3).

It is probable that more than one dyke of pitchstone occurs on this slope of Glas Bheinn Mhòr, for, at a spot not far north of the last, two pitchstone boulders were found in the drift of Strath Mòr, which differ from the variety just noted. One contains only scattered rectangular felspars about ⅛ inch long in a grey ground-mass. This has a patchy appearance from the intermingling of truly vitreous portions with others of somewhat duller, enamel-like aspect. The specific gravity of this rock is 2·34. A thin slice shows that besides the felspar phenocrysts there are, as usual, smaller ones of augite and a few grains of magnetite. The felspar is sanidine, and it encloses large patches of glass, besides crystals of augite and magnetite. The yellow and rather cloudy glass which forms the matrix owes its appearance to a crowd of minute globulites, barely resolved under a high-power objective. The other boulder from this place has a specific gravity 2·346. Under the microscope it shows a similar yellow glass, in which sanidine phenocrysts are embedded, and the yellowish turbidity is resolved with high magnification into a vast number of very minute rods and globulites. There are little clear spaces surrounding green microlites of larger dimensions, though still less than $\frac{1}{500}$ inch long, which tend to aggregate into roughly stellate groups, recalling some of the well known pitchstones of Arran.

Jameson[*] in 1800 recorded fragments of dark leek-green pitchstone on the slopes of Beinn na Caillich, and in 1818 discovered their source in the form of a "vein in a stream descending from that mountain," probably Allt a' Choire, above the farm of Coirechatachan (see Macculloch,[†] *passim*). Several pitchstone dykes, or dykes composed partly of pitchstone, intersect the granite of Beinn na Caillich. One high up on the northern face does not seem to be exposed, but fragments were found at an altitude of over 2000 feet. It is a deep olive-green glassy-looking rock, enclosing numerous little felspars and other crystals, and the specific gravity was found to be 2·35. A slice [6796] shows the little felspars to be mostly sanidine, but with some plagioclase. There are also some yellowish grains of augite and an occasional slender prism of a greener augite (extinction-angle 38°); and a few pyramidal crystals of quartz occur. The mass of the rock is a clear colourless glass full of little rod like crystallites, which in the neighbourhood of the porphyritic crystals have a marked fluxional arrangement. The largest of these minute rods just show a faint greenish tint, and they are presumably either augite or hornblende, the former being perhaps the more probable in view of the augite phenocrysts, though comparison with the Arran rocks forbids us to insist on this point.

Low down on the eastern slopes of the hill two or three dykes occur in the burn Allt a' Choire, which flows down to Coire-chatachan. A small water-fall at about 350 feet altitude is caused by a triple dyke running nearly E.–W. The two flanking members consist of compact quartz-bearing felsitic rocks which gave specific gravities 2·53 and 2·58 [8842]. The central member is a pitchstone of more subdued lustre than the preceding, but also of olive-green colour: its specific gravity was found to be 2·30. Porphyritic elements are rare and of small dimensions: a thin slice [6794] shows that they are of sanidine with rather rounded outlines. The transparent colourless matrix of the rock is only partly glassy, and in large part crystalline, consisting of felspar. It is crowded, as before, with minute rod-like crystallites. Some larger ones show a greenish tint and a fibrous structure, and give extinction-angles

---

[*] *Mineralogy of the Scottish Isles*, p. 93; 1800.
[†] *Descr. West. Isl. Scot.*, vol. i., p. 401.

up to 16°, indicating hornblende. Each is surrounded by a clear space free from the smaller crystallites; a feature familiar in the Arran and other pitchstones (Plate XXIV., Fig. 2). Slices cut from the marginal portion of the rock showed some differences from the above. There are little bands wholly made up of closely-packed very minute spherulites, each giving the black cross. More complex, but less perfect, spherulitic growths of a brownish tint surround the few small porphyritic felspars, and form detached wisps. There is here less glass in the base of the rock, most of which shows depolarisation, especially evident in the clear spaces surrounding the hornblende crystallites [6795].

That rocks similar to the pitchstones of the Red Hills occur also in the Sleat district appears from a specimen collected by Mr Clough from a dyke at Allt Duisdale, near Isle Ornsay. It is a dark rock with a pitchy lustre, enclosing scattered felspars up to $\frac{1}{8}$ inch long, and having the specific gravity 2·36. It has a marked flow-structure, and also a rough platy or columnar fracture oblique to this. A thin slice [6130] shows that the porphyritic elements, only sparingly present, are, in the order of their crystallisation, imperfect octahedra of magnetite, light green prisms of augite, and clear untwinned crystals of sanidine, rounded and corroded. The rest is a clear colourless glass crowded with minute slender prisms with imperfect terminations. Some of these are of sanidine, but the majority have a greenish colour, and are found by their extinction-angles to be augite, perhaps with some hornblende.

The above pitchstones seem by their low specific gravities to be, at least in the main, of acid composition. This criterion is however not entirely satisfactory, and we have already remarked on the resemblance of one of the rocks to that of the Sgùrr of Eigg, which is of sub-acid composition. Published analyses of British Tertiary pitchstones show that those of truly acid nature have specific gravities ranging from 2·29 to 2·37, while the pitchstone of Barnesmore Gap in Donegal (with 64·04 per cent. of silica) gives 2·41, and that of the Sgùrr of Eigg (with 65·81 per cent.) 2·42. These sub-acid glasses are therefore very little denser than others containing 8 or 10 per cent. more silica.

Although pitchstones are of comparatively rare occurrence in Skye, there are in places very numerous dykes which, although not glassy, reproduce in other respects the characteristics of that group of rocks, and are perhaps to be regarded as devitrified and otherwise altered pitchstones. They are dykes of no great width, usually only a foot or two, exceptionally as much as six or even ten feet. Their direction is commonly about W.N.W.–E.S.E., but varies in extreme cases from W.–E. to N.–S. They are dull compact-looking rocks, often crowded at the margin with little spherules which show conspicuously on a weathered face; and these are sometimes alligned so as to give what Mr Clough has styled a "rodded" structure. A number of specimens were examined from the neighbourhood of Coire-chatachan and the slopes of Beinn na Caillich. Five of these gave specific gravities ranging from 2·45 to 2·54, with a mean of 2·50. For the sake of clearness we will refer to these presumably altered rocks as the *Coire-chatachan type*. Their local distribution is indicated in Fig. 76, above.

Before describing these dykes it should be observed that rocks of precisely similar characters are found in immediate association with typical pitchstones, and there have every appearance of an identical origin. Thus the dark green pitchstone of Glamaig, already described, passes into a dull grey compact rock, with fluxion-lines weathering out as slender ribs on an exposed face. A thin slice [8841] is very instructive. In natural light it appears practically identical with the pitchstone [8733], consisting of what looks like a pale yellow glass with scattered crystallites and enclosing little phenocrysts of sanidine and more rarely of green augite. With crossed nicols the appearance is totally different. What looked like a glass is found to be birefringent and to consist of a mosaic, the individual elements of which average about $\frac{1}{50}$ inch across. These elements, however, are not crystal-grains, for they give shadowy or "undulose" extinction, of a kind indicating a divergent fibrous structure. The birefringence is nearly equal to that of quartz. That this is due to devitrification of a once glassy rock is placed beyond doubt by another portion of the same slice. Here we have in natural light the same appearance of a glass, but with a patchy arrangement, little patches of pale yellow or yellowish brown tint, of irregular but rounded shape, being separated by nearly colourless and quite clear parts with a disposition like a network of veins. With crossed nicols we see that the yellow patches are still isotropic: the clear parts, however, structureless in natural light, break up into a mosaic comparable with that just described. The radiate structure of each element of the mosaic is here more developed, so as to give a perfect black cross. These clear doubly refracting parts evidently follow a system of cracks, partly with a general parallelism which corresponds with the platy jointing and flow-structure of the dyke. The evidence of devitrification seems in this instance to be complete.

Some of the Coire-chatachan dykes, though now devoid of vitreous matter, show so close a general resemblance to the rock just described that we may confidently assign to them a like origin. Good examples are afforded by a dyke (sp. gr. 2·54) about 1100 yards N.N.E. of the old house of Coire-chatachan and another (sp. gr. 2·53) in the lower part of Allt a' Choire. Slices [6785, 6793] closely resemble pitchstones when examined in natural light. There is a general cloudiness, due to a crowd of excessively minute crystallites (as in some well known pitchstones, such as that of Corriegills, Arran); and there are also larger crystallites, each surrounded by a narrow clear space and in the more altered parts by a ring of darker brown. Between crossed nicols the rocks show a microcrystalline structure, often with a confused "felsitic" appearance, but elsewhere consisting of evident grains of untwinned felspar. There is no black cross, and very little approach to a radiate arrangement such as is clearly, but it would seem exceptionally, developed in the Glamaig rock. Even in that case it is to be observed that no true spherulites, with defined boundaries, were formed in the process of devitrification. The spherulites there found [8733] are undoubtedly primary growths. In no rocks in Skye have we found any evidence of typical spherulites formed in connection with devitrification. Some of the Coire-chatachan dykes contain spherulites, or have contained them, but these structures seem to be in every case original, and, as we shall see, have often been destroyed by the secondary changes which the rocks have undergone. As an example of this we may take a one-foot dyke seen about 850 yards N.N.E. of the old house, a dull compact-looking rock with flow-lines marked by alternations of lighter and darker grey. A thin slice [6790] shows very numerous yellow spots, $\frac{1}{100}$ to $\frac{1}{20}$ inch in diameter, set in a paler, evidently crystalline, matrix. The spots are round and sharply defined: they have a darker border, and the larger ones have sometimes dark concentric rings. They seem certainly to represent spherulites; but, if so, they have doubtless had their structure wholly destroyed by recrystallisation, for they are now merely fine-textured granular patches. The paler matrix consists of elongated grains or imperfect crystals, up to $\frac{1}{50}$ inch long, extinguishing pretty accurately parallel to their length, and with the properties of orthoclase. Round the spherules they sometimes assume a radiating arrangement. Although the rock has now nothing of the characters of a pitchstone, comparison with other specimens suggests that such may have been its original state. Its composition is apparently that of a trachytic rock.

Other examples show what must be regarded as a more radical kind of alteration, probably affecting the bulk composition of the rock; and in such cases the term "devitrification" does not adequately express the changes undergone. A 10 ft dyke about 900 yards N. of the old house is of a dull compact rock with strong flow-structure, marked by closely alternating whitish and greenish grey bands: the specific gravity is 2·52. A slice [6784] shows the greenish tint to be due to little patches and streaks of chloritic and ferruginous matter. Some portion of this evidently replaces little crystallites like the larger of those seen in the pitchstones, and the cloudy, finely disseminated matter may perhaps be derived from the destruction of more minute crystallitic growths. The general mass of the rock has the confused "felsitic" structure noted in the other specimens, and where the elements of the aggregate are large enough to be identified, they are apparently orthoclase. There are, however, in addition, numerous irregular patches of clear quartz-mosaic, which from their manner of occurrence must certainly be set down as secondary, and seem to point to an introduction of silica from without. This appears more clearly in a dyke a little north of the preceding, and differing from it in general aspect only in being spherulitic. Distinct spherules and axiolitic bands formed by their coalescence make up a considerable part of the rock [6786], and some of them, preserving perfectly their radiating and tufted structures, must be nearly in their original state. Elsewhere there is considerable alteration evinced by the occurrence of abundant clear quartz in the form of sectors cutting into the yellowish brown spherulites and axiolites. They are often continuous with similar clear quartz occupying the interstices of the spherulites and forming streaks between the bands. In this case it appears that changes of a kind involving partial silicification have almost wholly destroyed the original nature of the matrix, and attacked to some extent the more durable spherulitic growths. The siliceous replacement must have been of a gradual kind, for both in this and in the preceding rock it is within the clear quartz areas that the forms of the little crystallites of the original rock are most perfectly preserved. The same remark applies to a rock in many respects resembling the last, occurring at the north-eastern base of Beinn na Caillich, about 550 yards N.W. by N. of the Lochain. It was found only in the form of abundant loose fragments, but evidently belongs to a dyke of this group. It has a lamellar jointing coinciding with a strong fluxion-banding and is crowded with little spherulites, which have the "rodded" arrangement.

A dyke seen on the coast to the N.N.E. of Corry Lodge, Broadford, has characters which in many respects resemble those of the more altered of the Coire-chatachan dykes, and is possibly like them a transformed glassy rock; but it is essentially different from them in its original nature. It contains abundant crystals of quartz, and must have been a rock of thoroughly acid composition.

CHAPTER XXV.

General Review of Tertiary Igneous Activity in Skye.

In the previous chapters we have given in detail the results of our study of the Tertiary igneous rocks of Skye, both in the field and in the laboratory. We have endeavoured to range them in natural groups, each belonging to a defined epoch, and these have in general been treated in chronological sequence. The departures from such order have in a few instances been dictated by convenience, to avoid repetition: more often they have been necessitated by the imperfection of the record or by our failure to decipher it. We have now to summarise the principal events during the prevalence of igneous activity in Skye in the earlier half of Tertiary time; at the same time touching upon certain considerations with respect to the origin and mutual relations of the rocks, which arise naturally from such a general review of observations already recorded. That the assemblage of igneous rocks described in the foregoing pages may be treated as a connected whole will be generally conceded without formal discussion, and has been implicitly assumed in the course of our account of the rocks. Our investigation therefore, though deficient in certain particulars, affords the requisite data for tracing to some extent the progress of igneous activity in its various manifestations from the earliest to the latest stage. The area studied, though but a small part of a vast region throughout which similar conditions prevailed contemporaneously, is wide enough to have furnished us with a large body of facts; it is in some respects a natural district complete in itself, especially as containing one of the principal centres of plutonic intrusions; and authorities, who differ widely in their interpretation of what is seen there, have agreed in regarding it as a pattern of the whole region.

One aspect of the subject upon which we have not yet touched is the relation subsisting between igneous activity and differential movements of the earth's crust, regarded as the expression of the forces by which they were brought about. The starting-point of any consideration of this kind is the general principle that important outbursts of igneous activity have always been closely bound up with great *crust-movements* in the same region and, in a broad sense, of the same age. As applied to the European area, this principle has been admirably worked out by M. Marcel Bertrand.[*] He points out that the Tertiary and post-Tertiary

[*] Sur la distribution géographique des roches éruptives en Europe. *Bull. Soc. Geol. Fra.* (3), vol. xvi., pp. 573-617; 1888.

igneous rocks of Central and Southern Europe stand in intimate relation with the folding which has given rise to the Alpine system of mountains. At the same time he recognises in addition an extra-Alpine suite of Tertiary eruptions, including those of the British Isles, which form part of a more or less continuous belt along the western border of the Old World. Bertrand associates these also with crust-movements, but with movements of a larger order than those which originated the Alps : he connects them with the depression of the Atlantic basin.

While this commends itself as a general conclusion to provisional acceptance, it must be remembered that the Alpine system of movements was felt at least in some degree in England, and we cannot assume that the Inner Hebrides lay wholly beyond the possible scope of minor disturbances of a like kind. The effect will be recognised there, if at all, only as a subordinate factor modifying the operation of the larger one, or, it may be, rising locally to the first importance. The significance of this point lies in the fact that the two systems of movements belong to different types, characterised by different manifestations of igneous activity. The Atlantic system is of the plateau-building type, consisting in differential movements in the vertical sense, which express themselves in monoclinal folding or (as in our case) faulting : the Alpine system is of the mountain-building type, involving more or less of the element of lateral thrust, and resulting in anticlinal folding or (if proceeding to an advanced stage) isoclinal folding and reversed faulting. In the Inner Hebrides we seem to recognise not only the former but, in an early stage of its development, the latter also ; the one affecting the region as a whole, the other making itself apparent in certain limited districts. To the former belong the voluminous fissure-eruptions, the numerous and extensive sill intrusions, and the great system of parallel dykes : to the latter belong the central volcanic outbursts, the plutonic intrusions forming bosses and great laccolites, the radial and other special groups of dykes, etc. In brief, recalling the distinction enforced in former chapters between regional and local groups of intrusions in our area, we connect these with the *regional and local systems of crust-movements* respectively.

We may conceive the crust of the earth in the British area as being during the earlier half of Tertiary time, or at frequent epochs during that time, in a state of strain ; and both crust-movements and igneous activity may be regarded as attempts to relieve that strain and restore internal equilibrium. The crustal strain was made up of two elements : firstly one of uniform type over the extensive region, and related doubtless to events of a large order, such as the Atlantic depression as suggested by Bertrand ; and secondly, superposed upon the first in certain places and there becoming paramount at certain epochs, systems of strain related to particular centres of disturbance.

Apart from possible vertical movements affecting the whole area in common and not to be detected by the survey of a small tract, the *regional* strain found expression in faulting and monoclinal tilting of the faulted blocks. But these were not the first nor the last events falling under this category. The normal result of the condition of strain, recurring many times, was the formation of sub-parallel (N.W. or N.N.W.) fissures, in which molten rock-magma rose forming dykes; and in the earlier part of the time these uprisings of magma reached the surface as volcanic eruptions. If at any later epoch the magma again found exit at the surface, no evidence of this is preserved in Skye. The dyke-fissures, of all ages, were apparently not lines of differential vertical movement : the earlier ones at least are never connected with faults. The faulting and tilting of the tract clearly belong, in the main if not wholly, to a subsequent epoch, later than the plutonic phase, and later too than the intrusion of the great group of sills ; * for the sills are broken by the faults and tilted in common with the bedded rocks. The strain then was relieved first by the uprise of molten magma through fissures communicating with the surface, then by the uprise of magma which did not find exit but was injected along bedding-planes ; only after this did bodily displacement of solid rock-masses come into play in the form of faulting and tilting.

One point which is perhaps of sufficient interest to warrant a short digression is the *relation of the Tertiary crust-movements to earlier movements in the same region.* Although the older rocks are concealed over the greater part of Skye, there are not wanting indications of pre-Tertiary movements of the plateau-building type, expressing themselves in considerable dislocations with the monoclinal arrangement. The effect has been to produce a general westerly dip with normal faults throwing down to the east. The most important of these pre-Tertiary faults actually exposed is that which our colleague Mr Wedd has laid down along the Abhuinn nan Leac valley and east of the Blaven range. In the system of movements thus brought to light we seem to find a foreshadowing of the like movements which have subsequently affected the Tertiary rocks themselves.

This point comes out more clearly when we turn from regional crust-movements to those which belong to the *local* category. Between the time of the great post-Silurian disturbances, when the Torridonian strata were thrust over the Cambrian, and the Tertiary volcanic period, with which our more immediate subject begins, there were at least two epochs of local differential elevation in Skye; one anterior, and the other posterior, to the deposition of the Triassic and Jurassic strata. In both cases the result was a relative upheaval of what are now the mountain districts.

As regards the pre-Triassic elevation, we note first the distribution of the Palæozoic rocks. The base of the Mesozoic in Skye rests usually upon the Torridonian. This is still true in part of the belt

* This is to be understood as applying to the regional, not to the local disturbances.

surrounding the gabbro and granite intrusions, when the relations can be examined.* When we come to the eastern Red Hills, however, we find indications that at some places the upper portion of the Torridonian had been removed prior to the deposition of the Mesozoic rocks, and at other places clear evidence that the whole of the Torridonian had been so removed. The Mesozoic rocks rest on the Cambrian on both sides of the Beinn an Dubhaich anticline, showing that that feature is in part of pre-Mesozoic date. The arrangement of the Mesozoic rocks themselves affords similar evidence, for the lower members of the succession in places overlap one another in the direction of the mountains. This again is most evident in the eastern part of the district. The Triassic conglomerate at the base is well developed on Raasay, at the N.W. corner of Scalpay, and in the country east and south of Broadford. Passing westward from this last locality, however, we find that between Beinn an Dubhaich and Glen Boreraig the conglomerate is overlapped by the Lower Lias, so that the limestones of this group, and finally the succeeding shales, come to rest on the Cambrian limestones. Farther north the evidence is very fragmentary, the boundaries being mostly faulted; but the conglomerate is not seen in the Beinn na Caillich district, and evidently dies out too towards Sligachan. Around the Cuillins the relations are almost everywhere concealed below the basalts, and in places below sea-level. The Trias conglomerate appears as a very small patch on the shore of the Sound of Soay, but is immediately overlapped by the Lias. Summarily, we see that there was a certain amount of elevation in pre-Triassic times, which may have affected in some degree the whole of the mountain district of Skye, but was at least most marked in the eastern part of the district, where at a later epoch occurred the boss-formed Tertiary intrusions, themselves attended by local uplifts.

By like evidence we can prove local elevation of the same general character at some epoch post-Jurassic but pre-Tertiary, or at least anterior to the oldest Tertiary rocks of Skye. The fact that the volcanic group rests on different formations in different places is of course attributable mainly to the regional system of disturbances (with concurrent erosion), but local elevations in what is now the mountain tract are also clearly indicated. As we travel towards the mountains, *e.g.* southward from Portree or northward and westward from Strathaird, we find that the Tertiary volcanic rocks rest first on the Oolites, then on the Lias. Still nearer to the mountains, *e.g.* on the shores of the Sound of Soay, they pass from the Lias to the Torridonian. To the north of Beinn na Caillich the basaltic lavas rest on the lower part of the Torridon Sandstone. On the site of Beinn na Caillich itself we find that even the Torridonian had been stripped away prior to the volcanic epoch, for in the enclosed patches within the granite the lavas are seen lying upon the Cambrian limestones; first upon the upper

* North and west of the Cuillins the base of the Mesozoic is nowhere exposed.

and then upon the lower of the zones of limestone present in the district. We infer that in this case too the elevation was most marked in that part of the area where subsequently occurred the boss-formed intrusions with their attendant uplift. Whether such post-Jurassic but pre-Volcanic elevation belongs to a single epoch or to two distinct epochs, one Mesozoic and the other post-Mesozoic, we are not able to decide. Cretaceous strata have been detected at two places near the border of the plutonic intrusions, viz. by Mr Clough on the Sound of Soay and by Mr Wedd in the southern part of Scalpay, and they rest unconformably on different members of the Jurassic; but these relics are of too fragmentary a nature to decide the question.

The correspondence between crust-movements of different dates becomes very apparent where the disturbance of the strata has taken the form of definite folds, as is partly the case in the eastern portion of central Skye. The clearest instance is seen in the curved anticline of Ben Suardal and Beinn an Dubhaich. Here the Cambrian and the overlying Torridonian, with the surface of overthrust dividing them, are thrown into a sharp anticlinal fold. This, as we have seen, is partly of pre-Triassic age. The Mesozoic strata, however, on the two flanks of the ridge also dip away from the axis, though at lower angles, proving a later folding on the same line. Possibly some part of this later folding was accomplished at the time when the granite was intruded as an elongated boss in the core of the anticline, but it seems in the main to have antedated the volcanic outbursts.* We see then that at this place there has been anticlinal folding on the same axis at two (or more probably three) widely separated epochs. The tendency of later folding to follow the same lines as earlier folding in a given district seems, according to Bertrand† and others, to be a law of considerable generality.

In Tertiary times there were repeated disturbances of the earth's crust at the old centres which seem to have been more or less clearly marked out before the close of the Palæozoic era; but these disturbances were now closely bound up with successive episodes in the igneous activity of the Skye focus. The nature of this relation, involving the question of how far the disturbances were the cause, how far the consequence of the igneous eruptions, is a subject not to be discussed here. In the most general view we may, as suggested, regard the two classes of events as alike the effects of a common set of causes.

We turn now from tectonic to *petrographical considerations*. Assuming all the Tertiary igneous rocks of Skye to belong to one connected suite, we must suppose them to have had in some sense

---

*The bedded volcanic rocks have been removed by erosion from this neighbourhood. The nearest lavas rest on the grits of the Lower Lias.

†See especially M. Bertrand, Sur la continuité du phénomène de plissement dans le bassin de Paris, *Bull. Soc. Géol. Fra.* (3), vol. xx., pp. 118-165; 1892.

a common origin; and the simplest form of this hypothesis is that which regards the various rocks as products of "differentiation" from one common stock, viz. a large body of fluid rock-magma initially of uniform composition and occupying an intercrustal reservoir at some unknown but probably very considerable distance beneath the surface. Such a hypothesis is not susceptible of deductive proof, but it is in harmony with conceptions now very prevalent among petrologists, and it will be provisionally adopted here as the starting-point for what follows.

The first and most obvious point concerning this initial homogeneous magma is that it must have been of thoroughly basic composition, at least if it is fairly represented by the rocks brought to light by erosion. Those which play the most important part as regards bulk are the basalt lavas and associated dolerite sills. If for the purpose of a very rough estimate we suppose these to make up three-fourths of the whole, and to be in equal amount, and if we divide the remaining quarter equally between gabbro and granite, then, on the basis of analyses already given, we find the mean composition of the whole to be that given below in column I. It is clear that by altering in any reasonable manner the estimated proportions of the several rocks, by allowing for the peridotites and the dykes, etc., no very material difference would be made in

	I.	II.	III.
SiO_2	49·36	49·49	58·98
TiO_2	1·86	1·60	0·52
Al_2O_3	16·45	15·87	15·41
Fe_2O_3	4·17	4·43	4·78
FeO	6·46	6·27	2·70
MnO	0·18	0·09	0·41
MgO	6·40	6·10	3·71
CaO	8·82	9·02	4·83
Na_2O	2·57	2·78	3·18
K_2O	1·25	1·50	2·77
H_2O	2·44	2·27	2·17
P_2O_5	0·11	0·11	0·21

I. Mean composition of Tertiary igneous rocks of Skye, calculated from 3 parts basic lavas, 3 parts basic sills, 1 part gabbro, and 1 part granite.

II. The same from the mean of 23 analyses taken without selection.

III. Mean composition of British igneous rocks of all ages, for comparison, being the average of 536 analyses taken without selection. The Fe_2O_3 is too high, and the FeO too low, the total iron having in many of the analyses been estimated as ferric oxide.

the result. Or if we simply calculate the mean of such analyses as we possess of the rocks, without selection,* we get practically the

* One only has been omitted, viz. that of a thin ultrabasic "schliere' in the banded gabbros, analysed on account of its peculiar composition, but not representing any important rock-mass.

same result (II.). For comparison we give in column III. what may be taken as the mean composition of British igneous rocks in general, calculated from a large number of analyses.* The great preponderance of basic types among the Tertiary igneous rocks is true not only of Skye, but of the other Western Isles, with Antrim, and of the much larger region of which the British area is only a fragment.

Another point in the general petrography of the suite of rocks is that they belong entirely to one of the two great branches of igneous rocks, viz. to what Iddings styles the "Sub-alkali" as distinguished from the "Alkali" Group. This appears in the analyses and equally in the mineral composition of the rocks. Types rich in alkali-felspars, without free silica, are of very exceptional occurrence; the "felspathoid" minerals, viz. leucite, nepheline, sodalite, and primary analcime, are almost, if not quite, unrepresented†; and an alkali-bearing amphibole is known from but one place in Skye and one other occurrence among British Tertiary rocks.

If the entire suite of rocks has originated from a common stock-magma, once homogeneous, we have to recognise that here typical acid rocks, such as granites, have been derived by processes of differentiation from a basic magma. Further the differentiation which gave these acid rocks was completed, as regards some portion at least of the magma, at a very early stage; indeed at an epoch antedating any known intrusion or extrusion in the area. This is proved by the oldest of all the igneous rocks dealt with above, viz. those which supplied fragments to the volcanic agglomerates of the earliest outbursts. We have already seen that the material of the agglomerates in certain parts of the island indicates the prior existence of both gabbros and granites which have not anywhere been brought to light as rock-masses. These rocks must have been consolidated either in some part of the primitive reservoir itself or as intrusions from that reservoir at lower horizons than those of any rocks exposed in the district. The acid rock, or part of it, must have been in some sense intrusive, for some of the gabbro fragments are traversed by granite veins; but this might conceivably happen within the original reservoir itself.

Acid rocks more or less closely resembling in composition the granite fragments in the agglomerates have been extruded or intruded within our area at several distinct epochs during the succeeding events. In proof of this we may adduce the local

---

* See Harker, On the Average Composition of British Igneous Rocks, *Geol. Mag.*, 1899, pp. 220-222. The figures here given are calculated in the same way, but include additional analyses.

† Nepheline is stated to be present in a thick sill in the Shiant Isles (Heddle, *Mineralogy of Scotland*, vol. ii., p. 46; 1901), and analcime occurs in a sill in the south of Arran (Corstorphine, *Tsch. Min. Petr. Mitth.* (N.S.), vol. xiv., p. 464; 1895). This latter mineral was regarded by the author named as secondary after nepheline, but to the present writer it seems more probably a primary constituent of the rock: see *Geol. N. Arran, Mem. Geol. Sur. Scot.*, pp. 112-114; 1903.

rhyolitic eruptions, the granite and granophyre intrusions of the Red Hills, and the later granophyric and felsitic dykes, etc.; to which may be added the xenoliths and xenocrysts of acid material enclosed in certain groups of basic dykes, such as those of the Suardal district. This recurrence of similar rock-types within a given area points to one of two explanations as *a priori* possible. Either differentiation has operated along identical lines, at the same centre, at wide intervals of time; or a considerable body of acid magma, separated at a very early stage, has remained throughout the whole time as an available source, which has been drawn upon at several distinct epochs. We may conceive this body of acid magma, or rather the unexhausted portion of it at any time, as contained within the primitive magma-basin or reservoir, and may further suppose a part or the whole of it to have been consolidated and re-fused more than once in that situation. Of the two alternatives, the latter, as thus qualified, has the advantage of simplicity, and is more in accordance with some of the special phenomena observed. It is probable, however, that we must further modify our conception by supposing that the processes which gave birth to the acid magma, though completed within a certain limited portion of the deep-seated reservoir at a very early epoch, enlarged those limits progressively during later stages. The granite fragments in the volcanic agglomerates, the granite and granophyre intrusions of the Red Hills, the later acid dykes, and the acid xenoliths in the later basic dykes indicate a gradual extension of the area involved from stage to stage.

Although we have appealed primarily to the distribution in time and space of the acid rocks, we might draw confirmatory testimony from other rock-types. Especially is this seen when we consider together the gabbro and the granite, rocks which in any view must be regarded as of closely cognate origin. We have already pointed out that the fragments of these rocks in the basal agglomerates show a certain defined areal distribution, which is in remarkable agreement with that of the later and somewhat more extended plutonic intrusions of like rocks. This seems to indicate a certain differentiation and separation in a lateral or horizontal sense, as between the gabbro and the granite, outlined at a very early time but persisting later. It is clearly traceable throughout the succeeding phase of minor intrusions.

We have then good reasons for supposing that differentiation to an advanced degree was effected in a part of the parent-magma of our rocks at a very early time in the Tertiary history of the region, and that rocks or rock-magmas of basic and acid composition coëxisted throughout a very long period in different parts of a deep-seated reservoir underlying the area; these being at certain times solid rocks, at other times fluid simultaneously or almost simultaneously, or perhaps solid in parts of the reservoir and fluid in other parts. Such a hypothesis, suggested by the simpler and more obvious relations of the rocks, is greatly strengthened by a consideration of some of the more peculiar phenomena, such as the occurrence of composite intrusive masses and mixed rocks, and the great profusion of xenoliths in several groups of intrusions. These *special* features must undoubtedly be regarded as highly characteristic of the great suite of igneous rocks under discussion, and we are in this view able to correlate them with *general* features, equally characteristic, which indicate that the principal differentiation was in great part effected at a very early stage. Further differentiation doubtless went on, both in the parent magma and in "partial" magmas drafted from it, at later stages; but on the whole the progressive march of differentiation is much less marked here than in many other connected suites of igneous rocks which might be cited.

The successive episodes which make up the history of Tertiary igneous activity in Britain will not fall into their places as parts of a connected whole unless we take into account the areal distribution, as well as the sequence in time, of the several groups of rocks. Certain groups are not connected with any special centre, but have a very wide distribution, coextensive perhaps in some cases with the limits of the "Brito-Icelandic province" itself. Other groups are more narrowly restricted in space, and stand related to defined foci of activity, one of which was situated in the central part of Skye. This Skye focus, which may doubtless be taken as a type of others in the province, was initiated at a very early epoch, prior to the outbreak of vulcanism. Once established, it became the seat of renewed activity at numerous epochs during the succeeding time. These local manifestations culminated in the plutonic phase of activity, when outbursts of the regional kind seem to have been in abeyance: the succeeding minor intrusions connected with the focus give evidence of waning energy.

We have already emphasised this distinction between regional and local groups of igneous rocks in our area in connecting them respectively with the two different types of crust-movements. The distinction is no less significant from the petrographical point of view, for the rocks belonging to the local groups collectively present a much greater range of variety than those which have a regional extension. The relation between localisation and specialisation is much too striking to be regarded as accidental, and it clearly proves that *the distinct foci at which activity was from time to time localised were also the principal centres of magmatic differentiation.* While the rocks of the regional series are all of basic composition, with a range of less than 2 in the silica-percentages of specimens analysed, those of the local series vary in different groups from ultrabasic to highly acid. Some differentiation there doubtless was in the former series; but the analyses already given show a much closer resemblance in composition among the basic lavas, sills, and dykes of regional distribution than among the local groups of basic rocks, such as the gabbros, the dykes of the Beinn Dearg type, and the inclined sheets of the Cuillins.

This fundamental distinction must be borne in mind in the general review of the sequence of events to which we now proceed. As regards certain of these events, the great region or "province" may be treated as a unit; as regards others, it must be viewed as an assemblage of distinct foci, at each of which development followed the same general lines. Episodes affecting the whole region alternated, and sometimes partly synchronised, with others related to the special foci; and the discrimination of these *two parallel series* is essential to a proper understanding of the sequence.

Here, as in numerous other areas and at various geological periods, igneous activity has manifested itself successively under *three different phases*, the Volcanic, the Plutonic, and the "Dyke Phase," or as we prefer to call it (in view of the important part played by sills) the Phase of Minor Intrusions. The epithet "minor" must be understood as applying to the individual intrusions, for the sills of the great group collectively surpass in volume all the plutonic masses. The three phases indicated embrace the actual manifestations of igneous activity in the form of extrusions and intrusions: as preface or prologue to the whole we may reckon those preparatory deep-seated operations, which are matters of speculation only, and have in part been briefly glanced at.

The earliest overt act, ushering in the *volcanic phase*, was of the local category, and consisted in the opening of several large volcanic vents within a limited area in the central part of the Island. The eruptions were of a violently explosive kind, and the vents, enlarged by successive outbursts, attained in some cases diameters of a mile or two miles. Only in one instance is the actual funnel now exhibited, cutting through the older stratified rocks; and here the structure is that of a sharp anticline, with the vent breaking through the arch. The material which fills the vents and extends for some little distance beyond them is, as regards its volcanic element, of basic composition; but there are abundant fragments of the disrupted country rocks and, in the heart of the district, débris of plutonic rocks, probably consolidated within the deep-seated magma-basin. At this earliest epoch then our area could boast great volcanoes, a feature repeated only in a single instance in the ensuing time. There can be little doubt that the eruptions were subaërial, the land standing higher above sea level than at present, and this state continued, probably not without considerable oscillations of level, throughout nearly the whole of Tertiary time.

The much more important eruptions which followed had a regional extension, and illustrated a totally different type in the mechanics of vulcanicity. They took the form of tranquil outpouring of lava in innumerable small flows emanating from a system of parallel fissures; and by prolonged extravasation of this kind a thick pile was built up over a vast extent of country, of which the plateaux of Skye are but a fragment. In many other regions of volcanic activity, of various geological periods, a regular succession is to be traced among the various types of lavas erupted, connecting itself with the hypothesis of progressive differentiation in a subterranean magma-basin. Thus, as Iddings has pointed out, a common sequence is one beginning with intermediate lavas and continuing with types on the one hand more basic and on the other hand more acid; *i.e.* showing an increasing divergence in opposite directions from the initial type. In our area the initial magma was not an intermediate but a basic one, and no wide departure from it on systematic lines is found. The pyroxene-andesites intercalated among the prevalent basalts do not indicate any ordered sequence. It is interesting to note that with this great outpouring of lava there were during the earlier part of the time a few small outbursts of the explosive type, and that these were more frequent and continued later in the immediate neighbourhood of the focus of central Skye.

At one place on the border of the central district there was, as we have seen, an outburst of the local series, and a central volcano was formed (Chapter V.). With this there was a resumption in part of the paroxysmal type of eruption. The products of this volcano were petrographically in strong contrast with the contemporaneous lavas of the regional series, exhibiting very considerable variety with progressive change. They were first trachytic (and andesitic) and afterwards rhyolitic. Taking into account the earlier local outbursts of basaltic nature, we have here an order of increasing acidity.

If any special circumstances attended the extinction of regional volcanic activity, the record is in this respect imperfect, for the summit of the basalt group has everywhere been removed by erosion. The volcanic phase was sharply marked off from that which succeeded, but the phenomena of metamorphism in the basalts suggest that the interval was not one of long duration.

In the *plutonic phase* regional activity was wholly in abeyance. Skye now became more clearly defined as a natural district, containing as it did one of the foci at which igneous energy was exclusively concentrated. This was included in the central part of the island, which had already experienced the local outbursts of the volcanic phase. Other centres were comprised in the neighbouring parts of Britain, the nearest being some fifteen miles distant, in what is now the Isle of Rum (Fig. 1, p. 3). The events of the plutonic phase fall into three well marked stages, characterised by ultrabasic, basic, and acid intrusions respectively. The law of succession indicated, that of decreasing basicity or increasing acidity, is one very general among associated plutonic rocks of all ages throughout the world.

The ultrabasic magma was intruded in the south-western part of the central area. It rose through fissures, and formed a number of laccolitic masses, the largest of which was at least $2\frac{1}{2}$ miles in diameter and 1500 feet in thickness. The most striking feature is extreme complexity of structure. The rock-types represented range from troctolite, through picrite, to dunite, and even to seams of pure picotite; and these have been intruded in part simultaneously, so that they alternate in bands, in part successively, so that a later rock veins an earlier or is crowded with débris of it. The intimate association of these rocks proves that they come from a common stock, viz. the general peridotite magma of the district. This being itself a product of differentiation, the rock-types met with must result from differentiation of a subsidiary order, and the great range of variety compassed in this way seems to be characteristic of ultrabasic magmas.

The peridotites were succeeded, apparently with little or no interval, by intrusions of gabbro, which were of much greater volume and affected a much larger area of central Skye. They assumed partly the laccolitic, partly the boss-form. The mechanical conditions which determined one or the other habit were probably complex. We have already given reasons for believing that the form of the boundary of a large intrusive body depends in part upon the nature of the country rock; but the distribution of crustal strain must also have been an important factor, and perhaps the prime one. It is very noticeable, in both gabbro and granite, that the laccolitic habit prevails to the west and the boss-like to the east, the latter being the quarter in which, as we have shown, the strain was most narrowly localised and most strongly accentuated. We have shown that the plutonic intrusions cannot be considered as in any sense representing the cores of volcanoes. The gabbro has no connection with the basaltic lavas other than the remote one of an ultimate common origin from the same great magma-reservoir. Nor does it extend indefinitely downward with plug-like habit or with a spreading form, although one intrusion has for a certain vertical distance assumed the shape of a boss with perpendicular walls.

The most important body of gabbro is that from which the Cuillins and the Blaven range have been carved out. Here the magma has risen through fissures and spread in laccolitic fashion in, or in places a little below, the basalt lavas. The horizon is not very different from that affected by the chief ultrabasic intrusions, and most of the peridotites, as well as numerous lenticles of the volcanic rocks, have been enveloped by the gabbro. The great laccolite had a diameter perhaps not less than 10 miles and a thickness of over 3000 feet. The shape of its base, as displayed diagrammatically on the sketch-map (Fig. 15, p. 36), shows (i.) a general inclination towards the centre; (ii.), modifying the preceding, a general inclination to S. or S.S.E.; (iii.), exaggerating this, a sharp rise at the N.N.W. border, about Bruach na Frithe; and (iv.) another sharp rise on the N.E. side, where part of the laccolite is missing. This last, being apparently connected with the granite intrusion of Marsco, etc., must be considered the result of subsequent deformation: the other features seem to belong mainly to the epoch of the gabbro itself, and to be connected with the circumstances of its intrusion. The inward inclination of the base may be interpreted as indicating a settling down of the floor, at the time of the intrusion, to close the space which would otherwise have been left at some depth below by the abstraction of the magma from its reservoir. If this be so, the intrusion need not have occasioned any important uplift of the basaltic lavas which formed its roof. The general inclination, to S. or S.S.E., which modifies the general inward slope of the base and throws the area where the gabbro is below sea-level towards that direction, is also an original feature, not due to subsequent tilting. The base of the basalts, which is very near sea-level at Loch Sligachan and Loch Harport, and presumably so between those places, comes to the sea-level also at Loch Scavaig; but, while the thickness of basalt below the gabbro is great on the north and north-west sides of the Cuillins, it is very small on the south side, and disappears altogether at places near Blath-bheinn. The laccolite then has for some reason made its way in a direction related, not to the horizontal plane, but to a plane inclined towards S. or S.S.E. The high altitude of the base of the gabbro on Bruach na Frithe, though partly connected with this general inclination, is due in part to the dying out of the lower component sheets of the laccolite towards the boundary. It may, however, be more than an accident that the rise coincides very closely with the site of the old trachytic and rhyolitic volcano.

The laccolite was built up by a multitude of distinct injections, which differed somewhat in composition, though not in this respect rivalling the peridotites. It is clear that in many instances a single intrusion has included various kinds of magma, which did not mingle, but have often been drawn out into a banded or ribboned arrangement. From a chemical point of view the subsidiary differentiation thus indicated did not always follow the same lines. In particular the extreme basic modifications show a special enrichment or "concentration" in some cases of magnesia, in others of iron-oxides and titanic acid. Both differ again from the special chrome-iron-alumina concentrations of the peridotite magma. All this differentiation seems to have been effected prior to intrusion: of differentiation in place there is little clear indication except in the "segregation veins." The comparatively uniform character of the gabbro of the Broadford boss is in accord with this, and we may note a contrast with some occurrences of gabbro in other regions, e.g. that of Carrock Fell in Cumberland. If again there was any progressive change in the average composition of successive injections of gabbro-magma in the Cuillin laccolite, such change must have been confined within much narrower limits than the variation set up in individual injections by the subsidiary differentiation, and it is thus difficult to verify. It comes out clearly only in the latest incident of the gabbro stage, which was the injection of various aplitic and felspathic veins of relatively acid composition, carrying out the general law of increasing acidity among our plutonic intrusions.

That in some parts of our area no interval of quiescence divided the gabbro-stage from the succeeding granite-stage is sufficiently proved by the phenomena described on Marsco. We may consider the dividing-epoch to be accurately marked by the intrusions of marscoite, representing a gabbro-magma modified before (and in places after) intrusion by granite material.

The granite, like the gabbro and presumably for the same reasons, assumed the laccolitic habit in the west and the boss-form in the east. In the former case it was intruded partly beneath and into the gabbro, which it lifted and partially invaded; but apart from this overlapping, the granite is found to the north-east of the gabbro, *i.e.* on the side away from the peridotite, indicating a displacement of the seat of activity in a north-eastward direction from stage to stage in the plutonic phase. Regarding all the plutonic rocks as derivatives from a common stock-magma, we may perhaps see in this distribution a sign of differentiation in the horizontal sense, and connect it with the fact that the granite itself seems to grow somewhat more acid towards the north-east and east. We may recall too that in the gabbro laccolite the relatively acid aplitic and felspathic veins are found chiefly in the eastern and north-eastern part.

The actual form of the large body of granite and granophyre cannot be made out with any precision. In the neighbourhood of Marsco and Meall Dearg, where it was doubtless thick, it has occasioned a very considerable uplift of the gabbro; while in the Blaven range, where it was thinning away, it has assumed the same synclinal form as the gabbro above. The granite does not maintain the laccolitic or sheet-like habit with the same regularity as the gabbro, but often shows a frankly transgressive junction, especially in its eastern part. Again, though it has undoubtedly been built up by distinct injections, these are less numerous than in the case of the gabbro, and show much more uniformity of composition. These differences, tectonic and petrographic, must be considered characteristic of an acid as contrasted with a basic magma.

The boss-formed masses of granite and granophyre in the eastern part of central Skye exemplify more than one fashion of intrusion. The Beinn an Dubhaich granite has risen through the core of an old anticline, and presents very remarkable relations to the dolomitic limestones which it intersects (pp. 132–135). The Kilchrist granophyre has found its way up the sides of the old volcanic funnel at that place. The larger mass, of generally elliptic outline, which forms Beinn na Caillich and its neighbours has also broken through on the edge of the old vent, but eccentrically, and it has partly invaded the earlier boss of gabbro. That igneous activity has thus been localised here at three distinct epochs is not surprising, for we have seen that this spot had been a special centre of strain (in the sense generally of upward pressure) since Palæozoic times. It is further interesting to notice that the strain was renewed after the intrusion of the granite boss, and was only relieved by a considerable relative upheaval at a later time. Owing to the narrow localisation of this upheaval, and perhaps in part to the nature of the surrounding rocks, the displacement in this case took the form of faulting. The north-western boundary is now a straight fault which cuts off the granite itself; and, as has been pointed out, this fault has its maximum throw in the middle part of its course and dies out both ways at or near the boundary of the granite, thus marking its connection with a vertical elevation of the granite boss. In its semicircular southern half the boundary of the granite is marked by a plexus of more or less tangential faults, the fracture here having occurred nearly along the junction of the relatively unyielding boss with the adjacent Liassic and volcanic rocks. On the eastern and north-eastern sides the granite was in intimate contact with a more stubborn mass, viz. the boss of gabbro, and the line of faulting here sweeps round at a wider radius (Fig. 28, p. 131), its curiously curved line from Strath Suardal to the Sound of Scalpay emphasising its relation to the granite boss with which it is concentric. The faults, and others connected with them, cut the composite sills and some minor acid intrusions; and the elevation of the Beinn na Caillich boss is thus referred to a somewhat late epoch. It was not accompanied by any igneous intrusions.

The plutonic phase does not seem to have been divided by any prolonged interval of time from that of the minor intrusions, and one remarkable group may be regarded as in a certain sense marking the transition from the one to the other. In various regions where the record of events during one complete suite of igneous eruptions can be followed it is seen that, while in the plutonic phase the succession of rock-types follows an order of decreasing basicity, in the "dyke phase" this order is reversed. This generalisation is applicable to Skye, provided that we confine our attention to those groups of intrusions which are related to the special focus of activity; the regional groups, which show little variation of any sort, being excluded. If, with this limitation, we may regard the reversal of order in the "dyke phase" as a general law, whatever be its significance and explanation, we may expect that between the plutonic phase and that which follows there will be a certain *critical epoch*, when, if intrusions occur, basic and acid magmas may be intruded almost simultaneously. It is precisely to this epoch that we refer those composite intrusions, consisting of basic and acid rocks in intimate association, which we have described under the name of the Cnoc Càrnach group (Chapters XII., XIII.). In this view they belong to a point of time accurately separating the plutonic phase from that of the minor intrusions, and evince a nicely balanced state which marked a turning-point in the mutual behaviour of basic and acid magmas at the Skye focus. The rarity of such remarkable composite intrusions in other regions we should then ascribe to the fact that the plutonic phase of activity and that which succeeds it are in general divided by a period of quiescence. As regards the areal distribution of the peculiar composite intrusions of this epoch in Skye, it is to be noticed that they occupy a semicircular belt of country, partly surrounding the granite tract of the Red Hills, but lying beyond it to the N.E. They are thus on the side remote from the gabbro of the Cuillins, and carry on a step farther that displacement northeastward of the centre of activity which we have noticed in the successive episodes of the plutonic phase. (*See* Fig. 58, p. 273.)

The *phase of minor intrusions* opened with a great revival of regional activity. There was an invasion of basic magma in the form of sills, collectively of enormous volume, intruded among the basaltic lavas and the underlying strata. This was apparently not a regional episode in the strictest sense of affecting the entire region alike; but it certainly had no connection with the Skye focus. If the sills of the great group in Skye are related to any centre, it must be to one lying towards the N. or N.W., in which directions the sills become thicker and more important, while they die out towards the S.E.

The intrusion of the great group of sills was followed by a long succession of episodes, which, as we have already insisted, fall into two parallel series, the local and the regional. The former was restricted to a limited area, including and surrounding the mountain tract of central Skye, and consisted of several distinct groups of intrusions, both dykes and sheets, with a wide range of petrographical variety. The latter comprised a vast number of basic intrusions, in the form of dykes with a predominant N.W. or N.N.W. direction, and is less easily divided into distinct groups. For this reason it will be convenient to consider the two series separately.

In the *local series of minor intrusions* we distinguish three principal stages, corresponding with those of the plutonic phase of activity but with an important difference. The sequence in the earlier phase was—ultrabasic, basic, acid: in the minor intrusions it is—acid, basic, ultrabasic; *i.e.* an order of decreasing acidity or increasing basicity. This reversal of order in the "dyke phase" has been recognised in other regions, and attempts have been made to explain it on general principles,[*] but a discussion of these would lead us too far from our main subject.

The minor acid intrusions constituting the first of the three stages took the form of dykes and sheets, not often maintaining the regular disposition of typical sills. Their epoch is well marked with reference to the regional as well as to the local sequence; for, while they were later than the great group of sills, they were earlier than the generality of the basic dykes which followed the sills over the whole region. The distribution of the acid intrusions in space is rather wide, but still clearly defined, including the Red Hills but extending for a considerable distance beyond (*see* sketch-map,

[*] *E.g.*, see Barrow, *Quart. Journ. Geol. Soc.*, vol. xlviii., p. 121; 1892.

Fig. 58, p. 273). The later acid intrusions are thus clearly related to the same focus as the granite, and indicate a resumption of activity at that focus, on a feebler scale but over a more extended area, after a lapse of time at least as long as that required for the intrusion of the great group of dolerite sills. It appears, however, that the crustal strain which provoked the new outburst was compounded of both local and regional elements, of which the latter exercised a powerful influence on the behaviour of the minor acid intrusions. The area affected by these intrusions, though centring in the granite focus, has an elongated outline with its long axis in the direction of the regional dykes, and the acid dykes themselves have in general the same direction.

In the absence of chemical analyses, the nature of these later acid rocks can only be inferred from their mineralogical composition. They appear to be somewhat poorer in ferro-magnesian constituents than the rocks of the granite group. If we suppose them to be derived from the granite-magma, or one of like composition, by further differentiation, we may look for a "complementary" group of basic rocks rich in iron and magnesia. The rocks to which we may most probably assign this rôle are the dykes of the Beinn Dearg group (pp. 324-326); which have the required petrographical characters, and present the peculiarity —otherwise anomalous—of a group of basic rocks whose distribution is closely bound up with that of the granite. We have included as aberrant members of the minor acid intrusions certain highly felspathic types with little or no free silica. These find their counterparts at earlier epochs in a rare syenitic modification of the granite, described as occurring below Creagan Dubha, and in the felsitic member of the composite sill of Rudh' an Eireannaich.

The minor basic intrusions of the local series followed the acid ones after an interval which must have been of long duration, for during this time were intruded a large proportion—perhaps the majority—of the regional basic dykes. This long pause, contrasted with the rapid succession of events during the plutonic phase, we must interpret as a sign of waning energy at the Skye focus.

Just as the minor acid intrusions showed a distribution about the Red Hills, so the minor basic intrusions (of the local series) are manifestly related to the Cuillin district. Here, however, the relation is of a stricter kind, for the rocks in question are scarcely found beyond the limits of the gabbro laccolite itself. Further, the directions of the intrusions have clearly been determined by some forces centring in or beneath the interior of the gabbro tract; the forms assumed being (successively or in part simultaneously) tangential dykes, radial dykes, and inclined sheets dipping towards the interior. The striking contrast between this disposition and that found in the minor acid intrusions is in some measure capable of explanation. During the interval between the two outbursts the regional crustal strain had been relieved by faulting on a very extensive scale, and the whole country broken up into separate strips or blocks. One block which thus became in some degree isolated included the gabbro laccolite and the immediately adjacent country, and it was of sufficient extent to allow of the development of a local system of strain in its interior. The precise nature of this strain, which provoked, and was relieved by, the minor basic intrusions of the Cuillin group, offers a mechanical problem of considerable difficulty, but we should picture it as a tendency to upheaval at the centre of the area. It is perhaps significant that the system is slightly eccentric, the point towards which the sheets incline being situated a little to the north-east of the centre of the laccolite (*see* Fig. 72, p. 367). If the magma of these intrusions was derived from the old gabbro-magma, or one originally of like composition, there must have been some further differentiation of this.

We cannot estimate precisely the interval which severed the intrusions just dismissed from the next well marked group, that of the minor ultrabasic intrusions. A considerable number of dykes of the regional series cut the former but are cut by the latter. Certain rocks in Skye which are petrographically on the border-line between basic and ultrabasic perhaps belong to this interval. This seems to be the case at least with a few rocks answering to this description which are found in the Cuillins, but as regards others (such as those of the Ben Aslak type) we are in doubt as to whether they belong to the local series or the regional.

The minor ultrabasic intrusions are collectively much inferior in importance to the basic group. The principal representatives are the later peridotite dykes of the Cuillins. In their radiate arrangement they recall the preceding group, and exceptionally at places in the heart of the district they assume the "inclined sheet" habit. Their distribution in space is interesting, the crescentic area which includes them covering the western and south-western parts of the gabbro laccolite, with some extension towards the south-east (sketch-map, Fig. 75, p. 375). This embraces only half a circle, viz. the south-western half, within which the much earlier plutonic peridotites were intruded. The three principal local groups of minor intrusions in Skye show thus an evident relation to the corresponding plutonic intrusions respectively, and the reversal of the order of succession in the final phase implies therefore a reversal of the direction of shifting of the centre of activity. If we take account of the shifting indicated in the old trachytic and rhyolitic volcano of Fionn Choire, the displacement throughout the three successive phases of igneous activity seems to have been of an oscillatory kind, as follows :—

    Volcanic, . . . from N.E. to S.W.
    Plutonic, . . . from S.W. to N.E.
    Minor intrusions, . . from N.E. to S.W.

Before proceeding to the minor intrusions of the regional series, we may briefly mention certain *subsidiary groups*, the precise relations of which to other members of the great suite we have not in all cases deciphered. They all belong to late epochs; but whether they are older or younger than the peridotites just considered, we have no means of ascertaining.* The trachyte and trachy-andesite dykes have been described in Chapter XXIII. Most of them, occurring near Broadford and in the Sleat district, have no close connection with the Skye focus, but belong to a group which has its chief area of distribution farther south-east, on the Scottish mainland. Like the great group of basic sills, it enters Skye from without, but from the opposite direction (Fig. 76, p. 387). The Drynoch group of trachytes seems to be of distinct origin, though still of late date; and to the same epoch we may conjecturally refer the mugearites and allied types (oligoclase- and orthoclase-basalts, etc.) noticed in Chapters XV. and XVIII. The dykes of augite-andesite and of acid pitchstone are scarcely numerous enough to afford a basis for any generalisation. We have seen indications (see p. 402) of an interesting relationship between the two types, but this does not come out so clearly in Skye as in Arran. The pitchstones seem in our area to have a very restricted occurrence, which might, however, be somewhat extended by including devitrified rocks perhaps referable to this group. The typical examples discovered have a distribution compatible with a relation to the granite centre. If this connection with the local series can be assumed, it is interesting, for it shows the oval area of distribution of the minor acid intrusions contracted during this final and feeble recrudescence of activity to little more than a line, following the usual direction of the regional dykes (Fig. 76, p. 387).

The sequence of the *regional series of minor intrusions* subsequent to the epoch of the great group of sills we have not succeeded in tracing out systematically from stage to stage. The difficulty of dividing the rocks into distinct groups and arranging these in order of chronological succession arises chiefly from three circumstances. (i.) The intrusions have almost exclusively the form of dykes. (ii.) A general community of petrographical characters runs through the whole series. (iii.) All the dykes have in general a common direction of strike; so that intersections, which might serve to determine the relative ages of different dykes, are not often found. A few remarks may be made on each of these three points.

The form and habit assumed by igneous intrusions at any epoch were directly dependent on the nature of the crustal strain at that epoch. During the earliest part of the phase of minor intrusions the regional strain had been such that the invading magma was injected in the form of very regular sills. This was also the case in varying degree with the local groups, viz. the peculiar composite intrusions of the Cnoc Càrnach group and the minor acid intrusions of the area surrounding the Red Hills. Shortly after the epoch of

* In Rum we have found the later peridotite dykes to cut the augite-andesites.

these last, however, occurred an event of the first importance in the geological history of Skye, viz. the principal faulting (of Tertiary age) in our area. To this is due the characteristic structure—that of a succession of gently tilted plateaux divided by lines of fault—which is the most striking tectonic feature over the greater part of the island. Its effect was no less important as altering the conditions under which igneous magmas were intruded. In the country thus shattered a new distribution of strains was set up, and the continuity of the strata (including the lava-flows and the dolerite-sills) was broken. Henceforth when molten magma again rose in fissures throughout the region—sometimes in the old fissures reopened—it was neither to spread laterally among the country rocks nor (so far as we know) to be poured out at the surface. The later dykes are in this sense self-sufficing intrusive bodies, neither the feeders nor the offshoots of other igneous masses. Such dykes differed functionally from those belonging to earlier epochs.

We have already insisted upon one conspicuous difference between the local and the regional series of rocks, a difference of a petrographical kind running through the entire suite in all phases of activity: the groups with regional distribution show nothing of the wide differentiation which we have had to notice in the local groups. This comes out strikingly in the chemical analyses here reproduced for comparison, though doubtless a more extended examination would discover greater variety than is apparent in these few examples. The basic dykes certainly present a remarkable monotony of petrographical characters when viewed as a whole, and we have found among them but few specific features which can be tentatively regarded as marking distinct natural groups or pertaining to defined epochs in the succession. Prophyritic dykes seem to belong in general to a rather late time, and the later dykes are also perhaps richer on the whole in xenoliths and xenocrysts. These points may possibly be significant (Chapter XX.). It is true there are certain subsidiary groups of which we have made mention, the trachy-andesites of Sleat and other types containing oligoclase and orthoclase, besides rocks on the other hand rich in olivine and carrying picotite; and some among these may possibly claim to be included in the regional series. We might rather say perhaps that there are certain subsidiary centres of activity in the region in addition to the chief foci, and these were also in a minor degree centres of differentiation. In any case the fact that all these special rocks, including also the pitchstones, etc., made their appearance at quite late epochs seems to show that, outside the principal local foci, any very important differentiation was arrived at only in the final stages of igneous activity in the region.

The general law of direction of the dykes has been sufficiently discussed in Chapter XVII. We recur to the subject here only to point out how the varying direction, as well as the varying frequency, of the regional basic dykes illustrates the mutual interaction of the regional and local elements of the crustal strain. The intervention of the regional influence in the behaviour of the

	I.	II.	III.
SiO_2	46·61	45·69	47·49
TiO_2	1·81	2·93	not det.
Al_2O_3	15·22	16·35	19·48
Fe_2O_3	3·49	6·09	5·02
FeO	7·71	7·70	9·05
MnO	0·13	0·26	not det.
MgO	8·66	6·10	5·29
CaO	10·08	8·27	10·05
Na_2O	2·43	2·80	} 2·39
K_2O	0·67	0·96	
H_2O	3·17	2·81	1·20
P_2O_5	0·10	0·15	not det.

I. Basaltic lavas (one analysis only).
II. Sills of the "great group" (mean of two).
III. Dykes of "regional series" (mean of two).

intrusions of the local series is apparent at more than one stage, and is most marked in the distribution and orientation of the acid dykes, intruded not long anterior to the faulting of the region. But a reciprocal influence is also to be observed. The energy displayed in the intrusion of the regional series of dykes seems to have attained its maximum in the neighbourhood of the gabbro focus. This appears in the extraordinary profusion of dykes in a broad belt of country surrounding the Cuillins, and especially in the distribution of multiple dykes, as already noticed (Fig. 52, p. 238). Further, there is (Fig. 63, p. 301) a decided tendency in the regional dykes to a radiate disposition about the chief centres of plutonic intrusions, a tendency discernible as a secondary influence modifying the primary principle of parallelism. This of course must be attributed not to the plutonic intrusions themselves, but to the local crustal strains with which these are intimately bound up; and accordingly the granite centres are attended by the same effects as the gabbro.

Despite the exception here implied, and generally away from centres of local disturbance, the dykes hold their normal course with a want of regard for geological structure and tectonic accidents which is very remarkable. Especially noteworthy is it that they have rarely taken advantage of the presumable lines of weakness offered by faults. The dykes are, it would seem, the expression of a larger law than that which is realised in the ordinary dislocations of strata. This independent behaviour characterises the Tertiary dykes of Britain as a whole.[*]

In conclusion we venture to suggest a question which may have more than a local application. One of the most remarkable circumstances brought out by a study of the basic dykes in the field, and one discussed at length in its proper place, is the manner

[*] *Cf.* Sir A. Geikie, *Trans. Roy. Soc. Edin.*, vol. xxxv., pp. 63-68; 1888: *Ancient Volcanoes of Great Britain*, vol. ii., pp. 116-171; 1897.

in which the intrusions have been controlled by the nature of the country-rock. The dykes, traversing some formations in vast numbers, show a singular reluctance to enter certain other formations. Whatever be the explanation of this behaviour, the fact has bearings which are possibly of some importance. On *a priori* grounds dykes which freely intersect one formation, but do not penetrate another overlying one, might with considerable show of probability be referred to an age intermediate between those of the two formations concerned ; but the results of our survey forbid us, in the area mapped, to attach any weight to negative evidence of this kind. Now in the northern, midland, and western counties of England and in parts of Wales there are numerous dykes and other intrusions of basic rocks, which intersect the Carboniferous and older strata, but not the New Red rocks ; and these intrusions have therefore generally been held to be of pre-Permian age. The facts which we have recorded suggest that an inference based on such grounds should be open to reconsideration. There is the more force in this suggestion since one dyke at Swinnerton Park in Staffordshire* does actually cut the New Red rocks ; while Mr Greenly† has found a similar case in Anglesey, and has put forward the opinion that a large number of dykes in that island, hitherto referred to the interval between Carboniferous and Permian, are in reality a part of the great Tertiary system of intrusions. If geological and petrographical evidence should be found to confirm and extend this conclusion, we may have to enlarge considerably the area admittedly affected by the latest suite of igneous intrusions in Britain.‡

To exhibit in one view some of the more important results summarised in this chapter, we append a table showing the sequence and in some degree the mutual relations of the chief groups of igneous rocks of the regional and the local series in Skye. The local episodes are indicated by separate tablets inserted in the table, their vertical spacing being intended to represent diagrammatically the time-intervals between the successive groups.

* Kirkby, *Trans. N. Staffs. Nat. Field Club*, vol. xxviii., p. 129 ; 1894.
† *Geol. Mag.*, 1910, pp. 160-164.
‡ On this subject see also Watts in Sketch of the Geology of the Birmingham district, *Proc. Geol. Ass.*, vol. xv., pp. 399, 400 ; 1898.

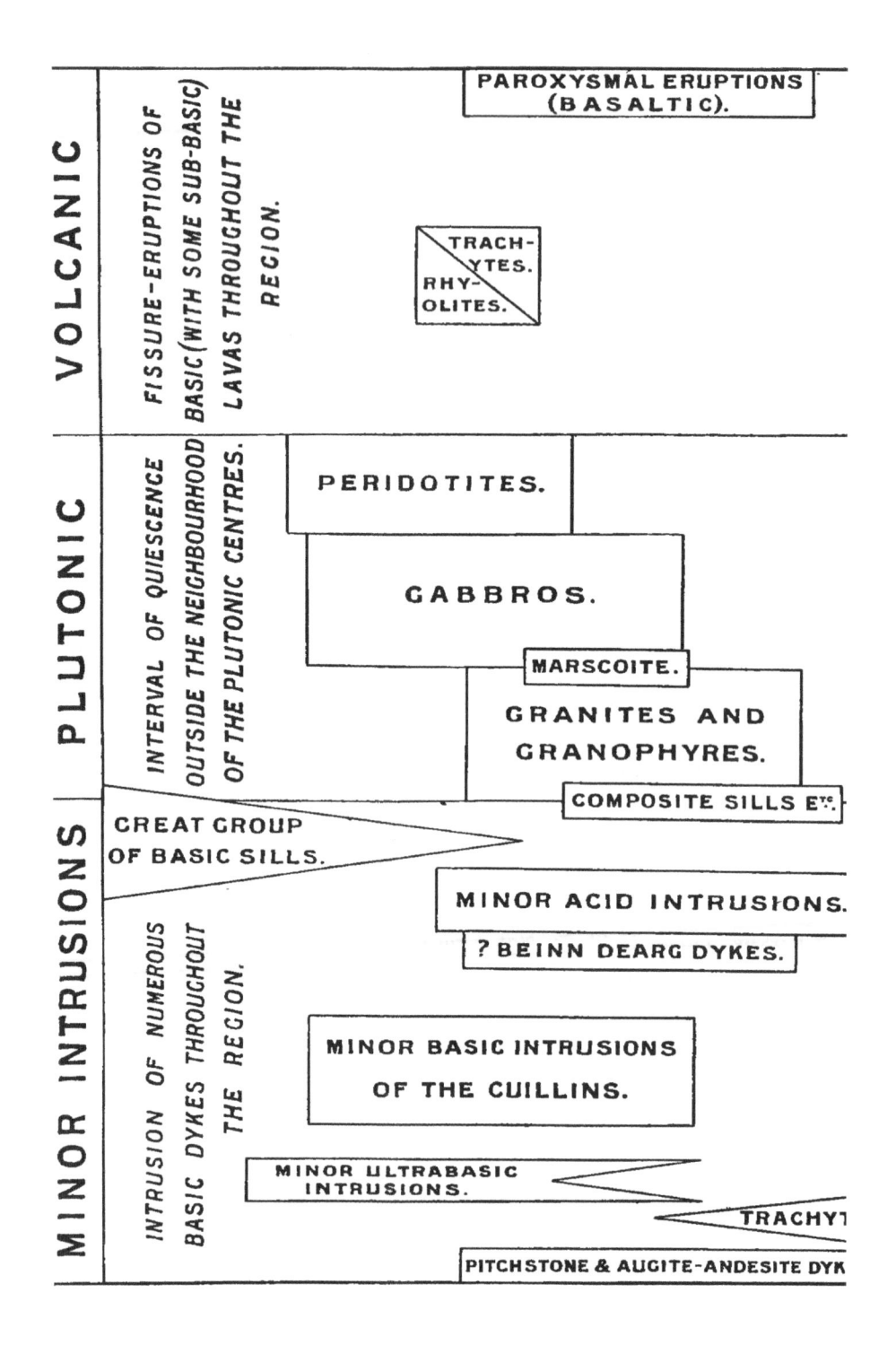

VOLCANIC	FISSURE-ERUPTIONS OF BASIC (WITH SOME SUB-BASIC) LAVAS THROUGHOUT THE REGION.	PAROXYSMAL ERUPTIONS (BASALTIC).
		TRACHYTES. / RHYOLITES.
PLUTONIC	INTERVAL OF QUIESCENCE OUTSIDE THE NEIGHBOURHOOD OF THE PLUTONIC CENTRES.	PERIDOTITES.
		GABBROS.
		MARSCOITE.
		GRANITES AND GRANOPHYRES.
		COMPOSITE SILLS ETC.
MINOR INTRUSIONS	INTRUSION OF NUMEROUS BASIC DYKES THROUGHOUT THE REGION.	GREAT GROUP OF BASIC SILLS.
		MINOR ACID INTRUSIONS.
		? BEINN DEARG DYKES.
		MINOR BASIC INTRUSIONS OF THE CUILLINS.
		MINOR ULTRABASIC INTRUSIONS.
		TRACHYTE
		PITCHSTONE & AUGITE-ANDESITE DYKES

CHAPTER XXVI.

Physical Features and Scenery.

The Western Isles of Scotland have often been cited in illustration of the enormous amount of material which has been removed by the agents of erosion and transportation during the latter half of Tertiary time. In this respect Skye does not yield in point of interest to any other part of the region. The basaltic rocks which build the north-western part of the island have been cut up into numerous hills and plateaux, divided by deep glens, while from the south-eastern part these rocks have been wholly stripped away. In the central tract erosion has gone still farther; for, not only have the basalts been removed, but the plutonic rocks, of later age and doubtless consolidated at considerable depths below the then surface, have been left standing out as mountains 2500 and 3000 feet high. In this final chapter we shall examine the manner in which the processes of erosion have been controlled by the geological constitution; so that the existing physical features and scenery stand related to the lithological characters, distribution, and arrangement of the various rocks. Such a discussion will derive a certain special interest from the fact that the rocks are, within the area to be more particularly considered, exclusively igneous rocks.

We have pointed out in some detail in the preceding chapter how the successive igneous eruptions in our area have been closely bound up with the development of strains in the earth's crust and the various ways in which these strains have from time to time found relief. From the same causes there also resulted, as we have seen, movements and deformations of the solid crust, sometimes of wide extent, sometimes rather narrowly localised. Such movements, taking in general the form of differential elevation (whether absolute or relative), have of course influenced the broader physical features of the country; and we can trace in the existing surface relief the interaction of the two elements—themselves closely connected—the distribution of the various igneous rocks and actual deformation of the earth's crust.

Disregarding the south-eastern portion of the island, where the Tertiary igneous rocks have had only a very small share in determining the existing surface-relief, Skye divides, for our present purpose, into three strongly contrasted tracts. To the north-west the basaltic country presents a well characterised, though monotonous, type of scenery. The central part of the island offers much greater diversity and, from the point of view of the artist, much more interest, possessing in the Cuillins a mountain-group without rival in the British Isles. This group, with which we must associate also the Blaven range, occupies the western portion of the central mountain-tract, where gabbro is the dominant rock. To the east we have the granitic " Red Hills," and the contrast in form between the two groups of mountains has been the subject of remark by numerous writers. We shall consider these three principal types of scenery in order.

In the *basalt plateaux* the determining element of the surface-relief is, from the lithological point of view, not the basaltic lavas but the great group of sills, to which all the strong features are directly due. At the same time the general arrangement of the features is the simple expression of the tectonic structure resulting from the (regional) system of crust-movements aleady described. These movements took the form of a shattering of the country by numerous faults and a tilting of the separate blocks or strips towards the west. There was at the same time a certain tilting of the whole country in the same direction. We may express this otherwise, from the point of view of the geological mapper, by saying that the cumulative throw of the faults towards the east is not enough to compensate fully the general dip towards the west; so that the base of the basalt group stands at a considerably higher altitude on the east side of the island than on the west. It has resulted from this that the highest ground in this part of the island occurs near the east coast, in the long and almost continuous range which may be regarded as the main escarpment of the basaltic group. It runs from Beinn Tianavaig, near Portree, northward to the Quiraing, culminating in the Storr (2360 feet).

We turn for a moment to the south-eastern part of Skye. This has clearly experienced, as a whole, since the volcanic epoch a greater elevation (or less depression) than the north-western tract. The greater relative elevation, however, is not sufficient to account for the fact that the basaltic group has here been totally removed. Indeed the average altitude of the surface at the present time is considerably lower here than in the plateau country. The removal of the basalts must be attributed mainly to another difference, depending on the distribution of the great group of sills. As we have seen, these were most developed towards the north and north-west, thinning away towards the south-east, and never reaching the Sleat district. Where the sills were in force, they not only greatly increased (probably doubled) the total thickness of the basalt group, but, by the interposition of sheets of hard rock at numerous horizons, enabled the whole to offer a much more effective resistance to erosion. In the south-east, where the sills were wanting, the much more perishable basaltic lavas were easily removed. It is interesting to notice that the effect of the general dip is nevertheless still indicated by the distribution of the higher ground, In the tract of Torridonian rocks which extends from Kyleakin to near the Point of Sleat, the greatest heights are found to the north-east (Sgùrr Coinnich, 2400 feet); the average altitude diminishes south-westward, and beyond Loch na Dal the country nowhere reaches the 1000-feet contour-line.

Returning to the basaltic tract, we may remark first that the coast-line affords admirable studies of the results of marine erosion. The finest display is on the west coast, especially between Loch Bracadale and Loch Brittle. Here the basalt group goes down below sea-level, and presents long ranges of precipitous cliffs, in many places practically vertical, rising 500 or 700 or even 900 feet out of the water. This greatest height is found at Beinn nan Cuitheann, to the south of Talisker. The cliffs have a very evident appearance of stratification, due to the alternation of lavas and sills; but in a vertical exposure the sills, with their pronounced cross-jointing, are no more durable than the lavas, and the whole presents one continuous face, in strong contrast with the effects of subaërial erosion inland. On the east coast the Jurassic strata emerge from beneath the basalts. Fortified by sills often more than 100 feet thick, they make in places strong sea-cliffs, especially towards the north, forming an advance-guard to the escarpment of the basaltic group behind.

This main escarpment runs generally parallel with the coast-line, but at a variable distance from it. In accordance with its structure, it presents a more or less precipitous face towards the east, with a characteristic broken appearance due to considerable land-slips, while the western slope is a gentle one. In the succession of plateaux west of the main escarpment we find generally a monotony of appearance due to iteration of the same type of structure. Such diversity as meets the eye results from the varying inclination, frequency, and thickness of the sills, which everywhere stand out in relief from the softer lavas. Where the dip is very gentle, as is sometimes the case on the west side of the island, a single sill may form the whole of the summit of a hill, and a remarkable flat-topped appearance is the consequence. This is especially striking in isolated hills * such as Macleod's Tables, the only points near the west coast which reach an altitude of 1500 feet. More usually there is a decided dip to the west, or some point near west. In this case the summit of a plateau is formed by several inclined sills, divided by abrupt steps, and the western slope also may consist in great part of broad dip-faces of other sills. The other slopes are terraced by the outcrops of numerous sills, which appear as so many escarpments separated by intervals of gentle inclination representing the intervening lavas. On the hill-sides bordering Glen Varragill, Glen Drynoch, Glen Eynort, etc., or facing the sea-lochs Harport, Eynort, and Brittle, as many as a score of such terraces may often be counted in the evening light (Fig. 79). Farther north, as the sills become thicker, the character of the landscape changes accordingly. A single sill may now be sufficient to form a considerable sea-cliff (Plate X.) or an

---

* In areas of Jurassic rocks a similar tabular summit may be made by an outlier of a strong sill. A good example is Dùn-can, the highest point of Raasay.

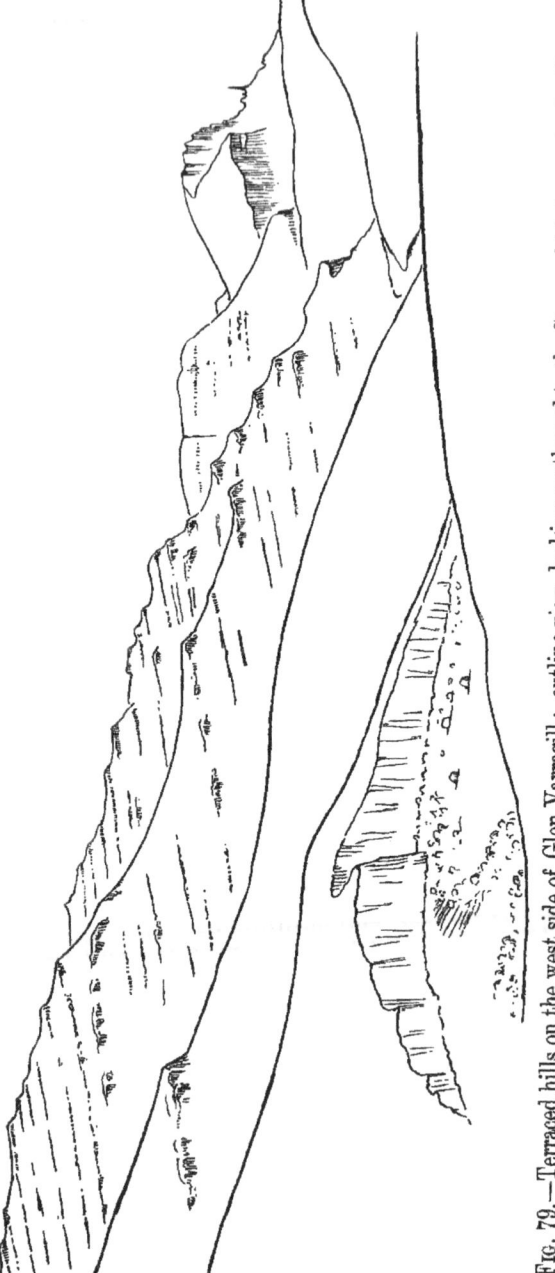

Fig. 79.—Terraced hills on the west side of Glen Varragill; outline view, looking northward to the Storr, which is seen in the distance (right). The terraces are caused by the very numerous intrusive sills intercalated in the basaltic lavas.

imposing inland escarpment. At the same time the columnar jointing of the sills becomes very pronounced, introducing a vertical element into the scenery; the long ranges of escarpment present perpendicularly fluted faces, and detached pinnacles and needles stand out in advance. In this way the plateau and terrace type of scenery, which in the central part of the island is only wearisome to the eye, becomes impressive farther north from mere exaggeration of scale. Especially is this the case in the main escarpment facing the east coast, where the Storr Rock and the Quiraing have long been included in the tourist's itinerary.

Next in importance to the basic sills as a factor in the detailed structure of the basaltic country come the basic dykes. A few of these, notably the large solitary dykes of coarse diabase, form salient features, a remark which is true also of the trachyte dykes of the Drynoch group; but the great majority have weathered more readily than the rocks which they traverse, and have often given rise to trenches, gullies, or even deep ravines. A glance at the Ordnance map shows how many of the smaller burns follow remarkably straight courses with a direction varying from N.N.W.–S.S.E. to N.W.–S.E. This is the case especially on moderately elevated and gently inclined stretches of moorland and on the slopes of the hills where these have something of a north-westerly or south-easterly aspect. Slopes such as those of Ben Lee towards Loch Sligachan, Brocbheinn towards Glen Drynoch, etc., are conspicuously scored by long straight parallel gullies, which have been determined by basic dykes, and often by multiple dykes (Fig. 80). On the higher ground, and especially where the basic sills attain a great thickness, dykes become less frequent, and the straight gullies cease to be so conspicuous a feature.

The weathering of the dykes into depressions, which are the channels of permanent or occasional streams, is not due to the rock of the dykes being intrinsically more perishable than its neighbours. Indeed the dyke-rock is in most cases very decidedly more durable than the lavas and often not inferior in this respect to the sills. It is the vertical posture of the dykes that has rendered them specially vulnerable to attack, and this is most markedly the case where a multiple dyke has presented several vertical planes of weakness (the junctions of the different members) in a short space. Any tendency to a platy fracture in an individual dyke tells in the same sense, and the much commoner cross-jointing also facilitates disintegration by allowing the dyke to divide into little horizontal prisms which are easily removed.

Unlike many other areas of somewhat similar geological constitution, the basaltic tract of Skye is remarkably sterile. Cultivation of any kind is possible only in some of the broader valleys, where the rocks are covered by a mantle of boulder-clay. Above the drift-line soil and subsoil are wanting. Several causes contribute to this result: the intractable nature of the sill-rocks, the scouring of the country by ice, the excessive rain-fall under existing conditions, and the prevalent covering of peat, which effectually protects the rocks from subaërial decay. Peat generally clothes the valleys and the less steep slopes, and often covers to a considerable depth the flat and gently sloping heights. The vegetation which gives rise to this accumulation is referable chiefly to *Sphagnum*, various species of *Scirpus*, *Juncus*, and *Carex*, and grasses such as *Nardus stricta*, but many other species also contribute.* Birch-bark and wood occur almost everywhere in the peat on the lower ground; and, although the country is now almost denuded of trees, it is clear both from existing relics and from the evidence of place-names † that much of it has once been wooded. The final destruction must be attributed to the cattle and sheep. Even now any inaccessible ravine, or an islet in any of the tarns, has an abundant, though dwarfed, growth of birch, alder, hazel, holly, rowan, oak, aspen, etc.

We have seen that on the basalt plateaux in general the lavas, which constitute the "country" rock, play nevertheless the least important part in determining the surface relief. There is, however,

FIG. 80.— Outlines of hills on the west side of Glen Brittle, seen from near Bealach a' Mhaim. The terraced appearance is due to the intrusive sills, and the long straight gullies are determined by the weathering of dykes.

a broken belt of country, immediately adjacent to the large plutonic intrusions of the mountains, in which the basalt scenery assumes a different character. Here the lavas, metamorphosed by the proximity of the gabbro and granite, become hard enough to offer a stubborn resistance to erosion, and form rough crags sometimes comparable with those of the gabbro itself. At the same time, and as a direct consequence of this induration of the lavas, the basic sills, which are the dominant feature of the plateau country, die out. The bedding of the lavas is usually very apparent, but does not give rise to strong ledges. The character of this sub-

* Among these may be mentioned such bog-plants as *Drosera anglica, D. rotundifolia, Saxifraga umbrosa, Lobelia dortmanni, Pinguicula vulgaris, Menyanthes trifoliata, Narthecium ossifragum,* and *Eriophorum polystachion,* Elsewhere the common heaths (*Calluna vulgaris, Erica cinerea, E. tetralix*) and other shrubby plants contribute to the formation of peat. Characteristic species on the higher moors are *Juniperus nana, Veronica montana, Vaccinium uliginosum, Armeria vulgaris* (var. *planifolii*), *Cochlearia officinalis* (var. *danica*), *Cladonia rangiferina,* etc.

† Such names as *Coille* (a wood) and *Doire* (a grove), besides the names of individual species of trees, are sometimes found where no trees now exist. The remark is doubtless applicable to much of the Highlands. It is noteworthy that many of the letters of the Gaelic alphabet are named from trees, and that the badges of some of the clans were sprigs of trees which would now be found with difficulty.

montane belt, interposed between the plateaux and the mountains, is well shown by Slat-bheinn and An Stac in Fig. 81, kindly drawn for us by Mr Colin Phillip. The eastern portions of Sgùrr nan Each and Belig belong to the same type. The rough crags of metamorphosed basalt are more striking when they occur in juxtaposition with the smooth slopes of the Red Hills, as on the summit and northern face of Glamaig and especially in Creagan Dubha, a spur of Beinn Dearg Mhòr (of Strath).

The chief interest in Skye to lovers of the picturesque attaches to the *gabbro mountains*. The astonishing indifference of the earlier travellers* to mountain scenery left the Cuillins † wholly unnoticed, and for a long time this part of the island was regarded as inaccessible. J. D. Forbes in 1836 first accomplished the ascent of Sgùrr nan Gillean, and the little sketch-map accompanying his valuable paper shows that he had also become acquainted with some of the peaks of the main range; but it was the late Sheriff Alexander Nicolson who made the district known to the general public.‡ The Ordnance Survey was made at a time when many of the summits had not yet been climbed,§ and the map leaves much to be desired as regards completeness and accuracy. In later years the explorations of members of the Scottish Mountaineering Club have accumulated a store of information, which is preserved in their *Journal*; but the mountains are still practically closed to the ordinary tourist, partly by the lack of accommodation but chiefly for want of knowledge.‖

We shall examine firstly the broad features of the topography and secondly the minor elements of the surface relief. The former are directly attributable to the form of the gabbro laccolite, while the latter are due chiefly to the dykes and intrusive sheets by which the gabbro is intersected, and to the peculiarites attending ice-erosion.

* Pennant, Johnson, Boswell, Jameson, and others either make no mention of the mountains, or refer to them incidentally in terms expressive of aversion, reserving their admiration for a wooded glen or a waterfall. Views of the Cuillins from Beinn na Caillich are given by Pennant and Jameson, but both are quite unrecognisable.

† The spelling Cuillin adopted here is that of the Ordnance Survey: the name is sometimes written Coolin. The Gaelic word is probably Cuilfhionn, as given by Nicolson, and to identify it with the name of the Ossianic hero Cuchullin seems to be purely fanciful. In older writers we find the forms Cuilluelum, Culluelun, Gulluin, Cullin, Quillin, Quillen, etc.

‡ See especially a series of articles in *Good Words* for 1875. The highest summit of the Cuillins has been named Sgùrr Alasdair in memory of the Sheriff.

§ Of about twenty peaks of 3000 ft and upward only seven have heights assigned to them on the map.

‖ The guide-books, which direct the tourist to devote a day to the Storr Rock and one or two days to the Quiraing, usually allow but a single day for a hasty visit to Loch Coruisk, and perhaps another for the ascent of Sgùrr nan Gillean, by no means the easiest peak of the Cuillins. Although a systematic study would necessitate camping, most parts of the mountains can be reached from Sligachan by a hardy pedestrian. Elgol also affords convenient access to the southern part of the district and Carbost to the western.

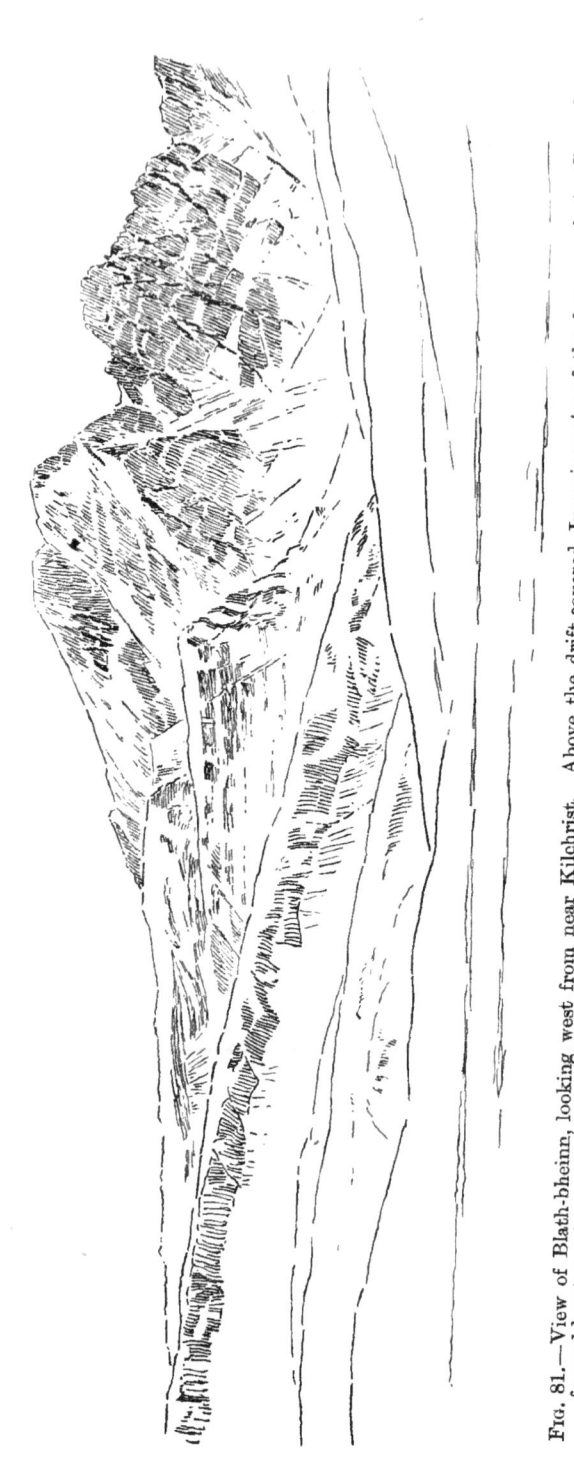

FIG. 81.—View of Blath-bheinn, looking west from near Kilchrist. Above the drift-covered Jurassic rocks of the foreground, An Carnach, formed by strong intrusive sills in the basalt group, illustrates the plateau type of scenery. Behind this rise Slat-bheinn and An Stac, in which the sills rapidly die out, and the indurated basalt lavas themselves constitute marked features, the bedding being sharply turned up towards the mountains. Blath-bheinn and Clach Glas in the background are characteristic gabbro mountains. (*Del.* C. B. Phillip.)

Especially interesting is the arrangement of the principal ridges and valleys of the Cuillins as dependent on the form of the gabbro laccolite. The laccolite is, as we have seen, of the nature of a thick sheet, thinning away towards its perimeter. The upper surface of the gabbro may therefore be assumed to have had a somewhat similar shape to that of the lower surface, as represented roughly by the contour-lines on the map given above (Fig. 15, p. 86). The covering of basaltic lavas which once overspread the whole island has been totally removed from the mountain area. What was the nature of the drainage-system during this earlier stage of the erosion it is not possible to discover; for that system has not been "superimposed" upon the gabbro from which the existing surface-relief is carved out. The gabbro so greatly surpassed the other rocks of the district in the resistance which it opposed to the agents of erosion, that, when in the course of denudation the upper surface of the laccolite was exposed, the drainage-lines at once began to adapt themselves to the form of that surface. On no other supposition can we explain the remarkable correspondence observed between the shape of the laccolite and the existing form of the ground. This correspondence comes out very clearly upon comparing the topographical map with Fig. 15, which for this purpose may be taken as representing very roughly the shape of the *upper* surface of the gabbro laccolite. The Coruisk basin has resulted from the broad syncline which occupied the south-western part of the area, and the main range of the Cuillins marks the south-western, western, and north-western limits of this syncline, coinciding nearly with the edge of the laccolite itself, which along this line dips always inward. The Druim nan Ramh, and Sgùrr na Stri ridges correspond with anticlinal flexures of the laccolite; and the former, branching off from the main range at Bruach na Frithe, must have been at one stage a more imposing range than now, having been considerably trenched upon by Harta Corrie. The Sligachan and Camasunary valleys coincide very closely with synclinal lines on the laccolite. The north-eastern portion of the gabbro is missing. We know that it was elevated by the intrusion of the granite magma, which invaded the earlier basic rock in a peculiarly intimate fashion. To what extent the gabbro was actually disintegrated by this attack is not certainly known; but the relics which can still be studied on Marsco suffice to show that the impregnation of the gabbro by the granite would greatly impair its durability under weathering agencies. The south-eastern limb of the gabbro laccolite thus came to be almost cut off, and surrounded by rocks much more easily destructible. It has, as we have seen, a synclinal structure, but it was too narrow a strip to originate an interior drainage, and so has given rise to the broken ridge extending from Blath-bheinn to Belig. The peculiar shape of the gabbro laccolite is due, as we have seen, chiefly to circumstances attending its intrusion. In so far as there was actual deformation at a later time, the overlying basalts would be partly affected in common with the gabbro; but it is probable that, when a drainage-system was initiated at the beginning of the erosion, the principal determining factor in this part of the area was not very different from a simple dome-like elevation of no very strong relief.

In a distant view the gabbro mountains at once assert themselves as a distinct geological unit with strongly marked characteristics. They present indeed a unique fragment of Alpine scenery among the mountain-groups of Britain. The spiry summits and acute, deeply-notched ridges are the more striking when seen across a foreground of the basaltic plateaux, or contrasted in the same view with the rounded outlines of the granite hills (Fig. 84, p. 449). Approaching the mountains by one of the large corries, or still better by Loch Scavaig, an observer is next struck by the contrast between the smooth surfaces of the lower slopes and the abrupt splintered forms of the peaks which overlook them (*see* frontispiece). The corries and interior valleys, with the slopes immediately enclosing them, are everywhere moulded by ice-action, and there is perhaps no district which exhibits more clearly the essential characteristics of glacial erosion. The present writer has discussed this subject in a separate memoir,* and has pointed out the significance in this connection of the peculiar form of the valleys, both in cross-section and in longitudinal profile, with their cirque-formed heads, tarn-basins, lake-basins, and other incidents. It is especially to be remarked that these features† are never related to anything in the structure or lithological constitution of the country. Indeed many facts observed in the Cuillins go to suggest that a surface-relief very little influenced by structure is a characteristic of direct ice-erosion. On the floor of any of the corries it is often impossible to decide that the eroding force has respected one rock more than another; for the gabbro, the enclosed patches of volcanic rocks, and the various dykes and sheets often figure together on one smooth rock-face.‡ As we pass up from the floor of the corrie, the inflence of structure declares itself with increasing prominence, and it is most marked on the actual ridges and peaks. This is partly because ice-erosion has there been less efficient, partly because the ridges have subsequently been subjected to prolonged weathering by frost-action. The débris resulting from this shattering action has been in part carried away on the glaciers, but in part it remains in the great taluses or screes which choke the heads of many of the glens. Without further considering the ice-worn valleys and corries, we shall have regard in what follows more particularly

* Ice-Erosion in the Cuillin Hills, Skye. *Trans. Roy. Soc. Edin.*, vol. xl., pp. 221-252; 1901.

† We are speaking here of the highly characteristic *forms* of the valleys, as now to be seen. The valleys themselves, as we have shown, are related to the broad structure of the district, and by far the greater part of the erosion was accomplished before the Glacial period.

‡ This of course implies, what is otherwise amply demonstrated, that under the present conditions erosion is almost completely checked. See Harker, Notes on Subaërial Erosion in the Isle of Skye, *Geol. Mag.*, 1899, pp. 485-491.

to those parts of the mountains in which the effects of differential weathering are clearly exhibited.

While the dominant rock is gabbro, there are, as we have seen, numerous enclosed patches of the volcanic group. In its highly metamorphosed state the basaltic lava is not greatly inferior to the gabbro in its resistance to destructive agents. Sometimes the gabbro stands out in relief from it, or the basalt may give rise to a depression in a ridge, as for instance on the col connecting Sgùrr Thuilm with Sgùrr a' Mhadaidh; but elsewhere, as on Sgùrr nan Gobhar, the basalt even forms salient features, and it builds several of the summits, notably those of Sgùrr Alaisdair, Sgùrr Tearlach, and Sgùrr Mhic Choinnich, which are among the highest peaks of the Cuillins. This metamorphosed basalt, however, with close texture and splintery fracture, disintegrates in a different manner from the gabbro, and it affords less secure holds for hand and foot. In this latter respect the gabbro, above the limit of ice-moulding, offers remarkable facility to climbers. It is even surpassed in some places by the picrite and peridotite group, owing partly to the extreme hardness and toughness of these rocks, partly to the pitted or embossed surfaces which they often present owing to the weathering of xenoliths. The relation of the form of the ground to these ultrabasic rocks is rather peculiar. The large laccolitic intrusion builds the prominent peak known as Sgùrr Dubh na Dabheinn, overlooking the tarn of Coir' a' Ghrundda; but the prolongation of the same mass, both eastward and northward, has been excavated into valleys. This seems to be connected with the very pronounced banded structure of the rocks, both in An Garbh-choire and in Coireachan Ruadha, which has hastened their erosion. Where banding is absent or inconspicuous, the rocks always form prominent features, as is well seen in An Sgùman and in the easterly spur of Sgùrr na Banachdich, the one due to a boss and the other to small laccolite of picrite.

It is, however, to the intrusive sheets and dykes, which traverse gabbro and basalt alike, that the mountains owe some of their most distinctive characters. In particular, the remarkable appearance of stratification often conspicuous upon the outward slopes is due to their being seamed by innumerable parallel sheets of dolerite and basalt. These rocks are of very durable nature, and are not often weakened by cross-jointing like the sills of the moorland country, so that they very frequently show in relief even against the gabbro. Elsewhere they have weathered more rapidly; but in either case they give rise to ledges running along the steep slopes, and in places these assume something of the character of a rude series of steps. This is seen on the outward slopes of the mountains only, because, as we have noticed, the intrusive sheets constantly dip inward.

The shapes of the ridges in different parts of the gabbro tract, and the marked difference often apparent between the opposed slopes, depend largely upon the direction of dip of the intruded basic sheets and the angle which the trend of the ridge makes with

View of Clach Glas from Garbh Bheinn.

the strike of the sheets. For example, in that part of the main or western range which comprises Sgùrr Dearg, Sgùrr na Banachdich, and Sgùrr a' Ghreadaidh the general direction coincides with the strike of the inclined basic sheets. Here the actual crest-line is usually made by one of the strong sheets of dolerite, dipping to the east in a perilous slope and then breaking away. The western slope is often steep, but is in many places rudely terraced at short intervals by ledges, which dip inward and afford secure 'traverses' to the mountaineer. The eastern slope is in places extremely precipitous, and where this is not the case the climber encounters broad slabs of smooth rock dipping outward and offering only precarious holds. These slabs are sometimes the surface of an intruded sheet, more often a surface of gabbro from which such a sheet has broken away. Approach is thus more difficult from the Coruisk than from the Glen Brittle side.* The character of the interior or eastern slope varies, however, according as its inclination in different parts is greater or less than the dip of the sheets. The outcrops of a group of strong sheets exposed at their upper edges may occasion a short and irregular subsidiary ridge parallel to the main one, or a bold easterly spur may have a summit encircled by the outcrops of a group of sheets. This later is illustrated by the fine peak known as Sgùrr a' Coir' an Lochain, which may be contrasted, e.g. with Sgùrr nan Gobhar, a westerly spur of the main range, where no such arrangement is possible. On the main range itself too is found here and there an abrupt prominence, formed either by a small outlying portion of a strong inclined sheet or by an outlier of gabbro resting on such a sheet. Examples are seen on the northern peak of Sgùrr a' Ghreadaidh and on Bidein Druim nan Ramh.

Corresponding with this part of the main range, but on the opposite edge of the gabbro tract, is the Blaven range, which from the scenic as from the geological standpoint must be regarded as an integral part of the Cuillins. Here the intrusive sheets dip in the opposite direction, i.e. still towards the interior of the tract, and the physical aspect of the mountains is in accord with this structure. Blath-bheinn itself on its steep western face has a steady slope (about 40°) nearly coinciding with the dip of the inclined sheets, and in consequence this face, disregarding for the present two or three deep gullies, has a very simple character. The same is true of the Clach Glas portion of the ridge, farther north, although there the summit is more precipitous, so that the outcrops of the sheets encircle it. The eastern side of the range is much more diversified in character, and is easier of access for reasons already pointed out (see Plate XIV.).

In contrast with the above, we may look at that portion of the Cuillin ridge which constitutes Sgùrr a' Mhadaidh, where the general trend, nearly E.–W., runs athwart the strike of the inclined sheets. Here there is no continuous crest-line. The ridge is

* This observation applies to the peaks themselves. Approach to the passes is often easier from the east, at least where extensive screes occur.

broken into a succession of small peaks, each presenting an abrupt drop towards the west and a steady slope towards the east, the latter always tending to coincide with the dip (about 40°) of the intrusive sheets to which this disposition is traceable. On the flanks of the mountain the same sheets are seen as ledges running obliquely down to the left as seen from Tairneilear (Plate XV.), or the right as seen from Coir' an Uaigneis (frontispiece). The same structure is exhibited on a ruder scale in Sgùrr Dubh, and again, with some modification, in other E.-W. ridges such as those of Sgùrr Sgùmain and Sgùrr nan Gobhar. In these latter examples alternations of basaltic lava with gabbro also contribute to the effect. It is to be noticed generally that the intercalated patches of basaltic lavas and agglomerates have in most cases the same inward dip as the inclined sheets, though not always in precise parallelism with them. It follows that where the occurrence of such enclosed patches has given rise to evident surface-features, these are in general agreement with the structure impressed upon the mountains by the inclined sheets. Gars-bheinn affords the best illustration of this. On the south-easterly ridge of this mountain, and in the shape of Coire Beag and Coir' a' Chruidh immediately adjacent, the general effect of a stratified group of rocks is very conspicuous, and is clearly indicated on the topographical map.

Not less important than the intrusive sheets as regards their part in controlling the erosion of the gabbro tract are the dykes. The only dykes which consistently make features in relief are the few composed of peridotites on Sgùrr Dearg, Sgùrr na Banachdich, etc. The ordinary basic dykes, and especially the latest ones which intersect the intrusive sheets as well as the gabbro, tend always to betray their presence by weathering out into depressions. In this way arise most of the deep gulleys which furrow the steep sides of the mountains, and become in wet weather the channels of mountain torrents. Less commonly a platform of gentler slope is trenched by a straight water-course of like origin, such as the deep gorge which drains Coir' a' Bhàsteir, north of Sgùrr nan Gillean. Sometimes the gullies are confined to the actual slopes, but very often they pass up into gaps in the ridge and are continued on the opposite side. Many deep notches, such as that which divides the twin peaks of Blath-bheinn and that named An Dorus (the door) between Sgùrr a' Mhadaidh and Sgùrr a' Ghreadaidh, have originated by the weathering out of dykes or groups of dykes. Distinct peaks, such as these which form Bidein Druim nan Ramh, owe their individuality in large measure to their being divided and cut off by dyke-notches; and it is in this way that the north-easterly ridge of Sgùrr nan Gillean is divided into a succession of graceful pinnacles (Plate XVI.). This latter and the much broken arête extending westward from the same peak[*] are instances of ridges in the most apt position to display such breaches of continuity, since they run nearly at right angles to

[*] See Geikie, *Ancient Volcanoes of Great Britain*, vol. ii., p. 338, fig. 333; 1897.

View from Coire na Creiche.

View of Sgurr nan Gillean.

Dykes as an Element in Mountain Scenery. 447

the dominant set of dykes in their neighbourhood. In most of the other minor ridges, however, the tendency is for the trend to follow the direction of the principal set of dykes. This is well seen in such small spurs as those running out from Sgùrr a' Ghreadaidh, and especially in the Sgùrr na Fheadain ridge which runs out from Bidein Druim nan Ramh towards Coire na Creiche (Pl. XV.). Even the long north-westerly ridge of Bruach na Frithe seems to have had its direction determined in some measure by the dykes. In a few places the breaking away of a dyke parallel to a ridge has occasioned for a short distance a vertical precipice. A more remarkable case is that of the isolated rock near the summit of Sgùrr Dearg known to climbers as the "Inaccessible Pinnacle." This is a relic of a wall-like mass of gabbro bounded on the two

FIG. 82.—The "Inaccessible Pinnacle" of Sgùrr Dearg, seen from near the summit-cairn. In the background the outlines of Sgùrr Sgùmain (right) and Sgùrr a' Coir' an Lochain (left).

sides by parallel dykes which have broken away. Since it is also of the nature of an outlier upon a strong inclined sheet of dolerite, and is extremely precipitous at the end facing the mountain, its shape is a singularly striking one * (Fig. 82).

We see that the dykes, like the inclined sheets, produce different effects according to their angle with the trend of the ridges. Other variable elements which enter are the comparative frequency of the dykes in different parts of the area and the occurrence in some parts of two or three distinct sets of dykes differing in

* The height of the pinnacle is about 60 feet, reckoned at the "short end," but the ascent by the "long end" is about 150 feet. It overtops the summit-cairn by quite 20 feet, and is a conspicuous object in a distant view.

direction. The main ridges, connected as they are with the deformation of the gabbro laccolite, must have been outlined from an early stage in the erosion of the region. Starting from this rough plan, the existing surface-relief has been developed largely with reference to the two leading structural elements which have been noticed, the intrusive sheets and the dykes. To the predominance of one or other of these elements, and to the ever-varying combination and interaction of the two, most of the mountain-scenery of the Cuillins in its ultimate analysis reduces. The noteworthy features in the landscape which do not fall under these heads are few. The behaviour of the rocks of the peridotite group has already been alluded to; and we may also recall certain special acid intrusions described on pp. 287, 288, which have occasioned the gap occupied by the "Alaisdair Stone-shoot" (Fig. 83) and the passes of Coire Labain and Coir' a' Ghrunnda.

FIG. 83.—Outlines of the Alaisdair group of mountains, seen from Sgùrr Dearg. The highest point is Sgùrr Alaisdair (3275 feet), separated from its neighbour, Sgùrr Tearlach, by the great stone-shoot. To the left is Sgùrr Mhic Choinnich, and to the right the broken ridge of Sgùrr Sgùmain with the outline of Sgùrr nan Eag behind.

The great toughness and strength of the gabbro itself is shown by the steepness which the mountain-sides may attain without breaking into precipices. The usual inclination of long continuous slopes varies from 35° to 40°, but on some of the minor ridges, such as Druim nan Ramh and Sgùrr na Stri—still excluding actual precipices—the angle of slopes more than 1500 feet high reaches 45° or even 50°. The ordinary slopes of the Cuillins are too steep either for screes or for vegetation, and accordingly the mountains consist in general of naked rock. The colour is derived from the augite of the gabbro, and ranges, with varying conditions of moisture and light, through every tone of purple; deepening to a velvety black in glimpses caught through a wrack of mist or brightening to burnished copper under the level rays of a cloudless sunrise. The sterility of the mountains is, however, relative rather than absolute. Even at 3000 feet and higher the narrow ledges and crevices nourish in places a small flora of Alpine habitat,* or even a scanty herbage which tempts the sheep from Glen Brittle to high up on some of the less difficult slopes and ridges. Permanent springs may occur up to as much as 2500 feet altitude, and there are some very copious ones at about the 2000 feet line.

The *granite mountains* do not require very detailed notice. The large body of granite, granophyre, etc., from which the majority of the Red Hills are carved out has, as we have seen, the general form of a great sheet or laccolite. It is, however, much more irregular in its behaviour than the gabbro of the Cuillins, and we are not able to trace out so close a correspondence between the broad features of the existing relief and the shape of the large plutonic mass. Nevertheless it appears that the western range of the Red Hills, from Ruadh Stac and Marsco to Glamaig, corresponds with an anticlinal curve in the granite mass, while Loch Ainort and the surrounding low ground coincide with a broad syncline.

The smooth slopes and flowing curves of the Red Hills are in strong contrast with the acute summits and deeply indented ridges

FIG. 84.—Contrasted outlines of the gabbro and the granite, as seen from Cnoc Càrnach. To the left is the Blaven range, with the southern Cuillins beyond and the basaltic plateaux of An Dà Bheinn and An Stac in front. To the right are the most easterly of the Red Hills, viz. Beinn Dearg Bheag, Beinn Dearg Mhòr, and Beinn na Caillich.

of the Cuillins (Fig. 84), and the reason of this difference is manifest. Just as the diversity of form in the gabbro mountains results from the complexity of their structure and the infinitude of sheets and dykes intersecting the dominant rock, so the simplicity of the surface-relief in the other case is mainly referable to the uniformity of geological constitution and the paucity of minor intrusions or other interruptions of the granite. Dykes are comparatively infrequent, and the inclined sheets of dolerite, which figured so prominently in the gabbro mountains are absent.

The variety of lithological characters met with among the acid rocks themselves is not often of a kind to express itself in the physical aspect of the ground, but instances of this kind might be cited; notably the precipice of Fiaclan Dearg, on Marsco, formed

* Among the common species are *Arabis petræa, Silene acaulis, S. inflata, Cerastium alpinum, Alchemilla alpina, Geum rivale, Sedum rhodiola, Saxifraga stellaris, S. oppositifolia, Antennaria dioica, Vaccinum myrtillus, Loiseleurea procumbens,* and *Oxyria reniformis.*

by a rock with marked columnar structure (*see* Plate VIII., above).*
As a rule any conspicuous departure from the characteristic smoothness of outline (apart from glacial cirques) is occasioned either by enclosed patches of older rocks or by younger dykes. The sheet of marscoite which forms Sròn a' Bhealain has already been mentioned (*see* Fig. 37, p. 188). In one or two places, as on the north-western slope of Ruadh Stac, small enclosed patches of gabbro make slight features; while, on the other hand, strips of gabbro impregnated by granophyre give rise to gullies, such as that on the north-west face of Marsco and that which crosses Druim Eadar da Choire. The rough northern half of the Beinn na Cro ridge is made by an enclosed patch of basalt lavas, with a thick sheet of gabbro below, which builds some prominent buttresses at the northern end. Another place where a considerable patch of the lavas makes a noteworthy feature is Meallan a' Bhealaich Bhric, on the east side of the Tormichaig valley, but this seems to be rather an exposed inlier than a portion truly detached and enveloped.

The basalt dykes which traverse the Red Hills weather out in relief against the granite. For this reason, but still more on account of their dark colour, they are conspicuous from a distance; *e.g.* on Beinn Dearg Mheadhonach as seen from Marsco, or Beinn Dearg Mhòr from Sligachan. Sometimes, as in Allt na Measarroch, to the north of Marsco, they have determined the course of a stream, but the channel is cut by the side of, not along, the dyke. In one place only, viz. on Beinn na Caillich, facing Broadford, does a dyke in the granite cause a strong feature: it is one of the large diabase dykes of solitary habit (Fig. 5, p. 17).

The granite hills are not only lower than those built of gabbro, but they are also less steep. The inclination of a long unbroken slope may rise to 30°, but never exceeds this by more than two or three degrees. When it declines a little below this, it falls within the angle of repose of loose material, and accordingly many of the slopes are encumbered by screes. The Red Hills also support vegetation much more than the Cuillins do, a result mainly of the more facile decay of the rock-surface. The rounded summits and ridges, when not grassed over, often have a thin layer of coarse quartz-sand derived from the subaerial waste of the granite. Whether consisting of naked granite or covered by screes of the same material, the slopes show something of the "red" tint implied in the name of these hills; but the colour is very changeable, varying from a cold greyish yellow in the dry days of early summer to a fiery crimson under an autumnal sunset. Permanent springs are not found so high, either absolutely or relatively, as in the gabbro mountains.

To the east of the large area of granite smaller intrusions in the form of bosses have caused the eastern Red Hills (Beinn na Caillich and its neighbours) and the more isolated Beinn an

* In the large acid intrusions of the Western Isles generally any pronounced columnar jointing seems to be rare. The best examples are Ailsa Craig and the west coast of Rum.

Dubhaich. We have pointed out that the prominence of the former is partly due to bounding faults. This, being a comparatively broad tract of granite, is trenched by deep corries and divided into three distinct hills; while the other boss, of narrow elongated form, has given rise to a simple unbroken ridge. It may be enquired why the gabbro boss north-west of Broadford has not caused any noteworthy eminence. On this question we may remark that there is no evidence of the intrusion having ever been prolonged upward with the boss form. At a short distance above the present surface of the ground it would pass from the Cambrian limestones to the Torridon Sandstone, and it is probable that it would then change to an irregular sheet of no great magnitude, as indeed it is actually seen to do at its northern extremity, on Creag Strollamus.

The granophyre hills of Carn Dearg, Beinn a' Mheadhoin, and Beinn a' Chairn reproduce on a small scale some of the features of the Red Hills. The other composite sills of the Cnoc Càrnach group give rise to more or less marked ridges, the more constant and massive acid rock being more in evidence in the thicker sills and the more durable basalt in the thinner. The numerous dykes which intersect the Cambrian limestone series are remarkable for the prominent fashion in which they stand out, often presenting the appearance of stone walls two or three feet high. A few, such as the large multiple dyke which runs S.E. from Loch Kilchrist, have given rise to very noticeable ridges. The dykes in the Lias are not often so prominent, except on the sea-shore, *e.g.* about Broadford, where they sometimes rise five or six feet above the soft shaly and calcareous strata. When we have recalled the volcanic agglomerate of the Strath vent, which in the low broken hills overlooking Loch Kilchrist presents a very characteristic appearance, we have almost exhausted the scenic aspects of the Tertiary igneous rocks in Skye.

APPENDIX.

BIBLIOGRAPHY OF THE TERTIARY IGNEOUS ROCKS OF SKYE.

[This list is meant to include all the more important works dealing exclusively or partially with the Tertiary Igneous Rocks of the island: mere compilations are excluded, and incidental references are cited only when they are deemed to be of some importance. In addition to general geology, petrology, and mineralogy, a few entries are given which have to do with allied subjects, such as metamorphism, rock-magnetism, the topography of the mountains, etc.

Papers contributed to Societies are, as far as possible, entered under the date of reading, that of publication being given after the entry.]

1774.

1. THOMAS PENNANT. *A Tour to Scotland and Voyage to the Hebrides, MDCCLXXII.*, 4to, pp. viii + 379, pl. XLIV.; Chester, 1774 [and later editions]. For extracts from other early travellers see W. Douglas, "Early Descriptions of Skye," *Scott. Mount. Club Journ.*, vol. v., pp. 205-230; 1899.

1800.

2. ROBERT JAMESON. *Mineralogy of the Scottish Isles; with Mineralogical Observations made in a Tour through different parts of the Mainland of Scotland, and Dissertations upon Peat and Kelp.* 2 vols. 4to, pp. xxvii + 243, iv + 289; Edinburgh, 1800. [A German translation by Heinrich Wilhelm Meuder, under the title *Herr Robert Jameson's Mineralogische Reise durch Schottland und die Schottischen Inseln.* . . . 1 vol. 4to, pp. xlviii + 257; Leipzig, 1802.]

1808.

3. [ROBERT] JAMESON. Mineralogical Queries, proposed by Prof. Jameson. *Mem. Wern. Soc.*, vol. i., pp. 107-125; 1808.

1811.

4. [ROBERT] JAMESON. On Porphyry. *Mem. Wern. Soc.*, vol. ii., pp. 217-220; pub. 1818.

1814.

5. J. MACCULLOCH. Miscellaneous Remarks accompanying a Catalogue of Specimens transmitted to the Society. *Trans. Geol. Soc.*, vol. ii., pp. 338-449, pl. 31-32; 1814.

1816.

6. JOHN MACCULLOCH. A Sketch of the Mineralogy of Sky. *Trans. Geol. Soc.*, vol. iii., pp. 1-111, pl. 1-4; 1816.

1817.

7. J. MACCULLOCH. Corrections and Additions to the Sketch of the Mineralogy of Sky, published in the third volume of the Transactions of the Geological Society. *Trans. Geol. Soc.*, vol. iv., pp. 156-192, pl. 9; 1817.

8. [ANONYMOUS.] Hypersthene Rock. *Phil. Mag.*, vol. xlix., pp. 464-466; 1817.

1819.

9. JOHN MACCULLOCH. A Description of the Western Islands of Scotland, including the Isle of Man: comprising an account of their Geological Structure; with Remarks on their Agriculture, Scenery, and Antiquities. 3 vols [2 8vo vols of text and 4to atlas of plates], pp. xv + 587, vii. + 589, 91 + XXXIII. plates and ten maps; London, 1819. [Skye, vol. i., pp. 262-419.]

1820.

10. AMI BOUÉ. *Essai géologique sur l'Ecosse* 8vo, pp. x + 521, with seven folding plates and two maps; Paris, no date [1820].

1823-4.

11. KARL CÆSAR VON LEONHARD. *Charakteristik der Felsarten.* 8vo, pp. lxxx + 772; Heidelberg, 1823-4.

1824.

12. JOHN MACCULLOCH. List of the Localities of some of the rarer Scottish Minerals. *Edin. Journ. Sci.*, vol. i., pp. 225-236; 1824.

13. JOHN MACCULLOCH. The Highlands and Western Isles of Scotland . . . in Letters to Sir Walter Scott, Bart., 4 vols 8vo; London, 1824. [Skye, vol. iii., pp. 370-484.]

1827.

14. RODERICK IMPEY MURCHISON. On the Coal-field of Brora in Sutherlandshire, and some other Stratified Deposits in the North of Scotland. *Trans. Geol. Soc.* (2), vol. ii., pp. 293-326, pl. XXXI., XXXII.; pub. 1828.

15. RODERICK IMPEY MURCHISON. Supplementary Remarks on the Strata of the Oolitic Series, and the Rocks associated with them, in the Counties of Sutherland and Ross, and in the Hebrides. *Trans. Geol. Soc.* (2), vol. ii., pp. 352-368, pl. XXXV.; pub. 1829.

1828.

16. ADAM SEDGWICK and RODERICK IMPEY MURCHISON. On the Structure and Relations of the Deposits contained between the Primary Rocks and the Oolitic Series in the North of Scotland. *Trans Geol. Soc.* (2), vol. iii., pp. 125-160, pl. XIII.-XVII. [Pl. XIII. is a Sketch of a Geological Map of the North of Scotland.]

1829.

17. [C.] VON OEYNHAUSEN and [H.] VON DECHEN. Die Insel Skye. *Karsten's Archiv für Min. etc.*, vol. i., pp. 56-104, pl. I.-III.; 1829.

1833.

18. [H.] VON DECHEN. [Eigenschwere basaltartiger Gesteine Englands.] *Neu. Jahrb. Min.* 1833, pp. 59-61.

1835.

19. WILLIAM KNIGHT. Account of the Granite Quarries of Aberdeenshire; and Remarks on Marble and Serpentine. *Trans. Highl. Soc.*, vol. x. (N.S. vol. iv.), pp. 54-80; 1835.

20. [ROBERT] JAMESON. Syenite or Granitel of Skye, Craig of Ailsa, St Kilda, Arran, etc. *Edin. New Phil. Journ.*, vol. xviii., p. 393; 1835.

1836.

21. THOMAS THOMSON. *Outlines of Mineralogy, Geology, and Mineral Analysis*. 8vo, 2 vols., pp. ix + 727, viii + 566; London, 1836.

1837.

22. J. CARMICHAEL. An account of the Principal Marble, Slate, Sandstone, and Greenstone Quarries in Scotland. *Trans. Highl. Soc.*, vol. xi. (N.S. vol. v.), pp. 398-416; 1837.

1840.

23. L. A. NECKER. Notes on some rare Scottish Minerals. *Edin. New Phil. Journ.*, vol. xxix., pp. 75-77; 1840.

23a. [JOHN MACCULLOCH.] *A Geological Map of Scotland by Dr MacCulloch, F.R.S., etc., etc., etc.* Published by order of the Lords of the Treasury. By S. Arrowsmith, Hydrographer to King. [Scale, 4 miles to an inch.]

1842.

24. WILLIAM RHIND. *The Geology of Scotland, and its Islands; with a coloured geological map, and numerous sections.* 8vo, pp. viii + 168: Edinburgh, 1842.

1843.

25. W. DELFFS. Analyse des Leonhardits. *Pogg. Ann.*, vol. lix., pp. 339-342; 1843. [? Skye.]

1844.

26. JAMES NICOL. *Guide to the Geology of Scotland; containing an account of the character, distribution, and more interesting appearances of its rocks and minerals.* With a geological map and plates. 8vo, p. 272, pl. X.; Edinburgh, 1844.

1845.

27. J. D. FORBES. Notes on the Topography and Geology of the Cuchullin Hills in Skye, and on the traces of Ancient Glaciers which they present. *Edin. New Phil. Journ.*, vol. xl., pp. 76-99, pl. IV., V.; pub. 1846. [Abstract in *Proc. Roy. Soc. Edin.* vol. ii., pp. 54-56; 1846. This paper has been reprinted, in full or in part, in guide books: see Black's "Guide to the Isle of Skye," 1854, and Maclure and Macdonald's "Oban to the Isle of Skye," Glasgow, no date [1874?].]

1851.

28. THOMAS ANDERSON. Description and Analysis of Gyrolite, a new Mineral Species. *Phil. Mag.* (4), vol. i., pp. 111-113; 1851.

29. EDWARD FORBES. On the Estuary Beds and the Oxford Clay at Loch Staffin, in Skye. *Quart. Journ. Geol. Soc.*, vol. vii., pp. 104-113, pl. V.; 1851.

1852.

30. A. J. SCOTT. Analyses of Indian Ores of Manganese, and of some Scottish Zeolites. *Edin. New Phil. Journ.*, vol. liii., pp. 277-284; 1852.

1855.

31. M. FORSTER HEDDLE and R. P. GREG. On British Pectolites. *Phil. Mag.* (4), vol. ix., pp. 248-253; 1855.

32. M. FORSTER HEDDLE. On Uigite, a new mineral (?). "*The Witness*," March 12th, 1856. [A paper read before the *Roy Phys. Soc. Edin.*, 1855; abstract in *Edin. New Phil. Journ.* (2), vol. iv., p. 162; 1856: paper reprinted in *Min. Mag.*, 1880, see below No. 79.]

1856.

33. J. W. MALLET. On a Zeolitic mineral (allied to Stilbite) from the Isle of Skye, Scotland. *Amer. Journ. Sci.* (2), vol. xxii., p. 179, and *Phil. Mag.* (4), vol. xii., pp. 406, 407; 1856.

34. [M. F.] HEDDLE. Note on the new Zeolite from Skye, analysed by Mallet. *Phil. Mag.* (4), vol. xii., pp, 552, 553; 1856.

35. M. F. HEDDLE. The Minerals of the Storr. *Trans. Edin. Geol. Soc.*, vol. vii., pp. 328-331; 1899. [Posthumous publication, in partly abridged form, of paper read before the Society in 1856.]

1857.

36. [M. F.] HEDDLE. On Mesolite and Faroëlite (Mesole). *Phil. Mag.* (4), vol. xiii., pp. 50-55; 1857.

37. A. GEIKIE. On the Geology of Strath, Skye. *Quart. Journ. Geol. Soc.*, vol. xiv., pp. 1-23, pl. I.; pub. 1858.

38. SAMUEL HAUGHTON. Notes on Mineralogy.—No. V. On Hypostilbite and Stilbite. *Phil. Mag.* (4), vol. xiii., pp. 509, 510; 1857.

39. ADMIRALTY CHART. No. 2498. Southern Part of the Sound of Raasay and Inner Sound. (Revised 1876, etc.)

1858.

40. ROBERT PHILIPS GREG and WILLIAM G. LETTSOM. *Manual of the Mineralogy of Great Britain and Ireland.* 8vo, pp. xvi + 483; London, 1858.

41. [M. F.] HEDDLE. On the Crystal-Form of Faroëlite. *Phil. Mag.* (4), vol. xiv., p. 28; 1858.

42. HUGH MILLER. *The Cruise of the Betsey; or a summer ramble among the fossiliferous deposits of the Hebrides. With the Rambles of a Geologist; or ten thousand miles over the fossiliferous deposits of Scotland.* 8vo, pp. ii + 486; Edinburgh, 1858. [Edited by W. S. Symonds from a series of articles in "The Witness".]

1859.

43. BALFOUR STEWART. On some Results of the Magnetic Survey of Scotland in the years 1857 and 1858, undertaken, at the request of the British Association, by the late John Welsh, Esq., F.R.S. *Rep. Brit. Assoc.* for 1859, pp. 167-190, pl. VI.; pub. 1860.

44. ARCHIBALD GEIKIE. On the Chronology of the Trap Rocks of Scotland (Abstract). *Rep. Brit. Assoc.* for 1859, Sections, p 106; pub. 1860: also *Edin. New Phil. Journ.* (2), vol. xi., p. 132; 1860.

45. SIR RODERICK I. MURCHISON. First Sketch of a new Geological Map of the North of Scotland; and Explanation of the Geological Map of the North of Scotland. *Quart. Journ. Geol. Soc.*, vol. xv., pl. XII., and pp. 419*-421*; issued 1860. [Scale not given, about 27 miles to an inch.]

1860-1.

46. ARCHIBALD GEIKIE. On the Chronology of the Trap-Rocks of Scotland. *Trans. Roy. Soc. Edin.*, vol. xxii., pp. 633-653, pl. XXXVIII. (map); pub. 1861. Abstract in *Proc. Roy. Soc. Edin.*, vol. iv., pp. 309-311; 1862.

1861.

47. ARCHIBALD GEIKIE. Additional Observations on the Chronology of the Trap-Rocks of Scotland. *Proc. Roy. Soc. Edin.*, vol. iv., pp. 453, 454; 1862: also *Edin. New Phil. Journ.* (2), vol. xiv., pp. 143, 144; 1861.

48. SIR RODERICK I. MURCHISON and ARCHIBALD GEIKIE. *First Sketch of a New Geological Map of Scotland with Explanatory Notes.* 22 8vo pp. and folding map [scale 15 miles to an inch]; Edinburgh, 1861.

1863.

49. T. STERRY HUNT. On the Chemical and Mineralogical Relations of Metamorphic Rocks. *Journ. Geol. Soc. Dubl.*, vol x., pp. 85-95; pub. 1864. [Skye, p. 95: see also p. 33 of "Chemical and Geological Essays," 2nd ed., 1878.

1864.

50. AMI BOUÉ. Ueber das saülenförmigen Gesteine, einige Porphyrdistricte Schottlands, so wie über die vier Basaltgruppen des nördlichen Irlands und der Hebriden. *Sitz. k. Akad. Wiss. Wien* (2), vol. xlix., pp. 439-452; 1864.

51. SAMUEL HAUGHTON. Geological Notes on some of the Islands of the West of Scotland. *Dubl. Quart. Journ. Sci.*, vol. v., pp. 93-96; 1865: also *Journ. Roy. Geol. Soc. Irel.* (2), vol. i., pp. 28-31; 1865.

1865.

52. ARCHIBALD GEIKIE. *The Scenery of Scotland viewed in connexion with its Physical Geology.* 8vo, pp. xv + 360, with geological map; London and Cambridge, 1865: 2nd ed. in 1887; 3rd ed. in 1901.

1866.

53. WILLIAM KING and T. H. ROWNEY. On the So-called "Eozoonal Rock." *Quart. Journ. Geol. Soc.*, vol. xxii., pp. 185-218, pl. XIV., XV.; 1866.

54. FERDINAND VON HOCHSTETTER. Ueber des Vorkommen von Eozoon im Krystallinischen Kalke von Krummau im südlichen Böhmen. *Sitz. k. Akad. Wiss. Wien, Math-Nat. Cl.*, vol. liii., part I., pp. 14-25; 1866 ["Hypersthenfels" of Skye].

1867.

55. ARCHIBALD GEIKIE. On the Tertiary Volcanic Rocks of the British Islands. *Proc. Roy. Soc. Edin.*, vol. vi., pp. 71-75; pub. 1869.

56. ARCHIBALD GEIKIE. Address by the President [of Section C, Geology]. *Rep. Brit. Assoc.* for 1867, Sections, pp. 49-54; pub. 1868.

1868.

57. TOWNSHEND M. HALL. *The Mineralogist's Directory: or A Guide to the Principal Mineral Localities in the United Kingdom of Great Britain and Ireland.* 8vo, pp. xii + 168; London, 1868.

1869.

58. WILLIAM KING and T. H. ROWNEY. On "Eozoon Canadense." *Proc. Roy. Ir. Acad.*, vol. x., pp. 506-551, pl. XLI.-XLIV.; pub. 1870.

1870.

58. FERDINAND ZIRKEL. *Untersuchungen über die Mikroskopische Zusammensetzung und Structur der Basaltgesteine.* 8vo, p. 208, pl. III.; Bonn, 1870.

60. T. STERRY HUNT. On Norite or Labradorite Rock. *Amer. Journ. Sci.* (2), vol. xlix., pp. 180-186; 1870.

61. [W.] KING and [T. H.] ROWNEY. On some Points in the Geology of Strath, Skye (Abstract). *Rep. Brit. Assoc.* for 1870, Sections, p. 78; pub. 1871.

1871.

62. FERDINAND ZIRKEL. Geologische Skizze von der Westkuste Schottlands. *Zeits. deuts. geol. Ges.*, vol. xxiii., pp. 1-124, pl. I.-IV.; 1871.

63. J. W. DAWSON. Note on Eozoon Canadense. (In Reply to Professors King and Rowney). *Proc. Roy. Ir. Acad.* (2), vol. i., pp. 117-123; 1871.

64. W. KING and T. H. ROWNEY. On the Geological Age and Microscopic Structure of the Serpentine Marble or Ophite of Skye. *Proc. Roy. Ir. Acad.* (2), vol. i., pp. 132-139, pl. XIV.; 1871.

65. W. KING and T. H. ROWNEY. On the Mineral Origin of the so-called "Eozoon Canadense". *Proc. Roy. Ir. Acad.* (2), vol. i., pp. 140-153; 1871.

1873.

66. JAMES BRYCE. On the Jurassic Rocks of Skye and Raasay. *Quart. Journ. Geol. Soc.*, vol. xxix., pp. 317-339, pl. XI.; 1873.

1874.

67. JOHN W. JUDD. The Secondary Rocks of Scotland. Second Paper. On the Ancient Volcanoes of the Highlands and the Relations of their Products to the Mesozoic Strata. *Quart. Journ. Geol. Soc.*, vol. xxx., pp. 220, 301, pl. XXII., XXIII.; 1874.

1875.

68. ALEXANDER NICOLSON. The Isle of Skye. *Good Words* for 1875, pp. 344-350, 384-392, 457-462, 561-568.

1876.

69. DAVID CORSE GLEN and JOHN YOUNG, JUN. List of Minerals and Rock Specimens found in the Central, Southern, and Western, Districts of Scotland: pp. 156-164 of *Catalogue of the Western Scottish Fossils*, compiled by James Armstrong, John Young, and David Robertson; Glasgow, 1876.
70. ADMIRALTY CHART. No. 2507. Ardnamurchan Point to Loch Bhreatal, Skye.
71. ARCHIBALD GEIKIE. *Geological Map of Scotland*. (Topography by W. and A. K. Johnston. Scale 10 miles to an inch); Edinburgh and London, 1876.

1877.

72. M. FORSTER HEDDLE. Chapters on the Mineralogy of Scotland. Chapter Second. The Felspars. *Trans. Roy. Soc. Edin.*, vol. xxviii., pp. 197-271, pl. XVII., XVIII.; 1877.

1878.

73. M. FORSTER HEDDLE. Chapters on the Mineralogy of Scotland. Chapter Fourth. Augite, Hornblende, and Serpentinous Change. *Trans. Roy. Soc. Edin.*, vol. xxviii., pp. 453-555; 1878.
74. HENRY HOW. Contributions to the Mineralogy of Nova Scotia. *Min. Mag.*, vol. ii, pp. 134-141.
75. ADMIRALTY CHART. No. 2561. Isle of Skye northward of Loch Ainneart and Sleat Sound with adjacent sounds and lochs.

1879.

76. M. FORSTER HEDDLE. Chapters on the Mineralogy of Scotland. Chapter Sixth. "Chloritic Minerals". *Trans. Roy. Soc. Edin.*, vol. xxix., pp. 55-118; 1879.

1880.

77. ARCHIBALD GEIKIE. The Lava-Fields of North-Western Europe. *Nature*, vol. xxiii., pp. 3-5; 1880. Reprinted in *Geological Sketches at Home and Abroad*, pp. 274-285; 1882.
78. [M. F.] HEDDLE. Field Meeting at Skye. *Min. Mag.*, vol. iv., pp. ix-xiii; 1880.
79. [M. F.] HEDDLE. On some Ill-determined Minerals. *Min. Mag.*, vol. iv., pp. 26-31, 1880.
80. [M. F.] HEDDLE. Preliminary Notice of Substances which may prove to be New Minerals. Part Second. *Min. Mag.*, vol. iv., pp. 117-123; 1880.
81. [M. F.] HEDDLE. Minerals New to Britain. *Min. Mag.*, vol. v., pp. 1-25; pub. 1882. Also a slip headed "Errata to No. 22" published with No. 23, 1882.

1881.

82. JOHN W. JUDD. *Volcanoes: what they are and what they teach.* 8vo, pp. xvi + 381; London, 1881.
83. W. KING and T. H. ROWNEY. *An Old Chapter of the Geological Record.* 8vo, pp. lvii + 142, pl. IX.; London, 1881.

1882.

84. M. FORSTER HEDDLE. Chapters on the Mineralogy of Scotland. Chapter Seventh. Ores of Manganese, Iron, Chromium, and Titanium. *Trans. Roy. Soc. Edin.*, vol. xxx., pp. 427-466; 1882.
85. [M. F.] HEDDLE. On a New Mineral Locality. *Min. Mag.*, vol. v., pp. 115-120; pub. 1883.
86. [M. F.] HEDDLE. [Note on the occurrence of wollastonite at Allt Ghoiridh.] *Min. Mag.*, vol. v., p. 279; pub. 1883.
87. [M. F.] HEDDLE. [Note on asphalte in the dolerite of Skye.] *Min. Mag.*, vol. v., p. 324; pub. 1883.

1883.

88. JOHN W. JUDD and GRENVILLE A. J. COLE. On the Basalt-Glass (Tachylyte) of the Western Isles of Scotland. *Quart. Journ. Geol. Soc.*, vol. xxxix., pp. 444-464, pl. XIII., XIV.; 1883.

1884.

89. F. HERWIG. Einiges über die optische Orientirung der Mineralien der Pyroxen-Amphibolgruppe. *Progr. d. k. Gymnas. Saarbrücken*, 1884. Abstract in *Zeits. Kryst.*, vol. xi., pp. 67, 68; 1886.
90. J. STARKIE GARDNER. On the Evidence of Fossil Plants regarding the Age of the Tertiary Basalts of the North-East Atlantic. *Proc. Roy. Soc.*, vol. xxxviii., pp. 14-23; pub. 1885.
91. JAMES WHITE. A Glimpse of Skye: with Remarks on Volcanic Action. *Trans. Geol. Soc. Glasg.*, vol. viii, pp. 105-111; pub. 1886.

1885.

92. JOHN W. JUDD. On the Tertiary and Older Peridotites of Scotland. *Quart. Journ. Geol. Soc.*, vol. xli., pp. 354-418, pl. X.-XIII.; 1885.
93. J. STARKIE GARDNER. Second Report on the Evidence of Fossil Plants regarding the Age of the Tertiary Basalts of the North-East Atlantic. *Proc. Roy. Soc.*, vol. xxxix., pp. 412-415; pub. 1886.
94. EDUARD SUESS. *Das Antliz der Erde*; Prag, 1885. [Skye, vol. i., pp. 204-206. See also French translation, *La face de la terre*, vol. i., pp. 201-203, 1897, with notes by A. Michel-Lévy.]
95. JOHN W. JUDD. On the Gabbros, Dolerites, and Basalts, of Tertiary Age, in Scotland and Ireland. *Quart. Journ. Geol. Soc.*, vol. xlii., pp. 49-95, pl. IV.-VII.; pub. 1886.

1887.

96. ARCHIBALD GEIKIE. On the Age of the Altered Limestone of Strath, Skye. *Quart. Journ. Geol. Soc.*, vol. xliv., pp. 62-73; pub. 1888.

97. CHARLES PILKINGTON. The Black Coolins. *Alp. Journ.*, vol. xiii., pp. 433-446; pub. 1888. See also a sketch-map of "The Cuchullin Hills" on the scale of two inches to a mile, based on the one-inch Ordnance map, with some of the peaks and ridges corrected; separately published. Heywood, Manchester, 1890.

1888.

98. ARCHIBALD GEIKIE. The History of Volcanic Action during the Tertiary Period in the British Isles. *Trans. Roy. Soc. Edin.*, vol. xxxv., pp. 21-184, pl. I., II.; 1888. Abstract in *Proc. Roy. Soc. Edin.*, vol. xv., pp. 344-348; 1888.

99. GRENVILLE A. J. COLE. On some additional Occurrences of Tachylyte. *Quart. Journ. Geol. Soc.*, vol. xliv., pp. 300-307, pl. XI.; 1888.

100. J. J. HARRIS TEALL. *British Petrography; with special reference to the Igneous Rocks.* Roy. 8vo., pp. viii + 469, pl. XLVII.; London, 1888.

101. E. REYER. *Theoretische Geologie:* Stuttgart, 1888. [Skye pp. 369-372.]

101a. MARCEL BERTRAND. Sur la distribution géographique des roches éruptives en Europe. *Bull. Soc. Géol. Fra.* (3), vol. xvi., pp. 573-617; 1888.

1889.

102. JOHN W. JUDD. On the Growth of Crystals in Igneous Rocks after their Consolidation. *Quart. Journ. Geol. Soc.*, vol. xlv., pp. 175-186, pl. VII.; 1889.

103. JOHN W. JUDD. The Tertiary Volcanoes of the Western Isles of Scotland. *Quart. Journ. Geol. Soc.*, vol. xlv., pp. 187-218; 1889.

104. A. W. RÜCKER and T. E. THORPE. A Magnetic Survey of the British Isles for the Epoch January 1, 1886. *Phil. Trans. Roy. Soc.* (A), vol. 181., pp. 53-328, pl. 1-14; pub. 1890.

1890.

105. JOHN W. JUDD. The Propylites of the Western Isles of Scotland, and their Relation to the Andesites and Diorites of the District. *Quart. Journ. Geol. Soc.*, vol. xlvi., pp. 341-384, pl. XIV., XV.; 1890.

106. JOHN W. JUDD. On the Relations between the Gliding Planes and the Solution Planes of Augite. *Min. Mag.*, vol. ix., pp. 192-196; 1890.

107. A. W. RÜCKER and T. E. THORPE. Preliminary Note on Supplementary Magnetic Surveys of Special Districts in the British Isles. *Proc. Roy. Soc.*, vol. xlvii., pp. 443-445: 1890.

108. A. W. RÜCKER. On the Relation between the Magnetic Permeability of Rocks and Regional Magnetic Disturbances. *Proc. Roy. Soc.*, vol. xlviii., pp. 505-535; 1890.

1892.

109. SIR ARCHIBALD GEIKIE. The Anniversary Address of the President [History of Volcanic Action within the area of the British Isles]. *Quart. Journ. Geol. Soc.*, vol. xlviii., Proc. pp. 60-179; 1892.
110. SIR ARCHIBALD GEIKIE. *Geological Map of Scotland* (Topography by John Bartholomew; scale 10 miles to an inch); with *Explanatory Notes to accompany a new Geological Map of Scotland*, pp. 23; Edinburgh, 1892.
111. M. FORSTER HEDDLE. On Pectolite and Okenite from New Localities: the former with New Appearances. *Trans. Geol. Soc. Glasg.*, vol. ix., pp. 241-255; 1893.

1893.

112. J. NORMAN COLLIE. On the Height of some of the Black Cuchullins in Skye. *Scott. Mount. Club Journ.*, vol ii., pp. 168-173; 1893.
113. SIR ARCHIBALD GEIKIE. On Structures in Eruptive Bosses which resemble those of ancient Gneisses. *Rep. Brit. Assoc.* for 1893, pp. 754, 755; pub. 1894.
114. JOHN W. JUDD. On Inclusions of Tertiary Granite in the Gabbro of the Cuillin Hills, Skye; and on the Products resulting from the Partial Fusion of the Acid by the Basic Rock. *Quart. Journ. Geol. Soc.*, vol. xlix., pp. 175-195, pl. II., III.; 1893. [See also remarks by A. Lacroix, p. 654 of *Les enclaves des roches volcaniques*, Macon, 1893.]

1894.

115. SIR ARCHIBALD GEIKIE. On the Relations of the Basic and Acid Rocks of the Tertiary Volcanic Series of the Inner Hebrides. *Quart. Journ. Geol. Soc.*, vol. l., pp. 212-229, pl. XIII., XIV.; 1894.
116. SIR ARCHIBALD GEIKIE and J. J. H. TEALL. On the Banded Structure of some Tertiary Gabbros in the Isle of Skye. *Quart. Journ. Geol. Soc.*, vol. l., pp., 645-659, pl. XXVI.-XXVIII.; 1894.
117. SIR ARCHIBALD GEIKIE. Annual Report of the Geological Survey and Museum of Practical Geology for the year ending December 31, 1894. Appendix E (pp. 267-300) to *42nd Report of the Dept. of Science and Art*; pub. 1895. [H. B. Woodward. p. 286.]

1895.

118. SIR ARCHIBALD GEIKIE. The Latest Volcanoes of the British Isles. *Trans. Geol. Soc. Glasg.*, vol. x., pp. 179-197; pub. 1896.
119. SIR ARCHIBALD GEIKIE. Annual Report of the Geological Survey and Museum of Practical Geology for the year ending December 31, 1895. Appendix E to *43rd Report of the Dept. of Science and Art*; pub. 1896. [A. Harker, pp. 30, 31; C. T. Clough, p. 31.]
120. GREENVILLE A. J. COLE, *Open-Air Studies: an Introduction to Geology Out-of doors:* 8vo, London, 1895. [Skye, pp. 208-212.]

1896.

121. ALFRED HARKER. On certain Granophyres, modified by the Incorporation of Gabbro-Fragments, in Strath (Skye). *Quart. Journ. Geol. Soc.*, vol. lii., pp. 320-328, pl. XIII., XIV.; 1896.
122. SIR ARCHIBALD GEIKIE. The Tertiary Basalt-plateaux of North-western Europe. *Quart. Journ. Geol. Soc.*, vol. lii., pp. 331-405, pl. XV.-XIX.; 1896.
123. SIR ARCHIBALD GEIKIE. Scottish Mountains, *Scott. Mount. Club Journ.*, vol. iv., pp. 113-125, with five plates; 1896.
124. H. ROSENBUSCH. *Mikroskopische Physiographie der Massigen Gesteine*, 3rd ed. 8vo., pp. xiv + 1360, pl. VI.; Stuttgart, 1896.
125. A. T. METCALFE. The Tertiary Lava-Fields of the West Coast of Scotland. *44th Ann. Rep. Nott. Nat. Soc.*, pp. 1-12; 1896.
126. GEOLOGICAL SURVEY OF SCOTLAND. Sheet 81 (Applecross) of the one-inch Geological Map of Scotland [including coast of Skye near Portree and part of Raasay: Tertiary igneous rocks by H. B. Woodward.]
127. SIR ARCHIBALD GEIKIE. Annual Report of the Geological Survey and Museum of Practical Geology for the year ending December 31, 1896. Appendix E to *44th Report of the Dept. of Science and Art*; pub. 1897. [A. Harker, pp. 73, 74; C. T. Clough, L. W. Hinxman, p. 74.]
128. JOHN W. JUDD. *The Student's Lyell: a Manual of Elementary Geology* [edited by J. W. J.]; London, 1896 [pp. 490-492, 518, 521, 530].

1897.

129. W. A. TILDEN. On the Gases enclosed in Crystalline Rocks and Minerals. *Proc. Roy. Soc.*, vol. lx., pp. 453-157, and *Chem. News*, vol. lxxv., pp. 169, 170; 1897.
130. W. DOUGLAS. Names, Heights, and Positions of the Coolin Peaks. *Scott. Mount. Club Journ.*, vol. iv., pp. 209-213; 1897. See also a map of "The Coolins, Skye," on the scale of four inches to a mile, reduced from the six-inch Ordnance map, with additional names and heights, issued with No. 25 of the Journal, January, 1898.
131. SIR ARCHIBALD GEIKIE. *The Ancient Volcanoes of Great Britain*. Roy. 8vo, 2 vols, pp. xxiv + 477, viii + 492, with seven maps; London, 1897.
132. M. F. HEDDLE. On Analcime with New Forms. *Trans. Edin. Geol. Soc.*, vol. vii., pp. 241-243, pl. XII.; 1897, issued 1898.
133. SIR ARCHIBALD GEIKIE. *Summary of Progress of the Geological Survey of the United Kingdom for 1897*; pub. 1898. [A. Harker, pp. 131-137; C. T. Clough, pp. 137, 138.]

1898.

134. C. T. CLOUGH and ALFRED HARKER. On a Coarsely Spherulitic ("Variolitic") Basalt in Skye. *Trans. Edin. Geol. Soc.*, vol. vii., pp. 381-389, pl. XXIII.; pub. 1899.
135. SIR ARCHIBALD GEIKIE. *Summary of Progress of the Geological Survey of the United Kingdom for 1898*; pub. 1899. [A. Harker, pp. 146-150.]

1899.

136. LIONEL W. HINXMAN. The Geology of the Scottish Mountains from a Climbing Point of View. *Scott. Mount. Club Journ.*, vol. v., pp. 269-286; 1899.
137. SIR ARCHIBALD GEIKIE. *Summary of Progress of the Geological Survey of the United Kingdom for 1899*; pub. 1900. [A. Harker, pp. 141-145; W. Pollard, pp. 172-174.]

1900.

138. ALFRED HARKER. Notes, Geological and Topographical on the Cuillin Hills, Skye. *Scott. Mount. Club Journ.*, vol. vi., pp. 1-13; 1900.
139. ALFRED HARKER. Magnetic Disturbances in the Isle of Skye. *Proc. Camb. Phil. Soc.*, vol. x., pp. 268-278, pl. XI., XII.; 1900.
140. SIR ARCHIBALD GEIKIE. *Summary of Progress of the Geological Survey of the United Kingdom for 1900*; pub. 1901. [A. Harker, pp. 126, 127; W. Pollard, pp. 156, 157.]

1901.

141. M. FORSTER HEDDLE. *The Mineralogy of Scotland* [posthumous publication], edited by J. G. Goodchild: 2 vols, roy. 8vo, pp. lviii + 148 and viii + 247, with many plates; Edinburgh, 1901.
142. ALFRED HARKER. The Sequence of the Tertiary Igneous Rocks of Skye. *Geol. Mag.*, 1901, pp. 506-509.
143. J. H. L. VOGT. Weitere Untersuchungen über die Ausscheidungen von Titan-Eisenerzen in basischen Eruptivgesteinen. *Zeits. prakt. Geol.*, vol. ix. [Skye, pp. 182, 186]; 1901.
144. J. J. H. TEALL. *Summary of Progress of the Geological Survey of the United Kingdom for 1901*; pub. 1902. [W. Pollard, pp. 86-88; A. Harker, pp. 131, 132, 147-149; C. T. Clough, p. 149; G. Barrow, p. 152.]

1902.

145. ALFRED HARKER. *Petrology for Students*, 3rd ed.; 8vo, Cambridge, 1902.
146. WILLIAM JOHNSON SOLLAS. A Process for the Mineral Analysis of Rocks. *Quart. Journ. Geol. Soc.*, vol. lviii., pp. 163-176; 1902.
147. J. J. H. TEALL. *Summary of Progress of the Geological Survey of the United Kingdom for 1902*; pub. 1903. [W. Pollard, pp. 60, 61.]

1903.

148. TEMPEST ANDERSON. *Volcanic Studies in Many Lands, being reproductions of photographs* . . . 4to, pp. xxviii. + 202, with cv plates; London, 1903. [Skye, pl. XCIII., XCIV.]

EXPLANATION OF PLATES XVII. TO XXVII.

PLATE XVII.

FIG. 1. × 20. Olivine-basalt lava, above schoolhouse, Braes, S. of Portree: showing olivine replaced by a mineral comparable with iddingsite. See p. 34.

FIG. 2. [6772] × 20. Olivine-basalt lava, Rudha Buidhe, near Braes, S. of Portree: showing another type of pseudomorph after olivine. See p. 34.

FIG. 3. × 40. Microstructures of the basic lavas.

    A. [8185] "Granulitic" structure in olivine-basalt, near bridge over Allt Fionnfhuachd, Drynoch; the rock analysed. See pp. 31, 36.

    B. [9246] Ophitic structure in hypersthene-basalt, lower part of Allt Dearg Mór, near Sligachan. A bastite pseudomorph after hypersthene appears in the lower left-hand corner. See pp. 36, 38.

    C. Ocellar structure in basalt at base of group, S. of Sgùrr nan Each: a type rich in augite and without olivine. See p. 37.

    D. [9366] Microlitic structure in augite-andesite, S. coast of Scalpay. the augite is mostly chloritised. See p. 37.

FIG. 4. [7460] × 10. Metamorphosed amygdule in basalt, close to granite on E. side of Blath-bheinn; showing a crystalline aggregate of new plagioclase felspar, partly with radiate grouping, replacing zeolites. See p. 51.

FIG. 5. [2700] × 10. Metamorphosed amygdule in basalt, near granite, Creagan Dubha, N. of Beinn Dearg Mhòr (of Strath): showing a granular crystalline aggregate of new felspar, derived from zeolites, with a border of epidote grains. See pp. 51, 52.

PLATE XVIII.

FIG. 1. [8731] × 20. Highly metamorphosed amygdaloidal basalt, near gabbro, N.E. of An Sgùman. The rock is completely reconstituted, and presents the appearance of some so-called pyroxene-granulites. The figure shows part of an amygdule, now consisting of alternate zones of augite and felspar. See pp. 52, 53.

FIG. 2. [9238] × 20. Anorthite-olivine rock (troctolite) in the peridotite group, lower part of An Garbh-choire: consisting simply of olivine and anorthite, the latter often traversed by numerous fine fissures, which radiate from the olivine grains. See p. 73.

PLATE XVII.

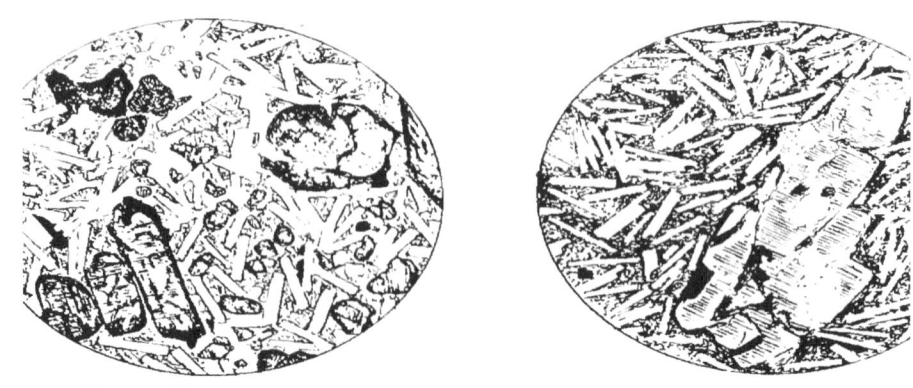

FIG. 1. Olivine-Basalt lava.

FIG. 2. Olivine-Basalt lava.

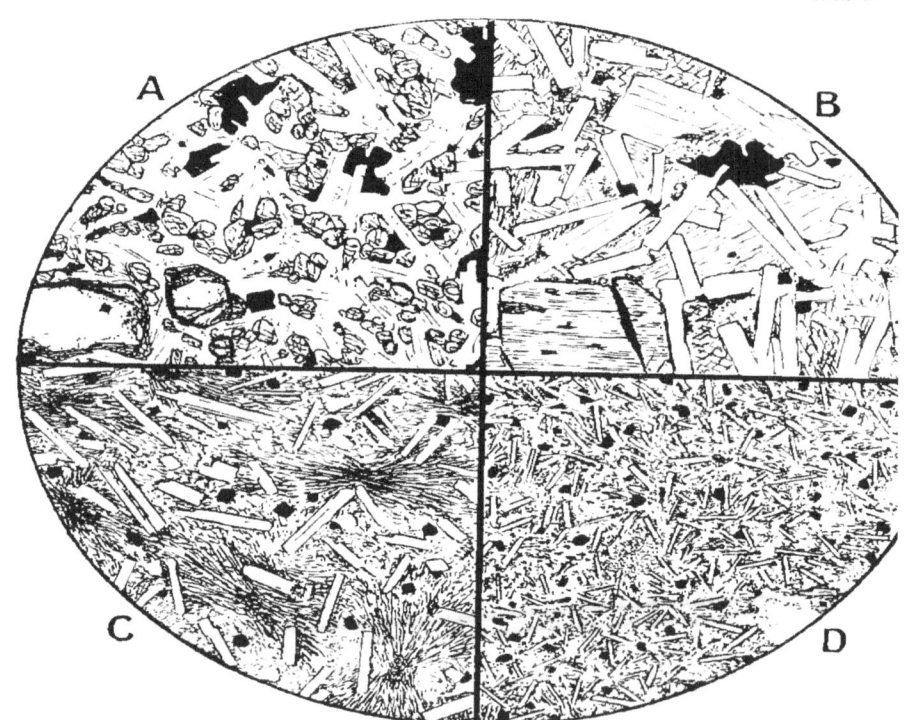

FIG. 3. Micro-structures of basic lavas.

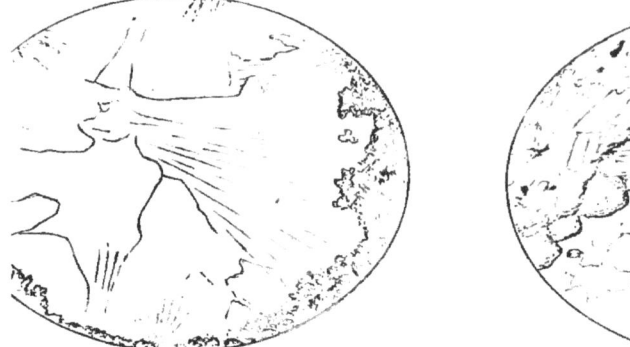

FIG. 4. Metamorphosed amygdule.

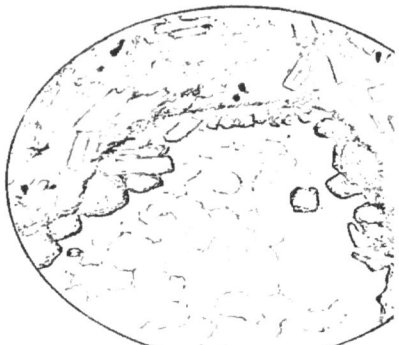

FIG. 5. Metamorphosed amygdule.

PLATE XVIII.

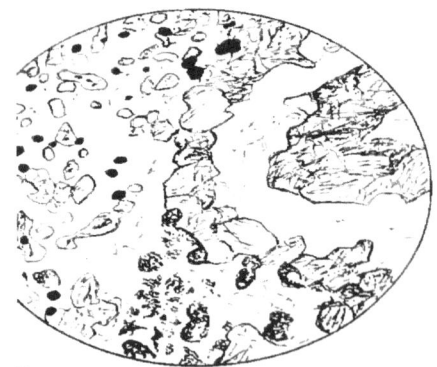

Fig. 1. Highly metamorphosed basalt.

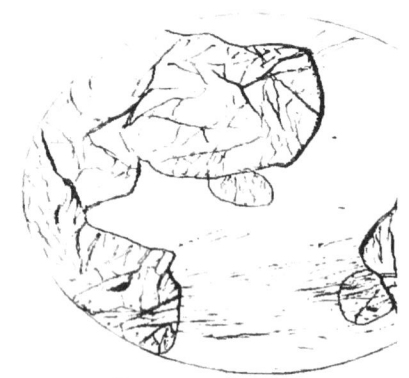

Fig. 2. Anorthite-olivine-rock.

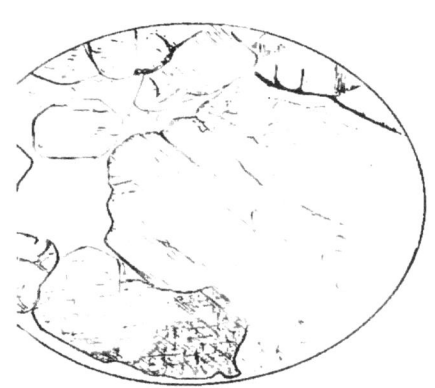

Fig. 3. Enstatite-anorthite-rock.

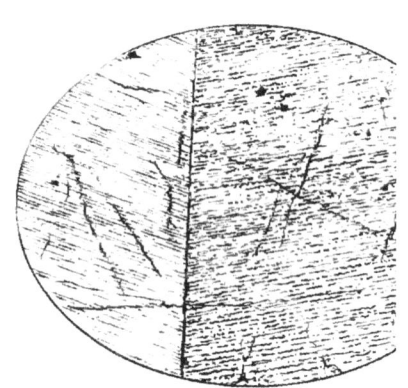

Fig. 4. Salite-structure.

Fig. 5. Diallage-structure.

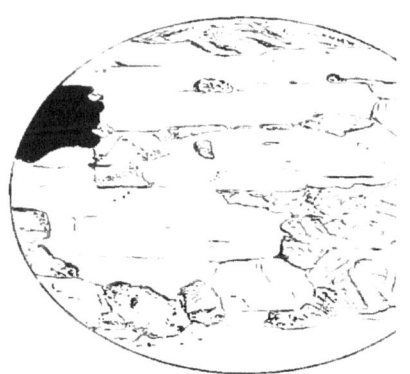

Fig. 6. Foliated gabbro.

PLATE X.

Fig. 1. Acidified gabbro.

Fig. 2. Micropegmatite phenocryst.

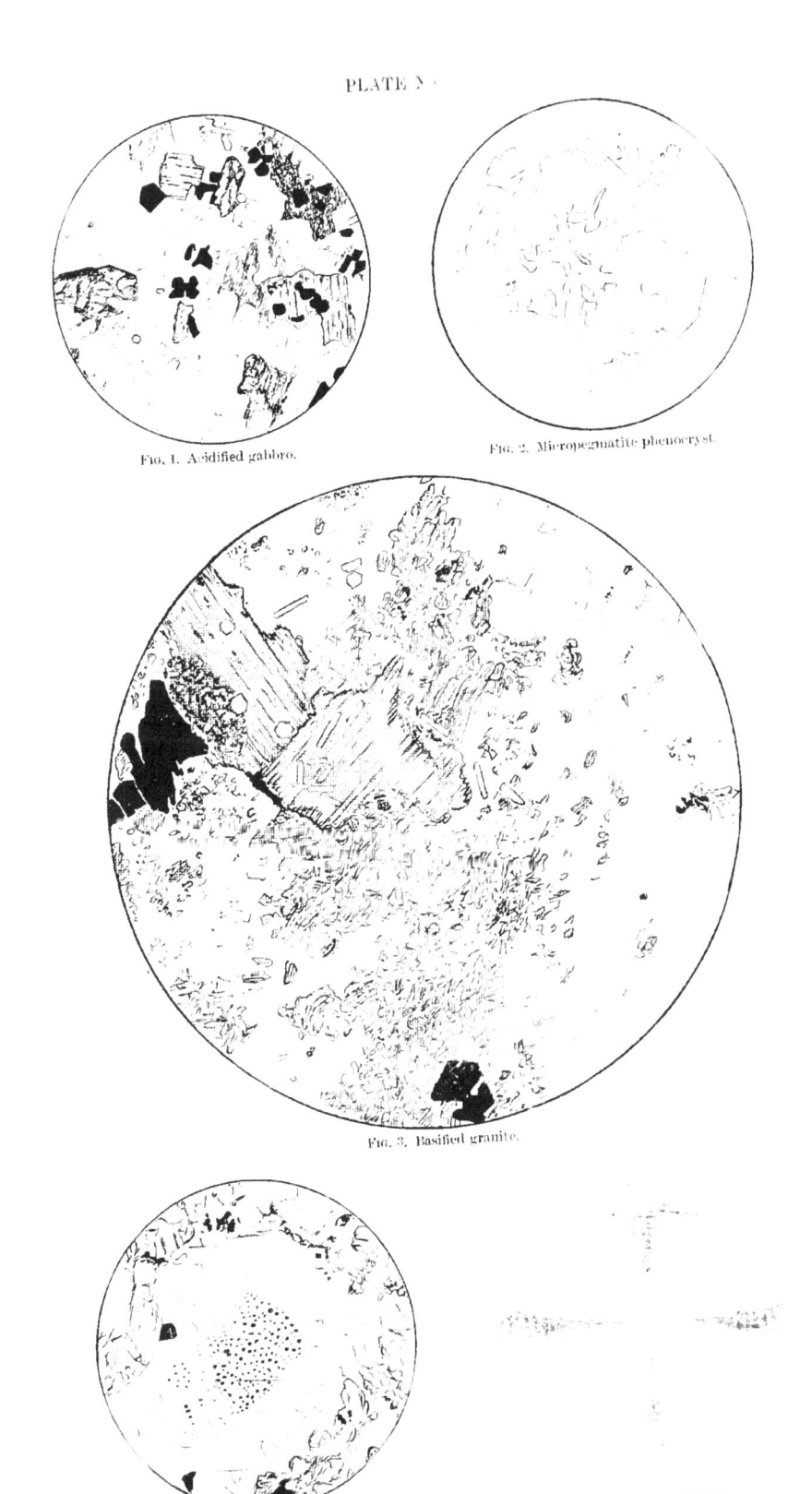

Fig. 3. Basified granite.

Fig. 4. Enlarged phenocryst.

Fig. 5. Spherulite in pitchstone.

PLATE XIX.

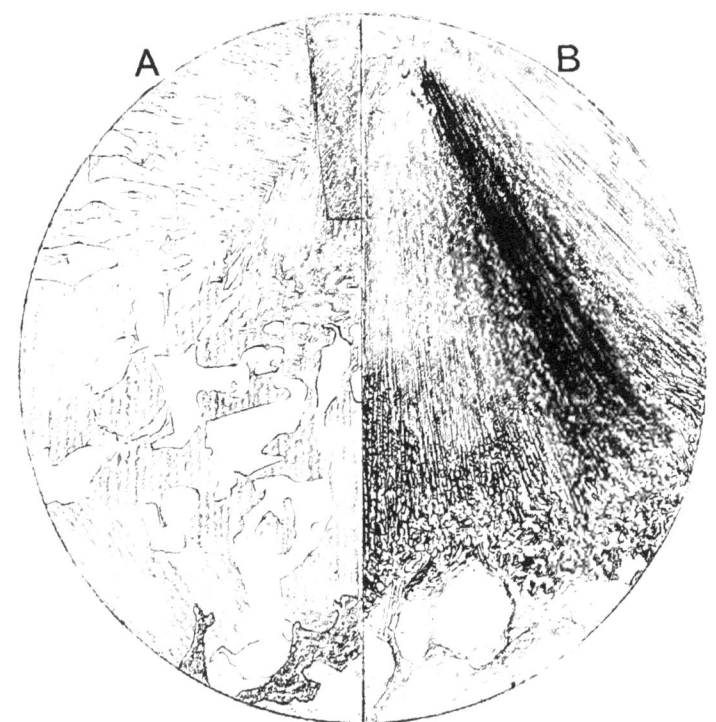

A B

Fig. 1. Granophyres.

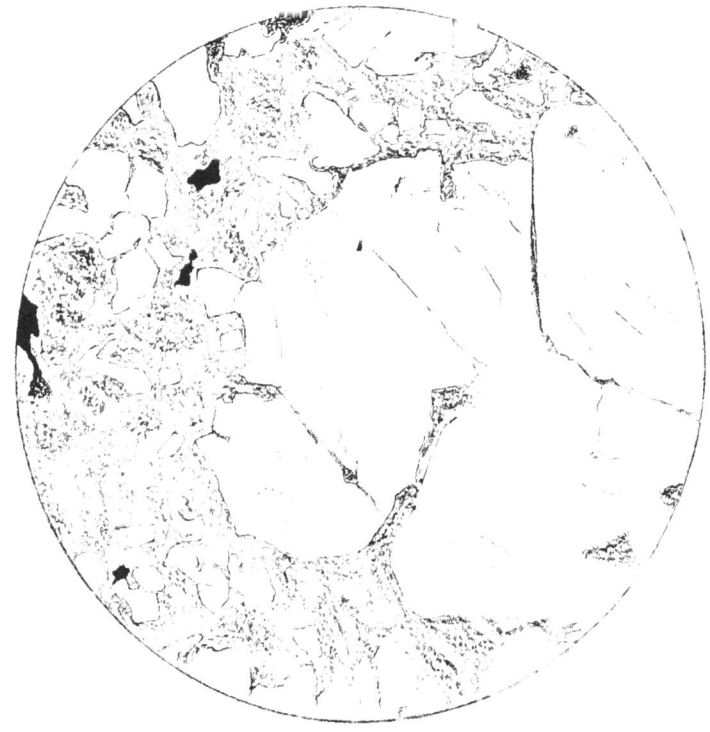

Fig. 2. Granophyre

FIG. 3. [8705] × 20. Enstatite-anorthite-rock (norite) in the peridotite group, N. of Sgùrr a' Coir' an Lochain, near Coruisk. The chief constituents are enstatite and anorthite, the latter interstitial to the former. At the bottom of the figure is a crystal, half of enstatite, half of diallage, and immediately to the left of this a crystal-grain of olivine. See p. 74.

FIG. 4. [7462] × 100. Augite of gabbro on the W. slope of Blathbheinn: showing the basal striation, accentuated by a fine "schiller" structure, and combined with the orthopinacoidal twin to give the "herring-bone" arrangement. See p. 109.

FIG. 5. × 10. Augite of gabbro at head of Loch Scavaig: showing the prismatic cleavage and diallage-structure. The latter, parallel to the orthopinacoid, is developed only in the marginal portion of the crystal. See p. 109.

FIG. 6. [7849] × 10. Foliated gabbro in the banded part of the group, Druim an Eidhne: showing a parallel orientation of the component crystals. See p. 119.

PLATE XIX.

FIG. 1. Graphic structures in granophyres; × 40, crossed nicols.

A. Roadside E. of Strollamus Bridge: showing micrographic intergrowth of striated oligoclase and quartz, and in the upper part of orthoclase and quartz, in connection with an orthoclase phenocryst. See p. 161.

B. Glas-Bheinn Bheag, near margin of intrusion: showing part of a single spherulite with the gradation from a cryptographic structure near the centre of growth to a visibly micrographic towards the periphery. See p. 281.

FIG. 2. [2667] × 40. Granophyric granite, Marsco: showing a rude micrographic growth round a grain of quartz. See p. 162.

PLATE XX.

FIG. 1. [8962] × 20. Gabbro partially fused and injected by the granite magma, gully on the N.W. face of Marsco. The minerals shown are felspar, partially destroyed augite, greenish brown hornblende, magnetite, apatite, and some interstitial quartz. Of the original constituents of the gabbro there remain relics of augite and some of the large crystals of labradorite. See p. 182.

FIG. 2. [5344] × 30. Phenocryst of micropegmatite in spherulitic dyke, Druim an Eidhne. It has served as the starting-place for subsequent spherulitic growths. See p. 284.

FIG. 3. [8694] × 40. Granite modified by absorption of gabbro material, S.E. ridge of Marsco. The figure shows aggregates composed of greenish brown hornblende with little scales of biotite, larger flakes of biotite enclosing apatite, and irregular grains of magnetite. The rest is of quartz, oligoclase, and orthoclase. See p. 184.

Fig. 4. [8188] × 20. Porphyritic Olivine-Dolerite, dyke on Roineval, two miles N of Drynoch: showing a felspar phenocryst enlarged by a later growth with crystalline continuity. See p. 329.

Fig. 5. [8733] × 50, crossed nicols. Spherulite in pitchstone, W. face of Glamaig: showing a concentric shell structure. See p. 404.

PLATE XXI.

Fig. 1. [7551] × 30. Xenolith of marscoite from the "spotted" granophyre of Allt Daraich, near Sligachan. The figure shows one of the large labradorite crystals, much fissured, in a ground-mass of hornblende, oligoclase, orthoclase, quartz, magnetite, and apatite. There has been some impregnation by the surrounding acid magma. See p. 195.

Fig. 2. [7858] × 100. Augite crystals replaced by fibrous green hornblende and granules of magnetite, in marscoite from the gully on the N.W. face of Marsco. See p. 186.

Fig. 3. [9982] × 100. Vitrified Torridonian grit, in contact with a dolerite sill, S. coast of Soay. Some relics of quartz-grains remain in a corroded shape. The rest is a clear colourless glass enclosing minute crystals of cordierite, magnetite, and a pyroxenic mineral. See p. 246.

Fig. 4. [9371] × 30. Corroded xenocryst of oligoclase in small sill above the composite sill of Rudh' an Eireannaich, near Broadford. The crystal, except at its centre, is greatly affected by secondary inclusions. In one place corrosion has eaten away the crystal, forming an inlet occupied by the ground-mass with its small felspar crystals. See p. 229.

PLATE XXII.

Fig. 1. [3200] × 20. Spherulitic felsite, above Boreraig: showing dense radiate spherulites, sometimes grown round quartz crystals, with interspaces having a granular structure. See p. 281.

Fig. 2. [8951] × 20. Dolerite, dyke at point E. of the mouth of Allt na Nighinn, 2 miles W. of Kyleakin. At the top of the figure is one of the shapeless later felspar crystals, enclosing numerous needles of apatite. See p. 322.

Fig. 3. [5389] × 40. Part of a large composite spherulite from an acid dyke cutting the gabbro of Druim an Eidhne. The centre of the spherulite is outside the figure, above and to the right. There are minor centres of radiation, which serves as the apices of conical growths directed outward, the axes of the cones conforming with the principal radiate arrangement. One such cone, cut along its axis, occupies the central part of the figure; while below, to the right, are others cut at some distance from their axes so as to present parabolic sections. The clear crystals are quartz, the opaque ones pyrites. See p. 286.

PLATE XXI.

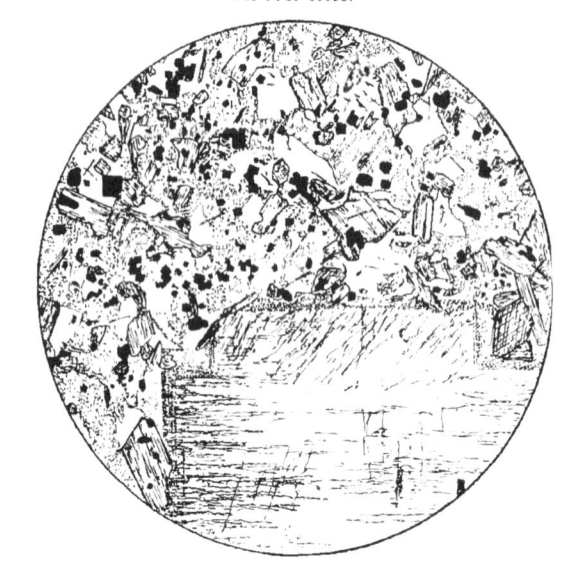

FIG. 1. Marscoite xenolith.

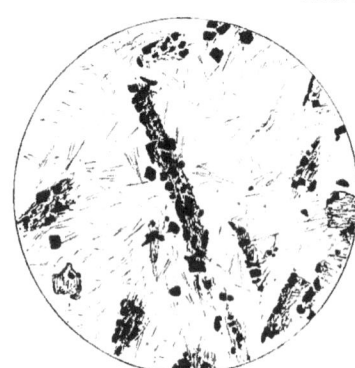

FIG. 2. Fused augites.

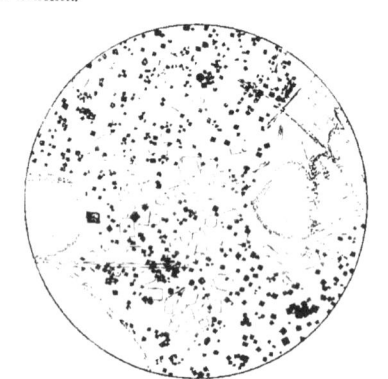

FIG. 3. Vitrified sandstone.

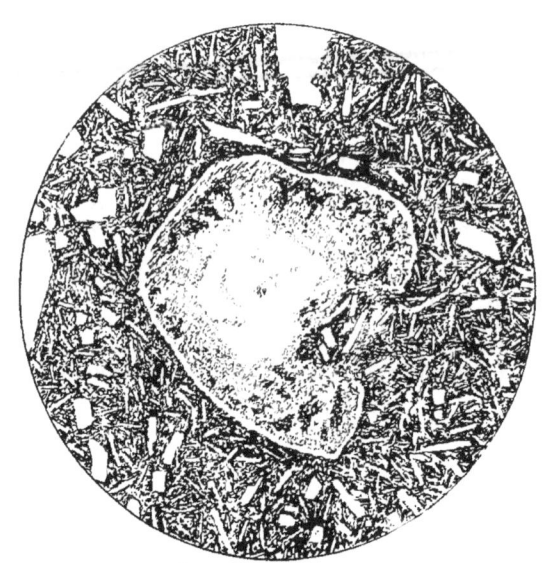

FIG. 4. Corroded xenocryst.

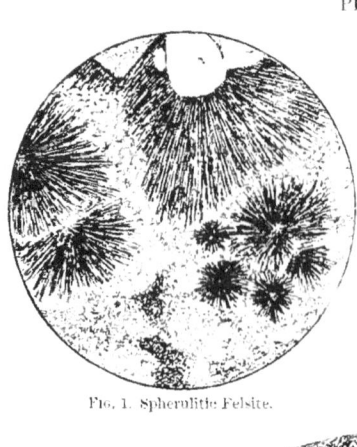

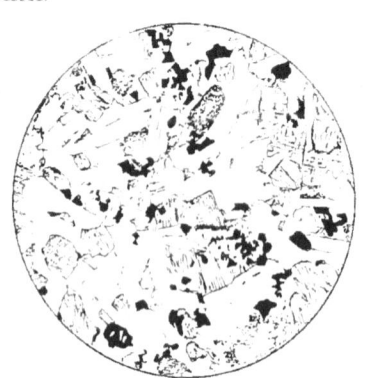

PLATE XXII.

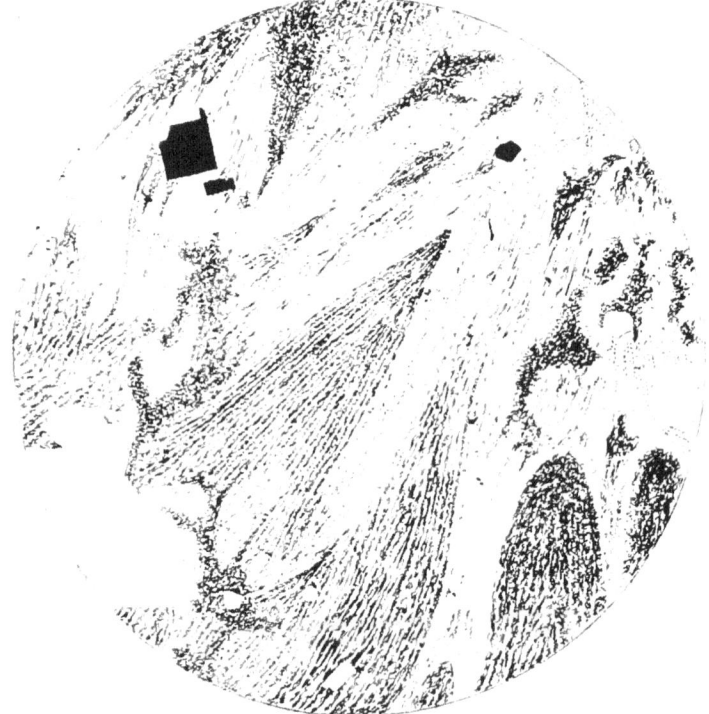

Fig. 1. Spherulitic Felsite.

Fig. 2. Dolerite.

Fig. 3. Complex spherulite.

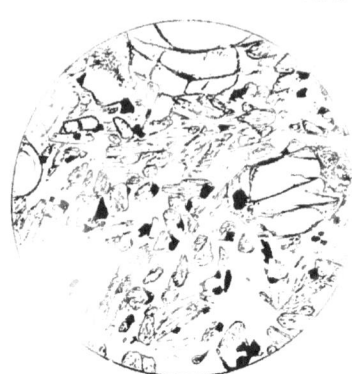

Fig. 4. Olivine-Dolerite.

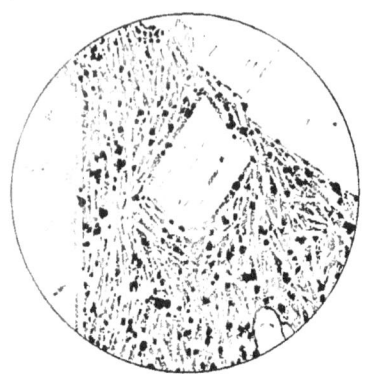

Fig. 5. Porphyritic Basalt.

PLATE XXI

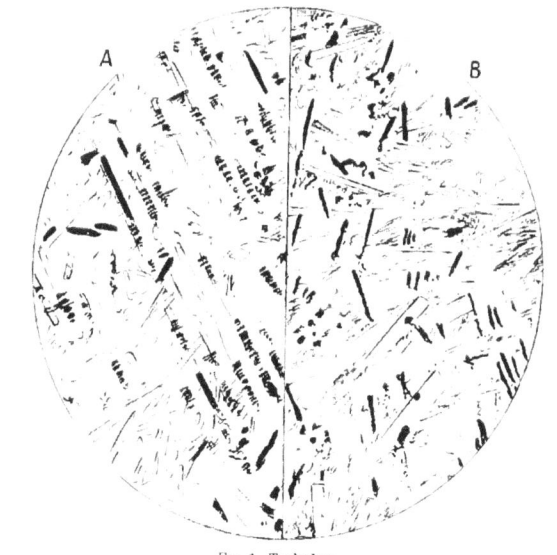

Fig. 1. Tachylyte.

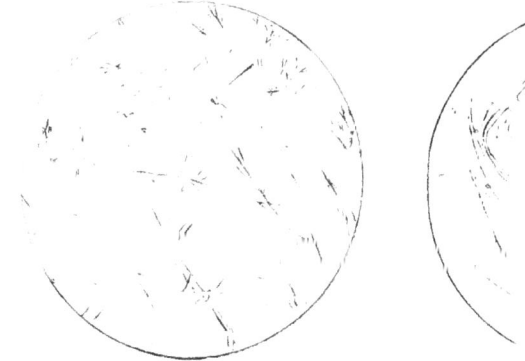

Fig. 2. Pitchstone.

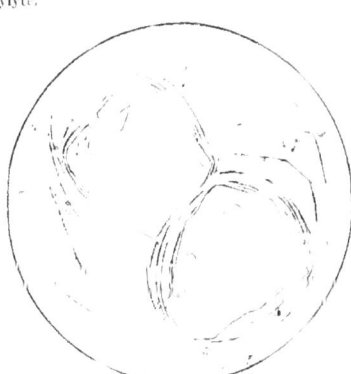

Fig. 3. Pitchstone.

Fig. 4. New-formed felspar.

PLATE XX

FIG. 1. Tachylytes.

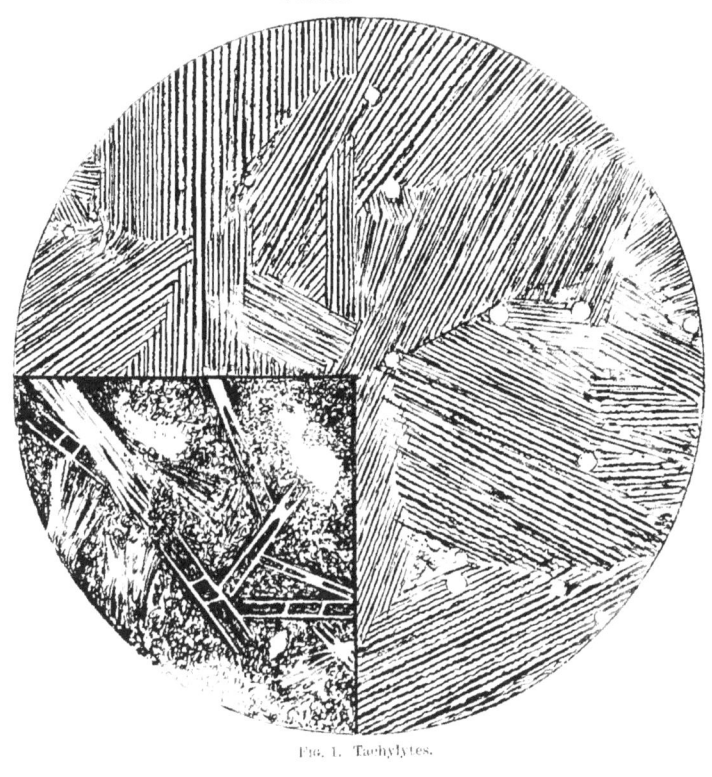

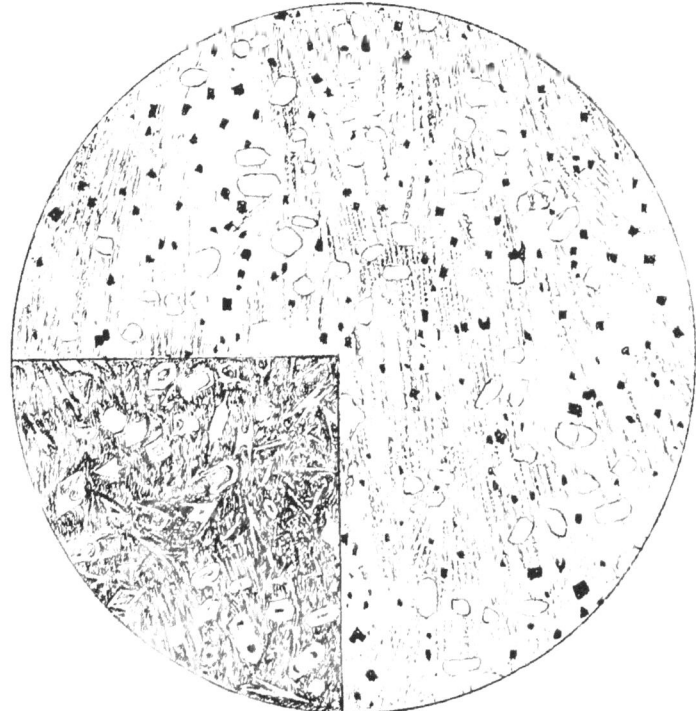

FIG. 2. Variolite.

Fig. 4. [7862] × 20. Porphyritic Olivine-Dolerite, dyke cutting the granite of Ciche na Beinne Deirge, 3 miles S.E. of Sligachan. This represents the Beinn Dearg type of dykes, and is the rock analysed. See p. 326.

Fig. 5. [6711] × 20. Porphyritic Basalt, dyke cutting Cambrian limestone ¼ mile S. by E. of Suardal, about 2 miles S.S.W. of Broadford. This rock illustrates one variety of the Suardal group of dykes, containing phenocrysts of labradorite and grains of olivine in a ground-mass of smaller felspars, abundant magnetite, and finely granular augite. See p. 327.

PLATE XXIII.

Fig. 1. A. (occupying three quadrants) [8849] × 40. Tachylyte, dyke ⅓ mile S. of Loch Ashik, near Broadford: showing the central part of the dyke, which consists of a clear colourless glass crowded with rods of magnetite in parallel groups. The small clear spaces are amygdules. See p. 349.

B. (lower left-hand quadrant) [8846] × 200. Basalt, largely glassy, with skeleton crystallites of felspar, central part of a thin dyke with tachylytic selvages, N. slope of Meall Odhar Beag, near Sligachan. See p. 345.

Fig. 2. × 40. Spherulitic or variolitic basalt, forming a sheet at Camas Daraich, Point of Sleat. See p. 347.

A. (occupying three quadrants) [7845]. Prevalent type, showing only part of one of the large spherulites.

B. (lower left-hand quadrant) [7846]. Marginal modification, largely vitreous, with olivine in the form of skeleton crystallites.

PLATE XXIV.

Fig. 1. [8850] × 150. Tachylyte, dyke ¾ m. N.E. of Kinloch, Sleat district: a quasi-spherulitic rock. See pp. 349, 350.

A. Outer portion of one of the large spherulitic bodies, showing parallel rods of augite, with some magnetite, embedded in a colourless glass.

B. Central part of a spherulite, showing abundant felspar, as well as augite and magnetite, with a smaller proportion of glassy base.

Fig. 2. [6794] × 20. Pitchstone, dyke in Allt a' Choire, above Coirechatachan, near Broadford: showing groups of crystallites, each surrounded by a clear ring. The turbid appearance of the rest of the glassy mass is due to a crowd of more minute crystallitic growths. See p. 407.

Fig. 3. × 20. Pitchstone, E. slope of Glas Bheinn Mhòr; showing perlitic cracks surrounding phenocrysts of quartz: also groups of crystallites, each surrounded by a clear ring. See p. 405.

2 F

470   *Explanation of Plates XVII. to XXVII.*

FIG. 4. [7479] × 30. Xenolith of quartzite from a basic dyke, S. end of Blath-bheinn. The figure shows the quartzite corroded by the basic magma and an inlet occupied by radiating fibres of new-formed felspar, probably oligoclase. See p. 352.

PLATE XXV.

FIG. 1. [9372] × 30. Porphyritic Dolerite, dyke 400 yards N.W. by N. of Scalpay House. The lower part of the figure shows part of one of the circular felspathic areas which represent vesicles filled by the oozing in of the residual magma. See p. 331.

FIG. 2; × 20. Xenoliths in basic dykes.

A. [7483]. Edge of gabbro xenolith in dyke in Abhuinn nan Leac, Strathaird; showing the earliest stage of breaking up by the formation of numerous fissures; also the development of secondary inclusions in both felspar and augite. See pp. 355, 361.

B. [6716]. Detached quartz-grain from granite xenolith in dyke on ridge N. of Ben Suardal, near Broadford: showing the earliest stage of breaking up by the formation of fissures, which here tend to run parallel to the outline; also incipient corrosion. See p. 356.

FIG. 3. × 20. Basic dyke carrying granite xenoliths, on shore N.E. of Corry Lodge, Broadford. See p. 357.

A. [6719]. The normal dolerite, where free from foreign material.

B. [6720]. Portion enclosing abundant débris of granite, of which two detached quartz-grains are shown, each with its corrosion-border of granular augite. The matrix, partly obscured by alteration, is of fine texture and of much less basic composition than the normal dolerite.

FIG. 4. [8723]. Picrite, An Sgùman.

A. (occupying three quadrants); × 30. Showing olivine, augite, anorthite, etc. The dendritic inclusions of magnetite in the olivine are conspicuous in the large crystal in the lower left-hand quadrant: in the crystal at the top of the figure they are cut at right angles to their plane, and so appear like rods. See p. 381.

B. (lower right-hand quadrant); × 110. Showing the dendritic inclusions more highly magnified. See pp. 68, 69, 381.

PLATE XXVI.

FIG. 1. [9980] × 32. Porphyritic Picrite, sill S. of Leac nan Faoileann, I. of Soay. The porphyritic elements are olivine and picotite. These recur also in a second generation, but the bulk of the ground-mass is of slender rods of felspar with sub-parallel arrangement and interstitial augite, the structure recalling that of some variolitic basalts. See p. 380.

FIG. 2. [7370] × 20. Ceratophyre (?), large dyke W. of Loch Gauscavaig, near Tarskavaig, Sleat: showing an aggregate of crystals of alkali-felspar with small crystals of augite and grains of magnetite. See p. 397.

PLATE XXV.

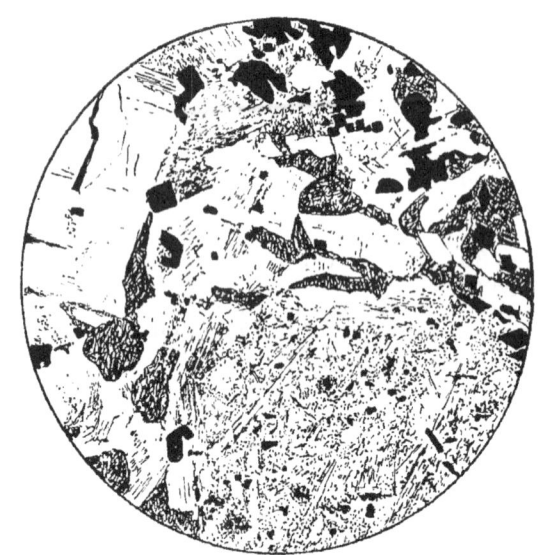

Fig. 1. Porphyritic dolerite.

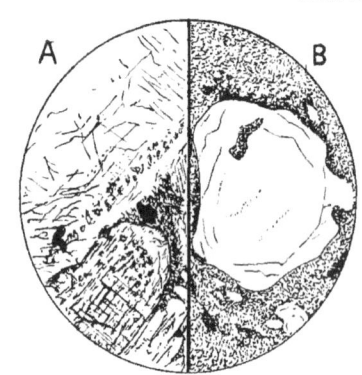

Fig. 2. Xenocrysts in dyke.

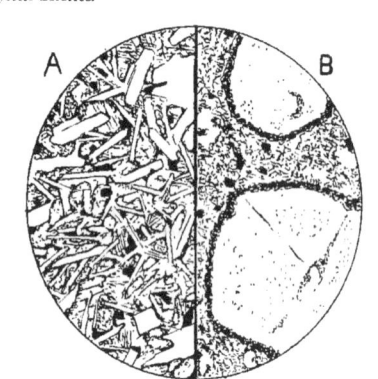

Fig. 3. Xenocrysts in dyke.

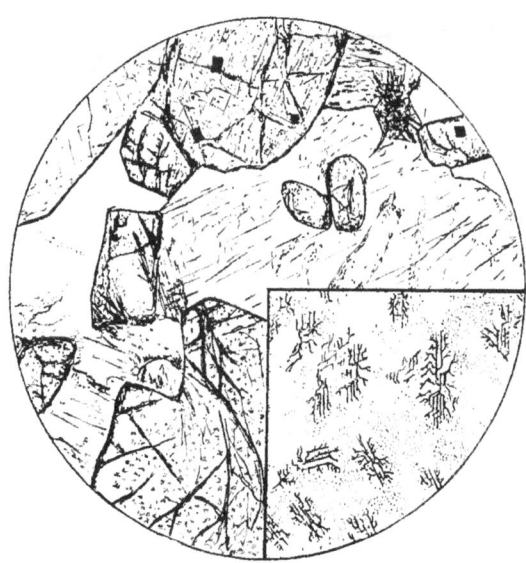

Fig. 4. Picrite.

XXVI

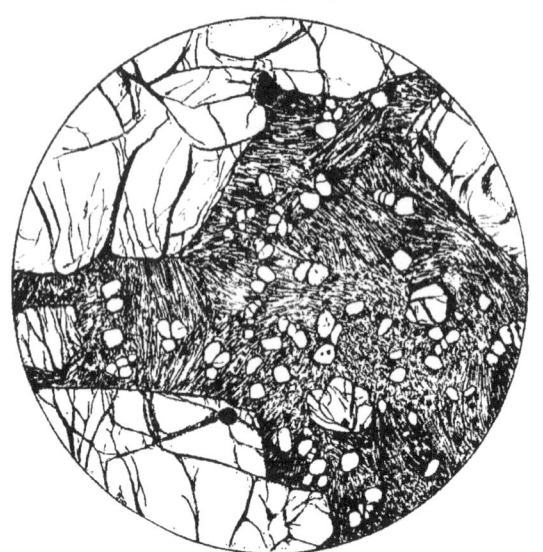

Fig. 1. Porphyritic picrite.

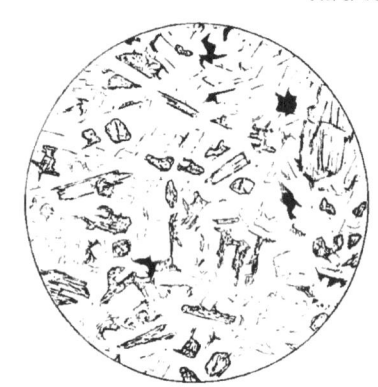

Fig. 2. Ceratophyre (?).

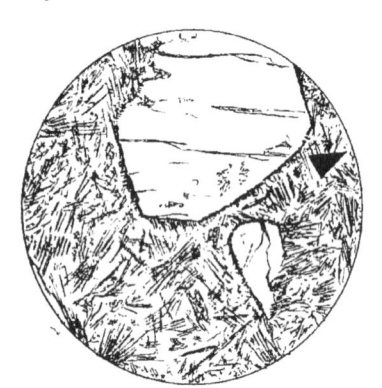

Fig. 3. Ceratophyre (?).

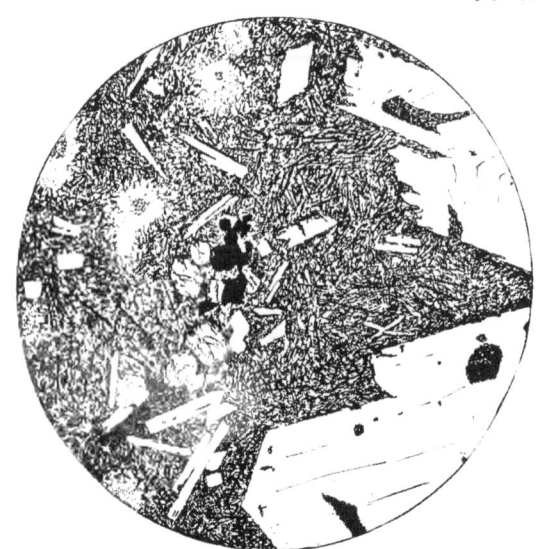

Fig. 4. Andesite.

PLATE XXVII.

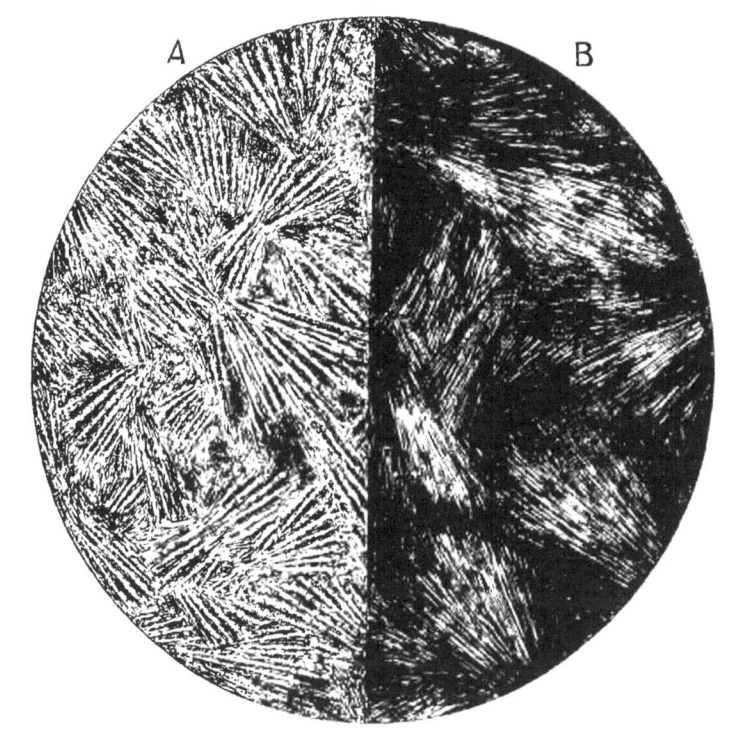

Fig. 1, Trachytes.

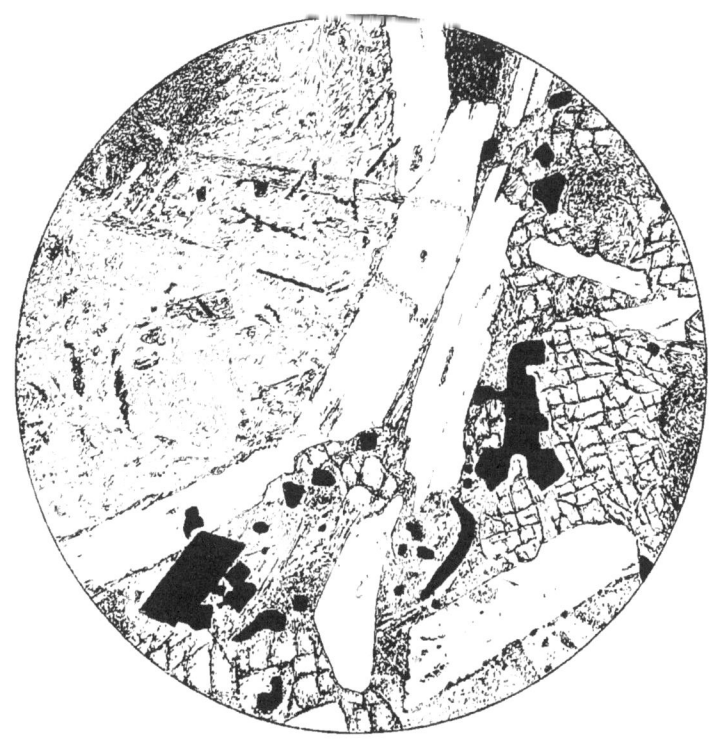

Fig. 2. Andesite.

Explanation of Plates XVII to XXVII. 471

FIG. 3. [6851] × 20. Ceratophyre (?), dyke nearly ⅔ mile N. by W. of Cnoc an Sgùmain, Armadale: showing phenocrysts of crypto-perthite in a ground-mass composed of an aggregate of crystals of alkali-felspar penetrated by very numerous needles of augite. See p. 397.

FIG. 4. [3201] × 30. Glassy Augite-Andesite, dyke on shore of Loch Eishort, W. of Boreraig: showing phenocrysts of felspar, augite, and magnetite in a ground-mass composed of clear glass crowded with crystallitic growths, largely in the form of minute rectangular gratings. See p. 401.

PLATE XXVII.

FIG. 1 × 40, crossed nicols. Micro-structure of the trachytic dykes of the Broadford and Sleat districts, showing the tendency to sheaf-like groupings of the felspars. See p. 394.

    A. [6749]. Dyke S.E. of Broadford.

    B. [5082]. Dyke in Allt Mòr, about 2 miles S.E. of Drochaid Lusa and 5 miles E. of Broadford.

FIG. 2. [5424] × 400. Augite-Andesite, dyke ⅓ mile S.W. of Rudha Guail, N.E. of Isle Ornsay. The structure is intersertal, and the figure shows also a part of a vesicle occupied by glass crowded with crystallites. See p. 401.

INDEX.

A

ABHUINN Ceann Loch Ainort, 167.
—— nan Leac, 355, 413, 470.
—— Lusa, 254.
Abnormal composition of hybrid rocks, 231.
Absorption of basic rocks by acid magmas, 172, 183, 193, 467; of acid by basic, 357, 359.
Accidental xenoliths, 351.
ADIE, R. H., 338.
Admixture of basic and acid rocks, 172, 177, 181, 183, 187, 192, 194, 231, 357.
Age of the igneous rocks, 1, 2, 5.
Agglomerates, volcanic, 16, 58; enclosed in gabbro, 89; dykes in, 293.
Ailsa Craig, 158, 450.
Alaisdair Stone-shoot, 273, 287, 448.
ALLPORT, S., 198.
Allt Aigeinn, 298.
—— Airidh Meall Beathaig, 201, 275.
—— Bealach na Coise, 307.
—— Cadha na Eglais, 153.
—— a' Chaoich, 64, 65, 70, 71, 72, 75, 76, 78, 97, 118, 119, 369.
—— a' Charn-aird, 314.
—— a' Choire, 171, 406, 408, 469.
—— a' Choire Ghaisteach, 54.
—— Clach an Geala, 202.
—— na Coille, 253, 320.
—— Coire na Banachdich, 25, 28, 94, 95, 123.
—— a' Coire Ghreadaidh, 123.
—— Coire Labain, 33, 38, 380.
—— Coir' a' Mhadaidh, 307.
—— Coire Riabhaich, 103, 115, 279.
—— Cùl Airidh Lagain, 388, 391-393.
—— Daraich (Sligachan), 187-189, 192-194, 201, 275, 305, 468.
—— Dearg Beag, 202, 320.
—— Dearg Mòr, 34, 39, 466.
—— an Doire, 27.
—— Duisdale, 276, 392, 407.
—— Evan, 334.
—— Fearna, 12, 131, 136, 159, 160.
—— an Fionn-choire, 59, 61.
—— Fionnfhuachd, 31, 466.
—— Geodh' a' Ghamnha, 26.
—— Grillau, 202.
—— an Inbhire, 319.
—— nan Leac, 19.
—— Leth-pheiginne, 28.
—— Leth Slighe, 83, 219, 383.
—— na Measarroch, 295, 450.
—— nam Mcirlach, 53.
—— a' Mhalm, 288.
—— Mhic Leannain, 103.

Allt Mòr an Finn-choire, 56, 59-61.
—— a' Mhuillin (Glen Brittle), 25.
—— na Nighinn, 322, 468.
—— a' Pairte, 208.
—— Réidh Ghlais, 390-393.
—— an t-Sithean (Broadford), 279; (Sligachan), 203, 208, 209, 211, 233, 282.
—— an t-Suidhe, 326, 355.
—— na Teangaidh, 166, 167.
—— Thuill, 311, 335, 336, 348, 383.
—— an Uchd Bhuidhe, 378.
Alpine flora of Cuillins, 449.
Am Basteir, 374, 446.
—— Bile, 331, 337, 338, 347, 360.
—— Fuar-choire, 156, 166.
Amygdaloidal structure in lavas, 30, 38, 42; gabbro, 96; sills, 247; dykes, 307, 308.
An Ceannaich, 10.
—— Carnach, 18, 441.
—— Dà Bheinn, 252, 355, 449.
ANDERSON, TEMPEST, 465.
—— THOS., 456.
Andesite lavas, 38, 58; dykes, 399; relation to pitchstones, 402.
An Diallaid, 374, 376, 378.
—— Dubh-sgeire (Soay), 66, 74, 79, 342.
—— Garbh-choire, 64, 72, 73, 75, 77, 334, 444, 466.
Anglesey dykes, 3, 432.
An Stac, 94, 101, 440, 441, 449.
—— Sgùman, 52, 68, 375, 380, 381, 444, 466, 470.
Antecedent xenocrysts, 223.
Antrim, 9, 10, 31, 47-49, 57, 248, 362.
Aodann Clach, 221, 382.
Aplitic veins of gabbro, 117; of granite, 166.
Ardmore Point, 10.
Ardnameacan, 308.
Ardnamurchan, 4, 55, 170, 199, 400.
Ard Thurinish, 335, 359.
Ardvasar, 360.
Armadale, 299, 317, 334, 392, 471.
Arran, 2, 18, 20, 153, 164, 170, 198, 199, 338, 340, 362, 385, 402, 404, 406, 417.
Augite-andesite lavas, 38; dykes, 399; relation to pitchstones, 402.

B

BAKER, T., 102, 315, 322, 382, 384.
Balmeanach, 8.
Banding in peridotites, 75; in gabbros, 90, 117.
BARROW, G., 383, 465.

Basalt lavas, age, 2; distribution, 3; extent, 6; dip, 7; from fissure-eruptions, 11; channels of supply, 12; thickness, 13; analysis, 31; component minerals, 32, micro-structure, 36; classification, 38: inclusions, 40; decomposition, 41; secondary minerals, 42; weathering, 46; metamorphism, 50; magnetism, 53; features in scenery, 439.

Basic dykes, 291; frequency and distribution, 292, 431; multiple, 296; eviscerated, 298; directions, 299, 431; interruptions, 302; width, 303; hade, 305; length, 306; amygdules, 307; margins, 308; jointing, 309; metamorphism by, 309; decay, 312; different ages, 315; petrography, 318, *etc.*; tachylytic selvages, 333, *etc.*; xenoliths in, 351, *etc.*; groups special to Cuillins, 364; influence on scenery, 438, 446, 450, 451.

—— secretions in granite, 166.

—— sheets of Cuillins, *see* Inclined sheets.

—— sills, distinguished from lavas, 29, 235; great group, age and distribution, 236; thickness, 237; multiple sills, 241; field-relations, 242; jointing, 243; magnetisation, 244; metamorphism by, 245; analyses, 248; component minerals, 249; microstructure, 250; xenoliths in, 251; minor groups of sills, 254; distribution, 255; double sills of Roineval type, 256; petrography, 261; porphyritic basalt sills, 269; sills as elements in scenery, 436.

Bauxite, 48.
Beal dyke, 333, 334, 337-341, 347.
Bealach Bàn (Scalpay), 353.
—— na Beinne Brice, 320.
—— na Beiste, 202.
—— a' Leitr, 128.
—— a' Mhalm, 402, 403, 439.
—— na Sgairde, 188.
Beerbachite, 116.
Beinn Bhreac, 24, 202.
—— Bhuidhe (Broadford), 126, 274; (Suishnish), 203, 217.
—— na Caillich, 2, 7, 17, 18, 126, 131, 142, 155, 167, 294, 296, 304, 320, 406, 408, 410, 414, 424, 449, 450.
—— a' Chairn, 153, 203, 204, 214, 216, 218.
—— na Cro, 83, 95, 101, 105, 122, 131, 137-139, 295, 450.
—— na Cuitheann, 47, 436.
—— Dearg, (Strath), 13, 17, 39, 126, 165, 325, 440, 449, 450; (Sligachan), 126, 166, 295, 325, 450; type of dykes, 325, 427, 469.
—— an Dubhaich, 126, 132, 133, 135, 143, 144, 148, 153, 155, 161, 166, 197, 292, 293, 301, 318, 319, 361, 414, 415, 424, 451.
—— an Dubh-lochain, 260.
—— a' Mheadhoin, 203, 204.
—— Reidh Beag (Scalpay), 289.
—— Tianavaig, 49, 435.
—— Totaig, 239.
Belig, 20, 24, 82, 83, 101, 124, 139, 202, 278, 440, 442.

Ben Aslak, 323, 383; type of sheets, 379, 383, 428.
—— Cleat, 374, 375, 378.
—— Lee, 248, 333, 341, 344 346, 438.
—— Meabost, 201, 279, 374, 378.
—— Suardal, 275, 294, 298, 301, 304, 309, 311, 312, 326, 327, 388, 392, 394, 395, 415, 470.
BERTRAND, M., 411, 415, 462.
Bidein Druim nan Ramh, 445-447.
Biod Mòr, 250, 251.
Blath-bheinn, 82, 83, 94, 127, 128, 130, 137, 141, 320, 351, 369, 372, 423, 441, 442, 445, 446, 466, 467, 470.
Blaven range, 82, 85, 87, 126, 128, 129, 292, 368, 413, 422, 445, 449; and *see* Blath-bheinn.
Bogha Charslice, 311.
Boreraig, 319, 400, 468, 471.
Boss-like habit of plutonic intrusions, 84; of gabbro, 97; granite, 131; peridotite, 380.
Bostonite, 227, 289.
BOUÉ, A., 1, 47, 199, 454.
Braes, 22, 247, 466.
Braigh Coille na Droighniche, 275.
—— Skulamus, 203, 204, 221.
Breccia, volcanic, *see* Agglomerate.
Brecciation of agglomerates, 28; lavas, 54; gabbro, 124; granite, 20, 167; peridotite, 77, 78, 383.
BRÉON, R., 363.
Brito-Icelandic province, 4; chemical characteristics, 416.
Broadford, 7, 82, 126, 136, 142, 144, 201-204, 212, 225, 255, 273-276, 282, 287, 296-298, 301-304, 357, 388, 392-395, 400 401, 410, 451, 468, 470, 471; gabbro boss, 82, 97, 100, 105, 293, 423, 401.
Broc-bheinn, 248, 250, 305, 320, 438.
BRÖGGER, W. C., 83, 230, 265.
Bruach na Frithe, 55, 57, 59, 86, 87, 89, 92, 422, 423, 442, 447.
Brucite-marble, 150.
BRYCE, J., 198, 245, 459.
BUCHANAN, J. T., 102.
Buile na h-Airidh, 260, 261, 267.
Bute, 199.

C

CAMAS Bàn, 22, 242.
—— Baravaig, 295.
—— Daraich (Point of Sleat), 256, 335, 346, 360, 469; (Tarskavaig), 334, 359.
—— Fhionnairidh, 139, 201, 309.
—— na Geadaig (Scalpay), 203, 207, 208, 233.
—— Malaig, 147-149.
—— a' Mhuillt, 302.
Camastianavaig, 10.
Camasunary, 87, 126, 129, 279, 292, 297, 309, 329, 442.
Cambrian limestones, 97; metamorphism of, 144; dykes in, 294, 296.
Canna, 10, 26, 269.
Carbonaceous seams in basalt group 10.
Carbost, 7, 8, 250, 311.

Index. 475

Carlingford, 2, 106, 142, 153, 154, 170.
CARMICHAEL, J., 455.
Carn Dearg, 203, 204, 208, 209, 211, 217, 375, 381-383, 451.
Carrock Fell, 2, 153, 156, 170, 338-340, 394, 423.
Cataclastic structures in gabbro, 124 ; in granite, 167 ; in peridotite, 383.
Central volcanoes, 4, 11, 420, 421.
Ceratophyre dykes, 396, 470, 471.
Chromium in rocks, 249.
Ciche na Beinne Deirge, 325, 469.
Clach Glas, 130, 141, 441, 445.
Clays in basalt group, 10, 47.
Cleveland dyke, 3, 295, 362.
CLOUGH, C. T., 19, 74, 101, 144, 245, 247, 254, 269, 270, 275, 295, 297, 299, 300, 302-304, 307, 309-313, 317, 319, 321, 327, 330, 334-337, 346, 359, 376, 379, 383, 384, 388-393, 395, 396, 407, 415, 463-465.
Cnoc Càrnach, 204, 205, 210, 211, 221, 255, 449, 451 ; type of sills, 203, 273, 425.
—— a' Chaise Mòr, 311, 336, 392.
—— nam Fitheach, 16.
—— Simid, 250.
—— an Sgùmain, 299, 396, 397, 471.
—— an t-Sithean, 209.
Coal in basalt group, 10 ; in agglomerate, 24.
Cognate xenoliths, 351, 353.
COHEN, E., 114.
Coireachan Ruadha, 64, 66, 72, 376, 444.
Coire na Banachdich, 96, 111, 116.
—— Beag, 64, 67, 72, 73, 76, 446.
—— Beithe, 2.
—— nam Bruadaran, 185.
Coire-chatachan, 167, 171, 393, 406, 407 ; group of dykes, 387, 408.
Coir' a' Chruidh, 371, 372, 446.
Coire Coinnich, 20, 22, 24, 127.
—— na Creiche, 202, 275, 447.
—— Gaisteach, 202.
Coir' a' Ghreadaidh, 365, 374, 376, 378, 379.
—— a' Ghrunnda, 64, 75, 444, 448.
Coire Labain, 25, 87, 96, 123, 287, 448.
—— nan Laogh (Gars-bheinn), 92; (Marsco), 166, 178.
Coir' a' Mhadaidh, 103, 373.
Coire Riabhach, 87, 93, 292.
—— nan Sagart, 54.
—— na Seilg, 20, 22, 83, 92, 127, 129, 139, 178, 180.
—— na Sgairde, 187.
Coir' an Uaigneis 143, 446.
COLE, G. A. J., 55, 199, 309, 333, 338-340, 348, 461-463.
COLLIE, J. N., 141, 463.
Columnar jointing in granite, 130, 450 ; basic sills, 243, 438 ; basic dykes, 309, 438.
Composite intrusions, 197, 425 ; literature, 198 ; unsymmetrical, 201, 297 ; symmetrical, 202 ; distribution, 203, 273 ; triple constitution, 204 ; imperfectly symmetrical, 212 ; petrography, 216, etc.
Conglomerates (fluviatile), 25.

Consequent xenocrysts, 223.
Contacts, two types of, 84 ; of peridotite, 79 ; gabbro, 94 ; granite, 137.
Corran a' Chinn Uachdaraich (Scalpay), 139.
COOMÁRA-SWÁMY, A. K., 281.
Corry Lodge (Broadford), 297, 357, 410, 470.
CORSTORPHINE, G. S., 199, 362, 385, 417.
Còruisk, 64, 86, 87, 368, 369, 442.
Country-rock, influence on dykes, 292, 432.
Cowal, 303, 389, 395, 396.
Creagan Dubha, 13, 18, 39, 131, 165, 440, 466.
Creag Bhriste, 222, 223.
—— Strollamus, 7, 12, 20, 27, 99, 100, 126, 136, 137, 155, 167, 171, 278, 451.
Crushing of volcanic agglomerates, 28 ; lavas, 54 ; gabbro, 124 ; granite, 20, 167 ; peridotite, 383.
Crust-movements, connection with igneous activity, 411 ; regional and local, 412 ; Tertiary and older, 413 ; local uplifts, 425, 428.
Cryptographic structure, 161, 280, 467.
Cuillin Hills, name, 440 ; gabbro of, 82 ; general structure, 85, 422 ; special dykes and sheets, 300, 364 ; erosion, 442 ; scenery, 443.
CULLIS, C. G., 277.

D

DANA, J. D., 46, 109.
DAWSON, SIR. J. W., 459.
DECHEN, H. VON, 1, 404, 455.
Dedolomitisation, 150.
Deformation of gabbro laccolite, 87, 422.
DELESSE, A., 199, 338, 340, 341.
DES CLOIZEAUX, A., 107.
Devitrified pitchstones, 279, 282, 407.
Differentiation of magmas, 417, 423.
Diffusion in magmas, 100, 172, 183, 185 232.
Doire Chaol (Soay), 270.
Dolerite sills and dykes, see Basic.
Dolomites, Cambrian, 97 ; metamorphism of, 144.
Donegal, 400, 407.
DOUGLAS, W., 464.
Down, 198, 199, 338.
Drochaid Lusa, 383-385, 471.
Druim na Cleochd, 157, 159, 160.
—— na Crìche, 256-268.
—— Eadar da Choire, 153, 180, 182, 296, 450.
—— an Eidhne, 21, 22, 53, 87, 88, 90, 92, 93, 115, 117, 124, 127, 128, 140, 143, 157, 158, 163, 271, 281, 283, 292, 368, 398, 401, 467 ; acid dykes of, 140 ; petrography, 277, 283, 468.
—— nan Ramh, 90, 96, 108, 123, 368, 371, 373, 442, 448.
—— na Ruaige, 166, 187, 188.
Drumfearn, 276.
Drusy structure, 42, 164, 175, 185, 218.
Drynoch, 31, 50, 253, 275, 328, 386, 405 ; group of dykes, 260, 386, 438, 466.

Dùn hill (Talisker), 261-263, 267, 268.
—— Merkadale, 250.
Dùnan, 131.
—— Earr an Sgùirr, 26.
Dunite, 71, 72, 76.
Dunvegan Head, 10.
Dyke phase, see Minor intrusions.
Dykes (acid), see Minor acid intrusions; (basic) see Basic dykes; (ultrabasic), see Peridotites; see also Andesite, Pitchstone, and Trachyte.
Dyke-feeders of fissure-eruptions, 12; of peridotite laccolite, 67; of gabbro, 92; of granite, 129; of composite sills, 210; of basic sills, 242; of inclined basic sheets, 369.

E

EARTH-movements, see Crust-movements.
Eas Mòr, 94, 95, 123.
Eigg, 55, 269, 396, 398, 405, 407.
Eilean Leac na Gainimh (Scalpay), 294.
—— Tioram, 22, 24.
Elgol, 201, 289, 398, 440.
Eocene flora, 2, 5.
Eozoonal structure, 147.
Erosion of region, 5, 434, etc.
Eskdale dyke, 199, 336, 402, 403.
ETTINGSHAUSEN, C. VON, 10.
Eutectic aggregate, 162, 281.
Eviscerated dykes, 298.

F

FAULTING, regional, 8, 9, 413, 427, 428, 430, 435; local, 425; relation to dykes and sills, 300, 302, 316, 317, 413, 430; pre-Tertiary, 413.
Fayalite in acid dykes, 286.
Felsite, 56, 61, 163.
Felstone lavas, 55.
Ferrite, 35, 262.
Fiaclan Dearg, 130, 178, 449.
Fingal's Cave, 248.
Fionn-Choire, 13, 55.
Fiskavaig, 49, 360.
Fissure-eruptions, 4, 11, 15.
Fissures of supply, see Dyke-feeders.
FLETT, J. S., 299.
Flora, Eocene, 2, 5; of peat, 439; of Cuillins, 449.
Fluviatile conglomerates, 25.
FORBES, E., 456.
—— J. D., 2, 85, 87, 440, 456.
Forellenstein, 73.
Forsterite-marble, 148.
Fragmental volcanic accumulations, 15.

G

GABBRO, distribution, 82; modes of occurrence, 83, 422; laccolite of Cuillins, 85; complexity, 88; banding, 90; feeders, 92; junctions, 94; Broadford boss, 97; its relation to limestones, 98; smaller masses, 101; analyses, 102; component minerals, 104; microstructure, 114; varieties, 115; petrography of banded varieties, 117; metamorphism of gabbros, 121; weathering, 123; crushing, 124; reactions with granite magma, 171, etc.; xenoliths in basic dykes, 355; scenery, 443.
Garbh-bheinn, 20, 82, 124, 127, 128, 130, 202.
GARDINER, J. S., 2, 10, 461.
Gars-bheinn, 66, 67, 77, 89, 92, 96, 294, 334, 371, 372, 374, 446.
Gases in crystalline rocks, 103, 154.
GEIKIE, SIR A., 2, 4, 9, 10, 11, 22, 23, 26, 46, 47, 55, 90, 91, 115, 117, 127, 140, 144, 152, 170, 199, 212, 237, 244, 245, 276, 291, 292, 295, 299, 306, 307, 319, 335, 336, 381, 385, 402, 405, 446, 457, 458, 460, 462-465.
Geur Rudha, 302.
Gheal Gillean type of dykes, 329.
Giant's Causeway, 248.
Gillean, 255, 310, 360, 396.
Glamaig, 53, 68, 82, 128, 139, 157, 187-190, 192, 278, 295, 375, 383, 403, 404, 449, 468.
Glas-bheinn Bheag, 126, 131, 143, 163, 467.
—— Mhòr, 129, 405, 469.
Glas Eilean, 201, 401.
GLEN, D. C., 460.
Glen Boreraig, 83, 134, 383, 414.
—— Brittle, 25, 290, 368, 386, 439.
—— Caladale, 50.
—— Drynoch, 436, 438.
Glenelg, 101.
Glen Eynort, 296, 436.
—— Sligachan, 83, 87, 90, 124, 126, 129, 130, 161, 368.
—— Varragill, 296, 436, 437.
—— Vidigill, 386.
Glomeroporphyritic structure, 250, 362, 371.
Gneissic structure, 185; and see Banding.
Granite, distribution, 126; modes of occurrence, 127; main body of Red Hills, 126; its complex structure, 130; boss of Eastern Red Hills, 131; of Beinn an Dubhaich, 132; smaller masses, 136; nature of junctions, 137; posteriority to gabbro, 140, 142; marginal modifications, 143, 271; metamorphism by, 144; analyses, 153; specific gravity, 155; component minerals, 156; microstructure, 160; varieties, 165; crushing, 167; absorption of gabbro material, 172, 183; xenoliths in basic dykes, 355; scenery, 449.
Granophyre, 152, 155, 215; microstructure, 161; with gabbro xenoliths, 172; with marscoite xenoliths, 194; minor intrusions, 280.
Granulitic gabbro, 53, 115.
—— structure in dolerites and basalts, 36, 52, 115, 322, 466.
Graphic structure, 161.
Great Group of basic sills, 236.
GREENLY, E., 3, 432.
GREG, R. P., 456, 457.
Gregarious dykes, 295.

Index. 477

Guillamon, 83, 279.
GUNN, W., 18, 199.

H

HADE of basic dykes, 305, 366.
Harrabol, 201, 304. 320, 399.
Harta Corrie, 87, 106, 108, 442.
HAUGHTON, S., 102, 106, 108, 153, 338, 457, 458.
Heast, 208, 210, 275, 350 ; road, 204, 221, 382, 388.
HEDDLE, M. F., 2, 35, 45, 47, 70, 76, 106, 108, 112, 150, 158, 262,¶263, 269, 310, 315, 333, 335, 338, 385, 417, 456, 457, 460, 461, 463-465.
HERWIG, F., 108, 110, 461.
HINXMAN, L. W., 464, 465.
HOCHSTETTER, F. VON, 458.
HODGKINSON, 338.
HOLLAND, T. H., 362.
Horizontal flow in dykes, 294, 37.
How, H., 460.
Huisgill, 260, 261, 266.
HULL, E., 199.
HUNT, T. S., 458.
Hybrid rocks, gabbro and granite, 181, 183, 185 ; marscoite, 175, 177, *etc.*; marscoite and felsite, 177 ; marscoite and granophyre, 194 ; porphyritic basalt and felsite, 288 ; basalt and granite, 357 ; abnormal composition of hybrids, 231 ; hybridism of second order, 196.
Hypersthene-basalt, 38, 466.
Hypersthenite, 107.
Hyskeir (Oighsgeir), 55, 398.

I

ICE-EROSION in Cuillins, 443.
Iceland, 4, 61, 363.
IDDINGS, J. P., 417, 421.
Iddingsite, 34, 112, 249, 262, 266, 466.
Imperfectly symmetrical composite dykes, 212, 305, 306.
Impregnation of gabbro by granite, 142, 181, 467.
Inaccessible Pinnacle, 373, 447.
Inclined flow in dykes, 294, 337.
Inclined sheets of Cuillins, 366, 427 ; distribution, 367 ; petrography, 370 ; as elements of scenery, 444.
Interruptions of dykes, 302, 306 ; of inclined sheets, 369.
Inver Dalavil, 327.
Inver Meadale, 244.
Iron, metallic, in gabbro, 102.
Iron-ore lumps, 90 ; seams, 120 ; lode, 159.
Isle Ornsay, 302, 307, 385, 401, 407, 471.

J

JAMESON, R., 243, 403, 406, 440, 453, 455.

Jointing, *see* Columnar.
JUDD, J. W., 2, 4, 5, 9, 11, 36, 39, 55, 71, 104, 107-112, 125, 140, 141, 199, 200, 216, 237, 250, 277, 278, 283-286, 309, 329, 333, 339, 340, 348, 362, 376, 385, 398, 400, 402, 459, 461-464.
Jurassic strata, pre-Tertiary surface, 7 ; sills in, 203, 235, 237, 436 ; dykes in, 294, 302, 451.

K

KAIBAB structure, 9.
KENDALL, P. F., 334, 335.
Kilbride, 16, 28, 148.
Kilchrist, 16, 126, 132, 143, 144, 159, 172, 296, 301, 304, 319, 424.
Kilt Rock, 244.
Kinloch, 254, 317, 334, 349, 383, 388, 392, 393, 469.
—— Ainort valley, 167.
KING, W., 147, 459, 461.
KNIGHT, W., 455.
Knock, 101, 295, 335, 336.
Kyleakin, 295, 301, 322, 435.
Kylerhea, 323, 328, 388.

L

LACCOLITIC habit of plutonic rocks, 83 ; of peridotite, 63 ; gabbro, 85 ; granite, 128 ; composite intrusion, 209.
LACROIX, A., 40, 77, 141, 361, 362, 463.
Lacustrine deposits in basalt group, 10, 49.
Lamlash, 338, 340.
Lamprophyres, 2.
Lava-flows, basaltic, 4, 11 ; trachytic and rhyolitic, 58, 59.
Leac Agamnha, 23, 49.
—— nan Faoileann (Soay), 270, 379, 470.
LEBOUR, G. A., 102, 315, 322.
Ledbeg (Sutherland), 144.
LEONHARD, K. C. VON, 454.
Lignite in volcanic series, 10.
Limestones, Cambrian, dolomitic, 97 ; metamorphism, 144 ; dykes in, 294, 296.
Linear variation, 121.
Lithophyses, 286.
Local and regional series, 5, 15, 419 ; crust-movements and strains, 419.
Lochain Beinn na Caillich, 98, 103, 131.
Loch Ainort, 128, 131, 155, 163, 196, 449.
—— Ashik, 332, 334, 348, 469.
—— an Athain, 141.
—— a' Bhasteir, 370.
—— Bracadale, 436.
—— Brittle, 24, 26, 47, 49, 375, 436.
—— Coir' a' Ghrunnda, 64, 76.
—— Coire Uaigneich, 320.
—— Coruisk, 66, 85, 90, 97, 102, 104, 111, 120.
—— na Creitheach, 88, 92, 137, 141, 142, 352, 398.
—— Cùil na Creag, 13, 27, 40
—— na Dal, 275, 335, 401, 436.
—— Doir' an Eich, 335, 359.

Loch Dubh, 130, 140.
—— Dunvegan, 47.
—— an Eilean (Heast), 210.
—— Eishort, 68, 127, 203, 211, 275, 309, 400, 471.
—— Eynort, 24, 26, 50, 250, 251, 436.
—— Fada (Suishnish), 211, 382, 383.
—— Gauscavaig, 312, 396, 470.
—— Ghlinne, 309.
—— Harport, 7, 8, 49, 50, 241, 250, 275, 296, 300, 311, 328, 386, 423, 436.
—— an Ime, 254.
—— Kilchrist, 16, 132-135, 145, 326, 355, 451.
—— an Leold (Scalpay), 213; (Suishnish), 211.
—— Lonachan, 146, 149, 151, 311.
—— Mhic Charmichael, 346.
—— a' Mhuillin (Scalpay), 213.
—— a' Mhullaich, 221.
—— Nigheann Fionnlaidh, 360.
—— Scavaig, 64-66, 70, 80, 87, 97, 103, 106, 108, 118, 119, 142, 369, 423, 443, 467.
—— na Sguabaidh, 278.
—— Slapin, 68, 126, 203, 368.
—— Sligachan, 203, 244, 248, 275, 282, 296, 300, 334, 423, 438.
—— na Starsaich, 210.
—— Staffin, 244, 245.
—— an Uamh, 254.
LOCKYER, Sir J. N., 32, 103, 248, 370.
Lòn Buidhe, 350.
Lota Corrie, 371, 373.
Lundy, 2.
Lusa, 302.

M

MACCULLOCH, J., 1, 10, 47, 76, 107, 110, 126, 127, 144, 165, 198, 235, 243, 294, 298, 333, 334, 381, 403, 404, 406, 453-455.
Macleod's Tables, 436.
MCHENRY, A., 55, 57.
Magnetism of basalt lavas, 53; gabbros, 113; dolerite sills, 244.
MALLET, J. W., 456.
Marble, 144.
Marginal modifications of granite, 130, 143, 163; of basic dykes, 308, 333, etc.
Market Stance (Broadford), 202, 212.
Marsco, 83, 92, 101, 128-130, 156, 158, 163, 166, 170, 176, 278, 295, 306, 334, 341, 345, 424, 449, 450, 467, 468.
Marscoite, 175; of Marsco, 177, 178, 180, 186; of Glamaig, 187, 188, 191.
Meadale, 239, 250, 328.
Meall Buidhe (Loch Ainort), 163; (Sleat), 255, 302.
Meall na Cuilce, 66, 97.
—— Coire Trusaidh, 16, 17.
—— Dearg, 126, 140, 153, 154, 157-159, 165, 368, 424.
—— na Gainmhich, 131, 320.
—— a' Mhaim, 320.
—— a' Mhaoil, 163, 164, 196.
—— Odhar, 56-58, 374, 378.
—— Odhar Beag, 333, 341, 345, 469.

Mechanical analysis, 104, 349.
Metamorphism of volcanic tuffs, 27; of basalt lavas, 50; of peridotites, 80; of gabbros, 121; of basic dykes, 319.
Metamorphism produced by gabbro, 97, 100; by granite, 144, 319; by dolerite sills, 245; by basic dykes, 309.
METCALFE, A. T., 464.
Miarolitic structure, see Drusy.
MICHEL-LEVY, A., 6.
Microgranite, 163.
Micrographic structure, 161, 280, 467.
Micropegmatite, 161, 280; phenocrysts, 282, 284, 467.
MILLER, H., 457.
Minor intrusions, phase of, 5, 426.
—— acid intrusions, 271; distribution, 273; petrography, 276; subacid types, 287.
—— basic intrusions, see Basic dykes, sheets, and sills.
Monadh Meadale, 239, 241.
—— Morsaig, 275.
Moorland flora, 439.
Mourne Mts, 2, 153, 164, 198.
Mugearite, 257; analysis, 263; petrography, 264; dykes, 331; tachylytes, 338, 347.
Mugeary, 257.
MUIR, T., 111.
Mull, 4, 10, 26, 55, 106, 112, 153, 170, 327, 334, 335, 338, 362.
Mullach an Achaidh Mhòir, 276.
—— na Càrn (Scalpay), 126, 274, 279, 353.
Multiple sills, 241; dykes, 296; distribution, 238, 431.
MURCHISON, Sir R. J., 333, 454, 455, 457, 458.

N

NECKER, L. A., 198, 333, 455.
NICOL, J., 456.
NICOLSON, A., 440, 459.
Norite, 74, 111, 467.

O

OB Allt an Daraich, 334.
Oban, 199.
Ob Gauscavaig, 295, 310, 313, 334.
—— Lusa, 302.
Ocellar structures, 37, 324.
OEYNHAUSEN, C. VON, 1, 404, 455.
Oighsgeir (Hyskeir), 55, 398.
Ophicalcite, 149.
Ophitic structure, 30, 115, 249, 322, etc., 466.
Ord, 302, 311, 359, 360, 392, 399.
Orkneys, dykes of, 299.
Orthophyre dykes, 288, 289.

P

PARALLELISM of dykes, 300-302, 431.
Paroxysmal eruptions, 15, 58, 420, 421.

Index.

PATRICKSON, 198.
PEACH, B. N., 18, 144.
Peat, flora of, 439.
Pegmatoid veins of peridotites, 78; gabbros, 116; granites, 166, 185.
Peinchorran, 8.
Pencatite, 145, 150, 151.
PENNANT, T., 243, 440, 453.
Peridotite, Sgùrr Dubh laccolite, 63; attacked by gabbro, 64; smaller laccolites, 66; dyke-feeders, 67; component minerals, 68; varieties, 71; banding, 75; xenolithic structure, 77; contact with sandstones, 79; later group, 67, 374, *etc.*; distribution, 375.
Permeation of gabbro by granite magma, 142, 181.
Petrographical province, 4; its characteristics, 416.
Phases of activity, three, 5, 420.
Phenocrysts, formed in place, 270; later growth, 329.
PHILLIP, C. B., 440, 441.
Picotite, 69, 72, 377, 384; analysis, 70.
Picrite, 72, 378, 380, 382.
PILKINGTON, C., 462.
Pitchstone dykes, 403, 429; distribution, 387; devitrified, 279, 282, 407.
Place-names in Skye, 82, 439.
Plant-remains in basalt group, 10.
Plateau structure, 9, 430; scenery, 436.
PLAYER, J. H., 23, 49, 118, 120, 396.
Plinthite, 47; analyses, 48.
Plutonic phase, 5, 421.
—— rocks, older (pre-volcanic) series, 11, 417.
Point of Sleat, 256, 295, 301, 321, 327, 330, 334, 335, 346, 360, 435, 469.
POLLARD, W., 31, 70, 102, 135, 146, 149, 151, 153, 216, 247-249, 261, 263, 315, 325, 370, 465.
Port a' Bhata, 337.
—— na Long, 299, 327.
Portree, 7, 10, 22, 23, 49, 242, 244, 247, 249, 331, 333, 337, 360, 435, 466.
POWELL J. W., 9.
PRATT, J. H., 71.
Predazzite, 150.
Pre-granitic dykes, 133, 135, 318; metamorphosed, 319.
Preshal Beg, 25, 243, 250.
—— More, 9, 25, 243, 244, 250.
Pre-Tertiary crust-movements and faults, 413; igneous rocks, 2; land-surface, 7.
Pre-Volcanic phase (early plutonic rocks), 11, 417.
Province, Brito-Icelandic, 4; its characteristics, 416.
Pyroclastic rocks, 15, 58, 59.

Q

QUARTZ-FELSITE, 163, 277, 278.
Quiraing, 8, 44, 47, 241, 263, 269, 333-335, 338, 341, 435, 438.

R

RAASAY, 126, 203, 340, 353, 385, 436.
Radial dykes of Cuillins, 300, 364; relation to crustal strain, 365, 428.
Radiate tendency of dykes, 300, 431.
Ramasgaig, 300.
RAMSAY, SIR A., 198.
RATH, G. VOM, 108, 111.
Red Hills, 126; granite, 127, *etc.*; minor acid intrusions, 272, 278, 283; basic dykes, 293, 295, 318, 324, 427; scenery, 449.
Regional and local series, 5, 15, 419; crust-movements and strains, 412.
REYER, E., 6, 462.
RHIND, W., 455.
Rhyolitic group, 55; tuffs, 59; lavas, 59; dykes, 280, 283.
Riebeckite-granophyre, 153, 158, 165.
Rivers of volcanic period, 25.
Rockall, 4.
Rodded structure, 389, 408.
Roineval, 256-262, 266, 268, 329, 468; type of double sills, 256; petrography, 261.
ROSENBUSCH, H., 116, 152, 280, 377, 400, 401, 464.
ROWNEY, T. H., 147, 459, 461.
Ruadh Stac, 126, 130, 180, 295, 449, 450.
RÜCKER, SIR A., 113, 462.
Rudha Bàn, 126, 129, 139, 141.
—— Buidhe, 244, 247, 466.
—— Chàrn nan Cearc, 255, 297, 335.
—— Chinn Mhoìr (Scalpay), 274.
—— nan Clach, 47.
—— Dubh Ard, 275, 302, 360, 392.
Rudh' an Eireannaich, 204, 207, 224-226, 276, 282, 287, 298, 468.
Rudha Gnail, 311, 334, 401, 471.
Rudh' an Iasgaich, 335, 337.
Rudha na Sgianadin, 304.
Rum, 4, 26, 70, 73, 74, 76, 170, 269, 376, 377, 421, 429, 450.

S

SAINT Kilda, 2, 4, 153, 170.
Sandaig (Glenelg), 101.
Satran, 387.
Scalpay, 8, 83, 126, 137, 139, 203, 207, 208, 212, 233, 255, 274, 279, 280, 289, 294, 305, 306, 330, 353, 466, 470.
Scenery of plateaux, 436; of gabbro mountains, 443; of Red Hills, 449.
Schiller-structures, origin, 109.
Sconser, 7, 278.
Segregation-veins in peridotites, 78; gabbros, 116; basic dykes, 308.
Serpentinous marble, 149.
Sgòrach Breac, 399.
Sgeir na Iasgaich, 322.
—— Mhòr (Torran), 298.
Sgiath-bheinn an Uird, 275.
Sgùrr Alaisdair, 87 287, 444, 448.
—— na Banachdich, 66, 124, 368, 374, 376, 378, 444-446.
—— a' Bhàsteir, 124, 371, 373.
—— a' Choire Bheag, 372.

Sgùrr Coiunich, 435.
—— a' Coir' an Lochain, 64, 74, 445, 447, 467.
—— Dearg, 123, 143, 372-374, 376, 378, 445-447.
—— Dubh, 63, 66, 72, 74, 76, 288, 444, 446 ; laccolite, 63, 71, 421.
—— an Duine, 24.
—— nan Each, 201, 440, 466.
—— nan Eag, 96, 143, 374, 448.
—— an Eidhne, 114, 127, 373.
—— na Fheadain, 447.
—— nan Gillean, 123, 128, 129, 202, 370, 374, 440, 446.
—— a' Ghreadaidh, 374, 379, 445-447.
—— nan Gobhar, 374, 376, 444-446.
—— na h-Iolaire, 255.
—— a' Mhadaidh, 143, 374, 444-446.
—— Mhic Choinnich, 64, 87, 143, 288, 444, 448.
—— Sgùmain, 446-448.
—— na Stri, 87, 94, 114, 372, 442, 448.
—— Tearlach, 87, 287, 448.
—— Thuilm, 56, 59, 61, 372, 374, 379, 444.
—— na h-Uamha, 128.
Sheath and core structure, 336.
Shiant Isles, 71 237, 385.
Sills, acid, 272-275 ; see *also* Basic sills and Composite.
Skulamus, 275.
Slat-bheinn, 94, 250, 252, 320, 355, 441.
Sleat, 295, 297, 300, 302, 304, 313, 321, 327, 330, 334, 359, 388 ; group of trachyte dykes, 389, 420, 430 ; distribution, 387.
Sligachan, 39, 166, 209, 233, 253, 276, 305, 383, 440, 468 ; River, 87, 103, 115, 127, 129, 139, 279, 442, 466.
Soay, 63, 66, 67, 74, 245, 247, 269, 294, 342, 375, 376, 378, 379, 395, 468, 470.
Solfataric action on basalts. 41, 45.
Solitary dykes, 295, 303, 305, 320.
SOLLAS, W. J., 73, 77, 104, 142, 170, 349, 400, 465.
Sound of Scalpay, 7, 425.
—— of Soay, 7, 19, 328, 414, 415.
Specific gravity of granites, 155 ; anomalous, of tachylytes, 340.
Spectra of igneous rocks, 23, 103.
Spherulitic structures in rhyolitic lavas, 61 ; granite margins, 130, 163, 467 ; acid dykes, 280, 284, 468 ; tachylytes, 336, 343-350, 469 ; trachyte dykes, 389, 394, 471.
Spotted granophyre, 187, 193, 194.
Springs in mountains, 449, 450.
Sròn a' Bhealain, 166, 187-189, 191, 193, 194, 450.
Staffa, 31, 244, 248.
Steinscholl, 249.
STEWART, B., 457.
Stockval, 9.
Storr, 8, 44, 47, 436-438.
Strathaird, 7, 10, 18, 201, 237, 255, 275, 289, 294, 296, 300, 320, 329, 330, 374, 375, 378.
Strath Beag, 126, 131.
Strath na Creitheach, 21, 93, 127, 128, 130, 141, 271, 292, 295, 368.

Strath Mòr, 105, 126, 405.
STRENG, A., 248.
Strollamus, 40, 467.
Struan, 241.
Suardal, 146, 148, 395 ; type of dykes, 326, 355, 469.
Subacid dykes, 287.
Subaërial origin of volcanic series, 9 ; weathering of basalt lavas, 47 ; of gabbros, 123 ; of basic dykes, 312.
SUESS, E., 461.
Suishnish, 68, 126, 203, 208, 211, 217, 381, 382.
Syenite, as modification of granite, 165.
SYMES, R. G., 199.
Symmetrical composite intrusions, 198, *etc.*

T

TACHYLYTE selvages, 269, 308, 333 ; distribution, 334 ; special structures, 336 ; analyses, 338 ; specific gravity, 339 ; microstructures, 342, *etc.*
Talisker, 9, 14, 25, 33, 37, 38, 44, 45, 47, 48, 243, 244, 260, 262, 264, 266, 268, 436.
Tangential dykes of Cuillins, 365.
Tarneilear, 293, 446.
Tarskavaig, 254, 255, 308, 310-312, 330, 334, 359, 360, 396.
TEALL, J. J. H., 90, 91, 104, 107, 109, 115, 117, 120, 144, 148, 150, 158, 162, 165, 362, 363, 400, 402, 462, 463, 465.
Terrestrial deposits in volcanic series, 10, 49.
Tertiary age of rocks, 1, 2, 5 ; volcanic action reviewed, 420, *etc.*
Thermal metamorphism, *see* Metamorphism.
THOMSON, T., 455.
THORPE, T. E., 462.
TILDEN, W. A., 102, 154, 464.
Tobar nan Uaislean, 56, 57, 59.
Tokavaig, 313.
Tormichaig, 128, 450.
Tormore, 295, 304, 312, 321, 360.
Torran, 149, 197, 295, 298, 304, 311, 318, 319.
Torridon Sandstone, contact with peridotite, 79 ; with gabbro, 99, 100 ; with granite, 137 ; with basic and ultra-basic sills, 245, 376 ; dykes cutting, 294, 295.
Torvaig, 337.
Trachyte lavas, 55 ; petrography, 58 ; dykes, 289, 386 ; rodded structure, 389 ; petrography, 393.
Trachy-andesite dykes, 386, 394.
Triple composite sills, 202, *etc.* ; dykes, 210, 298.
Troctolite in peridotite group, 73, 466 ; in gabbro, 82.
Trotternish, 237, 245.
Tuffs, basic, 15, 17, 21, 23 ; rhyolitic, 56, 57, 59.
Twin-lamellation, secondary, in felspars, 124.
Tynemouth dyke, 362, 363, 400.

U

ULFHART Point, 328.
Ultrabasic rocks, *see* Peridotites
Unsymmetrical composite dykes, 198, 297.

V

VANADIUM in rocks, 249.
Variolitic structure in basalts 347, 469; in trachytes, *etc.*, 394.
Varragill River, 253, 275.
Vents of volcanoes, 16, 19.
Vesicles occupied by ground-mass, 331, 342.
Vikisgill Burn, 201, 275.
Vitrified sandstones, 79, 245, 376, 468.
VOGT, J. H. L., 78, 119, 121, 465.
Volcanic vents, 16, 19.

W

WATTS, W. W., 432.
Weathering of igneous rocks, 47, 123, 312.
WEDD, C. B., 383, 413, 415.
WHITE, J., 461.
Wolf Rock (Cornwall), 4.
WOODWARD, H. B., 49, 126, 353, 463, 464.

X

XENOCRYSTS, in granophyre, 173, 195; in marscoite, 186, 191; in composite sills, 209, 219-224, 229, 233; in basic dykes, 351, 359; of second order, 195; antecedent and consequent, 223; source discussed, 361.
Xenolithic granophyres, 172, 183, 194.
Xenolithic structure in peridotites, 77, 377, 381; gabbros, 121; granites, 166.
Xenoliths, cognate and accidental, 350; sandstone in basalt, 40; gabbro in granophyre, 172, 183; gabbro in marscoite, 193; marscoite in granophyre, 187, 194, 468; basalt in granophyre, 208, 218, *etc.*; basalt in basalt, 224; gabbro in dolerite sills and sheets, 251, 373; quartz in basic dykes, 351; gabbro and granite in basic dykes, 355; probable source and significance, 363, 418.
Xenoliths within xenoliths, 224.

Y

YOUNG, J., 460.

Z

ZEOLITES in basalt lavas, 42-46; metamorphosed to felspars, 51, 466.
ZIRKEL, F., 2, 33, 35, 104, 107, 108, 112, 157, 270 354, 381, 404, 459.

GLASGOW; PRINTED BY JAMES HEDDERWICK AND SONS,
FOR HIS MAJESTY'S STATIONERY OFFICE.

EXPLANATION OF FOLDING MAP.

Geological Sketch-Map of Central Skye, with the adjacent smaller islands, on a scale of $\frac{1}{2}$ inch to a mile.

This is intended to present in one view the general geological relations of a large part of the tract principally dealt with in the foregoing pages. It will also serve to make most parts of this Memoir intelligible, even in the absence of the maps of the regular one-inch series and of the special six-inch maps selected to illustrate the Memoir more fully.

The superficial deposits which often conceal the solid rocks are omitted; as are also the sub-divisions of the Torridonian, Cambrian, and Mesozoic strata, which are for the most part without significance for our purpose. The Tertiary igneous rocks, with which we are more immediately concerned, have been simplified by omitting the great majority of the minor intrusions—sills, sheets, and dykes. Of the great system of dolerite sills in the basaltic tract a few have been inserted to suggest the distribution of the group and the character of the outcrops as dependent on the form of the ground. Of the innumerable dykes, chiefly of basic composition, a few only are given, which will suffice to indicate the general direction of the dykes in different parts of the area. The width of these is of course greatly exaggerated.

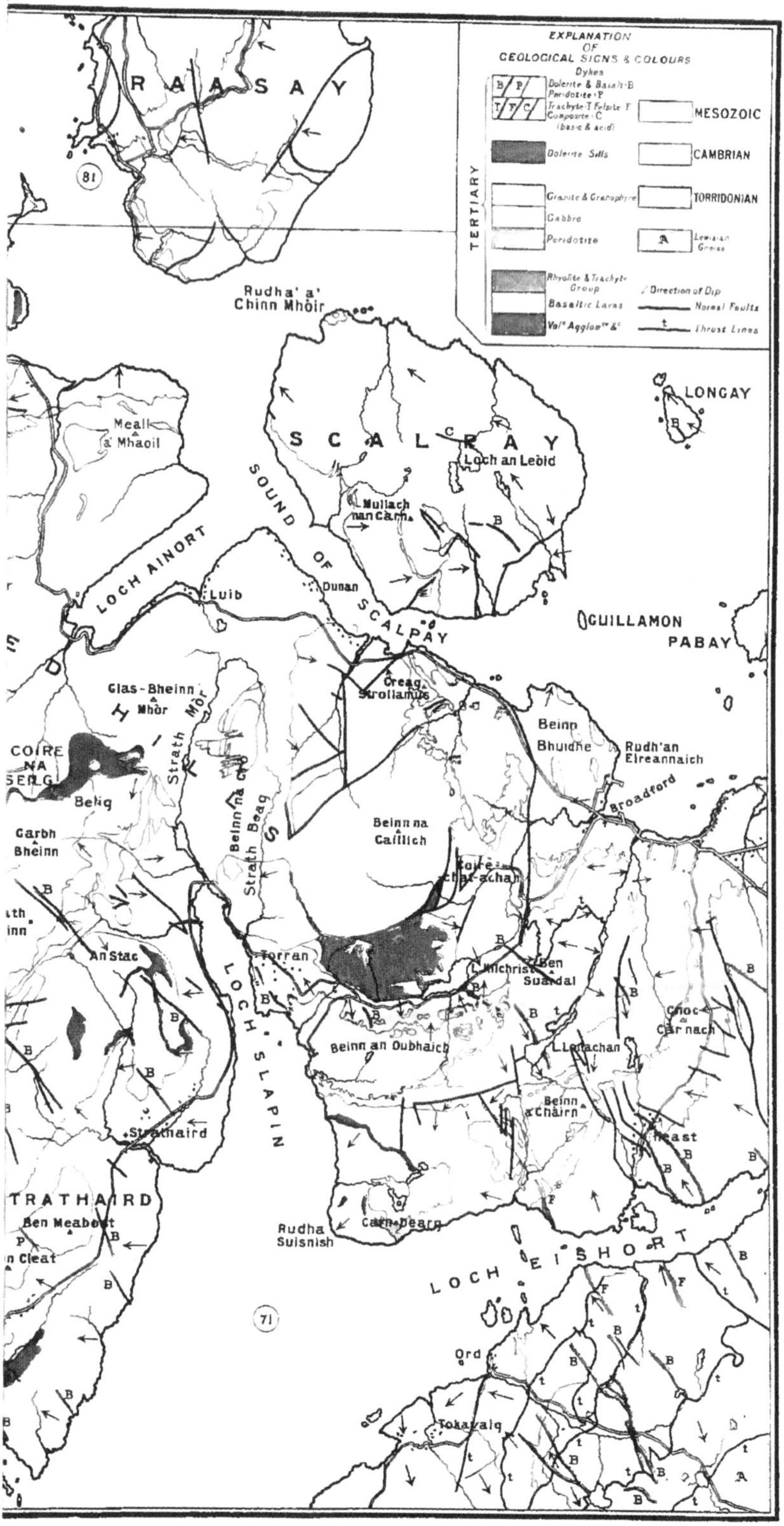
EXPLANATION OF GEOLOGICAL SIGNS & COLOURS
Dykes
Dolerite & Basalt · B
Peridotite · P
Trachyte · T Felsite · F
Composite · C (basic & acid)
MESOZOIC
Dolerite Sills
CAMBRIAN
TERTIARY
Granite & Granophyre
TORRIDONIAN
Gabbro
Peridotite
Lewisian Gneiss
Rhyolite & Trachyte Group
Direction of Dip
Basaltic Lavas
Normal Faults
Thrust Lines
RAASAY
81
Rudha' a' Chinn Mhòir
LONGAY
SCALPAY
Loch an Leòid
Meall a' Mhaoil
SOUND OF SCALPAY
Mullach nan Carn
LOCH AINORT
Luib
Dunan
GUILLAMON
PABAY
Glas-Bheinn Mhòr
Creag Strollamus
Beinn Bhuidhe
Rudh'an Eireannaich
COIRE NA SEILG
Belig
Strath Mòr
Broadford
Garbh Bheinn
Beinn na Cro
Strath Beag
Beinn na Caillich
Coire-chat-achan
An Stac
Torran
Kilchrist
Ben Suardal
LOCH SLAPIN
Cnoc Càrnach
Beinn an Dubhaich
L. Lonachan
Beinn a' Chàirn
Strathaird
Heast
STRATHAIRD
Ben Meabost
Rudha Suisnish
Carn Dearg
LOCH EISHORT
71
Ord
Tokavaig

ImTheStory.com

Personalized Classic Books in many genre's

Unique gift for kids, partners, friends, colleagues

Customize:

- Character Names
- Upload your own front/back cover images (optional)
- Inscribe a personal message/dedication on the inside page (optional)

Customize many titles Including
- Alice in Wonderland
- Romeo and Juliet
- The Wizard of Oz
- A Christmas Carol
- Dracula
- Dr. Jekyll & Mr. Hyde
- And more...

Emily's Adventures In Wonderland

Ryan & Julia